thai food

Renowned chef David Thompson first went to Thailand by mistake: a holiday plan had to be changed at the last minute and he ended up in Bangkok, where he was seduced by the people, their culture and cuisine. Since that fateful trip some 20 years ago, Thailand has become his second home.

Working alongside cooks who had perfected their craft in the Thai royal palaces, he began to document the traditional recipes and culinary techniques that have been handed down from generation to generation – before they were eroded, altered and modernised beyond all recognition. The result is *Thai Food*, the most comprehensive account of this ancient and exotic cuisine ever published in English.

David Thompson writes with passion and conviction about a unique style of cooking that he believes to be one of the world's greatest cuisines. Complemented by Earl Carter's superb photography, *Thai Food* captures all aspects of this diverse culinary culture.

Widely acclaimed as an expert on Thai food, David Thompson is one of Australia's foremost chefs, restaurateurs and cookery writers. He is also an eloquent ambassador for Thai culture.

His Sydney restaurants, the acclaimed Darley Street Thai – now closed – and the perennially popular Sailors Thai, have increased the awareness and appreciation of authentic Thai cooking. In July 2001 he opened nahm, in London's Halkin Hotel. Seven months later, it gained a Michelin star, making nahm the first Thai restaurant to attain such an award.

Currently David Thompson is consulting with the prestigious Suan Dusit College in Bangkok on the preservation of Thai culinary heritage.

david thompson

with photography by earl carter

thai food *arharn thai*

PAVILION

First published in the United Kingdom in 2002 by
Pavilion
43 Great Ormond Street
London WC1N 3HZ

First published in Australia in 2002 by Penguin Books Australia

A CIP catalogue recod for this book is available from the British Library

Designed by Melissa Fraser
Illustrations and map by Graham McArthur
Set in Johanna MT
Colour reproduction by Splitting Image, Australia
Printed and bound in China by RR Donnelley APS

10 9

ISBN 978-1-86205-514-8

www.pavilionbooks.com

FOR TANONGSAK YORDWAI

CONTENTS

ACKNOWLEDGEMENTS

This book has taken quite a few years to write. During this time I have come to recognise the importance of certain people, whose patience and indulgence have supported me throughout.

I must thank all the staff who worked at both Darley Street and Sailors Thai restaurants during my absences and distractions while writing. Their professionalism and skills maintained standards that I could only have hoped for in myself. Among so many, I would like to mention in particular: in the kitchens, David King, Max Mullins, Damien Jones, Ross Lusted, Martin Boetz, Dean Samut, Justin McGrigor, Jordan Theodore, Michael Voumard, Ben Thomas, Khun Pacharin Jantrakool ('Air') and Khun Bhum; and on the floor, Ray Moore, Leeta Collins, Colin Nelson, Khun Wandee Iamyoung ('Lek') and Charles Leong.

Little of this would have been possible without the understanding of my business partners, Maureen O'Keefe and Peter Bowyer. Peter has been with me from the start and only with him could we have made such a success of the restaurants. Without him, this book could not have been written.

Frank and Eileen McEwan provided great support during the initial stages.

Sadly, during the writing, two people instrumental to my career, and thus this book, died. Firstly, my dearest mother, whose profound inability to cook perhaps compelled me into cooking and whose implicit support and sweetness were only matched by my father's. Secondly, Bernard Appleton, who financed Peter and myself into Darley Street Thai in Kings Cross. It launched us onto a bigger stage than the back of a pub in the then sometimes insalubrious Sydney suburb of St Peters. Barney was a generous man in more ways than just finance.

During my 14 years cooking Thai food I have amassed a substantial collection of Thai cookbooks and memorial books. Some managed to confound, others to elucidate. All have given me a rare access to an exotic culinary culture. Without these books, without these authors – mainly women, and a few men – this book would have been impossible.

The writing of this book has been an interesting, prolonged experience. It was first commissioned by Julie Gibbs, who patiently – and I suspect with disbelief – saw the project change from a small book on Thai snacks to what follows. Although this has taken some time, I hope that it justifies the wait.

I had the rare luck to have been assigned an editor of formidable talents: her ability to wade through the original manuscript and yet make sense of it was remarkable. Her understanding, belief and support have been miraculous – although at times I thought it a mixed blessing. It is only through Clare Coney's patience and dogged persistence that this book has managed to be completed. Clare triumphed over the improbable, realised and gave form to the unlikely, and dismissed the impossible. I am in awe, adore and am eternally grateful.

Alison Cowan added the final polish to the book. As the last to edit – and the one to oversee the transformation from manuscript to book – she offered insights that improved the text, making it leaner and more accessible to the reader. Although I initially resisted such improvements and trimming, they have produced, I believe, a more concise, focused book. I am also grateful to Melissa Fraser for her inspired design and for taking everything in her stride, and to Carmen De La Rue for coordinating the book's production.

Earl Carter's arresting photographs have captured the essence of *Thai Food* quickly and elegantly. In comparison to his vision, my writing, I am afraid, seems laboured and blurred. I must also thank the Tourism Authority of Thailand, especially Khun Phornsiri Manoharn and Khun Wasawadee Sanpradith, for their generous assistance during Earl's assignment in Thailand.

Finally to my partner, my darling Tanongsak Yordwai, who throughout the 16 years of our relationship has been an unwavering beacon of hope, calm and support. Tanongsak made many suggestions, specifically in the desserts chapter, but more generally has patiently assisted in research, translated those confounding passages, clarified techniques and recipes, offering insights and explanations – sometimes too lucidly – and with rare forbearance overlooked my absences, preoccupations and frustrations.

All of these people have contributed to this book in some way, either by giving their time or knowledge – or allowing me to research and write away from my restaurants. This book's merits are due to them; whatever shortfalls it might contain are mine.

David Thompson
July 2002

INTRODUCTION

I first went to Thailand by mistake, but it was a mistake I have never regretted. A holiday plan had to be changed at the last minute, and I ended up in Bangkok. There I basked in the agreeable life of this exotic land, and quickly became seduced by the people, their culture and cuisine. What enamoured me most was the easy and open-hearted hospitality of the Thai people. Coy and playful, proud yet reserved, they approached life and the world in a very distinct way.

Thailand has a majestic past, with all the travails that ancient cultures are heir to, yet the Thai are not overwhelmed by their legacy. The past sits very happily with the present in Thailand, and the Thai live easily with both. I resolved to live there.

Within a year I moved to Bangkok. The reality of living in this sprawling city was vastly different from my holiday in the sun. I recognised that the grace with which the Thai have adapted to the stresses of the modern world was admirable. Within two or three generations they had left their paddies to embrace the tumult of urban existence and had successfully done so while maintaining aspects of their traditional culture.

I soon had the good fortune to meet someone who would have an enormous influence on me: Sombat Janphetchara, affectionately called Khun Yai, 'Grandmother'. She was the wife of a high-ranking bureaucrat and the daughter of a *kon chao wang* – a person who lived in a palace. She was thus an heir to Thailand's ancient tradition of cooking, where fine craftsmanship and sharply honed skills were prime considerations.

Her cooking transformed my understanding of Thai food, *arharn thai*. Before then I had considered it an agreeable cuisine, but in her hands the agreeable became extraordinary. She cooked in the old-fashioned Siamese manner, where the best ingredients are assembled, then deftly cleaned, sliced or pounded before being combined and seasoned with an adroit cast of the hand. Her approach to cooking was instinctive; she disregarded cautious weighing and measuring, along with the dictates of any recipe, preferring to follow her own experience and taste. Her cooking was truly unique.

Initially I was disconcerted by such a loose approach to cooking, having trained for some years in the more rigorous discipline of French cuisine. But soon I began to appreciate that hers was not a culinary bedlam, but a responsive and intimate way of cooking and seasoning. I became a convert.

I cooked for several months with Khun Yai – pounding pastes with a mortar and pestle, sweating over woks, sneezing over curries – and slowly began to gain some insight into this remarkable cuisine. I tried to analyse it with a keenness that only a convert can have. But I was uncertain of my grasp.

There is a custom, unique I believe to Thailand, of having memorial books published and distributed at the cremation of the deceased. Such books record their family, their genealogy (if noble), their life and achievements, their habits and interests. This practice dates back to the cremation of one of the major wives of King Rama V in 1881. At a time when there were few books in the country, the king expressed his wish that this example might encourage people to publish accounts of the Siamese.

When books were published for women, particularly ones who had lived in palaces, they often included a wealth of recipes. I avidly read these funeral books and from such sources I began to gain a more solid understanding of Thailand's remarkably complex cuisine.

Thai cooking is at odds with the modern world, where speed and simplicity are paramount. Thai is not an instant cuisine, prepared with the flick of a knife and finished with a toss of a pan. It needs the cook's attention, it expects time and effort to be spent and it requires honed skills, but it rewards with sensational tastes.

This book aims to give an understanding of all Thai food. It does, however, have a bias, reflecting my own interests: I believe that Thai cooking reached an apex in the last decades of the nineteenth century. The only recorded recipes of this high point were those of the upper classes. Historically, the best food of any country has always been centred around the court, and this was certainly true of Siam and its many palaces. The development of Thai cuisine was clearly driven by those who did not have to cook or sully their hands with manual labour, otherwise they would not have demanded so much. The result, however, was sublime. Not that regional and peasant food is to be dismissed; it presents a living record, having remained unchanged generation after generation, and is still being cooked today. This book tries to capture all aspects of this diverse culinary culture.

Therefore, one reason I have written *Thai Food* is to describe this ancient cuisine, in English, before it is eroded, altered and modernised. I want to acknowledge the generations of Thai who have evolved a unique style of cooking that is, I believe, among the world's great cuisines. To do them justice, this book contains some recipes that are difficult, calls for some ingredients that are hard to find, and places some demands on the cook, but I have included such recipes in order to show the extent to which Thai cooks are prepared to go to produce their sophisticated cuisine. Substitution and short cuts when describing the food would be not only disrespectful but debasing.

However, this book is not meant to be an unyielding tract, dictating dogged adherence to interminable techniques and bizarre ingredients. This would be unrealistic and arrogant – and I hope that you will enjoy both cooking and eating the food. I have, though, tried to give a rounded view of Thai cooking, and not just a number of recipes. First, I describe the cuisine and rice in the context of Thailand's history, culture and regions; I then explain the techniques and types of dishes that are peculiar to Thai cooking, both ancient and modern. Next, I have put together combinations of recipes in a series of sample menus, to show how a Thai meal is composed and cooked today. I hope that by doing so you will be able to see how the food should be cooked – and, most importantly, understand *why* it is done in a particular way. Then there is a section on the snacks and street food that play such a lively, entertaining role in Thai life. And, finally, a chapter on desserts, which some Thai cooks believe to be the pinnacle of their cuisine.

If I succeed in giving a firm appreciation of Thai taste and an understanding of the techniques, then I will have fulfilled some of my intentions when writing this book. I hope I will also equip you with sufficient knowledge and confidence to *explore* the possibilities inherent in this compelling cuisine. So you will not simply follow the recipes, but will understand their underlying mechanics and be able to cast this book aside with a certain rebellious aplomb. And then begin to cook instinctively, just as good Thai cooks – or any other, for that matter – do.

At first I expect you will experiment tentatively, and then with increasing confidence, following your senses and employing intuition. The recipes should certainly be a guideline, but not adhered to as gospel. This was, after all, the standard manner of the cooks of Siam: when I first began to translate recipes from the older memorial books I was astonished at their vagueness. Ingredients were listed without quantities, a brief line would indicate the most complex of methods, or a whisper when seasoning was suggested. There was a certain assumption – indeed, expectation – that a cook would be sufficiently skilled to alter the recipe according to the availability of ingredients and whim.

Initially it was daunting, trying to make sense of this nebulous cuisine and its capricious cooks, but slowly and gradually, after many attempts, my understanding began to coalesce, and what was once baffling became an invitation to interpret. And so the process is the same with these recipes, although I have rather kindly listed quantities! However, at this stage I must add that alteration and adaptation of the recipes is not an invitation for culinary carte blanche. New ingredients must be apposite and judiciously chosen. But by understanding Thailand and its culture, by practising the techniques and by appreciating the tastes of Thai cuisine, you should be able to introduce successful variations. If this is done, then I will have achieved my aims.

This book does ask for some effort from those who follow its recipes, but I feel that it is one of my responsibilities to encourage and expand the capacities of the cook, rather than succumb to easier options. To do less would be a grave disservice to the modern cook, to those ancient cooks and to good Thai cooking.

AUTHOR'S NOTES

THAI TRANSLITERATION

The official transliteration of Thai to English script is based on a system devised by King Rama VI. My transliterations are phonetic; I believe it is more important to pronounce the Thai words correctly, which is not always possible when following the accepted version. However, when a dish, word or place is well known, the familiar transliteration is used.

SERVINGS

The recipes in Part Two of this book are generally designed to work within the context of a meal. For a complete Thai meal with rice, four dishes – a relish with a few of its accompaniments, a soup, a curry (perhaps with a side dish), and a salad – will easily serve 4 people.

Suggested combinations of recipes suitable for 4–6 people are given in the 'Menus' chapter, together with some guidelines on preparing and eating a Thai meal.

Part Three deals with food considered by the Thai to be outside the meal proper. Most of the recipes in 'Snacks and street food' are single-plate dishes: they are not shared, although the Thai will still eat together. There is also no assumption that rice will be served with them – but it might well be. Likewise, in the 'Desserts' chapter, recipes make enough for a single plate, but several may be combined to make a dessert platter.

part one

thailand and food

part one   thailand and food

T hai cooking is a singular cuisine that is easily distinguished even from its nearest neighbours. Yet this distinctiveness is not the result of an insular, unaccommodating attitude that refuses novel ideas and dismisses new ingredients. Throughout Thailand's long history, the resilience of the culture has allowed it to accept the unfamiliar without fear of compromise. The incorporation of the chilli into the cuisine is a most potent example of this. In Europe, it took 200 years for the tomato to be considered anything more than a poisonous apple, yet Siamese cuisine completely absorbed the chilli within a century. And now Thai cooking is inconceivable without it.

The true genius of Thai cuisine is its ability to incorporate the unfamiliar, whether it be ingredient or technique, and absorb it so completely that it becomes an integral component; to 'Siam-ise' it to a degree that it becomes indistinguishable from the indigenous. The history and character of the Thai have afforded this extraordinary synthesis of cooking, ingredients and circumstances to create a vital cuisine that is the embodiment of a remarkable people and their culture.

Thai food is intertwined with all aspects of Thai culture. Since ancient times, dishes have been offered to the many gods and spirits that inhabited the Thai world and the Thai psyche. Such offerings placated the deities and ensured their aid in times of uncertainty. Today no celebration is complete without a meal, and the offering of food to monks is a sure way to obtain merit. Food offers more than nourishment alone; it is sustenance for the country and the soul.

The diverse terrain of Thailand imposes its own marked characteristics on the cooking. The many physical barriers – uplands, mountains, deep ravines, rivers and ragged coastlines – are set in a landscape that was, until only recently, sparsely populated. These factors have inevitably led to vast regional differences in culture and cuisine. Only in the late nineteenth century did the idea of a united country begin to develop; before then, Thailand was the sum of its many parts.

Rice plays a pivotal role in Thailand: its cultivation has altered the countryside and created a culture that is uniquely Thai. This primacy is reflected at the Thai table where, no matter how refined, delicate or complex dishes may be, they are merely accompaniments to the rice. Without rice, a meal would be incomprehensible – and Thailand, as it is today, would not exist.

1

A HISTORY

The various tribes who would eventually become the Thai originated in the cloud-covered mountains and deep gorges beyond the lower reaches of the Yangtze River in Yunnan, where they were recorded as a distinct people by Han Chinese chroniclers in the first century BC. At this time the area was a semi-independent region different from the Han-occupied country to the north, having more in common with regions farther to the south. Its monsoonal climate created an ancient rice-growing culture and a sturdy, self-reliant people, the T'ai.

T'ai describes the broad ethnic and linguistic group that spread from the south of China to the border of modern Malaysia, and from the north of Vietnam to the Brahmaputra River in north-eastern India. In the north-east, surrounding the Mekong River, these people are called the Lao; farther north, in modern Vietnam, the T'ai Yuan; to the west, along the Salween River, the Shan or T'ai Yai; and in the south, in the central plains of modern Thailand, they became the Thai or, as others would have it, Siamese.

In southern China, the T'ai flourished. However, over several centuries, the Chinese migrated into this fertile region from farther north and, by the ninth century AD, the autonomy of the T'ai was compromised. After many attempts to maintain their independence, the disaffected T'ai began to move southwards. Their migration clung to the contours of the low-lying land, along the valleys of this mountainous region, away from the steeper hills where rice growing was barely sustainable. The initial wave crossed the Mekong River and reached the area that would become modern Thailand in about the tenth century. Some historians suggest that several centuries before this, communities of T'ai were already established in the area, being the vanguard of the movement southwards. Moreover, the group of tribes historically called the T'ai was a loose association that shared similar heritage and language, who moved gradually but independently into the Chao Phraya basin; they had as much in common with the local Mon and Lawa peoples as they did with the people remaining in the fractious tribal kingdoms of the Nan Chao and Sipsongpanna. These primitive cultures shared the same needs and methods of survival, and had perhaps not yet reached the stage where there was any appreciable cultural divergence. This allowed for easy intermingling between the newcomers and the more established peoples.

Before the advent of the Thai – as they came to be known – onto the central plains surrounding the Chao Phraya basin, this region was sparsely inhabited by the indigenous, peaceful and agrarian Mon people, who lived under the tenuous control of the once mighty, but by then declining, Khmer kingdom of Angkor. Increasingly, the area inhabited by the Mon fell under Thai control. As the Thai encroached they absorbed some of the customs and rituals from the remnants of the Mon ancient Dvaravati culture that had flourished several centuries before, and from the more sophisticated Khmers of Angkor. The Thai now began to intensively cultivate paddy rice in the fertile and alluvial plains; one Khmer government dispatch observed they would 'turn forest into rice fields'.

The food of these people was primitive, probably similar to the food of the primitive hill tribes of northern Thailand and Laos today. These tribes – the Hmong, Akha, Lahu, Lisu, Mien and Karen – cling to the high hills, by-passed in many ways by the passage of both time and the Thai who progressed south. One of these ancient meals might have consisted of a pile of steamed sticky, or glutinous, rice and a pungent paste made from dried soy beans, salt and sour leaves. People ate simply with their fingers, rolling balls from a central, shared mound of the rice, which they then dipped into or mixed with the coarse paste.

MUANG THAI

The Thai have always formed groups, called *muang*. This is a hard term to define, yet important to understand, because it has accompanied the Thai throughout the long trek of their history. The word is used for village or community, but its usage is not confined to its literal meaning – *muang* came to encompass the complex network of social and economic relations, commitments, obligations, dependencies and commonly shared values and beliefs that mesh and knit kith to kin. It includes mutual dependency between families and the hierarchical relationship between the leader or chieftain and the group, and individual to individual, superior to inferior. *Muang* is the gel of Thai society.

Originally, a small group of families would bond to form a *muang*. This structure was reproduced in every village and farming community. As these semi-autonomous communities expanded, they became loosely strung together under one dominant leader. So, as the Thai evolved from nomadic farmers, through the exotically alluring and cosmopolitan Siamese kingdom of Ayuthyia to modern-day Thailand, the concept of *muang* remained firmly rooted in their culture, maintaining a familiar structure that allows the Thai to respond to and embrace new influences from an assured and confident base. Even today, its inhabitants call Thailand *muang thai*.

About the tenth or eleventh century the loose confederation of *muang* began to bond together, forming the basis of several independent T'ai kingdoms: Nan Chao in Yunnan and the central Laotian hills, then, later, Chiang Saen and Yonok on the Mekong River, and Chiang Mai in northern Thailand.

SIAM

The Thai have always described themselves as *kon thai*, 'Thai people', and whatever area they inhabited as *muang thai*, 'the community of Thai'. However, throughout their history, they have had many names conferred on them by outsiders, the most common being 'Siam'. The origin of this word is shrouded in a mist of uncertainty. Some historians believe it was a convenient geographical appellation, as dispatches describing the Thai to the neighbouring, more established kingdoms – the Khmer, Mon and Peguan – refer to the area they inhabited as Shien. It is easy to see how those who lived in that area were simply, but indiscriminately, called Shien, later corrupted to Syam. Other historians plausibly argue that Siam may derive from the first two syllables of Suvannannabhumi, the mythical city where Buddhism was first received in the Chao Phraya valley. Its Sanskrit name means 'land of gold', and healthy fertility has always been enjoyed by the people who have occupied this area. The equivalent Malay word, *syam*, means 'gold', 'bronze' or 'brown'. Malay was the original lingua franca of the region before the arrival of the Europeans, and thus it may have been in Malay that the Siamese were first described to outsiders.

The names 'Siam' and 'Siamese' continued to be used by all groups that subsequently came in contact with the Thai, and 'Siamese' eventually became the accepted name for these people who dominated the central plains. Even the Thai's capital cities – most notably, Ayuthyia – were sometimes referred to as Siam, regardless of their actual names. It is one of the remarkable and telling characteristics of the Thai that they have never been chauvinistically insistent on others using the words by which they refer to themselves.

Whatever its derivation, 'Siamese' was used to describe these people until the middle of the twentieth century. The country's name was changed to Thailand in 1949, in a burst of nationalism that rejected the imposed name. To my ears there is still an alluring connotation to 'Siam': it suggests the exotic in a way the literal, more prosaic 'Thailand' does not.

THE RISE OF SUKOTHAI

As Angkor's power waned during the twelfth century, it maintained influence not so much by ruling as by marrying the daughters of Khmer nobility to the increasingly independent and fractious Thai chieftains, in order to preserve their allegiance. As a result, the rough and energetic culture of these fringe-dwellers of empire was tempered and refined by the genteel ladies of the Khmer court. But soon neither bonds of marriage nor deference to the Khmers' superior culture was sufficient to hold the Thai under Angkor's sway.

By the middle of the thirteenth century, the Thai threw off the shackles of Angkor. Sukothai, regarded as the first independent Siamese kingdom, was established; the Thai refer to this era as 'the dawn of happiness'. Sukothai lay amid three powerful kingdoms: to the west, the Burmese kingdom of Pegu; to the east, Angkor; and to the south, Srivajava, on the island of Sumatra, which ruled over the Malay peninsula. Under its greatest king, Ramakhamhaeng (who reigned from 1279 to 1298), Sukothai rapidly won the allegiance of numerous small fiefdoms and principalities. Ramakhamhaeng was suzerain over a vast area, from north-eastern Laos through the central plains of the Chao Phraya River down into the Malay peninsula. King Ramakhamhaeng, whose name literally means 'Rama the Bold' – he was so called because of his prowess in battle – is considered to be the father of the Thai people and nation. To confirm his triumph, Ramakhamhaeng ordered stone pillars to be carved describing the kingdom and its king. The following inscription was found in abandoned ruins in 1833 by a monk-prince of Siam who would later become its king – Mongkut. The language on this pillar was strange to the Siamese and it took some fifty years to decipher it. Once finally translated, it proclaimed a promising bounty:

> When I caught game or fish . . . When I picked acid or sweet fruits that were delicious and good to eat . . . In the time of King Ram Khamhaeng this land of Sukothai is thriving. There is fish in the water and rice in the fields. The lord of the realm does not levy toll [too heavily] . . . whoever wants to trade . . . does so . . . They plant areca groves and betel groves all over this *muang* . . . coconut . . . jackfruit . . . mango and tamarind groves are planted in abundance. King Ram Khamhaeng, lord of this kingdom . . . planted . . . sugar palm trees.

Any description of the type of food that was eaten in Sukothai can only be conjecture, but it is likely that both sticky and non-sticky rice were consumed. Although the above inscription records coconut groves around Sukothai, it is unlikely that coconut cream was used in cooking at that time. Sukothai is at the northernmost edge of the coconut zone and so coconuts would have been a rare and novel fruit to these recently arrived people from the north. Probably coconut was first used in ceremonies as sweetmeats for the gods; one authority, Dr Kanit Martarbhorn, suggests that the oil extracted from coconuts was used to make votive candles. Coconut oil might also have been used in some purification rites, much as ghee is used in Hindu rituals.

The late Mom Ratchawongse Kukrit Pramoj, a Thai gourmet of renown, believed that Thai food of this period was not unlike modern northern food, based around steamed glutinous rice served in a basket. The accompanying dishes would be:

- a relish – a simple paste of shallots pounded with galangal and peppercorns
- a soup – simmered pieces of pork and vegetables
- vegetables – some cultivated, as well as ferns, shoots and creepers that were gathered where they grew wild in nearby fields, along canals and in more distant forests
- meat – wild boar, small mountain deer, wild birds, frogs and various freshwater fish and prawns, cooked by grilling or boiling.

Any excess meat or fish, or an abundant harvest of vegetables, was salted, dried, pickled or fermented, in order to preserve this bounty for a time of need. The cuisine was firmly rooted in the land and the society.

Although much Sukothai court ritual and structure was influenced by Angkor, the kings of Sukothai were more accessible to their subjects than the Khmer rulers had been. While the kings' power was absolute and all within their domain – people, animals and land – were their chattels to dispose of as they willed, their rule was paternal. The obligations and strictures of Buddhism prevented too arrogant a dominion over their people.

Buddhism was not the only religious influence in Sukothai. From the Indianised Khmer state the Thai had assimilated the important role of Brahmin priests as intermediaries between the king and the Hindu gods, ensuring the maintenance of the state by their ancient and arcane rites. Many traditional festivals and customs originate from this time, when the Thai first consolidated their culture and kingdom. Thai society was distinct from that of the Khmers, and probably more attractive to its neighbours than the imposing, impersonal and decaying rule of Angkor. Steadily the dominion of the Thai increased.

AYUTHYIA

Around 1350 a new kingdom, Ayuthyia, arose to the south of Sukothai. Over the next four centuries it grew to be one of the wealthiest and most cosmopolitan kingdoms of South East Asia. Ayuthyia was far removed from the gentle, more accessible *muang* of Sukothai. The material expression of this can be seen by comparing the ruins of the two cities: there is a humanity of scale in Sukothai that is in stark contrast to the grandeur of Ayuthyia (pictured over the page).

Ayuthyia expanded in both area and might and in 1431 it conquered the Khmer kingdom. The city of Angkor was sacked. Its royal regalia and most of the court, including Brahmins, monks, scholars and cooks, with their knowledge and skills, were removed to Ayuthyia. Thus many of the highly formal practices of the ancient kingdom of Angkor were absorbed into Ayuthyia, conferring Angkor's stamps of succession, continuity and ritual on this flourishing kingdom. It irrevocably altered the nature of Thai society.

In Ayuthyia the early Thai model of kingship changed. The king became deified and now a commoner could look upon the monarch only on pain of death. Even the highest-born had to crouch, head bowed, in his presence. A new language – *rachasap* – evolved; it was based on a mixture of Pali (the ancient ecclesiastical language of Thai Buddhism, closely related to Sanskrit) and Khmer and was used only when talking to or about the king and high nobles. Just as Ayuthyia absorbed the Khmers' rarefied court practices, the new Thai kingdom's preparation and service of food became less functional and more formal. Instead of two or three simple dishes at a meal, several more would arrive, befitting the status of the recipient. Embellishment became as important as the substance. Sumptuous display became indicative of status.

Ayuthyia was one of the greatest cities of its time. It was larger than most fifteenth-century European cities and had greater stability of government. Its wealth was based on the trade between India and China: Indian merchants traded spices, opium, scented wood and hides with their Chinese counterparts for silks, tea, porcelain and gold, while the Siamese bartered elephant tusks and rhinoceros horns, precious stones, rattan, beeswax and, with royal licence, surplus rice.

THE ARRIVAL OF THE EUROPEANS

Europeans also arrived at this market, trading in guns, textiles, religion, glassware and spices. Trade – especially in spices – lured the Europeans from their cold northern corner to the ends of the world. They wished to break the monopoly that the Arabs and Venetians enjoyed in the spice trade. Their ambition was not always matched, however, by their skill in navigating. The Portuguese, followed some decades later by the Dutch then the English, rounded the Cape of Good Hope towards the end of the fifteenth century, establishing toe-holds at Goa on the western coast of India in 1510 and later in Calicut and Cochin. Clinging tentatively to the shore, these intrepid, acquisitive mariners and merchants followed ancient trade and Buddhist pilgrimage routes from Ceylon through the Straits of Malacca, where the Portuguese captured the trading port of Malacca from its sultan in 1511. As the sultanate had been a tributary of Siam, the Portuguese sent emissaries to Ayuthyia to placate the Siamese. It was Siam's first encounter with Europeans.

Some countries, like China, remained haughtily closed to Westerners; others, like Japan, violently expelled the European adventurers. In Siam, however, they found a haven – a place where they could trade freely with other countries, relatively unimpeded by government restrictions. Ayuthyia fostered such trade by designating areas outside the city walls where these foreigners could reside and establish their trading posts. Chinese, Malay and Persian – as well as Siamese – administrators served as intermediaries to supervise agreements, ensure their compliance and levy tax. The Europeans were generally referred to as *farang*, a word borrowed from Persia, which had encountered these strange pale people centuries before. The Siamese employed many foreigners: Indian officials, Khmer governors, Dutch advisors, French generals, Japanese mercenaries and English administrators were all engaged in various government departments. Their abilities determined their positions and they were often regarded as more trustworthy and loyal to the monarch than their Siamese counterparts, who were enmeshed in internal power struggles in the Machiavellian court of Ayuthyia. Their professionalism was often in contrast to the indolent Siamese in their sinecures.

A recurring method used by the Siamese to effect control was to encourage an individual, group or country at the expense of the others – the classic divide-and-rule. Fractious individuals were dealt with in a pleasingly Siamese way: by being burdened with costly honours, such as court positions that bound them irrevocably to the king and were onerous to maintain; being offered a daughter's hand; or being sent to govern distant provinces with an equally fractious population. This pattern of manipulating rivalries was extended to the Europeans. When Siam believed that the Portuguese influence was too strong, the Dutch were encouraged. With the incorporation of the Dutch and later English East India companies, the Portuguese were soon eclipsed in the commerce of the region, and the Siamese began encouraging the French and English.

THE GLORIES OF AYUTHYIA

Most foreign chroniclers remarked upon Ayuthyia's glittering temples and palaces, and the network of canals reminiscent of Venice, which were flanked by broad, shady trees that brought relief from the tropical heat. All recalled the size of the city, its bustling commerce, its diverse population and the opulence and beauty of its temples, faience-encrusted spires or *chedi* housing important religious relics, and scrolling *naga*, gracefully tapering temple awnings that resemble a serpent, the Buddhist symbol of wisdom. Some sense of this exotic and fantastic metropolis can be gained today by looking across the Chao Phraya River in Bangkok to the Grand Palace complex, which consists of replicas of several temples and palaces from Ayuthyia.

The flamboyant Abbé de Choisy recorded his visit to this thriving city in his *Journal of a Voyage to Siam*. He entered in his diary for 27 October 1685:

> We went for an excursion outside the town. I am never tired of admiring this very large city on an island surrounded by a river three times bigger than the Seine, full of French, English, Dutch, Chinese, Japanese and Siamese vessels, and an uncountable number of barges and gilded galleys with sixty oarsmen. The king is beginning to build ships in the European manner; three have recently been launched on to the waters. But something still more admirable is that on both sides of this island are the quarters or villages inhabited by the different nationalities; all the wooden houses are in the water . . . The streets are alleys of fresh flowing water as far as the eye can see, under huge green trees, and in these tiny houses there is a great crowd of people. Slightly beyond the villages are broad landscapes of rice which one passes through by boat. The rice is always above the water; and the horizon is limited by big trees, above which one sees here and there the shining towers and pyramids of the pagodas covered with two or three layers of gilding. I do not know if I am presenting your imagination with an attractive view, but certainly I have never seen anything finer, though with the exception of the pagodas everything is still of natural simplicity.

The Siamese have always been a curious people – it is one of the hallmarks of their culture – while their confidence in themselves allows them to explore foreign ideas without fear that their way of life will be compromised. Indeed, the genius of their culture is that it can absorb new ideas and influences, digesting, incorporating, then expressing them in a uniquely Siamese style. During the reign of King Narai the Great (1656–88), this interaction reached a fevered pitch. At this time there were emissaries in Ayuthyia from many countries: Persia, Portugal, India, China, Japan, England and Holland. Hungry for treaties and trade, these countries opened embassies. The city became an entrepôt.

One Greek adventurer, Constantine Faulkon, originally employed by the English East India Company, was washed ashore with a Siamese ambassador after a shipwreck in the Gulf of Siam. Through good luck, determination, great skill, acumen, betrayal and much ingratiation, he eventually became a government minister in charge of the country's exchequer and foreign affairs for the last three years of King Narai's reign.

Prince Damrong, a son of King Rama V, sombrely reflected in the early twentieth century on an alternative view of some of the fruits of trading:

> during that period the Portuguese appear to have brought to the Siamese three things, namely the art of making fire-arms, the way to use fire-arms in warfare, and the adoption of fortification against fire-arms . . . Perhaps there were other things that the Portuguese brought to the Siamese . . .

Indeed there were. The Portuguese introduced a new spice to Thai cooking. It was readily absorbed into the cuisine, to such a degree that Thai food today is inconceivable without it – the chilli. One reference, admittedly unsupported, remarkably suggests that Portuguese mariners ate chillies as a fierce anti-scorbutic, because – like limes and sauerkraut – their high vitamin C content prevented scurvy. The chilli arrived in Thailand sometime after 1511, the year the first Portuguese envoy came to Siam.

No doubt the chilli was originally eyed with some suspicion (as was the tomato in sixteenth-century Italy) but soon this new, fiery ingredient was incorporated into Siamese cuisine with gusto. Perhaps it was assimilated so readily because a similar taste already existed in Siamese cooking – that of the fresh green peppercorn or, when out of season, a combination of white pepper pounded with dried galangal and salt.

The late seventeenth century was a high point for Siamese cooking. It was a period of prosperity and security, two prerequisites for a flourishing cuisine. Moreover, there were new influences and ingredients that stimulated innovation. For example, a Siamese journal of that era records an extraordinary dish of ground and deep-fried fish mixed with sugar and salt, served with fresh and deep-fried shallots and, improbably, watermelon.

European chroniclers of the time commented: 'There are no people more frugal than the Siamese. The common people only drink water and are content to eat rice, which they cook, some fruit and a little dried fish in the sun', wrote Nicolas Gervaise, a French Jesuit missionary in the late seventeenth century. Indeed, throughout the history of Siam and Thailand, little seems to have altered in the diet of the common farmer; it is determined, as it always has been, by what can be grown or caught near the paddy. Gervaise continued, in his book *The Natural and Political History of the Kingdom of Siam*:

> they mix with all their stews a certain paste made of rotten prawns, called capy in Thai . . . which has a pungent smell that nauseates anyone not accustomed to it. It is said to give meat a certain zest which whets the appetite . . . so that to make a good sauce in the Siamese manner salt, pepper, ginger, cinnamon, cloves, garlic, white onions, nutmeg and several strongly flavoured herbs must be mixed in considerable quantities with this shrimp paste. At banquets the dishes are served all higgledy-piggledy and in no particular order, with fruit and rice in vessels of gold, silver and porcelain.

In response to a French diplomatic mission to Siam in 1685, King Narai sent three envoys to the court of the Sun King the following year. They caused great excitement at the newly completed palace of Versailles, with their exotic dress and even stranger manners. During the audience, Louis XIV bade them rise from the floor as they had 'come from too far not to be permitted to see Us', but they refused, as in their own court this impudent breach of etiquette would result in banishment or perhaps even death. The Siamese chief ambassador, Chao Phraya Kosaparn, recorded his travels. His impressions of the French and their manners, Versailles and Catholicism make interesting reading and they are certainly a refreshing counter-balance to the Western journals of the time. On French food, Kosaparn observed that wine, 'helps give taste to the food which otherwise be insipid to our palates; here are few spices and much meat, and an attraction of quantity replaces piquant wholesomeness'. Touché.

Ayuthyia was at its alluring pinnacle. The sumptuous display in this golden city enticed many European adventurers and privateers. Their rapaciousness and reckless manners, combined with the arrogance of their diplomats, soon gave the Siamese cause for concern and regret. Sadly, but inevitably, this period of openness came to a close in 1688, due to the machinations of various European powers who were trying to ensure favourable trading agreements with the Siamese.

The French not only vied for trade but for souls too, seeking to convert King Narai to Catholicism. Outraged at such temerity, the more conservative elements at court staged a coup d'état on the king's death. Those associated with the previous regime were removed from power or executed: Constantine Faulkon was beheaded, many foreigners were expelled and the court became more rigid, traditional and insular. In one of the small ironies of history, Kosaparn, who had written so tellingly of his time in France, commanded the siege of the French garrison fort at a small village called Bangkok. The French soon surrendered, were expelled and departed for India.

Siam, however, did not completely rebuff the outside world as China had, nor close itself off like Japan, but it did want to stem the tide of Europeans and control their flow. Siam remained quite unresponsive to the West for several generations.

THE FALL OF AYUTHYIA

Throughout its history Siam was regularly, almost consistently, at war with one of its neighbours. Siam was in fact a loose conglomeration of provinces and fiefdoms, with borders and allegiances in a constant state of flux. During the four centuries of the Ayuthyian kingdom there were only two periods of peace, altogether a total of 130 years. Occasionally Ayuthyia fought with the neighbouring Laotian and Vietnamese kingdoms. Most often it was at war with the Burmese kingdom of Pegu. It was also necessary for Siam to keep in check the virtually independent nobles and chieftains at the periphery of its territory – sometimes even in its heartlands. To support these incessant battles a system of compulsory labour was established. The corvée system brought all eligible males between 18 and 60 under the direct control of the capital. The traditional period of duty was six months per year; later, in the eighteenth and nineteenth centuries, this was reduced to four months or a fee charged in lieu. In time of war or necessity, such service would be at the king's prerogative.

Although most men were pressed into the army, other tasks were allotted: digging irrigation canals and removing built-up silt; sowing, harvesting and milling rice; the supervision of the king's elephant herds. A man's wrist was tattooed for corvée, clearly indicating his government department and position. Those conscripted could be moved anywhere around the country; for instance, Laotians from Vientiane were relocated to the central plains in a vain attempt to divert the Chao Phraya River to increase the rice harvest. As recently as 1870, the population of a Laotian village was moved from the Mekong deep into the central plains for two years until their assigned task of irrigation works was completed. Today, the Thai will often greet each other with an easy *bai nai* or *bai nai maa*, 'Where are you going?' or 'Where have you been?'. These innocent inquiries belie their darker origin, when the conscripts asked each other earnest questions regarding where they were being sent or where they had worked.

Siam had been invaded many times, but in 1569 Ayuthyia fell to the invading Burmese armies after a prolonged and debilitating war that saw betrayal at court and the defection of allies and major regional vassals, the ravaging of loyal provinces including, eventually, Ayuthyia itself, and finally the subjugation and stagnation of the country. A Thai quisling, Maha Thammaracha, was installed as king and his son, Naresuan, was sent to the Burmese court to ensure the amenability of his father. For 23 years Siam floundered, vulnerable to all. Even its erstwhile vassal, Cambodia, invaded and regained territory.

In 1590 Naresuan rallied the Thai army and over the next three years restored confidence in Ayuthyia and dominion over rebellious provinces of Siam: the central plains, Laos, Cambodia and part of the Isthmus of Kra. After a few successful skirmishes, Naresuan engaged the Burmese at Nong Sarai. In an episode that is regaled with pride in the annals of the Thai, Naresuan issued a personal challenge to the Burmese crown prince to fight a duel on elephants. They engaged and, after a few thrashing manoeuvres, the elephants locked together. A gruesome, bloody swordfight ensued. Naresuan triumphed, slaying the prince, whose army fell into disarray and retreated. Siam's independence was re-established.

Another war had been fought in the mid-fifteenth century, when the Burmese king of Pegu became envious of the large number of white elephants owned by the Siamese king. Although this may seem an insufficient, somewhat petulant *casus belli*, in South East Asia albino elephants are auspicious and an august manifestation of prestige – Buddhist scriptures recount

that the penultimate incarnation of the Buddha was as a white elephant. They therefore hold a very respected position. When one was found in Siam there was much celebration. Such elephants were brought to the capital and installed with much ceremony in their own palace and kept in great state, often at ruinous cost, having cooks and servants to attend them, including a human wet nurse for the unweaned. So esteemed were these beasts that one later diplomatic dispatch described a bewitching Queen Victoria thus: 'her eyes, complexion and, above all, her bearing are those of a beautiful and majestic white elephant'. For a monarch to have one was a vindication of celestial favour; to have several signified inestimable merit. As a corollary, for one to die – or, even worse, for the king to have none – implied a spiritual deficit on the part of the monarch, which could threaten his mandate, and thus the state.

Constant skirmishes over elephants eventually led to a war with Pegu that resulted in the fall of Ayuthyia in 1767. Such was the magnitude of this defeat that, according to some estimates, only 10,000 of the city's 300,000 inhabitants were left free. Art treasures, monks, cooks, elephant and horse 'medicine men' and, intriguingly, 'coiffeurs and nautch girls' were among the booty taken to Pegu, just as the Siamese had plundered Angkor some 300 years earlier. The city was totally razed, its records burnt in the conflagration. Thus, sadly, most accounts of Siam before this time must rely on the sometimes disingenuous observations of foreigners.

Ayuthyian society was left in utter devastation. Desecrated Buddhas still forlornly survey the ruins of Ayuthyia today (pictured on previous page). The king, although claiming sanctuary in a temple, was killed. The Burmese wanted revenge and loot: nobody was spared and little remained. Describing the calamitous aftermath, one disconsolate monk, Somdet Phra Wannarat, later wrote:

> The populace was afflicted with a variety of ills by the enemy. Some wandered about, starving, searching for food. They were bereft of their families, their children and wives, and stripped of their possessions and tools . . . They had no rice, no fish, no clothing. They were thin, their bodies wasting away. They found only the leaves of trees and grass to eat . . . In desperation many turned to dacoity . . . They gathered in bands, and plundered for rice and paddy and salt. Some found food, and others could not. They grew thinner, and their flesh and blood wasted away. Afflicted with a thousand ills, some died and some lived on.

Those in such an atrocious position were not of the lower classes, accustomed to the vicissitudes of fate, but nobles and courtiers, who had been certain of their superior position and now were robbed of place and privilege.

A NEW BEGINNING

Although Ayuthyia and its surrounding area were despoiled, the remainder of the country was largely untouched. Ayuthyia had unified a vast and culturally diverse area and after its destruction the kingdom fell into total disarray, fragmenting into fiefdoms with several rival claimants to the throne and their respective supporters vying for power. One of the larger remnants of the city rallied under General Taksin who, with a battalion of soldiers fortuitously saved from the catastrophe, repaired down the Chao Phraya River to Dtonburi, opposite Bangkok. There Taksin assumed the monarchy and, after a series of brilliant and rapid campaigns, regained almost all the territory previously allied to Ayuthyia. In battle he was a successful warrior; in peace, however, he became a deluded and vengeful autocrat – he believed he was the incarnation of the Buddha and that he could fly, executing those who demurred. Eventually he was deposed, accused of madness and heresy. One of his generals, Chao Phraya Chakri, became king, moved the capital across the river to what is now Bangkok and established the current dynasty.

All kings of this dynasty are styled Rama after the hero prince of the *Ramayana*, an epic tale known throughout all of southern Asia. Rama ruled over the sacred city of Ayodhya and was renowned for his courage and piety. He was believed to be the incarnation of Vishnu, the god of royalty. Rama was also the name of the first kings of Sukothai and Ayuthyia, Ramakhamhaeng and Ramathibodi respectively, which conferred even greater prestige on this dynastic title. Each king was named Rama, and his reign was distinguished by a number.

King	Personal name	Reign
Rama I	Phra Phutthayotfa	1782–1809
Rama II	Phra Phutthaloetla	1809–24
Rama III	Phra Nangklao	1824–51
Rama IV	Mongkut	1851–68
Rama V	Chulalongkorn	1868–1910

King	Personal name	Reign
Rama VI	Vajiravudh	1910–25
Rama VII	Prajadhipok	1925–35 (abdicated)
Rama VIII	Ananda Mahidol	1935–46
Rama IX	Bhumibol Adulyadej	1946–

To ensure continuity with the past, to salve and reassure the Siamese after their violent disloca-
tion, and perhaps to consolidate his control, Rama I created his new capital in the image of
Ayuthyia. Even the stones were transported from the old city. Canals were dug to replicate the
island capital and the Grand Palace was based on recollections of the one in Ayuthyia. Court
ritual and etiquette were reinstated. This was all to reproduce the environment in which the
Siamese had previously thrived and so allow the continuation of their culture and tradition. At
times of threat, confusion or consolidation, the Thai have always become culturally introspec-
tive, seeking answers – or at least comfort – in their past. The conflict between responding
to the new and relying upon the old creates a fundamental dynamic in Thai culture.

Bangkok – meaning 'village of the hog plum' – is in fact the name of the
village where the new capital was founded. In Thai, however, the city has an extraordinarily
long, formal name: Krung Thep Maha Nakorn Amorn Ratanakosindra Mahindrayudhya
Mahadilokpop Noparatana Rajdhani Burirom Udom Rajanivet Mahastan Amorn Pimarn
Avatarn Satit Sakkatuttiya Vishnukarm Prasit. This translates as 'The City of Angels, the Great
City, the Residence of the Emerald Buddha, the Impregnable City of the God Indra, the Grand
Capital of the World Endowed with the Nine Precious Gems, the Happy City, Abounding in
Grand Palaces that Resemble the Heavenly Abode of the Incarnated God, a City Dedicated
to Indra, Built by Vishnu'. Mercifully, it is normally abbreviated to Krung Thep.

When the Temple of the Emerald Buddha (pictured opposite), the royal
temple in the Grand Palace, was consecrated in 1809, some 2000 monks took part in the ceremony. This was a time of great celebration as it was believed that, with this inauguration, the
dignity of the Siamese state was finally being restored after 50 years of disarray. The official
chronicle describes the chanting of the monks and the subsequent feast. A grilled sausage of
pork and crab, a *panaeng* curry of chicken, salted duck eggs and ground fish with watermelon
were among the delectable savoury dishes. Desserts followed – a coconut and egg custard,
jade-coloured glutinous rice, and 'golden strands' made from duck eggs.

The West began to engage with Siam again during the reign of Rama II, 150 years after the debacle under King Narai. Although encounters with the West had never been entirely absent during the intervening time, they had been insignificant, with only the Dutch maintaining an official embassy. One early nineteenth-century English envoy, John Crawfurd, who was sent to re-establish contact with the Siamese, described the prospering city of Bangkok thus:

> Numerous temples of Buddha with tall spires attached to them, frequently glittering with gilding, were conspicuous among the mean huts and hovels of the natives, throughout which were interspersed a profusion of palms, ordinary fruit and the sacred fig (*po*) . . . The face of the river presented a busy scene, from the number of boats and canoes of every size and description that were passing to and fro. The number of these struck us as very great at the time, for we were not aware that there are no or few roads in Bangkok and that the river and canals form common highways, not only for goods but for passengers of every description. Many of the boats were shops containing earthenware, and *blanchang* [*gapi*], a fetid condiment in very general use composed of bruised shrimps and small fish. Vendors of these several commodities were hawking and crying them as in a European town.

King Rama II was a great aesthete, whose inheritance today can be seen in many of the buildings in the Royal Palace. He was also quite probably the only ruling monarch ever to have written an epic poem on love, food, women and their foibles: the Boat Songs. These were composed to inspire the oarsmen of his royal barges to work harder and in unison – it is very typical of the Thai to sweeten their labour by dreaming of delights.

Mussaman geng gao dtar	Mussaman curry is like a lover
Horm yii raa rot rorn reng	As peppery and fragrant as the cumin seed
Chai dai day gleun geng	Its exciting allure arouses
Reng yark hai fi fan haa	I am urged to seek its source

Latiang kit dtiang norng	Latiang is like the pillow on which I dream
Norng dtiang tong tam meung bon	And to the heavens from which I rise,
Lot lang chan chorp gon	Yet upon my unsettling return
Yorn yark nit trar kit naep norn	I find close comfort only with you

Sangkaya nar dtang kai	The rich custard
Kao nio sai sii soek sadtaeng	On the grains of rice shows its sallow
Ben nai mai kleuap klang	Silent sadness all too clearly
Jang war jao sao soek leua	Broken, like my heart, for the love of you

WESTERN OVERTURES

The mid-nineteenth century was a dangerous time for Siam. As the two great imperial powers of Europe, Britain and France, colonised Asia, the Siamese were obliged to resume closer diplomatic relations with Europeans. Rama III assumed the throne at a time when the English had just annexed part of Burma and were encroaching on Siam's southern borders at Kelantan. The French were gaining footholds in Cochin China.

Rama III rejected most diplomatic approaches by the West for fear of the consequences, but Rama IV made several treaties with Westerners, beginning with the British in 1855, then with the French and Americans, Portuguese, Prussians, Dutch and Scandinavians – all of whom sued for trade concessions. While the concessions made by Siam were considerable, King Rama IV and his advisors knew that to reject them might lead to Siamese sovereignty being compromised, and eventually to the surrendering of independence. Siam may only have managed to maintain its sovereignty because of this complex maze of diplomatic treaties and understandings. The result of the myriad agreements was such that no European power could dominate without infringing upon the position of another. None dared move; there was a political impasse. Yet, surprisingly, in this tense diplomatic atmosphere, the Siamese prospered.

The Bowring Treaty of 1855 had vast ramifications, as it set Siam on the path of economic development but at the same time allowed the erosion of its domestic industries. It reduced the import tariff rate to 3 per cent and soon foreign, cheap, manufactured products flooded the market, undermining locally made goods. For example, the fragile earthenware pots made in every large provincial town and traditionally used to cook rice and curries were replaced with sturdy metal pans from the United States, Prussia and England. At the same time, however, one area of the economy expanded. The Siamese traded the crop that grew so very well – rice. Bangkok prospered as rice was exported, its revenue doubling between 1850 and 1868. New markets for rice opened all over the world. Siam became increasingly dependent on this grain as its main source of revenue – at the cost of its economic independence. Most merchants were either Chinese or European. The Europeans, mainly English, controlled all shipping and the markets to which the products were sold.

As further treaties were signed, embassies were opened. There were more Westerners – diplomats, government advisors, traders and missionaries – in Siam than there had been in Ayuthyia during its golden days. King Mongkut employed Western officials in his government and even his palace, the most famous of these being Anna Leonowens, governess to his children and the author of a somewhat disingenuous account of her stay in Siam, *The English Governess at the Siamese Court.*

THE MODERNISATION OF SIAM – AND ITS PLACE IN THE WORLD

Until this time there were few roads in Bangkok, all commercial buildings and most residences hugged either the Chao Phraya River or were situated on the canals that served as highways and gave rise to one Western name for Bangkok in this era, the Venice of the East. Anything that needed to be transported could easily be taken by boat. Rice was floated downstream on large, sinister-looking barges to the warehouses of Bangkok's Chinatown; fresh vegetables, fish, ducks and chickens were sent to the main market that still services Bangkok today. During the rainy season, most of Bangkok was – and still is – submerged under the deluge, making roads useless and canals the only means to move about the city. However, the increasing European population was uncomfortable with this practical, but for them unfamiliar mode of transport. Certain of the superiority of their ways, the Europeans petitioned the king to build a road parallel to the river that would allow them to conduct themselves in the manner to which they were accustomed. Within a decade, there were roads crossing and surrounding the city. There were even sufficient business travellers to warrant the building of a gracious hotel, the Oriental, which opened in 1876. Under Rama IV and his son, Bangkok was transformed from a medieval backwater to the capital of a prospering kingdom.

Siam had always thought itself a major power in the region, which in the terms of its understanding meant the world. It considered itself second only to China. The Siam of Rama I extended from northern Laos and Cambodia to Singapore. Some of this area was truly Siamese, but much was surrounding territory that paid tribute to Siam. Such tribute might be in money or trade, wives or even golden trees, which were a symbolic gesture of allegiance. Sometimes such a client province found no conflict in paying tribute to two dominant states, and yet still felt itself to be independent. Control of outlying regions was at best tenuous. Officials or hereditary rulers of these states had little interference from Bangkok – or earlier, Ayuthyia. This loose confederation of allegiances was the modus operandi of Siam.

The encroaching Western empires, accustomed to chauvinism and set national borders, were at first confused by such laxity but soon exploited this uncertainty. They began to exert their influence in the region, removing piecemeal provinces, towns and regions from Siam's control. Within 40 years over one-third of Siam's traditionally held territories had been ceded to the exacting French and pragmatic English. As Lord Rosebery, the then English Foreign Secretary, memorably observed, Siam was like an artichoke, 'devoured a leaf at a time'.

During the reign of Rama V (Chulalongkorn), Siam continued to engage with Western powers. Unprecedentedly, the king twice left the country to travel to Europe, in 1897 and 1907, with the aim of cementing diplomatic agreements and securing the most advantageous treaties possible. This probably helped to ensure the sovereignty of Siam, unique in Asia during this imperialistic age. Another factor in Siam's independence may have been the need for France and Britain to have a buffer state between their respective colonies.

The king's aim was to equip his country to face the modern world and protect it from foreign 'usurpation', but diplomacy was only one aspect of this programme. Until the reign of Chulalongkorn, Siam's system of government and its administration had remained largely unchanged since Ayuthyia's heyday. If Siam were to become a modern state, Rama V believed he needed to fundamentally reorganise the government. He relied on his brothers, especially princes Damrong and Devawongse, to assist him. Within 30 years the Siamese system of administration was transformed from a medieval suzerainty into a viable state. Bangkok asserted control over its traditional areas of influence. Semi-independent rulers were sworn to the state yet retained their ceremonial position, or were removed from power. Railways were built to the north and south, allowing fast transportation of goods and, if necessary, troops. Telegraph connected the distant provinces to Bangkok, so that communication could be effective and swift. The lower Chao Phraya delta was cleared with farmers who were encouraged to grow rice for export. It was a radical transformation – the Chakri Revolution – orchestrated from the very pinnacle of society.

King Chulalongkorn created new, effective ministries along Western lines, headed by his sons, many of whom were educated overseas – several in England, some in France, a few in Germany and even one in Russia. One prince, Chirapravati, spent 11 of his first 20 years abroad. Tension grew between the progressives and the conservatives, those educated overseas and those not. Rama V's style of government was oligarchic – his immediate family assisted in the ruling of the country, and they deferred to him. But this sowed seeds of disaffection as traditional paths to power for the nobility were closed. However, given the character and ability of the king, little dissension occurred during his reign.

The princes were often assisted in government by Western advisors who resided in Siam, just as foreigners had assisted the kingdom of Ayuthia. Trading companies, diplomats, travellers, missionaries and businessmen were mostly based in Bangkok; many of these wrote journals during their stay. Charles Buls reported in *Siamese Sketches*:

> The Royal Palace, bordered by its picturesque, sparkling white, crenellated wall immediately attracts attention. It forms the nucleus of the city and it is surrounded by the first canal. Then come[s] the royal quarter, also encircled by a broad wall, cut by towers and covered with climbing plants. A canal runs outside this second enclosure. Finally, a third canal encircles the rest of the metropolitan area . . . Formerly the palaces, the temples and the houses, which are situated along these canals, had no other access and all traffic was by barge . . . The present King, Chulalongkorn, has created large streets, avenues planted with trees, in all directions . . . From the heights of our observation post we contemplate the extraordinary liveliness that reigns on the dazzling stream . . .
>
> From the royal quarter rise the triple roofs and triple arrows, golden, sparkling, flaming, characteristic elements of Siamese architecture. Then, surrounding them, there is a forest of white, golden or enamel spires, flanking the numerous temples. The effect is overcoming for the newcomer. This is the Indies of which one dreams with its fantastic palaces, its golden minarets, its perfumed gardens, concealing pavilions, that are inlaid with mother-of-pearl and precious stones, the mysteries of the harem.

THE INFLUENCE OF WESTERN CUSTOMS

Siam was a very fertile country, able to grow almost any produce. New vegetables were soon planted to accommodate the needs of the foreigners, such as asparagus, beloved vegetable of the nineteenth century and called in Thai 'Westerner's bamboo'. The comfortingly familiar peas and carrots – the latter called 'orange long turnips' in Thai – also appeared fresh on the tables of Westerners living in Siam. Meat, traditionally eschewed by Thai Buddhists, was now sold in the marketplace.

As Siam flourished, even faced with the spectre of imperialism, it embraced more Western customs and accoutrements, as if to indicate its status as a civilised country in terms that the West could recognise. The traditional manner of eating with hands was discarded by the upper classes, as first spoons and then forks were adopted. Glass and tableware became symbols of wealth and prestige to the status-sensitive Siamese.

King Rama V was a great gourmet who loved to relax and idle over food. He welcomed a simpler style of Thai cooking, in contrast to the exquisite heights of Siamese cuisine that were often served to him at his court. When Chulalongkorn travelled to Europe he kept a diary, recounting his experiences, his impressions of the European courts and the industry and society of those countries; he also detailed their customs, entertainments and food. His account of his European sojourn is filled with entries fondly recalling his country and longing for the things he most loved: shrimp paste relish (*nahm prik gapi*), deep-fried dried fish with pickled garlic – and his wives. Tantalised, he dreamt of salted duck eggs, red curries soured with kaffir lime juice, deep-fried prawn cakes and cucumber relish, but instead he was served bortsch, roast beef and Yorkshire pudding.

At the turn of the century, Western food was often served at Siamese state functions, which were attended by many Western diplomats and advisors. This was not just for reasons of statecraft – the Siamese recognised that European cuisine, with its steady progression of courses, was more suited to formal occasions than Siamese cuisine and its manner of eating. They also realised that adopting it was a diplomatic tool reflecting the level of sophistication and modernity of Siam. There was, too, an element of innate courtesy in serving it: the Siamese understood that some of their Western guests found Siamese food not just unpalatable but inedible. Moreover, the Siamese were genuinely delighted with this different cuisine and novel manner of eating, which offered them an array of new tastes to savour in a way that entertained yet also allowed the business of diplomacy to be performed.

A menu for a dinner at the Grand Palace on 23 February 1900 included: *poisson de mer, sauce au beurre*; *pâté aux doves*; *poulet, sauce chaud-froid*; *aspic de foie gras* and, somewhat further down the menu, *plats Siamois*. One noblewoman recorded in her journal how enterprising ladies of the court transformed and 'Siam-ised' the *poulet* with *chaud-froid* sauce from poached chicken coated with jellied stock enriched with a velouté sauce to minced chicken dressed with Asian citron juice, pickled garlic and ground roasted rice, set in a coconut agar-agar.

Sophisticated though European food was acknowledged to be by the Siamese — and in this appraisal they were far more open-minded than their European counterparts — it was still a delicious second to their own cuisine. During another court function the menu consisted solely of Siamese food, a re-creation of Rama II's Boat Songs. There were 35 savoury dishes and 30 desserts.

The reign of Chulalongkorn marked another high point in Siamese culture, and consequently its food. Siam's prosperity encouraged enterprise and the incorporation and adaptation of ideas from the outside, both by the state and in its cuisine. Siam was led by a monarch who ruled strongly and wisely, and who naturally commanded respect. Like his father Mongkut before him, Chulalongkorn guided Siam safely through perhaps one of the most dangerous times in its history. While the area of the country diminished, Siam's sense of nationhood greatly increased; it was the only country in South East Asia not to be colonised.

THE TRANSFER OF POWER

Successions to the Siamese throne were rarely smooth. There were always power struggles as various prospective and ambitious sons — usually only those of high-born mothers who were considered acceptable candidates — manoeuvred into likely succession by aligning themselves with powerful families, such as the Bunnark, Singhaseni and Siriwatthanakun, and their factions. Prince Mongkut's suit to become King Rama IV was ensured by powerful Bunnark support. His son, Chulalongkorn, struggled under the regency of another member of the Bunnark clan.

A fundamental constituent of the political history of Siam was the continuing power struggle between these great families and the throne. The Chakri Revolution centralised power in the king, his family and Bangkok. The influence of the ancient families was curtailed for the next 50 years, until the absolute monarchy was toppled in 1932 by the disaffected scions of the new élite.

By the time of King Rama V's death in 1910, Siam was fully engaged with the West. The new king, Vajiravudh, had been educated at Eton and was thoroughly Westernised – to the extent of appearing affected in the eyes of some of his conservative courtiers. The many years of prosperity meant that not only had the sons of the king and high nobles been educated overseas, but also those of the rising economic élite, both Siamese and Chinese. The oligarchic government by the sons of the king, although satisfactory when instituted some 40 years before, was now seen to be antiquated. More of the élite wished to be involved in the business of government; the fruits of education had begun to ripen. However, they were excluded from most aspects of government. Only one avenue was open to these families – the army, which was set to play a greater role in the fortunes of Siam than it had in the past.

Late in the First World War, Siam joined the Allies, not only because of the beliefs held by its Anglophile monarch but also in the hope that, when the war was over, some redress would be made for the unfair and onerous treaties imposed on it during the previous century. After protracted negotiations, this was finally achieved in the mid-1920s and was accompanied by a surge in national pride. Yet, at the same time, the export price of rice reached unprecedented lows, and this was compounded by a series of disastrous rice crops. The dichotomy between national pride and economic turmoil rent the fabric of society.

In 1925, King Rama VI's only child, a daughter, was born. Two days later, he died and was succeeded by one of his brothers. King Prajadhipok was the seventy-sixth son of Chulalongkorn and was not expected to assume the crown. By nature intelligent but shy, he was untrained. Worse, he inherited an unstable economy, a privy purse that was empty, and an élite clamouring for a greater share of power.

As the economy had grown over the previous half-century, for the first time a Thai urban class had appeared. Thai are traditionally rice farmers, not traders. The traders of Siam came from a group not attached to the land – almost invariably, the Chinese. From the time of Sukothai and Ayuthyia, the Chinese had been the merchant class and had prospered in the cities. One keen observer, Malcolm Smith, described the hierarchy of Bangkok, in *A Physician at the Court of Siam*, in the following terms:

> The number of Chinese living there was greater than the number of
> Siamese, a somewhat surprising affair until one considers the structure of
> the community which formed the city. The Chinese were the shopkeepers
> and merchants, and nearly all the trade of the city was in their hands.

> The Siamese, on the other hand, were the administrators, men drawn
> from every rank, whose whole existence centred around the Court, each
> one dependent for his living upon the man above him. Princes, nobles,
> lesser officials, underlings, servants to name them in a descending scale,
> formed together a giant pyramid, on the summit of which sat the King.

This new urban élite, unlike that of previous generations, did not derive its wealth or position from the patronage of the king or his court, so they had less allegiance to the crown. The king, while hardworking, did not inspire great loyalty at this time of economic uncertainty. And the situation was exacerbated by the Wall Street crash.

These factors led inexorably to a coup d'état. On 24 June 1932, a bloodless coup ended the absolute monarchy of Siam. In a manner typical of the Thai, while the king's prerogatives were curtailed, the king himself was not removed. But over the next two years relations steadily deteriorated between the new government and the king and, in March 1935, Rama VII abdicated. He was succeeded by a young boy, Rama VIII, who spent the next nine years in Switzerland completing his education before returning to Siam, only to die in mysterious circumstances six months later. In 1946 his brother – the current king, Bhumibol – acceded to the throne.

MODERN THAILAND

The influence of the monarchy and court has been eroded in modern Thailand. In the sixth reign, society changed also, but in a rather different way. Then the king actually led the Westernisation of society and the discarding of traditional customs. He instituted surnames; before this time all Thai people were simply known by their first name or a nickname. Furthermore, Rama VI was instrumental in the development of a system to transcribe English letters for the Thai alphabet. Since Rama VII had only one wife (previous kings had had an inordinate number), the high culture of the court and its ladies went into rapid decline. The rising élite considered the court's traditional customs quaintly anachronistic and, having less allegiance to the court, felt little commitment to maintaining such antiquated practices. By the 1950s, this Siamese manner of living was all but extinct.

In the 1940s and 1950s, the government embarked upon a bizarre programme of legislation designed to hasten the Westernisation of the country – at least in appearance. In 1949, the country's name was changed from the exotic Siam to the more prosaic Thailand.

The chewing of betel nuts, a national addiction, was banned. Even more peculiarly, the government attempted to force public demonstrations of affection between the sexes, a strange and surprising piece of legislation, as the Thai have always been, and still are, reticent. Hats became de rigueur, too.

Later, during the Vietnam War, Thailand was filled with American troops on leave. Hamburgers, ketchup and Coke abounded. One memorable dish of the time was American fried rice – rice with tomato sauce. This marked the beginning of the commercialisation of Thailand, as society and cooks began to cater to the American presence.

Although the urban Thai indulged in Western food and Western manners, this was merely the superficial expression of their break with the past. Significantly, I think, while all was changing around them, people still relished traditional food, finding it a source of certainty and comfort.

The Thai have always relied upon their strong culture to maintain their sense of identity and community. At times of threat or change their traditions become a source of reassurance and inspiration, as the Thai find succour in their past. What is unique about the Thai is their ability to balance the past with the present. This type of continuity braces the community against change, and comforts and affirms when things are most uncertain. The Thai are indeed fortunate to have such a deep well of cuisine and culture.

2   CULT

JRE AND SOCIETY

History is the passage of the past to the present; culture, then, is the reflection of this journey – it expresses the beliefs of the past in the present. The bonds that unite a nation are the result of an accumulation of incidents, beliefs and prejudices. Over a long and eventful history the Thai experience has resulted in a singularly powerful culture, strong in the confidence of its past and able to respond with flexibility to new influences. Like bamboo, the Thai symbol of resilience, it bends with the wind but never breaks. The daily observance of age-old customs and rituals defines and reaffirms Thailand's unique character, giving dimension and meaning to these practices.

THE IMPORTANCE OF BUDDHISM

Buddhism coheres all aspects of Thai culture and society. Monks are present at every milestone in the life of a Thai, and at every occasion that recalls a prominent episode in history. Birth, death, marriage, the building of a house, the coronation of a king, the signing of a new diplomatic treaty or even the commissioning of an aeroplane: all are blessed by monks. No occasion has worth or merit without them. Buddhism stamps its imprimatur on all things Thai.

Monks chant sacred texts in Pali at every event, edifying those present. Such is the power of the words that, although the language is incomprehensible to most, the listeners' spirits are still nurtured and illuminated. After such rites, monks are fed. This is an act of merit that improves the karma of the donor. All Thai, from the king to the poorest peasant, regard the monks as the soul of the country.

Understanding karma is essential in order to understand the inherent structure of Thai society. All Thai have an allotted position in a hierarchy where no one is equal. Age, wealth, education and birth all help to determine one's standing in relation to others. Such inequality may be repugnant to Westerners, but to the Thai it is ordained. As Buddhists, they believe that the circumstances surrounding their current incarnation are determined by karma. If they have been meritorious in their previous life, the benefits are realised in this one. Conversely, if their last life was reprehensible, their present life will be arduous.

Karma is immutable, so one must accept one's current circumstances with gracious resignation. To rail against them invites worse to come. The aim of Buddhism is to reduce and ultimately end the suffering that is an inevitable part of living, as its followers will eventually attain enlightenment, ending the cycle of reincarnation. To reach enlightenment, however, may take myriad reincarnations. Buddhism attempts to quell the passions that distort reality and disturb one needlessly in the brief interlude called life. It teaches that one should tranquilly accept whatever happens. It encourages tolerance by accepting that others are also on the path to enlightenment, although at different stages and therefore with different understanding. By such resignation one becomes less attached to the transient illusion of life; this begets serenity and so the cycle of life can be observed imperturbably. Perhaps this is why the Thai are so relaxed, gentle and warm, and may also help to explain two of their most endearing traits: the enjoyment of all things (*sanuk*) and the refusal to be too disturbed by problems (*my ben rai*).

Paradoxically, Buddhism also teaches that one must accept responsibility for oneself. Right-mindfulness and Right Action are two basic tenets of Buddhist teaching. Right-mindfulness is the capacity to perceive the truth with equanimity and then to achieve it. Every right thought improves the mind's ability to understand. It obliges concentration solely on the moment, unfettered by the past and unconcerned for the future. Right Action is the realisation of Right-mindfulness. Every action should express the best intention and strive for the best result, focused on what is at hand. Everything therefore should be done as skilfully as possible. Action or ritual creates, evolves and indicates an insightful mind. All actions should reflect this.

This is, I believe, the fundamental motivation behind skilled Thai craftsmanship. Not every action performed is considered to be a religious act, but the effect is, nonetheless, the same. Every job should be executed as perfectly as possible. The Thai aspire to, and delight in, excellence in all aspects of their culture – and their cooking is a delicious manifestation of this.

It is the obligation of every Thai male to become a monk for at least three months, usually around the age of 20, during the rainy season – which is concurrent with the Buddhist Lent. This interlude from the world sustains Buddhism in Thailand by acquainting all men, if only for a brief period, with its basic principles. It is also the rite of passage from childhood to adulthood, conferring prestige and reaffirming ancient cultural traditions. Until a boy has been a monk, he is not considered a man – that is, mature and trustworthy. It is believed that the merit accrued during these three months is often transferred to the mother of the monk, as women are unable to amass merit by such an action. A poor family will often send a young boy to the temple to attend the monks. In return, the monks will educate the boy in the precepts of Buddhism and also give him a secular education, sometimes even to university level, ensuring a better future than would otherwise be possible. Moreover, such service attracts great merit for the boy and his family.

Buddhism proscribes lying, stealing, committing adultery and the consumption of alcohol, but perhaps the most important Buddhist commandment is not to take life. However, the Thai do not maintain a strict vegetarian diet and this has always posed some problem to Buddhists of other nations. The Thai believe that eating meat does not necessarily involve the *taking* of life, as they are not actually killing the animal themselves. Thai fishermen, for example, justify their livelihood by the somewhat evasive reasoning that all they do is catch the fish and remove it from the water. The fish itself then chooses to die. Buying or consuming meat once it has been killed means that the purchaser is not directly responsible for the death of the animal; it is already dead. In Bangkok and larger cities, most butchery is performed by Chinese and Muslims, for whom the taking of an animal's life does not present such quandaries. In the remote countryside, few farmers can afford the luxury of such scruples: what animals they eat, they must kill.

The Thai also believe that the larger the beast, the more spirit it contains and therefore the greater the sin occasioned by the taking of its life. Thus they are reluctant to eat larger beasts, such as water buffalo, but have fewer qualms with smaller animals like birds or fish. This may also be one reason why most flesh is chopped or sliced very finely – in order to turn it into a less disturbingly familiar form.

More strict Buddhists do abstain from eating meat and there is a strong tradition of vegetarianism. Meat does not have a primary role in the cuisine and most Thai will forgo it without great discomfort for a special occasion, to make merit for themselves or another, and may do so once a week over a prolonged period – or completely for a few weeks, even a whole year.

FOOD FOR THE MONKS

It is the duty of every lay person to support the monks by feeding and maintaining them and their temples. Every morning throughout Thailand, at dawn and then again a little before noon, the monks leave their temples and walk along the muddy roads, around bamboo groves, to the green edges of the rice paddies, where they receive food. Even today, in their saffron robes, they wend their way through the mayhem of Bangkok's gridlocked streets, through the din and pollution, past palaces and skyscrapers, possessed of an unswerving tranquillity that transcends the clamorous city.

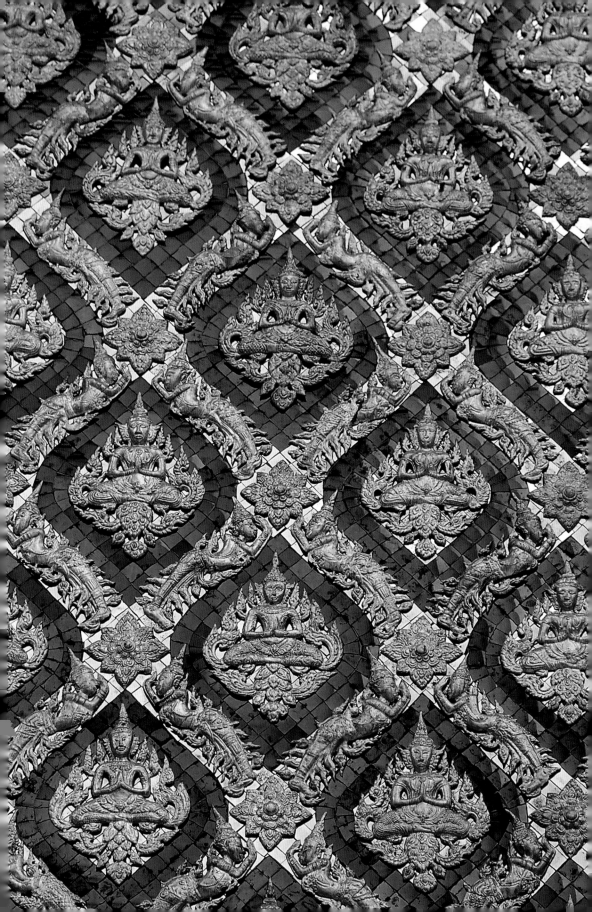

Monks must eat no more than is sufficient to sustain life. Any more would be sinful gluttony. Though they must accept what is given to them – refusal would be arrogant and thus generate bad karma – they might not necessarily eat it, but instead give some to the temple boys, or reserve it to be eaten later. Monks normally eat twice a day, at sunrise and before midday. They are forbidden to eat after midday, although they may drink water throughout the day. Some ascetic monks will eat only once a day.

Ideally, everything should be made especially for the monks. The rice must be freshly steamed, the relishes newly pounded and the curries fried at the time, as any less effort is somewhat unfitting and so results in less merit. Mostly, the food that is offered to monks is the same as the household would eat, though more care is taken, expressing the regard in which the monks are held. Even the poorest farmers offer what they can daily; however, this may just be a part of their own meagre meal, which they serve first to the monks, eating the remainder later.

When offering the monks food, one should be slightly bent over, then afterwards give the traditional sign of respect, the *wai*, by raising both hands with the palms joined and held at eye level – the higher the hands, the greater the respect. While the monks themselves are admired as humans willing to forgo the world and aspiring to enlightenment, it is in fact the saffron robe that is revered as a symbol of the Buddha, his protective aegis and pervading wisdom. The monks must not be touched, for this is impolite – a breach of etiquette. Women are forbidden to hand anything directly to monks; they must first place the item on a piece of cloth on the ground for the monk to pick up. The offering is completed by libation, pouring water over the fingers onto a plate.

Thanpuuying Pliang Pasonagorn, a descendant of Rama II, was the wife of a government minister in the late nineteenth century. She wrote in great detail about the proper etiquette, appropriate to her exalted milieu, of offering food to monks, gods and kings, in a series of small volumes that later became the first published Thai cookbook, *Mae Krua Hua Bark*. One volume included many dishes purported to have been served at the ceremony and subsequent feast inaugurating the Temple of the Emerald Buddha in the Royal Palace in 1809.

There were four trays of food, served in the following order. The first tray contained food for the monks and offerings to the Buddha, while the second, third and fourth trays comprised the meal to be consumed after the ceremony.

The first set, or tray of food, consisted of the 'rice bowl' and 'dishes served on the lid of a monk's bowl'. The 'rice bowl' contained rice for the monks. Only the topmost layer from a pot of steamed rice was used, and this was spooned into a special bowl reserved for serving monks. Then the rice was offered to the monks; a small bowl was also presented to the statue of the Buddha.

The accompanying 'dishes served on the lid of a monk's bowl' were prepared in advance for each monk that attended the ceremony, to take away for later consumption or to be given to the temple boys. A spoonful of rice was put into each monk's bowl and the various dishes put onto the lid of the bowl. Again, a tray was offered to the statue of the Buddha. These dishes, served in small banana-leaf cups, were:

- steamed salted duck eggs or a small grilled crab and pork sausage
- a sponge-like cake or jade sticky rice
- one hand of small bananas, the black stems removed so that nothing imperfect was offered.

The second tray, known as the rice set, held 12 dishes:

- pork and crab sausage
- minced pork bound with roasted rice and pickled garlic (*naem*)
- a mixed salad including prawns, eggs, cucumber and mint
- minced prawns wrapped in egg nets
- stir-fried red curry
- minced chicken and prawn dumplings
- stir-fried dried ground fish served with watermelon or pineapple
- grilled pork with chilli jam
- sweet pork
- a relish of minced pork dressed with roasted coconut and shallots
- stir-fried pork
- deep-fried battered pork.

The third tray held accompanying dishes, served in covered bowls:

- red curry of chicken or beef
- yellow bean and star anise stew with bamboo shoots or lily stalks
- an offal curry with lemongrass
- soup with either pineapple or mangosteen

and, if the host was a farmer, a further dish was served:

- thin rice noodles dressed with wild ginger and minced fish.

Finally came the dessert tray, containing 16 dishes:

- an egg-yolk pastry drenched in sugar syrup
- 'golden strands', made from duck eggs
- yellow bean pudding or peanut pudding
- a layered tapioca pudding
- crystallised coconut
- steamed cup cakes
- candied coconut wrapped in rice-flour pastry
- steamed cakes
- mung bean paste wrapped in egg noodles
- small fruit-like mung bean paste dumplings dipped in agar-agar
- taro paste
- sweetened jade rice
- agar-agar flavoured with fruits
- deep-fried pastry
- tapioca and coconut cream paste
- Asian citron in iced sugar syrup.

Women of Thanpuuying Pliang's rank would prepare all the food themselves, out of respect for the monks and to acquire extra merit for themselves and their households. This immense offering would be served in small enamel bowls on silver trays reserved especially for monks. The portions would be minute, to accord with religious dietary rules. Thanpuuying Pliang helpfully suggested that in reduced circumstances or on a lesser occasion eight items would suffice on the rice tray, with one accompanying dish and five or so desserts.

Food is used as a vehicle to express devotion to the monks and the Buddha. It is not simply a matter of the food alone. Since striving to the utmost of one's ability creates merit, conversely there is less merit if one is lax. The corollary is that the preparation of food has intrinsic value in accruing merit. If a greater array of dishes increases the benefit to the donor, then it follows that increasingly complicated techniques used to produce the food are also of worth. The production of the best, most varied and sophisticated offerings becomes an opportunity to gain more merit. This constant quest for excellence is a further reason, I believe, why Thai food has developed into the immensely complex cuisine it now is.

While the offering of food is meritorious, its primary function is to feed the monks – not to placate gods and idols, as in other rituals. Therefore the symbolic significance of ingredients used in such rites is of less importance than another, more human requirement – taste. Usually, extra food was prepared for a ceremony so that after the monks had been fed the remainder would be shared among those attending. Guests, family and neighbours would all be invited to partake of the splendid repast. Often a little was put aside to make yet another offering to the household's gods and spirits.

TRADITIONAL FAITHS

Although profoundly Buddhist, the Thai have not abandoned the ancient spirits and gods that inhabit their land. Buddhism is a system of beliefs and practices that assists people to attain enlightenment. It does not proscribe other religions; it simply professes to be the most truthful as it tolerantly accepts the validity, to varying degrees, of other beliefs.

On their journey through history, the Thai have come in contact with many creeds. Firstly, animism – the traditional belief in spirits and gods that inhabit trees, rivers, fields, mountains and the skies – combined with ancestor worship. All things contain a vital spiritual essence, *khwan* in Thai, which needs to be carefully tended by special ceremonies marking important moments in the passage of life and small everyday rituals that acknowledge the abiding presence of spirits inhabiting and affecting all quarters of this world. These ensure the continuing presence of the *khwan*. To scare, shock, insult or ignore this vital essence can cause it to leave, then whatever it once inhabited sickens, withers and may even die. The very young and the very sick are especially susceptible – their *khwan* is feeble.

In a person, the *khwan* is believed to reside in the highest part of the body, the head. A Thai will always slightly lower his or her body when passing elders or walking through a group of people, to ensure that deference is shown to their superiors and their *khwan*. Should one accidentally knock the head of a Thai, one must always apologise for the slight, even *wai* to make amends. To deliberately commit such an act is arrogant. Conversely, the least significant, lowest part of the body is the feet. To point is rude. To point with the feet is a breach of acceptable behaviour intended to insult. And to place the feet above anyone's head is a serious provocation.

The *khwan* is invoked in a variety of ceremonies determined by the nature of the object or the circumstances of an ailment, and it is offered sweetmeats and fruits as an inducement to stay and flourish. There is a special ritual for blessing a newborn elephant in which flowers, a whole steamed chicken, sweetened glutinous rice, bananas and rice wine are offered to the elephant's *khwan*, asking it to accept domestication. After the ceremony, the head of the chicken is broken open. If its beak and jaw are straight, it augurs well: the elephant will not rail against its fate and may also bring wealth to its new owner. If the beak and jaw are crooked, the elephant may pine and die.

The second religious belief that has influenced the Thai is the northern, or Mahayana, school of Buddhism with its pantheon of gods, demons and tantric rituals, as practised by the Khmers of Angkor and most of northern Asia, from whence the Thai originated. This approach relies on the aid of the good spirits that inhabit the heavens to obtain benefits and understanding, while mandalas and talismans are employed in these supplications. It has much in common with Hinduism. Even in Thailand today, many faithful Buddhists use flags, amulets and magical spells in the hope of obtaining their wishes.

Thirdly, the Thai encountered southern, or Hinayana, Buddhism. During the Mon Dvaravati period, from the sixth to eleventh centuries, animism, Hinduism and northern Buddhism were all practised concomitantly in the Chao Phraya basin – statues of Brahma, Indra, Vishnu, Ganesha and the Buddha have been found in many archeological excavations. Although Buddhism was still the pre-eminent religion, its purity had been compromised and it went into slow decline. Around the thirteenth century, at the invitation of King Ramakhamhaeng of Sukothai, missionaries arrived from Sri Lanka to reform and revitalise religious life with the southern form of Buddhism. Its simpler, less convoluted practices relied on individual accountability to attain enlightenment by rigorous effort. This evolved into the Theravada, or 'vehicle of the elders', Buddhism of today's Thailand.

Finally, Brahminism, with its highly formalised rituals acknowledging ancient Hindu gods, was imported from India through Angkor and is still the basis of many rituals that surround and affirm the position of the king and his court. Brahmin ceremonies seek to ensure the welfare of the king and consequently the state by enlisting the support of the Hindu gods, especially Vishnu and Shiva. Thus Brahmins, the priestly intermediaries between the Hindu gods and humanity, conduct the king's coronation rites.

THE THAI KING – AND REGAL TABOOS

Once installed, anointed and crowned, the king is considered a sacred vessel. His individual personality is subsumed beneath the sanctity of his position and he becomes the earthly incarnation of Vishnu and Shiva, the Hindu gods of royalty. Traditionally, Buddhists believe he is a Bodhisattva – one who has attained enlightenment but has chosen to return to the world to guide others.

Many taboos surround the king and, to a lesser degree, those associated with him. For example, knowledge of the personal name of the king was once taboo. It was only during the fourth reign that his personal name was made known. Before then, it was recorded in state chronicles after his death – although it could never be spoken. King Mongkut lifted the taboo, posthumously conferring names upon his predecessors and publicly revealing his and their names. Apart from his many formal titles in Pali and Sanskrit, a living king is still commonly known as 'The Lord Over Our Heads' or 'Lord of Life', while after his death he is referred to as 'The Lord in the Urn'. This last, peculiar title is surprisingly apt. The elaborate funeral rites of a king, often lasting several years, ensure his apotheosis in the spiritual realms. The deceased king is bathed, anointed, wrapped in 500 layers of white cloth, adorned with jewels, and then stored in a golden reliquary urn. Throughout this lying in state, monks chant and Brahmins invoke the aid of their gods. The cremation can only occur once these obsequies are completed and on a day determined as auspicious by the court astrologer. During this time, the king's favourite food is served daily in front of his urn.

To look upon the king's person was also taboo. The Danish adventurer Engelbert Kaempfer described his experience in 1690:

> When the King of Siam goes abroad, everybody must keep out of the way . . . All windows are shut and not the least noise is to be heard. If one happens to chance to meet the King or his Wives, or the Princess Royal in the open fields, he must prostrate himself with his face flat to the ground, turning his back to the Company, till they are out of sight.

Perhaps the most remarkable feature of the Siamese court, certainly the aspect that was described by all foreign observers, was the manner in which the king was attended. They were enthralled by the spectacle of hundreds of courtiers, each one prostrate in a highly stylised *wai*, lying on one side with five points of their body touching the ground – the forehead, two palms and both knees. This is the most deferential form of the *wai* and was reserved only for the Buddha and the king. Performing it literally ensured that the king was 'The Lord Over Our Heads'. Even today, the Thai approach the king with great deference – crouched on their knees, with joined hands raised to the forehead. In the past, strict decorum was insisted upon when approaching the royal precinct. All were obliged to dip their parasols and slightly lower themselves, while boatmen reefed their sails as they approached the palace, otherwise archers on the parapets would pelt the offenders with balls of clay.

Nothing could be passed directly to the king. Anything given to him had to be transferred by golden bowl, as his person was inviolate. The penalty for contravening this could be death. This taboo was extended to anything that belonged to the king, so his family and wives were all treated as sacrosanct, too – sometimes with tragic consequences. Queen Sunanda, the premier wife of King Rama V, drowned when her boat capsized in 1880 on the way to the summer palace of Bang Pa In, near Ayuthyia. Although surrounded by many ladies-in-waiting and guards, these retainers were unable to come to the queen's aid when the boat foundered and she was thrown into the water. Forbidden to touch her, they watched in helpless agony as the queen struggled and then sank beneath the waters of the Chao Phraya River.

All food sent to the king was sealed and only opened in his presence. Often his clothes were covered in jewels, as gems were believed to be antidotes to any poison – rubies, pearls and emeralds were considered particularly efficacious. During some reigns, the food was eaten only after it was tasted by an official – sometimes by the cook – to ensure it was both safe and of the highest standard. The rice that the king ate was tended with special care in paddies near Bangkok, and cooked either by the women of the palace or by royal pages. Covered and placed on a silver tray, along with other dishes belonging to the same 'set', it was then wrapped in a white cloth and sealed. A poem was often attached to the package to identify its contents and to entertain. Perhaps the procession of covered trays reminded one delighted recipient, King Rama II, of a fleet of royal barges fully bedecked – and thus provided the inspiration for his Boat Songs.

Describing a relish of marinated prawns dressed with shredded ginger and kaffir lime juice, the king mused:

Dtai pla sae saeng wa	The savour of this dish
Dut wa jark grabot grabuan	Reminds me
Bai sorrok bork	Of the piquant
Sorrok krawn	And lingering heartache
Hai pii saera jao duang jai	That your leaving creates

Thanpuuying Pliang related this poem in full, and proposed some 35 savoury dishes to be served at a formal banquet, followed by 30 desserts. All had accompanying stanzas. It was a greater array than that offered to monks, as the king had no dietary restraints. His splendour was reflected by the sumptuous variety offered; it was an affirmation of his position in the world and the heavens.

All the strictures surrounding the king were to ensure his dignity and state were properly maintained. However, in private the king lived a far more relaxed and agreeable life. While not treated like the god-king his formal persona required, he was still the object of great reverence. Brahminism gave him a godlike status, Buddhism reminded him he was a man, and being Thai ensured he was not overawed by his own position.

The 'difficult' Anna Leonowens, recounting her experiences during the reign of King Mongkut in her book *The English Governess at the Siamese Court*, observed:

> In an antechamber adjoining a noble hall, rich in . . . carvings and gildings, a throng of females waited, while his Majesty sat at a long table, near which knelt twelve women before great silver trays laden with twelve varieties of viands – soups, meats, game, poultry, fish, vegetables, cakes, jellies, preserves, sauces, fruits, and teas. Each tray, in its order, was passed by three ladies to the head wife or concubine, who removed the silver covers, and at least seemed to taste the contents of each dish; and then, advancing on her knees, she sat them on the long table before the king.
>
> But his Majesty was notably temperate in his diet, and by no means a gastronome. In his long seclusion in a Buddhist cloister he had acquired habits of severe simplicity and frugality . . . [later] he chatted

with his favourites among his wives and concubines, and caressed his children, taking them in his arms, embracing them, plying them with puzzling or funny questions, and making droll faces at the babies: the more agreeable the mother, the dearer the child. The love of children was the constant and hearty virtue of this forlorn despot. They appealed to him by their bounty and their trustworthiness, they refreshed him with the bold innocence of their ways, so frolicsome, graceful and quaint.

The kings of Siam always had many wives: to cement ties, to bestow and receive honour, to sire children and occasionally for pleasure. Mongkut, King Rama IV, had 108 wives of various rank and 82 children of according rank – impressive for a man who spent 27 years in a monastery and only began his obligations to the state when he was 46. His son Chulalongkorn, equally indefatigable, had 153 wives, on three of whom was conferred the unprecedented status of queen. Other wives of royal birth had the title of celestial consort bestowed on them; the remainder – most in fact – were nominal wives of comparatively minor status. His last surviving wife, Chao Chom Sabad, died in 1983. Chulalongkorn had 77 children, 43 of whom were daughters; they, being unable to find spouses of equal rank, remained unmarried and confined to the palace all their lives. Princesses entering morganatic marriages relinquished their rank and title, with all the privileges these entailed, although they were still held in high honour. So from these two reigns alone more than 500 Siamese nobles were produced in the first generation, whose dignity demanded that they be kept in high state.

'THE INSIDE'

The royal wives, the high-born and favourites, lived with their children in the Grand Palace until the end of the nineteenth century, when the Chitralada Palace and surrounding smaller palaces were built by Rama V to house his extensive entourage. These people were *chao wang*, 'people of the palace', or simply of 'the inside', paragons of their culture serving those at its pinnacle. Malcolm Smith was appointed physician to the court of Rama V, and so was privy to 'the inside' at its height. His observations were not only rare in what they described but also unusual in their warm regard for the Siamese – or at least in their lack of the note of condescension so prevalent in most Europeans' journals of the time:

The harem was a town complete in itself, a congested network of houses and narrow streets, with gardens, lawns, artificial lakes and shops. It had its own government, its own institutions, its own laws, and law courts. It was a town of women, controlled by women. Men on special work of construction or repair were admitted, and doctors when they came to visit the sick. The King's sons could live there until they reached the age of puberty . . . But the only man who lived within its walls was the King.

The population of 'The Inside' was enormous. Each Queen had her own household of between 200 and 300 women . . . Each minor wife had a fairly large retinue; if she became a mother it increased. Each one had a separate establishment, the size of which was in proportion to her rank. Altogether the population of 'The Inside' numbered nearly 3000 people.

When a Siamese king died, all his wives who resided in the principal palace were assigned to dowager palaces or returned to their families, depending on the will of the late king. This ensured that the wives of the new king could be installed in their proper state without the complications of determining rank and precedent that could otherwise paralyse the court.

THE NOBILITY OF SIAM

The Siamese system of nobility is very complex and is determined solely by relationship to the king – the ranking of nobles is often revised accordingly on the accession of a new king. The various grades of nobility diminish with each subsequent generation. To explain as simply as possible: there are seven ranks, beginning with the king; then come his children, styled *somdet chao faa* ('celestial prince or princess'), or a variation of this depending on the rank of the mother; then *pra ong chao*; a child of *pra ong chao* is *mom chao*. All these are ranked as royalty, with its attendant privileges and courtesies – a special language, *rachasap*, is even used when addressing such aristocrats. Lesser titles follow: *mom ratchawongse* and finally *mom leuang*, which is the lowest degree of nobility before a person is considered a commoner.

This system, from king to commoner in seven generations, ensured that Siam was not congested with royalty. Nevertheless, Siam was certainly cluttered with nobles, an old saying observing, 'If you throw a stone in Siam you will either hit a prince, a monk or a dog.' And no matter whom the stone might hit, it would probably land in a palace. Bangkok in the late nineteenth and early twentieth centuries was a city of palaces, the households of royalty and other nobles, descendants of previous kings, high ministers of state and the rich.

These palaces were the bastions of high Siamese culture, where gentle and ancient arts were taught to the next generation. The princesses sponsored this inheritance – a custom dating from the time when Khmer princesses had helped civilise the ancient Thai. In this rarefied milieu traditional arts were maintained and refined. The curriculum of culture would include preparing betel nuts, cooking, braiding flowers, weaving and making perfumes. It was delicate work that entertained and diverted, but often was worth nothing more than the delight it brought. The hallmarks of success and culture were painstaking skill and dexterity. The complicated became admired and difficult tasks were aspired to. A girl as young as three years old might be admitted to a palace, and during her life would rarely leave it, unless to marry. Thus her inventiveness and skills, while highly developed, were often without any reference to the outside world.

THE SKILLS AND CUISINE OF THE PALACES

Each palace prided itself on its reputation for skill and zealously upheld it. Every task its inhabitants undertook would be an indication of this. Competitions were often held between palaces, to stimulate and increase the complexity of various skills. These were quite famous and even 'the outside' would learn their outcome and the names of the winners, who were so adept at their crafts. Sometimes children were sent to those triumphant palaces specifically to learn from famed practitioners. This would, of course, enhance the reputation of the palace and the prestige of its owner.

In the palaces, great store was put on teaching the art of mixing and rolling betel nuts in just the right proportions to obtain a lingering savour. Poor or rich, all Thai indulged in chewing betel nuts, a national habit since time immemorial. The areca nut is boiled, dried, sliced and mixed with pink hydrolysed lime, then smeared onto a betel leaf that is finely rolled. When chewed slowly, the betel nut releases its tingling, astringent and addictive taste. This slightly narcotic pastime has the unprepossessing result of making the teeth appear like shiny ebony, and staining the mouth and lips a bloody rouge. Often the Thai, enamoured by early portraits and daguerreotypes of European women, were beguiled by the colour of their lips, assuming that this was due to betel nuts.

One particularly daunting culinary skill involved removing the seeds of a custard apple and then reassembling it. Difficult enough once peeled, but the competition evolved to such levels that the more dexterous women could remove the seeds without having to peel the fruit. Only the smallest slit of skin would be lifted, then the seeds would be removed with a splinter of bamboo, so the custard apple would be left seedless but with its skin miraculously intact. Meals were prepared with the same awesome prowess.

Although the ladies of the court were confined to 'the inside' and far removed from the worldly concerns of the nearby outer court of the king and his government, they were aware of matters of state and proceedings at court. Increasingly, banquets were held in the Western manner, with a stately progression of course after lavish course. The cuisine was French, in the opulent style of the belle époque, and a menu could include such dishes as grilled venison with caper sauce or goose with beetroot. Intrigued by this novel way of cooking, the ladies attempted to cook some of the dishes, but with decidedly peculiar results. Western cooks were engaged to teach this strange cuisine, and soon the various dishes were being interpreted in a singularly Siamese way. Unorthodox creations included pork liver mousse, served with rice cakes as an hors d'oeuvre or spooned into clear soups; braised ox tongue and potatoes with star anise; and, to finish, coconut or lemon basil seed ice-cream.

Traditionally the daytime meals in palaces were quite insubstantial, as the enervating tropical heat reduced eating to a mere nibble. When the day began to cool, appetites were rekindled. Around four in the afternoon, the first of a series of ornate snacks left the kitchens. These were complicated sweetmeats designed to delight and stimulate: crisp-skinned coconut cup cakes topped with minced prawn, pork or chicken stir-fried with curry paste; jade-coloured glutinous rice covered with sweetened dried fish; rice perfumed with flowers and garnished with salted shrimp. Perhaps an exquisitely refined dish of iced perfumed rice with several complicated garnishes might be served, or sweetened glutinous rice with egg custard, or black glutinous rice dressed with caramel. To these ladies the mixing of sweet and savoury flavours, which were served simultaneously or even in the one dish, was a delicious, entertaining pleasure, not a confusion.

Dinner was served in the cool of the evening, at sunset. It was the culinary highlight of the day. Rice was served with several exquisite accompanying dishes. An elegant curry, a pungent relish, a soothing soup and a salad would be eaten. In the rarefied atmosphere of the palaces of Siam, the normal was transformed into the extraordinary: this is what so distinguishes this food from that of 'the outside'. All the ingredients were of premium quality –

the rice was harvested from the best areas, seasonal fish were freshly caught or perfectly preserved. Strange and exotic tastes were eagerly sought to surprise and satisfy cultivated palates. The food was cooked with great skill and care, and with full regard to the rank of the people for whom it was prepared. Finely sliced and shredded ingredients were combined and cooked with precision, the tastes and textures were refined and enhanced and then the final seasoning was deftly executed, delicately calculated to balance and draw the cooking to a poised conclusion.

Great delight was taken in combining food into new and unusual combinations, like a red beef curry garnished with a small dish of deep-fried clams, or a green peppercorn curry served with crisp-fried salted squid. Vegetables that accompanied a relish were intricately carved, so that cucumbers resembled small mango leaves and eggplants blossomed like flowers. A gentle, clear soup might be served in a small, sculpted melon casing. All these dishes were accompanied by rice, which would arrive glisteningly white, unseasoned and unadorned.

Desserts, for some the pinnacle of the cuisine, arrived on a separate platter – tender and golden threads of duck egg yolk perfumed with jasmine flowers, a rich pudding redolent with coconut cream and palm sugar, and fruit simmered in fragrant coconut cream or glistening in iced sugar syrups.

The art of perfuming was considered an essential skill for the women of the palaces. They created alluring colognes, primarily to infuse clothing – but these also came to be used in cooking. Ingredients included fragrant herbs, flowers and barks, such as pandanus, kaffir lime leaves, jasmine, ylang ylang, hibiscus, eaglewood, sandalwood and camphor from the northern forests; and essential oils from animals, such as beeswax, even *chamot*, the secretions from Burmese and Chinese civets and musk oils from stags – the basis of most traditional perfumes.

The already refined cooking of 'the inside' reached new heights when it was an adjunct to celebration and ceremony. Mom Leuang Neuang Ninrat recorded the excited anticipation of the ladies as they prepared for Songkran, the Thai New Year. This was not the boisterous and often hilarious water festival that now saturates modern Thailand. Originally it was a gentle affair to welcome in the lunar year. The palace was cleaned and food prepared in readiness. Smoked rice biscuits were made to please the departed ancestors, and coconut toffee for the living. In the morning, food was presented to monks, and then the forehead of each person was anointed with perfumed lustral water by the head of the house, to cleanse them of their previous year's transgressions. Sometimes a palace would receive visitors, relatives mainly, coming to pay respect. After such formal courtesies were completed, the guests were often invited to eat.

This challenged the kitchen, as all its expertise was called upon. Mom Leuang Neuang recalls a dish where salted chicken was braised with sugar cane, finely shredded and then dry-fried in a brass wok over a very low heat while the meat was picked and teased apart by hand until it was a dried floss of diaphanous caramelised strands. When cool, it was tossed with deep-fried shallots before being sprinkled over thin, shapely slices of rice cake. Rose petals were individually dipped into thick, perfumed syrup, cooled, then reassembled into a fleetingly crisp bloom, a remarkable decoration for a plate of confectionery.

Although there were distinct and very different standards of living between palace and paddy, much of Thai cooking, its styles, ingredients and recipes, was similar. Palace food only differed from that of other classes in the intricate techniques employed, the refined tastes and the elaborate presentations. A green curry, for example, would have been – and still is – immediately recognisable wherever it was cooked, regardless of its presentation.

In the legislative past of most countries there have been 'sumptuary laws' regulating the indulgences of the rich. Clothes, jewels and glassware have at some time been subject to such laws. Food, too, has been subject to such restrictive, often puritanical laws. In Europe during the fifteenth century, the ingredients, the array of dishes and the ostentatious display that could in all propriety be allowed during a meal were set out in law. All ranks had their rights and privileges duly prescribed. Furthermore, gaming, poaching and, later, enclosing laws ensured that certain foods – or at least their provenance – remained in the exclusive domain of the propertied classes.

Similar laws were proclaimed in Siam during the reign of Rama III. Tellingly, they concerned the display of food – not the ingredients, but the accoutrements on which dishes were served. Solid gold or sterling silver were for those of very high rank, but these laws were, in fact, rarely enforced as usually only those of the appropriate rank could afford to eat off gold. All Thai were free to eat any ingredient, if they could afford it.

PEASANT LIFE AND FOOD

For more than a thousand years rice has tied the peasants to the paddy and committed them to its inexorable cycle, attuned to the land and the passage of the seasons. From day to day, month to month, the only significant changes in the flat, unrelenting pace of the farming life have been the seasons. While everything else remains constant, the weather in Thailand can change violently. The rains burst upon the country in a deluge that can turn villages and surrounding valleys into lakes, yet at the same time guaranteeing the water necessary to grow rice and make the countryside literally teem with life. Then comes the cool aftermath, when the rice ripens and is harvested, a time of plenty and of festivals. This leads to the hot season, three months of fierce sun that bakes the earth and drains the canals and rivers. When all is parched and wizened, the rains come again. For the earth to be at its most generous, the sky's yield must be predictable and consistent. Any disruption is calamitous: the crops fail, privation occurs. Or worse, starvation.

In the past, although life was hard and farmers usually lived only just above subsistence, they were content, working in harmony with their land. The outside world rarely intruded upon the peasants and their fields. The rains came, rice grew and the harvest was gathered, in a continuous and unchanging cycle. They were unaware that there was any other way of life; their world was small, its boundaries fixed by the paddies they had to tend. Only after a certain age – around 13 – would children truly begin to work. Before then, they would assist with chores around the house, or tend buffalo, but nothing too arduous. As they grew older, they would help in the paddies. At some stage the boys might have some lessons at the temple, as long as it did not interfere with their work.

Farmers today, *chao naa* (literally, 'persons of the fields'), spend all day in the paddies during the growing season, often beginning at 4 a.m. and toiling until sunset, amid steadily rising waters and among intermittent but torrential rain. Should the gods smile and the rain be plentiful and timely, other problems may beset the farmers, the worst perhaps being the land crabs. These unlikely crustaceans simply nip the stalks of rice at water level, eventually drowning the plant. When this pest appears in plague proportions, it is disastrous: often the crops over large areas are wiped out. When they appear in manageable proportions, however, the crabs themselves are harvested by the farmers, grilled and eaten with chilli or crushed with a pestle and mortar as an ingredient in *som dtam* – the famous green papaya salad of north-eastern Thailand – or boiled to a murky paste in the north, to preserve them for later use.

Another pest is the water beetle, or rice roach. Though not as detrimental to the crop as the crabs, to the farmers they are even more delectable. They are deep-fried and eaten as a crisp and enticing snack, used in salads, or infused in fish sauce that is then used as a seasoning; they have a somewhat bitter taste and pungent aroma. Any excess of this upcountry delicacy is ploughed into the earth of the large paddies, where it fertilises the soil.

At the peak of the rainy season, the whole of the Chao Phraya river system floods. The land is awash, with water spilling into the paddies and filling the dams, creating

the conditions for rice to grow. As the clouds burst, and the paddies turn green, life teems in the bounteous overflow. The farmers take advantage of this and catch various types of fish, prawns, frogs and birds. After the feast, the women preserve the remainder for a leaner, drier time. Prawns and small fish, for example, are cured in salt to make the two elemental components of Thai cuisine: shrimp paste (*gapi*) and fish sauce (*nahm pla*). Later in the season, when the fish or prawns are too big or, rather, have too much meat to waste on such fermentation, they are dried or salted, thus preserving them in a recognisable form. All this happens with extraordinary speed, life bursting and brimming. It must, for this fertile season is short.

The traditional diet of the farmer consisted of food at hand, prepared in as little time as possible – time that had to be diverted from tending the paddies. In Thai this is called *gin ngai gin yuu* ('eat simply, live easily'). A meal, therefore, would mainly comprise a spicy relish (*nahm prik*), served with raw or boiled vegetables, such as purple Siamese watercress, green beans, the tips, stalks and leaves of various plants and trees and almost any vegetable that was grown or gathered from nearby canals or groves. This would perhaps be supplemented with a fresh fish, grilled simply, slowly and smokily over a few embers, and a broth of boiled bamboo shoots and pork ribs. With rice aplenty. Occasionally, a little of the green rice was harvested to make what has now become a rare dessert – pounded young, soft green rice with pandanus leaves, simmered with water until thick, then sweetened with sugar.

HARVEST TIME

During the rice harvest, it was necessary for families to rely upon the larger community through the ties of the *muang* to enable the rice to be harvested in time – although the planting was staggered, so at least paddies ripened sequentially. Apart from reciprocated assistance, people also repaid this help by cooking vast quantities of food to feed all those involved in the massive task of harvesting. This became a traditional time of celebration. Huge pots filled with a stew of a freshwater carp-like fish with salt and sugar cane, perhaps accompanied by a fried spicy relish with fresh tamarind, and a soup of preserved mustard greens, were prepared by old women, then transported to the rice fields to feed the hungry and weary. Since all the family joined in the harvest, it was a time when young men and women would be allowed to meet, even court. There would be a general air of relief, gratitude and, with luck, festivity – since by this stage it would be known if the year was successful or not. Along with courtship, music was in the air; an old man might play a reed-like flute to soothe the burdens of savage heat and heavy load. In the cool of the night, the farmers would continue the music and courtship in bucolic revelry.

Just before the end of the harvest, the Thai celebrate Loy Grathong, the candle festival. At this festival, which originated in Sukothai, the river goddess, Pra Mae Kongka, is invoked and permission is sought for the continued use of her river water. A raft or boat of banana leaves is fashioned with a candle in it, and a coin inserted into its folds. This raft is launched onto a river or canal and, with it, the hopes for a good year ahead and the transgressions of the previous one are both dispatched. The festival coincides with the end of the rainy season, when the waters are at their height, and the twelfth full moon, which is the largest of the year. Some women believed that bathing at midnight on the festival night would make them as alluring and bewitching as the round silvery moon that shone on them. This was especially desirable given the proximity of harvesting farmers over the following weeks.

In larger towns, life moved at a faster pace but, with the exception of Bangkok and Chiang Mai, most towns were little more than a market place where business was transacted. Trips to the market were uncommon, and farmers went only to purchase things that they could not supply or make; in remote areas it may have taken a full day's walk to get there. The market was exciting: it bustled with strange people and new things. People closer to town could rely on it to supply their daily needs, but those at a greater distance – the majority – had to rely on their own skills or do without, except on rare occasions.

Although the farmers were equal to their tasks, they were also acutely aware of the things beyond their control, such as weather or pestilence. In order to ensure the success of their crops, they performed many rituals to propitiate the local gods, goddesses and spirits. These ceremonies, whether they worked or not, at least granted some peace of mind and a certain security. The countryside is still considered to be the domain of many spirits, some beneficial, others harmless and a few positively malicious to susceptible, vulnerable farmers, who fearfully placate these often capricious entities.

THE SUPERSTITIONS OF THAILAND

The Thai are inveterately superstitious. They regularly consult astrologers, palmists and other prognosticators to reveal their future, discover past transgressions and ascertain what ritual must be performed to make amends. One text to which all Thai soothsayers refer is *sawatdi raksa*, a guide to safeguarding one's welfare by living in agreeable harmony with the changing heavens, the whim of the gods, the sweep of nature and the caprice of humankind. It is a compendium of many cherished axioms, age-old customs and hoary sayings, which were put into verse in the early nineteenth century by a favourite of King Rama II – his court poet, Sunthorn Bhu. He rather solemnly advises that they are:

> . . . observances fit for persons of rank and dignity. In observing them, one will meet enduring luck, long life, numerous descendants, increased happiness and might. Do not forget to uphold your welfare in accordance with the teachings of the ancients.

Often the 'fit practices' he suggests are sage advice, common sense and good manners; others, however, seem quaint and are now given little credence. He advises that one should pay respect to any monk, or mishaps will follow. One should never curse the sun, rain or wind, otherwise they might withhold their bounty:

> Do not hasten the day to come to an end. Pay respect every daybreak and dusk to the sun and moon.

Washing hair on a Saturday prevents calamity, as does cutting nails on Mondays and Wednesdays. And wearing a loincloth tucked to the right happily ensures no future encounter with the teeth and claws of a crocodile. (Guaranteed, no doubt, to urge all gentlemen to dress to the right.)

Facing east when eating makes for a contented life; south guarantees popularity; to the west, happiness and health will ensue; but facing the north, ill-luck can only result. However, a kitchen should always face north and, idiosyncratically, a stove's position in the kitchen should be determined by the day on which the cook or owner was born.

Outside every house in Thailand there is a small spirit house, the residence of the spirit of the land that the house has displaced. Daily offerings of flowers, incense, candles and sweetmeats are made for its pleasure, thus maintaining the prosperity and happiness of the household. Certain trees, flowers and shrubs are considered lucky or unlucky and are accordingly planted near the house or outside the compound. For instance, cannas are believed to bring good luck by association, as their name in Thai, *phutaraksa*, means 'the protection of Buddha'. The banyan tree, however, is rarely planted near houses, usually being found in temple grounds; it is the auspicious tree under which the Buddha attained enlightenment. Even today, yellow robes are wrapped around the broad trunk of this splendidly shady tree as a reminder of its sacred role. A banyan tree can grow to a venerable age, when respectful villagers will trim and whitewash bamboo poles and place them around it as supports in its dotage. The hibiscus is never planted in the compound, for in the past its scarlet flowers were the sign of a harlot; condemned convicts on the way to public execution had these notorious blooms placed behind their ears as a sign of their crimes and impending death. Banana trees are planted freely throughout the compound; their fruit and leaves are used constantly. The one exception is the *gluay tani* variety, as it is believed to harbour a capricious spirit, *nang tani*, who revels in scaring the unwary. However, by following a certain ritual, the imp can be seduced into revealing one's future wife. When the tree is about to bud, a man will flirt with the tree to attract *nang tani*. It might take several days of courting to gain this coy spirit's attentions. Once obtained, he cuts a small piece of the root of the tree and, while reciting a magical formula, carves it into the figure of a woman. This is then hidden. That night, it is believed the spirit will appear in a dream, in the form of his future wife. Permission has to be sought from *nang tani* to marry this real woman; otherwise, like the proverbial woman scorned, she will wreak a furious revenge.

The permission of other spirits, the *phii sua* of the forests and fields, streams, mountains and skies, is always sought when using their domain. The *chao phii* and *pra phum* are the tutelary spirits that inhabit and own various areas of the house and the countryside, and ceremonies must be performed to ensure that no disfavour is incurred by ignoring them. It is important to supplicate these spirits, else some mishap will doubtless strike. The everhelpful Thanpuuying Pliang proposes the preparation of two tables covered with white cloths. On each one should be set a pig's head on a banana leaf, with its trotters and tail forming an ephemeral silhouette, a boiled chicken complete with head and feet, and a bowl of chilli jam, together with seven sticks of incense and a large candle.

Offerings are also made to obtain the spirits' consent for the use of property. When passing through a doorway, for example, the Thai step over the threshold, not onto it, as they believe that to do so will offend the spirit of the door. If such a transgression occurs, propitiation ceremonies are required. The grander the house, the greater in dignity the spirit and thus the more elaborate the atonement rites.

For a hovel, a *wai* was sufficient. However, if a threshold in the royal palace was accidentally trodden on, the guards insisted upon an involved procedure, including an enforced prostration, the offering of prayers with several sticks of incense and perhaps a few oranges to placate the spirit's ire. Even today, if an unknowing tourist errs, he or she must re-enter the door – the spirits, it would seem, are more accommodating to a *farang*. Rarely do the Thai commit such a trespass.

Witches, succubae and incubi, wraiths and spectres, the ghosts of suicides, women who have died in childbirth, infants, and all those who have died unshriven and who have not been cremated are condemned to roam the countryside, wreaking their mischief on the living. One particularly unsavoury ghoul, *phii graseu*, is believed to feed upon the entrails of newborn babies and their placentas to replace the dripping entrails of her own torso-less body. In the absence of such ghastly delights, human excrement is her preferred dish. Those supped upon by this ghost die a wasting death, and anything that withers is believed to be her victim. Her partner, *phii grahang*, has wings and a tail and flies in pursuit of his gory food; his legs and tail resemble the long pestles used for pounding unhusked rice.

The Thai are so afraid of provoking these marauding spirits that the newborn are given pejorative nicknames in order not to invoke their animosity: *muu* ('pig'), *uan* ('fatty'), *nuu* ('rat'), *kliang* ('empty') and the more modern but sinister *bern* ('gun') are used to divert their attention. The resourceful Thanpuuying Pliang recommends a steamed fish curry, some skeins of rice noodles, a few betel nuts, a roll of fermented tea leaves, and a bottle of whisky to mollify these vengeful spirits. Babies' proper names, bestowed on them by monks, their parents or sponsors, are infrequently used, normally on formal occasions; they are rarely known by anyone outside the immediate family.

THE THAI FAMILY

Each person in the extended family plays an integral role in the maintenance of that family. As no one is equal, the complicated interdependence needs to be designated with precision. Standing is determined primarily by age, then whether they are paternal or maternal family, and finally by gender.

Status in Thailand is maintained even to the degree that the personal pronoun 'I' alters according to the person to whom one is speaking. Other words can change too, according to circumstances. For instance, there are six words meaning 'to eat', and these are used depending on the rank of the person who is eating: monks *chan*, the king and high nobles *sawoei*, lesser nobles and seniors *raprathaan*, parents *thaan*, friends *gin* and children or inferiors *dtak*.

Each person in a Thai family has a specific title, which also determines the use of their own personal pronoun:

bpuu, yah paternal grandfather, grandmother		*dtaa, yai* maternal grandfather, grandmother	
luun, baa father and mother's older brothers and sisters	*por, mae* father, mother	*ah chai, ah sao* father and mother's younger brothers and sisters	
pii chai, pii ying older brothers and sisters	*pom, dichan* self (male, female)	*nong chai, nong ying* younger brothers and sisters	

These designations are used as a prefix to a person's name. They declare the exact relationship between people, thus ensuring the proper respect can be shown. Often, however, the designation alone is used, rather than the personal name. This pattern extends beyond the immediate family into the village and on. All are encompassed in this familial structure: a crouched old woman selling green papaya salad in the market place is called 'grandmother'; a slow-walking, wizened old man, 'uncle'; an inquisitive female neighbour, 'auntie'. Those roughly equal refer to each other as either older or younger brother or sister, depending on age. Once acquainted, all will refer to each other as intimately as brother or sister, followed by the nickname. Thus all Thai are included in this 'extended family', *muang thai*, and assigned a position that implies a relationship in an engaging and meaningful way. Rarely, however, are foreigners included in this network and they are referred to as *khun*, a very polite but detached term.

THE CHINESE MERCHANTS

Bangkok in the nineteenth century was really two distinct cities: a city of commerce and a city of government. Bangkok engaged in trade, bringing wealth to the kingdom, prospering on the export of rice and the import of manufactured goods, but the Siamese saw themselves primarily as farmers and eschewed trade, believing it to be a somewhat tainted occupation.

Commerce was the province of the Chinese, the merchants of the Orient. From the time of Sukothai, the Chinese have formed a sizeable community in Thailand's larger towns, supplying the needs of farmers and administrators. Unconstrained by the system of forced labour that prevented free movement of the Thai from their allotted districts, the Chinese could travel throughout the country and so were able to dominate trade.

In the mid-nineteenth century, Rama III – sometimes referred to as 'the Merchant King' – invited a group of Chinese to occupy an area in the south of Bangkok, to stimulate economic growth. By the late nineteenth century, the population of Bangkok was 50 per cent Chinese, and two-thirds of all Chinese in the kingdom lived in Bangkok.

Not only were the Chinese culturally and socially distinct from the Siamese, they were physically distant too. The Siamese lived around the Grand Palace and the temples to the north of Bangkok. The Chinese area, Yaorawat, was farther south and was devoted to commerce. Visitors remarked upon its *klong* (canals), lined with open-sided shops. Major warehouses bordered this section of the river, where ships were sometimes berthed three deep. Yaorawat was a bustling commercial hub, pulsing with energy – unlike other areas of the city and country, which were more attuned to the agreeably languid attitude of the less commercial Thai.

The Chinese merchants prospered. They maintained their families in traditional style, bringing wives from China. And they ate Chinese food, with chopsticks from bowls rather than by hand from plates as the Siamese did. The once distinctly Chinese dishes of roast duck, pork braised with star anise, fish dumplings, noodles, soups, fermented soy beans and rapid stir-fries eventually became incorporated into the Thai repertoire.

Not all the Chinese who came to Siam prospered, however. The coolies were the hard-working urban poor who had left China in the hope of finding a better life. Regrettably they found not only similar hardships and squalor but also loneliness in a foreign country. They soon began to marry Siamese women and gradually forsook their Chinese identity.

THE BUREAUCRACY OF BANGKOK

Bangkok was also the city in which the king resided, surrounded by his court, and increasingly by government ministries and bureaucrats. The Outer Palace was where the business of state occurred. Ambassadors were received, banquets held, ceremonies performed invoking aid for the state, and the ministries enacted their policies.

The ministries were feudal institutions with ancient customs, which until the nineteenth century had remained largely unchanged for 300 years. In effect, these were small states within the kingdom and were controlled by great, bureaucratic, intermarried families – the Bunnark, Singhaseni, Siriwatthanakun. These families accumulated enormous wealth, lived regally, wielded great influence and dispensed patronage through the almost inherited control of 'their' ministries. Nepotism was rife in these administrative fiefdoms, as son succeeded father and nephew followed uncle, brother deputised for brother and daughters married, building tremendous power blocs. Notably, most of these families were originally descended from foreigners employed by the Siamese monarchs – Persian, Brahmin, Chinese and Mon. However, over generations they had been 'Siam-ised', and most were related to the various kings of the Ayuthyia and Bangkok eras.

The Bunnark family was descended from a Persian envoy to the court of Siam in the late sixteenth century. Over subsequent centuries, it grew in power and stature to become the second family of the kingdom. Its pre-eminent position was assured by contracting innumerable, sometimes almost incestuous, marriages with various ruling dynasties through-out Ayuthyia and, later, Bangkok. Many of Rama I's consorts were Bunnarks, one being the mother of King Rama II, who in turn had several Bunnark spouses. Rama III was a first cousin of the heads of several Bunnark-controlled ministries. The Bunnark family became so entrenched that for just over a hundred years, from the establishment of Bangkok to the late nineteenth century, it had unbroken control of the ministry in charge of the western and southern provinces – and effectively of the military, foreign affairs and trade.

The king conferred honorary titles on high government officials: *somdet chao praya*, *chao praya*, *praya*, *pra*, *leuang* and *khun*, in descending order. Although these titles were earned by merit and had less standing than inherited titles, their owners often wielded greater power. Some old sepia photographs of these men show them gazing confidently at the camera, formally attired, invested and bejewelled with distinguished insignia of state; others capture them happily relaxing among their wives and children. Just like King Mongkut.

The élite of Siam were closely interrelated: to try to chart the relationships and genealogy of these families is to enter a labyrinth of numerous wives, countless children and untold bastards. These high officials had names conferred on them linked to their appointed roles in government; these titles would change according to new positions or responsibilities. Such high officials were referred to only by their titles, and no record was kept to associate several changes of name that might occur during a career.

THE SIAMESE CHARACTER

One of the peculiarities of Siamese society is its insistence on assigning names and titles and establishing relative positions, yet once established these formalities are easily disregarded and the Thai revert to their informal nature. For example, the formal, obscure and changing titles of the king and his high ministers, and the reluctance to use personal names for them, is paralleled by the custom of using nicknames rather than given names to deceive hostile spirits. Bangkok is actually a sobriquet for the city of Krung Thep. Siam is the imposed name for *muang thai*. The Thai feel a need to establish a relationship, but once having done so, have loose regard for it. After all, this life and all its attachments are an illusion, a mere passing phase. One should aspire to perfection but not divest oneself of humanity – that defeats the purpose. This dichotomy is one of the interesting and revealing quirks of the Thai. They somehow retain their humanity despite all the pomp in their culture, tradition and history. Their light-hearted character overcomes the weight of ritual. This is the charm of the Thai.

Until the late nineteenth century, Bangkok, although acclaimed as the celestial abode of the gods and the Venice of the East, was in fact a medieval backwater, riddled with palaces, *klong* and cholera. It was very little more than a large market place and an administrative base. However, as Siam responded to the modern world, the town grew, spreading wide boulevards where once there were *klong* and paddies. The city began to attract people from the countryside. After the reign of Rama V, in the early part of the twentieth century, the gilded palaces rapidly went into decline. By the 1930s their exotic way of life was almost as extinct as it was obsolete in the modern world. The exquisite cuisine of the palaces also disappeared, alas, compromised by modern needs. Time, labour and cost – three of the least considered ingredients in these kitchens – became increasingly important commodities in the rapidly developing city. Thus, in modern Thailand, cooking has become more standardised, less involved and reflective of status, less singularly Siamese than the food of the past. The Thai are aware of the existence of their culinary treasure, but sadly are often unsure of its content.

Cuisine remains, nonetheless, an important aspect of Thai culture. It evokes profound beliefs and ancient rituals, forging an intricate society with highly involved conventions. It is the accumulation of knowledge and experiences, giving meaning to the past. Cuisine out of its cultural context is disembodied – doomed, like the unfulfilled *phii* and ghouls that roam the Thai landscape seeking substance. Thai cuisine is firmly rooted in the land, sitting deeply in the psyche of its people: it is the epitome of Thai culture.

3 REG

The map of Thailand (see page 79) resembles the silhouette of an elephant's head. The north and north-east of the country are its two ears, the central plains its head, with Bangkok at the mouth, of course, while its trunk – the Isthmus of Kra – descends sinuously to the south. From the misty foothills of the Himalayas in the north to the arid plateau of the north-east, along the verdant expanses of the central alluvial plains, down to the shimmering Gulf of Thailand and beyond, this country is a land of immense contrasts.

The various regions of Thailand have their own traditions, customs, festivals, dialects and cooking styles. These diverse cultures reflect their distance from the historical heartland of the Siamese – the central plains. Ever since the establishment of Sukothai, this region has been the core of Thai polity and culture, and its recipes form the basis of the major part of this book. Despite the differences, there is a shared culture and history throughout Thailand: rice, monarchy and religion bind the country into a singularly cohesive nation.

The differences in topography and climate of the regions naturally have an effect on the plants and animals found in these areas and therefore the cuisine. For example, among the mountainous areas of the north, west and north-east, the rain is not as heavy as it is farther south, there is a long dry season (particularly in the north-east, where the land becomes arid at that time) and most of the indigenous plants are tropical, deciduous types. To the south grow verdant evergreens and lush virgin forests, while mangroves line the coasts of the Gulf of Thailand and the Andaman Sea.

A century ago over 95 per cent of the land area was covered by dense forest. Today, only just over 25 per cent remains so. Some of this clearance is a result of the slash-and-burn agriculture of the hill tribes, but most is due to the rapacious logging that began in the nineteenth century and sadly continues – illegally – today. Of course, some forest has also been lost as the population has increased, from about 5 million in 1850 to its current level of over 60 million.

Remote provinces in the far north and north-east have only opened to the world in the last 20 years. Such isolation has until recently preserved the profound cultural differences that exist between various ethnic groups in Thailand. The Hmong, for instance, would find the southern Malay Muslims incomprehensible, while the primitive Mlabri have more in common with the Semang of the south than with the Thai. The ethnic Thai – whether from the north, the Lao of the north-east, or the Siamese of the central plains and the south – comprise almost 80 per cent of the population. The Chinese, mainly third or fourth generation, make up another 11 per cent of the population, with ethnic Malays at 4 per cent, and Mon, Khmers and hill tribes the remaining 5 per cent.

THE CENTRAL PLAINS *park glang*

Central Thailand is one broad alluvial plain, consisting of the Chao Phraya River and parts of the Ping, Wang, Yom, Nan and Pa Sak rivers, touching the basins of the Mae Klong and Bang Pakong rivers. All the rivers come together at the delta to create the Chao Phraya basin. As this area has the most fertile soil in Thailand and plentiful water, it has attracted the most settlement and has become the economic and political centre – the 'heart of the country'.

The area has been permanently settled for at least 2500 years. It was at the hub of ancient trading routes, and its maritime culture extended into the hinterlands where people traded forest products, like ivory, perfumed woods, spices and gemstones, for more sophisticated items, such as pots, urns, lamps and beads. The influence of the port and river cities thus spread, although they never controlled the interior. Thailand's major cities, such as Ayuthyia, rose in the central plains, and Bangkok now dominates the Chao Phraya basin. The plain rises gradually northwards but is mostly flat except for occasional outcrops around Lopburi. It is densely populated and large towns are located on the rivers, which either connect naturally or by canals dug to facilitate transportation and allow irrigation for crops; together the canals and rivers form an extensive network. As the canals were dug into the marshland, farmers, rice and Thai culture followed.

The effects of human habitation are everywhere: vast green paddies stretch across the plains, which are criss-crossed by waterways and dotted with many small villages and larger market towns. This agricultural landscape appeared only when rice began to be intensively cultivated in this region for export, rather than domestic use. Where the land is too dry for rice, alternative crops, such as maize, peanuts and taro, are grown.

The Chao Phraya basin is surrounded by highlands, which influence rainfall. There are two distinct seasons: the wet and the dry. Surprisingly, the bitter Siberian weather builds high-pressure systems that drive dry and relatively cool winds southeastward during winter, and thus Bangkok was once comparatively chilly during November, December and January. Now, due to deforestation and urbanisation, it is always infernally hot. During March the airflow reverses and hot, moist air from the south initiates the rainy season. April is the hottest month, when temperatures soar, to an average of 39°C (102°F) in some districts, and people eagerly, longingly, await the first rains, the 'mango showers'. Between May and October an average of 1400 millimetres (55 inches) of rain falls and rivers rise, as does the risk of flooding.

THE FOOD OF THE CENTRAL PLAINS

The cuisine of this region is the most complex in the country, reflecting its wealth, diversity and the many influences of the past. The fertile land supports the cultivation of foods not only from this region but, since there is migration from the other parts of Thailand, from those areas too. The dominance of Bangkok and its sophisticated palace cuisine has bestowed a wide repertoire of dishes on the central plains, using a great variety of ingredients. This is the Thai cooking that most foreigners are familiar with.

Long grain is the preferred rice, and most of the land is given over to rice production. With much of the land cleared, there is little access to wild ingredients, in contrast to the north. Most vegetables are cultivated, although they were once gathered along the many rivers and irrigation canals that meander through the region. The people of the central plains often refer to their vegetables in two categories, 'water' and 'land', depending on where they are grown. 'Water' vegetables include Siamese watercress, both the purple-stemmed variety used in sour orange curries and the more common green variety that is stir-fried with yellow beans, garlic and small prawns; lotus shoots that are simmered in coconut cream with small mackerel or a few briny salted land crabs; and the delicious sour yet nutty water mimosa, stir-fried with minced pork and peanuts or simmered in curries.

'Land' vegetables, such as the fern-like *cha-om*, appear in omelettes and rustic curries with frogs, snails and eels; the tobacco-like leaf of *bai yor* is shredded in red curries, imparting a slightly bitter flavour. Many shapes, varieties and colours of eggplants – pea, apple, fuzzy and long – are available in the market. Several types of bamboo shoots are sliced and then either boiled or fermented to use in soups and curries, or stir-fried with pork or fish. The food of the central plains uses all the classic aromatics of Thai cooking: galangal, lemongrass, kaffir lime, mint and coriander, as well as Thai, holy and lemon basil.

Few forests mean that little game is caught in this region so pork, chicken and duck are the most common meats. However, the many rivers teem with life, prawns are abundant and even in the dustiest of markets they can be purchased fresh – often still alive. Many freshwater fish, including *pla chorn* and the muscular catfish, are readily available; crabs and molluscs are also plentiful. Most of these ingredients are found dried, too. A particularly popular fish is threadfin, which is lightly salted and dried in the sun for a day before being deep-fried and dressed with a green mango salad. Beef and pork are often treated in a similar manner. There are many pickled vegetables and fruit which are occasionally eaten alone, but mostly accompany relishes and curries, for example pickled Siamese watercress, eggplants and limes or green mango pickled with honey.

The broader range of flavours and dishes in the central plains compared to other parts of Thailand means there is a broader range of seasoning, although hot and salty are the dominant tastes. Some of the more complicated dishes, such as crispy noodles and the various *miang* (snacks rolled in 'betel' leaves), may be hot, salty, sweet and sour in varying degrees. All types of chillies are used and while this region's food is not as hot as that of the north-east or south, it is much hotter than the food of the north. Green bird's eye chillies are used to make the justly famous green curries that have their origin here. Fish sauce is the main salty seasoning, although fermented fish sauce (*nahm pla raa*) is still used in very ancient dishes and in the northern parts of the region. Both white and palm sugars are used. Dishes are soured by lime juice in all types of hot and sour soups; and also by tamarind water in sour orange curries; by vinegar in sour ginger soups; and by fruit, such as green mango, *madan* (sour cucumber), hog plum and tamarind pods. Spices are used carefully, with white pepper, coriander seed and cumin being the most ubiquitous, while mace, nutmeg and other spices are employed less commonly.

Shrimp paste (*gapi*) is a fundamental component of this cooking. It is used in most curry pastes, many soups and a few salads and stir-fries, and is crucial in making most of the relishes of the region. The favourite dish of the central plains, perhaps the national dish, shrimp paste relish (*nahm prik gapi*), is based on it. People of this region also simmer coconut cream until it is thick and enrich it with various ingredients, like minced prawns or yellow beans, before serving with a plate of raw vegetables and other accompaniments.

Soups comprise a comforting array of simple broths and the legendary hot and sour soups, especially *dtom yam gung*, which is made with prawns. Almost as well known are the coconut- and galangal-infused soups, peppered with chillies and lime juice and made with many ingredients, such as fish, wild mushrooms or chicken. Rich coconut soups, seasoned with lemongrass and kaffir lime, are also eaten with fresh fish or crisp smoked fish.

The region has many varieties of curries. Most are boiled and stock-based – a sour orange curry, usually made with a freshwater fish and one or two vegetables, being the most traditional. But perhaps the most ancient is a light curry of dried fish and vegetables perfumed with lemon basil and white pepper. Notably, there are also many fried curries. For jungle curries, the spicy paste is fried in oil with meat or fish before being moistened with stock and finished with plenty of vegetables. To make the more familiar red and green curries, the paste is fried in separated coconut cream. The many 'foreign' curries reflect the diverse influences in this region, such as the luscious *mussaman*, a sweet and sour curry combining poultry or beef with potatoes; and the delicate, turmeric-infused yellow curry, which is usually served with a sweet and sour cucumber relish.

Salads from the central plains are perhaps the most versatile and easy style, with simple, spicy dressings made from fresh lime juice, fish sauce, some sugar and lots of chillies – or based on chilli jam. They can be made of blanched squid, wing beans, smoked fish, grilled beef, chicken feet or grilled long eggplants. Sliced red shallots, mint and coriander are regular aromatic accompaniments.

The strong Chinese influence means that there are many brisk stir-fries and rice noodle dishes. Street dishes are also often of Chinese origin: Chinese chive cakes and braised dishes – mostly of pork and duck with bean curd, Chinese broccoli and star anise.

THE NORTH   *park neua*

The north is a proud region with a venerable heritage. It was the pathway along which the Siamese travelled on their journey south: ancient cities, crumbling temples and historical chronicles are a testament to this past. Lamphun, Chiang Saen and Chiang Rai were important northern kingdoms that predated Sukothai on the central plains.

Chiang Mai, the major city of this region, has a long and varied history. It was established by the legendary King Mangrai in 1297 and has at various times been independent, conquered by the Burmese and in allegiance with Ayuthyia. Only in the late eighteenth century, after 200 years of Burmese rule, did Chiang Mai come under the control of Siam. Its distance from Bangkok, however, meant that this control was tenuous and administrative only, and daily life was undisturbed. Its remoteness was such that it took a month to travel from Bangkok to Chiang Mai using the only means possible – boat and elephant. In 1921 a rail connection was built and in 1928 King Rama VII became the first Siamese king to visit this distant, but sizeable and wealthy region. The advent of the railway increased Bangkok's control over the area and was followed by trade with the south of Thailand, and use of the national currency.

The north is really a series of upland valleys. To the east is the Mekong catchment; to the west, the Salween in Burma (Myanmar). Most rivers drain into the Chao Phraya, following the fall of the land at Nakorn Sawan, where two rivers converge; the sight is memorable, as their waters are of different colours – both are muddy but one is redder than the other.

The landscape of this region is mountainous – covered with evergreen forests that once sustained monkeys, deer, wild cattle, boar, tigers and even bears – and lined with deep valleys, rivers and lakes beside wide tablelands. The mountains are still mostly covered with forests – except around hill-tribe settlements, since their slash-and-burn agriculture clears substantial areas of surrounding land. Towns and farming communities are spread over the narrow plains and along valleys. The teak and other hardwood trees that covered this low-lying land were a major source of wealth in the late nineteenth and twentieth centuries, but so much of the timber has been exploited that 75 per cent of the land area is now deforested. The high, exposed and stony terrain of the north rises to about 1600 metres (5250 feet), while the valleys that run north to south gave easy passage to the Thai on their way to the central plains over a thousand years ago. The myriad small, isolated *muang* that define and characterise this region developed within these valleys. The densely forested mountains separating the valleys meant that there was little communication between the *muang*, giving rise to distinct yet parallel cultures. The distance, for example, between Lampang and Chiang Mai is only 100 kilometres (62 miles) and today it takes a mere 90 minutes by car, yet before roads were built the journey took up to seven days, travelling on foot or by horse, raft or elephant. This effectively put Lampang beyond the control of Chiang Mai – and certainly outside that of Bangkok.

The climate is variable in these mountains. The wet season usually lasts from May to October; it is followed by a cold, dry season from November to February and then a hot, dry season from February to May. The lowest average temperature is in January, 14.5°C (58°F), while April is the hottest month, averaging 37°C (99°F).

THE PEOPLE OF THE NORTH

The people of the northern regions of Thailand are often referred to as *kon muang*, 'people of the principalities'. The name encompasses a wide range of people and ethnic groups, giving some indication of the cultural diversity, physical isolation, political autonomy and historical complexity of the region. Some Lao are picturesquely referred to as black-bellied Lao – these northerners have heavily tattooed stomachs, as opposed to their Laotian and Thai north-eastern cousins, who are unmarked and are thus known as the white-bellied Lao.

The indigenous inhabitants of the Chiang Mai region are the Lawa. Archeological evidence places them here from the fifth century AD. The Lawa lived mainly around Chiang Mai and were once the dominant group, but with the arrival of the Mon and later the Thai, they were displaced to the hills and edges of their old kingdom. The remnants of the population now live, marginalised, in the mountains of northern and western Thailand.

The Haw Chinese traders from southern Yunnan have plied the mountainous trade routes between Thailand, Burma, Laos and Vietnam for hundreds of years. Mule caravans carried porcelain, cooking pots, silks and lamps from China, which were bartered for rice, tea, cotton, opium and gemstones. Although the Muslim Haw had traded for centuries in the northern provinces of Chiang Mai, Chiang Rai and Mae Hong Son, only after the Muslim Rebellion of Yunnan was crushed by the Chinese in 1855 did they move into Laos, Burma and Thailand.

Other ethnic groups in northern Thailand include the Kui, whose origins may have been in the lowlands of Thailand and Cambodia, and the Karen, who arrived in the eighth century. Most of the hill tribes, like the Hmong and the Mien, moved into the region during the nineteenth century, compelled by political pressures, civil wars or the need to expand their settlement areas. Coming from Laos, Burma or the southern reaches of China, their cultures vary in their level of sophistication but most practise slash-and-burn agriculture.

Around Nan and Phrae, in northernmost Thailand, live the Mlabri, who migrated from Laos in the mid-nineteenth century. Called 'the ghosts of the golden leaves' by other Thai, they have a simple hunting and gathering lifestyle, building makeshift shelters from banana branches; when these turn yellow, it is taken as a signal that it is time to move on. Since they avoid other people, their discarded housing is usually the only sign of their presence. 'Mlabri' is the word they use to refer to themselves and simply means 'people of the forest', but other hill tribes once considered the Mlabri harmful spirits and shot them on sight.

The Mlabri used to gather wild bamboo shoots, yams and palm shoots, mushrooms and wild fruits such as bananas and mangoes; they collected honey and boiled the beeswax to make candles. They picked herbs for medicine and believed in the curative value of fire, spreading ashes onto wounds. Skilled hunters, they took boar, deer, elephant, bear, wild buffalo and monkey with spears, although monkey was traditionally their staple meat. They collected rats, lizards, snakes, birds and their eggs and caught fish, crabs, other crustaceans and molluscs. They grilled their catch over embers – either whole or cut into strips and packed into bamboo lengths. However, their rudimentary manner of living is rapidly disappearing as they come into contact with other hill tribes and the Thai.

Chiang Saen

Chiang Rai

Chiang Mai   Nan

THE NORTH

Phrae

LAOS

MEKONG

VIETNAM

PING

Nong Khai

Sukothai   Udon Thani   Nakhon Phanom

Phitsanulok

Mukdahan

THAILAND   Khon Kaen

CHI   Yasothon   MEKONG

THE
CENTRAL   Nakhon Sawan   THE NORTH-EAST
PLAINS

ChaiNat   MUN   Ubon Ratchathani

Lopburi
CHAO PHRAYA   Nakhon
Ratchasima   Surin
Kanchanaburi   Ayuthyia   (Khorat)

Bangkok

Ratchaburi   Chonburi

Siracha   CAMBODIA
Phetchaburi   Pattaya   THE SOUTH

Hua Hin   Ko Samet   Chanthaburi

Laem
Ngop

Prachuap   Ko Chang
Khiri Khan

VIETNAM

Chumphon

GULF OF THAILAND

Similan   Ban Hin   Ko Samui
Lat

Surat Thani

Khao Lak

Nakhon Si
Thammarat

Phuket   Krabi   THE SOUTH

Trang   Phatthalung

Songkhla

Ban Pak Bara   Hat Yai   Pattani

Yala   Narathiwat

MALAYSIA

BURMA (MYANMAR)

0   50   100   150   Kilometres
     50   100   Miles

Another fascinating ethnic group in Thailand's north is the Padong of Mae Hong Son province. They are commonly referred to as the 'long neck' or 'giraffe' people, since the women often wear brass rings around their necks, aspiring to a maximum of 32 coils.

THE FOOD OF THE NORTH

Northern food is not as extreme in taste as that of other regions of Thailand. The traditional abundance meant there was no need to have piercingly hot dishes so that a small amount of pungent food could be mixed with copious rice to satisfy the appetite. Sticky rice is the preferred rice and is sold in the market both raw and already steamed, wrapped in banana – or traditionally teak – leaves, or in bamboo baskets.

Coconut is seldom used in the north as the region has too temperate a climate for the palms to grow. Most dishes are moistened by water or stock, and the seasoning of dishes is generally less intense than in other regions. It is as if the comparative gentleness of the climate has had a mitigating effect on the food. Rendered pork fat is the traditional frying medium, imparting a wonderfully rich, silken quality. It is, however, wonderfully rich in cholesterol too, and vegetable oil is now more commonly used.

The primary seasoning characteristic is hot and salty. Heat, of course, comes from chillies, but also from dried and powdered galangal and other rhizomes and spices; white, black and long peppers; and the dried berries of prickly ash (*macquem*), which have a delicate mandarin perfume and an agreeable heat. The saltiness comes mainly from light soy sauce and plain salt. The most ancient seasoning is *tua nao* – soy beans fermented in brine, puréed and dried into cakes then wrapped in banana leaves. When *tua nao* is needed, it is grilled then added to curries and relishes, very much as shrimp paste is used on the central plains. A primordial fermented fish, *pla raa*, is also used, both in its undiluted form as a base for curries and relishes or simmered with water and aromatics as a general seasoning. Another peculiar base is pounded land crabs simmered with lemongrass until thick, black and murky, before being used in salads and relishes. Traditionally shrimp paste was rarely used, although it is now available in markets to cater to the tastes of southern Thai living in the north. Fish sauce is also a comparatively recent addition to the northern repertoire, but its milder taste is finding favour with a new generation of northern cooks who can be confronted by the robustness of some of the traditional local pickles.

Additional seasoning is obtained from the ingredients employed, rather than the balancing of sugar and lime juice or tamarind water as happens farther south. These come from the wide range of vegetables and fruit that are cultivated or gathered in this agreeable climate. Rosella or tamarind leaves, mango shoots, hog plums, *madan* (sour cucumber), or small and quite sour orange cherry tomatoes impart a complex and unusual sourness to dishes. Sugar is an uncommon seasoning in northern food – any sweetness is again derived from the natural sugars in fruit and vegetables.

One taste in northern food that is not commonly encountered elsewhere is bitterness, produced by a variety of leaves, shoots and plants collected from the nearby mountains and forests. Wild and astringent, they are used in curries and soups, and raw or blanched as an accompaniment to relishes. Intriguingly, just after the rainy season many species of wild mushrooms are gathered, including turmeric mushrooms, golden chanterelles and *het kone*.

Pork is an especially popular meat – northern Thai eat all cuts in all ways. It is grilled, deep-fried, simmered in soups and curries, dried, salted and fermented. Freshwater fish, especially catfish and eels, are popular. Frogs and game, like deer and boar, are also found in local recipes. Away from larger towns the food is often more rustic – jungle food. Here restaurants serve hare, deer, snakes, turtles, lizards, ants; and sometimes dogs, cats and gibbons, but not their apocryphal brains. Surreptitiously, some endangered species such as barking deer, Asian tigers and the small Asian bear are even on offer, although wildlife services now make regular crackdowns on such operations.

It is notable that little food is eaten raw in this region; even the vegetables used in salads and as accompaniments to relishes are often cooked. Certainly, it reduces spoilage in the tropical climate. However, other regions, which are doubtless equally scrupulous, have fewer cooked dishes in their repertoire. I think this is because fuel is readily obtainable in the heavily forested north. The southern regions are given over to vast paddies, cleared of most forests, while the north-east is arid and wood is difficult to find. Easy access to fuel affords the northerners the luxury of cooking almost all their foods; it also gives them a greater choice of cooking techniques.

Deep-fried foods abound as this region consumes a lot of pork and thus has an excess of pork fat: deep-fried chicken, deep-fried pork with garlic and peppercorns, and deep-fried pork skin – the last a particular favourite that is eaten as a snack, in soups, salads, with and in relishes and curries. All fish are subject to this treatment as well, being fried in very hot oil, or simmered in oil for up to half an hour, from which they emerge crisp and fragrant. Even young bamboo shoots are deep-fried. They are first shredded and then stuffed with pork and garlic, sometimes dipped into a simple batter, and deep-fried until golden.

Grilling is a fundamental technique, and grilled foods are always included in a northern meal, whether fresh fish, prawns, game or mushrooms; skewered and grilled pork or its liver is especially popular.

Plenty of fuel also makes steaming, simmering and braising popular techniques. In the markets of the north, cauldrons are filled with pork belly simmered with pickled mustard greens, scrawny but flavoursome chickens with lemongrass and red shallots, and steamed serpent fish in broth with Asian celery and pickled red Chinese plums. Braised pork hocks with star anise bubble in huge brass woks, testament to the Chinese migration throughout the kingdom.

Stir-frying over rapid heat is also a Chinese introduction; the indigenous version of a stir-fry, *krua*, is much gentler, the ingredients being almost simmered in the oil. These dishes straddle the boundary between curries and relishes: a paste is briefly fried and then finished with other ingredients to make, for example, a chicken curry with green melon and *macquem*. If a *krua* is to be eaten as a relish, then it is made less moist and the vegetables are eaten as an accompaniment. An ancient version is one made from a paste of yellow beans simply heated in oil with red shallots, then sprinkled with coarsely chopped coriander.

Relishes are almost without exception cooked, unlike those of the south. Ingredients are either grilled before being pounded into a pungent paste, such as Chiang Mai chilli relish, or puréed before being simmered, as in Chiang Mai pork and tomato relish. All these relishes are eaten with vegetables, usually grilled or boiled, and, almost invariably, deep-fried pork skin.

Soups of the north are usually gentle, very simple broths – often just minced or cubed meat simmered with vegetables, such as pork simmered with bamboo shoots. Hot and sour soups are enhanced with charred red shallots, garlic and chillies and perfumed with shredded herbs. Very often there is little distinction between spicy northern soups and curries; furthermore, charred ingredients are often pounded to form a relish paste, which is then dissolved in simmering stock, in a very curry-like manner.

Curries of the north are mostly boiled, the paste being dissolved in simmering liquid: examples include jackfruit and pork curry, minced rabbit curry, and taro shoot curry with minced fish. Sometimes the paste and the ingredients for the curry – fish, prawns, bamboo shoots or even wild mushrooms – are mixed and then wrapped in banana leaves and grilled. Fried pastes are rare in northern curries and occur mainly in dishes of foreign derivation, such as Burmese pork curry or the more familiar red and green curries from the south.

Salads are not as popular in the north as they are in other regions. Usually all the components are cooked, albeit briefly. Sliced apple eggplants are soaked in salted water to remove their bitterness before being combined with smoked fish and grilled chillies, or dressed with a mixture of grilled chillies and shallots pounded with salted beef and sprinkled with dried prawns. In another style of salad, the ingredients are pounded together using a pestle and mortar and eaten with fresh vegetables. Perhaps the most popular is pomelo dressed with fresh prawns, lemongrass and crab paste, then eaten with fresh 'betel' leaves.

Street food and other snacks are popular. Cured pork (*naem*) is the most famous. In its basic version, minced pork is cured with sticky rice and garlic and presented wrapped in a banana leaf. Pork ribs or freshwater fish are often treated in the same way. Perhaps my favourite is the uncommon and unlikely but extraordinarily delicious deep-fried cured chicken cartilage – ambrosial with beer. Chiang Mai sausage (*sai ouah*) is sold everywhere. It is grilled over a low heat, impregnated by the smoke then deep-fried. It can be eaten hot or cold, but is always accompanied by slices of fresh ginger, bird's eye chillies and sprigs of coriander.

Kao soi, Chiang Mai's favourite curried noodle dish, is believed to have arrived with Muslim Chinese traders, the Haw. Consequently, it is usually made with either beef or chicken. Fermented rice noodles, *kanom jin*, are dressed with a relish that traces its roots to the Shan – made from pork, tamarind, chillies and deep-fried shallots. *Miang* is now used as a general term to describe the central plains snack rolled in 'betel' leaves, but its original meaning was a fermented wild tea-leaf eaten after a northern meal to refresh and stimulate. *Miang warn* includes caramelised coconut and soy beans, while *miang som* is a somewhat astringent version eaten with ginger; a third kind is eaten with salt as a puckering palate-cleanser.

Local desserts are few in number, but are reflections of what the ancient Thai would have eaten. Steamed sticky rice is dressed with coarse palm sugar, grated coconut and perhaps sesame seeds; or raw sticky rice is mixed with bananas and peanuts before being wrapped in banana leaves and steamed.

Carl Bock, a Norwegian explorer and naturalist, recounted a journey through northern Thailand and Laos in *Temples and Elephants*, published in 1884. He described the food of Chiang Mai thus:

83

[They] take their meals twice a day, at about seven in the morning and towards sunset. They sit in a circle on the floor, or on mats, with a lacquer or brazen tray before them, on which were placed a number of saucers or small bowls containing dried or boiled fish, bits of buffalo-meat stewed, a salted egg, or a piece of the favourite pork: all these meats are invariably served with rice and curry. For vegetables they eat stewed bamboo shoots – not at all a bad substitute for asparagus – beans, plantains, tamarinds, and powdered capsicums. Pervading everything is the inevitable fishy flavour, which, like the garlic among the Spaniards, is never absent. This is imparted by adding to the dishes a small quantity of rotten fish – the ngapee of the Burmese [*pla raa* or *gapi*] – the preparation of which is as much an art among the Laosians and Siamese, Burmese and Malay, as the anxious endeavour on the part of the European housewife to keep her fish fresh. The rice, simply boiled or steamed, is served separately to each person in a small basket . . . From the basket of dry rice a small quantity is taken with the fingers and rolled between the hands into a ball, which is then dipped into one or more of the various curries and flavouring dishes.

In the north there was also a very traditional and formal manner of eating, the *kan dtok*, where the dishes were served on a teak platter. The dishes on the platter might have included Chiang Mai pork and tomato relish or Chiang Mai chilli relish, deep-fried pork skin, Chiang Mai pork curry, mixed curry, a *larp* salad with raw vegetables, smoked sausage and deep-fried pork. To one side would be a bamboo basket of steamed sticky rice, and a fingerbowl of perfumed water as the food was eaten by hand. Afterwards a small platter of desserts would be served.

At a modern *kan dtok* meal the guests arrive in a candlelit room or large garden, where a small plate of betel nuts and leaves to be chewed and savoured is waiting. The platters are set in front of the guests: one platter, depending on its size, is for four or eight people. With the platters comes the rice. Historically, there would often be a dance performance during the meal; traditionally the wives or servants of the host would perform, but today the dancers are professionals. Finally the desserts arrive – sweet sticky rice, crispy caramelised rice, a dumpling and some *miang*.

THE NORTH-EAST   Isarn

Deriving its common Thai name, Isarn, from the Sanskrit for north-east, this plateau sits some 200–300 metres (650–1000 feet) above sea level. Although it is hemmed in by mountain ranges to the west and the south, the plateau itself is quite level, unlike the northern and western regions of Thailand. The Mun and Chi rivers flow down to the Mekong, which forms much of the boundary of Isarn with Laos and Cambodia. The very flat land means the rivers meander and form lakes.

Until very recently, this region was isolated at the best of times and cut off completely for several months during the rainy season. The Phetchabun mountain range prevented easy communication. Further, the fact that the rivers in the area flow eastward to the Mekong and thence down through Laos or Cambodia to the southern provinces of Vietnam, rather than west into the central plains of Thailand, means the usual Thai method of transport – by water – is not possible here.

Until the nineteenth century Isarn was, and had been from time immemorial, covered with dense impenetrable forests filled with abundant game. The Mekong was the only means of trade with, and access to, the outside world. Travellers such as Gerard van Wusthof in 1641, and the Frenchman Garnier in the late nineteenth century, recorded the deep forests and primitive life. Hugh Clifford, in his epic tale of the exploration of South East Asia, *Further India*, written in 1904, imaginatively describes Garnier's journey along the Mekong from Phnom Penh to Ubon at the onset of the monsoon in July 1866:

> On each bank of the great river rose marvelous tangles of untouched
> forest – giant trees with buttress roots, treading on one another's toes,
> standing knee deep in striving underwood, their branches interlocked
> and each to each by vine and creeper, shaggy with ferns and mosses,
> draped with hanging parasitic growths and set here and there with
> delicate stars of orchids. Between these sheer cliffs of vegetation the
> great river rolled, sullen and persistent . . .

Of the present population of Isarn, only 10 per cent live in towns. And although three-quarters of the plateau is devoted to rice production, Isarn produces only 34 per cent of Thailand's rice. Yields are unreliable: the rainfall is often insufficient for rice, and the soil is notoriously poor.

Irrigation can offset such problems to a degree, and has allowed for an increase in the production of rice, but ultimately rain determines output – and drought can quickly devastate crops and desiccate the land. The people of the north-east often seem caught in a cycle of poverty: two-thirds of the rice they produce is eaten and the balance is kept for sowing the next year's crop, so little is left to sell.

Extremes of wet and dry are a continuing pattern in this region, which cannot rely on the moderating influence of the sea. Changes of season can be drastic. Little rain falls in December; in May, rockets are fired into the heavens at festivals to try to coax rain from the sky; yet by September, the landscape is mostly flooded. There is 60 times more water in the Chi River in October than there is in March. The swollen rivers burst and flow across the plains. Such is the volume of the floodwater reaching the Mekong that the river chokes and the water backs up, increasing the extent and duration of the flooding. The unfortunate and lasting effect is that the forests, groves and thickets in the area are waterlogged. Beyond the floodplains, however, the land remains quite dry, with only remnants of the deciduous forests that once supported diverse fauna, including wild cattle, boar and deer.

Deforestation and silt flows have also greatly increased the extent of flooding, making the flat lands of the north-east a precarious place in which to settle. Marshes have encroached as trees became swamped, destroying the cover of the land and, as a consequence, its wildlife. Slightly to the west, the extreme results of the floods are mitigated and the inundation is beneficial, fertilising the land. It is here, along the gentler tributaries and slopes, that the first communities were recorded. Currently, however, erosion has taken its toll and this area is arid, with thin soils.

This region has been under the control of a succession of kingdoms or empires during the last two millennia. The earliest may have been Funan, an empire based around the Mekong delta. In the sixth century, the region was ruled by Chen-la, which was contemporaneous with the Dvaravati kingdoms around the Chao Phraya basin. The Khmer empire held sway over this region for two centuries longer than it did over the rest of the country, but with the decline of Angkor, the Lao and Siamese influence in the area increased.

Depending on their position, north-eastern *muang* gave allegiance to Bangkok or Hué, the royal capital of Vietnam. Little is known of the interior of Isarn, for throughout most of its long history very few towns or communities were mentioned in the state chronicles either of the Siamese or the Lao. It was considered a backwater of scant political or economic significance – although the principal exports from Isarn during the

Ayuthyian period included fragrant woods used for incense, rattan, rhinoceros horn and ivory. In the nineteenth century the main tribute presented to Bangkok was cardamom.

A layer of salt forms one of the lower soil strata of the plateau – hence the infertility of the region. Isarn survived in early times on trade in salt, iron and forest products, but the extraction of salt and iron both require large amounts of labour and fuel, and so can deplete the forest. It is possible that such early deforestation resulted in today's poor soil. And the general isolation of the region further retarded settlement.

THE PEOPLE OF THE NORTH-EAST

Both Khmer and Mon have long been present on the plateau, at its eastern and western edges respectively, with the Thai arriving from the tenth century onwards. The Lao settled at the same time, advancing into the region over several decades, and engaging in commerce and agriculture with the Mon and Khmer, whom they considered inferior peoples. From the eighteenth century the advance was no longer gradual but quite rapid – possibly led by peasants in need of land to cultivate.

An early-nineteenth-century missionary, Monsignor Jean-Baptiste Pallegoix, visited Isarn during the reign of King Mongkut, and in his book, *The Description of the Thai Kingdom or Siam*, published in 1854, he observed:

> The Lao are peaceful, deferential, patient, sober, confident, gullible, superstitious, loyal, simple and naïve. By nature they abhor theft. It is said that one of their kings fried thieves in a boiler with boiling oil.
>
> Their food consists of sticky rice, fresh fish, chickens, pork, deer or wild buffalo meat and abundant vegetables. But their favourite dish is fish which they let spoil in the sun and then put into brine [*pla raa*]. They make a paste of this and mix this with their rice, adding red peppers. For them, snakes, lizards, bats, rats and whole frogs are delicate game. They consider seasoning superfluous and are satisfied with roasting the animals on a fire.
>
> Among the common people it is rare to find earthenware or porcelain pottery. They eat from baskets woven with tiny rotan [rattan?] and if one excepts a wooden casket containing their pretty dresses, one does not see any other furniture among them than rotan or bamboo

baskets. No chairs, benches or beds. A few used mats serve at the same time as chairs, table and bed.

The entertainment they love most is hunting and fishing, I have often admired the skillfulness of children piercing fish with a long javelin in the clear water of torrents coming back to their huts loaded with their prey in the evening. The weapons they use for hunting are rifles, crossbows, and blow pipes consisting of a long hollow bamboo from which they blow arrows which rarely miss their targets.

Soon the Lao became the major ethnic group of Isarn, settling the area from the Mekong to midway between the Chi and Mun rivers. The second largest group, the Khmers, occupied the area south of here to the Cambodian border. The third ethnic group was mainly Siamese, and was found around the administrative capital, Nakhon Ratchasima or Khorat. Mon and small ethnic groups also co-existed here, and there was an easy interchange between all these groups. Slowly, though, the Thai became dominant throughout Isarn. Nakhon Ratchasima became the first town under the absolute control of Bangkok, and this control soon extended to other townships.

Several other ethnic groups live in Isarn, such as the Bru, who occupy the borderlands along the Mekong between Laos and Thailand in the Ubon Ratchathani province. An ancient people, they once filed and painted their teeth, tattooed their faces, pierced their ear lobes and inserted wood or pewter to stretch them. The Bru live in a complex spiritual world; they are profoundly animist and place great store on placating gods of the sky, the forest, rice and the village. The Bru worship their ancestors. Each family has a small altar on which raw rice, cooked rice and a bowl of water are proffered. Sorcerers, shamans and magicians assist in the Bru's negotiations with the supernatural; sacrifices are also used, but these may be as simple as an egg given for the slaying of a buffalo, along with rice, whisky, bananas and coconuts. The sacrifices follow the cycle of the seasons and the agricultural calendar. Blood and meat are important elements in a sacrifice to placate the spirits and these are often displayed in bowls and pans.

THE FOOD OF THE NORTH-EAST

There is an ethnic boundary in Isarn between the Lao area and the Khmer area, running midway between the Chi and Mun rivers. Ethnic culture and diet are distinct. The southernmost limit of the Lao marks another boundary: north of it, glutinous or sticky rice is mainly grown but beyond, where the Siamese settled, long-grain rice predominates.

Significantly, long-grain rice is served in most restaurants in the larger cities of the region. Those who migrate to the cities usually change their preference; glutinous rice is the rice of the countryside, eaten by those who grow it. Coincidentally, coconuts share the same geographical distribution as long-grain rice, and thus are used in the south of the region but not the north.

The traditional cuisine was once diverse but has become reduced as the area has become deforested. The struggling farmers eke out an existence, and the food reflects this: it is not a cuisine of great complexity or diverse flavours, but it is distinctive. North-eastern food is hot, very hot. Because it is such an impoverished area, only a small amount of food is available to dress rice – and therefore the food is extremely pungent. Small dried red chillies are used to season most dishes. Mineral salt is harvested from the region and exported throughout the country. During the annual floods fish are caught and preserved in salt and rice to make the fundamental seasoning of this region, *pla raa*. Other dried spices are rarely used; cardamom was an export product only.

Since there are very few trees and thus little fuel, a lot of food is eaten raw or cured, such as pickled or raw fish or a *larp dip* (a salad of minced meat or fish). Surprisingly, the people of the north-east eat buffalo, a meat that is disliked elsewhere in Thailand, but they do so from need and lack of choice rather than preference. Most foods that are cooked are either grilled or boiled, as little fat is available. Many fresh herbs are used to counterbalance the intense heat of the cuisine: dill is especially popular, used almost as prominently as coriander is on the central plains. Relishes are hot and salty, based on *pla raa* or boiled fish, with any sourness being obtained from accompanying items, such as hog plums, tamarind and red ants.

North-eastern soups are simple, stock-based assemblies of dried or fermented fish with wild vegetables gathered from the remaining forests. Occasionally they are enriched with a few grilled items such as chillies, shallots and even coconut. Sometimes these ingredients are pounded together and dissolved in a soup, becoming virtually indistinguishable from curries. To the south, there are also some coconut curries and soups.

Insects like locusts and crickets, frogs and lizards, are also consumed, and red ant eggs are considered a great delicacy. The idea of such food may seem repugnant to a Westerner, but all too often it is the idea rather than the taste that repels. However, having tried deep-fried locust, I have to admit that its taste and the idea of eating it swirled and swarmed together and I was not converted – perhaps because while the exterior was crunchy, the insides were not.

Formal eating is similar to the northern *kan dtok*, but is called *kao laeng*; several dishes arrive on a platter, but without much ceremony. On this platter there might be a grilled chilli and *pla raa* relish, a curry of boiled wild mushrooms with dill, a spicy salad with mint and roasted rice and a plate of fresh raw vegetables. Sticky rice would be served to accompany the dishes.

THE SOUTH *pak dtay*

The south of Thailand can be regarded as two distinct areas: the low-lying provinces to the south and south-east of Bangkok, which were once lowlands covered by dry deciduous forests, but are now ricefields; and the Isthmus of Kra.

Peninsular Thailand – better known as the Isthmus of Kra – is a long, narrow strip dominated by a spine of hills with a coastal plain to the east and west. At its narrowest, it is only 40 kilometres (25 miles) wide. The hills are covered with evergreen forest, and the western plain is fringed with mangroves.

The isthmus is subject to the longest period of monsoonal weather in Thailand, for the western coast and hills are exposed to the south-western monsoon from May to October, while the eastern side receives most of its rain during the north-eastern monsoon, from October to December. The eastern plains are somewhat broader and sandier than the western and have several secure anchorages. Many small rivulets course from the hills; those flowing to the east carry silt, building large deltas as they reach the sea. Despite the heavy rainfall, the area grows little rice. Instead, there are substantial plantations of coconuts and bananas and a fishing industry that is the region's main source of income. Tin mining was once the most prominent industry and timber was also important.

There are many islands off the isthmus: in the Gulf of Thailand around Surat Thani are the Samui, Pa-ngan and Anthong islands. The Andaman Sea coast, on the western side, is renowned for its beauty, with islands including Phuket and the Similan group, where tourism is now a major industry. The Andaman Sea coast differs from the rest of Thailand. The rugged coastline hides fishing villages in small emerald bays, which alternate with sheer limestone cliffs covered with dense tropical vegetation. The granite Tenasserim (or Phuket) mountain range runs in a north–south direction and often extends right down to the Andaman Sea. Mountain streams join and form small rivers, creating alluvial floodplains as they flow into the sea. Most of the coastline is lined with mangrove swamps, broken by long white beaches of quartz and coral. The magnificent limestone mountains in the province of Phangnga, about halfway down the isthmus, were formed by glaciers some ten millennia ago. There are caves in the mountains, some with prehistoric rock paintings, but they are also the source of the nests of tiny forktail swifts – once so relished that they were exported to Ayuthyia and China, and later Bangkok, as tribute from the area. Inland from the coastal fishing villages, tropical rainforest is interspersed with paddies, rubber and pineapple plantations, and coconut and cashew nut groves.

The Isthmus of Kra has a history of contact with the outside world. In the past, the west coast was the first point of contact for merchants and mariners from the West – whether it be India, Arabia or, later, from Europe – and archeological excavations have revealed the remains of ancient ports and trading villages.

THE PEOPLE OF THE SOUTH

The division between Buddhism and Islam pervades the culture of the south today, with 34 per cent of the population of south Thailand being Muslim. In the Isthmus of Kra the majority of Muslims live on the seaboard, while most of the Buddhist Thai live inland and are farmers. Various feasts reinforce the Muslim community: to celebrate marriages; to mark important moments in life, such as naming ceremonies, births and deaths, as well as religious occasions like the Prophet's birthday – and especially the day after Ramadan, the month of fasting. A feast is an important social affair, and the more guests or the more prestigious the guests attending, the greater its success. Refusal to attend is a great insult.

For a feast chickens and goats are slaughtered in the morning, and then only the best dishes are prepared, like goat curry, pineapple curry of fish, and saffron rice. When people arrive the men sit in the house, the women in the kitchen. The men recite relevant verses from the Quran, after which the participants are sprinkled with talc and perfumed water and blessings are requested from Allah. This is followed by a community meal, and each guest contributes a cash gift to the host. Each household will hold a feast at least once a year, building the bonds of community, 'a web of relationships in which favours and obligations are reciprocated', as Olli-Pekka Ruohamäki observes in his book *Fisherman No More? Livelihood and Environment in Southern Thai Maritime Villages*.

While the Muslims recognise that their religion does differentiate them, they also acknowledge many shared values and traditions that ensure their belonging – their 'Thai-ness'. They refer to themselves as 'Thai people upholding Islam' – and, except in the southernmost provinces, they speak the same language. Farther south, however, there is some ethnic tension as the Muslims are Malay rather than Thai.

There are smaller ethnic groups, too. The Semang are negroid pygmies who live in the distant south, near the border with Malaysia, and are believed to be the aborigines of South East Asia. The Semang inhabit the dense rainforest-covered foothills and mountains of southern Thailand and northern Malaysia, where their way of living has remained unchanged over thousands of years. Like the northern Mlabri, the Semang are a shy people, occupying virtually inaccessible areas that can only be reached by arduous treks along precipitous and narrow mountain paths. Their traditional clothing is made from the bark and leaves of trees and vines. They file their teeth with sandstone, and cover themselves with dirt and soot, first rubbing their bodies with fat then sleeping in the ashes of a warm hearth, and thus are crusted with a greyish skin. On ceremonial occasions they paint their faces white with clay. On their infrequent excursions down to the plains to barter rare woods, honey and medicinal herbs for salt, tobacco and knives, they wear less traditional garb, although their stature and hair make them easily identifiable. They are nomadic, building temporary shelters of leaves and branches that are demolished when game becomes hard to find or when strangers intrude. They hunt birds, deer, wild boar and monkeys with poisonous blowpipes, and catch fish with poisoned spears. One group in the Yala region is much feared as they have the belligerent habit of shooting intruders in the back with poisoned darts from their blowpipes.

Another recognised group are the sea gypsies, Mawken and Moklen, people of the sea who range down the west coast of the Isthmus of Kra along the Andaman Sea. They live on their boats or in floating villages, spending most of their life at sea. They harvest the sea and barter for rice and other essentials with its bounty. Oysters are especially important to them since, even if these do not contain a pearl, Chinese merchants will happily barter for their mother of pearl. The Mawken also collect edible birds' nests from sea caves for lucrative trade, clambering up vertiginous, flimsy bamboo ladders.

Sea gypsies will come ashore to collect wild fruit, berries and honey, and occasionally to hunt small game. During a bad rainy season, they may have to survive on what they can obtain from the forests. Some of the sea gypsies practise Islam, a few are Buddhist but most are animists and thus make sacrifices for aid and protection. During such ceremonies, rice, shells, roots, stewed chicken and blood are placed in bowls, and a candle is lit.

THE FOOD OF THE SOUTH

Vivid red turmeric colours southern Thai food and shrimp paste gives it depth. The many varieties of chillies make the food from this region the spiciest in Thailand; small dried bird's eye chillies are used in almost every curry, in place of the kinder long dried chillies used to the north. Coconut cream and its oil are used heavily in the south, but because the food is balanced with astringent turmeric, powerfully hot orange chillies, sour fruit – unripe pineapple, 'assam', tamarind and *madan* (sour cucumber) – and highly salted or fermented relishes, it does not cloy. A side plate of raw vegetables, or occasionally of vegetables simmered in coconut cream, accompanies every meal. These add texture and savour, as well as mitigating the extreme heat of the food. Vegetables include the shoots of mango, hog plum and rose apple. Many ferns and roots are collected from densely forested hills, most of them having a pronounced taste that balances the intensity of the dishes. Herbs are usually astringent, and sometimes sour: dill, lemon basil and 'betel' leaves.

Unsurprisingly, seafood plays a major role in the cuisine of this coastal region. There are myriad varieties, sizes and colours of prawns, clams, oysters, mussels, scallops and crabs. Especially delicious is the seasonal softshell crab from Trang, stir-fried with black pepper and lemongrass, while Phuket is famous for its colourful crayfish. Squid and cuttlefish are freshly caught, grilled, deep-fried or dried in the sun.

The Gulf of Thailand is a perfect area to catch fish, including the favourite fish of the Thai, a small mackerel called *pla tuu*, which is cleaned, washed in seawater and then salted before being steamed in bamboo baskets and sent overnight to almost every market in Thailand. Other fresh fish – for example, sea bass or barramundi and red emperor – are grilled and served with a spicy chilli, lime and garlic sauce, or deep-fried with garlic or fresh turmeric. Further ways of cooking seafood are roasting on salt in an earthenware pot, stir-frying with freshly pounded chillies and garlic, or adding to pungently hot and sour yellow curries with green papaya or pickled bamboo shoots.

Much of the catch, however, is dried in the fierce sun. Whole villages are occupied in this task, filling the air with a truly memorable scent. The beloved shrimp paste (*gapi*) is made, as well as dried prawns and a fermented fish sauce. Relishes are hot, very hot, and always based on shrimp paste. Small salted prawns are dried and grilled on a skewer and made into a pungent relish with shrimp paste, served with *petai* beans grilled in their large spiralling pods and cucumbers. A local delicacy is prawns mixed with salt, sugar and a little cooked rice, then fermented for a week before using. This can be eaten as a salad with red shallots, mint and chillies, or pounded into a *nahm prik* relish. Another intensely concentrated relish of chillies, garlic, turmeric and fish innards – much more delicious than it sounds – is eaten with crisp, raw vegetables.

Stir-fries are hot, sometimes fiercely hot. Soups are perfumed and coloured with turmeric, and are either based on coconut cream, or are similar to a golden version of a hot and sour soup. There is a simple and delicate coconut soup of mackerel with lemongrass, shallots and tiny, young, purple-skinned lotus stalks boiled with pineapple and ginger. A sizeable Chinese community means there are many noodle shops selling delicious noodle soups and stir-fried rice noodles, such as noodles in tapioca-thickened gravy with squid, pork or chicken. Barbecued meats, especially duck and pork, are served over rice or in noodle soups.

Most curries are boiled and are generally fish-based with a sour ingredient; the prevalent seasoning is hot, salty and sour. An incendiary yellow turmeric curry uses fish (whole or fillets), boiled, grilled or deep-fried, with various vegetables, such as bamboo shoots, cucumbers, heart of coconut or pieces of pineapple. The Buddhists of the region use coconut milk and cream. Familiar red and green curries appear, but with southern traits. Red curries are often made with small dried chillies plus a few fresh yellow chillies and always include red turmeric and often a larger proportion of shrimp paste. Green curries are made much hotter, using extra chillies and peppercorns, usually white; farther to the south, in Muslim regions, black pepper is sometimes added as well. Jungle curries are hot and golden with turmeric, and might include a small chicken with cucumber and wing beans, eel with fuzzy eggplants and heart of coconut, or fish with fleshy banana stalks.

The Muslim community of the south has different culinary preferences. They use only a little coconut cream, preferring stock, ghee and, surprisingly, yoghurt. Most Muslim curries are boiled, quite thick and redolent of cardamom and cumin. Seasoning depends on the province: in Pattani and Yala, the seasoning is hot and salty, but it is a little sweeter in Trang, on the Andaman Sea. Beef, mutton, goat and liver are stewed in complex yellow and *mussaman* curries. Seafood is eaten, but tends to be simply grilled. Sheep roam the streets of most villages and some towns in the Muslim south, where mutton is eaten in accordance with the Muslim diet. Beef is preferred, however, and pork is eschewed.

Smoky and nutty *kao larm*, sticky rice grilled in bamboo, is sold throughout the markets of the south – either white sticky rice or a mixture of white and black. In Trang there is a bizarre version where the rice is steamed in an insect-collecting pitcher plant; needless to say, the flower must be thoroughly cleaned first.

Grilled chicken, satay and grilled pork – marinated in honey and dried Chinese spices, five spice and torch ginger – are popular in the south. Among Buddhists, the satay is very similar to the central plains version. Farther to the south, the smoky Muslim version of grilled chicken is skewered and marinated in a rich sauce. Clams, chicken livers and oysters are also threaded onto skewers, dipped into marinade and grilled slowly over embers. *Madtarbark* is a common snack in the market places of southern Asia, and the Thai version is little different: chicken and potatoes are simmered in curry powder, onions, garlic and egg before being wrapped in a soft pastry and eaten with a cucumber relish.

4

RICE

The Thai are farmers and they farm rice. Rice is fundamental to every aspect of Thai culture and cuisine. It is an integral component of all the country's customs, traditions and ceremonies. The apotheosis of rice is Pra Mae Posop, who is venerated throughout rice-growing Asia under one name or another. In Bali she is called Dewi Sri and is believed to be the wife of Vishnu, one of the supreme gods of the Hindu pantheon. In Thailand her bounty is the source of life and the sustenance of both country and culture. So important is rice in Thailand that this goddess is included among the elemental forces, which the rest of the world believes to be fire, earth, wind and water. Pra Mae Posop is depicted as a young, long-haired woman with a diadem, seated on an altar. She wears the traditional dress of a classic Thai dancer, with a scarf wrapped around the left shoulder, leaving the right one bare, and she holds a sheaf of rice in one hand. The sides of the altar usually display images of rice plants, fish and lotuses.

The celebration of rice is the reason behind many Thai festivals. Rice itself is an indispensable ingredient in rituals – because rice is so necessary for human existence, it is considered an offering truly fit for the gods – and is at the heart of many Thai customs. At a child's birth, a banana-leaf receptacle is filled with a boiled egg and rice; the egg symbolises the new life, while the rice will sustain the child and is a symbol of its prospects. Rice nourishes the living, assuaging the spirits and gods in myriad rituals and ceremonies that mark the passage of life, and ensure its preservation. At the close of life, rice also performs a role. It is cast before a funeral procession, and in some regions a few grains are placed in a deceased person's mouth. Traditionally the floor of the room is strewn with rice before cremation, and no one can walk over it – it literally delineates the dead from the living.

During the rainy season, which corresponds with Buddhist Lent, itinerant monks who are normally free to roam are confined to their temples. Thai folklore maintains that the reason behind this is to prevent the precious rice seedlings from being crushed under the errant foot of a wandering mendicant – and thus life being taken.

Rice was also the agent of economic change that transformed ancient Siam into modern Thailand. 'Rice is not a crop that blends into the landscape. Rather, cultivation of rice sculpts the landscape to the crop's needs,' explains Jacqueline M. Piper, in her short but invaluable book *Rice in South-East Asia*. This transformation was not only economic; it also radically altered the environment, changing the vast tropical forests and wetlands, mountains and plateaux that comprised Siam into broad expanses of paddies – verdant and fertile. The countryside has nurtured this crop, which is all-consuming for the farmers tending it, and it has created a society, culture and cuisine that are uniquely Thai.

The central importance of rice to the Thai is also reflected at the table. All dishes other than rice are seen as an accompaniment to it; no matter how complicated, refined or delicious they may be, they are ancillary to the grain that has nourished the Thai, and ensured the cultivation of the land and its people. Rice has made the Thai Thai. Rice, Margaret Visser observes in her insightful book *Much Depends on Dinner*, is the

> creator and controller of human society. Where rice reigns, it governs power structures, technological prowess, population figures, interpersonal relationships, religious custom.
>
> The Thai . . . myths all insist on the delicate nature of rice . . . it is always easily offended or hurt . . . Rice, in other words, displays what is considered acceptable public demeanour by the people themselves. The ideal is to be unassuming, gentle, and sensitive. They feel deep shame when harsh words are used, and their feelings are easily offended by inconsiderate or ill-mannered behaviour. They concentrate on not letting unwanted violence erupt: there is no room for emotions getting out of hand. Rice is like themselves – and they have taken on these characteristics through their age-long devotion to rice and their adaptation to the crowded conditions which rice creates. The people have needed to cultivate the co-operative traits which suit rice best: sensitivity to wind, water, and weather, reciprocal neighbourliness, amenability to authority, patience, endurance, and the capacity to deal intelligently but ruthlessly with their own violent propensities.

THE RICE PLANT

Rice is a grass belonging to the same family – Graminae or Poaceae – as the other important grain crops of the world: wheat, maize, millet and barley. Rice, or *Oryza sativa*, is a cereal whose wild ancestor, *Oryza perennis*, was spread widely throughout southern Asia and parts of Africa. Rice is best described as an annual marsh plant; it is amphibious and extremely versatile, adapting to swampy valleys and paddies as well as hot, dry plateaux and cool, forested mountains.

It is hard to date the domestication of rice with any certainty. Most authorities believe that the wild grass *O. perennis* had its origins somewhere along the Asian fertile crescent – in what is now Upper Assam, Burma (Myanmar), Thailand, south-western China and northern

Vietnam. Fossilised grains have been located in the upper reaches of the Yangtze River, and have been dated between 5000 and 7000 BC. The first evidence of cultivated rice is in some Hoabinhian settlements around Lake Dongting, just south of the Yangtze, dating from some 8000 years ago (evidence of earlier cultivation is unlikely to be found, as rice cannot be expected to have survived the wet and tropical environment – whereas the ancestry of wheat in the drier regions of the Middle East can be traced back 10,000 years). The Hoabinhian peoples settled parts of southern China, northern Thailand and Vietnam between 10,000 and 4000 BC. They spoke a remote ancestral language of Mon, Khmer and Thai; indeed, this is probably where the Thai had their origin. Slowly the cultivation of rice expanded down the river valleys and across the plains – the same route followed by the Thai themselves on their migration southwards some 5000 years later.

At first rice was simply one of many grains collected, as it grew wild on nearby plains and at the edge of dense forests. Even when rice began to be cultivated, it was still possible to forage for wild rice, as the Thai had always done. The conversion from gathering to cultivation may have taken a few thousand years, during which time both practices would have continued, just as in Thailand today wild shoots, roots, leaves and animals are gathered or hunted to supplement cultivated vegetables and meats sold in the market.

THE DOMESTICATION OF RICE

Whenever and wherever rice was domesticated it was husbanded by farmers, and along the way evolved into an aquatic plant. In this new environment it was able to extract nutrients from water and yet not be drowned by it. Rice now had fewer weeds – and other plants – to contend with, and thus its yields increased substantially.

Before the domestication of rice, early communities of Thai were simple hunters of game and fish, and gatherers of tubers and fruit. A fundamental shift in society occurred when the Thai started to cultivate crops. They gradually became primitive farmers of taro and sago; these staples are still sometimes a desperate last resort when either rain or the rice crop fails, but in better times they are dismissed as food for the unsophisticated or the destitute. The population increased as food became assured; women had more children as they were better fed and not constantly on the move.

After rice became domesticated, aspects of society changed to support the cultivation of this demanding grain. People were harnessed to the rice paddy. Initially, rain and floodwaters alone served to saturate the paddy. However, as the population grew and became increasingly dependent on rice, consistent and sufficient water for the paddy could not always be guaranteed, due to the uncertainties of the weather and floods. Soon ways of controlling and channelling water were devised to ensure a plentiful supply – the rudiments of irrigation.

As Jacqueline Piper writes, in *Rice in South-East Asia*:

> Settled agriculture producing surplus foods eventually led to the development of civilizations, societies, and hierarchies of protectors and protected: kings, priests and soldiers, all fed by farmers. Where yields were good, some people could be spared from the rice-fields for the manufacture of arts and handicrafts. As societies developed, with élite groups of royalty, administrators and religious persons, the arts flourished and eventually attracted contact with a wider world.

Upon rice, great kingdoms were built. To the west, in Burma, Pagan flourished from the ninth to the thirteenth centuries; it was centred on a religious site in a bend of the Irrawaddy River. Later, between the fourteenth and eighteenth centuries, the kingdoms of Pegu, in the south of Burma, and Ava, in the north-east, rose – historically two of Siam's most indefatigable foes. The Khmer kingdom of Angkor was situated on the flat, fertile plain to the north of a vast lake in central Cambodia, Tonle Sap. Angkor's great temple complex had an intricate irrigation system to support it, begun by King Indravarman I, who reigned from 877 to 889 AD. Three centuries later, Chou Ta-Kuan, a visiting Chinese diplomat, observed that up to three crops of rice could be harvested in one year at Angkor, whereas in China at the time, one crop per annum was the norm. Even more unusually, he noted, a special variety of rice grown at Angkor kept pace with the floodwaters, even when they were a 'fathom' deep; this same variety is still grown on the central plains of Thailand.

Some of the traditional responsibilities of a king were to uphold the state and increase the wealth and contentment of his subjects. In rice-growing societies, this meant developing paddies and maintaining irrigation systems. Neglected canals silt up quickly and soon become unusable. Such disrepair, it has been suggested, led to the decline of Angkor and eventually its sacking by the Siamese. The aftermath was devastating: the subsequent silting of the canals caused the flooding of paddies and the water soon became stagnant breeding grounds for malaria, which struck the final blow to Angkor's ancient civilisation.

Inscriptions found at Sukothai laud the largesse of the king, the happy abundance of fish in its canals, and the fertile rice paddies irrigated by them. Chronicles of this period also record the trading of rice with the kingdom of Luang Prabang, in modern northern Laos, and southern China. In the sixteenth century Siam exported rice from the port of Malacca, then a tributary sultanate of Ayuthyia. Later, during the seventeenth and eighteenth centuries, there are records of a small rice trade with Europe.

At first, rice was viewed with some suspicion in Europe. It was initially believed to be poisonous – and certainly eating some raw grains would support such a fear. Soon it was considered medicinal, to be mixed with spices such as cinnamon and sugar, then simmered in milk and consumed as a carminative salve. Rice, kept under lock and key in the spice cupboard, was then a rare and expensive commodity. Later, it left the Elizabethan pharmacopoeia and entered into the receipts of the kitchen, where it was served in a similar manner, albeit to please rather than to cure.

THE RICE ECONOMY

Overseas trade of rice was the sole prerogative of the king, prohibited to others unless licensed by him. Only in times of abundance was trade permitted. This simple trading of excess changed with the arrival of the enterprising English in the mid-nineteenth century, who were eager for trade and anxious for new markets.

At the beginning of the nineteenth century, Siam's economy was diverse. Villages usually consumed what they produced and engaged in very limited trade. Some villages were renowned for crafts such as pottery, silverware or woodcarving; others for their salt, cotton or, along the coast, dried fish and prawns. All these products were bartered for rice. Bangkok was the regional trading centre for pepper, tobacco and cotton, along with such primary commodities as tin, rubber, teak, sugar and rice, but the boom ended when trade with China, Siam's principal trading partner, was interrupted by the First Opium War in 1841. Decline and disarray beset the Thai economy. New trade links had to be forged.

Rice was a commodity the world needed: increasingly it had become a staple cereal of industrial Europe, where it was seen as a quick and clean food to fuel industrialisation and feed the urban masses. The Georgian cook Hannah Glasse, in *The Art of Cookery Made Plain and Simple*, published in 1747, listed 20 rice dishes. Later, in 1861, the redoubtable Mrs Beeton included some 40 recipes involving rice in her *Book of Household Management*. Slowly this grain was incorporated into the European diet. But not without exception, for Brillat-Savarin rather sweepingly opined in his *Physiology of Taste* that rice 'softens a man's fibres, and even robs him of courage . . . [those] who live almost exclusively on rice . . . have never resisted any attempt to subjugate them . . .'

By the latter part of the nineteenth century, rice had become the principal trading commodity of Siam. This was not only due to its quality, but also to increased demand; the supply from traditional sources had been disrupted, the Indian Mutiny of 1857 having interrupted English trade with India. A decade later, the American Civil War and its blockade suspended the trade from the Carolinas. Merchants looked farther afield, to Indo-China, to secure their rice, at a time when there were vast improvements in transportation. Siam's once diverse economy diminished to become mainly dependent on a single commodity – rice. As a consequence, rice exports increased 25-fold between 1850 and 1930, supplanting all other crops in economic pre-eminence. In 1850 only 5 per cent of exports were of rice, yet by 1920 the figure was 80 per cent. Rice supported Siam's economic viability during a period when it was most vulnerable. This signified more than just mere revenue. It showed, in a way the West could understand during an age of commercial progress and imperial conquest, that Siam could manage its own affairs and maintain its sovereignty. Rice secured Siam's future, just as it had sustained its past.

Thus the stability of Siam was, and is, due to the constant trade in rice. Never in the history of Thailand have there been serious, national food riots – although there have been skirmishes, dissatisfaction being vented over price, and sometimes supply. Seldom does the crop fail. However, in the 1930s, a series of inadequate rice harvests and falling prices for exports contributed to the Siamese elite and military expressing their disaffection by toppling the absolute monarchy.

Today Thailand produces over 20 million tonnes of rice per annum; it exports a quarter of that, making it the world's fourth largest exporter of rice. The remainder is consumed domestically, 60 per cent of it within 50 kilometres (30 miles) of where it was grown. Although the changes that have occurred in the rice industry have rendered traditional practices almost obsolete, over 40 per cent of employment in Thailand is still connected in some way with rice – its growth, sale or export.

A GRAIN OF RICE

The grain of rice is the seed of the plant. About 80 per cent of it is starch, which is converted into glucose and feeds the plant as it germinates and takes root. Each grain contains two types of starch, amylose and amylopectin. These starches are encased by a third one, cellulose, which is harshly indigestible when raw; when cooked, however, the cellulose denaturises and becomes edible, preventing the grains from becoming a sticky, gluggy mass.

The essential difference between glutinous and long-grain rice is the proportion of the two starches in the grain. The greater the amount of amylose, the drier and fluffier the rice is when cooked. Amylopectin breaks down when cooked, and so rice high in this starch becomes sticky.

Rice contains no vitamins A or C, but many B group vitamins, such as thiamine, riboflavin, niacin and folic acid. It also contains trace amounts of the minerals phosphorus, zinc, copper and iodine. Although all the husk and most of the bran is removed during commercial milling of white rice, cooked rice contains a considerable amount of resistant starch, which some authorities believe compacts during cooking and acts like fibre when digested. Rice bran is believed to reduce cholesterol levels in the blood by raising the proportion of high-density lipoproteins to low-density lipoproteins.

Most Thai prefer to use rice within a year of its harvesting. New season rice does not have as 'toothsome' a character as older, drier rice. When new rice is boiled it appears to be quite sticky, because the outer casing of cellulose dissolves slightly. Usually a farmer has sufficient of the previous year's crop to feed his family for three or four months into the new season before using the current 'vintage'.

Rice is believed to be at its prime three or four months after harvesting, when it is drier. It remains firm throughout cooking and the grains stay separate. One authority uses the charming analogy that good rice should be like brothers: close, but not too close. As rice gets older, it intensifies in flavour, and it needs additional water – albeit only slightly more – to cook.

Most rice is consumed within 18 months of harvest. Some connoisseurs, however, believe that older rice – which is somewhat musty in flavour – is superior to new rice. Not only can such gourmands taste the difference between new and old, but they say they can distinguish fast-growing from slow-growing rice. Some discriminating connoisseurs prefer rice from one province to another, indeed even down to the paddy. They demand as much provenance from their grain as does the oenophile from his communes in Burgundy.

GROWING RICE

Rice takes between 100 and 210 days to mature, depending on the climate and the variety. The grain is first soaked in water overnight to stimulate its germination. Submerged, its shoots develop quickly in a quest for air. Although rice flourishes in water it needs oxygen to survive, or it will drown. The starch in the grain feeds the growing shoot during this stage. The plants obtain oxygen through pores above water level on the shoots, and later the stems. Bubbles of air soon surround the submerged roots and stalks, providing another means for the plant to breathe. Agitation, either from flooding or rain, further aerates the water.

As rice grows, it forms small clumps of roots that then throw off side shoots or tillers. The stem grows 50–150 centimetres (20–60 inches), depending on the variety and environment. On each stem there is one flower, which has about 100 small, green spikelets, each destined to become a grain of rice. Immature grains are light green but, as they ripen and the plants yellow, they turn a golden ivory. Rice is self-pollinating, ensuring homogeneous offspring, so it rarely relies on breezes for fertilisation and thus there is no need for the flowers to develop intense colour or scent to lure birds or insects – although a subtly haunting perfume wafts across the paddies for one or two days when the rice plants are in flower. Farmers are nonetheless cautious of wild or mutant varieties lurking on the edges of their paddies as these may corrupt the planted type. Should these ancient, undomesticated varieties cross-pollinate with cultivated ones throwbacks will be produced, reducing the yield and quality of the grain – traits that have been steadily bred into cultivated rice. Rice usually matures between four and five months, although some varieties ripen in as few as three months, while others take up to seven months. Usually several cultivars are planted: some fast-growing or 'light' rice (*kao bao*); others, being slower to mature, called *kao nak* or 'heavy' rice; while the remainder is 'middle' rice (*kao glang*). This enables the harvest to be staggered.

In the past, farmers saved the more resilient seeds that did not ripen too early or shatter during harvesting to be sown the following year. Over time, other criteria were also used for selection: taste, cooking qualities, size and colour. Thus rice has been adapted over count-less generations. Now there are thousands of varieties of rice, each suited to and flourishing in a specific environment – temperate mountains or torrid plains, in areas afflicted with poor soils, floods or droughts – and adapted to diverse cultural preferences and culinary needs.

There are three main kinds of rice. *Indica* grows in tropical monsoonal areas and is tolerant of extreme conditions, both drought and flood. Though its yield may be moderate, it produces the best-quality grain, such as Thai jasmine and basmati rice. The grains are long and slender and the plants tall and leafy, which poses a problem for modern machine farming, as the plants tend to fall onto their sides, creating difficulties at harvest time. *Japonica* strains produce a broad, thick grain with a high yield. They are shorter than *Indica* plants, suited to more temperate climates and to mechanised cultivation. Both white and black sticky rice belong to this variety. *Javanica*, an equatorial species, produces a stubby grain with low yields and is susceptible to drought.

Rice is cultivated in two different ways in Thailand, either by 'shifting' cultivation or in paddies.

SHIFTING, OR SLASH-AND-BURN, CULTIVATION

This is the most primitive method of rice cultivation. It is still practised among the hill tribes of northern Thailand, where farmers rely only on rainfall to grow rice in cleared areas of forest. There are no paddies with embankments to contain a reservoir of water. Rice, mostly glutinous – along with all other crops and vegetables – is grown in small plots for several years before the farmers move on. The farmers leave the land because it is exhausted, so rarely does the forest regenerate its natural cover. This ancient practice degrades once lush land, leaving exposed slopes that are prone to landslides, and causes soil erosion in the rainy season and desiccation during the dry.

Slash-and-burn creates an undistinguished landscape, but there are compensations. The forest can replenish itself – although not completely if over-exploited. Farmers still have access to forest tracks, and thus additional food and fuel. As the farmers use the forests for needs other than rice, they do not destroy the trees wantonly, nor is the community too dependent on rice. Societies that grow rice like this are mostly animist and pay homage to the gods, acknowledging their ownership of the forest by carefully seeking permission of the spirits to use it. Although slash-and-burn is the most primitive method of agriculture, it still demands an intrinsic understanding of the land, the crop and the weather. This leads to an intricate pattern of beliefs and rituals, to explain and propitiate the caprice of the gods and nature. Society has become organised around these concerns to ensure the success of the crop and the survival of the community.

Yields can be quite good from slash-and-burn cultivation, which can support up to 50 people per square kilometre (about 250 acres), but this puts a lot of pressure on the land. It can result in farmers returning to previous plots of land before the forest has had time to recover. Or they may be compelled to adopt a new approach to cultivation – paddy rice.

PADDY, OR WET RICE, CULTIVATION

This type of cultivation has a drastic effect on the landscape. 'Paddy' is a Malay word for unharvested or unhusked rice, or the area in which it is grown. On the central plains of Thailand it has created an unnaturally flat and vast terrain. The original cover of woodland and groves of bamboo has been replaced by broad cultivated expanses. Fruit and palm trees – especially coconut and sugar – line irrigation channels to prevent them washing away during torrential rains or floods. Regular inundation provides sufficient water for growing rice over a wide area and, with irrigation, an even greater area.

In broadcast cultivation the seed is cast where the plant is to grow. The yield may not be as high as for transplanted rice, which is enclosed in smaller, irrigated paddies, but broadcast rice can be grown over a larger area with less effort. Both methods of growing paddy rice demand time and labour. Transplanting yields better results, but the labour is more intensive. As farmers are increasingly leaving their paddies for the cities, those who remain are reverting to the older method of production, since it requires less labour, but increasing the crop by planting improved varieties and adding fertilisers. Sometimes two harvests are possible in a season, the first transplanted, the second broadcast.

BROADCAST RICE

This type of farming was the norm where land was cheap and some natural flooding could be relied upon. This was a precarious manner of growing rice, as farmers depended on consistent rainfall to ensure the crop's success. They had to determine when sufficient rain had fallen, not necessarily locally, but at the headwaters of the flooding river, which could be a considerable distance from the paddy.

From painful and costly trial and error a system of prediction evolved, based on the cycles of the moon. If this was misinterpreted and seed was broadcast too early, or insufficient rain fell and the fields did not flood, the crop would fail. Conversely, as very little irrigation was used to control and channel the floodwaters, sometimes serious flooding could occur.

As the population of Thailand increased, a family's holdings were generally divided by inheritance, ever diminishing in area, so the sprawling method of broadcast agriculture became less viable. The smaller growing areas were then enclosed by a series of dykes or bunds, shored up by groves of fruit and coconut trees; these tree-lined canals also fed the paddies with water. Buffaloes helped to prepare the paddy and seed varieties adapted to these new circumstances were developed.

TRANSPLANTED RICE

Where there is plenty of labour, rice is grown by a different method. The rice is first soaked to encourage germination, then broadcast into a small nursery paddy. After a week, the seedlings are 'thick on the ground' and already as tall as 5–8 centimetres (2–3 inches). After 40 days, the seedlings are carefully lifted from the soil, stacked and wrapped in damp, protective leaves. They are then transported to the flooded main paddies that have been prepared by ploughing; if they are left for too long before transplanting, the crop yield is considerably reduced.

The rice crop requires heavy rains – apart from the initial days after planting. At this early stage, too much water will wash the seedlings away; too little and the rice will be stunted and eventually die. A depth of almost 2 metres (6 feet) of water is necessary to cultivate rice but Thai farmers can only reasonably rely on 1–1½ metres (3–5 feet) of water from natural rainfall. The rest must come from a flooding river or, more trustworthily, irrigation. After the shoots and roots have been trimmed and pruned, they are planted by dibbing in rows. Sowing, transplanting and tending the rice is arduous. About a month after transplanting, the rice begins to turn golden as it ripens, ready for harvest. If planted sequentially, not all the rice needs to be harvested at the same time. The harvesting should then be, if not completely manageable, at least not too overwhelming.

The farmers will always begin the harvest in the field in which the first ceremonies and plantings occur, even if other paddies are just as ripe or more conveniently located: it is the right order of things. Traditionally the rice is 'laid' when harvesting, that is, the plant is pushed to the ground in one orderly direction to make the harvesting much easier. At the end of each day's cutting, the different types of rice are stored separately: the seed rice, for next year's crop; rice to be consumed throughout the coming year; rice to be sold; and, finally, glutinous rice.

LEGENDS AND CEREMONIES

Rice cultivation is closely associated with animism. Rice has a soul, *khwan*, and ceremonies respecting rice ensure its growth. All rice farmers acknowledge this by major rituals and constant small ones. When rice pollinates and swells it is said to be pregnant and, in the province of Ayuthyia, offerings such as an orange, a banana and sliced sugar cane were made to the rice goddess, similar to those made to a newly pregnant woman. Powder, perfume, oil and a comb were also proffered. The head farmer then combed the 'hair' of the rice plant, its fronds and leaves, as a gesture of comfort. The farmer wished her well and promised to guard the rice from anything untoward. In other provinces, slightly different ceremonies were performed.

At no time can any impoliteness occur in the presence of the rice goddess or she will be offended and flee, thus threatening the crop. Rice was traditionally harvested by hand, with a small, sharp blade hidden in the palm of the hand. This, it was believed, would not frighten the spirit of the rice, which might otherwise shed its grain prematurely.

Traditionally – although this is now rarely practised – before a meal a small ball of cooked rice was placed outside as an act of merit to other living beings. During religious festivals, the faithful leave small offerings of rice at the base of a stupa, a venerated reliquary monument or a sacred banyan tree, as an acknowledgement of both the Buddha and the rice goddess. Then monks are fed. After a meal, children raise joined palms and *wai* in thankfulness to Pra Mae Posop.

'Rice is not only the basic sustenance for the body, but also for the soul of man, incorporating the male and female creative forces, as earth and water both unite to give rice,' writes Jacqueline Piper in *Rice in South-East Asia*. Thai peasants are more pragmatic and robust: they believe that the bran of the rice is male, and its pearly inside is female. The bran protects the delicate rice, and therefore is associated with the masculine characteristics of resilience, toughness and strength. The rice itself is attributed feminine qualities, as it feeds and nurtures the Thai.

A northern hill tribe, the Akha, has a Persephone-like legend about the origin of rice that involves a poor widow and her daughter, who gathered taro to survive. One day the daughter disappeared and was later found as the wife of the lord dragon who lived in the river. The lonely daughter asked her mother to live with them. Soon, however, the mother became restless and wished to return to her own home. As a parting gift, the dragon gave the woman some magical rice seeds, wrapped in a leaf inside a hollow reed, saying that if she planted them she would always have enough to eat. This she did, and soon the magical seeds produced such an overwhelming crop that she was unable to carry the bounty home. She returned to the river and asked the dragon for guidance. He told her to stand in the field and whistle and clap three times. The yield was reduced to a manageable amount, sufficient for her daily needs. This legend not only explains the origin of rice, but also why all ceremonial rice must be carried in leaves and hollow reeds – and why the Akha never whistle or clap their hands in a rice paddy lest the crop be diminished.

Farther south, on the Isthmus of Kra, farmers believe that once, in the mythical past, rice never needed to be harvested. Every day, a single grain of rice would appear and proceed to the pot. The farmer's wife knew how to cook the rice grain, but it was taboo to look into the pot while it was cooking. If she kept the taboo, the pot would be miraculously full of cooked rice by the afternoon. Unfortunately, one of her children became inquisitive and lifted the lid. Inside the pot crouched a small girl, the rice spirit. Indignant at this outrage, she left. And ever since, people have been compelled to work for food – the price of impudence.

THE CYCLE OF RICE AND CALENDAR OF FESTIVALS

Thai farmers traditionally use the stars as a seasonal clock to determine when to clear and sow their fields. As in most agrarian societies, their festivals follow a lunar calendar.

The farming year can be said to begin during the waxing moon of the fourth month (early May), when the farmers begin to prepare for ploughing ceremonies. The auspicious day is now determined by astrologers and is recorded on every agrarian calendar in the kingdom. Usually, it is an odd-numbered day.

Peasants used to determine the correct day by consulting monks. They would include their own birth year in the calculation, ensuring that the time was the most propitious for them. The Thai, who follow a similar astrological system to the Chinese, believe that the year of one's birth plays a significant role in determining the fate of the individual. In some places farmers might follow their headman's choice of day and time, or 'stage' (before clocks the traditional Thai way to estimate the time was by 'stages', where the farmer would measure the length of a shadow with his foot).

In the past, a small bamboo shrine was erected to the guardian spirit of the land on the first ploughing day, and offerings were made. These depended on what was available to the peasants – whatever they ate, they offered to the spirits first – but rice was never omitted. Just as when offering food to monks, the rice came from the uppermost layer in the cooking pot. The offerings were always presented on banana leaves, a custom perhaps derived from the Indian caste system, where higher castes ate from the leaves to ensure that their food was not tainted by being handled by members of a lower caste. More practically, the Thai used banana leaves because they were readily obtainable and easily disposable. Candles and incense were also offered. This was a simple ceremony asking the spirit to protect the rice grown on its land from predators, both natural and supernatural. The rice and earth goddesses were enlisted to aid in this and flags were raised to delineate the area to be protected. At every stage, the gods were beseeched for support.

The rural Thai believed the success of the crop depended on the gods and took these ceremonies very seriously. Among the northern Akha, those negligent in their obligations threatened the survival of the whole community and were therefore expelled. Even in modern Thailand, the doubting still perform the ceremonies, not just as a custom but also perhaps out of caution.

The state celebration of ploughing is more spectacular. The Royal Ploughing Ceremony takes place in mid-May every year at Sanam Luang, outside the walls of the Grand Palace. It is often repeated in several major regional cities. This ancient Brahmin ritual predicts the prospects for the coming year's rice crops and initiates the planting season. During the time of Sukothai, the king played a leading role: there are many examples in both myth and religion where the monarch wields the plough himself.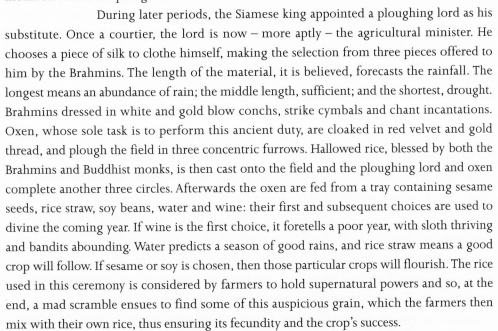

During later periods, the Siamese king appointed a ploughing lord as his substitute. Once a courtier, the lord is now – more aptly – the agricultural minister. He chooses a piece of silk to clothe himself, making the selection from three pieces offered to him by the Brahmins. The length of the material, it is believed, forecasts the rainfall. The longest means an abundance of rain; the middle length, sufficient; and the shortest, drought. Brahmins dressed in white and gold blow conchs, strike cymbals and chant incantations. Oxen, whose sole task is to perform this ancient duty, are cloaked in red velvet and gold thread, and plough the field in three concentric furrows. Hallowed rice, blessed by both the Brahmins and Buddhist monks, is then cast onto the field and the ploughing lord and oxen complete another three circles. Afterwards the oxen are fed from a tray containing sesame seeds, rice straw, soy beans, water and wine: their first and subsequent choices are used to divine the coming year. If wine is the first choice, it foretells a poor year, with sloth thriving and bandits abounding. Water predicts a season of good rains, and rice straw means a good crop will follow. If sesame or soy is chosen, then those particular crops will flourish. The rice used in this ceremony is considered by farmers to hold supernatural powers and so, at the end, a mad scramble ensues to find some of this auspicious grain, which the farmers then mix with their own rice, thus ensuring its fecundity and the crop's success.

When the dry season is at its height, the Thai farmers invoke the gods to hasten the downpour. Of the rain-making ceremonies throughout Thailand, perhaps the most suggestive is the rocket festival of north-eastern Thailand, with its phallic symbolism: rockets are fired into the cloud-laden sky to seed rain and as a pointed reminder to the rain god, Wassakam, that it is time to soak the earth. In other parts of Thailand, farmers believe that the rockets will prod Pra Taen, the god of the sky, into action. Cats also seem to be proficient at bringing rain. In northern Thailand, cats are saturated with water to hasten the inundation – a case of sympathetic magic without too much concern for the cat! The caged feline is paraded through the streets, then dowsed with water while an appeal is made: 'Hail *nang maew* ("Miss Pussy") give us rain, give us rain to pour on *nang maew*'s head.' There is even a special breed of cat that stars in this drenching role – the Siamese Silver Blue, or Khorat. Cats, in general, symbolise the uncertainty of almost domesticated nature, while this breed's grey coat suggests the colour of rain-laden clouds and its green eyes are the colour that most symbolises life, growth and the verdant paddy.

Once the rain has come, more ceremonies are needed, this time to curtail the flood. During the Ayuthyian period, when the waters had reached their peak – around the time of the famous candle festival, Loy Grathong – the king would proceed by royal barge into the centre of the Chao Phraya River and smite the waters three times with a golden sword, commanding them to recede.

After the harvest, old men remain at home to prepare an area for threshing the grain. Traditionally – and to the less rustic, somewhat distastefully – the ground is smeared with a mixture of buffalo dung and water (clearly Pra Mae Posop is less squeamish about some things than others). Once dried, this prevents the rice being soiled by dirt and mud, especially if it rains. Any grain that has fallen by the wayside during the harvest is regarded as belonging to Pra Mae Posop, containing her *khwan*. A new set of clothing, and food – consisting of white and red rice dumplings and a hand of bananas, a sliced duck egg, cooked rice and, in some areas, a dried coconut – are offered. The clothing is laid out on the ground or folded in the paddy. The farmers then offer the food to Pra Mae Posop, saying: 'You have come out and borne the sun and the rain for a long time in the fields. Do you return to the cool shade of the threshing ground and house?'. The peasants return to the house and fashion the loose rice, the awns and stubble into a small, rough doll-like figure of the goddess, which is then dressed in ceremonial clothes; thus she is welcomed into the threshing area. The rice doll is stored in the upper portion of the barn until the next sowing season, when it is combined with rice from the ploughing ceremony for the new year's planting. Meanwhile, some of the harvested rice is cast into the paddy to feed the birds and thus make merit.

Threshing is always begun with the rice from the first paddy. Either the rice is flailed using wooden poles or, if the threshing is communal, it is trodden by buffalo. Winnowing is the next process, in which all the bran and rice dust is blown away. When this is finished there is a feast, including jungle curries of minced ricebird, braised fish with sugar cane, grilled frogs, stir-fried wild boar with chillies and holy basil, bananas simmered in coconut cream, and sweet sticky rice. The next morning, monks are fed on the threshing ground, after which they chant and sprinkle the rice with holy water.

MILLED AND POLISHED RICE

In the past, and sometimes even today in the countryside, rice was pounded with a huge wooden pestle and mortar, and then winnowed to remove the husk and bran before it was cooked. This was normally done every day. It was a tedious task, but the resulting rice tasted different from commercially milled rice as a little of the flavoursome bran was still attached. There was a greater vitamin content as well. However, rice that was hand-milled or pounded was far more susceptible to spoilage than commercially milled rice, since its germ and part of the bran, which contain volatile oils, quickly became rancid.

Commercial milling of rice began in the middle of the nineteenth century, using hard metal rollers that crushed the rice and removed most of the bran and germ. The next process polished the rice, removing any remaining bran. Around this time an unprecedented disease appeared, baffling physicians. Sufferers of beri-beri developed muscular weakness due to nerve damage, leading to an inability to walk. Most doctors believed the ailment to be caused by a germ, but Dutch researchers sent to Java to investigate the disease noticed that hens fed leftover polished rice displayed similar symptoms, yet other birds, fed on unhusked rice, did not. The chief doctor, Christian Eijkman, conducted further research. As a result, the importance of previously unknown components of food was established: vitamins. Beri-beri was recognised as a deficiency of vitamin B or thiamine, which was attributable to the super-efficient rice-milling processes.

During the nineteenth and early twentieth centuries, many countries held world fairs and exhibitions of engineering or agriculture to display the progress and prowess of their industry and their nation. Siam, too, held annual agricultural fairs, although on a very small scale. This is yet another example of how the country wished to display to the world its steady development in a way that Westerners could understand. During one such fair, in 1907, King Rama V held a competition to encourage the improvement and standardisation of Thai rice – at a time when rice was crucial to the nation's economy. Strain Kao Dork Mali 105 was voted to be the best. This was not only due to its flavour, but also because of its high yield, its resistance to disease and other excellent qualities. As a result of its royal sponsorship, this winning grain became the prototype strain of all today's Thai rice.

RICE ON THE TABLE

Vital to Thai life and integral to its culture, rice is also at the centre of the Thai table. In colloquial Thai one easy greeting is '*gin kao ruu yang*', which is commonly translated as 'how are you going?', but literally means 'have you eaten rice yet?'. It shows the intrinsic hospitality of the Thai, who associate well-being with rice, and do so by offering an acquaintance a meal – rice. As most Thai people are too reticent to impose upon others, the invitation is rarely accepted and so the literal meaning has become redundant. However, the implication is that if one is not hungry, then one has eaten rice and so all is well with the world.

To the Thai, rice *is* the meal; food in Thai is called *kao*, which is also the word for rice. When referring to uncooked rice, the Thai say *kao jao*, literally 'lord rice', as an acknowledgement of its essential role in their culture and cuisine. Cooked rice is often called *kao suay*, 'beautiful rice'. Exquisite curries, robust relishes, assuaging soups and piquant salads, delicious though they may be, are subordinate to the rice. Such dishes are given the generic name *gap kao*, 'with rice', plain and simple.

The ancient diet of the Thai was predominantly sticky rice. Today it is still the prevalent rice in the north and the north-eastern areas of the country, where the Lao and other ethnic groups remain loyal to their glutinous rice – although they will grow a little long-grain. The other half of the country, comprising the central plains and the south, is under the sway of the long and slender grain but, again, they will grow a little sticky rice for desserts. Long-grain rice was the rice grown by Mon farmers before the arrival of the Thai onto the fertile alluvial plains of the Chao Phraya basin. Initially in the minority, the newly arrived Thai still ate their traditional grain. Slowly, however, they adopted the rice of the region – perhaps because it was the variety of the élites at the time, the Khmers and Mon. The transfer of allegiance was a gradual process, taking perhaps as long as a thousand years. Certainly by the sixteenth century long-grain was the chosen variety. In the past, rice of either sort was seasoned with very pungent relishes to give it savour. As the culture developed, supplementary dishes were added to the table, but the primacy of rice has never been supplanted.

part two

fundamentals
of thai cooking

part two   fundamentals
           of thai cooking

T hai cooking is the opposite of Western cuisine, where two or three flavours are blended in an elegant way to arrive at a distillation of the requisite flavours. Thai food creates a locus of flavours within each dish, through its components, producing a complexity that can be dazzling.

This section introduces the main categories of Thai food and describes their development and diversity. First there is an introduction to the Thai kitchen, its recipes and cooks, and the importance of balance and seasoning in Thai food. The 'Ingredients and basic preparations' chapter discusses the basic ingredients that are used throughout Thai cuisine. Then come chapters covering the four fundamental classifications of Thai cooking – relish, soup, curry and salad – from their earliest, simple beginnings to later, more evolved versions.

The spicy relish, *nahm prik*, is the root of Thai cooking and from it stem other branches. *Nahm prik* and its gentler offshoot, *lon*, are served with accompaniments that should have contrasting textures and tastes. These can be as simple as a plate of raw vegetables, but may be much more complicated. Soups not only contribute flavour, they soothe and refresh; soup is an indispensable part of the meal, countering complexities and often assuaging heat. The curry chapter reveals a huge range of flavours and techniques, showing that there is far more to Thai curries than the hot green or red generic versions that most people are accustomed to. Salads are the easiest of dishes to prepare and their vibrancy invigorates the meal.

A formal meal usually consists of one of each of these dishes, with rice. In addition to these central dishes, a stir-fry or grilled meat or fish may be included; some examples of such meals are given in the 'Menus' chapter. However, the Thai way of understanding their cooking is not so rigid or codified; they use techniques where appropriate and ingredients when available. How to do so correctly is instinctively under-stood, as are most aspects of culture. In order for me to understand the intricacies of Thai cooking, however, it was helpful to form a model. Like any model, it should be used as a guide – to help devise a menu, to assist in appreciating the complexities of these culinary categories. In practice, Thai cooking is inherently fluid and the boundaries are blurred.

In these chapters there are few concessions in the recipes, as they are included to act as references. Traditional recipes and methods are used, with modern alternatives included. Tastes and seasonings are described, so that if an alternative ingredient is used, a similar taste can be achieved. In order to innovate, I believe a sound knowledge is a fundamental prerequisite. Recipes can be simplified and adapted but, in order to do so without debasing the cuisine, one must have a full appreciation of what is to be altered before it can be adapted successfully. Thus the recipes should become a starting point, the beginning of possibilities, a departure.

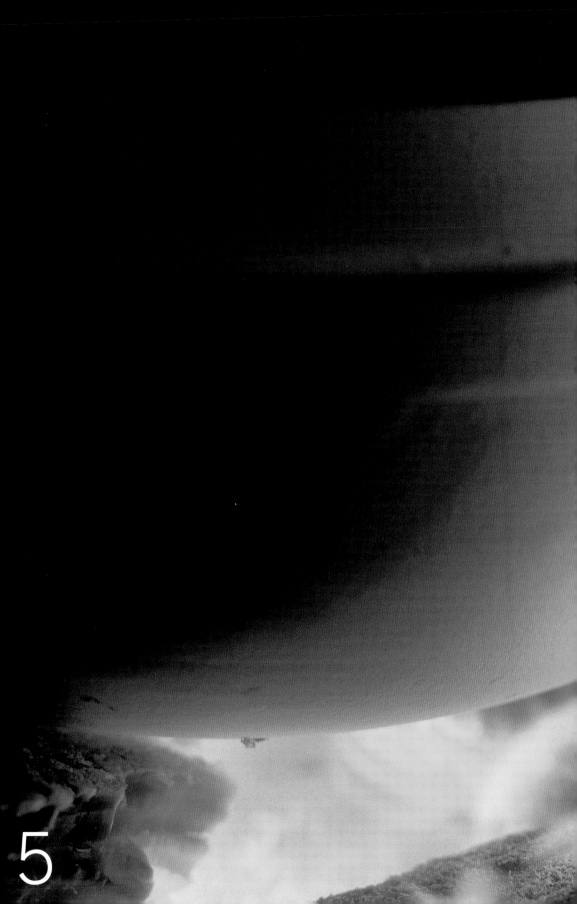

5

THE THAI KITCHEN

In all cuisines, the methods used to cook are determined by the available fuel, equipment and utensils. Thai cooking uses simple equipment. It is important to appreciate this in order to understand the techniques employed, which are the logical outcome of circumstances. The evolution of Thai recipes has always been tempered by the constraints of environment, culture and technology.

THE TRADITIONAL THAI KITCHEN

The kitchen was once a small room – often separate from the main house and usually faced auspiciously to the north, taking advantage of a full day's sun. It was well ventilated, as the walls were made from slatted bamboo or rattan; they could be rolled up during cooking, ensuring that even the most pungently explosive fumes did not overwhelm the cook.

The main piece of equipment was the stove (*mae dtow*). This consisted of a large clay cooking surface positioned over burning embers of charcoal or wood; two large holes allowed two dishes to be cooked simultaneously. The clay stove-top was also a perfect place to keep food warm before serving. Alternatively, a smaller 'single' stove was used – and these can still be seen today, at street and market stalls and occasionally in homes. Poorer households used clay pots supported by metal tripods instead of a stove, with hot embers underneath. The poorest households would cook over an open wood fire.

The position of the stove in the kitchen was determined by the day of birth of its owner, according to the traditional manuscript of Thai lore, *sawatdi raksa*. The correct placement of the stove ensured happiness and prosperity for the cook and the household.

To ensure popularity for those born on Sunday, the stove should be to the west. A stove to the north-west guaranteed happiness for those born on Monday, while for those born on Tuesday, the south conferred protection. Prosperity and abundance was assured to those born on Wednesday should they also place their stove to the south. South-west, and peacefulness would descend on those born on Thursday. Friday's child would be less full of woe if the stove were in the north-west. An easterly direction would further the career of those born on Saturday. Such placements squared one with the world.

EQUIPMENT AND UTENSILS

A modern Thai kitchen is virtually indistinguishable from a Western kitchen.

To produce good Thai food only a few specialised utensils are needed – the pestle and mortar being the most important.

PESTLES AND MORTARS

Stalwart pestles and mortars, made from hard stone, usually granite, are used throughout most of South East Asia, but nowhere, in my understanding, are they more integral to the cuisine than Thailand. They are used daily to make *nahm prik* relishes, sauces and curry pastes, to grind spices and pound fish and prawns into purées. Heavy and large, they have been and still are indispensable. Some of the earliest mortars and pestles were huge pieces of equipment that were used to pound rice to remove its husks for a whole village. The same principle, in a smaller version, was then employed to pulverise fibrous ingredients to a paste. The most ancient type of mortar was made from clay and was used with a wooden pestle, the best being made from the sugar palm tree. Only since the early Bangkok period have mortars and pestles been made from granite. Today both types are found in Thai kitchens. The clay and wood type is used only for making salads, especially green papaya salad (*som dtam*). The stone version is a general implement, used to produce pastes, relishes and sauces. The Thai believe that the character of a person is revealed when using a mortar and pestle: a regular rhythm is indicative of an even temper and consistency.

A pestle and mortar should be large, the larger the better, as these versatile pieces of equipment can be used for – and can accommodate – everything, from making curry pastes and relishes to grinding spices and milling roasted rice. While a food processor can be used to do much the same job quickly and cleanly, a pestle and mortar is always a sound investment.

POTS AND WOKS

Recent excavations from Kanchanaburi in the west of Thailand and Ban Chiang in the north-east have revealed that people of these regions have used clay pots and bowls for 3000 years. Thai soil makes excellent clay: it is hard and not too porous.

The most traditional Thai pot, the *mor din*, was earthenware, large and rounded at the bottom and narrowing at its neck, opening out at its rim. It was used to cook rice: the narrow neck ensured minimal evaporation, and allowed excess water to be poured out easily; it also reduced the chances of ash dropping into the cooking pot. Being of unfired clay, it was less likely than a fired pot to shatter when exposed to a naked flame. All other kitchen pots were made the same way, although of differing shapes. Curry pots were large and rounded, but only narrowed slightly at the neck; they had a wide rim with two large handles. These were used for almost every style of cooking: boiling, deep-frying and occasionally stir-frying. The Thai wok (*grata*) was also terracotta and was a slightly modified and later version of the curry pot, with a wider base and no neck or rim.

Generally, foods were made or kept in earthenware pots or containers: shrimp paste (*gapi*) was stored, mustard greens or bamboo shoots fermented, and rice wine made in them. Otherwise, produce was stored on bamboo wicker trays, in woven bamboo leaf sacks or wrapped in banana leaves.

Later, during the Ayuthyian period, brass woks began to be used. One source suggests that the Portuguese introduced cooking utensils made of this alloy of copper and zinc. Not only were brass woks symbols of wealth and status, but they were sturdy and could conduct heat well. As a consequence they allowed a different, faster type of cooking than before. Most Thai cooks now prefer to use brass woks for making desserts, while some use them for all their cooking. Brass woks come in various sizes but are all the same shape – hemispherical with two large, rounded handles.

Brass is comparatively inert, which means it does not react with the acids in fruit or taint fresh coconut cream; it also heats evenly, so syrups and candies can be prepared without scorching. It does however, oxidise and thus discolour. The traditional way of maintaining brass woks is to rub them with a piece of brown tamarind pulp. Its acid cleans and shines the soft metal, yet its soft pulp ensures that the metal is not scratched. The wok is then rinsed out with water that has had a little charcoal ash dissolved in it. This softens the water and removes any residual acid left by the tamarind; it also makes the surface alkaline, so that it will not unduly react with ingredients and impart a metallic, somewhat oily taste. More modern cooks can use half a lime or lemon to clean their brass wok, then rinse it in soapy water. Salt or other abrasives should never be used, as they can scratch the soft metal.

Although tin utensils became available in the mid-nineteenth century, it was only after the Second World War that they – and aluminium – made any inroads into the provinces. These novel pots, woks and kitchen spoons were generally cheap and robust, and soon almost completely replaced the outmoded, but often beautiful, traditionally crafted cooking utensils.

GRATERS AND KNIVES

The other traditional piece of equipment in Thai kitchens is the coconut grater – a lifesaver in Thai cooking. I used to prise the meat from a coconut, which I then peeled and whirred in a blender. This works very successfully, but takes a while. Now I recommend a traditional coconut grater – not a little ornamental bench with a small grater on one end (called a 'rabbit'), but the larger kind, a hand-cranked rotating spindle that clamps onto a surface. A quick wallop, several spins, a squeeze or two and you have good coconut cream.

All Thai kitchens contain a multitude of knives. Some are most delicate, exquisite pieces of craftsmanship with the curved blade wrought from brass and the handle from teak. Usually quite small, these knives are used to carve fruit and vegetables. Other knives are more menacing, huge and heavy, being used to peel bamboo shoots and sugar cane, and to husk and cleave coconuts. Notably, Thai cooks always peel away from themselves, never towards, as is the more common practice in the West.

Thai techniques are employed with a dexterity as deliberate as the placement of the stove in the traditional kitchen.

KNIFE WORK

Most food is chopped or minced in order to ensure quick cooking. In rustic cooking, little knife work is used apart from rudimentary cutting and slicing. More refined cooking relies a great deal on honed knife work. Often intensely flavoured ingredients are finely shredded so that they will not dominate; and with so many being used, this allows each ingredient to be tasted. Sharp knives are essential for this. The item should be cut into the required length before being sliced to the desired thickness and then finally shredded.

Mincing (grinding) of meat or fish is achieved using a very sharp, heavy knife or even a cleaver. When these ingredients are minced in a machine they are torn, squashed and heated as they are forced through the grate of a mincer – most probably some good time before they are bought. Mince made like this will probably have been oxidised by its exposure to the air, and therefore will taste flat and fatty. Hand-chopped mince is almost fluffy in comparison, and it tastes more defined. Mostly pork, chicken, prawns or fish are minced, and they should be chopped quickly with a knife or cleaver until clearly, cleanly and plainly minced. A sprinkle of salt while doing so will sweeten the meat or fish as it cooks. I also like to add a point of garlic – a small piece that literally sits on the point of a sharp knife – to give a certain richness.

ROASTING AND GRINDING SPICES

With the exception of peppercorns, all spices are roasted before use to revitalise their fragrance. Each should be roasted individually, as they take different times to roast. Spices are roasted by heating them very slowly in a heavy pan or wok, tossing regularly to prevent scorching, which would impart an acrid finish. When the spices begin to crackle, toast and colour, they are ready. Grind spices very finely, preferably in a spice grinder; if grinding in a mortar, use the pestle in a circular movement. Always sieve the result to remove any chaff.

All dried spices should be kept in an airtight, dark container – ideally refrigerated – to extend their life. It is best to roast and grind spices when needed, although any leftover spice mixture can be rejuvenated by heating it through over a low heat. This, however, should be a last resort, not general practice.

MAKING PASTES

Traditionally, all Thai pastes are made with a mortar and pestle. Individual ingredients are added gradually, in a given order, from the hardest and driest to the softest and wettest, with each being reduced to pulp before the next is added. As the ingredients are pounded they release their fragrance; the balance of the paste can be perceived in this aroma, and is adjusted while being made. The recipe is used as a guide, not gospel, and so can – and should – be altered to achieve a balance. Traditional recipes are vague regarding quantities, as it is expected that the cook will alter the ingredients according to what actually happens in the mortar.

Pastes for *nahm prik* relishes, and other simple pastes, are always made with a pestle and mortar and can be fairly coarse (see page 188 onwards for details of *nahm prik* ingredients and recipes). However, a curry paste should be puréed as finely as possible. Because of the volume of ingredients in some curry pastes, a blender or mincer can be an expedient solution (see page 280 for detailed instructions on making curry pastes), but purists insist that a hand-made paste is quite superior – both in texture and taste – to one made in a food processor. The ingredients are smashed, crushed and pounded with a pestle and mortar, not ripped, torn and shredded; the tastes are balanced and layered, rather than whirled into a pulp.

PRESERVATION: DRYING, PICKLING AND FERMENTING

The Thai kitchen employs many techniques to preserve ingredients when they are plentiful for use in times of need. Perhaps the simplest is by salting and drying. The ingredient – usually fish or prawns, but occasionally meat – is rubbed with salt or marinated in brine, fish sauce or soy sauce for a period of time before being dried in the sun. Sometimes food is preserved just by steeping in salt or sugar without being dried. Alternatively, it may be pickled in a brine or syrup made from salt, sugar, or both, dissolved in water or vinegar.

Fermented products are used in all types of Thai cooking: in soups, relishes and curries. Most notable are the two ancient fermented ingredients of fish sauce and shrimp paste, without which Thai food would be fundamentally different. One of the most elemental ways of fermenting is in rice-rinsing water – that is, water that has been used to wash rice before cooking – since dissolved enzymes in the rinsing water encourage fermentation. This is effectively controlled spoilage: once the food has sufficiently fermented, it is preserved.

COOKING METHODS

Certain cooking methods are universal – boiling, grilling and deep-frying – but others are peculiar to a single cuisine, especially one as ancient as Thai.

Historically, the material and shape of the cooking utensil effectively determined the type of cooking that was possible. And with the clearing of forests for the ever-expanding paddies, fuel became increasingly scarce (except in the north of the country and in mountainous areas farther south). Consequently, cooking methods evolved to use precious fuel most efficiently: brief cooking times over gentle heat and slow, lingering grills over dying embers. If an intense burst of heat was required, the embers would be fanned or stoked.

boiling *dtom*	Cooking in a liquid, usually salted, over a medium heat. Mostly vegetables are boiled; meat and seafood toughen if subjected to a rapid boil.
stewing or simmering *ruan*	Minced (ground) meat, fish or other small items, such as prawns, are simmered in a little liquid or oil in a wok with some salt, stirring over a low to medium heat until just cooked. Traditionally this technique prevented items from spoiling in the tropical heat, but it is now used to ensure they are not overcooked or toughened. I find this the most satisfactory way to cook mince. *Larp* salads are the best example of this cooking method.
cold-blanching	Not a traditional Thai method, but one that I employ with good results. The food is placed in cold, salted water and brought to the boil. The longer it takes to come to the boil, the more the item is cleaned, reducing excessive pungency or oiliness. A little vinegar or lime juice can be added to assist this process. Pork is especially improved by cold-blanching, as are bitter vegetables such as cassia leaves and bitter melon. Sometimes it may be necessary to repeat the blanching in order to make the ingredient palatable.
blanching *luak*	The ingredient is plunged into boiling liquid, often being dipped several times. The liquid is not allowed to return to the boil – generally the pot is taken off the heat. Alternatively, the item is allowed to sit in the liquid until it has changed colour or firmed before being removed. This method is used for ingredients that require little cooking; to remove a raw, coarse flavour or aroma; and for items that tend to toughen when subjected to other methods of cooking – mainly seafood.
slow-blanching *hung*	This is especially good for starchy ingredients – like bamboo shoots, potatoes, taro or cassava – where some of the excess starch is sloshed away with the discarded water. The ingredient is brought to the boil in plenty of water, then skimmed or the scum poured off along with some of the water. The heat is reduced and the food is simmered until cooked. This is the traditional way to cook rice. Sometimes the discarded water is replaced by cold water and, once returned to the boil, the process may be repeated.
steaming *neung*	Although the Thai have steamed rice, especially sticky rice, from time immemorial – originally in a perforated clay 'lid' attached to the top of an earthenware pot, but now more commonly in a woven bamboo conical basket – the steaming of other ingredients may have been introduced by the Chinese. Steaming is now used throughout Thailand, but less commonly in the remote countryside, and is often employed for special occasions or to cook celebratory dishes, such as a whole fish. Food is placed in a steamer over boiling water, then the lid is quickly replaced, sealing the item and ensuring that it steams over a rolling boil. Be careful if steaming on a plate, as the underside of the food will take longer to cook.
double-steaming *dtun*	Double- or indirect-steaming ensures melting tenderness. The food, usually cut into large pieces, is put into a bowl, often with some aromatic ingredients. It is covered with a boiling liquid, sealed, then placed in a steamer for several hours. This method is used to extract flavour from items that can sustain prolonged cooking, and when incorporating Chinese medicine into food.

GRILLING

grilling or **toasting** *bing*	Grilling over a low to medium heat or coals until the food is golden or crisp, but not necessarily completely cooked – as for *pla grop* (crisp fish). Often the item toasted is already cooked, and this method invigorates its perfume and flavour while slightly crisping it.
grilling *yang*	Grilling over a low heat until cooked – for example, catfish might be grilled slowly over embers for hours until it is impregnated with smoke and honey-golden. Other items are not always subject to such prolonged cooking.
chargrilling *pao*	This form of grilling is done over a high heat until the exterior is blackened. Unpeeled shallots or garlic, for example, are charred, cooled and then peeled. Charring imparts a smoky, redolent taste. The longer something takes to cook, the smaller it should be cut, for if too large the outside will burn before the food is cooked through. The interior should remain moist or even slightly undercooked.
dry-grilling *siap*	Ingredients are threaded onto skewers and then dried in the sun before being grilled.
grilling in **bamboo** *larm*	Ingredients are sealed inside a hollow bamboo segment, then grilled slowly (traditionally the bamboo is placed in embers). Although the bamboo blackens, the food inside remains un-charred but is smokily perfumed by the bamboo. Rice, usually sticky and moistened with coconut cream, or vegetables to be served as an accompaniment for *nahm prik* relishes, are often prepared this way. Typically lunch or peasant food is cooked like this and may be carried, still in its bamboo casing, to be eaten in the fields. Use only old bamboo stalks, which can occasionally be found at garden nurseries, and soak them in water for several hours before use.

FRYING

dry-frying or **roasting** *krua*	Items such as rice, dried chillies, shredded coconut and spices are often roasted in this manner. In a wok, with no oil or water, they are dry-fried over a low to medium heat, stirring regularly, until golden, fragrant or crispy.
stir-frying *pat*	Traditional Thai stir-frying was not the fierce and furious cooking method of the Chinese, but gentle frying over radiant heat in an earthenware pot. Stir-frying in the contemporary sense of quickly cooking sliced items in oil over a very high heat in a metal wok, while stirring or tossing constantly, is a Chinese technique that has been incorporated into the Thai repertoire. One of the characteristic tastes of a good stir-fry is a slight smoki-ness. This can only be achieved by cooking at an intense heat. The wok should be tempered before its first use: heat the wok until almost white hot, then wipe with a cloth – when slightly cooled – before reheating for use. This not only seals the wok, preventing items sticking, but also imparts the desirable smoky tinge. It is important to make sure the wok is hot *before* adding the oil, so the latter does not burn or overheat while the wok is heating up.
crisp-frying *jiaw*	Sliced or shredded items are deep-fried in hot oil, stirring regularly, until crisp, fragrant and golden – as for deep-fried shallots or garlic.

deep-frying *tort*	Historically, deep-frying was a luxurious technique, since rendered pork fat or coconut oil – the traditional deep-frying mediums – were not plentiful, and the earthenware pots could not withstand the high temperature needed. Shallow-frying was more common, cooking food partially immersed at relatively high temperatures, then turning it over to complete the cooking. Today most Thai cooks deep-fry in the Western manner – although still in a surprisingly small amount of oil – by immersing the item in hot oil and frying over a high heat until just cooked. Sometimes, however, the item is deep-fried at a low heat for a surprisingly long period until it is very crisp, almost dried, such as *pla grop* (crisp fish).

TRADITIONAL RECIPES

Thai cookbooks per se are only comparatively recent: to my knowledge, the first was published in the late nineteenth century. Before then, most recipes – and perhaps this is too precise a term – were handed down orally from generation to generation, mother to daughter, cook to assistant. Most cooks were female; most Thai believe that women make the best cooks, as only they have sufficient patience and dexterity to deal with intricate and time-consuming techniques.

Ancient recipes were vague, loose affairs, often listing the ingredients required but not their quantities because the amounts could be varied as the recipe coalesced. In fact, written recipes were most likely incomprehensible to these often illiterate cooks. They would work their way through a recipe, for example a curry paste, stopping to sniff the developing aroma of the paste in the mortar after the addition of each ingredient and then adjusting accordingly. Very often, they were enjoined to cook *hai horm*, 'until fragrant'. The recipes' brief cooking instructions – whether oral, remembered or written – used colour and aroma as indicators of readiness. It was assumed that experienced cooks would interpret such instructions according to the ingredients being used and their intentions. The implication was that cooks had to be familiar with the ingredients and techniques to the extent that they would know when and how to alter them to attain the desired results without affecting the integrity of the dish. This takes not only a deft hand but a knowledgeable one, too – something, I fear, that can only be achieved by trial and error. Regular cooking builds up a vocabulary of taste and a confidence in techniques. Surely this is the definition of good cooking, regardless of cuisine – just as the women of old Siam knew.

Given the lack of written recipes, some might contend that it is difficult to guarantee truly authentic – or at least consistent – Thai cooking, due to the possibility of infinite variations, and few agreed standards or explicit methods. In fact there are conventions – established practices and flavour preferences – that give a certain, albeit elastic, continuity to the cuisine. Such culinary customs ensure that a dish can be faithfully reproduced in taste, if not precisely then approximately.

Any variation would be due only to the preference of the individual cook; but such a cook would be one who had been rigorously tutored in the 'correct' taste – in Thai called *rot tae*. Taste is a conservative sense. The familiar becomes the accepted and expected; the unfamiliar is viewed with suspicion and distaste. With an almost inherited skill, successive generations of Thai cooks have learnt by the side of the cook, and in both the gilded palaces and meanest hovels the manner of teaching was the same. Only what was taught differed. Day after day, tastes were instilled in this time-honoured manner.

Yet within this pattern different traditions – tastes, 'recipes' and their methods – coexisted. Within a region, a city, a class, or even a large family, there can be great differences, inspiring heated debate. Such arguments over the finer points of a dish result in a vital and creative food culture where alteration and innovation are points for discussion, to be appraised, then accepted or rejected.

Distinctive culinary styles began to develop, so that by the late nineteenth century, many palaces – or noble families – were recognised as different 'schools'. Tracing these lines of descent (*sai*) gave authority to contentious practices and dishes. It also gave greater meaning to recipes: a dish might be the favourite food of a king, princess or great hero; it might be eaten at a certain time to recall a historical or mythical event or during a time of celebration – marriage, ordination or Thai New Year. This suffused the cooking with meaning, placing cuisine firmly within the context of culture.

In this vibrant atmosphere, reputations of individual cooks were made, along with the palaces and the schools they represented. The late nineteenth century became a high point of Thai culinary art as cooks strove to develop their craft to rarefied heights. Food from these palaces became increasingly removed from that of the nearby rice farmers. However, palace and peasant dishes still shared many characteristics, making them familiar to all – and decidedly Thai.

EARLY THAI MEMORIAL BOOKS AND COOKBOOKS

In the late nineteenth century, when memorial books first began to be published, those of high-ranking women would often include a collection of recipes.

A steadfast source of such recipes, Thanpuuying Pliang Pason-agorn, was descended from King Rama II; born into the cultured Xuto family, she married into the powerful Bunnark family in the middle of the nineteenth century. She wrote the first Thai cookbook, *Mae Krua Hua Bark*, which was originally compiled for her own household, but became so popular that it was later published. In it are many extraordinary recipes that reveal the delicious complexities of Thai cuisine. Like many woman of her milieu, she encountered Western food and often adapted recipes – tongue braised with potatoes and star anise was one she proposed. Perhaps Thanpuuying Pliang was introduced to codified recipes by a Western cook brought to Siam to train such ladies in this novel cuisine, as she was one of the first to quantify recipes using Chinese measurements, to ensure that they could be faithfully reproduced.

Thanpuuyiing Pliang was the grandmother of another famous cook of the middle of the twentieth century, Jip Bunnark, who taught Khun Sombat Janphetchara, who in turn introduced me to good Thai cooking. Khun Sombat was over eighty years old when I met her and had exacting culinary standards – everything was made by hand. Her cooking was instinctive and spontaneous, relying upon taste and smell, not slavish adherence to relentless cup and weight measures. I was confronted with uncertainty, strange ingredients and extreme tastes when taught by Khun Sombat. The vagaries of older recipes, while whetting my appetite, did little to increase my understanding of actual methods and proportions.

At this stage, I needed to follow set recipes, to begin to understand – or frankly, to unravel – the mechanics of a dish, its tastes, textures and seasonings. However, once I became familiar with these elements I began to understand the somewhat nebulous nature of traditional cooking, with its implicit invitation to adapt and alter, develop and improve – albeit within certain constraints. My approach to cooking has since discarded Western rigidity and become looser, more instinctive, relying on taste and smell rather than a written, prescribed amount. A true conversion!

Little is known of most of the great cooks of Thailand. While appreciated, they remained in their kitchen. It was their domain. However pleasing and influential they were in this world, sadly little remains other than their names, and occasionally the regard in which they were held. Throughout the following sections, there are many references to these Siamese women and their recipes. It is some small acknowledgement of their lives, their contribution as cooks in the maintenance of Thai cuisine, and their role in giving dimension to the content of this book. An extensive list of these women – and occasional man – is included in the bibliography.

CHARACTERISTICS OF THAI FOOD AND SEASONING

To my understanding, Thai food has three levels or tiers. Firstly, the taste of the ingredients used; secondly, the texture of those ingredients; and, finally, the seasoning. The complex and vibrant qualities of Thai cooking are based on the interplay of these components.

Thai cooking is a paradox: it uses robustly flavoured ingredients – garlic, shrimp paste, chillies and lemongrass – and yet when these are melded together during cooking they arrive at a sophisticated and often subtle elegance, in contrast to their rather coarse beginnings. Often the ingredients employed in a recipe can be an extraordinary, bewildering array of up to 20 items in a single dish. In any other cuisine this would guarantee a cluttered and confused finish, yet in Thai cooking these disparate ingredients are transformed into a seamless whole – the honed result of generations of fine Thai cooks. This does not mean that all the tastes are blended into an indistinguishable unity, but that the diverse flavours work harmoniously in concert – rounding, contrasting and supporting each other.

Although perhaps not a critical element, the texture of the various ingredients plays a much greater, more defining role in Thai cooking than in other cuisines. Chillies have a surprising characteristic: they sensitise the palate to texture, despite their initial impact. In a simple stir-fry of green vegetables, for example, texture is crucial to the character and therefore the pleasure of the dish. In other recipes, texture plays a less apparent role but is still a feature – for instance, the crunch of deep-fried shallots or peanuts in salads. The garnishes of chillies, torn or shredded kaffir lime leaves, crunchy and pleasantly bitter eggplants, or the leaves of various basils, not only perfume but add texture, since these garnishes are usually meant to be eaten. Perhaps the most obvious example is the raw vegetable accompaniments to relishes (*nahm prik* and *lon*). All have texture that is played against the background of rice.

Seasoning is the considered application of flavours: sweet, sour, hot and salty. Two, three, or occasionally all four of these primary tastes create the ultimate level of taste that so distinguishes Thai cooking. Balance is paramount. If the principle of European cooking is 'keep it simple', then the Thai dictum is 'keep it balanced'. A dish that is palatable can be transformed into the memorable by the deft employment of seasoning. It does not disguise the ingredients but imbues them with a greater dimension. Thai food strives to achieve a balance where the tastes, textures and seasonings are assembled in every dish to the intended degree, enhancing and defining it. This is *rot chart* – *rot* meaning 'taste' and *chart* meaning 'proper', 'unified', 'balanced' or 'appropriate' – and is quite simply the epitome of Thai cooking.

Each region has a customary preference; each dish its requisite seasoning; and each cook their own predilection. It is this agreed sequence, followed by countless Thai cooks, that maintains proper – or at least consistent – Thai taste. In the recipes in this book, the description of the overall seasoning at the end of the method indicates the relative dominance of these components, in both order and intensity; thus the first taste mentioned should be the strongest, the second and third seasoning tastes following accordingly.

While there is an accepted combination of seasonings, perhaps, not surprisingly, there is also latitude according to personal preference. Old written recipes often conclude with the injunction *brung rot dtam jai chorp* ('season according to your heart's desire') – an open invitation to change. This involves making mistakes, but is all part of the process of developing skills and understanding the underlying mechanisms, combination of techniques and seasoning. Only then can recipes be adapted and ingredients used freely, seasonally and successfully while still achieving *rot chart*.

All Thai believe that each cook has a seasoning tendency: salty, sweet, hot or sour. I am unashamedly sweet in my preferences, although I do tend to like a few chillies! Some would doubtless say too sweet, therefore 'season according to your heart's desire' in all the recipes. But this is not to incite culinary carte blanche – it must be exercised with discretion.

Whatever one's ultimate preference, rarely should it conflict with standard seasonings, although it will alter them slightly; it should enhance the finish, not overwhelm it. The cook who achieves this is said to have *fii meu*, a sure talent and deft skill in cooking and assembling the requisite balance of tastes, texture of ingredients and in the ultimate seasoning.

SERVINGS

Most of the recipes in Part Two of the book are designed to work within the context of a meal. For a complete Thai meal with rice, four dishes – a relish with a few of its accompaniments, a soup, a curry (perhaps with a side dish), and a salad – will easily serve 4 people.

Suggested combinations of recipes suitable for 4–6 people are given in the 'Menus' chapter, together with some guidelines on preparing and eating a meal.

A NOTE FOR VEGETARIANS

While there are very few specifically vegetarian Thai dishes, most recipes can easily and successfully be adapted for the strict vegetarian; in this cuisine, dietary requirements are not a limitation or restriction but an opportunity. Simply use a good vegetable stock, season with light soy sauce rather than fish sauce, and omit any meat or fish ingredients. There is a wonderful versatility about Thai cooking, where adaptation is not necessarily compromise but merely reflects the availability of ingredients, the season and the preferences of the cook.

Remember that rice is the principal part of the Thai meal; everything else is used to add savour. The meat is merely one of many components that comprise the soup, curry or whatever – which is itself only one dish in a meal consisting of several dishes. The Thai simply place less importance on meat than Westerners do.

STANDARD MEASUREMENTS

1 teaspoon	5 ml
1 tablespoon	15 ml
¼ cup	60 ml
⅓ cup	80 ml
½ cup	125 ml
1 cup	250 ml

SOME USEFUL QUANTITIES AND EQUIVALENTS

Fresh long chillies	1 tablespoon = ¼ fresh chilli	6 g
	1 cup = 4 fresh chillies	100 g
Dried long red chillies	1 tablespoon = 1 dried chilli, deseeded and soaked	2 g
	1 cup = 15 dried chillies, deseeded and soaked	25 g
Bird's eye chillies (scuds)	1 teaspoon = 3 bird's eye chillies	2 g
	1 cup = 30-odd bird's eye chillies	90 g
Lemongrass	1 tablespoon = ⅓ small stalk of lemongrass	6 g
	1 cup = 6–10 small stalks of lemongrass	90 g
Galangal, ginger, turmeric	1 tablespoon = 10 thin slices	10 g
	1 cup	150 g
Red shallots	1 tablespoon = 2 small shallots *or* 1 large	10 g
	1 cup = approximately 15 small *or* 8 large	150 g
Deep-fried shallots	1 tablespoon = 4 small shallots *or* 2 large	15 g
Garlic	1 tablespoon = 2 medium cloves of garlic	10 g
	or 5 cloves of Thai garlic	
Deep-fried garlic	1 tablespoon = 3 medium cloves of garlic	15 g
Coriander root	1 teaspoon = 1 medium coriander root	4 g
	1 tablespoon = 3–4 medium coriander roots	12 g
Kaffir lime zest	1 teaspoon = zest of approximately ¼ kaffir lime	8 g
Shrimp paste	1 tablespoon	22 g
White peppercorns	1 teaspoon = 7–8 peppercorns	3 g
	1 tablespoon = 20 peppercorns	10 g
White sugar	1 tablespoon	16 g
	1 cup	230 g
Palm sugar	1 tablespoon	22 g
	1 cup	340 g

6   BA

NGREDIENTS AND
C PREPARATIONS

In order to make authentic-tasting dishes, use authentic Thai ingredients. These aren't always easy to find outside Thailand, so I've often indicated substitutes, but do make an effort to visit Asian groceries and source as many Thai ingredients as possible. Having said that, alternatives can be used in almost every Thai dish with an easy versatility. Indeed, Thai cooks would consider it madness not to use the best ingredient available – as should any good cook. They would refuse to use a second-rate ingredient just because it was specified in the recipe, if there was a higher-quality alternative. Therefore, the Western cook should feel free to substitute the best and freshest ingredients available. However, before a substitute ingredient is decided upon, consider the taste of the original dish, that of possible alternatives, and the other dishes with which it is to be eaten.

Thai cooks have no qualms about buying many prepared products. Curry pastes, coconut cream and relishes are all purchased with ease in the market – and they are always fresh: the curry pastes and relishes might have been made the day before, but the coconut cream will be made to order. What cook would not avail themselves of such products? Regrettably, there are few such market places outside South East Asia, so I've included recipes and techniques in this chapter to enable you to make these basic preparations for yourself.

ACIDULATED WATER

This is water to which lemon or lime juice has been added. Acidulated water is used to prevent fruit and vegetables oxidising – turning brown – after they have been prepared. It is also sometimes used to clean offal.

AGAR-AGAR *wun*

Agar-agar is a gelatin-like substance obtained from seaweed. It is sold in sheets and strands, but more commonly in powdered form. I believe the sheets or strands are better, as they have a greater capacity to set – and sometimes the powdered form is adulterated with gelatin. If using the sheets or strands, soak in water to soften, before adding to boiling liquid. The powder is simply whisked into simmering liquid, in the proportions given on the package. Whatever type is used, it must be simmered for at least 10 minutes to activate the setting agents, otherwise the jelly will never become adequately firm.

Unlike gelatin, agar-agar can set at temperatures as high as 32°C (90°F), which makes it viable in hot and humid kitchens without refrigeration. Like gelatin, however, the jelly becomes tougher the longer it is kept after being made – it stays at its best for about 12 hours.

ASH MELON *see under* **GREEN GOURDS**

ASIAN CELERY *see* **CELERY, ASIAN**

ASIAN CITRON *see* **CITRON, ASIAN**

ASIAN PENNYWORT *see* **PENNYWORT, ASIAN**

ASSAM *som kaek*

This uncommon ingredient looks like a thin slice of dried apple, and is used in southern Thai food. 'Assam' is Malay for sour and it is usually sold under this broad description, as 'sour wood apple', or sometimes *gelugor*. It should be soaked in water for a few minutes then rinsed before being added either whole or sliced to sour curries, or it can be shredded and tossed into salads.

AUBERGINE *see* **EGGPLANT**

BAI CHAMPLUU *see* **'BETEL' LEAVES**

BAI DTAMLEUNG

A green, spinach-tasting, maple-shaped leaf used in stir-fries, salads, soups and curries. It cooks very quickly. Snow pea shoots or young spinach are alternatives.

BAMBOO SHOOTS *nor mai*

Traditionally one of the most important and versatile plants in South East Asia, bamboo is used for building houses and furniture, and crafting utensils for cooking and eating. Segments of larger stalks are used as buckets for carrying water, the leaves are used for wrappers, and dried poles secure funeral pyres. An added boon is that its shoots are edible. Each variety has a slightly different flavour, but they share a crisp, slightly nutty bitterness. Fresh bamboo shoots are becoming increasingly available, normally from early summer to early autumn. More rarely, young shoots sometimes appear in the market for a few weeks in mid-spring. Try to choose shoots that are firm and not too long. Old or long bamboo shoots are wooden in texture and taste; stale shoots will be quite yielding to the touch and may have developed some mould on the base – they have no other taste than rank bitterness.

Bamboo shoots are at their best when just harvested, but soon deteriorate as the hydrocyanic acid they contain reacts with the sugars and starches in the plant, making it increasingly bitter. Cooking removes this taste and arrests the deterioration, and so should be done as soon as possible.

Beware of the small black bristles on the outside of the sheaths: they irritate the skin and can stick to clothes for days. Wearing a pair of gloves, use a sharp knife to cut deeply along the length of the shoot, then peel off the outer layers until the white, hairless and fleshy core is revealed. Continue until the whole length is cleaned. Store in salted water until ready to cook.

If the bamboo shoots are old – and mostly they are – slice them before cooking, as this will help to remove bitterness, then blanch from a cold-water start in salted water. Old recipe books suggest the addition of either a little sugar or a 'betel' leaf or two in the blanching water. Boil, refresh and repeat – it may be necessary to blanch two or three times. Be careful not to blanch for too long, though, as part of the attraction of bamboo shoots is their crisp bitterness. After blanching, allow to cool in the water; the bamboo shoots can then be kept for several days, as long as the water is changed every other day.

Canned bamboo shoots save much labour but will never have the subtlety of the freshly cooked product. If using, rinse in several changes of water before blanching in salted water from a cold-water start (to remove the processed taste), then proceed as per recipe.

See also fermented bamboo shoots.

BANANAS gluay

Banana plants accompany the Thai from the cradle to the grave: the first solid meal a baby has is often stewed bananas, and at a funeral the deceased is laid upon a bed of banana leaves.

As many as 28 varieties of bananas are used in Thai cooking, each with its own characteristics and taste. Not all varieties are interchangeable. For instance, the small sugar or Ducasse bananas, of which the Thai are so enamoured, are best for deep-frying or grilling, but turn to stone when poached in sugar, for which long Cavendish bananas are better.

BANANA BLOSSOMS hua blii   These are the rusty purple buds that contain the sterile flowers of the banana plant. The taste is astringently sappy, yet when prepared properly, slightly and creamily bitter. Banana blossoms are normally shredded and added to salads or curries. The unshredded but separated leaves are sometimes served raw as a garnish for a lon relish or sweet fish sauce, where their pleasant bitterness works as a delicious foil.

When purchasing, choose a firm, large bud with a good, even colour. Open one or two of the outer leaves: if the inner leaves are beginning to discolour, then choose another. There is quite a lot of wastage, with two-thirds of the bud being discarded in cleaning. Only a stainless steel knife should be used, as the flesh discolours the moment it touches any other metal. If the banana blossoms are to be grilled, char them whole and then discard the outer blackened leaves before cleaning.

To prepare the blossoms, remove the outer coarse and coloured leaves to reveal the creamy white heart. Quarter the heart lengthwise, rub quickly with lemon or lime juice, remove the core and shake out the very bitter stamens by flapping the quarter against the palm of your hand, then immediately place in salted acidulated water. Repeat with remaining quarters. Do not slice more than half an hour in advance or the blossoms will discolour, despite the acidulated water.

A fast and pleasing way to pickle cleaned banana blossoms is to wash them in salted and acidulated hydrolysed lime water, before squeezing to extract the bitter sap, and then marinating in a strong solution of lime juice, salt and sugar for 2–3 hours. Rinse before use.

BANANA LEAVES *bai dtong*   These are used to wrap foods – mostly for grilling, but occasionally to hold desserts. The softer leaves are best, but should only old, tough leaves be available, quickly blanch or grill them before use. A little heat is all that's necessary to soften these recalcitrant leaves and make them bend to your will.

BASIL

The Thai use three types of basil leaves to perfume and augment food. These delicate tropical herbs can lose their fragrance very quickly, so it is best to buy them on the day of use. Generally, they should be stored upright in a little water, covered. Refrigeration ruins the flavour of basil.

HOLY BASIL *bai grapao*   In Thailand there are two types of holy basil – red and white. The red variety has purple stalks and is more pungent; the white version, with green stalks and a less intense flavour, is normally used with seafood and fish. The leaves of both are pointed and slightly variegated, with a fragrance redolent of cloves. The taste is sharp and hot; when very fresh, it can actually numb the tongue. Both types of holy basil are mainly used in stir-fries, especially hot and spicy ones.

LEMON BASIL *bai manglaek*   This basil has small, light green leaves and an almost palpable, sticky citrus fragrance. It should be kept covered, but not in water. Lemon basil is used mainly in wet dishes: it is indispensable for mild *geng liang* curries.

LEMON BASIL SEEDS *luk manglaek*   These small, black seeds of the lemon basil plant look like poppy seeds, but when soaked in water they develop a slippery, mucilaginous coating. This frogspawn-like substance is used to garnish iced syrups and occasionally in ice-creams.

THAI BASIL *bai horapha*   A purple-stemmed, green-leaved herb with a heavy aniseed fragrance and a strong liquorice flavour, Thai basil sweetens and perfumes any dish in which it is used. The leaves are used in red and green curries, soups and stir-fries. Sprigs of Thai basil also often accompany pungent *nahm prik* relishes – their slightly anaesthetic effect smooths and soothes.

BEAN CURD   *dtor huu*

There are several varieties of bean curd, from firm to soft. I prefer to use the softest kind, which is sometimes called silken bean curd. It is deliciously tender and can be used in most Thai dishes.

See also fermented bean curd.

BEANS, SNAKE *see* **SNAKE BEANS**

BEANS, YELLOW *see* **YELLOW BEAN SAUCE**

'BETEL' LEAVES *bai champluu*

Closely related to true betel, these large, tender green leaves are often known outside Thailand as 'betel' or sometimes piper leaves. They are indispensable when making *miang*, a perennially popular snack. Torn leaves are also added to some curries.

BITTER MELON *see under* **GREEN GOURDS**

CARDAMOM *luk grawan*

Cardamom is an uncommon spice in the Thai repertoire, used primarily in a few curries of Muslim origin. The cardamom used in Thailand is not the common green one found in Indian curries, but a small off-white pod the size of a pea, with four black seeds. Thai cardamom can be bought in Chinese medicine shops. Generally, the whole pod is roasted before being broken open and the seeds used in a curry paste, but it can be left whole, bruised and then added to finish a curry.

Green cardamom can be used, but it is more pungent, so reduce the quantity by a third.

CASSIA BARK *op choey*

Cassia bark is related to cinnamon, but has much larger and coarser quills, with a richer and oilier flavour. It is readily obtainable in Chinese shops.

CASSIA LEAF *bai grawan*

Dried cassia leaf is used in *mussaman* curries and occasionally in beef soups. It is often sold under its Indonesian name, *daun salam*. Although unrelated and with a different fragrance, a Western bay leaf is often used as an alternative.

See also Siamese cassia flowers and leaves.

CELERY, ASIAN *keun chai*

Asian celery is stronger and more aromatic than regular celery. It is a leafy plant with thin, long stalks – a bunch of Asian celery could be mistaken for flat-leaf parsley – and is usually available in Chinese food shops. Washed and sliced, it makes a flavoursome and crisp addition to stir-fries and soups. It combines especially well with seafood and beef, and cleans and reduces pungent oiliness in dishes.

CHA-OM

A fern-like green sometimes found in Thai and Chinese shops, *cha-om* is bitter and nutty to the taste and has a strong, pervasive, almost unpleasant smell. There is no substitute.

CHIANG MAI CURED PORK *naem*

This cured pork, made by fermenting pork and sticky rice with garlic, is perhaps the most famous preserved meat from northern Thailand. *Naem* is available in some Thai food shops, but store-bought has little of the robust depth of flavour of home-made (see recipe on page 522).

CHILLI SAUCE *sauce prik*

A delicious chilli sauce – sometimes called Sauce Siracha – often accompanies grilled and deep-fried dishes. Named after a seaside village on the eastern coast of the Gulf of Thailand, just near Pattaya, this sauce is red in colour and full-bodied in flavour. It is readily available and comes in varying degrees of heat; I think medium-hot is the most versatile. A recipe for a homemade version, which can be made hot or mild to taste, is given on page 450.

CHILLIES *prik*

Many chilli varieties, not always the same as Western ones, are used in Thai cooking. As a rule of thumb, the smaller or thinner-skinned the chilli (whether dried or fresh), the more memorable it will be.

See also roasted chilli powder.

LONG CHILLIES *prik chii faa*   These chillies are about 5 centimetres (2 inches) long and come in various colours, mainly red and green. Long red chillies have a richer, fuller flavour than green, which are sharper and more herbaceous. I also find green chillies hotter than their riper, red comrades. Whether the seeds are removed is a matter of preference and heat tolerance – other than for curry pastes, where aesthetic considerations favour deseeding.

Normally only red chillies are grilled; green or unripe chillies are harder to peel. Chillies should be chargrilled – or can be blackened over an open flame – then cooled, peeled and deseeded before use. Grilling creates a smoky, hot, yet suggestively sweet flavour, with a slightly reduced fieriness.

BIRD'S EYE CHILLIES *prik kii nuu suan*   The smallest and certainly the most memorable of the Thai chillies – I often refer to them as 'scuds'. These thin green, or occasionally red, chillies form the basis of green curries and most *nahm prik* relishes: the green chillies are unripe and have a sharper flavour. Apart from in green curries, where the colour is a defining characteristic, either colour can be used. Deliciously addictive, they are viciously hot, yet have a wonderfully floral aftertaste. Some cooks prefer to nip off their stalks but leave the buds, believing this increases their fragrance.

Scuds are available from South East Asian providores. While any other hot chilli can be substituted, it will not have the same depth of flavour or fragrance. Dried bird's eye chillies (see page 146) should not be used in place of fresh ones.

DRAGON'S EYE CHILLIES *prik kii nuu sun yaew* These are larger than scuds and, mercifully, not as hot. They are thin and crooked, about 4 centimetres (1½ inches) long – and, most importantly, have the most wonderful, slightly sour flavour. Similar chillies are occasionally available in Indian food shops.

BANANA CHILLIES *prik yuak* These large, mild, yellow-green chillies (sometimes called corn peppers) are generally used in salads or stir-fries. In this book, I have also used them – often in combination with long chillies – to approximate the flavour of a thin, lime-green chilli that is difficult to find outside Thailand.

ORANGE CHILLIES *prik leuang* These orange, slightly sour-tasting chillies are uncommon outside Thailand. They are about 3 centimetres (1¼ inches) long, thin-fleshed and of extraordinary heat. They are mainly used in southern Thai dishes. Long chillies can be used instead.

DRIED CHILLIES *prik haeng* There are two varieties of dried chillies: long and bird's eye. Dried long red chillies form the basis of red curries, while dried bird's eye chillies are used mainly in southern dishes and for roasted chilli powder (see page 174). When buying, always look for the darkest-coloured ones.

If the recipe calls for soaked dried chillies, soak them in cold salted water for 10–15 minutes; if you are in a rush, soak them in warm salted water for 3–4 minutes. Dried long red chillies are often deseeded before soaking: cut off the stem and cut down the pod, removing the seeds and the membranes attached to them (some may prefer to wear gloves for this), then rinse the chillies under running water. Dried bird's eye chillies are rarely deseeded before soaking – ensuring that they are unforgettable.

CHINESE RICE WINE *lao jin*

Although alcohol is rarely used in Thai cooking, rice wine is sometimes used in dishes of Chinese origin. When called for, use the best-quality Shao Hsing wine. Most Chinese rice wine is intensely flavoured and is reminiscent of dry sherry, which makes a good substitute.

CILANTRO *see* **CORIANDER**

CITRON, ASIAN *som sa*

The Asian citron is a small, green-skinned orange with slightly yellow flesh. The zest has a delicious fragrance and the juice is quite sour. Mandarin and tangelo, especially if not too ripe, make excellent alternatives.

CLOUD EAR MUSHROOMS *het huu nuu*

Also known as wood ears and tree ears, these small, brown, somewhat bizarre-looking mushrooms are believed to be beneficial for the blood and circulatory system. They have little flavour, but are prized for their cartilaginous texture. Mostly they are bought dehydrated, and are easily reconstituted by soaking in water for 20 minutes or so – they swell to triple their size.

COCONUT *mapraow*

When buying a fresh coconut, always choose one that is quite heavy for its size: this means that there is more flesh in the coconut and therefore it will yield more cream. Shake the coconut: if there is water inside, the flesh is less likely to be fermented. Coconut is used in many ways, grated or shredded, and sometimes roasted.

GRATED OR SHREDDED COCONUT *mapraow krut* For grated coconut, hold the coconut in the palm of the hand, eyes towards thumb or little finger, and with the back of a heavy cleaver, crack the coconut deftly down the centre with a hefty wallop. Lift the cleaver quickly, so as to shatter the husk. Repeat, rotating the coconut. Two, three or four times should do it. Do this over a bowl to catch the liquid. The coconut water – when fresh – is the most thirst-quenching of liquids; however, it sours very quickly, and is often used to ferment vegetables or make vinegar.

The coconut halves are washed and then grated. Traditionally, the Thai use a grater called a 'rabbit' – actually a small stool with a sharp-pronged grater at one end. However, a hand-cranked spindle grater or even a zester works better, in my experience. For long strands, drag the utensil all the way across the coconut half. For shorter shreds, start from the centre of the coconut half and work your way to the rim. Turning the coconut regularly helps ensure even strands.

ROASTED COCONUT *mapraow krua* Roast the scraped or grated coconut in a very low oven, checking and turning often, until golden, fragrant and nutty.

YOUNG COCONUT *mapraow orn* Young coconuts can be readily bought, normally frozen, from most Asian suppliers. Sometimes the cleaned flesh with some of its water can be bought ready to go in a small plastic bag. If the coconut is in its shell, pierce the husk twice with a steel skewer to drain the water, then cleave in half and remove the soft, gelatinous flesh with a spoon. Shave the brown inner skin from the flesh before using.

Keep the husk, which is used in various desserts, especially Coconut Ash Pudding (page 608). In Thailand, there are also special 'grating' coconuts (*mapraow teun teuk*), which are not quite mature and so have tender flesh that is perfect for using fresh in desserts.

The taste of fresh coconut cream is incomparably luscious, with a complexity and depth of flavour that, I think, justifies the labour required to produce it.

Although grated coconut can be worked by hand with an equal amount of hot water for a few minutes, I have had greater success with a food processor. The coconut can be simply scored or cut into segments to make it easier to prise from the shell, and the brown inner skin peeled away and discarded. The flesh is then chopped and blended in a food processor with water, before being squeezed to extract the cream and milk.

Always extract the cream and milk by squeezing through muslin – or a very clean tea towel – into a glass, china or plastic bowl (metal taints the cream). Leave to separate for at least 20 minutes. The cream is the thicker, opaque liquid that separates and floats on top of the thinner liquid, which is the milk. No matter how much water is added, the yield of cream will always be the same, as the cream separates from the milk. Normally one good coconut yields about a cup of coconut cream. Often the squeezing process is repeated, but this second pressing will yield more milk than cream.

Both cream and milk are best used within a few hours. They can be kept refrigerated, but they will harden and become difficult to use. One Thai trick is to add a bruised chilli to retard the hardening. Coconut cream sours within a day or two, depending on the quality of the coconut. To arrest this process, the coconut cream and milk can be simmered for a minute – but this is, in effect, pasteurisation, which destroys some of the lush, sweet creaminess that so distinguishes fresh coconut cream from its canned cousin.

CANNED COCONUT CREAM   Canned coconut cream has been pasteurised and homogenised and, as a result of the canning process and long storage, I believe, bastardised. If using in a curry, do not shake the can, as the plug on the top can be used to fry the paste – though you'll probably need to add a tablespoon of oil to help things along. If using for soups or salads where a rich cream is required, then shake to mix before use.

'CRACKED' OR SEPARATED COCONUT CREAM   Curries that are fried in coconut cream often call for the cream to be 'cracked' or separated. This involves simmering the cream until most of the water evaporates; the cream then separates into thin oil and milk solids. Once separated, coconut cream lasts indefinitely. The separated oil can also be used for deep-frying and the solids are sometimes used in desserts when a weighty sumptuousness is required.

CORIANDER *pak chii*

Coriander plants arrived with Arab and Indian traders in the south of Thailand over a thousand years ago. The Thai use all the plant, so when buying make sure that the stems have roots attached. The picked leaves (sometimes called cilantro) are used in salads and soups; the stems are added to stocks, while the roots are a common ingredient in sauces and curry pastes.

CORIANDER SEEDS *luuk pak chii* Thai coriander seeds are much smaller, darker-coloured, more fragrant and a lot sharper in flavour than regular coriander seeds. They are easily obtainable from any South East Asian providore.

CRISP FISH *see* **PLA GROP**

CURRY PASTES

A curry paste should be puréed as finely as possible (see page 280 for detailed instructions on making curry pastes). Leftover paste can be happily stored for up to two weeks, cartouched – that is, sealed tightly with plastic wrap pressed against the surface of the paste – and refrigerated in an airtight container. Do not freeze a paste as, when thawed, the shallots and garlic will become bitter and the paste insipid as it weeps.

RED CURRY PASTE
This recipe is for a basic red curry paste (*geng dtaeng*) that can be used for dry curries, especially those made with seafood, or added to Fish Cakes (page 494).

10 dried long red chillies, deseeded, soaked and drained
large pinch of salt
1½ tablespoons chopped galangal
3 tablespoons chopped lemongrass
2 teaspoons finely chopped kaffir lime zest
1 tablespoon scraped and chopped coriander root
1 tablespoon chopped red shallot
2 tablespoons chopped garlic

Gradually pound the ingredients together using a pestle and mortar, adding one by one, until smooth.

CURRY POWDER *pong gari*

The Thai prefer a light curry powder. Since dried spices are so irregularly used in Thai cooking, even the most exacting Thai cooks buy prepared curry powder from the market. There are many commercial curry powders available, and if their quality and freshness are assured then, without hesitation, use them. I think curry powder is another instance where store-bought can sometimes be better than homemade (but see page 241 for a curry powder recipe that's especially good with beef). If the powder is a little stale, spread it on a plate and leave in the sun or a very low oven for a few hours to invigorate it; alternatively, it can be briefly dry-fried in a pan or wok over a low heat.

DAIKON *see* **SALTED WHITE RADISH; WHITE RADISH**

DEEP-FRIED GARLIC *see under* **GARLIC**

DEEP-FRIED SHALLOTS *see under* **RED SHALLOTS**

DRIED FISH *pla haeng*

Drying is the most ancient method of preservation, and dried fish are used extensively in Thai cooking. Throughout the country, especially near water – the seaside, rivers and canals – fish are left in the sun to dry. Happily, in Thailand a completely sunny day can normally be guaranteed. Good dried fish is quite difficult to find and yet it is easy to make (see recipes below).

Semi-dried fish (*pla dtat dtiaw*) is not truly preserved and will last only a day or two unrefrigerated, a week or so chilled. To use, the fish can be either deep-fried or grilled, and is perfect in a salad with a sour fruit, as a garnish for a *nahm prik* relish, or in a pineapple curry.

Leaving it out to dry longer will result in a drier, harder fish that can be used as the base for a fried *nahm prik*, in a *krua* curry paste, or toasted and pounded in a salad.

See also salted fish; smoked fish.

SEMI-DRIED FISH

Semi-drying concentrates the flavour of the fish and makes it slightly oily.

200 g (6 oz) fillet of salmon or any oily-fleshed fish, such as mackerel, swordfish or bonito
2 tablespoons fish sauce
1 teaspoon white sugar
a little sea salt
pinch of white pepper

Clean the fish. Mix fish sauce, sugar, salt and pepper and marinate fish in it for at least 3 hours or overnight. Remove fish and set on a cake rack over a tray lined with foil in a warm, dry place for several hours, until the fish is semi-dried. Turn once or twice during this process.

DRIED FISH

The best fish to dry is quite full-flavoured, like mackerel, swordfish or bonito, but any fish will do.

200 g (6 oz) fish fillet
1 teaspoon salt
pinch of white sugar
3 tablespoons fish sauce or light soy sauce

Clean the fish. Marinate with salt, sugar and fish sauce or light soy sauce overnight. Remove from marinade and dry on a cake rack in a warm place for at least 1–2 days. Alternatively, the fish can be dried in a low oven for several hours.

DRIED LILY STALKS *dork mai jin*

These are the dried stamens of lilies, and taste a little like raisins or sultanas. They are always rehydrated in water for 20 minutes or so, then tied into a small knot to prevent them breaking up during cooking.

DRIED ORANGE PEEL *piw som haeng*

Used mainly in soups and braises, this aromatic ingredient can be purchased in any Chinese providore. You can also make your own: simply dry orange zest – ensuring all pith is removed – in the sun or a warm place until completely dried. Store in an airtight container in a dark place.

DRIED PRAWNS *gung haeng*

Try to find a shop that has a good turnover of dried prawns, and buy those that have the deepest red colour and smell the sweetest. Once purchased, they are best kept in the refrigerator. If ground dried prawns are required, briefly grind in a clean coffee grinder or spice mill. Store-bought dried prawns are certainly more convenient than drying prawns at home, but the latter tastes undeniably better (see recipe below).

DRIED PRAWNS

10 large uncooked prawns (shrimp)
1 teaspoon salt
3 tablespoons fish sauce or light soy sauce
pinch of white sugar

Peel and devein prawns, then wash them. Mix salt, fish sauce or soy sauce and sugar; pour over prawns and leave to marinate overnight.

Place prawns on a cake rack over a foil-lined tray (this makes for easier cleaning). Ideally, they should be dried for a day or two in direct sunlight, covered by muslin or a tea towel to prevent anything untoward joining them. Otherwise, dry in a very low oven – either overnight with just the pilot light on, or for around 4 hours at 90°C (195°F) with the door ajar – until dried but not brittle. Once dried, the prawns will keep for several weeks refrigerated.

DUCK EGGS, SALTED *see* **SALTED DUCK EGGS**

DURIAN *turian*

Perhaps the most notorious fruit in Thailand, if not the world, is the durian. It is a fruit that provokes passion – either devotion or disgust and nothing in between. Some say it's like eating custard in a toilet, others like New York in summer. I am addicted to it, and will follow its alluring, mesmerising aroma wherever it may lead. Fresh durian is incomparable; it is sometimes available in Thai and Chinese shops.

The Thai use several kinds of eggplant (aubergine) in their cuisine, and it is believed that eggplants originated in Thailand. They should only be cut with a stainless steel knife, as any other metal will instantly discolour the flesh; if sliced eggplant is not used straightaway, it should be steeped in salted water to prevent it turning an unsightly black.

APPLE EGGPLANT *makreua prao* Apple eggplants are green, yellow, orange or purple in colour and round in shape. It is of the utmost importance that they are fresh, because then they taste crisp and clean, nutty and almost sweet; the flesh is virtually white. If they are old and wizened, they will be musty and quite bitter. They are normally used in salads and curries, or as a vegetable accompaniment to a relish. They are eaten raw or just cooked.

FUZZY EGGPLANT *maeuk* This eggplant is uncommon outside Thailand. It is round, 1 centimetre (½ inch) in diameter and surprisingly sour; its fuzz needs to be scraped off before use. Cape gooseberries can be used as a substitute.

LONG EGGPLANT *makreua yaew* This eggplant looks very similar to a long baby (Japanese) eggplant, except that it is green in colour. Long eggplant is normally served grilled or in green curries.

PEA EGGPLANT *makreua puang* These are pea-sized berries that grow in clusters. Eaten alone they have a somewhat bitter taste, but this is a pleasant foil to the richness of some curries.

ERYNGO *see* **PAK CHII FARANG**

FERMENTED BAMBOO SHOOTS *nor mai dong*

Only freshly peeled and sliced bamboo shoots can be successfully fermented. Older, wizened shoots have deteriorated to the degree where they cannot ferment – they simply rot in the rice water. Usually, fermented bamboo shoots are rinsed before use; however, I like the intense sourness and use them as they are, often including some of the fermenting liquid to reinforce their flavour.

FERMENTED BAMBOO SHOOTS

While fermented bamboo shoots can be safely stored at room temperature, I cautiously store them refrigerated until needed; they last for a very long time. And although they can be eaten immediately, in my experience they improve if matured, refrigerated, for at least a week. This process is natural fermentation and sometimes the unexpected and undesirable may occur: if the product turns blue or smells foul then – not surprisingly – discard it!

2 fresh bamboo shoots – roughly 1 kg (2 lb)
2–3 tablespoons salt
2 stalks lemongrass, bruised
4 slices galangal
3 kaffir lime leaves, torn
1 long red or green chilli
1 teaspoon palm sugar
pinch of salt
rice-rinsing water (see page 128), to cover

Wearing gloves, use a sharp knife to cut deeply along the length of the shoots, then peel off the outer layers until the fleshy core is revealed – you should have about 400 g (12 oz) bamboo shoots. Slice lengthwise very finely. Rub with the salt and leave overnight in a colander set over a bowl, to draw out some of the bitterness.

Next day, rinse bamboo shoots thoroughly to remove excess salt, which would hinder fermentation. In a sterilised glass jar, combine with lemongrass, galangal, lime leaves, chilli, palm sugar and pinch of salt (a little salt must be present to kill any bacteria).

Pour in rice-rinsing water, making sure that the bamboo shoots are completely immersed or the exposed part will rot and spoil the rest. Put on a tightly fitting lid and leave in a warm place for 7–15 days, until quite sour and fragrant. Check every few days, and refrigerate when the desired degree of sourness is reached.

FERMENTED BEAN CURD *dtor huu yii*

Originally of Chinese origin, this unctuous product is truly delicious. It is made by fermenting slightly dried bean curd with a red rice mould over several months.

Some aficionados eat fermented bean curd simply mixed with warm rice and seasoned with shredded ginger. Often other ingredients, such as wine, sesame oil or chilli, are added to create an extra dimension of colour and flavour; to my taste, it is one of the few ingredients that can be successfully combined with Chinese wine. It should be used sparingly to prevent the finished dish being cloying.

Fermented bean curd is available in small jars and comes in two varieties: very red, or creamy white veined with pink. The former imbues everything with its vivid colour; the rich marbled colour of the latter makes it more versatile, certainly more subtle and therefore, to my aesthetics at least, preferable.

FERMENTED FISH *pla raa*

Pla raa is an evil thing, leering out from its murky distant past. It is made by salting freshwater fish for several days then drying it in the sun. Next, the fish is fermented with either boiled or roasted rice, or sometimes even its bran, for at least 8 months before use. *Pla raa* is astonishingly, breathtakingly pungent by itself – although some culinary thrill-seekers eat it deep-fried and dressed only with a little lemongrass and green mango. However, when mixed in the right proportion with other ingredients its malevolence dissipates and it becomes a silken and suave undertaste, vastly different from its primal state.

For some, life is too short and the world too small to make *pla raa*, especially since it can be easily and odourlessly purchased from Asian food shops. However, for those who must pursue authenticity to its extreme . . .

FERMENTED FISH

1 kg (2 lb) freshwater fish fillets, such as trout or perch
1 cup good-quality salt
banana leaves
½ cup ground roasted rice (see page 159)
extra 3 tablespoons salt
rock salt

Wash the fillets and mix with the cup of salt. Marinate, covered, for at least 3 days (some brews are left at this initial stage for up to 3 months), then rinse the fish completely to remove the salt and dry for a few hours in bright sunlight. Cover fish with banana leaves, place in a colander, weigh down and leave for 3 days to extract any excess liquid. Mix fish with ground roasted rice and the extra salt, then pack tightly into a narrow-necked earthenware pot. Press strips of bamboo down onto the fish to keep it completely immersed. Finally, cover fish with water and then with a layer of rock salt before sealing pot. Leave to ferment in the shade for at least 8 months.

FERMENTED FISH SAUCE *nahm pla raa*

The robust precursor of fish sauce, *nahm pla raa* is still used in the north and north-east of Thailand – most commonly in a diluted form, simmered with various aromatics to round it out. Fermented fish sauce is used to season curries, soups and some *lon* relishes. It has the remarkable characteristic of being extremely pungent when eaten alone, yet when combined with other ingredients, it retreats into the background.

FERMENTED FISH SAUCE

Do not make this sauce standing downwind (even some Thai find the flavour too strong, and happily use regular fish sauce in its stead).

3 stalks lemongrass
5 red shallots
3 coriander roots, scraped *or* a handful of coriander stalks
1 jar (225 g or 7 oz) fermented fish (*pla raa*)
1 whole kaffir lime *or* 4–6 kaffir lime leaves
10 slices galangal

Bruise the lemongrass, shallots and coriander. Combine all ingredients in a pot and cover with water. Simmer until the fish has dissolved – at least 10 minutes. Strain and leave to cool. Refrigerated, this keeps indefinitely. I often add the bones of *pla grop* (crisp fish) or dried fish to give extra flavour, or a few fish heads to give extra body.

Fermented rice is a sweet, slightly alcoholic product that is sold in small plastic containers in most Asian providores. It is used in savoury food, especially mild coconut relishes, to counterbalance any extremes of taste or seasoning, sourness or saltiness, and is also used in desserts.

FERMENTED RICE

The yeast used to ferment rice is a special dried yeast sold in Chinese grocers in small tablets. It is different from normal yeast as it contains powdered dried galangal. I also like to add a pinch of palm sugar to assist fermentation.

300 g (10 oz) white sticky rice
15 g (½ oz) ground dried yeast
1½ tablespoons white sugar

Soak rice overnight. Drain and steam for 15–20 minutes, rinse and drain again. Stir in yeast and sugar. The rice is traditionally wrapped in banana leaves, but a sterilised, sealable glass jar will do fine. Leave to ferment in a warm place for 3–7 days.

FERMENTED SHRIMP PASTE *see* **SHRIMP PASTE**

FERMENTED SIAMESE WATERCRESS *pak bung dong*

Fermented Siamese watercress makes an excellent ingredient in sour orange curries and coconut soups, and is also used as a garnish for rich relishes.

FERMENTED SIAMESE WATERCRESS

Many other green leafy vegetables can be treated in this manner, although Siamese water-cress tastes the best. It is absolutely delicious – I think it has a pronounced sultana-like flavour. Thai cooks always rinse it before use, but I like to add a little of the fermenting liquid to recipes in which it is used, to reinforce its flavour.

1 bunch Siamese watercress
around 4 cups rice-rinsing water (see page 128)
large pinch of salt
1 tablespoon palm sugar

Clean the watercress. Remove coarse ends and cut into 2–3 cm (1 in) lengths. Steep in water for a few hours. Lay out in the sun or a warm place for a full day until wilted, in parts almost wizened and beginning to brown. Mix rice-rinsing water with salt and sugar, stir to dissolve. Place watercress in a sterilised glass jar, cover with the liquid and close the lid. Leave in the sun for at least 5 days – until it tastes quite sour. Refrigerate for another week or so to mature before using; this lasts for a few months if kept refrigerated.

FERMENTED SOY BEANS *tua nao*

Tua nao is an ancient fermented product once used extensively in northern Thai cooking. It is not so common now, having largely been replaced by shrimp paste. Before *tua nao* is used in a recipe, it is grilled or toasted, then ground.

FERMENTED SOY BEANS

This is the traditional way of making this paste. Fresh soy beans are its normal base, but fresh yellow lentils are occasionally used. Since these are not readily available, a viable alternative is to use Chinese fermented beans from yellow bean sauce (see page 185).

2 cups fresh soy beans or rinsed and drained yellow bean sauce
1 tablespoon salt
2 garlic cloves, peeled
large pinch of ground white pepper

Wash and soak soy beans overnight. Bring to the boil in plenty of water and simmer for 3 hours. Strain, wrap in banana leaves and place in the sun to ferment for 3–4 days. Then pound beans with salt, garlic and white pepper to make a paste, smear onto banana leaves and dry in the sun. Once dried, it lasts indefinitely.

FISH, DRIED *see* **DRIED FISH**

FISH, FERMENTED *see* **FERMENTED FISH**

FISH, SALTED *see* **SALTED FISH**

FISH, SMOKED *see* **SMOKED FISH**

FISH SAUCE *nahm pla*

Fish sauce is a vital ingredient in Thai cuisine; it is the salty element in the seasoning that balances all savoury dishes. Fish sauce is an unusual condiment: it smells and tastes extremely pungent, yet when combined with other ingredients it melds into the whole, supports other flavours and is unobtrusive. Chinese or Japanese soy sauce should not be used as substitutes – although light soy sauce can be used as a vegetarian alternative to fish sauce, with varying degrees of success.

Fish sauce should not be too harsh; some cooks even dilute it. The better ones are traditionally made – from fish or prawns – and the very best comes from Ranong, on the east coast of the Gulf of Thailand. Sadly, the finest fish sauce is rarely available outside Thailand, but most commercial brands are perfectly acceptable.

FLATTENED RICE *kao mao*

Two types of flattened rice (sometimes sold as rice flakes) are available: that made from white, unbleached rice; and a green one, which has been coloured, traditionally with pandanus. Flattened rice is used in desserts, normally to make a batter or crust – it imparts a subtle, nutty taste and has a delicate, crunchy texture.

GALANGAL *khaa*

This rhizome is extensively used in Thai cuisine. When young, it has creamy white skin with pink sprouts, and is best used in soups. As it matures the skin thickens, the flavour becomes more pungent and peppery, and the colour changes to a musty gold or even a burnished red; then it is ideal for curry pastes. Galangal is available at most South East Asian food shops, and should be stored in the refrigerator, in a plastic bag to prevent dehydration.

Powdered galangal can also be easily purchased, but is simple to make. Peel and slice some galangal and dry over several days, preferably in the sun, then grind in a spice grinder. I prefer to store it refrigerated.

GAPI *see* SHRIMP PASTE

GARLIC *gratiam*

Thai garlic is much smaller and less pungent than most of the garlic that is available in the West. Use young, new season garlic where possible to approximate Thai garlic.
See also pickled garlic.

DEEP-FRIED GARLIC *gratiam jiaw*   Deep-fried garlic can be bought, but there is no guarantee of its quality or age. It is incomparably better to fry your own.

For garlic to be deep-fried successfully, a certain amount needs to be fried – usually at least a cup – otherwise it is difficult to control the cooking, and it can burn easily and all too quickly. Slice the garlic lengthwise into very thin, even slices. It is important to slice the garlic lengthwise, so that the slices deep-fry evenly and crisply, rather than becoming knotted disks. The slices should also be as fine as possible – almost paper-thin – so that they cook quickly and evenly, becoming crispy and golden; if they are too thick, the edges will burn while the inside remains undercooked.

Heat oil in a wok until moderately hot, then add garlic and reduce the heat a little. Deep-fry, stirring constantly with tongs. When the garlic starts to lose its sharp, peppery aroma and smells nutty, and starts to turn amber and then a light honey-gold, remove it from the oil. Drain and spread out on absorbent paper to cool. Pass the oil through a sieve to collect any scraps before re-use; the garlic-infused oil can be used for deep-frying or stir-frying. The garlic will keep for 2–3 days in an airtight container.

MINCED DEEP-FRIED GARLIC *gratiam sap jiaw*   Often minced deep-fried garlic is left to cool in the oil and then it, along with a little of the perfumed oil, is spooned over soups and braises. Therefore, it is especially important not to overcook it.

Mince, pound or coarsely purée 10 garlic cloves with a large pinch of salt. Deep-fry over a low to medium heat, stirring regularly until just turning golden. Remove from the heat. Drain if beginning to overcook, and return once the oil has cooled. This keeps well for 2 or 3 days in an airtight container.

GRILLED OR ROASTED GARLIC *gratiam pao* Traditionally this is done over an open flame, but an easier way is to 'roast' the unpeeled garlic cloves in a wok with a little water, until the water has evaporated and the skin is charred. This ensures that the garlic is completely cooked and quite smoky but without any bitter, blackened parts. When cool enough to handle, peel, chop and add to the dish.

GINGER *king*

Mature ginger is used in soups and a few curry pastes, mostly with fish or strongly flavoured meats, to counteract their pungency. Young ginger, with its white, translucent skin and pink sprouts, is generally preferred in Thai cooking and is used in salads, curries and soups. Buy only firm and unwrinkled rhizomes and store in a plastic bag or airtight container to prevent dehydration. If the ginger is old or pungent, rinse in water to remove its sharpness before use.

See also pickled ginger.

DRIED GINGER *king haeng* Older, wizened ginger is best peeled, sliced and dried in the sun. It can then be stored in an airtight container in the dark, and ground in a spice grinder as required; it makes unsurpassed powdered ginger.

GINGER WATER *nahm king* Ginger water is made by simmering bruised ginger and a little white sugar in water for several minutes; cool and strain before use.

GOURDS *see* **GREEN GOURDS**

GRACHAI *wild ginger*

Sometimes known as lesser galangal or Chinese keys, *grachai* is a cluster of pencil-like rhizomes with a thin, brown skin. There is no accepted English name, but for the sake of convenience I have dubbed it wild ginger. Its earthy, peppery, camphor-like flavour is favoured in jungle curries and fish dishes.

Fresh *grachai* is becoming available, but failing that it can be readily purchased pickled in brine – before using the latter, rinse, then soak in water that has been sweetened with white sugar to remove some of the preservative's taste.

GREEN GOURDS

Many types of green gourd, which are of Chinese origin, are now used extensively in Thai cuisine.

ASH MELON *fak gwio* This is called ash melon because of the white powder on its skin. The Thai believe it cools the body and so often use it in soups, especially with other Chinese medicine.

BITTER MELON *mara*   In Thailand there are several types of bitter gourd, including a very small, oval one called *mara kii nok*, which graphically translates as 'bird droppings melon' but tastes relatively mild. The regular one, Chinese bitter melon, is easily obtainable from any Chinese providore; it is longer, light green in colour and has a knobbly skin. The Thai, like most Asians, enjoy the bitterness of this melon, believing it to be a mild purgative. Others find the taste repellent, no matter how beneficial the melon is supposed to be.

One way to reduce its bitterness is to rub the chopped, deseeded melon with salt and leave for a few hours to leach out some of the bitterness. I find this insufficient – it is still too bitter for my taste – and take the additional precaution of blanching from a cold-water start. To ensure that the flesh survives such prolonged treatment, steep the cleaned and salted melon in hydrolysed lime water for 10 minutes before blanching. The melon is still bitter after all these processes, but not unpalatably so.

SNAKE GOURD *boap nguu*   This vivid green, ribbed gourd is named for its length and curvaceous form. It has a mild flavour and is often used in simple broths and soups.

GROUND ROASTED RICE   *kao krua*

Most commonly, ground roasted rice is used as a textural binder in salads, especially minced spicy salads (*larp*) and grilled meat salads (*nahm dtok*). Occasionally it is used as a thickener in rustic curries.

To make ground roasted rice, dry-fry white sticky rice over a low heat in a wok or pan, stirring regularly until golden and fragrant. Sometimes a few slices of galangal and kaffir lime leaves are added to enhance the delicate perfume. The rice must smell nutty and cooked, and look lightly toasted. If it is insufficiently roasted, it is not only indigestible but unpalatable. Leave to cool, then grind in a spice grinder to a medium to fine powder.

HOG PLUM   *makrok*

Hog plums are small, tart green fruits. They are available in many Asian fruit and vegetable shops; if you can't find them, green mango is a good alternative.

HYDROLYSED LIME WATER   *nahm bun sai*

This is made from lime powder (obtained from fossilised shells) and water. There are two types: red and white. Red lime is dyed using the mahogany-coloured heartwood of the cutch tree. It is eaten as an adjunct to betel nut – it imparts a spritzig astringency – and is traditionally used in hydrolysed lime water, imbuing it with a slight pink tinge. I prefer colourless, bleached white lime, which is made without the addition of cutch.

To make hydrolysed lime water, dissolve a teaspoon of lime powder in 4–5 litres (4–5 quarts) water and leave overnight until it has precipitated; if only a small amount is required, simply add a small pinch of powder to a cup of water. Only use the treated water and not the lime at the bottom; strain before use.

Hydrolysed lime water keeps for several weeks, and is used mainly in desserts, but also for batters and deep-frying. Traditionally an ingredient (especially tender fruit) is soaked in hydrolysed lime water to tighten its cell membranes, enabling it to survive prolonged simmering without dissolving or toughening. Experienced cooks will often alter the proportion of lime paste to water to take into account the qualities of the ingredient. The soaking time also depends on the nature of the item: usually 30 minutes is enough, but to truly preserve something an overnight dip may be required. Always rinse thoroughly in running water.

JACKFRUIT *kanun*

This large fruit is used in both savoury and dessert cooking. The smaller, hard unripe fruit is added to curries, while the larger, pungently perfumed ripe fruit is used mainly in desserts.

JASMINE *mali horm*

These small, highly perfumed, ivory-coloured flowers are steeped in water overnight to make perfumed water, which is then used in desserts. It is believed that the flowers should be picked at sunset, for this is when their fragrance is most pervasive.

KAFFIR LIME *bai makrut*

The leaves of this citrus fruit are used extensively throughout Thai cuisine. Fortunately fresh leaves are now readily available outside Thailand; dried or frozen ones are comparatively useless as all the fragrant, volatile oils will have been lost. Kaffir lime trees are available in garden nurseries, so should access to shops that carry these leaves be inconvenient, buy a tree, thus ensuring a ready supply.

Some Thai believe that the kaffir lime wards off evil spirits and hang them outside their homes; others, more prosaically, wash their hair in the juice to ward off another type of evil that is often more pernicious – dandruff.

The fruit (*luk makrut*) is often difficult and expensive to obtain. It is mainly used for its zest in curry pastes, and occasionally the juice is added to salad dressings. If zest is called for, scrupulously avoid the white pith, for it is very bitter. When fresh limes are unobtainable or out of season, frozen can be used, but be warned – the pith becomes even more bitter on thawing. It is easier to remove the zest from frozen limes while the fruit is still hard, neither completely frozen nor thawed. Once thawed, the zest is very fragrant, but only for an hour or so; aim to use it promptly. Do not use the juice of frozen limes – except, perhaps, in the final rinse!

KECAP MANIS *see* **SOY SAUCE**

LANGSART

This is a deliciously sour, slightly bitter, lychee-like fruit with mottled yellow skin. Any small, tart, fleshy fruit, such as longan or loquat, can be used in its place.

LARD *see* **RENDERED PORK FAT**

LEMONGRASS *dtakrai*

This blade-like plant is used in curries and soups, especially hot and sour *dtom yam* soups. Lemongrass is very fibrous, so remove the outer sheaths and green, woody top third of the stalk before using. (Offcuts can be used to make stock or delicious lemongrass tea – or even boiled in water to produce a natural insect repellent that can be poured around plants to discourage bugs.) It is easily grown by striking the bulb in water, then planting in a large pot with a tray of water beneath to keep the soil very moist.

LIMES *manao*

Thai limes are smaller and slightly sweeter than their Western counterparts. Ideally lime juice (*nahm manao*) should be squeezed as needed. Its succulence, vibrant colour and vitamin content dissipate quickly when exposed to air and light. Lemon juice is not a satisfactory substitute – it is a last resort.

See also pickled limes.

LIMES, KAFFIR *see* **KAFFIR LIME**

LONG-LEAF CORIANDER *see* **PAK CHII FARANG**

LONG PEPPER *diplii diplii*

Long pepper is a small, cylindrical, spike-like spice that tastes like a cross between pepper and cassia. It is most often found in Indian spice shops, where it is known as *peepar*.

LOTUS STALKS *sai bua*

These crunchy stalks are occasionally sold fresh. The skin – in some varieties pale green, in others flecked with purple – must be peeled before the stalks are cut into lengths. Mild, even bland to taste, they are normally simmered in coconut cream.

LYCHEE *linchii*

Thai lychees can be very large indeed, with a small seed and a luxurious amount of gloriously flavoured flesh. They are used in many ways – in salads, with dried fish, in curries and desserts.

MACE *dork jan*

The outer sheath of the nutmeg, mace is sometimes used in curry pastes – especially with fish and in *mussaman* curries.

MACQUEM prickly ash

This uncommon northern Thai spice – the dried seeds of white prickly ash – is used in *larp* salads and some curries, imparting a mandarin-like fragrance. Thai from the central plains sometimes call it 'fragrant pepper', *prik horm*. It can occasionally be found in Asian shops, or Szechuan peppercorns may be substituted.

MADAN sour cucumber

In the absence of a common English name for this unusual fruit, I use 'sour cucumber'. It is as small as a cornichon, with the same slightly ribbed, elongated oval shape, lime-green skin and a core of small seeds. *Madan* are best when unripe – the flesh is then soft and tastes very tart. When overripe, it is mushy and has an unpleasant, slightly fermented taste.

A fresh, tart, unripe, peeled tamarind pod is a more available alternative, as are green tomatoes or green mango.

MALTOSE *bae sa*

This viscous syrup with a sweet and toasty flavour is the product of germinating or malting rice bran. Maltose is readily available in Chinese grocery stores, but honey, glucose or corn syrup can be used instead.

MANGO *mamuang*

At one time every household in Thailand had its own mango tree – and in many ways the mango is a perfect example of the resourcefulness of the Thai, for they use everything the tree provides.

During the rainy season when the young leaves and shoots sprout, they are used as an accompaniment to a *nahm prik* relish. When the comparatively cold winter winds from China blow, small green mangoes often drop off the tree; these are gathered and eaten with shrimp paste relish, or simply with salt and chillies. As the fruit mature, the fully grown but not yet ripe mangoes are added to a *nahm prik* relish or dressed with sweet fish sauce. If there is a glut of unripe fruit, they will be preserved in brine to be eaten as a snack or for use when the fresh fruit is no longer available.

The mangoes ripen fully during March, which is the season for luscious mango and sticky rice, but the Thai also eat the fresh fruit on its own, as an accompaniment to a *mussaman* curry or with rice. If there are still mangoes left, the remainder of the crop is turned into a dessert of mango paste or sliced into sheets and dried in the sun for snacks.

MELON *see* **GREEN GOURDS; WATERMELON**

MINCED DEEP-FRIED GARLIC *see under* **GARLIC**

MINT *bai sarae nae*

The Thai normally use a fragrant, small-leafed variety of mint, very similar to common garden mint.

MOOLI *see* **SALTED WHITE RADISH; WHITE RADISH**

MUNG BEANS *tua leuang*

There are myriad varieties of these ancient legumes – green, gold, red and black – but beneath the skin they are mostly ivory-coloured. In Thai cuisine, they are mainly used in desserts, and occasionally to add texture to a noodle dish.

ROASTED AND GROUND MUNG BEANS *tua leuang krua* Green or yellow mung beans are often roasted and ground before being added to dishes. Rinse beans and soak overnight, or for at least 30 minutes, then drain. Roast in a low oven or in a wok over a very low flame, stirring, until golden. Some recipes recommend sprinkling the grains with water to ensure the starch is completely cooked as it roasts – the result is certainly more fragrant. Allow to cool and grind coarsely.

MUSHROOMS *het*

Thai cuisine includes many varieties of mushrooms. The most common is the straw mushroom (*het fang*), which has a slightly bitter taste when raw, but tastes sweet and nutty when cooked. Fresh straw mushrooms are uncommon outside Asia; do not use the canned product, but rather a fresh alternative, such as oyster mushrooms.

During the rainy season, particularly in the north, the Thai gather a lot of wild mushrooms, such as cèpes, chanterelles and several varieties of russula. Perhaps the most widespread is the fawn-coloured, umbrella-shaped *het kone*, which has the peculiar characteristic of souring when it has been salted for a few hours. Like most other mushrooms, it is used in almost every style of Thai cooking – soups, relishes and curries, but especially salads.

See also cloud ear mushrooms; shiitake mushrooms.

MUSTARD GREENS, PICKLED *see* **PICKLED MUSTARD GREENS**

NAEM *see* **CHIANG MAI CURED PORK**

NOODLES

Rice noodles (*sen gwi dtiaw*) are simply a paste of rice flour and water steamed in large trays to form deliciously fleshy, yielding, white noodles that are cut into various widths: wide noodles, *sen yai*, which are normally about 2 centimetres (1 inch); thin noodles, *sen lek*, small strands less than ½ centimetre (¼ inch); or *sen mii*, vermicelli, so thin that they are always dried – these noodles are used in the famous *pat thai*. Wide and thin can be used interchangeably – it is simply a matter of preference.

Most Thai eat rice noodles freshly made; they are readily obtainable at any Chinese market. Unrefrigerated, they are quite soft and stay at their best for 2–3 days, becoming harder as they get older. Although they can be refrigerated, this toughens them and they then need to be reheated slightly before being used – steam until just warm to soften. Fresh noodles need only moments to cook in a dish.

Dried rice noodles are reconstituted by soaking in water until soft before draining and using. Although they have a different texture and taste, they can easily be used instead of fresh noodles.

KANOM JIN These tender, white, spaghetti-like noodles are made from rice flour. Once, every village in Thailand had a special noodle mill made from heavy teak expressly for making them. On one of the black and gold walls of the lacquer pavilion in Suan Pakkard palace, which dates from Ayuthyia (but is now in Bangkok), there is a depiction of a group of women forcing these noodles through a sieve-like drum set over a cauldron of boiling water.

Although genuine *kanom jin* are only available in Thailand, there are many very satisfactory alternatives. Fresh Vietnamese noodles are the nearest equivalent, but there are also dried versions in Asian shops.

EGG NOODLES *ba mii* These delicious, wheat-based strands come in various sizes. They need to be blanched in boiling water, for as little as 20 seconds, before use.

OIL *nahm man peut*

The traditional Thai frying medium is rendered pork fat or coconut oil: using pork fat results in a rich silken texture, while coconut oil gives a nutty finish. However, both of these options are distinctly unhealthy – the first is dripping with cholesterol and the second laden with saturated fats.

For most dishes, regular vegetable oil is an easy choice, and it works well. Where an oil with more character is desired, a reasonable compromise is to mix a small amount of pork fat or coconut oil with vegetable oil.

ORANGE PEEL, DRIED *see* **DRIED ORANGE PEEL**

PAK CHII FARANG long-leaf coriander

This is an uncommon herb that may be found in Asian shops; it is also known as eryngo or sawtooth herb. *Pak chii farang* is quite delicious, with serrated leaves about 5 centimetres (2 inches) long. It has a succulent taste, not dissimilar to coriander, and an inviting, herbaceous fragrance.

PANDANUS LEAF *bai dtoei horm*

Pandanus has a long, green, blade-like leaf, normally sold in bunches. The fresh leaves are not uncommon in Asian shops, and they are readily available frozen. They are used to perfume desserts or rice (insert a leaf into a pot of freshly cooked rice and leave for several minutes before serving). Their flavour, released only on heating, is resinous and nutty. Charmaine Solomon has described pandanus as the vanilla bean of Asia. I can only agree.

PEANUTS *tua lii song*

Peanuts are available in many forms – from the unshelled to the salted and roasted – but the more prepared they are, the less versatile they are. Buying shelled and peeled, but unroasted, peanuts is probably your best bet. They can then be simply roasted in a low oven or, more appropriately for Asian food, deep-fried.

DEEP-FRIED PEANUTS *tua lii song tort* Peanuts should be deep-fried over a medium heat, otherwise they will burn on the outside before they are ready. For economy's sake, it is best to use oil that has been used before – such as for deep-fried garlic or shallots – as the starch from the peanuts thickens the oil, rendering it unusable for further deep-frying.

Blanch 2 tablespoons of peanuts from a cold-water start, drain and cool on a tray. (This swells their fibres so that when they are fried they crisp beautifully.) When dry, deep-fry in plenty of oil over a medium heat until light golden. Drain and cool on absorbent paper. Store in an airtight container and grind as needed.

Cashew nuts can be treated in the same way.

CARAMELISED PEANUTS *tua grajop* Caramelised peanuts are sold everywhere in Thailand, and are used in salads, sauces and desserts. They are easy to make and keep indefinitely. Humidity is their enemy – it makes the sugar weep – so store in an airtight container.

I like to blanch peanuts before caramelising to draw out some of the bitterness, but this is a matter of taste. If doing so, make sure the peanuts are completely dry before proceeding. Melt 2 cups of white sugar in a heavy pan. Add 1 cup of peanuts and stir until they have coloured and have a glorious fragrance. (Some cooks also like to add a large pinch of sesame seeds.) Pour onto a lightly oiled tray to cool and harden. To remove, turn the tray upside down and, with one swift hit on the base of the tray, the caramel should fall off in a block. Crush, if necessary, to fit into an airtight container.

Mogens Bay Esbensen, a Danish chef who lived in Thailand for 16 years, caramelised peanuts in a very different way. After blanching them, he would roll them in sugar as they were drained; the steam caused the sugar to stick to the nuts. Then he would deep-fry the cooled peanuts in plenty of hot, clean oil, stirring them once they began to caramelise, before removing and setting them aside on a tray to cool. The advantage of this method is that the caramelised peanuts can be separated to make an attractive garnish.

PENNYWORT, ASIAN *bai bua bok*

These green, fleshy, clover-like leaves are occasionally used in salads or as a side dish for a spicy *nahm prik* relish, but mostly are juiced and served with sugar and ice as a delicious, quenching and cooling drink.

PEPPERCORNS *prik thai*

The Thai use only two types of peppercorns: white, which are used as a seasoning; and fresh green, which are used as a garnish, as well as in jungle curries, dry red curries and stir-fries. Black peppercorns are very rarely used.

Thai white peppercorns are *not* identical to the Western ones: they are slightly smaller, and are not completely white, having small black markings. Ground white pepper, coriander root and garlic pounded together is one of the oldest and most frequently used seasoning pastes in Thai cuisine.

Buy only a small amount of fresh green peppercorns at a time, as they blacken quickly (within a week), and their taste changes from sharp, moist and peppery to a lingering, bitter and musty flavour. They should be kept refrigerated, but not too cold, and they do not freeze – or rather thaw – successfully. Green peppercorns in brine are an alternative, but one I am reluctant to use as they lose most of their pungency and bite; they should always be well rinsed before use.

See also long pepper.

PETAI BEAN *sadtor*

The deliciously rich petai bean is also unbecomingly known as stink bean. Grilled in its pod, it is served as an accompaniment to a relish, or is sometimes added to curries. It is mostly used in the south of Thailand, where its pungent flavour is balanced with shrimp paste and an excess of chillies.

PICKLED GARLIC *gratiam dong*

Pickled garlic is available in Asian food stores, lasts indefinitely and is as good as homemade (see recipe on page 385). It is used for many purposes, but its main role always seems to be one that addresses excess – preventing the palate from being overwhelmed by fatty foods, relieving heat, balancing sourness or cutting sweetness. The syrup from pickled garlic is also sometimes used in Thai recipes.

PICKLED GINGER *king dong*

Pickled ginger is readily available in jars or can be made from scratch (see recipe on page 385). Its most common use in Thai food is as an accompaniment to curries.

PICKLED LIMES *manao dong*

Pickled limes are easily purchased and are very satisfactory to use. Two varieties are usually available — one sweet and the other salty. Generally the salty one is preferred, although it is really a matter of taste. It is important to use pickled limes whole — not split, squashed or broken — or they will impart an unattractive bitterness, tainting whatever dish they find themselves in. Those with time on their hands can pickle their own limes (see recipe below); they will last for many a year refrigerated.

PICKLED LIMES

For pickling, try to choose small, thin-skinned limes during the height of the season; they are more succulent and have only a thin layer of pith. Pricking and steaming the fruit further reduces the bitterness of the pith, which could otherwise ruin the pickle.

15 small limes
4 cups water
3 tablespoons salt
1 cup white sugar
½ cup white vinegar

Prick limes all over with a fork and steam for 1 hour until soft. Leave in the sun (or a warm place) to dry for a day, then place in a sterilised glass jar. Bring water to the boil with salt, sugar and vinegar. Pour over limes, cool and cover. Leave in the sun or a warm place for at least a month — they seem to be at their best after 6 months.

PICKLED MUSTARD GREENS *pak gart dong*

Bought pickled mustard greens are generally prepared with very coarse chemicals. Although making them at home (see recipe on page 387) reduces the concentration of the pickle, they should still be well rinsed before use; I occasionally like to add some of the homemade brine to give dimension to a dish.

There are two types of pickled mustard greens — one salty and sweet, the other salty and sour. The sweet version can be used as an accompaniment to rice soup, or in a salad with dried prawns and red shallots. Sour mustard greens can be used as a vegetable in a sour orange curry, to accompany a curry, or in soups.

PICKLED RED SHALLOTS *horm dong*

These are a common accompaniment to relishes and curries. They can be bought at Asian shops, but are best made from scratch (see recipe on page 386).

PLA CHORN

This pink-fleshed freshwater fish abounds in Thailand and its cuisine, but is unknown outside South East Asia. I think trout makes an excellent alternative, although any fish, from perch to barramundi, or even prawns (shrimp) and lobster, can be used.

PLA GROP crisp fish

Pla grop is a favourite ingredient that has been used by the Thai for several hundred years. This small fish is preserved by smoking very slowly over charcoal and coconut husks until impregnated with smoke and quite dry. It keeps indefinitely, but should be briefly grilled before use – not for too long, however, as it burns very quickly. The fish is then skinned, boned and ground. When fried, *pla grop* tastes surprisingly like smoked bacon; it is really quite delicious.

> *Pla grop* is usually sold on a skewer or a brace, and is normally available frozen – and this is not to its detriment – in Asian food stores. The dedicated can make their own from freshwater fish (see recipe below). I think hot-smoked trout is the nearest and most convenient Western substitute, although any type of dried fish will do. Dried prawns also make a delicious alternative.

PLA GROP

3 trout *or* 1 Murray perch *or* 1 pike – approximately 300 g (9 oz)
1 cup light soy sauce
1 tablespoon white sugar
2 cups grated coconut
1 cup uncooked rice
1 cup white sugar
oil for deep-frying

Clean the fish, scaling if necessary. Marinate in soy and the tablespoon of sugar overnight. Line a wok or a heavy cast-iron pan with foil. Mix grated coconut and rice with the cup of sugar and pour onto the foil. Turn heat to high. Remove fish from marinade and place on a Chinese metal steamer inside the wok or pan. Cover and smoke the fish over medium to high heat for at least 1 hour. Allow to cool. Heat oil in a wok and deep-fry the fish at a medium heat for 20 minutes or so, until very crisp and golden – make sure it does not burn. Drain.

PLA RAA *see* FERMENTED FISH

PLA SALIT

This is a small freshwater blue gourami. Rarely eaten fresh, it is normally dried or cured. It is deliciously oily and salty but has little meat and is quite bony; it is available frozen in Asian shops. Once thawed, it is usually grilled or deep-fried to concentrate its robust flavour.

MOCK PLA SALIT

This recipe is an attempt to approximate *pla salit* at home.

1 gourami or silver perch – approximately 400 g (12 oz)
3 tablespoons salt
2 cups grated coconut
1 cup rice
½ cup white sugar

Clean the fish, trim the fins and remove the head. Rub with salt and leave overnight. Next day, wash the fish and pat dry. Line a wok or a heavy cast-iron pan with foil. Mix grated coconut and rice with sugar and pour onto the foil. Turn heat to high. Put fish in a Chinese metal steamer of a similar diameter to the wok or pan. Cover and smoke the fish over a low to medium heat for at least 1 hour. Then leave in a warm place – ideally in the sun – for several days until completely dried, turning every day. Once dried, it will last indefinitely in the refrigerator.

PLA TUU

This small frigate mackerel is the national fish of Thailand. It is usually sold slightly salted and steamed in woven bamboo baskets, but is not always available in the West. Sardines or mackerel are the closest approximations, but any freshwater fish will do.

POPPED RICE *kao dtork*

Made by pounding and dry-frying young rice until the air in the grain expands, popped rice has a mild toasty flavour. It is sometimes found in Indian providores under the name of Poona rice. Popped rice is used in ceremonial desserts and sweetmeats. Mixed with perfumed flowers, it is strewn across the path of a welcomed and honoured guest; it is also the rice that is cast across the floor when a person dies.

PORK *muu*

Pork is a Thai favourite – especially in the north of the country, where rendered pork fat (see page 171) is the traditional cooking medium.

Pork skin is also greatly enjoyed: deep-fried pork skin (page 400) is a steadfast accompaniment to most northern Thai relishes and curries, while boiled pork skin is primarily used in salads. Shredded boiled pork skin (*nang muu*) can be purchased ready-made in Asian food stores; however, it does look – and, I am afraid, taste – like rubber bands. Luckily it is quite easy to prepare (see recipe below).

SHREDDED BOILED PORK SKIN

200 g (6 oz) pork skin
2 tablespoons lime juice
½ teaspoon salt

Wash pork skin and remove excess fat. Bring a pot of water to the boil, add half of both the lime juice and the salt. Add pork skin and boil until it is tender and translucent – about 1 hour. Cool, then scrape any excess fat from the skin and very finely shred it. Steep in remaining lime juice and salt for a few minutes. Rinse and pat dry.

PRAWNS *gung*

Devein prawns either by using a small skewer to hook out the dark vein, or by slicing each prawn lengthwise along its back and scraping out the vein. Rinse well and dry.

See also dried prawns; tomalley.

RAMBUTAN *ngor*

This fruit is truly spectacular, its skin flaming red and covered with small spikes. However, I often find the taste of the lychee-like fruit inside to be disappointing.

RED SHALLOTS *horm dtaeng*

One of the most important vegetables in Thai cooking, shallots are used in curry pastes, in salads and to perfume soups. Red shallots are very similar in taste to normal brown or grey shallots, but their skins are light purple in colour. They can be found in Asian stores and some supermarkets.

See also pickled red shallots.

DEEP-FRIED SHALLOTS *horm jiaw* These are an important garnish in Thai cooking. Although they can be bought in stores, it is much better to fry your own. At first this may seem a little daunting, but after one or two attempts initial trepidation is overcome and the results are worthwhile.

You'll need to fry at least a cup of shallots at a time, in order to control their cooking; they can burn easily and all too quickly. Slice the shallots lengthwise into very thin, even slices. Heat oil in a wok until moderately hot, then turn up the heat and add shallots – be careful, the oil will bubble up. When the oil has recovered its heat, turn down slightly. Deep-fry, stirring constantly with tongs, until the shallots begin to colour. Make sure the oil remains quite hot throughout, otherwise the shallots will absorb oil and become soggy.

Remember that the shallots will continue to cook for a few moments after they have been removed from the oil, so when they have lost their onion-like aroma and begin to smell enticingly nutty, are becoming golden and starting to stick to the tongs a little, drain and spread out on absorbent paper to cool. The shallots should crisp as they begin to cool, retaining surprisingly little oil. (Pass the oil through a sieve to collect any scraps; the shallot-perfumed oil can be used for deep-frying or stir-frying.)

The shallots will keep for 2 days in an airtight container.

GRILLED OR ROASTED SHALLOTS *horm pao* Traditionally shallots are grilled over an open flame, but an easier way is to 'roast' them in a wok with a little water, unpeeled, until the water has evaporated and the skin is charred. This ensures that the shallots are completely cooked and quite smoky but without any bitter, blackened parts. Once cool they are peeled, sliced and added to the dish.

RENDERED PORK FAT *nahm man muu*

The traditional cooking medium in the north of Thailand, rendered pork fat imparts a wonderfully rich, silken quality; it is, however, wonderfully rich in cholesterol, too. Vegetable oil is more commonly used now.

For those who insist on living dangerously, pork fat can be rendered as follows. Wash and mince some pork fat. Put in a pan, cover with water and add salt. Heat over medium heat, stirring occasionally, until the fat has rendered and the water evaporated. The fat begins to colour as it crisps and fries: be careful, for if burnt it is unusable. Stir regularly over a gentle heat until the scratchings – that is, the solids remaining as the fat renders – are lightly golden brown, and smell nutty and toasty. I often perfume the almost-rendered fat with a few leaves of pandanus, a little ginger or garlic. These remove its sometimes unctuous aroma, but don't add them too early or they will burn. Strain oil into a metal bowl. Cooled and refrigerated, rendered pork fat keeps for several weeks.

Keep the scratchings separately – to be eaten as a snack, or added to relishes and salads – although they will only last for a day or two.

RICE *kao*

The favourite rice of Thai from the central plains is long-grain jasmine rice. There is no substitute for this slender, delicious grain that when cooked has an elusive scent. In Thai it is known as *kao horm mali*, which translates as 'rice fragrant jasmine'. Some believe that this is because the unique scent of the cooked rice is reminiscent of jasmine. In fact, the aroma – *horm* – of the rice is redolent of pandanus; *mali*, the jasmine reference, relates to the pearl-like sheen of the grain and has little to do with its scent.

White sticky rice is the ancient grain of Siam. It is now considered by those who live on the central plains as being primitive – the food of the poor – but is still the preferred rice of north and north-east Thailand, where the thin soils on the mountainous slopes, the sharper, shorter growing season and the erratic rainfall suit its needs better. Black sticky rice has a tinted bran, and is used only for desserts (see page 593).

See also fermented rice; flattened rice; ground roasted rice; noodles; popped rice; rice flour; rice liquor.

BOILED RICE *kao suay* Wash jasmine rice in several changes of water. (One engaging tradition has it that devout Buddhists wash rice three times while repeating the triple gems of faith, taking refuge in the Buddha, his law and the monkhood.) Comb your hands through the rice in the water to remove any husks, insects or anything untoward. With cupped hands, gently rub the grains together. Drain and repeat two or three times until the water is clear; this prevents gluggy rice. The rice-rinsing water may be used for fermenting a range of products.

Put rice in a rice cooker or a heavy pot – tall rather than wide for small amounts, yet the converse for larger amounts – and cover with cold water, traditionally about an index-finger joint above the rice. Surprisingly, this joint is almost always the same length! For the less traditional, and for doubting Thomases, the proportions of approximately 2½ cups of rice to 3½ cups of water give you plenty of rice for 4 people. Significantly, rice is not seasoned with salt – the accompanying dishes are sufficiently seasoned. Cover pot with a tightly fitting lid, bring quickly to the boil then turn heat to very low and cook for 10–15 minutes. Remove from the heat and let rice rest, covered, for 10 minutes or so; a pandanus leaf may be added to enhance the rice's perfume. The rice will remain quite warm for 30 minutes in the pot.

Do not stir rice during cooking, as this breaks down the grains, releasing starch and making it gluggy. If the rice on top is dry at the end of cooking, sprinkle with a little warm water and cover with a piece of banana leaf or greaseproof (parchment) paper. Return to a low heat for a few minutes, and the top rice should be cooked.

Most Asian cooks now use electric rice cookers, which make perfectly cooked rice simple and almost failsafe. However, take care not to overfill: one-third full is enough; any more and the rice might cook unevenly.

STEAMED RICE *kao neung*   In the past, rice was steamed in a woven bamboo basket tied with a cloth. Having no method of timing, a stick of incense was lit and placed near the sealed steamer; when the incense had burnt, the rice was cooked.

First wash jasmine rice, then cover with the proverbial index-finger-joint's depth of water in a bowl (see 'boiled rice' above for amounts). Cover the bowl and put into a steamer. It is best not to have the rice too deep, or the bottom layers might become mushy while the top layer remains undercooked and dry. Cook for 30–50 minutes, depending on the strength of the heat beneath the steamer.

Alternatively, rice can be truly steamed, in which case it is soaked in water for several hours before cooking. Drained, it is then steamed for at least 45 minutes; again, timing depends on the level of heat – or the length of the incense stick!

TRADITIONAL THAI RICE *hung kao yang rin nahm ting*   The traditional Thai method of cooking rice is in a clay pot, usually over embers. Rice cooked like this is softer than that cooked by absorption, with a greater purity of flavour. This method also avoids the problem of gauging the varying proportions of water to rice required due to the different ages, quality and varieties of the raw grain. Certainly, this method reduces the vitamin content, but if one's nutrition is dependent on discarded rice water, then one's diet is fundamentally inadequate.

Rinse jasmine rice, then cover with double its volume of water. Bring to the boil over high heat, skimming any froth from the surface. Boil, stirring regularly to prevent rice from sticking, but taking care not to break the grains. After 10 minutes, when almost cooked, completely drain. Cover pot and leave over the lowest possible heat until cooked. After about 10 minutes, turn off heat and let rice rest for a minute or so.

STEAMED WHITE STICKY RICE *kao niaw neung* Sticky rice is always soaked for several hours before cooking. (Traditionally this was the last chore of the night, before sleep.) Pile the drained and rinsed rice into a mound on a bamboo or metal steamer, then place over boiling water, cover and steam for about 20–25 minutes. Surprisingly, only a few grains fall through the holes of the steamer. For the doubtful, a banana leaf or a cloth under the rice adds security – but the rice does take longer to steam this way. Do not pile sticky rice onto a plate to cook as this will intercept the steam. To check if rice is completely cooked, lift and separate the 'cake'. If it is tender in the centre, it is cooked. Steamed sticky rice must be kept covered, if only with a cloth, to prevent it cooling, drying out and becoming tough.

WHITE STICKY RICE COOKED IN BAMBOO *kao larm* This ancient method of cooking sticky rice – grilled in bamboo segments – is perhaps one of the oldest extant methods in the Thai repertoire. Cooked in this manner, the rice developed a wonderfully smoky, redolently nutty and slightly bitter flavour. It was first steeped in water overnight. The next day it would be drained and packed into a bamboo segment. Enough coconut milk mixed with salt and sugar was then poured in to cover the rice. After being sealed with banana leaves, the rice-filled bamboo was slowly grilled over glowing embers for at least an hour.

RICE FLOUR *blaeng kao*

Rice flour is used mainly in desserts. Fresh rice flour is made by soaking rice overnight and then grinding it slowly in a heavy stone mill. Dried rice flour, however, is far more common, and is readily available in Asian providores. The freshly ground rice paste is simply dried quickly in the sun; once dried, it lasts for several weeks. Jasmine rice makes the lightest rice flour, while white sticky rice flour is the heaviest, resulting in a denser dessert. Black sticky rice flour is used mainly for the colour it dyes desserts; it is not as starchy as its white cousin.

RICE LIQUOR *lao kao*

A potent by-product of leftover sticky rice fermented with sugar and water is a lethal but loved brew, rice liquor. It is known by several other names including *nahm kao*, *sato*, *ou* and *chaang*, but these are all usually made the same way and certainly have the same results. The lingering after-effect is of cheap tequila and stale frothy beer that percolates through every pore of the body.

Rice liquor is drunk in small nips, neat, and in quick dizzying succession. It is an upcountry liquor that, while now illegal to make, is commonly drunk with abandon at festivals and parties, especially in the far north and remote north-east of the country. Moonshine from the south is milder and gentler to the soul the morning after. Legendary Mekong whisky and San Thip are the comparatively refined, commercial versions of the above rice mulch. Both are drunk avidly in Thailand, straight or mixed with ice, soda or cola. Rice liquor is rocket fuel; the unsuspecting must beware being left amid the sheer vertigo of leglessness.

See also Chinese rice wine.

ROASTED CHILLI POWDER *prik bon*

This is a ubiquitous condiment in Thai cuisine, being used to flavour soups, salad dressings and noodle dishes. To make it, roast a cup of dried bird's eye or dried long red chillies in a wok or pan over a medium heat, stirring regularly to prevent scorching, until they have changed colour and are beginning to toast. Cool, then grind to a coarse or fine powder, as preferred, using a pestle and mortar or a clean coffee grinder. It keeps well in an airtight container.

ROASTED RICE *see* **GROUND ROASTED RICE**

ROSE APPLE *champuu*

A small pear-shaped fruit, sometimes lime green or occasionally red-skinned. Frankly, most are a little bland, but they have a pleasing crisp texture and are very quenching.

ROSELLA LEAVES *bai grajiap*

These ribbed, dark and leathery leaves make a deliciously tart addition to soups and curries. They can often be found in Indian grocers. An alternative, tasty leaf, although of a very different texture, is sorrel.

The rosella plant also produces a sour, small, spiked red fruit that is puréed to make a refreshing drink or glacéd in sugar.

SAFFRON *yaa farang*

Although not a traditional Thai flavouring, saffron is sometimes used to add a depth of flavour and a golden colour to some rice dishes and desserts.

SAFFRON WATER *nahm yaa farang*   Used in Muslim cooking to add colour and flavour, saffron water is made by steeping a pinch of saffron threads in hot water until cool.

SALT *gleua*

The Thai use both mineral salt and sea salt. The north-east of the country was once covered by ocean and thus has vast salt beds; for thousands of years, salt has been mined here and traded with other regions. Along the coast, salt is harvested from the sea by evaporation: in markets in the south of Thailand, it is still possible to find small stalls selling freshly harvested salt – it is usually quite damp and darkly coloured, but delicious. Always use the best-quality salt.

SALTED DUCK EGGS *kai kem*

Originally, eggs were immersed in brine for several weeks to preserve them, and eventually their resulting, altered taste became desired. To the uninitiated, salted duck eggs taste astoundingly and unnaturally salty, but those accustomed dote upon them. Their saline pungency makes them ideal in Thai dishes, especially relishes, and as an accompaniment. They can be dressed with dried prawns, sliced red shallots and bird's eye chillies; mixed with steamed rice; or eaten with rice soup or porridge.

Salted duck eggs are readily obtainable from Asian food stores, but can also be made at home (see recipe below). Chicken – even quail – eggs can also be salted, but the salting time is decreased according to their size; the time required also varies depending on the freshness of the egg and the ambient temperature. As a guide, duck eggs normally take 3 weeks to salt, chicken eggs 2 weeks and quail eggs about 1 week.

Salting makes the egg whites viscous and the yolks surprisingly firm – they can be cut in half when raw! Generally just the egg yolks are used, and the whites (which absorb most of the salt from the brine) are discarded, though I use them in batters to produce a crisp saltiness. Salted duck eggs are usually bought raw. When ready to use, steam the eggs for 20 minutes. Cut the unshelled eggs in half with a sharp knife, then scoop out the halves with a spoon.

SALTED DUCK EGGS

This is the traditional manner of preserving eggs in Thailand – the durian husk ash gives the preserved yolk its yellow-orange colour. When sufficiently salted, they are removed from brine and kept in a dry, airy place, where they will last for 2 months.

125 g (4 oz) salt
4 cups water
1 teaspoon durian husk ash – optional
4–5 duck eggs

Bring the salt and water to the boil. Allow to cool and add durian husk ash, if using. Immerse the eggs for 3–4 weeks – any longer would impregnate the eggs with too much salt, making them inedible to all but salt diehards.

SALTED FISH *pla kem*

The Thai would normally buy this preserved fish – usually grouper or rockfish – in the market. While salted fish can be bought in Asian stores outside Thailand, it is coarsely salty and not nearly as good as the ones in the market.

Fortunately, it can easily be made at home (see recipe on next page).

SALTED FISH

This is probably the most authentic recipe for salted fish. It comes from the north of Thailand and ideally calls for meaty freshwater fish. The best-quality salt must be used. This elemental recipe relies solely upon the quality of the ingredients, which will be reflected in the result.

300 g (10 oz) fish fillet – trout, perch, carp, mackerel or bonito
30 g (1 oz) best-quality salt

Vigorously massage salt into fish, but don't destroy the flesh. Leave overnight, traditionally at room temperature, or more cautiously – but therefore for half a day longer – refrigerated. Rinse excess salt away in plenty of water. Dry fish in sun for 2 days, or in a warm place for 4 days, until quite dry.

Unrefrigerated, this keeps safely for a week; refrigerated, the fish will last for a few weeks.

SALTED WHITE RADISH *hua chay poa*

Sometimes white radish (see page 185) is used shredded and salted, and this can be purchased at Chinese food shops. I prefer whole ones, which can be cut into whatever size is preferred. Always rinse before use.

For those who must know how to make it, a recipe follows.

SALTED WHITE RADISH

3 large white radishes, peeled
coarse salt
palm sugar

Wash the radishes and work coarse salt vigorously into the flesh. Leave overnight. Next day, rinse and weigh the radishes. Measure out 20 per cent of their weight in salt and work into the radishes, then leave to dry in the sun or a warm place for 1 day. Put radishes into a cloth bag, weigh down with a large, heavy object to extract as much water as possible, and leave for 3 days.

Bring enough water to cover radishes to the boil, and dissolve the same volume of palm sugar in it. Cool, then steep radishes in this syrup for a few hours, drain and leave in the sun or a warm place, covered, for several days until dry.

SANTOL *grathorn*

This fruit has a hard, golden-yellow, rough and slightly ridged skin. Inside is the firm meaty white 'pith', which tastes slightly pear-like. Then there is an inner fleshy, sour and translucent segment that surrounds the seeds. Once the thin skin is peeled, it must be immersed in acidulated water or the flesh will oxidise and turn brown. A few deep cuts are made to help leach out some of the raw fruit's astringency. So prepared, santol is cut into slices and used in curries, soups and salads.

SAWTOOTH HERB *see* **PAK CHII FARANG**

SHALLOTS, RED *see* **RED SHALLOTS**

Dried shiitake mushrooms must always be rinsed to remove any dust and then simmered until tender (about 10 minutes) before use. In traditional Chinese cooking, a piece of pork fat is often added; sometimes I include a star anise and a pandanus leaf to augment the flavour of the mushrooms. After removing the tough, inedible stalks (which can be used to add flavour to stocks), store the mushrooms in their braising liquid, refrigerated. This prevents them dehydrating and thus they can be kept for several days; if brought to the boil every third day, they last much longer. Always add a few tablespoons of their stock to dishes, along with the mushrooms – it imparts a wonderful depth of taste. I have found that Japanese dried shiitake mushrooms are consistently good.

SHRIMP *see* **PRAWNS**

SHRIMP, DRIED *see* **DRIED PRAWNS**

SHRIMP PASTE *gapi*

Gapi is the soul of Thai food. It is made from planktonic shrimp that have been salted, fermented and then dried in the sun for up to a year. From this unpromising beginning comes an essential component that imparts 'Thai-ness' to Thai cooking.

Shrimp paste can be used either raw or slightly roasted to enhance its flavour. Traditionally, it is wrapped in banana leaves and roasted over embers for a few minutes. Instead it can be wrapped in foil and dry-fried in a heavy pan over a low flame or in an oven, or very quickly microwaved in a bowl covered with plastic for 30 seconds or so. This is not essential, but it does invigorate the paste, making it more fragrant. Take care not to overcook or it will scorch, becoming bitter and hollow.

Thai shrimp paste differs from similar pastes in surrounding countries, being less dry and more fragrant. Although good-quality shrimp paste can be easily bought – mercifully, in an airtight container – and keeps forever in the refrigerator, I've included a recipe for the culinary daredevil (see below).

SHRIMP PASTE

This *gapi* does not turn the familiar murky aubergine, but a chalky white, because the shrimp or prawns used in it are quite large in proportion to their iodine-dark eyes. In Thailand the preferred variety of shrimp is very small, so the eyes form a large percentage of their weight. This gives the paste a murky, muddy colour that ripens to a deep purple as it ferments and matures.

Any shrimp or prawns, regardless of size or quality, are satisfactory for this recipe – after all, they will be fermented for 6 months. Plenty of time and sun and a little salt are then all that is needed. It is best to make shrimp paste during the summer months.

The dark liquid that is the by-product of this process can make the most excellent fish sauce. Bring to the boil, with a piece of sugar cane or palm sugar, and then pass through several layers of muslin (cheesecloth) to trap any sediment before storing in a sterilised glass bottle. Leave for several days in the sun or a warm place before using. Use sparingly, perhaps as a sauce alone, as it is too good to waste in highly spiced dishes. It has a sweetness of taste and elegance – if that is the right word for such a revolting process – that belies its origins, and somehow epitomises the paradox that is Thai cooking.

1 kg (2 lb) shrimp or prawns
½ cup salt

Mix shrimp or prawns with salt and leave overnight in a warm place. Next day, pound or purée, then form into a coarse disc and dry in the sun or a warm place for 2 days. Purée one more time before rolling into a ball (this time wearing gloves!) and placing in an earthenware or glass jar. Push down the mass and seal the surface with plastic wrap, then close and seal lid. Leave in the sun or a warm place for no less than 2 months and for up to 6 months – the longer, the better. Remarkably, after this time, the *gapi* will smell quite rich, meaty and sweet – not at all as might be expected!

When fermentation is complete, remove from jar, drain excess liquid and dry paste in the sun or a warm place for a day or two. It will then last indefinitely in the refrigerator, but make sure it is firmly covered: its fragrance has the capacity to swamp any ingredient stored with it!

SIAMESE CASSIA FLOWERS AND LEAVES *dork lae bai kii lek*

This is not the same as the hard cassia leaf, similar to a bay leaf, that is used in curries (see page 144). Siamese cassia has soft, fleshy, khaki-green leaves. The immature flowers and buds, which are the same colour as the leaves, are sold together in Thailand. They are very bitter and thus are always blanched once or twice, or even simmered. Thus prepared, they taste almost like tea leaves.

SIAMESE WATERCRESS *pak bung*

A leafy green with hollow stems and heart-shaped leaves, Siamese watercress is called *pak bung* in Thai, *kang kong* in Malay and *ong choy* in Chinese. There are several names for it in English – morning glory is one of my favourites, but water convolvulus and water spinach are also common. It is used extensively in Thai cooking as a vegetable accompaniment to relishes, and as an ingredient in soups, curries and stir-fries.

See also fermented Siamese watercress.

SMOKED FISH *pla lom kwan*

Strictly speaking, there is no such thing as smoked fish in Thai cuisine. The following recipes are an approximation of a Thai method of preservation whereby fish are grilled slowly over embers for several hours. As the oils from the fish drip down onto the coals, the fish is effectively hot-smoked. Without an open fire, the best way to replicate this is by lightly smoking the fish in a Chinese steamer.

See also pla grop; pla salit.

SMOKED FISH

1 Murray perch, catfish, perch or pike – about 500 g (1 lb)
2 cups grated coconut
1 cup jasmine rice
½ cup palm sugar

Clean the fish and diagonally score the flesh, cutting right to the bone, to enable the smoke to penetrate. Line a heavy wok with foil. Mix the coconut, rice and sugar together and place on the foil. Put the fish, with its 'wings' spread, on a Chinese metal steamer or wok rack.

Place wok over a high heat and, when it begins to smoke, fit with the steamer or rack, cover with the lid and turn down the heat to low to medium. Smoke for at least an hour, until golden-coloured. If it stops smoking, turn up the heat again.

DRIED SMOKED TROUT FILLET

Slightly drying the fish concentrates its flavours and hydrolyses its oils, so that when it is smoked it turns a most appetising golden hue.

2 river trout
1 cup desiccated coconut

Wash and fillet the trout. Remove any remaining bones with a pair of tweezers. Dry in the sun or a warm place for 3 hours.

Line an old wok or pot with foil. Turn on the heat and pour in the desiccated coconut. When it begins to smoulder, cover with a rack or Chinese steamer lined with a banana leaf. Place the fish on rack or in steamer, turn off the heat, cover wok and let it smoke gently for an hour or so. Should the coconut go out, simply turn on the heat until it begins to smoke again. Smoke for around 2 hours until the fish is coloured.

Remove from the steamer and dry once more in the sun – or a warm, airy place – for several hours until crisp and dry.

SNAKE BEANS *tua fak yao*

Also known as yard-long beans, these sinuous beans are much used in stir-fries and as a garnish for spicy *nahm prik* relishes and *larp* salads. They are best eaten young and very fresh.

SNAKE GOURD *see under* **GREEN GOURDS**

SOUR SNAKESKIN PEAR *rakam*

This oval fruit has a large central seed. Beneath its strawberry-coloured, snake-like skin lies very sour, white flesh. It is quite uncommon, but either unripe pineapple or green papaya can be used as an alternative.

SOY SAUCE *nahm siu uu*

Thai cooks generally prefer to use a lighter-style soy.

Sweet Indonesian soy sauce (*kecap manis*) is occasionally used in Chinese-style braises; I also use it to briefly marinate ingredients before deep-frying to give them a wonderful golden colour and a caramelised flavour.

SPRING (GREEN) ONIONS *dtom horm*

This is a problematic vegetable, for it is known by many names: spring or green onions, scallions or Chinese shallots. Whatever its name, it is the long green stalks with white bases that all Asian shops – and most supermarkets – sell.

STOCK *nahm cheua*

The best stock to use in Thai cooking is the simplest and lightest. With so many other flavours and ingredients normally added, a stock that is too fully flavoured might introduce unwelcome elements – confusing or disrupting the balance in the finished dish. Some Thai cookbooks, old and new, suggest water as an easy alternative to stock.

To my taste, chicken makes the lightest, cleanest stock while pork makes a rich and weighty stock. The latter, having a more decided flavour than chicken stock, is less versatile. I often add a pork bone to chicken stock, to give it extra body but not too unctuous a taste. Fish stock is rarely made in the Thai kitchen. If required, I think the best stock is made from fish or bones that are simmered in water with some ginger, salt and a little Asian celery. Although not a Thai precaution, I also think it best to simmer these only for 20 minutes or so, otherwise the stock becomes slightly bitter and takes on a stewed taste.

Basic stock recipes are given on page 225.

SUGAR

Sugar cane is native to south Asia, probably around the Bay of Bengal, and has been growing wild farther east for at least a thousand years. At first sugar cane was simply peeled, pounded and boiled to extract its sweetness. It was also peeled and whittled into a skewer for grilling, thereby perfuming and impregnating the food with a subtle sweetness.

SUGAR CANE *ooy* Even today, sugar cane is enjoyed in its unprocessed state. In every market in Thailand, there is a stall that sells sugar cane juice – a welcome, thirst-quenching nectar in enervating tropical heat. The cane is cleaned and fed into a mangle to extract the juice, which is sweet and just slightly, greenly bitter. The fibrous pulp that remains is used to feed animals.

Traditionally, farmers would chew a peeled piece of cane after eating. The sweetness satisfied after a pungent meal and freshened the breath, while the fibre cleaned the teeth.

PALM SUGAR *nahm dtarn bip* This sugar has a rich flavour and a creamy sweetness that is not too cloying. Palm sugar is concentrated from the sap of the palmyra and sugar palm trees. Young agile boys climb up the trunks and beat the trees over a few days to stimulate the flow of sap. Incisions are then made into the trunk and a bamboo pipe is inserted to channel the flow; the tree is bled overnight. The sap is boiled to evaporate the water and sold as a thick syrup, or poured into a coconut husk and further dried in the sun.

The amount of reduction and concentration may vary, but beyond the control of the villagers are the seasons. During the rainy season, a palm becomes flushed with water so the sap obtained is dilute. During the dry, the opposite occurs. Thus the appearance and flavour of palm sugar may change between batches – production is still a cottage industry. Sometimes a little raw sap is left to ferment for several hours to make toddy, an intensely intoxicating drink. But its joys are transient – within a day, fermentation renders toddy sour and undrinkable. And if too much is drunk, then the next day is unthinkable. The dried sugar, however, keeps well.

Once concentrated and dried, the divergent characteristics of the sugars from the different palms are evident. Sugar from the palmyra palm is dense and nutty, while that from the sugar palm has a richness that greatly enhances any food it seasons.

Palm sugar can be bought at some supermarkets as well as Asian food shops. Often it is as hard as rock and difficult to use: either pound in a mortar until soft, then store in an airtight container, or microwave for 30 seconds. Before microwaving, ensure that any wax seal has been removed – and be careful, microwaved palm sugar is molten. Stir in a little water once the sugar is hot and it will remain soft when it cools.

COCONUT SUGAR *nahm dtam maprao*   To make this sugar, the coconut tree is 'bled' of its sap; this depletes its nutrients and, as a consequence, the coconuts themselves are of inferior quality, or sometimes do not form at all.

Coconut sugar is much lighter in flavour than palm sugar, and is generally used in desserts. Most coconut sugar is dark brown or black; sometimes it is available bleached white, but this type has little flavour.

WHITE SUGAR *nahm dtam sai*   White sugar is the watery sap of sugar cane boiled down to a thick syrup, bleached with lime, skimmed and then crystallised. The more refined the sugar is, the whiter it is – and the less character it has.

When white sugar is called for in dressings and sauces, it is best to use castor (superfine) sugar as it dissolves quickly and thoroughly.

YELLOW ROCK SUGAR *nahm dtam gluat*   This Chinese version of sugar is believed to be a tonic, and is good for relieving coughs and sore throats. In cooking, it is used in braised or steamed dishes of Chinese origin. While it does not taste different from white sugar, it imparts a glossy sheen to the sauce of a finished dish.

Fresh tamarind is an uncommon delight. The brown-skinned, slightly green-fleshed fruit is puckeringly sour and available for 3–5 months a year. The fresh pods should be firm yet supple, not brittle to the touch, and must be peeled and deseeded before use. Pare off the skin with a small, sharp knife, then cut the pod in half lengthwise, prise out the seeds and cut out the lining that encased the seed. If preparing in advance, steep the tamarind flesh in salted water to prevent discolouration. Tamarind flesh is used in relishes and soups – and can even be eaten raw, as the Thai do, with some salt mixed with sugar, ground dried prawns and roasted chilli powder.

For several months in the year, a sweet variety of tamarind (*makaam warn*) is also available. It is usually sold in its skin, which sometimes may have begun to crumble. The flesh looks like regular tamarind pulp but it is surprisingly sweet, and yet sour. It is eaten as if it were a sweet treat.

TAMARIND LEAVES *bai makaam* The very tender, purplish white shoots and leaves of tamarind are used in soups, relishes and curries. They taste remarkably like sorrel, which can be used as a substitute.

TAMARIND PULP *makaam bliak* By far the most common version of tamarind is in pulp form, when the flesh has ripened and been dried in the sun, which results in a chocolate-brown pulp. The best quality has few seeds.

TAMARIND WATER *nahm makaam bliak* This is one of the major souring agents in Thai cooking. While it can be purchased ready-made, this has little of the tart plumminess of freshly made tamarind water and, to my taste, is too salty and not very sour. Tamarind water can be made a few days in advance, as long as it is kept in the refrigerator. After this time it may begin to ferment. The Thai often boil tamarind water to prolong its life, but I find this alters its date-like sweetness.

To make tamarind water, break off an amount of the pulp, rinse to remove any surface yeasts, then cover in a similar amount of warm water and leave for a few minutes to soften. Squeeze and work the pulp to dissolve it, then strain the liquid to remove any fibres or seeds. It is best to make it quite thick, as this can always be diluted later, but very thin tamarind water added to a curry, soup or relish may over-dilute it.

TAPIOCA *saku*

Tapioca is used as a thickener in quite a few Thai dishes, as well as in desserts. Buy the best quality as some unscrupulous manufacturers adulterate the pearls with cheaper starches. Do not clean tapioca by rinsing in water, as the pearls will clump together forming a gluggy, irretrievable mass. Toss in a sieve and then blow away the dust.

TAPIOCA FLOUR *blaeng man*

Extracted from the cassava root, tapioca flour gives a malleable, silken and dense texture to pastries. It is rarely used alone, but rather to lend elasticity to rice flour pastry. Tapioca flour is also used to thicken some soups and stir-fries, and a small amount may be added to dumplings to give them a more toothsome texture.

TARO *peuak*

This rough, brown-skinned, starchy root vegetable is of ancient provenance – and was probably farmed even before rice was cultivated. It is now mainly used in desserts, where its slight bitterness imparts a desirable complexity.

TOMALLEY *man gung*

This is the coral or mustard squeezed from the heads of prawns, or the roe of crabs, lobster, etc. Tomalley should only be used if it is absolutely fresh. Only tomalley from fresh shellfish (never that from thawed frozen seafood) should be used, and it should be cooked as soon as possible or it becomes dark and quite bitter.

TOMALLEY PASTE

Raw tomalley is, quite frankly, disgusting, tasting rankly of iodine, but when cooked it is transformed into the essence of seafood and is rich and sweet in flavour. Tomalley paste (*man gung brung*) can be made in advance – refrigerated, it lasts for a week or so.

tomalley from 6 large uncooked king prawns (jumbo shrimp), crab, yabbies or freshwater
    crayfish – about 3 tablespoons
1 garlic clove, peeled
1 coriander root, scraped
pinch of white pepper
pinch of salt
1 tablespoon oil or rendered pork fat
2 tablespoons white sugar
1 tablespoon fish sauce

Pound garlic with coriander root, white pepper and salt. Heat oil in a pan, fry garlic paste until golden and add tomalley. Simmer until tomalley has changed colour and lost its raw, eggy smell. Season with sugar and fish sauce, and continue to simmer for another minute or so.

TURMERIC *kamin*

This rhizome, related to ginger, grows throughout South East Asia. A huge variety of turmeric is available in Thailand, ranging in colour from the familiar deep, bloody orange to an unsettling blue. In the north, old women collect these roots for a multitude of reasons – culinary, medicinal and even for casting the odd spell. Turmeric has a role in many Brahmin and Buddhist ceremonies throughout Asia; in Thailand, it is used to ritually cleanse novices and prepare them for their ordination as monks.

For cooking purposes, however, only a few varieties are used. Fresh and powdered turmeric have quite different tastes; they are not interchangeable. When dried turmeric powder is called for, be cautious – all too often it is adulterated with tapioca or rice flour, and tastes bitter and musty. Either dry and grind your own (peel, slice and dry in the sun, then store in airtight containers and grind when required), or use half the specified amount of ready-prepared turmeric powder.

RED TURMERIC *kamin leuang* Fresh red turmeric is used in curry pastes, especially those from the south of Thailand. Mainly included for its colour, red turmeric has a strong, almost medicinal smell and should be added to recipes with discretion. Prepare it carefully, for it stains everything; wash knife and chopping board in hot soapy water immediately after use.

SUGARCANE TURMERIC OR ZEDOARY *kamin ooy, kamin chan* This looks similar to red turmeric but its flesh is the colour of light brown sugar. It is usually shredded and added as a final flourish to a green or jungle curry or stir-fry made with a strongly flavoured ingredient, like eel or frog. Medieval Europeans believed that this root could cure the plague.

WHITE TURMERIC *kamin kao* This turmeric is uncommon outside Thailand. It is a variety that is young, crisp and full-flavoured, with white juicy flesh and a thin skin. It is especially delicious peeled and sliced to accompany a *nahm prik* or *lon* relish.

VINEGAR *nahm som*

The Thai use a white vinegar based on fermented coconut water. Good varieties can be purchased at Asian food stores, or you can make your own (see below). Regular white vinegar makes a very acceptable alternative if slightly diluted with water.

In dishes of Chinese origin, Chinese black vinegar, sometimes called Chin Kiang, may be required. It is made from wheat and malt and tastes remarkably like balsamic vinegar.

COCONUT VINEGAR
This is a recipe for traditional Thai coconut vinegar (*nahm som mapraow*). The yeast used is an Asian dried yeast usually sold in Chinese food stores: it differs from Western yeast in that it is flavoured with a little dried galangal. Some galangal can be mixed with brewer's yeast to achieve a similar effect.

3 cups coconut water
½ cup white sugar
1 rounded teaspoon yeast

Bring coconut water and sugar to the boil. When dissolved, strain through muslin and cool. Add the yeast and pour into a sterilised jar, leaving some space at the top to allow the vinegar to ferment and froth. Leave for at least 15 days, until it stops frothing. Skim and then strain. Leave for a few more days to mature before use.

WATER MIMOSA *pak grachet*

An aquatic, fern-like plant. The only edible part, the fronds, is slightly sour and crunchy. It has a high iron content, which gives it a distinctive taste, and is used in stir-fries and especially in sour orange curries.

WATERMELON *dtaeng mor*

This is one of the more cooling, quenching fruits in Thailand's climate. It is eaten by itself; with the traditional but bizarre combination of ground fish, deep-fried shallots, sugar and salt; or dressed in a spicy salad with smoked fish.

Thai watermelon is usually much smaller than its Western equivalent, with sweeter, hot-pink flesh. Nothing is wasted: its seeds are used for desserts and snacks, and its woody pith is glacéd to make a sweetmeat or added to sour orange curries.

WHITE RADISH *hua pak gart kao*

This long, white and fleshy root is used throughout Asia. It is often known by its Japanese name, *daikon*, or its Indian name, *mooli*.

See also salted white radish.

WING BEANS *tua pluu*

These are succulent beans with four ruffles running along their sides. They are used in salads and stir-fries, and either blanched or raw with *nahm prik* relishes. The best beans are small, about the length of a finger – any longer and they begin to become tough. And the fresher they are, the better, since within a day or two the ruffles turn an unsightly black.

YARD-LONG BEANS *see* **SNAKE BEANS**

YELLOW BEAN SAUCE *dtow jiaw*

This is a sauce based on yellow soy beans, which are salted and then fermented with a rice mould. It sounds disgusting but tastes delicious, very much like Japanese *miso*. Yellow bean sauce is used in sauces and soups, and normally indicates a dish with Chinese influences.

There are two types: the first, and more traditional, is creamy white; the more common one is honey-brown. There are various grades, too, ranging from whole beans through broken beans to a paste. The best contains unbroken beans which have been fermented in brine, with a little roasted rice. Although not absolutely necessary, rinsing the beans results in a much purer flavour.

7

RELISHES

Relishes – *nahm prik* and *lon* – are the very core of Thai cooking and have fed the Thai from their distant past to the present. These pastes, called *kreuang jim* in Thai, are produced from pungent ingredients using simple techniques. They are served in small bowls and eaten with vegetables and strongly flavoured accompaniments. The consequent balance of tastes and contrasting textures is honed by the seasoning and makes relishes, I believe, the epitome of Thai cooking.

Most *nahm prik* are redolent of shrimp paste and chillies. Traditionally they were eaten with copious amounts of rice, so that their extremes of heat and flavour were diffused and hunger could be satisfied. In essence little has changed – this is still how a Thai meal is eaten today. *Lon* were introduced much later to the repertoire, only after the Thai had become established on the central plains. *Lon* incorporate intensely flavoured, normally preserved ingredients whose effects are mitigated by being simmered in rich coconut cream.

A relish and its accompanying dishes are a compilation of tastes and textures that may begin quite simply, with just the relish and a few raw vegetables, but incrementally becomes more complex with the addition of more ingredients to the relish and more elaborate side dishes. The Thai manner of developing tastes is not to make a dish so subtle that it becomes bland or diffuse, but to expand its flavours. Great pride is taken in refining the taste of a relish, or devising new and interesting accompaniments to it that reflect the talent, knowledge and skill of the cook.

NAHM PRIK

A *nahm prik* is perhaps the most ancient style of Thai dish: ingredients are combined using the primitive crucible of this cuisine – the pestle and mortar – to create a textured purée. The original seasoning of a *nahm prik* was rudimentary: a sharp, dry heat from peppercorns, and a rich and salty flavour from fermented soy beans, possibly rounded by a few smokily charred shallots. The taste might then be augmented by a souring agent – some leaves pounded into the paste, later perhaps lime juice, fresh tamarind or its dried pulp, even a sour fruit like green mango, star fruit or the tart *madan* (sour cucumber).

As the Thai progressed southward so their cuisine expanded, absorbing the produce of the newly encountered regions: coconuts, palm sugar and fermented fish and shrimp paste. Their food became enriched by its new environment, embodied with fuller and more rounded flavours as it incorporated these ingredients. Fermented soy beans (*tua nao*) accompanied the Thai from their original homeland in the dry mountainous plateaux of Yunnan, and this paste is still the basis of some northern Thai and Laotian relishes today. Descending from those high plateaux, the Thai crossed the mountains, gorges and rivers of Laos. Here they first met fermented fish (*pla raa*), a breathtaking speciality of the northern Mon and Khmers, made by preserving the seasonal abundance of freshwater fish by salting and fermenting them with rice over several months. This intense pickle soon super-seded fermented soy beans in relishes, becoming the fundamental seasoning of the Thai kitchen. *Pla raa* is still widely used northwards from the upper central plains and in the north-east of Thailand, where its pungency is savoured.

Gapi, the now-beloved Thai shrimp paste, was probably first encountered around the fourteenth century. The indigenous Mon, on the southern reaches of the Chao Phraya delta, may have been first to use this ancient paste, due to their extensive trading connections with the sea. In the south, along the seaboard, prawns of various sizes were caught. Some were eaten fresh. Most, however, needed to be preserved – salted, dried or fermented into a dark paste. As the Thai settled around the lower reaches of the Chao Phraya River, shrimp paste usurped its ancient predecessors in their cuisine.

The simplest *nahm prik* are uncooked. Development occurs as new ingredients are introduced, either as a new season begins or, historically, as the Siamese absorbed new regions. In more complex *nahm prik* recipes, the paste is cooked in some way – boiled, grilled or fried – then seasoned.

NAHM PRIK INGREDIENTS

The quintessential ingredient in most *nahm prik* is shrimp paste (*gapi*), which imparts a deep, fecund sweetness that encompasses the ingredients with which it is used. Too much and the relish will be murky; too little and the relish will be disjointed, the tastes jostling.

Garlic opens up the relish, giving it a rich and sweet flavour and body. The salt in the relish is not only used as a seasoning but also as an abrasive: it helps to break down the garlic, which in turn prevents the shrimp paste from making the paste too heavy and oily. Salt also 'sweetens' the garlic and removes its pungency. Once the garlic and shrimp paste have been pounded with the salt, chillies are added to the mortar. Using more chillies increases the heat of this relish, naturally enough, but pounding the chillies to a pulp also makes the relish hotter. For a less fierce relish, add the chillies at the end and pound only until they have broken. They will thus flavour the relish without making it too ferocious. Beware, however, the little pods of pleasure that will be lurking whole and menacingly in the relish.

Bird's eye chillies (scuds) are used in some fiery relishes. Frankly, it is too difficult to remove their seeds – and, as these chillies are generally used when an incendiary heat is required, it is also a pointless exercise. Fresh long chillies are very occasionally used and can be surprisingly hot. Either red or green can be used; green are often preferred for their extra pungency and sharpness. I prefer to deseed them, but the reckless may not. If grilled chillies are called for, it is vital that the skin is removed, but the seeds can be included in the relish.

When dried long red chillies are used in a *nahm prik*, they should be deseeded and soaked in cold salted water for 10–15 minutes (or in warm salted water for 3–4 minutes), then drained and squeezed dry. Sometimes, dried long red chillies are grilled after soaking.

The *nahm prik* is finished by seasoning with lime juice, a little palm sugar and, if necessary, some fish sauce. It should taste hot, salty, slightly sour and slightly sweet. The structure of the tastes should be seamlessly poised. The garlic prevents the shrimp paste swamping the dish; the chillies sharpen the taste and hone the palate; the shrimp paste, the principal ingredient, enriches with its redolence and prevents the disparate tastes pulling away from each other. The seasoning then tightens the various tastes: the fish sauce lengthens and concentrates the flavour, the sugar rounds and smooths any abrupt tastes, while the lime juice finally cleans and reveals the finished product.

NAHM PRIK ACCOMPANIMENTS

Nahm prik are never eaten alone, but are always accompanied by *kreaung kiam* (side dishes), ranging from a simple plate of raw vegetables to an omelette or deep-fried pork; recipes for these are given in the 'Side dishes and accompaniments' chapter, starting on page 379.

There are three types of *nahm prik*: one is meant to be eaten with raw vegetables; another with cooked – that is, boiled, grilled or deep-fried – vegetables; and the last with pickled vegetables. The type of vegetables that are served as an accompaniment will also affect the seasoning and consistency of the *nahm prik*.

A relish to be eaten with raw vegetables should be hot and salty, rounded by a little sweetness and sharpened by lime juice.

If the *nahm prik* is served with boiled vegetables, it should maintain the seasoning balance as for raw vegetables, but be diluted with a tablespoon of water – perhaps the water or coconut milk in which the vegetables were boiled. These vegetables have a different flavour from, and less texture than, raw vegetables; consequently, diluting the relish restores its balance with its accompaniment by preventing the relish from tasting too cloying and thick.

Grilled vegetable accompaniments add complexity. A relish to be served with them should include a teaspoon of ground *pla grop* (crisp fish) or smoked fish, and be seasoned with sour fruit, such as green mango, fuzzy eggplants or cape gooseberries, sour snakeskin pears or a little kaffir lime juice.

If a *nahm prik* has as its accompaniment deep-fried vegetables, the relish should be in equal parts hot, salty, sweet and sour, to counterbalance the batter or oil. Reduce the salt or fish sauce and increase the sugar to achieve this.

Finally, if a *nahm prik* is to be eaten with pickled vegetables, it should be quite thick, hot and salty, and only slightly sour with little sweetness, as the pickling liquid already contains these flavours. Reduce the lime juice and palm sugar accordingly.

SHRIMP PASTE RELISH

nahm prik gapi

This is perhaps the most fundamental relish in the Thai repertoire and is the basis upon which many other *nahm prik* are built. As shrimp paste became the preferred base for Thai relishes, garlic became a more successful and delicious partner than the sharper, more austere taste of the red shallots used in older recipes. An even more sensational addition was the chilli. A chilli's heat hits the centre of the palate, rather than rasping at the back of the throat as pepper does.

The basic shrimp paste relish recipe is very often adapted and improved by adding other ingredients, determined by the skill and whim of the cook. Sometimes, if the shrimp paste is too strong, a little scraped coriander root is added as a counterbalance. I like to include one or two charred and peeled red shallots, which add redolence. And dried prawns may be used to extend it, giving body and texture and rounding out the richness of the shrimp paste. In any case, the seasoning should always be tasted and altered in order to maintain the balance.

    4 garlic cloves, peeled
    pinch of salt
    1 tablespoon shrimp paste (*gapi*), raw or roasted
    3–7 bird's eye chillies (scuds)
    1 teaspoon–1 tablespoon palm sugar
    1–1½ tablespoons lime juice
    a little fish sauce – optional

Using a pestle and mortar, pound garlic with salt and shrimp paste into a fine paste. Add chillies, pounding until fine or merely bruising, depending on level of heat desired – the more the chillies are pounded, the hotter the relish will be. Season with palm sugar and lime juice and then finish with fish sauce, if required. The relish should taste rich, salty, hot and sour.

Eat with:

— Raw Vegetables (page 380), such as apple eggplants and cabbage
— Steamed Eggs (page 388) or boiled eggs
— Omelette (page 390), either plain or with thinly sliced long eggplants
— deep-fried fish – *pla tuu* (a small Thai mackerel), sardines or mackerel.

OLD-FASHIONED TAMARIND RELISH

nahm prik makam boran

A variation of uncooked *nahm prik* is one made with dried red chillies. It is not too common, but it is delicious. It is thicker than a normal *nahm prik* and the flavour is intense. Interestingly, this relish is not seasoned with fish sauce but with salt alone. This, the use of dried chillies and the overall simplicity of the recipe suggest to me that it is very old.

The original recipe, by Thanpuuying Pliang Pasonagorn, called for equal amounts by volume of all the ingredients except salt and sugar; this makes a very salty, pungent relish. I think the tamarind pulp she used must have been more intense than the pulp that is now normally available. Importantly, only the pulp is included in this recipe – no water is added.

10 dried long red chillies
1½ cups tamarind pulp
1 teaspoon salt
3 tablespoons minced garlic
3 tablespoons ground dried prawns (shrimp) – ideally freshly made (see page 151)
1–2 tablespoons palm sugar

Deseed and soak chillies in warm salted water for 3–4 minutes. Drain and squeeze dry. Rinse tamarind pulp, flatten with a pestle and remove seeds and fibre to obtain 1 cup of useable pulp. Using a pestle and mortar, pound the chillies with salt. When puréed, add garlic and, when that is puréed, the dried prawns. Mix in palm sugar and then strenuously work in the tamarind pulp, ensuring it is well incorporated. This relish should taste equally hot, salty and sour.

Serve with some of the following:
- raw young ginger and white turmeric, peeled and sliced
- slices of bitter melon, salted, rinsed and blanched
- pickled ginger
- pickled red shallots
- Steamed Salted Duck Eggs (page 391)
- Crispy Fish Cakes (page 393)
- Deep-fried Trout Dumplings (page 395)
- Salted Pork with Coconut Milk (page 397)
- Sweet Pork (page 397)
- Pork Cooked in Two Styles (page 399).

CRAB ROE RELISH

nahm prik kai bpuu

Circumstances and ceremony have also played a part in the evolution of Thai food. A son of King Rama V, Prince Paribatra, a naval minister at the beginning of the twentieth century, visited the seaside province of Samut Songkarn, where he was entertained by the mayor with a *nahm prik* made from a rare delicacy, crab roe. Here is the recipe from the wife of the host, Nang Ratchayaadtiraksaa.

The roe is only found in the female crab – there are stalls in large Thai markets that specialise in sexing this beast. The roe runs down the centre of the crab and the inside of its shell. Roe deteriorates quickly when raw and is very pungent; I recommend cooking it promptly, as for tomalley (see page 183). Alternatively the cooked, solid tomalley – the innards of every crab – can be scraped out and used in this relish. The cooked crabmeat can be added to the relish or dressed with some coconut cream to make a very apposite accompaniment.

    1 small female crab, weighing around 300 g (9 oz)
        or 3 tablespoons crab roe or 100 g (3 oz) crabmeat
    3 garlic cloves, peeled
    large pinch of salt
    1 teaspoon shrimp paste (*gapi*), raw or roasted
    3–8 bird's eye chillies (scuds)
    pinch of palm sugar
    1 tablespoon lime juice
    1 tablespoon fish sauce
    1 small green mango, shredded

If using a whole crab, steam or boil for 10–12 minutes. Cool, remove the meat and scrape out the roe. Pound garlic with salt and shrimp paste. Add crab roe or crabmeat and then the chillies, bruising them only. Season with palm sugar, lime juice and fish sauce. Mix in the mango. The relish should taste hot, salty and sour.

Serve with a selection of the following:
— Raw Vegetables (page 380), such as cucumber, banana blossoms, white turmeric and young ginger
— sprigs of Thai basil and coriander
— *pla grop* (crisp fish), grilled or deep-fried
— Freshly Salted Beef (page 402).

SHRIMP PASTE RELISH WITH DRIED PRAWNS
nahm prik gung haeng

This recipe for a more elaborate shrimp paste relish comes from a renowned cook of the 1940s, Mom Chao Jongjittanorm Disakul, who was the daughter of the influential brother of King Rama V, Prince Damrong, the Interior Minister for two crucial decades leading up to the First World War. She remembered presenting this *nahm prik* as a young girl to her elderly uncle.

The original recipe called for a teaspoon of salt. I find this makes it extremely salty; a large pinch of salt is usually sufficient. Perhaps the shrimp paste she used was of a better, sweeter quality than the modern, commercially produced ones.

The pea eggplants impart a delicious bitterness to the relish. Occasionally these eggplants are grilled before being added, altering their taste and making them wonderfully nutty. Simply wrap them in banana leaves – or foil – and grill until they are tender. This recipe also calls for Asian citron (*som sa*). The zest has a delicious fragrance and the juice is quite sour. Mandarin juice, especially if the fruit is not too ripe, is an excellent alternative.

1 tablespoon dried prawns (shrimp)

pinch of salt

3 garlic cloves, peeled

2 teaspoons shrimp paste (*gapi*), roasted

4–10 bird's eye chillies (scuds), fewer if also using orange chillies

a few orange chillies – optional

1 tablespoon palm sugar

1½ tablespoons lime juice

squeeze of Asian citron or mandarin juice – optional

a little fish sauce

2 tablespoons pea eggplants

3 scraped sour fuzzy eggplants or cape gooseberries, finely sliced – optional

2 tablespoons julienned green mango

a little very finely sliced Asian citron or mandarin flesh

a little julienne of Asian citron or mandarin zest – optional

Using a pestle and mortar, pound dried prawns and salt into a paste. Add garlic and continue to pound until fine. Add shrimp paste and, when incorporated, add chillies. Season with sugar and lime juice, and the citron or mandarin juice, if using. *Carefully* add a little fish sauce to taste – do not add too much as there is already a lot of salt present. Finally, mix in eggplants or cape gooseberries (if using), green mango, and Asian citron or mandarin flesh and zest, if using.

This *nahm prik* should be quite thick, hot and salty, sour and sweet.

It can be served with:
— Raw Vegetables (page 380), such as apple eggplants, asparagus, cucumber, Siamese watercress, young wing beans or green beans, young ginger, white turmeric, rocket (arugula), iceberg lettuce, witlof (Belgian endive)
— Boiled Vegetables (page 381), such as cabbage, pumpkin, baby corn, bitter melon, okra.

This relish can also be served with Deep-fried Vegetables (page 383), but, if so, Mom Chao Jongjittanorm cautions against adding the eggplants to the relish; or Pickled Vegetables (page 383), adjusting the seasoning accordingly. Another good accompaniment is Pork Cooked in Two Styles (page 399).

SHRIMP PASTE RELISH WITH DRIED PRAWNS

SALTED DUCK EGG RELISH

nahm prik kai kem

After sampling Crab Roe Relish (page 192) during a seaside sojourn, back in Bangkok Prince Paribatra bade his palace chef re-create the unusually delicious dish. Although the capital is not too far from the sea, it did take some time to travel between them in the early 1900s, so fresh crabs with roe were uncommon. The prince's chef improvised by using the yolks of salted duck eggs instead of the roe and tomalley to make a relish that, while not as rare, proved almost as satisfactory. Even today, the supply of crab roe is limited, so salted duck egg yolks are used as an alternative or to supplement this delicacy. Traditionally, just the rich yolks are used in a salted duck egg relish, pounded with grilled long red chillies and shallots to replicate the appearance of the dark crab roe.

Only occasionally do some Chinese shops sell just the salted egg yolks. Consequently, this version uses the salt-laden egg whites as well: use some or all, as preferred, and be careful when adding fish sauce in the final seasoning – if the relish is too salty, increase the palm sugar and lime juice to counterbalance this.

2 salted duck eggs
handful of pea eggplants
3 garlic cloves, peeled
pinch of salt
1 coriander root, scraped – optional
1 teaspoon shrimp paste (*gapi*), roasted
1 tablespoon ground dried prawns (shrimp)
4–8 bird's eye chillies (scuds)
a little stock or water, to moisten – as necessary
1 tablespoon palm sugar
1 tablespoon thick tamarind water
2 teaspoons fish sauce
1 small green mango, shredded
1 tablespoon lime juice

Steam or boil the eggs for 15 minutes. Cool. Cut in half lengthwise, spoon the egg from the shell and coarsely chop.

Wrap pea eggplants in foil or banana leaves and grill, dry-fry in a heavy pan or roast in the oven until tender, turning regularly to prevent scorching.

Pound garlic with salt and coriander root, if using, into a fine paste. Add shrimp paste and dried prawns. Continue to pound until puréed, then add chillies, and bruise or purée depending on the level of heat desired. Mix in the chopped eggs. Moisten with stock or water, if required. Season with palm sugar and tamarind

water, then carefully add fish sauce – remembering that the eggs are quite salty. Stir in the pea eggplants and green mango. Finish with the lime juice. The relish should taste rich and salty, hot and sour – adjust accordingly.

Serve with some of the following:
- Raw Vegetables (page 380), such as cucumber, fennel, white turmeric, pomelo and rose apple
- Pickled Vegetables (page 383), especially ginger
- sprigs of coriander
- grilled, steamed or deep-fried fish
- Crispy Fish Cakes (page 393)
- Sweet Pork (page 397).

CHILLI AND FERMENTED FISH RELISH
jaew bong

This primitive paste echoes the taste of early Thai food. Interestingly, such remnants from the culinary past are found in the northern half of Thailand along the path taken by the Thai on their movement south. This recipe includes *pla raa*, the fermented fish condiment that is normally sold in open buckets in the market places, where its fragrance permeates the air; outside Thailand it is available in jars.

1 piece fermented fish (*pla raa*) – roughly 4 tablespoons of flesh
4 red shallots, grilled and then peeled
3 garlic cloves, peeled
2 cm (1 in) piece galangal, peeled
pinch of salt
10 bird's eye chillies (scuds), sliced

Wrap fermented fish in a banana leaf or foil and heat through in a heavy pan; cook for a few minutes on each side.

Unwrap fish and chop it. Finely slice shallots, garlic and galangal, then chop together with the fish. Sprinkle with salt. Add sliced chillies.

Eat with:
- Raw Vegetables (page 380), such as cucumber and iceberg lettuce
- Boiled Vegetables (page 381), such as cabbage and green beans.

CHIANG MAI CHILLI RELISH
nahm prik num

The specific chilli used in this relish is uncommon outside northern Thailand. It looks like a thin, lime-green banana chilli, but tastes more like a cross between a capsicum or bell pepper and a fresh long chilli. Hence the combination in the following recipe.

This relish comes from a restaurant in Chiang Mai, Heun Khun Pen, run by a remarkable woman called Wipah Burupat. Her nickname is Pen, meaning 'moon'. I called her Aunty Moon – most people do. The way she ran her restaurant was truly admirable: everything was cooked to order. A rare thing, I have found, in many restaurants. Ingredients were peeled, scraped, poached and sometimes even killed to order. Khun Pen ruled her roost with a firm hand, ensuring the quality of the food, and all was done according to her exacting standards. This recipe is drawn from my notes of the time I spent in her kitchen.

5 red shallots, unpeeled

4 garlic cloves, unpeeled

4 large Chiang Mai chillies *or* 2 banana chillies and 2 long chillies

1 tablespoon fermented fish (*pla raa*) or shrimp paste (*gapi*)

pinch of salt

pinch of sugar

1 tablespoon chopped spring (green) onion

1 tablespoon coriander leaves

Grill or roast shallots, garlic and chillies until charred, then cool and peel. Wrap fermented fish or shrimp paste in a banana leaf or foil and heat through in a heavy pan; cook for a few minutes on each side, then unwrap and chop.

Pound shallots, garlic and chillies with salt using a pestle and mortar. Add sugar to taste. Sprinkle with spring onion and coriander. The relish should taste salty and hot.

Accompany with:

— raw cucumber, cut into lengths

— sprigs of coriander and mint

— Boiled Vegetables (page 381), especially cabbage and snake beans

— Vegetables Simmered in Coconut Milk (page 382), especially pumpkin and cabbage

— Deep-fried Pork Skin (page 400).

GRILLED COCONUT RELISH

nahm sup kry

This relish is from the south of Thailand. A special type of coconut is used – one that is somewhere between a young green coconut and an old, dry coconut. It is easy to grate and is not too tough. Normally it is used for desserts, but is ideal in this relish.

1 tablespoon palm sugar

1 cup grated coconut

banana leaves or foil

paste

4 tablespoons sliced lemongrass

large pinch of salt

7 red shallots, peeled

5 garlic cloves, peeled

1 tablespoon chopped turmeric

1 tablespoon picked green peppercorns

5–15 bird's eye chillies (scuds)

1 tablespoon shrimp paste (*gapi*)

Pound all paste ingredients using a pestle and mortar. Season with palm sugar and mix in the coconut. Wrap the paste in the banana leaves, if using, and grill over a low heat until the outer banana leaves are charred to produce a wonderfully fragrant relish. (Wrapping the relish in foil and then searing in a pan will approximate this.)

Eat with:

— Raw Vegetables (page 380), especially banana blossoms, 'betel' leaves
  and pomelo

— sprigs of coriander

— sprigs of Thai and lemon basil

— grilled or steamed fish, prawns (shrimp) or crab.

CHILLI JAM

nahm prik pao

This kind of *nahm prik* keeps indefinitely. There are two ways of making chilli jam: one by grilling all the ingredients, the other by frying them. The grilled version is by far the older method, but this fried version produces the chilli jam most frequently included in Thai recipes. It can be used in a multitude of ways: as a *nahm prik*, in salad dressings, to enrich hot and sour soups and as a base for a stir-fry.

Since it is quite time-consuming to make but lasts well, it is probably better to make a large amount (this recipe makes 5–6 cups). Be careful not to simmer the seasoned paste for too long, otherwise it will seize as the sugar caramelises and, when cooled, will be impossible to use. To add extra texture, reserve a handful of the deep-fried garlic, shallots and chillies and fold them into the paste just before serving.

oil for deep-frying

4 cups red shallots, sliced lengthwise

2 cups garlic, sliced lengthwise

½ cup dried prawns (shrimp), rinsed and dried

1 cup dried long red chillies, deseeded and chopped

10 slices galangal

1 teaspoon shrimp paste (*gapi*), roasted

1 cup palm sugar

½ cup thick tamarind water

3 tablespoons salt *or* ½ cup fish sauce

Heat oil in a wok and separately deep-fry shallots, garlic, prawns, chillies and galangal until golden. Blend them all in a food processor, with the shrimp paste, moistening with some of the oil used for deep-frying (up to 1 cup) to facilitate the blending.

In a pan, bring the mixture to the boil and season with palm sugar, tamarind water and salt or fish sauce. Simmer until quite thick, stirring regularly. The resulting 'jam' should taste sweet, sour and salty.

If using as a relish, serve with:
- banana blossoms, separated into leaves and steeped in acidulated water
- sprigs of Thai basil
- steamed squid
- Crispy Fried Pork (page 399).

CHIANG MAI PORK AND TOMATO RELISH

nahm prik ong

The small Thai tomatoes used in this relish are quite sour, even though ripe. Given the quality of most tomatoes, this should pose no problem. However, if the tomatoes are particularly sweet and ripe, add a green tomato or a little tamarind water. Simmer the paste with the tomatoes and pork until quite rich but not too dry.

Originally from the north, this delicious relish is now very popular throughout Thailand. On the central plains, the paste may often include a little galangal, and be garnished with tart Chinese red dates – sometimes called jujube.

2 garlic cloves, peeled

pinch of salt

3 tablespoons oil or rendered pork fat

150 g (5 oz) minced fatty pork

2 tablespoons fish sauce or light soy sauce

pinch of palm sugar

a little stock

paste

5 dried long red chillies, deseeded, soaked and drained

large pinch of salt

1 tablespoon chopped lemongrass

3 tablespoons chopped red shallot

2 tablespoons chopped garlic

1 disc fermented soy beans (*tua nao*)

   or 1 teaspoon shrimp paste (*gapi*)

1 cup coarsely chopped tomato

First, make the paste: pound chillies with all the other paste ingredients, in the order given.

Separately pound garlic with salt to make a coarse purée. Heat oil in a pan or wok. Add garlic purée and fry until fragrant and golden. Add paste and continue to fry over a medium heat for several minutes until fragrant. Stir regularly. Add minced pork and stir to prevent it clumping. When pork is cooked, season with fish sauce or soy sauce and palm sugar. If necessary, moisten with stock.

The relish should be quite dry, hot, sour and salty – and slightly sweet from the tomatoes.

Eat with:

— Boiled Vegetables (page 381), especially cabbage and green beans

— freshwater fish or prawns (shrimp), poached or grilled

— Deep-fried Pork Skin (page 400).

NAHM PRIK OF FRESH TAMARIND, PRAWNS AND PORK
nahm prik makaam sot

This *nahm prik* is a cooked type where the unseasoned paste can be boiled or fried, then seasoned. If fresh tamarind is unavailable, simply increase the tamarind water in the final seasoning. Or increase the green mango to make this a green mango relish.

3 tablespoons stock or water

1 teaspoon fish sauce

2 uncooked prawns (shrimp), peeled, deveined and minced

50 g (2 oz) minced fatty pork

extra 2 teaspoons fish sauce

1 teaspoon palm sugar

2 tablespoons tamarind water

squeeze of lime juice

a few extra bird's eye chillies (scuds), bruised – optional

paste

3 garlic cloves, peeled

large pinch of salt

1 tablespoon dried prawns (shrimp)

1 tablespoon *pla grop* (crisp fish) or hot-smoked trout – optional

1 tablespoon shrimp paste (*gapi*)

2 tablespoons cleaned and chopped fresh tamarind

4–10 bird's eye chillies (scuds)

1 tablespoon pea eggplants – optional

1 small green mango, shredded

First, make the paste: pound garlic with salt using a pestle and mortar. In order, add dried prawns, fish (if using), shrimp paste, tamarind and chillies, pounding to produce a very fine paste. Add eggplants (if using) and green mango and crush coarsely.

Bring stock or water to the boil, add fish sauce, then the minced prawns and pork, stirring constantly to prevent clumping. When these are almost cooked – surprisingly only a matter of seconds – add the paste and stir until fragrant. Season with extra fish sauce, palm sugar and tamarind water. Finish with lime juice and more chillies to taste. The result should be hot, sour, salty and smoky.

Serve with a selection of vegetables and accompaniments:
- Boiled Vegetables (page 381), ideally snake beans, cabbage and pumpkin
- Steamed Eggs (page 388)
- Crispy Fish Cakes (page 393)
- Sweet Pork (page 397).

RELISH OF GRILLED PRAWNS AND GREEN MANGO

nahm prik gung mamuang

Any sour fruit or leaf can be used if green mango is not available: hog plums, cape gooseberries, tamarind leaves or blanched sorrel. The taste of this *nahm prik* should be sour and salty to equal degrees and then hot. The bitterness of pea eggplants works well with the interplay between the palm sugar and green mango.

As with so many Thai dishes, there is great versatility in how this recipe can be adapted. The hot-smoked trout is not traditional, but it works. Sticklers for tradition can use *pla grop* (crisp fish), any dried or salted fish, boiled fish, or an increased amount of dried prawns. The paste can be fried with some crispy pork belly; and any seafood will work with this relish – crab, freshwater crayfish or grilled fish. However the seasoning must be adjusted accordingly.

3 medium uncooked prawns (shrimp), unpeeled

3 garlic cloves, peeled

1 teaspoon salt

1 teaspoon dried prawns (shrimp)

½ teaspoon shrimp paste (*gapi*)

3–5 bird's eye chillies (scuds)

2 tablespoons shredded *pla grop* (crisp fish) or hot-smoked trout

1 tablespoon pea eggplants – optional

1 small green mango, julienned

2 teaspoons palm sugar

1 teaspoon tamarind water

1 tablespoon lime juice

1–2 tablespoons fish sauce

Devein the prawns: either use a small skewer to hook out the vein or slice each prawn lengthwise along its back and scrape out, then rinse and dry. Grill in their shells until just cooked. Cool, peel and shred. Pound garlic with salt, dried prawns and fresh prawn meat. When fine, add shrimp paste and, when well incorporated, the scuds. Work the shredded trout into the paste, then add eggplants (if using) and green mango. Season with sugar, tamarind water, lime juice and fish sauce – it should taste hot, sour and salty. Mix well and maybe finish with a few extra scuds.

Serve with the following:
- Raw Vegetables (page 380), such as cucumber and white turmeric
- Boiled Vegetables (page 381), especially okra
- sprigs of coriander and Thai basil
- Steamed Eggs (page 388) or Steamed Salted Duck Eggs (page 391)
- Omelette (page 390), with *cha-om* or sliced long eggplants
- small fish – such as red spot whiting, tommy ruff or sardines – deep-fried until crisp
- Crispy Fish Cakes (page 393).

EMBARKING RELISH

nahm prik long reua

Garnishes – *kreaung kiam* – can play such an important role that they make the dish what it is. The following recipe is a prime example of this.

This recipe comes from the memorial book of Chao Chom Sabad, a remarkable woman who was one of the last links with the truly exotic character of Siam. She died at the venerable age of 93 in 1983. More remarkably, she was the last remaining wife of King Rama V, who reigned from 1868 to 1910. As a very young girl,

she was brought to the Grand Palace to be taught the finer points of culture. Later her languorous beauty attracted the attention of Chulalongkorn and she married him in 1907, at the age of seventeen.

At the time, all consorts and concubines of the king were confined to the harem, just behind the Grand Palace, and were rarely allowed out. When the king and his court left Bangkok during the oppressively hot months of April and May for Bang Pa In, 50 kilometres (about 30 miles) to the north, just near Ayuthyia, his harem followed. There they were obliged to entertain the king, but happily were released from the hidebound etiquette of the palace.

The journey could take as long as a fortnight, travelling by boat; roads were uncommon and untrustworthy, whereas water guaranteed safe travel and was the most traditional way. The frantic preparations would take weeks, and nothing could be forgotten, as this would be to the detriment of the household's reputation. Furniture, kitchens, dancers and musicians all had to be moved. Food also had to be prepared in the palace kitchens and cooked in makeshift kitchens on the shore during the journey. And so this recipe assembled ingredients that were at hand: sweet pork, shrimp paste, chillies, ground fish, pickled garlic and salted duck eggs.

4 garlic cloves, peeled

pinch of salt

1 tablespoon rendered pork fat or oil

1 tablespoon tamarind water

1 tablespoon lime juice

a little fish sauce

1 apple eggplant

5 cloves pickled garlic, sliced

1 salted duck egg yolk, cut into 8 pieces

1 piece Crispy Fish Cake (page 393)

handful of coriander leaves

sweet pork

100 g (3 oz) pork belly or ribs

1 teaspoon rendered pork fat or oil

2 coriander roots, scraped

pinch of salt

5 white peppercorns

3 garlic cloves, peeled

3 tablespoons palm sugar

2 tablespoons fish sauce

a little stock

chilli paste

1 coriander root, scraped

pinch of salt

5 long red chillies – deseeded, if desired

1 heaped teaspoon shrimp paste (*gapi*)

For sweet pork: wash pork and slice into small pieces, about 1 cm × ½ cm (½ in × ¼ in). Heat rendered pork fat or oil in a wok and fry pork over a low flame until beginning to colour, stirring occasionally to ensure that it does not stick. Meanwhile, pound coriander roots with salt, peppercorns and garlic in a pestle and mortar to produce a fine paste. Add this to pork and fry until fragrant and golden. Add palm sugar and simmer until almost caramelised. Moisten with fish sauce and then cover with stock. Simmer until pork is tender, about 30 minutes, skimming regularly. The sweet pork can be made a few hours before the rest of recipe.

Make chilli paste by pounding coriander root with salt using a pestle and mortar. Add chillies and pound until puréed, then work in shrimp paste.

Pound or mince garlic with salt. Heat rendered pork fat or oil in a small wok or saucepan and fry garlic until golden. Add chilli paste and continue to fry over a medium heat until fragrant, stirring regularly. Pour in sweet pork and simmer for a few minutes. Season with tamarind water, lime juice and, if necessary, fish sauce. It should taste richly salty, hot, sweet and sour.

Finely slice apple eggplant and stir into the relish. Pour into a serving bowl. Sprinkle with sliced pickled garlic and salted duck egg pieces, partially crumble the crispy fish cake over the relish and then finish with the coriander.

Serve with slices of cucumber and steamed prawns (shrimp).

GREEN PEPPERCORN RELISH

nahm prik prik thai orn

This relish is an interesting latter-day version of one of the primeval *nahm prik* that used peppercorns as their base. Be quite generous in the seasoning – the rich nature of this dish requires it. This *nahm prik* will keep for some time, as it is preserved with rendered pork fat. When reheating to serve, it may be necessary to adjust the seasoning. Like the original *nahm prik* of northern Thailand, this relish is very good mixed with warm rice and served with grilled or deep-fried fish and raw vegetables.

100 g (3 oz) pork belly

3 garlic cloves, peeled

large pinch of salt

3 tablespoons picked green peppercorns

1 tablespoon shrimp paste (*gapi*)

3 tablespoons dried or smoked fish – *pla salit*, *pla grop* or hot-smoked trout

a few bird's eye chillies (scuds)

½ cup mixed shredded sour fruit and vegetables – such as green mango, fresh
  tamarind pods, sorrel, fuzzy eggplant or cape gooseberries

3 tablespoons rendered pork fat or oil

2 apple eggplants, destemmed and cut into sixths

1 tablespoon palm sugar

2 tablespoons fish sauce

1 tablespoon tamarind water

squeeze of lime juice

Wash the pork belly. Blanch from a cold-water start, with plenty of salt. Bring to the boil, refresh and repeat. This time simmer the belly for 10 minutes or until cooked before draining and refreshing. Allow to cool completely before cutting into small pieces – about ½ cm (¼ in) cubes.

Pound garlic with salt and 2 tablespoons of the peppercorns. Add shrimp paste, fish, the chillies and half of the sour fruit. Continue to pound into a very fine paste.

Heat a pan. Add rendered pork fat or oil and fry pork until golden and crisp. Add paste and continue to fry over a low heat for several minutes until fragrant. Add apple eggplant and remainder of sour fruit, and continue to cook for a few minutes more. Moisten, if necessary, with a little water.

Season with palm sugar and fish sauce and finish with remaining table-spoon of green peppercorns, tamarind water and lime juice. It should taste salty, hot from the pepper, then sweet and just slightly sour.

Serve with some of the following:

- Raw Vegetables (page 380), such as cucumber, rocket (arugula) or green beans
- Pickled Vegetables (page 383), especially cucumber and red shallots
- prawns (shrimp), steamed or deep-fried
- Steamed Eggs (page 388)
- Deep-fried Fish with Pickled Garlic (page 423).

FRIED CHILLI RELISH

nahm prik pat

Authentically, any dried fish can be used for this relish. However *pla grop*, a small, dried and smoked fish usually sold on a skewer or a brace, is the most popular. Normally it is available frozen in Asian food stores. Hot-smoked trout or dried prawns make delicious alternatives.

When making the paste ensure that it is well puréed, as this is the hallmark of a well-made *nahm prik*. The paste needs to be cooked over a low heat for a considerable time to enable the flavours of the smoked fish to develop and the raw heat of the chillies to diminish. It has a rich taste from the bacon-like *pla grop*, rounded by the garlic and shrimp paste, sharpened by the chillies and enriched by the pork fat. No one flavour dominates another, all work in concert. The seasoning should be salty and rich from the pork fat and then hot.

The recipe can be made on the day or, like other relishes of this type, it can be made in advance. It will last for quite some time once cooked, with the fat acting as a preservative – as it does in the French *confit*. To refresh after a long period of storage, a little pounded garlic can be browned in some fat or oil before adding the *nahm prik* to reheat, but it will then need to be re-seasoned.

100 g (3 oz) minced pork fat *or* 6 tablespoons oil

1 teaspoon salt – only if using pork fat

6–12 dried long red chillies, deseeded, soaked and drained

6 garlic cloves, peeled

7 red shallots, peeled

1 teaspoon salt

2 tablespoons *pla grop* (crisp fish), dried fish, dried prawns (shrimp)
   or hot-smoked trout

1 garlic clove, pounded

1 teaspoon sugar

1–2 tablespoons fish sauce

If using pork fat, wash and put in pan; cover with water and add salt. Place over medium heat, stirring occasionally, until the fat has rendered and the water evaporated. The fat begins to colour as it crisps and fries. Be careful, for if burnt it is unusable. Stir regularly over a low heat until the scratchings – that is, the solids remaining as the fat renders – are lightly golden, brown and smell nutty and toasty. Strain into a metal bowl. Cooled and refrigerated, the rendered pork fat keeps for several weeks. Keep the scratchings separately, although they do not store as well.

Using a mortar and pestle, pound chillies, garlic and shallots with salt. When puréed, add fish, pound until smooth and set this paste aside. Heat 6 tablespoons of pork fat or oil in a wok. Add pounded garlic and fry until golden. Add paste and continue to fry until quite dark and fragrant from the fish. (It may be necessary to moisten with a little water.) Season with sugar and fish sauce and cook until dry again. The balance should be hot and salty. Traditionally, 1–2 tablespoons of the pork scratchings are added after the seasoning.

This relish has an intensely concentrated flavour; consequently, nutty vegetables counterbalance it:

— Raw Vegetables (page 380), ideally white radish, witlof (Belgian endive), sorrel, green mango and green tomatoes >

- Boiled Vegetables (page 381), especially green beans and okra
- Vegetables Simmered in Coconut Milk (page 382), such as cabbage and pumpkin
- Pickled Vegetables (page 383), especially ginger and cucumber
- Steamed Eggs (page 388).

LON

Lon are the gentler, kinder side of relishes. '*Lon*' means to simmer or stew, normally in coconut cream. *Lon* can be rich and sumptuous while also being pungent and salty, as they are nearly always made with a fermented, salted or pickled ingredient. This is because coconut cream affords the *lon* great scope in taste and seasoning.

Lon are not as ancient as *nahm prik*. I believe they date from the time of Sukothai – from the thirteenth century, when the Thai first entered the regions where coconuts were grown. The first type of *lon* was most likely made by simmering fermented fish (*pla raa*) with coconut and other aromatics. The coconut may have been extracted cream or simply grated flesh. Although an ancient preserve, *pla raa* is a product of the northern half of Thailand. These two products first met at Sukothai.

LON INGREDIENTS

A *lon* can be made from fermented yellow beans; salted, fermented or dried fish or prawns; cured pork; fermented bean curd; even ants' eggs. This main ingredient is simmered in coconut cream – generally the thicker the better, although a little stock might be used to lighten the relish and to prevent it from separating unduly. All the other additions are simply to highlight the principal ingredient.

Minced pork or prawns are often added to give body and substance to the *lon*, and also to soften the pungency of the principal ingredient; traditionally minced pork fat was used. After the ingredients have been simmered for some time the *lon* is seasoned, although not too strongly, with tamarind water, palm sugar and fish sauce. Thick tamarind water should be used so as not to dilute the *lon*. And caution should be exercised with palm sugar and fish sauce, both of which can overwhelm the subtle flavours. I like to add a pinch of salt along with the fish sauce, to ensure that not too much of the latter is used.

Then the *lon* is garnished with red shallots, fresh long chillies and chopped coriander leaves. The shallots should be sliced just a little thicker than usual so they won't wilt, while the chillies should be cut into ½ centimetre (¼ inch) rounds and soaked in water for a few moments to reduce their heat; rarely are the seeds removed. Coriander, sprinkled over just before serving, adds freshness and succulence. Among other garnishes, shredded *grachai*, green mango or galangal may be employed as a welcome contrast to a rich, silky *lon*. These should also be added at the last moment, so they retain their flavours and textures.

LON ACCOMPANIMENTS

Raw vegetables usually accompany *lon*, as their crispness offers a textural contrast to the simmered coconut cream. Pickled vegetables, with their sweet and sour syrup, also make an excellent accompaniment.

The same wide range of side dishes (*kreaung kiam*) that contrast with and parallel *nahm prik* are also suitable for *lon*; recipes for these are given in the 'Side dishes and accompaniments' chapter, starting on page 379.

FERMENTED FISH RELISH

lon pla raa

Probably the first *lon* was made with fermented fish sauce (*nahm pla raa*), simmered with coconut cream and pounded galangal until quite thick. *Nahm pla raa* is, to my taste at least, immeasurably improved by the addition of coconut cream. The robust becomes rich, velvety and suave — it is an extraordinary transformation. Some recipes include a drizzle of honey and a pinch of turmeric when simmering the coconut cream.

2 cups fermented fish sauce (*nahm pla raa*)

2 cups coconut cream

1 tablespoon palm sugar

200 g (6 oz) freshwater fish – catfish, trout, salmon, zander – coarsely minced

2 tablespoons shredded galangal

3 tablespoons finely sliced lemongrass

2 tablespoons coarsely sliced red shallot

1 teaspoon shredded kaffir lime zest

2 tablespoons shredded *grachai* (wild ginger)

2 tablespoons kaffir lime juice or regular lime juice

extra palm sugar and fish sauce, to taste

extra 3 tablespoons coconut cream

2 kaffir lime leaves, finely shredded

Bring fermented fish sauce and coconut cream to the boil. Simmer and reduce until quite thick. Add the tablespoon of palm sugar and the minced fish. Stir in galangal, lemongrass, shallot, kaffir lime zest and *grachai*. Season with lime juice, more palm sugar to taste and, if necessary, fish sauce. Enrich with the extra coconut cream and serve sprinkled with shredded lime leaves.

This pungent *lon* needs strong accompaniments. Serve with a few of the following:

— Raw Vegetables (page 380), such as 'betel' leaves, pomelo, rose apple, cucumber, green or half-ripe mango, green beans, apple eggplants, young ginger and white turmeric >

- Boiled Vegetables (page 381), especially bamboo shoots and apple eggplants
- sprigs of *cha-om* and coriander
- grilled fish
- steamed prawns (shrimp)
- *pla grop* (crisp fish)
- Crispy Fish Cakes (page 393)
- Deep-fried Pork with Spices (page 400).

MINCED PRAWNS SIMMERED IN COCONUT CREAM

lon gung

This is a refined dish with a purity of taste that displays the best characteristics of a *lon*: rich, balanced and elegant – a reflection of the milieu from which it comes. Mom Ratchawongse Dteuang Sanitsawongse, a descendant of King Rama II and a daughter and a sister of government ministers of the fifth and sixth reigns, was a renowned cook during the first half of the twentieth century. Her recipes are often included in the memorial books of others because they are believed to be classics, and this recipe is indeed one.

This *lon* is from Bangkok where prawns were plentiful. I like to add a little Tomalley Paste (page 183), as it imparts a subtle hue and a pleasant depth to this beautiful relish. Fresh crabmeat is an agreeable alternative to prawns.

1 cup coconut cream

½ cup stock

1 teaspoon salt

2 tablespoons cleaned fresh tamarind – if available

1 tablespoon minced pork fat *or* 2 tablespoons minced fatty pork

1 tablespoon palm sugar

1 tablespoon fish sauce

1–2 tablespoons thick tamarind water

4 large uncooked prawns (shrimp), peeled, deveined and minced

2 red shallots, sliced

1 long red chilli, sliced into rounds

handful of coriander leaves

extra 3 tablespoons coconut cream

Bring the 1 cup coconut cream to the boil with stock and salt. Add fresh tamarind, if using, and minced pork fat or pork. Stir regularly to prevent it clumping. Simmer for a minute. Season with palm sugar, fish sauce and tamarind water. Add prawns. Simmer until cooked – around a minute. Finish with shallots, chilli and coriander. Enrich with the extra coconut cream. The *lon* should taste creamy, salty, sour and slightly sweet.

Serve with some of the following:
— Raw Vegetables (page 380), especially cucumber
— Pickled Vegetables (page 383)
— fresh or dried fish, deep-fried
— Crispy Fish Cakes (page 393)
— Sweet Pork (page 397).

CURED PORK SIMMERED IN COCONUT CREAM

lon naem

This relish is rich, subtle and sumptuous.

1 cup coconut cream
½ cup stock
1–2 tablespoons palm sugar
1 tablespoon tamarind water
2 tablespoons fish sauce
pinch of ground white pepper
100 g (3 oz) Chiang Mai cured pork (*naem*)
50 g (2 oz) minced uncooked prawns (shrimp) – optional
3 red shallots, sliced
1 small long red or green chilli, sliced into rings
1 tablespoon coriander leaves

Bring coconut cream and stock to the boil. Season with sugar to taste, tamarind water, 1 tablespoon of the fish sauce and pepper. Crumble in the cured pork and, when the liquid has returned to the boil, add prawns and turn down the heat. When prawns are cooked – about a minute – add remaining ingredients. Check seasoning: the relish should taste creamy, sour, salty and sweet – it may need a little more fish sauce.

Serve with some of the following:
— Raw Vegetables (page 380), such as cucumber, young ginger, spring (green) onions, white turmeric, witlof (Belgian endive)
— Boiled Vegetables (page 381), especially green beans
— Grilled Vegetables (page 382), especially apple eggplants and bamboo shoots
— Deep-fried Vegetables (page 383), especially 'betel' leaves and Siamese watercress
— sprigs of Thai basil and coriander
— pickled ginger
— pickled red shallots
— grilled squid, cuttlefish or octopus
— Crisp Fish Skin (page 392)
— Deep-fried Pork Skin (page 400).

SHRIMP PASTE SIMMERED IN COCONUT CREAM

lon gapi

This is a luscious *lon*. The similarity between curry and *lon* pastes can be seen here at its closest, not only in the ingredients but also in the method employed. The recipe may seem to include a disproportionate amount of *grachai*, smoked fish and raw shrimp paste, but as this paste cooks, the fetid and pungent becomes rich and earthy.

The *grachai*, initially piercing, becomes smooth and helps to clean the shrimp paste of its earthiness. The fish prevents the paste from becoming too oily. The cooking transforms the heavy paste into a redolent and rich relish that can be enjoyed unadorned, mixed with rice, or with dishes that develop, complement and complete this *lon*. Of course, a transformation occurs as items cook in every cuisine, but I think it happens no more dramatically or satisfyingly than in Thai cooking.

For an extravagance, a few chopped prawns can be added just before serving; or some prawn tomalley can be stirred in. Alternatively, instead of adding them to the relish, the deveined prawns can be grilled or steamed in their shells, then peeled before serving with the *lon*. Grilled or steamed fish, such as a piece of salmon, can also be served on the side.

2 cups coconut cream

3 tablespoons palm sugar

2 tablespoons tamarind water

2 tablespoons fish sauce

1 cup coconut milk

½ cup mandarin juice

1 red shallot, sliced

1 long red chilli, sliced into rounds

1 tablespoon coriander leaves

paste

4 dried long red chillies, deseeded, soaked and drained

1 teaspoon salt

3 tablespoons chopped lemongrass

1 tablespoon chopped galangal

¼ cup chopped *grachai* (wild ginger)

2 tablespoons chopped red shallot

3 tablespoons chopped garlic

¼ cup *pla grop* (crisp fish), hot-smoked trout, dried fish or dried prawns (shrimp)

¼ cup shrimp paste (*gapi*)

First, make the paste: gradually pound the ingredients together using a pestle and mortar, adding one by one, until smooth.

In a pan, separate the coconut cream over medium heat, then add paste and fry over a medium to low heat for at least 10 minutes until it is fragrant with fish or prawns and *grachai*. Season with palm sugar, tamarind water and fish sauce. Simmer for several more minutes, adding the coconut milk and continuing to simmer until thick but still quite oily. Finish with mandarin juice, shallot, chilli rounds and coriander leaves.

Serve with:
— Raw Vegetables (page 380), such as cucumber, witlof (Belgian endive), iceberg lettuce, young ginger, white turmeric, green mango, green tomatoes
— Pickled Cabbage (page 387)
— Crispy Fish Cakes (page 393)
— Sweet Pork (page 397).

LON OF SEMI-DRIED SALMON

lon pla salmon dtaet dtiaw

Salmon, although not a Thai fish, is exemplary when used in this recipe. Fermented rice is used quite often in Thai cookery, to enrich with its silken sweetness and to counterbalance oiliness.

200 g (6 oz) semi-dried salmon fillet (see Semi-dried Fish, page 150)
1 cup coconut cream
½ cup coconut milk
2 tablespoons fermented rice – optional
1 teaspoon palm sugar
1 tablespoon tamarind water
a little fish sauce
1 tablespoon finely sliced lemongrass
2 red shallots, sliced
1 long red or green chilli, cut into 1 cm (½ in) slices
1 small green mango, julienned
a few coriander leaves
1 kaffir lime leaf, finely shredded
1–2 tablespoons salmon roe (or more, if truly indulgent) – optional

Grill fish for 2 minutes each side over a very high heat, or fry in a little oil. Leave to rest for 10 minutes. Heat coconut cream and milk together. Add fermented rice, if using, and simmer for a minute. Season with palm sugar, tamarind water and fish sauce: it should be creamy, sweet and sour, but not too pronounced. Flake in fish and add lemongrass; continue to simmer for a minute or so. Take off the heat and garnish with remaining ingredients. If using roe, add it last – it must not be allowed to boil, otherwise it toughens and becomes tasteless. Check seasoning: it should be salty, sweet and sour.

Serve with some of the following:
- Raw Vegetables (page 380), such as cucumber, fennel, witlof (Belgian endive), sorrel, young spinach, banana blossoms and banana chillies
- sprigs of Thai basil
- steamed prawns (shrimp).

SOUTHERN-STYLE SHRIMP PASTE

geng koie kreuang

Koie is a type of shrimp paste made from the small planktonic shrimp that abound in the Gulf of Thailand. Unusually, this relish is thickened with an egg.

2 cups coconut cream
1 tablespoon white sugar
1 tablespoon tamarind water
2 tablespoons fish sauce
1 egg, lightly beaten
3 kaffir lime leaves, torn

paste
30 dried red bird's eye chillies, soaked and drained
1 teaspoon salt
1 tablespoon chopped lemongrass
1 teaspoon chopped galangal
1 teaspoon finely grated kaffir lime zest
1 tablespoon chopped turmeric
2 tablespoons chopped red shallot
1 tablespoon chopped garlic
3 tablespoons shrimp paste (*gapi*)

First, make the paste: gradually pound the ingredients together using a pestle and mortar, adding one by one, until smooth.

Separate coconut cream by heating gently. Add paste and fry over a medium heat for several minutes until fragrant. Season with sugar, tamarind water and fish sauce. Stir in the egg and simmer until cooked. Add lime leaves.

Serve with plenty of Raw Vegetables (page 380), such as cucumber, ginger, white turmeric and apple eggplant.

MINCED PRAWNS SIMMERED IN COCONUT CREAM AND CHILLIES

nahm prik lon pak ruu

This unusual relish is a combination of a *lon* and a *nahm prik*. Even the Thai name questions where it belongs. It comes from the recipe book of the unfailing Thanpuuying Pliang Pasonagorn.

3 large uncooked prawns (shrimp), peeled and deveined

3 large dried prawns (shrimp)

2 garlic cloves, peeled

pinch of salt

5 fuzzy eggplants or cape gooseberries, sliced

1 small green mango, shredded

5–10 bird's eye chillies (scuds), washed in salted water then bruised

½ cup coconut cream

2 tablespoons fish sauce

1 tablespoon white sugar

2 tablespoons tamarind water

1 tablespoon lime juice

1 tablespoon Asian citron juice or mandarin juice

Chop the fresh prawns. Pound the dried prawns with garlic and salt. Mix with fuzzy eggplant or cape gooseberries, mango and chillies. Pour coconut cream into a medium pan, add fish sauce, sugar and tamarind water, then the dried prawn, fruit and chilli paste. Heat until paste is dissolved. Add fresh prawns and simmer until they just change colour. Finish with lime juice and citron or mandarin juice.

Eat with Raw Vegetables (page 380), ideally apple eggplants, banana blossoms and young ginger.

OTHER RELISHES

Several other dishes are served and eaten in a similar manner to *nahm prik* and *lon*, although they are prepared quite differently.

KAFFIR LIME JUICE DRESSING WITH GRILLED PRAWNS

saeng wa gung pao

This relish, which in my previous book I included as a salad, is typical of the heights to which Thai cuisine can climb. It has an unusual combination of flavours and textures that stimulates a flagging palate.

KAFFIR LIME JUICE DRESSING WITH GRILLED PRAWNS

All the garnishing ingredients need to be finely shredded to ensure that there is not a preponderance of one flavour at the expense of another. This balance is the aim of all Thai food, and it is achieved by careful cooking, proper seasoning and appropriate knife work. The amount of shredding and the uncommon ingredients in this recipe suggest that this was originally royal food.

6 large uncooked prawns (shrimp), unpeeled
2 bird's eye chillies (scuds), pounded
3 red shallots, sliced
1 tablespoon finely sliced lemongrass
4 kaffir lime leaves, shredded
2 tablespoons julienned young ginger
1 tablespoon julienned long red or green chilli
handful of mixed mint and coriander leaves

dressing
2 tablespoons kaffir lime juice or regular lime juice
2 tablespoons Asian citron or mandarin juice
1 tablespoon castor (superfine) sugar
2 tablespoons fish sauce

Devein the prawns, then rinse and dry. Grill or roast in their shells. Cool, peel and shred. Combine the dressing ingredients and dress the prawns. Then combine prawns with the remaining ingredients.

Serve with a few of the following:
— Raw Vegetables (page 380), especially cucumber and sorrel
— Boiled Vegetables (page 381), such as apple eggplants, green beans and cabbage
— sprigs of coriander and Thai basil
— Crispy Fish Cakes (page 393)
— Sweet Pork (page 397).

SEASONED PRAWN RELISH

man gung brung song kreaung

Prawn tomalley is a most unlikely delicacy – but only tomalley from very fresh prawns should be used, and it should be cooked as soon as possible One of the best ways to enjoy this exotic ingredient is in the following recipe. The initial paste can be made well in advance – refrigerated, it lasts a week or so – then reheated and finished with marinated prawns. The acid from the pungent kaffir lime juice cooks the prawn meat.

If fresh kaffir limes are unavailable, do not use frozen fruit as its juice will be too bitter; use mandarin, tangelo or even ordinary lime juice instead. Although these will reduce the paste's savoury complexity, they still result in a most enjoyable dish. The addition of coconut cream is optional but does enrich the relish.

    6 uncooked king prawns (jumbo shrimp), unpeeled
    1 garlic clove, peeled
    1 coriander root, scraped
    pinch of ground white pepper
    pinch of salt
    1 tablespoon oil, rendered pork fat or coconut oil
    1–2 tablespoons white sugar
    1 tablespoon fish sauce
    3 tablespoons coconut cream – optional
    pinch of salt
    2 tablespoons kaffir lime juice
    2 red shallots, coarsely sliced
    1 long green chilli, finely sliced

Peel and devein prawns. Squeeze the heads to extract the tomalley – as much as possible of the innards should be dragged out of the head. There should be about 3 tablespoons. Pound garlic with coriander root, pepper and salt.

Heat oil in a pan. Fry garlic paste until golden and add tomalley. Simmer until tomalley has changed colour and has lost its raw, eggy smell. Season to taste with sugar and fish sauce, and continue to simmer for another minute or so. Moisten with coconut cream if desired.

Meanwhile, coarsely chop the prawn meat and bruise lightly. Work in the salt and lime juice. Marinate for 3 minutes or until the flesh turns white and the acid has 'cooked' the prawns, then add them to the paste. Simmer for a moment but do not cook for long or the prawns will become surprisingly tough. The relish should taste rich, sour and sweet. Garnish with shallots and chilli.

Serve with some of the following:
- Raw Vegetables (page 380), such as cucumber, fennel, spring (green) onions, rocket (arugula), sorrel, spinach, white turmeric
- Boiled Vegetables (page 381), especially cabbage and wing beans
- sprigs of coriander.

8

SOUPS

Thai soups are not confined to a single, separate course, as in a Western meal. Instead, they play an integral part in a meal, to be sipped and savoured throughout, as desired. They are more than just a complementary dish – soups restore the palate after the onslaught of chillies and revive it for the next round.

At its most basic, a Thai soup is little more than boiling water poured over shredded ingredients or some chopped meat boiled with a vegetable – reflecting its primitive origins. Slightly more sophisticated are the simple stock-based soups, known in Thai as *geng jeut*, literally but unappetisingly translated as 'bland liquids' and perhaps better referred to as broths. Since the essence of such a soup is simplicity, only a few ingredients should be added to perfume the stock. For once, I recommend restraint. A little ginger, a clove of garlic, a leaf of cabbage, some coriander and spring onions are all that is needed.

Stock is used more as a base for Thai soups than a flavouring agent. Therefore the best stock to use is the simplest and lightest (see recipes opposite). Some Thai cookbooks, old and new, suggest water as an easy alternative to stock. While fats have their uses in other areas of Thai cuisine, they play little or no part in stocks or soups – any fattiness or cloudiness will mar their clarity. And seasoning should be done judiciously, so that the result is neither insipid nor affronting.

Deep-fried garlic (see page 157) is an important seasoning element that is used to perfume many soups, adding a rich and nutty dimension and a golden complexion. Although sliced deep-fried garlic can be crushed over the soup, usually garlic meant for soup is minced before it is deep-fried. Often the garlic is left to cool in the oil and then it, along with a little of the perfumed oil, is spooned over: it should be used with discretion; a mere drizzle is sufficient. It is not used in every *geng jeut* – although, I must admit, I like it in most simple broths.

Thai food is an incremental cuisine, producing its effects by adding an ingredient here and a garnish there. Soups are no exception. Over time, these clear soups have developed in complexity through the addition of ingredients and the inclusion of a simple paste of garlic or red shallots in the broth. Other soups have evolved into a drier version – a thick, almost hearty braise, which itself can be accompanied by a light broth.

Perhaps the most singular style of Thai soups are the hot and sour variety, *dtom yam*. They are for many people the most identifiable; they are certainly the most memorable. The seasoning ingredients for hot and sour soups are bruised using a pestle and mortar before being simmered in the broth. Occasionally, the ingredients are even pounded into a paste before being dissolved in the soup, making the dish a primitive form of curry. The final style of soups in this chapter are the luscious coconut-based ones. These are the richest, the hardest to make and the most difficult in which to balance the seasoning.

Simple though they may be in technique, Thai soups encompass an enormous array of tastes and textures.

VEGETABLE STOCK

nahm cheua jae

Stock is best made on the day it is to be used, but it can be frozen for convenience. The following suggested list of ingredients is rather vague – it really depends on what vegetables are at hand. All that is required is a good flavour.

handful of mushroom stalks
a few outer leaves of Chinese cabbage
handful of spring (green) onion offcuts
1 white radish, cut into chunks
1 onion, cut into chunks
2 celery stalks
a few coriander stalks
3 slices ginger
a few garlic cloves, bruised
pinch of salt
pinch of white sugar

Cover vegetables with water, add salt and sugar, bring to the boil and simmer for 1 hour. Strain.

CHICKEN STOCK

nahm cheua gai

One way to revitalise older stock, or stock that has been frozen, is to add a piece of ginger when reheating; skim often and remove ginger before use.

1 kg (2 lb) chicken bones – of course, a whole chicken could be used
pinch of salt
1 small piece of ginger, bruised
1–2 garlic cloves, bruised
offcuts from spring (green) onions, cabbage, coriander stalks – whatever is at hand

For everyday use, simply cover stock ingredients with cold water, quickly bring to the boil and then simmer for at least 30 minutes, skimming as needed.

But I find a cleaner stock is achieved by washing the bones, removing any skin or fat, then blanching, draining and rinsing the bones to remove any scum. (The chicken skin can be rendered and, when crisp and golden, drained. The fat can then be used for stir-fries and the nutty scratchings are great with a beer.) Crush bones slightly with a pestle or heavy object before covering with cold water. Add salt and bring to the boil, allow to simmer for 20 minutes, then add vegetables. Simmer for 2 hours, skimming as required, then strain. >

Skim stock as it cools, to remove any impurities and fat. One technique to ensure a clean stock is to add a handful of ice cubes to the strained stock. This rapidly cools the stock, causing most impurities to rise to the surface. Skim off the top layer of congealed stock and fat before the ice melts completely.

A SOUP FROM THE PAST

geng nok

A *geng nok* is an ancient dish that gives a glimpse of the Thai culinary past. This soup must be among the oldest in the Thai repertoire, being primitive in technique, rustic in taste, and using easily available fresh or dried ingredients – food people could prepare and eat conveniently. *Pla chorn* is a common fish which thrives in the rivers that course through the countryside of the north, while groves of mangoes lined the valleys of ancient Siam.

1 dried *pla chorn* or Dried Smoked Trout Fillet (page 179)
1 small green mango, shredded
4 red shallots, sliced
2 cups water
2 tablespoons fish sauce

Grill fish until fragrant. Cool and coarsely shred. Combine with mango and shallots in a bowl. Boil water then pour over fish and mango and season with fish sauce.

PRAWN SOUP WITH SLICES OF LIME

geng jeut dtom gung manao

This soup is an exercise in simplicity and thus the ingredients need to be of prime quality – freshly made chicken stock, sweet prawns and just-sliced lime. The lime cleanses the stock, as well as imparting a pleasing citrus perfume and slightly bitter flavour. Any seafood can be used instead of prawns. A slightly more complicated version might include some shredded ginger with clams, scallops or small oily fish, such as sardines, deep-fried until quite crispy. I think that salmon, fresh or slightly salted and grilled, would be a very agreeable alternative.

4 cups chicken stock
large pinch of salt
pinch of white sugar
3 thin slices lime
100 g (3 oz) small uncooked prawns (shrimp), peeled and deveined
pinch of ground white pepper
1 tablespoon coriander leaves

Bring stock to the boil. Season with salt and sugar, and add lime slices. Add prawns, skim and when they are cooked – a few moments only – serve sprinkled with pepper and coriander. The soup should taste slightly salty and just a little bitter and sour.

PORK RIB AND BAMBOO SHOOT SOUP
dtom sii krong muu gap nor mai

This is another primitive soup, which for all its simplicity is truly delicious. The crisp bitterness of the bamboo shoot is countered by the richness of the pork ribs. Although stock can be used, it does cloud these simple tastes. I often double-blanch the pork ribs from a cold-water start, then rinse them before adding to the soup. The best cut of ribs to use is the one with soft cartilage rather than bones.

The success of these types of soups is based on the quality of the ingredients. Fresh bamboo shoots have a rich nutty bitterness that canned versions simply lack. Wild mushrooms or bitter melon and its leaves, or even green mango or melon, can be simmered with the pork ribs. Alternatively, shredded salted beef; fresh, deep-fried or grilled fish; *pla grop* (crisp fish) or even dried prawns can stand in for the pork to form a rustic but delicious mélange.

200 g (6 oz) fresh bamboo shoot
6 cups water
pinch of salt
pinch of sugar
100 g (3 oz) pork ribs, cut into 2 cm (1 in) pieces
2 tablespoons light soy sauce
1 teaspoon minced deep-fried garlic
1 tablespoon coriander leaves
pinch of ground white pepper

Wearing a pair of gloves, use a sharp knife to cut deeply along the length of the bamboo shoot. Peel off the outer layers until the white, hairless and fleshy core is revealed. Continue until the whole length is cleaned. Store in salted water. Cut into 2 cm (1 in) lengths, then shred. Blanch from a cold-water start with salt. Repeat to further reduce the bitterness, if required. Allow to cool in the water. The bamboo shoot will keep for several days at this stage, if the water is changed every other day.

Bring the 6 cups of water to the boil with salt and sugar. Add bamboo shoot and pork ribs and simmer until the ribs are tender, around 20 minutes. Skim regularly and replenish with water if necessary. The soup must be light and clean, flavoured by rich and pungent ingredients. Season with soy sauce. It should now taste rich, salty and bitter. Serve sprinkled with garlic, coriander and pepper.

BREAM SIMMERED WITH PICKLED GARLIC SYRUP

dtom pla nahm gratiam dong

Thanpuuying Gleeb Mahiton was born in 1876. She was sent to be educated in the palace of her aunt, a concubine of Rama III. As she grew up, she became renowned for her poise and beauty, attracting the attention of King Rama V, who indicated to her parents that he desired her to become his concubine. Unwilling to allow his daughter to be subjected to the scorn of the principal wives, her father moved Than Gleeb to the provinces. There she remained until she married a lawyer who later became a government minister, Chao Praya Mahithon. Despite the king's unfulfilled desires, Than Gleeb was welcomed back to court without any ramifications.

As a minister's principal wife, she was responsible for many banquets and entertainments for which she became as famous as she had earlier been for her beauty. The following is one of her recipes – except that she would have used *pla chorn* and not bream or trout. Than Gleeb did suggest that pickled ginger syrup could be substituted for the pickled garlic syrup.

4 cups stock
pinch of salt
½–1 cup pickled garlic syrup (leftover liquid from a jar of either bought or
    homemade pickled garlic)
100 g (3 oz) bream or trout fillets, finely sliced
a little fish sauce
a little lime juice
handful of chopped spring (green) onion
pinch of ground white pepper
1 tablespoon coriander leaves

Bring stock to the boil. Season with salt and pickled garlic syrup. Add bream and poach until just cooked – about 1 or 2 minutes. Check seasoning: it might well need fish sauce or a little lime juice. Sprinkle with spring onion, pepper and coriander. The soup should taste equally salty, sour and sweet – but not overwhelmingly so.

SIAMESE WATERCRESS AND CHICKEN SOUP

geng jeut pak bung

In effect this is a vegetable soup, the shredded chicken merely being a garnish that adds texture. Small dried or fresh prawns, freshwater crayfish and shelled mussels make enticing alternatives to the chicken. Siamese watercress is readily obtainable in Asian shops, but any leafy Asian – or Western – vegetable can be used. Sometimes I enrich the soup with a couple of tablespoons of yellow bean sauce.

> 1 small bunch Siamese watercress
> 4 cups chicken stock
> pinch of salt
> 50 g (2 oz) skinless chicken breast or thigh fillets
> pinch of white sugar
> 3 tablespoons light soy sauce
> a few slices of deep-fried garlic

Cut off coarse lower stems of watercress and chop into 2 cm (1 in) lengths. Soak in water to dislodge any soil or grit. Drain.

Bring stock to the boil and add salt. Poach chicken, remove and cool, then shred somewhat coarsely. Return stock to the boil and add Siamese watercress and sugar. Simmer for several minutes until watercress is wilted and soft, almost overcooked – this gives the soup a delicious nuttiness, which is further enhanced by the deep-fried garlic. Season with soy sauce and deep-fried garlic. The soup should taste nutty and salty. Add chicken, let it warm through and serve.

CHINESE BROCCOLI AND CRISP EGG SOUP

geng jeut pak kanaa

The pleasant bitterness of the broccoli imparts an alluring taste to this soup, but any full-flavoured Chinese greens can be substituted. To give greater body to the soup, simmer a few shiitake mushrooms – or wild mushrooms – in it and add a few small prawns or a little shredded chicken. Or make the stock by poaching some duck, coarsely shred it and add it to the soup with a little duck liver, giblets and perhaps some crabmeat too.

The salted duck egg is made into a thick batter which is deep-fried in some oil until crisp and golden. If the batter is too salty, add a little more sesame oil and sugar to it or, if the batter is already cooked, to the soup. A plain egg, whisked, seasoned and then fried in oil – a Thai omelette – makes a fine and simple alternative.

1 salted duck egg

2 tablespoons rice flour

pinch of palm sugar

pinch of ground white pepper

dash of sesame oil

oil for deep-frying

2 stalks Chinese broccoli

4 cups stock

pinch of salt

pinch of white sugar

1 tablespoon light soy sauce

a little oyster sauce, to taste

1 teaspoon minced deep-fried garlic

extra dash of sesame oil

Separate the egg. In a bowl, sprinkle the flour with a little water to moisten. Break up the egg yolk and work into the flour. Mix a teaspoon of water into the egg white and then stir into the flour. Incorporate well. Season with sugar, pepper and sesame oil.

Heat oil in a wok, ladle in the batter and deep-fry until crisp and golden. Remove, drain and cool before cutting into pieces.

Wash and trim broccoli; peel coarse lower stems, if necessary. Cut into elegant pieces. Bring stock to the boil, season with sugar, salt, soy and oyster sauces, then add broccoli and simmer until well cooked. Add egg, deep-fried garlic and sesame oil.

SOUP OF MINCED PORK AND CELERY

geng jeut bachor

It is well worth chopping the pork by hand (see page 127) to make the mince for this soup – its clean-cut freshness will be immediately evident, as it cooks without coagulating. When a soup is so simple, this extra attention to detailed technique shines through, achieving a superior result.

Cabbage, spring onions, *bai dtamleung* – a young spinach-like leaf – and Siamese watercress are all agreeable, but certainly not the only, partners to the minced pork in this *geng jeut*. Peeled asparagus, Chinese flowering chives, cubes of pumpkin, rounds of white radish, sweet corn, shredded bamboo shoots, mushrooms of most kinds, and sliced cucumber or gourd are also delicious prospects. The vegetable should be added either before or at the same time as the meat, depending on how long it takes to cook.

4 cups stock

pinch of salt

1–2 tablespoons light soy sauce

pinch of white sugar

50 g (2 oz) Asian celery or spring (green) onions, diagonally sliced

a few mushrooms (oyster or shiitake, for example), torn

100 g (3 oz) minced pork

1 tablespoon coriander leaves

pinch of ground white pepper

Bring stock to the boil, season with salt, soy sauce and sugar, add celery or spring onions and mushrooms. Bring back to the boil and add pork, stirring to prevent the meat clumping. Do not overcook the pork – a moment or two is sufficient, or it will toughen and become oily. Serve sprinkled with coriander and pepper.

SOUP OF BITTER MELON WITH MINCED PORK

geng jeut mara yord sai

This recipe is from the memorial book of Nang Oonreuan Pipatgun, who was born near Pattaya, in the south-eastern province of Chonburi in 1908. Although raised in an affluent family, she received little formal education and was taught the traditional arts considered appropriate for women of her generation and milieu – including cooking, at which she became particularly adept. Eventually Khun Oonreuan's culinary talents gained such renown that she opened a small cooking school to train the daughters of wealthy families in her province.

An elegant balance of flavours is achieved in this soup, where the bitterness of the melon cleanses the palate. Any green melon, cucumber or gourd can be used. One delectable variation is to stuff cleaned squid with the seasoned pork mixture and poach it in the soup, adding some Asian celery and shiitake mushrooms or a few wild mushrooms. The only thing to remember is that a *geng jeut* is a soup, not a stew, and such an accumulation of ingredients must not result in a thick clutter. Alternatively, the stuffed melon rounds can be steamed, rather than poached in stock, to make a refreshing side dish.

I often like to enrich this soup by simmering a few small fresh prawns in it, adding some shredded poached chicken or some blanched chicken liver just before serving and then sprinkling the soup with a few drops of sesame oil.

1 large or 2 small bitter melons

pinch of salt

150 g (5 oz) minced fatty pork

2 tablespoons light soy sauce

1 teaspoon palm sugar

4 cups stock

extra 2 tablespoons light soy sauce

pinch of white sugar

pinch of ground white pepper

1 tablespoon coriander leaves

garlic paste

2 coriander roots, scraped

pinch of salt

3 garlic cloves, peeled

10 white peppercorns

Wash bitter melon and cut into 2 cm (1 in) rounds. Remove seeds and surrounding white pith with a spoon. Rub melon rings with salt, then leave for an hour in a colander. Rinse. Blanch from a cold-water start, refresh. Taste the melon; if it is still too bitter, carefully blanch again.

Using a pestle and mortar, make the garlic paste by pounding the ingredients together one by one. Mix with the minced pork in a medium bowl and season with soy sauce and palm sugar. Gather the meat into a ball and throw it into the bowl; repeat this slapping process several times until the mixture becomes smoother and firmer. (This helps to hold the meat together during the cooking.) Check the seasoning by boiling a little of the mixture in water, then taste and adjust seasoning, if necessary. It should be agreeably rich and salty.

Stuff melon rounds with pork mixture. Bring stock to the boil and season with soy sauce and white sugar. Add melon and poach gently for 10 minutes. Serve sprinkled with pepper and coriander.

ROAST DUCK AND CRABMEAT SOUP WITH TAPIOCA

geng jeut saku

Tapioca is used as a thickener in this soup. Buy the best quality as some unscrupulous manufacturers adulterate tapioca with cheaper starches. Either small or large beads can be used, but in this dish I prefer the larger, more distinct ones.

The Thai way of cooking tapioca is to boil it until a dot of uncooked starch remains in the centre – medium rare, as it were, looking like frogspawn. While the smaller beads may be toothsome cooked this way, the larger ones become both gooey and starchy – inedible, to my taste. I prefer to simmer the tapioca until it is completely cooked and translucent.

3 tablespoons tapioca pearls, large or small

5 cups chicken stock, perhaps with a few bones from the roast duck included

pinch of salt

1 tablespoon oyster sauce

1–2 tablespoons light soy sauce

large pinch of palm sugar

100 g (3 oz) crabmeat

100 g (3 oz) roast duck meat, sliced

1 bunch *bai dtamleung*, snow pea shoots or young spinach leaves

2 spring (green) onions, chopped

1 tablespoon chopped coriander leaves

1 teaspoon deep-fried garlic

pinch of ground white pepper

drizzle of sesame oil

Clean the tapioca of any dust by tossing in a sieve. Bring plenty of water to the boil and whisk in the tapioca, stirring regularly to ensure that it neither clumps nor sticks to the bottom of the pot. Simmer until translucent – about 15 minutes for small tapioca pearls, 30 minutes for larger ones. Drain in a sieve.

Bring stock to the boil and season with salt, oyster sauce, soy sauce and sugar. Skim. Add tapioca, crab, duck and *bai dtamleung*, snow pea shoots or spinach. Heat through, taking care that the soup does not boil. Serve sprinkled with spring onions, coriander, garlic and pepper. The soup should taste salty and a little nutty. Drizzle with sesame oil.

RAMBUTAN AND PORK SOUP WITH CRAB

geng jeut gorn gaew

This recipe is from the unfailing Thanpuuying Pliang Pasonagorn. Its literal name is 'exquisite morsels' or 'precious jewels'. Most of the elaborate dishes from the palaces of Siam were given fanciful names that were meant to amuse and entice with their poetic allusions.

Rambutans are an ideal fruit to be used as a 'casing' in this soup. They are relatively easy to deseed, are not too delicate to stuff and can be cooked without deterioration. I have always found rambutans to have an insipid flavour – as opposed to their spectacular appearance – and so I do not feel that they are spoiled by such treatment.

Recipes such as this require the cook to lavish much time and skill, placing great store in complicated presentation and subtle technique. This is what made the palace cuisine of Siam so remarkable – the triumph of craftsmanship over efficiency. If time is scarce however, rather than dismissing this fine recipe, adapt it by simply rolling the minced pork into small dumplings and poaching them in the soup along with the deseeded rambutans.

50 g (2 oz) minced fatty pork

1 tablespoon light soy sauce

pinch of white sugar

30 g (1 oz) cooked crabmeat

12 rambutans

5 cups chicken stock

pinch of salt

extra 1–2 tablespoons light soy sauce

extra pinch of white sugar

4 spring (green) onions, cut into 2 cm (1 in) lengths

a little minced deep-fried garlic

1 tablespoon coriander leaves

paste

1 coriander root, scraped

pinch of salt

1 garlic clove, peeled

1 slice ginger

5 white peppercorns

a little grated nutmeg

First, make the paste: gradually pound the ingredients together, adding one by one, until smooth. Place pork in a spacious bowl and mix in the paste, seasoning with soy sauce and sugar. Roll the mixture into a ball, pick it up and throw it back into the bowl. Continue until the mixture becomes smoother and firmer. Mix in half the crabmeat. Check seasoning by boiling a little of the mixture in water, then taste and adjust seasoning, if necessary.

Peel the rambutans. With a sharp, small paring knife, tunnel out the seed from the top. Roll the pork mixture into an elongated oval and stuff the rambutans, or use a forcing bag with a medium nozzle to pipe the mixture into the rambutans.

Bring stock to the boil and season with salt, soy sauce and sugar. Add rambutans and poach until firm, a sure indication that the filling is cooked. Finally, add spring onions, deep-fried garlic and remaining crabmeat. Taste for seasoning – it should be salty and rich – and adjust accordingly. Serve sprinkled with coriander.

PORK, CHICKEN AND DRIED PRAWN SOUP FROM CHIANG MAI

geng hang huay

During a formal northern Thai dinner, this rustic soup is often a companion to a dry Chiang Mai Pork Curry (page 324).

4 cups chicken stock

pinch of salt

50 g (2 oz) skinless chicken breast fillet

50 g (2 oz) minced fatty pork

1 tablespoon best-quality dried prawns (shrimp) – ideally homemade
  (see page 151), rinsed

1 small white or brown onion, cut in half and sliced

1 tablespoon sliced Asian celery

1–2 tablespoons fish sauce

pinch of white sugar

1 cup coarsely chopped rosella or sorrel leaves

Bring stock to the boil. Season with salt, add chicken and poach until cooked – about 10 minutes. Remove, cool and then finely shred along the grain. Bring stock back to the boil, skim and add pork, stirring to prevent from clumping. Simmer for a few moments, then add dried prawns, onion, celery and shredded chicken. Season with fish sauce and sugar. Add chopped rosella or sorrel and serve as soon as the leaves are wilted.

CHICKEN, SHIITAKE MUSHROOM AND YOUNG COCONUT SOUP

geng jeut mapraow orn

Sweet young coconut, the nuttiness of deep-fried garlic, the meatiness of fresh shiitake mushrooms, the heady aniseed of Thai basil and the delicacy of chicken gently poached in stock perfumed with pandanus combine to make this soup perhaps the most suave of broths. Delicious as it is, alternatives to the chicken include blanched, shelled yabbies (freshwater crayfish) or crisp deep-fried fish, such as trout or perch. And if the season is right, try some wild mushrooms, like pine mushrooms, blewits, cèpes or the 'turmeric' mushroom of northern Thailand – the chanterelle – in place of the shiitake mushrooms.

3 cups chicken stock

pinch of salt

1 pandanus leaf

1 chicken leg

4 large fresh shiitake mushrooms

1 young green coconut

   or 1 cup coconut flesh and 1 cup coconut water

2 tablespoons light soy sauce

1 teaspoon oyster sauce

pinch of palm sugar

2 teaspoons deep-fried garlic

large handful of Thai basil leaves

Bring stock to the boil. Add salt and pandanus leaf and poach the chicken over a low heat until just cooked, about 20 minutes. Remove, cool, discard skin and shred meat. Slice the mushrooms.

If using a young coconut, remove any excess husk and pierce two holes through the coconut's eyes with a metal skewer. Drain the flavoursome coconut water and set aside. Strike the coconut with the back of a heavy cleaver until it splits in half, then spoon out the soft, gelatinous flesh. With a small knife, pare off any brown, bitter skin and slice the flesh into elegant strips.

Return stock to the boil and skim. Season with soy sauce, oyster sauce and palm sugar. Add mushrooms, simmer gently for a minute, then add all remaining ingredients, including reserved coconut water. This delicate soup should be salty, slightly sweet from the coconut water and pleasantly fragrant from the basil.

MUSLIM OXTAIL SOUP

sup hang wua

This soup comes from the south of Thailand. Various other parts of the beast can also be added to the soup – muzzle, ears, tripe, shank and feet. I like to blanch the oxtail once, even twice, from a cold-water start. This cleans the meat so that it does not cloud the stock, and also considerably reduces the cooking time – by up to 2 hours.

The curry powder used in this soup is excellent for all beef recipes, but for convenience a good-quality bought curry powder can be substituted. Uncommon in the rest of Thai cooking, ghee is often used for frying in the southern Muslim region near the Malay border.

3 kg (6 lb) oxtail, cut into segments and blanched

5 white or brown onions, chopped

5 cups ginger water

pinch of salt

a few bird's eye chillies (scuds), to taste

pinch of ground white pepper

1 tablespoon chopped coriander leaves

3 tablespoons deep-fried shallots – ideally, deep-fried in ghee

lime wedges

curry powder

1 tablespoon black peppercorns

3 tablespoons coriander seeds

3 tablespoons cumin seeds

1 tablespoon cloves

1 tablespoon fennel seeds

20 Thai cardamom pods

15 long pepper – optional

3 tablespoons chilli powder

5 tablespoons ground home-dried ginger

or 2½ tablespoons bought ground ginger

7 tablespoons ground home-dried turmeric

or 3½ tablespoons bought ground turmeric

First, make the curry powder. Wash whole spices, remove any loose husks and chaff, then briefly toast in a heavy pan. Grind using a pestle and mortar or clean coffee grinder, and combine with the chilli, ginger and turmeric powders. Pass through a sieve.

Wash oxtail and place in a pot with the onions. Add 4 heaped tablespoons of the curry powder (store any excess in an airtight container for later use), the ginger water and salt. Cover with water, bring to the boil and simmer until tender, around 3–4 hours. Skim occasionally. The onions should be completely dissolved by the time the oxtail is cooked; if not, lift out and pass through a sieve. If preferred, remove the oxtail from the stock and, when cool enough to handle, take the meat off the bones, return to the soup and gently reheat.

Serve the soup seasoned with chillies, pepper, coriander and deep-fried shallots – it should taste aromatic and rich – and with wedges of lime on the side.

SOUP OF SNAKE GOURD AND EGG

geng jeut buap nguu

This is a simple, cooling soup: a perfect counterbalance to any spicy dish. The best gourd for this soup is called a snake gourd, as it is long, ribbed and curvaceous. Peeled and simmered, this gourd – or any other – blends well in this gentle soup.

1 tablespoon chopped garlic

pinch of salt

1 tablespoon oil

4 cups stock

1–2 tablespoons light soy sauce

pinch of white sugar

1 medium snake gourd (about 150 g or 5 oz), peeled and diagonally sliced

1 egg, very lightly beaten

1 tablespoon dried prawns (shrimp)

1 tablespoon coriander leaves

pinch of ground white pepper

Make a coarse paste with the garlic and salt. Heat oil in a pan and fry garlic until golden. Pour in stock and season with soy sauce and sugar. Bring to the boil, add gourd and simmer for a few minutes, skimming often. When gourd is soft, add egg and dried prawns; continue to simmer until egg is just scrambled. Serve sprinkled with coriander and pepper.

TAMARIND LEAF SOUP

geng jeut dork makaam

This is a refreshingly tart soup made with fresh tamarind leaves and pods. Common in the tropics, these can be difficult to find elsewhere. Sorrel makes an eminently acceptable alternative. To give further depth to the soup, the shallots can be grilled before being added to the paste.

4 cups stock

3 peeled green tamarind pods – optional, but desirable

pinch of salt

large pinch of palm sugar

2 tablespoons light soy or fish sauce

1 cup tamarind leaves *or* 3 cups torn sorrel leaves

100 g (3 oz) uncooked prawns (shrimp) and fish, cleaned and sliced

tamarind water, to taste

1 tablespoon deep-fried garlic

paste

1 tablespoon scraped and chopped coriander root

pinch of salt

2 tablespoons chopped red shallot

½ teaspoon shrimp paste (*gapi*), roasted

6 white peppercorns

First, make the paste: gradually pound the ingredients together until smooth.

Bring stock to the boil with the tamarind pods, if using, and season with salt, palm sugar and soy or fish sauce. Simmer for several minutes. Skim. Dissolve the paste in stock and boil for a moment. Add tamarind leaves, prawns and fish, and poach until cooked. The soup should taste deliciously sour and slightly salty – adjust the seasoning with a little tamarind water, if necessary. Finish with deep-fried garlic.

GLASS NOODLE SOUP WITH PRAWNS, PORK AND CLOUD EAR MUSHROOMS

geng rorn wun sen

This soup from the north of Thailand is an accumulation of tastes and textures that work in concert with each other. In many other cuisines, such a number of ingredients would only clutter and confuse the palate, but here it is simply delicious. If all ingredients cannot be assembled, simply use what can be found; it really won't diminish the quality of the soup. Noodles are rarely eaten with rice in Thailand – this soup is an exception.

1 tablespoon oil or rendered pork fat

4 cups chicken stock

2 tablespoons fish sauce or light soy sauce

pinch of white sugar

50 g (2 oz) minced pork

50 g (2 oz) small uncooked prawns (shrimp), peeled and deveined

50 g (2 oz) glass noodles, soaked in water and then cut into 2 cm (1 in) lengths

6 fresh or rehydrated cloud ear mushrooms, sliced

1 piece of bean curd skin, rehydrated and sliced

2 tablespoons dried lily stalks, rehydrated and then tied in a knot

1 spring (green) onion, finely sliced

1 tablespoon coriander leaves

pinch of ground white pepper

paste

1 teaspoon scraped and chopped coriander root

pinch of salt

1 tablespoon chopped garlic

5 white peppercorns

First, make the paste: using a pestle and mortar, gradually pound the ingredients together until smooth.

Heat oil or rendered pork fat in a pan and fry paste until golden. Add stock and bring to the boil. Season with the fish or soy sauce and sugar. Add pork and simmer, stirring to prevent it clumping. Add prawns and, when they have changed colour, add all remaining ingredients except pepper. Check seasoning – the soup should taste rich and slightly salty. Sprinkle with pepper and serve.

BEEF AND MANGOSTEEN SOUP

dtom neua kho gap mangkut

Fruit is used in all aspects of Thai cooking. At first, it can be unsettling to see fruit combined with meat or fish – sometimes both – yet I know of no other cuisine where such unlikely combinations work so deliciously well. Santol, unripe star fruit (carambola) and even flowers are simmered with pork, chicken, prawns or occasionally beef. One of my favourite versions is a soup of pork ribs simmered with santol, Asian celery and dried prawns.

A little roasted shrimp paste and grilled red shallots can be included in the paste to give this soup another dimension.

100 g (3 oz) beef rump or sirloin
1 tablespoon oil
2 tablespoons fish sauce
4 cups chicken stock
2 tablespoons light soy sauce
pinch of white sugar
3 mangosteens
pinch of ground white pepper
1 tablespoon coriander leaves

paste
1 teaspoon scraped and chopped coriander root
pinch of salt
1 tablespoon chopped garlic
5 white peppercorns

First, make the paste: using a pestle and mortar, gradually pound the ingredients together until smooth.

Cut the beef into small cubes, about 2 cm × 2 cm (1 in × 1 in). Work the paste into the meat and marinate for an hour or so.

Heat a wok, add oil and stir-fry beef briskly and briefly over a very high heat. Add fish sauce, remove meat and set aside to rest.

Bring stock to the boil and season with soy sauce and sugar. Peel and segment mangosteens, and add to the pot, together with the beef. Do not boil, as this will toughen the meat and spoil the colour and savour of the mangosteen. Serve sprinkled with pepper and coriander.

TROUT BRAISED WITH CARAMEL, CELERY AND FISH SAUCE
dtom kem pla sy keun chai

This recipe was included in my first book, *Classic Thai Cuisine*, but it is such a delicious and delicate dish that I must give it again. It is a recipe by Mom Ratchawongse Dteuang Sanitsawongse, whose memorial book has been a steady guide in my unravelling of the complexities of Thai cuisine.

Dtom kem are dishes that can be served either 'wet' or 'dry': they can be served in a lot of the stock or just a little. I am enamoured by the elegance, the taste and the ease of the *dtom kem* style. Although *kem* means salty, this is not the sole taste, as the garlic and pepper paste imparts a nutty pepperiness and the caramelised palm sugar gives a rich, sweet depth to the dish.

The original recipe calls for *pla chorn*, a pink-fleshed freshwater fish that abounds in Thailand and its cuisine but is unknown outside South East Asia. I think that trout makes an excellent alternative, although any fish, from perch to barramundi, or even prawns and lobster, can be used. Rather than celery, peeled and sliced fresh sugar cane can be used to introduce a rich, raw sweetness to the braise – but then reduce the palm sugar by half.

1 tablespoon oil

3 tablespoons palm sugar

3 tablespoons fish sauce

stock or water

1 medium trout, brook trout or Murray perch – about 250 g (8 oz) – whole or filleted

2 tablespoons chopped Asian celery

2 red shallots, peeled and finely sliced

1 tablespoon coriander leaves

pinch of ground white pepper

paste

2 teaspoons scraped and chopped coriander root

pinch of salt

1 tablespoon chopped garlic

10 white peppercorns

First, make the paste: using a pestle and mortar, gradually pound the ingredients together until smooth.

Heat oil in a pan then fry the paste until fragrant and golden. Add sugar and when it has begun to caramelise – be careful, it burns very quickly – add fish sauce. Add stock or water to cover and, when it has come to the boil, add fish and celery. Cover with extra boiling liquid and just barely simmer on a very, very low

heat until cooked: 2–3 minutes for a fillet, 5–10 minutes for a whole fish. Remove from heat and allow to rest for a few minutes in a warm place. Check seasoning – it should taste salty and sweet – and adjust accordingly. Serve sprinkled with shallots, coriander and pepper.

DUCK AND SPRING ONION SOUP
bpet dtom bai horm

This soup is a good deal more complex than the preceding recipes. The addition of pungent, roasted coriander seeds to the paste, the sweet sharpness of spring onions and the tartness of vinegar give the soup a greater dimension, enabling it to handle the richness of the simmered duck. Braising the bird on the bone gives flavour to the broth and prevents the meat shrinking during its cooking; deep-frying the meat gives a deep mahogany colour to the skin and removes excess fat.

200 g (6 oz) duck on the bone, roughly chopped into 2 cm (1 in) cubes
2 tablespoons sweet soy sauce (*kecap manis*)
oil for deep-frying
6 cups chicken stock
pinch of salt
2–3 tablespoons white sugar
4 tablespoons coconut vinegar
2 tablespoons fish sauce
1 small bunch spring (green) onions, diagonally cut into 2 cm (1 in) lengths

paste
2 teaspoons scraped and chopped coriander root
pinch of salt
2 tablespoons chopped garlic
10 white peppercorns
2 teaspoons coriander seeds, roasted

First, make the paste: using a pestle and mortar, gradually pound the ingredients together until smooth.

Marinate duck in soy sauce for about 10 minutes. Deep-fry in plenty of oil until golden, remove and leave to rest. Meanwhile, fry paste in a tablespoon of the oil until fragrant and golden. Add stock and bring to the boil. Season with salt, add duck and, when the soup has returned to the boil, add sugar, vinegar and fish sauce. Simmer, skimming regularly. When duck is almost cooked (about 25 minutes), add spring onions and continue to simmer until they have wilted. The soup should taste rich and just slightly sweet, sour and salty – adjust seasoning accordingly before serving.

MURRAY PERCH AND MUSHROOM SOUP WITH YELLOW BEANS

dtom het dtow jiaw

In Thailand after the rainy season, the north abounds in mushrooms; one variety, *het kone*, is eaten with great pleasure in salads, curries, and soups such as this one. As it is not commonly available outside Thailand, any mushroom can be used in this soup, but make sure it has some character and flavour – like a pine mushroom, cèpe or other wild mushroom.

A small frigate mackerel, *pla tuu* – the national fish of Thailand – is most often used for this soup, but is not always available elsewhere. I think a Murray perch or cod is the best substitute; salted beef or pork, fresh chicken, frog or yabbies (freshwater crayfish) can also be used.

oil or rendered pork fat for deep-frying

150 g (5 oz) Murray perch or cod fillet

2 tablespoons yellow bean sauce, rinsed

large pinch of palm sugar

5 cups chicken stock

handful of shredded young ginger

100 g (3 oz) mushrooms, torn into bite-size pieces

splash of light soy sauce, tamarind water, lime juice or vinegar – optional

2 spring (green) onions, chopped

1 tablespoon chopped coriander leaves

paste

1 tablespoon scraped and chopped coriander root

pinch of salt

2 tablespoons chopped red shallot

10 white peppercorns

First, make the paste: using a pestle and mortar, gradually pound the ingredients together until smooth.

Heat oil or rendered pork fat and deep-fry fish until crisp and golden. Put to one side. Drain all but 2 tablespoons of the oil and fry the paste until fragrant. Add yellow bean sauce and continue to fry, at a lower heat, until it too is fragrant. Season with palm sugar and, when beginning to colour, add stock. Bring to the boil, add ginger and mushrooms and simmer for a few minutes. Check the seasoning: the soup should taste of ginger and yellow beans, but not be too salty. (If more salt is needed, add light soy sauce – and perhaps a little tamarind water, or a drop of lime juice or vinegar to clean up the flavours.) Add fish and finish with spring onions and coriander.

PORK SHIN WITH PEANUTS

geng hong khaa muu gap tua lii song

This style of soup, a *geng hong*, shows how close Thai soups can be to thick braises. Sometimes a clear and fragrant broth is served in the same meal as this soup – any *geng jeut* would be appropriate. This may seem surprising until this rich, thick and slightly bitter dish has been tasted. The richness is counterbalanced by the bitterness of the peanuts. Both nutty and sumptuous, this soup is a perfect foil to the heat and fury of other dishes; it calms the palate and works well with hot or sour foods.

Traditionally this dish is made with pork hocks. Hocks pose a problem for some cooks, however: they can be quite fatty; the skin can separate from the meat during braising; and while some may have plenty of meat, others are just skin. They need attentive preparation before the actual cooking of the soup. As briefly as possible, here is the elaborate technique we used at Darley Street Thai restaurant. First, blanch the hocks twice from a cold-water start. Allow to cool, then deep-fry the hocks and immediately plunge them into cold water. This swells the skin and helps prevent it bursting during the braising. Next – but this is optional – deep-fry the hocks a second time to improve the colour of the meat, so the finished soup does not look too pale. Braise for 1–1½ hours, and then the hocks are ready for the recipe.

A simpler, more convenient ingredient is pork shin. Other variations include chicken braised in the same base but garnished with knotted Chinese lily stalks; or a freshwater fish, like trout or Murray perch, with bamboo shoots.

100 g (3 oz) peanuts

200 g (6 oz) pork shin *or* 1 pork hock, prepared as described above

1 tablespoon oil

1 tablespoon palm sugar

2 tablespoons light soy sauce

3 tablespoons Chinese rice wine – optional

1 cup stock

1 tablespoon coriander leaves

paste

1 tablespoon scraped and chopped coriander root

5 slices ginger

3 slices galangal

1 teaspoon salt

3 cloves garlic, chopped

2 red shallots, chopped

10 white peppercorns

½ star anise, roasted and ground

2 tablespoons yellow bean sauce, rinsed

Soak the peanuts in salted water for 30 minutes, then rinse in several changes of water. Blanch from a cold-water start, drain and allow to cool. Deep-fry in oil until golden; this is optional, but it gives the peanuts a good colour.

If using pork shin, blanch and refresh, then remove the shinbone and cut meat into medium cubes. If using a blanched, deep-fried and braised hock, take the meat from the bone and cube.

Make the paste: using a pestle and mortar, gradually pound the ingredients together until smooth. Heat a pot, add the oil and fry the paste until the garlic is golden and fragrant. Season with palm sugar, light soy sauce and, if using, the Chinese wine. Add pork and peanuts. Cover with stock and braise, covered, until all is cooked – about 1 hour. Add extra stock if necessary.

Check seasoning: the soup should taste rich, slightly bitter and not too salty. Serve sprinkled with coriander.

MUSSEL AND GINGER SOUP

dtom som hoi malaeng puu

A *dtom som* is a soup of gentle complexity, full of the hearty taste of ginger, although sometimes pineapple or another sour fruit is used – *som* means 'sour'.

Any freshwater fish or seafood works admirably in this soup. The fish can be dried, salted, deep-fried, grilled or just left plain before it is added to the simmering, seasoned stock. Clams, any other shellfish, pork, chicken, mushrooms, fermented bamboo shoots or bean curd can also be used, individually or perhaps in a medley. In northern regions, *grachai* is substituted for the ginger. Occasionally the soup is finished with deep-fried shallots. A well-rounded seasoning is the only thing to remain constant in this most versatile of soups.

1 tablespoon oil or rendered pork fat

2 tablespoons palm sugar

2 tablespoons tamarind water

2 tablespoons fish sauce

2 cups chicken stock

½ cup shredded ginger

200 g (6 oz) mussels, cleaned and debearded

3 spring (green) onions, cut into 2 cm (1 in) lengths

1 tablespoon coriander leaves

pinch of ground white pepper

paste

1 teaspoon scraped and chopped coriander root

pinch of salt

1 tablespoon chopped garlic

1 tablespoon chopped red shallot

1 tablespoon chopped ginger

¼ teaspoon shrimp paste (*gapi*)

10 white peppercorns

First, make the paste: using a pestle and mortar, gradually pound the ingredients together until smooth.

Heat oil or rendered pork fat and fry paste over a moderate heat until fragrant and beginning to turn a light golden colour. Add sugar and simmer for a minute, then add tamarind water and fish sauce. Pour in stock and add half the ginger. When the soup has come to the boil, add mussels and turn down the heat to a simmer until they have opened (discard any that remain stubbornly closed). Add the other half of the ginger and the spring onions. Check seasoning – the soup should taste equally sweet, sour and salty – and adjust accordingly. On serving, sprinkle with coriander and pepper.

BARRAMUNDI, GINGER AND GREEN MANGO SOUP

pla grapong kao dtom king brung

This soup is an example of the degree of complexity Thai soups can reach. Sour, hot and salty is the simple seasoning guide, but that doesn't do justice to its intricacies of taste. It is a poised balance between the pungently flavoured pickled vegetables, the succulence of green mango and the sweetness of pickled garlic.

200 g (6 oz) barramundi, sea bass, salmon or trout fillets

2 tablespoons fish sauce

1 tablespoon white sugar

pinch of ground white pepper

2 teaspoons scraped and chopped coriander root

pinch of salt

1 tablespoon chopped garlic

6–10 white peppercorns

6 long red or green chillies

oil for frying

4 cups stock

1–2 tablespoons palm sugar

2 tablespoons tamarind water

2 tablespoons fish sauce

½ cup pickled garlic syrup

5 cloves pickled garlic, finely sliced

1 cup Pickled Siamese Watercress (page 388) or pickled mustard greens, rinsed

2 tablespoons shredded ginger

1 small green mango, julienned

3 tablespoons minced deep-fried garlic

1 tablespoon coriander leaves

Clean the fish, then marinate in fish sauce, sugar and pepper overnight. Remove and dry on a rack in a warm place or in the sun for several hours.

Using a pestle and mortar, gradually pound coriander root, salt, garlic and peppercorns together until you have a smooth paste.

Lightly pound chillies to break the skin, so they won't explode when they are cooked. Grill, deep-fry or shallow-fry the dried fish and the chillies separately, then set aside.

Heat 1–2 tablespoons of oil, add paste and fry until golden and fragrant. Pour in stock and season with sugar, tamarind water, fish sauce, pickled garlic syrup and cooked chillies. Simmer for a few minutes, then add pickled garlic and pickled vegetables. After another minute, add the fish, crumbling it into the broth, together with the ginger, green mango and deep-fried garlic. Check the seasoning: it should taste salty, sour and hot. Serve sprinkled with coriander.

CHINESE TONIC SOUP

gai dtam dtun yaa jin

This next category of soup is of Chinese extraction, and was made popular in Thailand by migrants who arrived in Siam over several centuries. The method itself is quite simple: the requisite ingredients are assembled, then covered with boiling stock and steamed for several hours. This technique is called *dtun* and, significantly, is called the same in Thai and Chinese.

The prolonged method of cooking was developed to extract as much goodness as possible from the ingredients. A black-skinned bantam chicken is the standard chicken for this soup; it is believed to be more nutritious than other breeds. Most Thai subscribe to the Chinese medical philosophy, seeing food as a palliative medicine. Often some Chinese medicine is added to the soup: go to a herbalist and have a specific medicine prescribed, or just ask for a general tonic at a Chinese medicine shop.

This is a suave soup – and medicine has never tasted so good.

5 dried shiitake mushrooms

1 teaspoon oyster sauce

2 slices ginger

pinch of palm sugar

1 small black silky chicken, spatchcock, poussin or Cornish game hen –
    about 400 g (12 oz)

2 garlic cloves, unpeeled

1 coriander root, scraped

1 star anise

1 small piece dried orange peel

1 small green gourd, peeled, cubed and steeped in hydrolysed lime water

pinch of salt

1 tablespoon crushed yellow rock sugar

½ pandanus leaf

1 small packet Chinese medicine or general tonic

1 tablespoon oyster sauce

2 tablespoons light soy sauce

6 cups boiling stock or water

drizzle of sesame oil

1 tablespoon chopped spring (green) onion

1 tablespoon coriander leaves

pinch of ground white pepper

Rinse dried mushrooms and put in a pan with the teaspoon of oyster sauce, one slice of the ginger and the palm sugar. Cover with water, bring to the boil and simmer for 10 minutes or until tender. Cool and destem the mushrooms (keep the stalks for stock), reserving the braising liquid.

Remove the legs from the chicken and cut each into three. Remove breast cage from backbone and chop in half lengthwise. Cut each half into three.

In a pan, combine the chicken, garlic, the remaining slice of ginger, coriander root, star anise, orange zest, gourd, salt, sugar, pandanus leaf, Chinese medicine or tonic, the tablespoon of oyster sauce and the soy sauce. Pour in the boiling stock or water and reserved mushroom liquid, cover and simmer for 1½ hours. If the bird is then tender and the broth clear and fragrant, it is ready; if not, simmer for a little longer. Allow to rest for a few minutes and skim off excess fat (although the Chinese would not).

Serve sprinkled with sesame oil, spring onion, coriander and pepper.

DOUBLE-STEAMED DUCK SOUP WITH PICKLED LIMES

bpet dtun manao dong

There was an old Chinese restaurant near Lumpini Park in Bangkok that was renowned for cooking this style of soup. Steamer after steamer lined the entrance, and each contained a different version of this comforting, efficacious soup: chicken with lotus seeds and dried orange zest, tripe and red dates, venison with cassia bark, goose in Chinese wine, pork with bitter melon, bêche de mer with seaweed and dried fish with ginger.

DOUBLE-STEAMED DUCK SOUP WITH PICKLED LIMES

Sadly, it has been demolished. In the quest to modernise Bangkok, many of its culinary landmarks – ramshackle food stalls selling the most pungently authentic Thai food and musty Chinese restaurants with their exotics – have been closed.

2 duck legs *or* 1 whole duck

3–4 tablespoons sweet soy sauce (*kecap manis*)

1 star anise, ground

oil for deep-frying

1–2 cabbage leaves

1 small green gourd, peeled, deseeded and chopped into 5 cm (2 in) pieces

1 pickled lime, with ½ cup of pickling liquid

5 cm (2 in) piece cassia bark, roasted

1 piece dried orange peel

6 cups boiling chicken stock

3 tablespoons light soy sauce

1 tablespoon oyster sauce

small piece yellow rock sugar, crushed

pinch of ground white pepper

1 tablespoon coriander leaves

Chop each of the duck legs into three pieces. If using a whole duck, remove the legs and do the same, then cut down the bottom of the rib cage and remove the back-bone. Chop the breast in half lengthwise and then cut diagonally into three. Marinate duck in the *kecap manis* and ground star anise for about 5 minutes.

Deep-fry duck until dark brown, to enrich the soup; don't worry if it looks burnt – it's just the *kecap manis* caramelising. Drain. (The deep-frying is optional, but it helps to prevent the duck looking too anaemic in the finished soup.) Line a large, deep bowl with cabbage leaves and add the duck, gourd, whole pickled lime, cassia and orange peel. Cover with boiling stock and season with soy sauce, oyster sauce and sugar. Cover tightly with foil and steam for 2–3 hours, checking the water level in the steamer at regular intervals.

Serve sprinkled with pepper and coriander.

HOT AND SOUR PRAWN SOUP

dtom yam gung

To most people *dtom yam* is this ubiquitous hot and sour Thai soup of prawns, but *dtom yam* in fact encompasses a vast range of dishes, from the extremely basic to the highly complex – *dtom* simply means to 'boil' and *yam* to 'mix' or 'toss together'. At its most easily identifiable, a *dtom yam* is a soup that is flavoured with lemongrass, perfumed by kaffir lime leaves, and seasoned with lime juice, fish sauce and chillies, usually resulting in a balance that is salty, sour and hot.

Perhaps the dish that is most widely associated with Thai cooking, this soup seems to appear on every Thai restaurant menu throughout the world. When done well, it is very easy to understand why it has become a culinary classic. Sadly, when poorly executed the soup is little better than a culinary cliché. This can be avoided simply by using good ingredients: freshly squeezed lime juice, pungent bird's eye chillies, fresh kaffir lime leaves and lemongrass. One important technique I have learnt is to season the soup in the serving bowl – this way, the lime juice is never boiled and thus remains vibrantly sour. As with all *dtom yam*, the seasoning is hot, sour and salty, although this can be adjusted to suit individual preferences.

This recipe and the one for Hot and Sour Barramundi Soup (page 259) both come from a distant cousin of Queen Sirikit, Mom Ratchawongse Gidtinakdaa Gitdtiyargon, a cook of some renown. He suggests making a prawn stock by boiling the shells and especially the flavoursome prawn heads. He believes that simmering them in water with some salt will extract a deeper, richer flavour from their delicious tomalley. As a result, an attractive red-hued oil will float and dapple the surface. This, Khun Gidtinakdaa counsels, is a very desirable thing.

Khun Gidtinakdaa also suggests an alternative, where the cleaned prawns are placed in the serving bowl and briefly marinated in the lime juice, fish sauce and chillies. The boiling soup is poured over them and then the seasoning adjusted. The prawns are thus barely cooked and have a delicious texture.

10 uncooked prawns (shrimp), unpeeled

4 cups water

large pinch of salt

1 tablespoon fish sauce

3–7 bird's eye chillies (scuds)

2 stalks lemongrass, chopped

3 kaffir lime leaves, torn

3 tablespoons lime juice

extra fish sauce, to taste

handful of coriander leaves

Peel and devein the prawns, reserving the heads and shells. Give these a quick rinse and put them in a pan of salted water. Bring to the boil and simmer until the stock has a red hue and there is a smear of oil floating on top – but do not cook for longer than 15–20 minutes, or the flavour will be dulled. Strain, pressing the shells against the sieve to extract as much of the stock as possible. Return stock to the boil and season with fish sauce. Bruise the scuds and then the lemongrass using a pestle and mortar. Add lemongrass to the stock, along with lime leaves. Add prawns and simmer until they have just changed colour. In a serving bowl, mix together the lime juice, extra fish sauce, bruised chillies and coriander. Ladle in the soup and check the seasoning – it should be salty, sour and hot.

HOT AND SOUR SOUP OF CLAMS WITH CHILLIES AND LIME

dtom yam hoi nahm sai

In Hua Hin, on the gulf coast of southern Thailand, I had a *dtom yam* of austere simplicity, a clear liquid that highlighted the prime quality of its ingredients. Stock was brought to the boil, a little salt and some freshly caught clams were thrown in, then it was finished with lime juice and a chilli or two. Each ingredient worked with every other one. It was not fiery, as the chilli was used only to add a hint of piquancy. There was no fish sauce – that would have been too strong – just salt. Lime juice was used to define the flavours, not as a strong flavouring in itself. Altogether, it was an exercise of restraint in seasoning. Here is my version of it.

> 200 g (6 oz) clams, mussels or pipis
> 4 cups stock
> pinch of salt
> pinch of white sugar
> squeeze of lime juice
> a few bird's eye chillies (scuds), bruised
> 1 tablespoon coriander leaves

Scrub the clams. Bring stock to the boil, add salt and sugar to taste, then add clams and simmer until just opened (discard any that remain closed). Season with lime juice and bruised scuds. The soup should taste salty, sour and hot. Serve scattered with coriander.

HOT AND SOUR BARRAMUNDI SOUP

dtom yam pla grapong kao

This soup is Mom Ratchawongse Gidtinakdaa's pride – he has cooked it for the King of Thailand.

What is unusual about this recipe is that flesh from the bones, tail and head of the fish is scraped off after the stock has been made and then puréed and returned to the simmering soup to enhance the flavour and thicken it slightly.

If barramundi is unavailable, use sea bass, snapper, whiting or Murray cod. The chilli jam adds an attractive hue and greater depth of flavour – do not stir it into the soup, just let it float on top.

250 g (8 oz) whole barramundi or sea bass

1–2 tablespoons salt

4 cups water

a pinch of white sugar

1 tablespoon tamarind water

pinch of roasted chilli powder

3 stalks lemongrass, chopped and crushed

3 kaffir lime leaves, torn

2 tablespoons fish sauce, plus extra to taste

3 tablespoons lime juice

2–6 bird's eye chillies (scuds), pounded

1 tablespoon Chilli Jam (page 200)

Fillet and finely slice the fish. Wash the fish bones and rub vigorously with plenty of salt. Leave for several minutes then rinse. Bring water to the boil, add fish head and bones and boil until the flesh is cooked – no more than 20 minutes. Strain, retaining stock. When fish head and bones are cool enough to handle, scrape flesh from them and pound into a paste.

Return stock to the boil, season with sugar, tamarind water and chilli powder, then add 2 tablespoons of the fish paste, lemongrass, lime leaves and the 2 tablespoons of fish sauce. Put finely sliced fish into a sieve and dip into the simmering stock several times, until the flesh is just cooked.

In a serving bowl, mix the extra fish sauce with lime juice and chillies, add the fish and then ladle over the soup. Check the seasoning, and adjust to your taste – my preference is salty and sour and hot. Add the chilli jam.

HOT AND SOUR SOUP OF SHREDDED CHICKEN AND LEMONGRASS

dtom jiw gai

4 cups chicken stock

pinch of salt

pinch of palm sugar

4 slices galangal

2 stalks lemongrass, trimmed

3 red shallots, peeled

2 kaffir lime leaves, torn

200 g (6 oz) skinless chicken breast or thigh fillets

3 tablespoons lime juice

3 tablespoons fish sauce

4 bird's eye chillies (scuds), bruised

3 tablespoons finely sliced lemongrass

2 tablespoons finely sliced red shallot

5 kaffir lime leaves, finely shredded

1 tablespoon coriander leaves

Bring stock to the boil and season with salt and sugar. Add galangal, whole lemongrass and shallots and torn lime leaves. Simmer for a few minutes, add chicken and simmer until cooked – about 5 minutes. Remove, cool slightly and then coarsely shred. Strain stock, discarding the aromatics, and return to the boil. In a serving bowl, combine lime juice, fish sauce and chillies. Add chicken and pour over the boiling stock. Stir in sliced lemongrass and shallots and shredded lime leaves. Check the seasoning: it should taste equally hot, sour and salty.

Serve sprinkled with coriander.

HOT AND SOUR CRAYFISH SOUP WITH TAMARIND LEAVES

dtom klong gung nahm jeut

A *dtom klong* is very similar to a *dtom yam*, except that it is seasoned by sour fruit or leaves, but never with lime juice. It is quite rustic and was traditionally made only with shallots and a dried fish, *pla salit*. To make the authentic version, grill the *pla salit* along with the other ingredients, then fillet it before adding to the soup. This can be done quite quickly by standing the fish upright and pressing down on it with the side of a large knife or cleaver. The meat pulls away from the bone and can be lifted off.

Pla grop (crisp fish) also makes a delectable soup, as does Dried Smoked Trout Fillet (page 179) or prawns. However, since this soup has its origins in the northern central plains, I think freshwater crayfish or yabbies are ideal.

12 large freshwater crayfish or yabbies

4 dried or fresh long chillies

2 stalks lemongrass, trimmed

5 red shallots, unpeeled

4 cups stock

pinch of salt

1 bunch washed tamarind leaves *or* 2 bunches sorrel

palm sugar, to taste – optional

2 tablespoons tamarind water

2 tablespoons fish sauce

Blanch the crayfish or yabbies in plenty of salted boiling water. Refresh in very cold or iced water. Shell and devein. Scrape out any tomalley from heads and purée. Grill the chillies and lemongrass until charred and the shallots until soft. When cool enough to handle, peel the shallots. >

Bring stock to the boil and add salt, chillies, lemongrass, shallots, tamarind or sorrel leaves and the yabbies or crayfish with their tomalley. Season with sugar, if using, tamarind water and fish sauce. The soup should taste salty, sour and as hot as desired.

SPICY CHICKEN SOUP WITH COCONUT

dtom gai maprao pao

In the markets of Thailand, young coconuts of every variety are always available. Sometimes they are even roasted in embers, which gives a delicious smoky, sweet and nutty flavour to the meat. Desirable though this is, it can be dangerous since coconuts have been known to explode as they roast. Here is a recipe that approximates the taste and is certainly safer.

> 1 young coconut
> 2–5 bird's eye chillies (scuds), bruised
> 3 cups chicken stock
> pinch of salt
> 5 large oyster mushrooms, torn
> 4 kaffir lime leaves
> 200 g (6 oz) skinless chicken breast or thigh fillets, sliced
> 2 tablespoons coarsely shredded *pak chii farang* (long-leaf coriander)
> 1–2 tablespoons fish sauce
> large pinch of palm sugar
> 2–3 tablespoons lime juice

Open the coconut, reserving its water. Coarsely chop the coconut flesh and grill or dry-fry to colour the surface. At the same time, grill the chillies. Bring stock to the boil and add salt, coconut water and flesh, mushrooms, lime leaves and chicken. Simmer until chicken is cooked – about 2 or 3 minutes. Season with *pak chii farang*, chillies, fish sauce, sugar and lime juice; the soup should taste hot, salty, smoky and sour.

MUSHROOM SOUP WITH CHILLIES

dtom het bpa gap prik dam

This recipe shows how close Thai soups can be to simple curries, especially those from the north. Interestingly, the paste in this dish can either be dissolved in the broth or served as a sauce to be eaten with the simmered mushrooms. If the paste is eaten on the side, I like to add a handful of shredded ginger to the broth. Mushrooms are generally simmered with salt, rather than fish sauce, since the Thai believe that mushrooms all too easily acquire a fishy taint from the sauce.

In Thailand, edible fungi come mainly from the northern half of the country, from the hills, forests and nearby streams, clustered around trees in their cool shade. There myriad varieties grow, mainly russula and boletus. Some grow in ash or rice straw, others on termite mounds; some varieties are oval and dark and covered in fine fuzz; others, however, look more comfortingly familiar, like a champignon. They are collected in the morning, and some varieties are so perishable that they must be eaten for lunch on the day they are gathered. Very often they are simply rubbed with salt and wrapped in banana leaves with some lemon basil, then grilled and eaten with a sauce. Depending on the variety, they may also be used in a salad, relish or curry, or even this soup.

100 g (3 oz) assorted mushrooms – pine, cèpe, chanterelle, chestnut, for example
4 cups stock
pinch of salt
handful of shredded ginger – optional
handful of chopped coriander leaves
handful of chopped spring (green) onion

paste
3 dried long red chillies
3 red shallots, unpeeled
2 garlic cloves, unpeeled
4 slices galangal
½ teaspoon shrimp paste (*gapi*), roasted
pinch of salt

First, make the paste. Grill chillies, shallots, garlic and galangal until golden. Peel shallots and garlic; deseed chillies if desired. Using a pestle and mortar, gradually pound all the ingredients together until smooth.

Tear or cut mushrooms into bite-size pieces. Bring stock to the boil, add salt, mushrooms and ginger, if using, and simmer until cooked. Dissolve paste in stock and simmer for a moment. Check seasoning: the soup should taste salty, smoky and a little hot. Serve sprinkled with coriander and spring onion.

DRIED PRAWN AND COCONUT SOUP WITH PUMPKIN
geng dtom gati fak tong

The final style of Thai soup is enriched with coconut cream. There are two kinds, *dtom gati* and *dtom khaa*, literally meaning 'boiled coconut cream' and 'boiled galangal'. Such soups are less highly seasoned than *dtom yam* or *dtom klong*, in order to maintain their lusciousness. They are delicious – creamy yet tart.

This a simple yet sumptuous soup. If using fresh prawns, you might want to make a prawn stock, following the recipe for Hot and Sour Prawn Soup (page 256). However, a light chicken stock is best with dried prawns.

3 cups coconut milk

1 cup stock or water

pinch of salt

pinch of white sugar

½ cup cubed pumpkin

10 best-quality dried prawns (shrimp), rinsed

    or 10 fresh uncooked prawns (shrimp), peeled and deveined

pinch of ground white pepper

paste

1 tablespoon ground dried prawns (shrimp)

pinch of salt

4 red shallots, chopped

3 coriander roots, scraped and chopped

8 white peppercorns

First, make the paste: using a pestle and mortar, gradually pound the ingredients together until smooth. Bring coconut milk and stock or water to the boil. Season with salt and sugar, then dissolve the paste in it. Add pumpkin and, if using, the dried prawns. Simmer until both pumpkin and prawns are tender. If using fresh prawns, add them just before serving and simmer until they change colour. Check seasoning – the soup should taste creamy, salty and just a little sweet – sprinkle with pepper and serve.

LOTUS STALK, MACKEREL AND COCONUT SOUP

dtom gati sai bua

The lotus plant is one of the main symbols of Buddhism, expressing the path of knowledge. The bulb is rooted in the dark, thick mud at the bottom of a river or lake. As it grows, the stalk progresses through murky water heading towards the light. When it surfaces and is exposed to the sun, the plant bursts into magnificent flower. Lotus plants line the rivers and canals of the countryside and, while respectfully aware of their symbolism, the Thai also have healthy appetites and the succulent crunchiness of the stalks proves irresistible. Happily no blasphemy is committed when the stalks are eaten – they are normally sold in the market in reels, a few lengths being wound together. Eaten alone, lotus stalks have a spongy texture and nondescript taste. However, when simmered in richly seasoned coconut cream, the stalks absorb the flavours.

To counterbalance the rich, sumptuous taste of simmered coconut cream, various sour fruit and vegetables are regular components in this style of soup. An unusual item in this recipe is the fresh *madan*, a small, sour cucumber-like fruit. More readily available alternatives include fresh, unripe, peeled tamarind pods, tamarind or rosella leaves, fermented bamboo shoots or pickled *madan*. In the south, this style of soup is coloured with fresh turmeric and soured with assam or green pineapple. Often fresh cashew nuts are added.

100 g (3 oz) fresh lotus stalks
3 cups coconut milk
2 small *madan* (sour cucumber)
   or 2 fresh tamarind pods, peeled and bruised
pinch of salt
1 tablespoon white sugar
3 red shallots, bruised
150 g (5 oz) mackerel
1 cup coconut cream

Peel the lotus stalks by simply stripping the skin off with a sharp paring knife, chop into 2 cm (1 in) lengths then steep in fresh water. Bring coconut milk to the boil, add *madan* or bruised tamarind pods. Simmer until the *madan* have dissolved, or, if using the tamarind, simmer for several minutes while it releases its sourness (before serving, remove seeds or pods with a spoon). Add salt, sugar, red shallots, mackerel and lotus stalks. Simmer until fish is cooked – about 5 minutes. One of the important characteristics of this soup is that the coconut milk should not sepa-rate; if it looks as if it is about to, pour in some water or stock to prevent this. Finish with the coconut cream.

The soup should taste sweet, creamy, salty and sour.

RED EMPEROR, TURMERIC AND COCONUT SOUP
dtom gati pla grapong dtaeng

This is a rich southern Thai version of this style of soup, tempered by *som kaek*, a sour, semi-dried fruit readily available in Asian food stores, where it is normally sold under the name 'assam'. Should it be unobtainable, try shredded green mango, green pineapple, green papaya, soured banana blossoms or fermented bamboo shoots.

Turmeric, a signature ingredient of southern Thai food, imparts a golden colour and a slightly bitter or medicinal taste. I sometimes add a few torn 'betel' leaves to this soup, which not only provide a colour contrast but also a pleas-ing spiciness. Red emperor is ideal but any firm-fleshed ocean fish will go well in this soup, as would prawns, scallops, mussels or clams.

2 cups coconut milk

1 cup chicken, vegetable or fish stock

2–3 teaspoons white sugar

pinch of salt

2 stalks lemongrass, trimmed and cut into lengths

1 cm (½ in) piece fresh turmeric, peeled

3 red shallots, peeled

2 garlic cloves, peeled

5–10 bird's eye chillies (scuds)

100 g (3 oz) fillet of red emperor, turbot or red mullet

5 slices 'assam' (*som kaek*) – optional

1 cup coconut cream

a little fish sauce

Bring coconut milk and stock to the boil. Season with sugar and salt. Using a pestle and mortar, bruise lemongrass, turmeric, shallots, garlic and chillies, then add to simmering stock. Add fish and assam, if using, then simmer until cooked. Before serving, enrich soup with coconut cream. It should taste hot, creamy, sour and salty. Add fish sauce, if necessary.

SMOKED FISH AND COCONUT SOUP

dtom gati pla grop

This soup should taste smoky and rich from the coconut cream simmered with the *pla grop*. There should be a pleasant, slight bitterness from the banana blossom, and a perfume from the addition of the aromatic kaffir lime leaves and lemongrass. Sometimes the soup is enriched with a coarse chilli paste made from three grilled red shallots pounded with three grilled garlic cloves and four grilled dried red chillies; a more refined addition is Deep-fried Chilli and Garlic Sauce (page 271).

5 *pla grop* (crisp fish)

1 banana blossom – raw, grilled or pickled, as preferred

1 cup coconut cream

2 cups coconut milk

1 cup water or stock

2 stalks lemongrass, trimmed and cut into lengths

3 red shallots, peeled

4 kaffir lime leaves, torn

pinch of salt

2 tablespoons fish sauce

a little palm sugar, to taste

1–2 tablespoons tamarind water

Toast *pla grop*, then fillet and set aside the flesh. Shred banana blossom quite finely on an angle and place in acidulated water.

Combine coconut cream, coconut milk and water or stock in a large pan. Bring to the boil. Bruise lemongrass and shallots using a pestle and mortar, then add to soup, along with the lime leaves. Season with salt, fish sauce, palm sugar and tamarind water. Add fish and simmer for 5 minutes or until it is tender.

Drain shredded banana blossom, squeezing to extract as much water as possible. Add to soup and continue to simmer for a few more minutes.

CHICKEN AND GALANGAL SOUP

dtom khaa gai

This is one of the best known of Thai soups, and deservedly so. There is a wonderful interplay between the richness of the coconut cream – which is slightly separated by being boiled – the peppery galangal and the sour finish. Although this soup's name means 'boiled galangal', it has become associated in most people's minds with chicken. However, many other ingredients can be used in a *dtom khaa*: fish, shellfish, mushrooms of all kinds, quail and pork are some possibilities.

2 cups chicken stock

1 cup coconut milk

1 cup coconut cream

pinch of salt

1 teaspoon palm sugar

2 stalks lemongrass, trimmed

3 red shallots, peeled

2 coriander roots, scraped

2–3 bird's eye chillies (scuds)

10 slices galangal

3 kaffir lime leaves

100 g (3 oz) chanterelles, straw or oyster mushrooms, torn

100 g (3 oz) skinless chicken breast or thigh fillets, sliced

2–3 tablespoons fish sauce

1 tablespoon lime juice

extra 4–5 bird's eye chillies (scuds), bruised

1 tablespoon coriander leaves

In a pan, combine stock with coconut milk and cream. Bring to the boil, season with salt and sugar. Bruise lemongrass, shallots, coriander roots and scuds using a pestle and mortar. Add to boiling stock, along with galangal and lime leaves. Simmer for a few minutes, then add mushrooms and chicken, turn down the heat and continue to simmer until chicken is cooked. In a serving bowl, mix fish sauce, lime juice, extra scuds and coriander. Ladle in the soup, stir and check seasoning – it should taste rich, salty, sour and hot.

COCONUT AND GALANGAL SOUP WITH TROUT

dtom khaa pla

This final version of a *dtom khaa* pounds the main ingredients together to form a paste, which is then dissolved in the soup. At this stage, it becomes quite hard to distinguish between what might be described as a curry and a soup such as this. The boundaries become increasingly blurred.

This recipe is from Mom Chao Janjaroen Rachani; unfortunately there is little information about her, except that she was a descendant of the last *uparaja*, or Second King of Bangkok. Her original recipe called for chicken, but I have successfully made it using pheasant, rabbit and trout.

2 cups coconut milk

1 cup stock

pinch of salt

1 tablespoon palm sugar

10 slices galangal

4 kaffir lime leaves, torn

150 g (5 oz) trout fillet, sliced

1 tablespoon fish sauce

3 tablespoons lime juice

3 bird's eye chillies (scuds), crushed

1 tablespoon coriander leaves

paste

20 slices young galangal

pinch of salt

2 tablespoons chopped lemongrass

1 tablespoon scraped and chopped coriander root

2 tablespoons chopped red shallot

1 tablespoon chopped garlic

7 white peppercorns

First, make the paste: using a pestle and mortar, gradually pound the ingredients together until smooth.

Combine coconut milk and stock and bring to the boil, season with salt and palm sugar, then dissolve the paste in it. Add galangal, lime leaves and fish. Simmer until cooked.

In a serving bowl, mix together the fish sauce, lime juice, scuds and coriander. Ladle in the soup and stir to incorporate – it should taste sour and salty and hot.

DEEP-FRIED CHILLI AND GARLIC SAUCE

nahm jim prik jiaw

Mom Chao Janjaroen Rachani suggested spooning this chilli jam–like paste over a galangal soup to season and add colour contrast. I have found it can be used to season many hot and sour soups with equal success.

Once made, it lasts for several months.

8 garlic cloves, peeled
pinch of salt
oil for deep-frying
4–6 dried long red chillies, deseeded if preferred
3 slices galangal

Coarsely pound the garlic with the salt. Heat the oil. Deep-fry the garlic, chillies and galangal separately until fragrant and golden. Allow to cool before pounding into a paste; moisten with a little of the deep-frying oil. Check seasoning – the sauce may need a little extra salt, otherwise it will taste somewhat hollow and bitter.

9

CURRIES

Wherever you go in Thailand – province, region or village – everyone has a favourite curry, which they firmly believe to be superior to all others. Thai curries are diverse, and the range can be both bewildering and at times contentious. This huge array is the delicious outcome of the availability of ingredients, the changing seasons, regional variations, different techniques, personal tastes and local customs. Thai curries are thus altered incessantly. So an ordinary red curry, for instance, which should be agreeably familiar, becomes a source of controversy embroiling all: ingredients are included or excluded, considered necessary, incidental or unacceptable, and argued over with hungry passion.

The Thai word for curry, *geng*, has a far wider application than the English approximation suggests. It means any wet savoury dish enriched and thickened by a paste. Curries are more specifically called *geng ped*, or 'thickened spicy liquids', while the remainder are *geng jeut* – that is, unspiced, literally 'bland liquids' or soups. The late Mom Ratchawongse Kukrit Pramoj, an expert on Thai culture and history, speculated that the original, most primitive type of curry was simply a broth into which a spicy relish (*nahm prik*) had been dissolved. This, he proposed, was done to alleviate what would otherwise have been a monotonous diet of a dry relish, accompanied by vegetables and fish, eaten with soup and rice.

Curries range from the very simple to the highly complex. The earliest version of curry, according to Than Kukrit, was a *geng liang*, a mild dish made using very simple techniques with easily obtainable and indigenous ingredients: a paste of red shallots, white peppercorns, *grachai* (wild ginger) and fish dissolved in boiling liquid, then finished with various leaf vegetables and perfumed with lemon basil. More evolved versions of curry range from the familiar green and red curries, to the highly spiced aromatic curries (*geng gari*) and elaborate *mussaman* curries. Regional variation also plays an important role. In northern areas of Thailand, which have been more influenced by the Burmese and as a consequence the Indians, more dried spices are employed than in the heartlands of the central plains. And the Muslim south embraces dried spices in their curries, which are redolent of cumin and cardamom.

A Thai curry has three elements that define it: first, the ingredients in the paste; second, the way it is cooked and seasoned; and third, the ingredients in the curry. Although these final ingredients have the most obvious effect on the flavour and appearance of the curry, they are *not* necessarily the principal, distinguishing element. They are certainly the most salient aspect of a curry and hence the easiest way to describe the finished dish, but from the Thai cook's point of view, each of the three components is equally important, and together they determine what kind of curry it is.

To give further dimension to their curries, the Thai serve them with small side dishes (recipes for these are given in the 'Side dishes and accompaniments' chapter, starting on page 379). Perhaps the simplest accompaniments are fresh raw vegetables, but pungently flavoured pickled vegetables, salted eggs or dried or salted fish are also often eaten with curries.

Curry pastes have been developed and refined over centuries, as they are passed down from generation to generation. Most pastes use the same basic aromatic herbs and spices: chillies (fresh or dried), galangal, lemongrass, red shallots, garlic and shrimp paste. Their proportions vary in order to balance or enhance the character and strength of the other ingredients in the finished dish. Additionally, kaffir lime zest, coriander root, red turmeric, *grachai* and dried spices may be included.

In a good Thai curry, each flavour should be tasted to its desired degree and no one flavour should overshadow another. The striving for a complex balance of ingredients is nowhere more apparent than in curries: robustly flavoured ingredients are melded and blended together into a harmonious, yet paradoxically subtle and cohesive whole. To achieve this, it is important for the cook to recognise the flavours of the ingredients and to understand how they respond to cooking.

AROMATICS

It is vital that all the fresh ingredients be washed, peeled and finely chopped before being added to curry pastes. This may seem excessive, but the more preparatory chopping, the less work is needed. As each ingredient is pounded, the fragrance is checked and more of the current ingredient or the next one is added accordingly. This ensures that a gradual, composite and integral balance is achieved. Ingredients should be prepared as follows, and added to the paste in the order given.

CHILLI

The amount of chilli in a curry paste is variable – for example, a green curry is always much hotter than a red curry – and depends on, first, the type of curry being made; second, the other ingredients being used; and, finally, the preferred degree of heat. The colour of different types of chilli is also a distinguishing characteristic of curries. This is not just the obvious difference between fresh green and red chillies, but also between kinds of dried long red chillies: use the darkest, almost purple ones for intensely red curries; and lighter-coloured ones for sour orange curries and yellow curries.

Dried long red chillies are the most commonly used in curries, and are fruity and hot. However, in southern and sometimes in north-eastern curries, dried red bird's eye chillies are called for – these are simply hot. If the recipe calls for dried long red chillies, treat them as follows: cut off the stem, then cut down the pod, removing the seeds and the membranes attached to them (some may prefer to wear gloves for this), where most, but certainly not all, the heat of the chilli lies. Rinse the chillies under running water to remove any remaining membranes, seeds or other hidden surprises. Soak them in cold salted water for 10–15 minutes; if you are in a rush, you can soak them in warm salted water for 3–4 minutes. Dried red bird's eye chillies should be soaked in the same way, but are rarely deseeded beforehand – ensuring that they are unforgettable. Some of the chillies' colour and heat will be leached out by the soaking, but the flavour that remains is fuller and truer, without undue heat to overwhelm it (if you taste the water before it is discarded you will see how coarse it really is). Consequently, more chillies can be used in a paste, giving a greater depth of colour, flavour and heat to the curry. Soaked dried chillies must be squeezed to extract as much water as possible so that they do not dilute the paste or splatter when they are puréed.

Occasionally, fresh long chillies, both red and green, are used in curry pastes: deseed them and remove the fleshy white membrane. Small fresh bird's eye chillies – which I affectionately call scuds – are also sometimes used in curries; all the preparation they need is to be destemmed (although some cooks prefer to remove the stem but leave the 'bud' where it joins the chilli, believing it adds fragrance). The chillies are pounded or blended with salt and they should be completely puréed before any other ingredients are added.

SALT

Salt is used not only as a seasoning, but also as an abrasive to help grind the chillies and subsequent ingredients, and as a preservative. A freshly made paste needs less salt than one that is to be kept longer. Normally a large pinch, or about ¼ teaspoon, is the best amount to use in the recipes given. Any more and there is the likelihood of an overly salty curry; any less and the curry has a hollow, under-seasoned quality that cannot be redressed. Should the quantities in the recipes be multiplied to make a larger amount, the salt should be increased also – though not quite proportionally. With salt, as with dried spices, the effect of an increase is greater than its weight. A good-quality salt should be used.

GALANGAL

Galangal gives curries a peppery sharpness. Too much galangal and a curry will be slightly astringent, overwhelming the back upper palate with a rasping dryness; too little, however, and the curry will have no depth or length on the palate.

Old, but not wizened galangal is the best type to use in curries, as it has the right degree of concentration without too much water. If the only galangal that can be found is very old or dried, soak it in salted water for 5 minutes or so before use to soften it and remove some of its aggressive pungency. Dry thoroughly before chopping and adding to the paste.

LEMONGRASS

Lemongrass imparts a citrus quality to a curry, preventing it tasting too heavy or oily and cutting any fattiness. Too much lemongrass can dominate a curry, making it too lemony and sharp.

Peel off and discard the outer coarse sheaths, tough base and roots, and stringy top third of the stalk. Slice finely before pounding or blending.

KAFFIR LIME

Kaffir lime zest is used to add a floral flavour – it gives 'height' to the curry. Use cautiously: if too much is used, the curry will taste oily and resolutely bitter. Only the green zest should be used; the white pith tastes soapy. Chop or mince before adding to the paste. The juice of kaffir limes is sometimes used in sour curries.

CORIANDER ROOT

Coriander root gives curries a sweet freshness that lifts them. It should be used carefully as too much will make the curry leaden, with a muddy 'grassiness'. Scrape off the skin, soak in water for 5 minutes to loosen any stubborn dirt, then rinse in running water. Chop before adding to the paste.

Some cookery writers suggest adding coriander leaves and stalks, as well as roots, to a paste to produce a rich, green curry. I do not recommend this, as I have found it can make the curry taste heavy and muddy. Older Thai recipes suggest chilli leaves for added colour, if necessary, instead.

TURMERIC

Turmeric is used mainly to give colour to curries: a teaspoon added to a green curry paste will result in a verdant green colour. It is used most often in southern curries where lemongrass, dried bird's eye chillies and shrimp paste predominate. Use cautiously, as too much will render the curry acridly medicinal.

With rare exceptions, only fresh red turmeric is used in curry pastes. Peel and chop before adding to the mortar or blender – be careful, it stains everything. (Do not substitute powdered turmeric: no matter how little is used, it will produce a dry, musty flavour, pervading and spoiling the curry.)

GRACHAI

Grachai (wild ginger) makes a curry pungently peppery and prevents it becoming too oily or rich. However, too much makes a curry taste bitter and dirty. Soak in water before use, then scrape to remove the skin. It is usually shredded as a garnish for curries, but is occasionally added to jungle and green curry pastes.

RED SHALLOTS

Too few shallots in a curry and it will be ill-defined; too much and the curry will be overwhelmed by them, as they will blanket all the other ingredients. Peel, wash and chop before adding to the paste. Thai red shallots are smaller, sweeter and pinker than Western shallots. The latter or red onions can be used in curry pastes, but onions are more pungent, so adjust the recipe by slightly reducing the amount.

GARLIC

Garlic is an essential ingredient, acting like a bridge connecting all the other ingredients. Too little and the curry will taste thin, insipid and too sharp; too much and the curry will be oily, overly rich and almost sweetly over-pungent, with a lingering flavour.

Peel and wash garlic before mincing. Remove the green sprout, if present, as it can make the curry a little bitter and, if the curry is kept for a long period, may even cause fermentation.

SHRIMP PASTE

One of the most elemental of Thai ingredients, shrimp paste (*gapi*) is used in most curries. If too much *gapi* is added, the curry will be heavy and the *gapi* will smother all other flavours; not enough, and the curry will seem to have no anchor or base.

It may be briefly roasted to invigorate its taste and fragrance before being added to the paste, but if it is roasted for too long it becomes bitter.

FERMENTED FISH

Fermented fish (*pla raa*) is used in place of shrimp paste in some curries from the north and north-east of Thailand. Like shrimp paste, it can be used raw or roasted, and imparts a resonant character to the paste.

DRIED SPICES

Although dried spices have an important role in the composition of most curries worldwide, they play a surprisingly small part in most Thai curries. The Thai believe that they disguise the flavour of food and are somewhat suspicious of them, dismissing most as foreign. In the earliest Thai curries, the boiled ones, the only dried spice used is white pepper. In the more complex, fried red and green curries, three main spices are used: white peppercorns, coriander seeds and cumin seeds. Occasionally other spices – such as nutmeg, mace, cardamom, cassia and cloves – are sparingly added to give an elusive fragrance and to counterbalance the rich, meaty or gamy qualities of other ingredients.

Dried spices should be used gingerly in Thai curries. They are there merely to add a subtle piquancy, to support and give dimension to the taste and fragrance. The amount used varies according to personal taste, the other ingredients and the type of curry. With the exception of peppercorns, all spices should be roasted to revitalise their volatile oils – and each should be roasted individually, as they take different times to roast. The degree of roasting is also determined by their desired prominence in the taste of the curry: for example, a red curry of seafood demands lightly roasted spices, while the spices for a *mussaman* would generally be quite heavily roasted.

Spices are roasted by heating them very slowly in heavy pan or a wok, tossing regularly to prevent scorching (see page 127 for more on roasting and grinding spices). When roasting spices for a curry paste, take care neither to under-roast, which would result in a somewhat hollow echo of the spice rather than its rich perfume, nor to over-roast: remember that they will also be heated and fried as the paste is cooked. When the spices begin to crackle, toast and colour, they are ready. Grind spices very finely, and always sieve the result to remove any chaff.

When adding ground and sieved spices to a curry paste, do so gradually, as there are often marked variations in pungency. Before the dried spices are added, the paste should be buoyantly fragrant; afterwards it will be slightly heavier, more earthy and pungent – taste or smell the difference. Mix in half the amount suggested in the recipe first, then gradually work in the balance until the desired pungency is achieved. Do not over-spice – a spice-laden curry is not a Thai curry.

PEPPERCORNS

White peppercorns are rarely, if ever, roasted before being added to a curry – it can make the paste raspingly dry. This also results if too much pepper is used; too little can cause a lack of sharpness, precision even. If the pepper is stale, it may be invigorated by adding it to the roasted spices once they are removed from the heat, so that it is gently heated in the residual warmth.

Black peppercorns are occasionally used in Muslim and jungle curries, where their robust quality adds a diffused heat to the paste.

CORIANDER AND CUMIN SEEDS

Use Thai coriander seeds, if possible – they are smaller and less herbaceous in flavour. Roast gently until they begin to crackle and emit an orange-like fragrance. (If no fresh coriander roots are available when you are making a paste, compensate by slightly increasing the amount of coriander seeds.)

Cumin seeds should always be roasted separately, as they roast so quickly. The standard proportion in curry pastes is 2 parts coriander seeds to 1 part cumin seeds. If you add too much ground coriander to a curry, it will taste distorted and slightly hollow. If you add too much cumin, the curry will seem sharp and too bitterly direct; it is undisguisedly pervasive.

NUTMEG AND MACE

Nutmeg is used in most curries with beef, especially *geng panaeng*. It should be coarsely pounded before being very quickly roasted. Too much roasting, or an excess of nutmeg, will make a curry overly sweet, oily and musty.

Mace is rarely used. When it is called for, tread carefully; if too much is used, the curry will seem floral and oily.

CARDAMOM, CASSIA AND CLOVES

Cardamom is mainly used in *mussaman* curries: the pods are roasted before being cracked open to reveal the seeds, which are then ground and used in the paste. Thai cardamom has a finer taste than the more common Indian cardamom, but the seeds have a similar perfume; if using the more pungent Indian variety, reduce the quantity by about a third.

Cassia bark is grilled or roasted in a length before being ground.

Cloves are used mostly in Muslim-style curries, where their heady perfume counterbalances any heaviness. They must be used sparingly.

A curry paste should be puréed as finely as possible: although fibrous ingredients are used, by the end of the process it is the ingredients that should be tasted, not their texture. Such finesse is essential for a good curry paste. Once puréed, by whatever means, smell the paste. It should not be a muddled jumble of disjointed smells but be unified, complete, redolent, mellow and fully rounded – a surprising contrast to the manifold rawness of the ingredients. It should also be tasted: smear a little across the tongue, but be careful – its intensity can brutalise the palate. Khun Sombat, who taught me the rudiments of Thai cooking, always tested her pastes by sniffing them earnestly, believing it to be the most discriminating way to judge them. Fragrance, for her, was the best indicator, the most traditional and safest test.

Some of the following recipes make more paste than is needed for the individual dish. This is because a certain volume is required before the ingredients will purée successfully. And in fact, a surprisingly small amount of paste is produced compared to the unprocessed quantity – only half or even a third of the volume of the raw ingredients. Leftover paste can be happily stored for up to two weeks, cartouched – that is, sealed tightly with plastic wrap pressed against the surface of the paste – and refrigerated in an airtight container. Do not freeze a curry paste as, when thawed, the shallots and garlic will become bitter and the paste insipid as it weeps. It will be ruined, little better than canned pastes and a waste of the time and effort put into making it.

MAKING A CURRY PASTE WITH A PESTLE AND MORTAR

Traditionally, curry pastes are made with a pestle and mortar. Individual ingredients are added gradually, in a given order, from the hardest and driest to the softest and wettest, with each being reduced to pulp before the next is added. As the ingredients are pounded they release their fragrance; the balance of the paste can be perceived in this aroma, and is adjusted while being made. The recipe is used as a guide, not gospel, and so can – and should – be altered to achieve a balance. Sometimes, for example, shallots are more pungent or galangal sharper than usual.

The process of making a curry paste by hand is time-consuming, onerous and messy, but the result is quite superior – both in texture and balance of tastes – to one made in a food processor. Pastes made by hand have an integrity and intensity of flavour that machine-made ones do not possess. This is apparent when the paste is boiled; it becomes even more evident if the paste is fried.

MAKING A CURRY PASTE WITH A BLENDER OR MINCER

However, I wonder whether it is useful to be so exactly authentic if people are deterred from trying again after their initial attempt at pounding a paste. A convenient alternative is to use a blender, which is better for this purpose than a food processor. A blender has four blades that can cut and purée the paste quickly in the small well at its bottom, whereas a food processor has only two blades and works the paste in a much larger bowl, taking much longer with less success. Although neither a blender nor a food processor are quite as good as the pestle and mortar, a paste made in them is still much superior to a canned paste.

In a blender the ingredients are puréed, with a little water usually being added to facilitate the blending. Do not use oil to process a paste, as it will emulsify, turning the paste into a heavy, gluey ball, unlikely ever to separate again. One Thai recipe book suggests adding a little coconut cream or milk, but this should only be done if the paste is for a coconut-based curry. Be careful not to over-work such a paste, otherwise the coconut cream will curdle and the paste will not dissolve in the curry. Additionally, such a paste will not store longer than a few days, as it will begin to sour.

Do not overload the machine – it may be necessary to purée half the ingredients at a time. If this is so, press or strain the first batch to extract as much liquid as possible and then add this liquid to the second batch before puréeing. Thus the paste will be less dilute and will cook more successfully. Mix the batches well. Be patient as you make a paste – the blender, regrettably, was not created to make curry pastes and therefore may expire under such spicy exertion.

Do not overwork when blending and thus heat the paste, as this will begin to cook the paste too early, altering its taste and hastening the souring process. Three or four minutes should be sufficient for the blending. If the paste does not seem to be puréeing easily, add a little water and loosen the paste from the sides with a spatula. This breaks the vacuum that often forms at the bottom of the bowl. Naturally, turn the machine off when doing this, or beware the splatter.

Another method of making a paste is to use a mincer. Feed the ingredients twice or thrice – or as many times as it takes – through the machine until a fine consistency is achieved. Then change to a finer grate and feed through again to produce a smooth paste. The advantage of making pastes with a mincer is that no water is necessary and so the paste cooks more successfully.

BOILED CURRIES

Boiled curries are the simplest and the most popular of Thai curries. They are less refined than the more evolved fried curries, but just as varied and satisfying. Every region, village, market and house prepares these curries as everyday fare.

If the curry paste has been made using a pestle and mortar, it is often diluted with a little boiling stock, water or coconut milk before being poured back into the rest of the boiling liquid and dissolved in it. It is important that the liquid into which the diluted paste is added is boiling, otherwise there will be a difference in taste in the finished dish, albeit subtle to some; the Thai believe that the curry will 'smell', having been improperly cooked.

I have found it is best to lightly season the boiling liquid before using it to dilute the paste – with salt, a pinch of sugar and, if specified in the final seasoning, a little tamarind water. The diluted paste is then briskly dissolved in the seasoned liquid and simmered for a surprisingly short time, a minute or two only, until the paste has lost its coarse rawness. The paste will thicken and bind the liquid, thus making the curry. It should then be seasoned once more.

Finally the remaining ingredients are added, according to the time they take to cook. Most boiled curries use fish or seafood as their 'main' ingredient. I think it is best to poach rather than boil fish, and so reduce the heat after fish has been added. Many old Thai recipes tend to overcook fish; that is their culinary prerogative. Cook fish to the degree you prefer. Occasionally, fish is grilled or deep-fried before it is added to a Thai curry.

FISH AND VEGETABLE CURRY WITH WILD GINGER, WHITE PEPPER AND LEMON BASIL

geng liang pla

This curry is like the thickened soups of the past. Its primitive method – a paste dissolved in stock – echoes the first Thai curries. In Thai *liang* means 'at hand' or 'grown nearby', and that is precisely what is used. The main ingredients of a *geng liang* are indigenous to the north and the central plains: freshwater fish, shallots, *grachai*, peppercorns (perhaps once black, but now almost invariably white) and salt.

Although primitive, the curry is still very pleasing, as the fish thickens and creates a base with the pungently camphor-like taste of *grachai*, sharpened by the shallots, seasoned by the salt and pepper and perfumed by the lemon basil. Traditionally only freshwater fish is used – usually fresh but sometimes dried. Farther to the south, the same curry can include small freshwater prawns. Only three or four kinds of vegetable are used; any more would clutter the curry. Leafy or gourd-like vegetables are the best and most traditional choices, however asparagus, rocket (arugula) or spinach are also agreeable additions to this wholesome dish. Plenty of lemon basil and white pepper are essential.

If desired, extra trout slices, or fresh prawns, can be added to the curry with the vegetables. One unusual but delicious variant uses *pla salit* in a similar paste, which is then dissolved in coconut milk and simmered with pumpkin.

2 tablespoons trout, ground dried prawns (shrimp) or ground *pla grop* (crisp fish)

2 cups stock or water

pinch of salt

1 cup lemon basil leaves

1 teaspoon ground white pepper

a selection of 3–4 of the following vegetables – about 1 cup in total

pumpkin tendrils

banana blossoms

boiled bamboo shoots

wing beans

bai dtamleung, snow pea shoots or young spinach

oyster or straw mushrooms

baby corn

any peeled gourd

paste

3 tablespoons chopped *grachai* (wild ginger)

large pinch of salt

5 small red shallots, chopped

1 teaspoon white peppercorns

First, make the paste (see page 280).

If using trout, simmer in a little of the stock or water until just cooked. Remove fish, cool and pound into the paste. If using ground dried prawns or *pla grop*, simply add to paste. Bring remainder of stock or water to the boil and season with salt. Ladle several tablespoons into the mortar to dilute the paste, then dissolve paste in stock and continue to boil for a minute. Check seasoning. Add vegetables according to their cooking time. When all are cooked, finish with basil and pepper. This thin, soup-like curry should taste peppery and a little salty.

YOUNG JACKFRUIT CURRY WITH PORK RIBS

geng kanun orn

This curry comes from Chiang Mai, in the north of Thailand, where jackfruit is extremely popular. Alternative combinations include chicken with bamboo shoots, guinea fowl with pumpkin, and freshwater fish with banana blossoms.

The following recipe uses green jackfruit, which in fact is more like a vegetable than a fruit; at this unripened stage, it is starchy and sappy. The latex-like sap from unripe jackfruit is infuriatingly sticky. Traditionally the hands are rubbed with oil to protect them, but I find that everything still becomes dangerously gluey. Then, after it has dried, the sap becomes black and unsightly. Nail polish remover is the best solution. It *is* worth the effort.

3 cups water or stock

pinch of salt

pinch of white sugar

200 g (6 oz) pork ribs, cut into 2 cm (1 in) lengths

150 g (5 oz) young jackfruit

squeeze of lime juice

5 cherry tomatoes

a few torn 'betel' leaves – optional

a small bunch of *cha-om* – optional

paste

5 dried long red chillies, deseeded, soaked and drained

large pinch of salt

2 tablespoons chopped galangal

4 red shallots, chopped

3 garlic cloves, chopped

2 tablespoons fermented fish (*pla raa*) *or* 1 tablespoon shrimp paste (*gapi*)

First, make the paste (see page 280).

Bring water or stock to the boil. Season with salt and sugar. Wash the pork ribs and add to the pot. Simmer until almost tender – about 20 minutes – skimming regularly.

Meanwhile, peel and clean the jackfruit. Cut into 2 cm (1 in) cubes and steep in water acidulated with lime juice.

Dissolve 2 tablespoons of paste in the stock, then add jackfruit and tomatoes and continue to simmer until both are tender. Finish with 'betel' leaves and *cha-om*, if using. Check the seasoning: it should be salty, aromatic, herbaceous and slightly sour from the tomatoes.

Serve with:

— steamed prawns (shrimp)

— Salted Prawns (page 392).

MINCED RABBIT CURRY

geng oom gradtai sap

This curry comes from the north of Thailand, and uses the rudimentary boiling method typical of curries from this region. It is a very loose recipe with few prohibitions as to ingredients: meat, fowl or fish can be minced, chopped or sliced and simmered with almost any green or leafy vegetable – preferably ones that are slightly bitter or at least have a decided flavour (*oom* is a northern Thai word for green leaf).

Trout and plump green asparagus or quail with rocket (arugula) are inviting options for the Western cook, although to a Thai minced frog and 'betel' leaves or pork with *cha-om* and shredded banana blossoms would be more likely. *Nahm pla raa* is the preferred fish condiment in this recipe, but normal fish sauce is a convenient, less pungent alternative.

3 cups stock, ideally made from the rabbit bones

pinch of white sugar

2 tablespoons fermented fish sauce (*nahm pla raa*) or fish sauce

1 bunch Chinese broccoli, cut into 2 cm (1 in) lengths

   or 2 large handfuls of bitter melon leaves, snow pea shoots or young spinach leaves

   or 2 large handfuls of pumpkin tendrils, chopped into 2 cm (1 in) pieces

1 cup minced rabbit meat

paste

2 tablespoons dried red bird's eye chillies, soaked and drained

   or 6–12 dried long red chillies, deseeded, soaked and drained

large pinch of salt

2 tablespoons chopped lemongrass

1 tablespoon scraped and chopped coriander root

1 teaspoon chopped red turmeric

2 tablespoons chopped *grachai* (wild ginger)

2 tablespoons chopped red shallot

1 tablespoon chopped garlic

1 teaspoon shrimp paste (*gapi*) *or* 1 tablespoon fermented fish (*pla raa*)

First, make the paste (see page 280).

Bring stock to the boil, then season with sugar and 1½ tablespoons of the fish sauce. Dissolve 3 tablespoons of the paste in the stock. Add vegetable (if using broccoli, boil for several minutes until its colour begins to fade – the slight bitterness imparted improves the curry). Add meat, stirring to prevent it clumping, and cook for only a few seconds – until it has changed colour. Taste, and add remaining fish sauce if necessary. The dish should not be too thick and should taste salty, hot and just slightly bitter. This curry improves if it is allowed to sit for 5 minutes or so before serving. Reheat if desired.

This curry is often served with one or more of:

— pickled red shallots

— *pla grop* (crisp fish)

— Stir-fried Dried Mussels (page 396).

SOUR ORANGE CURRY OF SALTED FISH, WATERMELON RIND AND EGG

geng som bleuak dtaeng mor

Throughout the markets of Thailand narrow alleyways are lined with curry stalls, where old women sell prepared food: relishes, salads and curries, the most popular of which is the sour orange curry (*geng som*). Pot after pot of this style of curry is on offer – made from freshwater fish with Siamese watercress or fermented bamboo shoots; prawns with green papaya or heart of coconut; mussels with drumstick beans or water mimosa. Given the sourness of the curry, a fatty, meaty fish works best. Sometimes the fish is chargrilled until smoky, or deep-fried until crisp and crunchy, before being added to the curry – it is the fish in the paste that thickens the curry.

The hot-pink flesh of Thai watermelon is sweeter than its Western equivalent, but the fruit has a greater proportion of woody, slightly bitter, white pith. The Thai being a frugal people, the pith is not discarded but used in many guises: it can be glacéd and served as a dessert, or peeled, sliced and simmered in a sour orange curry. The small, green and rather tasteless pepino melon is an ideal alternative to Thai watermelon, as are unripe honeydews.

Unusually, this curry is finished with an egg: as well as thickening the curry, the egg's richness is a perfect foil to the curry's sourness.

3 cups chicken stock or water

a little palm sugar

2 tablespoons tamarind water

100 g (3 oz) salted fish, sliced

2 cups peeled and chopped watermelon rind – that is, white pith only

a little fish sauce, if required

1 egg

paste

10 red bird's eye chillies (scuds)

large pinch of salt

5 red shallots, chopped

2 garlic cloves, chopped

1 teaspoon shrimp paste (*gapi*)

First, make the paste (see page 280).

Bring stock or water to the boil and season with palm sugar and tamarind water to taste. Dissolve paste in the stock, then add fish and watermelon rind and simmer until the rind is tender. Check seasoning and adjust, if necessary, with fish sauce and more tamarind water. Lightly beat the egg and stir into the simmering curry. Check the seasoning: it should be salty, sour and hot.

Serve with Salted Beef (page 401), grilled.

SOUR ORANGE CURRY OF TROUT AND VEGETABLES

geng som pla

Sour orange curries are very simple to prepare, and yet are among the most versatile of curries: any fish or seafood can be used, teamed with almost any vegetable. Their antiquity is reflected in their simplicity – and their popularity may also be due to their long association with the Thai. This recipe is a version of sour orange curry from the central plains of Thailand.

3 cups stock
100 g (3 oz) freshwater fish fillets – such as trout, catfish, eel, carp or perch
3 tablespoons tamarind water
pinch of white sugar
2 tablespoons fish sauce

a selection of 2–3 of the following vegetables – about 1 cup in total
boiled and sliced bamboo shoots
snake beans or wing beans
Chinese cabbage
fresh or pickled Siamese watercress
'betel' leaves
white radish
asparagus – especially white
tomatoes
bai dtamleung, chard or spinach

paste
5 dried long red chillies, deseeded, soaked and drained
large pinch of salt
1 tablespoon chopped galangal
3 tablespoons chopped red shallot
2 teaspoons shrimp paste (*gapi*)

First, make the paste (see page 280).

Bring stock to the boil, add about a third of the fish. Simmer briefly until cooked, remove and drain, then work into the curry paste. Return stock to the boil, season with tamarind water, sugar and fish sauce. Add the paste. Return to the boil once again and add the vegetables according to their cooking time, then the remainder of the fish. This thin curry should taste salty, sour and hot. >

Serve with one or more of the following:
- ← Pickled Vegetables (page 383)
- ← Steamed Salted Duck Eggs (page 391)
- ← dried fish
- ← Sweet Shredded Skate (page 396)
- ← Salted Pork with Coconut Milk (page 397)
- ← Chiang Mai cured pork (*naem*)
- ← Deep-fried Pork with Spices (page 400)
- ← Salted Beef Simmered in Coconut Cream (page 450).

YELLOW CURRY OF CLAMS WITH PINEAPPLE

geng leuang hoi lai

In the south of Thailand, a decided amount of turmeric is used in pastes, which gives curries a rich golden-orange hue, like this yellow curry. This is an awesomely hot curry, perhaps the hottest in the Thai repertoire. The perpetrators – lethal, dried red bird's eye chillies and fresh orange chillies – are used with abandon, together with plenty of rich, earthy shrimp paste.

Given Thailand's expansive seaboard, mostly saltwater fish or shellfish are used in this dish; barramundi, sea bass, snapper and red emperor, bonito, mackerel, swordfish, lobster, large blue prawns (shrimp), mussels, clams and scallops are all suitable. Vegetables and fruit most favoured in this curry's home region are fermented bamboo shoots, green papaya, pineapple – either green or ripe – and assam. Here is one combination.

1 very small half-ripe pineapple

3 cups stock or water

large pinch of white sugar

2 tablespoons thick tamarind water

1 tablespoon fish sauce

200 g (6 oz) clams, purged of sand

2 tablespoons lime juice

paste

25 dried red bird's eye chillies, soaked and drained

large pinch of salt

1 tablespoon chopped galangal

2 tablespoons chopped red turmeric

4 tablespoons chopped garlic

1 tablespoon chopped red shallot

1 heaped tablespoon shrimp paste (*gapi*)

First, make the paste (see page 280).

Peel the pineapple and cut into quarters, discard the core and then coarsely chop the flesh. Bring stock or water to the boil and season with sugar, tamarind water and fish sauce. Dissolve 2 tablespoons of the paste in the stock and cook for a minute. Add pineapple and, when softened, the clams. Simmer until the clams have opened (discard any that remain stubbornly closed). Finish with lime juice. This should be quite a thin curry. Check the seasoning – it should be hot, sour and salty – and adjust accordingly.

Eat with a plate of cooling raw vegetables, such as cucumber, green beans, snake beans and young spinach.

CHICKEN AND VEGETABLE CURRY

geng kae gai

This thin, rustic curry comes from the mountainous, temperate north of Thailand and is relatively mild. Generally the paste is dissolved in boiling liquid, but occasionally the paste is briefly heated through in a small pot before being seasoned and the stock added. With this curry, as with many curries from the north and north-east of the country, either method can be used with success, although with slightly different results.

In the market places of Chiang Mai, a changing selection of herbs, shoots and small vegetables are bundled together and tied with a bamboo leaf for sale. These could include the soft inner stalks of banana trees or wild leaves collected from nearby groves and thickets – such as the tobacco-like *bai yor*, 'betel' leaves and *pak chii farang* – eggplants, bamboo shoots, holy and Thai basil. Also delicious in this recipe would be an array of wild mushrooms, such as yellow chanterelles.

100 g (3 oz) skinless chicken thigh fillets

2 cups stock

a selection of the following vegetables – about 2 cups in total

sliced mushrooms

torn 'betel' leaves

holy and Thai basil leaves

coarsely shredded *pak chii farang* (long-leaf coriander)

sliced bamboo shoots or banana stalks

long, apple or pea eggplants

wild mushrooms

snake beans

cha-om

paste

7–10 dried long red chillies, deseeded, soaked and drained

large pinch of salt

2 tablespoons chopped lemongrass

2 tablespoons chopped red shallot

1 tablespoon chopped garlic

1 tablespoon fermented fish (*pla raa*) *or* 1 teaspoon shrimp paste (*gapi*)

First, make the paste (see page 280).

Slice the chicken, combine with the paste in a heavy pot and simmer for a moment, until fragrant. Pour in stock and bring to the boil. Add vegetables and simmer until cooked. Check the seasoning: the curry should taste salty, slightly hot and bitter.

Serve with one or more of the following:

— grilled fish

— *pla grop* (crisp fish)

— Freshly Salted Beef (page 402).

STEAMED GUINEA FOWL CURRY WITH ROASTED RICE AND APPLE EGGPLANTS

hor neung gai heun

This curry comes from the north-east of Thailand. Any small game, chicken, meaty freshwater fish or eel can be used in place of the guinea fowl; shredded bamboo shoots or banana blossoms can replace the eggplants, and Thai basil can be used to line the banana leaves for extra perfume. The traditional way of folding banana leaves can be tricky, but after a few attempts it becomes quite easy. If stumped, simply line, fill and cover some small bowls with the leaves and then steam.

The additional steaming means that this curry lasts longer than usual, up to 2 days. Wrapped, it could easily be carried to the paddies to make a pre-cooked lunch with rice, or sold at a nearby market.

3 tablespoons stock or water

200 g (6 oz) guinea fowl meat or skinless chicken thigh fillets, finely sliced

1–2 tablespoons fish sauce

½ cup quartered apple eggplants, steeped in salted water

½ cup pea eggplants, steeped in water

2 tablespoons ground roasted rice

1–2 banana leaves

paste

10 dried long red chillies, deseeded, soaked and drained

large pinch of salt

1 tablespoon chopped galangal

1 tablespoon chopped lemongrass

1 tablespoon scraped and chopped coriander root

2 tablespoons chopped red shallot

1 tablespoon chopped garlic

1 teaspoon shrimp paste (*gapi*) *or* 1 tablespoon fermented fish (*pla raa*)

1 teaspoon coriander seeds, roasted

First, make the paste (see page 280).

Heat stock or water, add guinea fowl or chicken and simmer over a medium heat. When meat has firmed, add the paste and season with fish sauce. Drain the eggplants well and add to the curry. Continue to simmer for another 2–3 minutes, then sprinkle in the ground roasted rice. Mix well and after a further minute, as the curry thickens, remove from the heat and set aside to cool. Check the seasoning: it should be salty, hot, slightly bitter and nutty.

Cut the banana leaves into elongated ovals, about 8 cm (3 in) across and 12 cm (5 in) long. Wipe each side clean. Lay two leaves on top of each other, with shinier sides outermost. Place ½ cup of the cooled mixture in the centre. Bring the sides up to the level of the stuffing, but do not cover. Bring the ends up and over the stuffing to join together, folding over the ends to seal. Fold the corners around and secure with toothpicks. Repeat until all the mixture is used up – about 10 parcels. Steam for 15 minutes until firm. Allow to cool slightly before opening.

FRIED CURRIES – AND COCONUT-BASED CURRIES

Just as there are raw and fried *nahm prik*, there are boiled and fried curries – it is the next stage in their development. Most curries from the north are boiled; the few that are fried use rendered pork fat as the frying medium. Farther south, curries are fried in coconut cream, introducing a rich, sweet flavour. Traditionally, a curry paste was cooked in an earthenware pot over a few glowing embers. If a low simmer was required, the pot sat happily above the heat, while higher temperatures involved stoking and fanning the charcoal. This gives some indication of the heat required: a paste fried in oil is cooked at a much higher heat than one cooked in coconut cream, and so must be stirred more frequently.

For coconut-based curries, the paste is fried in coconut cream, which first needs to be simmered slowly until it separates and is quite oily. This is important as the paste must be *fried*, not *boiled* – it makes a marked difference to the final taste. The process is similar to clarifying butter, with the oil separating from the solids: the oil fries the paste, and the creamy solids give the curry substance.

Coconut cream can be separated in two ways. The first is to simmer the cream over a low heat, stirring regularly, until it is thick and is beginning to separate or 'crack'. For the second method, several cups of combined cream and milk are brought to the boil and, as the cream rises, it is skimmed off and simmered in a smaller, separate pan until it has cracked; I find this the more successful method. Either way, the paste is added to the oily, separated cream, worked in and then cooked. Sometimes, if large pieces of meat need to be poached, they are simmered in a coconut cream and milk mixture; the cream that rises is skimmed and used to cook the curry paste and the remaining liquid is used to moisten the curry, if required, after seasoning.

The problem with canned coconut cream is that it has been homogenised, and starch has been added to stabilise it, during its manufacture – making it almost impossible to separate. If using canned, add a little oil when frying the paste: this will replicate separated coconut cream.

FRYING THE PASTE

As the paste begins to cook, its fragrance begins to change. The ingredients that have the greatest water content normally start to release their aroma first: shallots, garlic and the rehydrated chillies begin to steam and, as their water evaporates, to fry. The paste needs to be stirred regularly, to prevent it from burning. The higher the heat, the more vigilant you must be – such is the price of speed. As more water evaporates, the paste begins to sizzle and change colour. As the colour deepens, the fragrance becomes more intense.

Each ingredient begins to cook at a different time according to the amount of water in it, and when each item fries its aroma becomes evident. The longer a paste is cooked, the more integrated and well bound the ingredients become.

As with all other aspects of Thai cooking, the ingredients themselves should inform you when they are ready. I find that when I can smell the ingredient that I want to taste most in the finished curry, then it is time to season. A hot jungle curry may, for example, be fragrant with lemongrass, while a red curry will have the perfume of kaffir lime, a *panaeng* will be rich with peanuts, and a *mussaman* curry pungent with cumin. Each curry has its own characteristic aroma.

Another sign that the paste is sufficiently cooked is its appearance. When the paste is worked into the hot oil or fat, it absorbs it. As the water in the paste begins to evaporate, the oil begins to separate from the paste once again. The paste then fries and, as more water evaporates, it becomes oilier. Each style of curry has a required amount of separation. Only a little oil is used cooking a jungle curry and none should be apparent in the finished product, whereas red and green curries use more and have a sheen. The dry red curry styles, like *pat prik king* and *panaeng*, contain quite a lot of oil, about 5 per cent of the total liquid. A *mussaman* curry has the most separation, as much as 10 per cent. The oil helps to line the mouth and stomach and thus prevents the chillies from burning – at least to some degree! It also ensures that the accompanying rice is not too 'dry'. When the finished curry is kept for some time, the oil rises to the top and forms an anaerobic barrier that helps it last longer – a necessary thing in tropical heat in the days before refrigeration.

All fried pastes have a scrambled appearance, which is the result of the requisite amount of separation. When they also have the desired aroma then they are cooked, ready to be seasoned and moistened. Experience and preference are the guidelines here. I realise this is vague, but with experience the cook will be able to respond to what is being cooked, as opposed to adhering unswervingly to a recipe, regardless of what occurs during the cooking. Initially, this may be daunting, but it soon creates confidence, and you can begin to cook according to your personal taste, which I think is ultimately a far more satisfying way of cooking.

A jungle curry paste may need as little as 3 minutes over a high heat to cook sufficiently (until you sneeze), whereas a *mussaman* paste, with its redolent spices, must simmer for at least 15 minutes before it can be seasoned. Curries using dried red chillies generally need to be fried for around 10 minutes over a low heat – longer if the curry is heavily spiced – and a curry using fresh chillies takes less time, around 5 minutes, before it is ready for seasoning.

SEASONING THE PASTE

It is best to begin the seasoning with the sugar, when called for, for several reasons. Firstly, the raw sweetness of palm sugar is transformed the longer it is cooked; secondly, it bonds with the paste, intensifying its effects on the palate; and thirdly, as the sugar cooks it begins to caramelise, raising the temperature of the mixture and thus cooking it more, while deepening the colour of the curry. Some curries, such as a *panaeng* or *mussaman*, are improved and made redolent by the sugar's prolonged simmering, while the pungent vibrancy of others, like a jungle curry, are diminished by similar treatment.

Care should be exercised when adding the fish sauce. Little can be done to regain a delicate balance if a dish has been aggressively over-salted, although some redress can be made by adding a little sugar or coconut cream. Remember that salt has already been added to the paste when it was made, and that during the frying, water has evaporated from the paste, intensifying its salty taste. In any recipe aim to add only half to three-quarters of the specified amount of fish sauce at this stage and leave the balance to the end of the cooking – to fine tune the seasoning. The longer the paste is simmered after adding fish sauce, the more water evaporates and the more the salty element develops; the hotter or richer the curry, the longer it is possible to simmer it after the fish sauce is added.

If tamarind water is required, use thick water so as not to dilute the curry and add it after the palm sugar and fish sauce. Then do not fry the paste for much longer – tamarind scorches quickly, irredeemably tainting the curry.

ADDING THE LIQUID

Another defining characteristic of a curry is the amount of liquid added to the seasoned paste. There are 'dry' and 'wet' curries. Some are always dry, and these are usually oily and quite thick – like a *pat prik king* or a *panaeng* curry. Others are always wet, and these can either be thick, like a *mussaman*, or thin, like a green curry. Still others are versatile, starting from a similar paste but then being made dry or wet by the addition of liquid, as with most red curries. Normally, curries made with dried red chillies are thicker than those made with fresh red or green chillies.

In my experience, it is best to season the cooked paste and simmer for a few minutes before adding any liquid. This results in a greater dimension to the finished flavour. Traditionally, whether coconut milk, water or stock is used depends upon what type of curry it is. Regardless, I am now beginning to prefer stock to coconut milk, which can sometimes cloy the curry, emulsifying it and preventing the desired degree of separation.

Once the liquid is added, quickly bring the curry back to the boil, then let it simmer for several minutes before adding the final ingredients. Allow to rest for a minute or so to enable the flavours to mature, then reheat, if necessary, before serving.

STIR-FRIED WILD PORK WITH BEANS AND GREEN PEPPERCORNS
pat prik king muu bpaa

In ancient recipes, *prik king* was the name given to any curry paste made with dried red chillies. A *pat prik king* curry is always cooked in oil or rendered pork fat, never coconut cream. This is a spicy, dry, yet oily curry. The paste must be cooked for some time to achieve this – very often the paste is cooked several days in advance, and simply reheated when required.

> 150 g (5 oz) loin of pork or wild boar
>
> 6 tablespoons rendered pork fat or oil
>
> stock or water to moisten
>
> pinch of white sugar
>
> 2 tablespoons fish sauce
>
> 50 g (2 oz) snake beans, blanched and cut into 2 cm (1 in) lengths
>
> 2 tablespoons shredded *grachai* (wild ginger)
>
> 4 kaffir lime leaves, torn
>
> 2 long red or green chillies, diagonally sliced
>
> 1 tablespoon fresh green peppercorns
>
> handful of holy basil leaves

paste

10–15 dried long red chillies, deseeded, soaked and drained

large pinch of salt

2 tablespoons chopped galangal

2 tablespoons chopped lemongrass

3 tablespoons chopped red shallot

3 tablespoons chopped garlic

1 tablespoon scraped and chopped coriander root

4 tablespoons ground dried prawns (shrimp), ground dried fish

   or *pla grop* (crisp fish)

First, make the paste (see page 280).

If using wild boar, grill to singe any remaining bristles. Scrape and wash the meat. Cut pork or wild boar into 1 cm (½ in) slices. Heat rendered pork fat or oil in a heavy wok and add 4 tablespoons of the paste. Fry over a medium heat until paste is fragrant and dry, yet with plenty of oil. Add meat and simmer until cooked – about 5–10 minutes. Moisten occasionally with a little stock or water, if necessary, but ensure the curry remains quite dry. Season with sugar and fish sauce. Add snake beans, *grachai*, lime leaves, chillies, green peppercorns and holy basil.

The curry should be quite dry and oily, and taste salty and hot.

STIR-FRIED CRISPY FISH CAKES WITH PORK AND SALTED EGGS
pat prik king pla fuu kai kem

The following version of a *pat prik king* is a very complex and refined one that comes from the recipes of Mom Ratchawongse Dteuang Sanitsawongse, and was popular during the fifth and sixth reigns. It reminds me of a *nahm prik* with all its garnishes rolled into one.

This curry is very spicy and intensely flavoured: not just hot from the chillies, but pervadingly aromatic from the holy basil and *grachai* and pungently salty from the salted eggs and dried prawns. Although teetering on the brink of excess, no essential ingredient is overwhelmed. The degree of heat can range from hot to very hot – this is a matter of preference – but it must be quite hot, otherwise the curry would taste too oily. The oil prevents the curry tasting *too* fiery.

100 g (3 oz) pork belly

2 salted duck eggs

7 tablespoons oil or rendered pork fat

large pinch of white sugar

2 tablespoons fish sauce

50 g (2 oz) snake beans, cut into 2 cm (1 in) lengths

100 g (3 oz) Crispy Fish Cakes (page 393)

2 tablespoons scraped and chopped *grachai* (wild ginger)

3 long green chillies, cut in half lengthwise and deseeded

handful of holy basil leaves

1 tablespoon shredded kaffir lime leaves

curry paste

6 dried long red chillies, deseeded, soaked and drained

large pinch of salt

1½ tablespoons chopped galangal

3 tablespoons sliced lemongrass

2 tablespoons chopped *grachai* (wild ginger)

1 tablespoon scraped and chopped coriander root

3 tablespoons chopped red shallot

3 tablespoons chopped garlic

3 tablespoons rinsed dried prawns (shrimp) or ground *pla grop* (crisp fish)

garlic paste

2 garlic cloves, peeled

3 stalks *grachai* (wild ginger), peeled

3–5 bird's eye chillies (scuds)

pinch of salt

Steam (or poach) the pork until tender – about 30 minutes. Remove, cool and cut into ½ cm (¼ in) cubes. Shell the salted duck eggs and cut the yolks in quarters (reserve the egg whites for another use, such as a batter).

Make the curry paste (see page 280). Heat 5 tablespoons of the oil or rendered pork fat in a heavy pot or wok and fry the paste over a low to medium heat until fragrant: this may take as long as 10 minutes. Add a little more oil if the paste seems too dry. Season with sugar and fish sauce. Set aside. Make the garlic paste by coarsely pounding all the ingredients using a pestle and mortar.

Heat the rest of the oil or rendered pork fat in a wok, add pork and fry over a medium to high heat until brown. (Be careful, it splatters.) Add the garlic paste and fry until it begins to colour, then add the beans and continue to fry until the garlic is golden and the beans have blistered. Add 3 tablespoons of the curry paste and mix well. Cook, stirring from time to time to prevent it burning, for 5 minutes. Adjust seasoning, if necessary.

Crumble in – but not too finely – the crispy fish cake and, once it has absorbed some of the oil from the paste, stir in the egg yolks, followed by the remaining ingredients. Taste, and add more fish sauce if needed.

Serve with Sweet Shredded Skate (page 396).

BARRAMUNDI OR SEA BASS CURRY WITH CUCUMBER

geng dumii

This thick, oily and highly seasoned curry is from the south of Thailand. Only seafood is used: lobster, prawns (shrimp), bonito, mackerel or sardines all make perfect alternatives to the barramundi or sea bass. As a delicious variation, sardines could be crisp-fried in the oil first and then set aside while the paste is fried in the fish-flavoured oil.

Traditionally, the curry paste would have been fried in coconut oil. This is made by simmering fresh coconut cream until it has completely separated, and lasts indefinitely once rendered. The solids are used mainly in desserts, such as Yellow Bean Pudding (page 624). Tasted alone, the coconut oil has a slightly harsh, liltingly bitter flavour, but when used in a strong curry gives depth.

3 tablespoons oil
large pinch of white sugar
2 tablespoons fish sauce
½ cup thick tamarind water
2 small cucumbers, peeled and cut into elegant pieces
200 g (6 oz) barramundi or sea bass fillet
a few 'betel' leaves, torn

paste
10–15 dried long red chillies, deseeded, soaked and drained
large pinch of salt
1 tablespoon chopped lemongrass
3 tablespoons chopped red turmeric
1 tablespoon chopped red shallot
3 tablespoons chopped garlic
1 tablespoon white peppercorns
1 tablespoon shrimp paste (*gapi*), roasted

First, make the paste (see page 280).

Heat the oil and fry 3 tablespoons of the paste over a medium heat for about 5 minutes – until it becomes fragrant and the colour deepens. Lower the heat and season with sugar, fish sauce and tamarind water. Add cucumber, barramundi or sea bass and 'betel' leaves and simmer until cooked. Check the seasoning – it should be sour, salty, hot and slightly sweet. Adjust accordingly.

Serve with Freshly Salted Beef (page 402).

JUNGLE CURRY OF DUCK

geng bpa bpet

A jungle curry is a very hot style of curry, as the heat of the chillies is not mitigated by the sweet richness of coconut cream. Jungle curries are favoured by people living outside major towns because they use ingredients that are easy to find, and the preparation takes merely a few minutes. Only a small amount of oil should be used, just enough to fry the paste, for a jungle curry is not an oily curry – any extra oil would swamp the dish, inhibiting its immediate pungency and thus its distinguishing qualities.

A jungle curry is usually seasoned only with fish sauce or its rustic forebear, fermented fish sauce, and perhaps a pinch of sugar. A wet curry, it is then moistened with stock – never coconut milk – and the end result should be a sharp, hot, salty and pungent curry. Rarely do jungle curries include dried spices – in fact I have never come across them in a recipe, apart from the occasional peppercorn. The most common jungle curries contain a variety of vegetables; this gives texture and flavour to the curry, preventing it from being just searingly hot. The vegetables may include baby corn, apple and pea eggplants, wing or snake beans and sliced bamboo shoots with plenty of shredded *grachai*. Jungle curries are usually perfumed with torn kaffir lime leaves and finished with holy basil.

> 150 g (5 oz) duck meat – including liver, giblets and heart, if possible
> bones from the duck
> 1 tablespoon oil
> 2 tablespoons fish sauce
> 2 cups stock
> 1 cup picked pea eggplants
> 3 apple eggplants, cut into sixths and steeped in salted water
> 50 g (2 oz) snake beans, cut into 2 cm (1 in) lengths
> 4 baby corn, cut into 2 cm (1 in) pieces
> ½ cup sliced bamboo shoots
> 5 stalks *grachai* (wild ginger), scraped and julienned
> 3 long green chillies, diagonally sliced
> a few chilli leaves – optional
> 3 kaffir lime leaves, torn
> handful of holy basil leaves
> 2 tablespoons fresh green peppercorns

curry paste

10–15 green bird's eye chillies (scuds)

large pinch of salt

1 long green chilli, deseeded and chopped

1 tablespoon chopped galangal

2 tablespoons chopped lemongrass

1 tablespoon chopped *grachai* (wild ginger)

4 tablespoons chopped red shallot

3 tablespoons chopped garlic

1 teaspoon shrimp paste (*gapi*), roasted – optional

garlic paste

1 garlic clove, peeled

pinch of salt

2 stalks *grachai* (wild ginger), peeled

3 bird's eye chillies (scuds)

Slice the duck meat into fine pieces, about 2 cm × ½ cm (1 in × ¼ in). Leave skin on or remove, as preferred.

Make a stock from the bones: wash, crush or chop them, blanch from a cold-water start, rinse and then cover with cold water, quickly bring to the boil and simmer for 30 minutes. Strain, allow to cool and remove excess fat.

Clean the offal: remove fat and gristle from the heart, slice and wash; discard any discoloured parts of the liver, slice; lift the red meat of the giblets away from the white gristle, and wash in salted, acidulated water.

Make the curry paste (see page 280).

Make the garlic paste by pounding the ingredients together using a pestle and mortar. Heat the oil in a wok or heavy saucepan and, when very hot, add garlic paste and fry over high heat until golden. Add 3 tablespoons of the curry paste and continue to fry, stirring vigilantly to prevent scorching, until it is so fragrant that it produces a sneeze – yes, a sneeze. Season with fish sauce. Add stock and bring to the boil. Add duck meat, offal and eggplants. Simmer until cooked – about 3 minutes. Add remaining ingredients. Check seasoning: the curry should taste hot and salty; adjust if necessary.

Serve with:

— pickled red shallots

— *pla grop* (crisp fish).

JUNGLE CURRY OF FISH WITH BREADFRUIT

geng bpa pla

Although it is standard to combine several vegetables in a jungle curry, sometimes only one or two are included. The following dish is an example of this. Alternatives to breadfruit are jackfruit, pumpkin, cucumber or long green eggplant. Almost always, however, fresh green peppercorns are used as a garnish – a reminder perhaps of the role this spice once played in Thai curries before the arrival of chillies.

Green breadfruit can be quite difficult to work with. Its sap is sticky, slightly smelly and is a nuisance to clean. Nail polish remover makes the clean-up job much easier.

1 green breadfruit
1 tablespoon oil or rendered pork fat
2 tablespoons fish sauce
100 g (3 oz) sliced *pla chorn*, trout or any freshwater fish
1 cup stock
2 tablespoons shredded *grachai* (wild ginger)
1 tablespoon picked green peppercorns
handful of holy basil leaves

paste

10–25 fresh red bird's eye chillies (scuds)
   or 10–25 dried red bird's eye chillies, soaked and drained
large pinch of salt
1 tablespoon chopped galangal
2 tablespoons chopped lemongrass
1 coriander root, scraped and chopped
2 tablespoons chopped *grachai* (wild ginger)
2 tablespoons chopped red shallot
1 tablespoon chopped garlic
1 teaspoon shrimp paste (*gapi*)

First, make the paste (see page 280).

Peel the breadfruit. Remove seeds and cut flesh into 1 cm (½ in) cubes – you need about 1 cup. Steep in salted, acidulated water, then bring to the boil and simmer until just tender.

Heat the oil or rendered pork fat, then fry 2 rounded tablespoons of the paste over medium heat for several minutes until explosively fragrant – cook until you can't help but sneeze! Season with most of the fish sauce, leaving a little for final adjustments. Add fish and breadfruit, moisten with stock and bring to the boil. Add *grachai*, peppercorns and basil and adjust final seasoning.

DRY RED CURRY OF LOBSTER

chuu chii haeng gung mangkorn

This kind of curry is mainly used for seafood: scallops, prawns, fish or any seafood
are ideal – of course, the cooking time will be much shorter than for lobster. The
seafood is fried and rested while the curry is being made and seasoned. It is quite
a dry, oily curry, very similar to the famous red curries. The difference lies in the
use of oil rather than coconut cream for frying.

Although this recipe is for a dry curry, it can also be made more
liquid simply by adding stock or water.

1 live lobster – about 1 kg (2 lb)

oil for deep-frying

large pinch of white sugar

2 tablespoons fish sauce

½ cup stock or water

5 kaffir lime leaves, finely shredded

handful of coriander leaves

paste

10 dried long red chillies, deseeded, soaked and drained

large pinch of salt

1½ tablespoons chopped galangal

3 tablespoons chopped lemongrass

2 teaspoons finely chopped kaffir lime zest

1 tablespoon scraped and chopped coriander root

1 tablespoon chopped red shallot

2 tablespoons chopped garlic

2 teaspoons shrimp paste (*gapi*)

First, make the paste (see page 280).

Cautiously wash the lobster and dispatch humanely. Cut in half, reserving
any liquid, tomalley or roe. Prise the meat away from the shell with a small paring
knife: this will ensure the flesh is easy to remove once it is cooked.

Heat the oil in a heavy wok. When quite hot, add the lobster, flesh side
down. Turn down the heat to medium and, after 2 minutes, turn the lobster. When
just cooked, remove and rest in a warm place.

Pour off all but 5 tablespoons of oil. Add 3 tablespoons of the paste and
fry over a medium heat for 5 minutes until fragrant. Season with sugar and fish
sauce. Continue to simmer until quite oily, moistening with any reserved liquid,
tomalley or roe from the lobster, and the stock or water. Check seasoning: it should
be salty, hot, rich and slightly sweet. Drain lobster of any liquid and place on a plate.
Cover with the curry and garnish with lime leaves and coriander.

Serve with:

- ← pickled garlic
- ← pickled ginger
- ← pickled red shallots
- ← Salted Beef (page 401), deep-fried.

CURRIED FISH INNARDS

geng dtai pla

It may come as some relief to know that fish innards can be bought ready to go in bottles from Chinese food stores. Do not be put off by such an unappetising ingredient: it is used only to flavour the curry and then discarded – and, once cooked, it becomes more than acceptable.

Originally served in the markets, this robust, thick, relish-like curry has gradually been incorporated into more formal meals, undergoing a sort of culinary gentrification along the way. This is a very popular dish among the Thai. Intense and powerfully flavoured, it is always served with vegetables.

1 cup stock

pinch of salt

1 cup fish innards (*dtai pla*)

1 tablespoon palm sugar

2 tablespoons fish sauce

2 tablespoons tamarind water

3 kaffir lime leaves, torn

handful of finely sliced green beans

5 slices galangal

a few slices white turmeric – if available

paste

3 tablespoons dried bird's eye chillies, soaked and drained

2 tablespoons fresh bird's eye chillies (scuds)

2 teaspoons salt

4 tablespoons chopped lemongrass

1 tablespoon chopped galangal

2 teaspoons finely grated kaffir lime zest

2 tablespoons chopped red shallot

2 tablespoons chopped garlic

1 tablespoon chopped red turmeric

15 white peppercorns

1 tablespoon shrimp paste (*gapi*)

½ cup boiled or grilled salted fish – ideally homemade (see page 176)

First, make the paste (see page 280). Bring stock and salt to the boil. Add the innards. Let stand for a few minutes, then strain. Return stock to the boil. Dissolve 3 tablespoons of the paste in stock. Season with palm sugar, fish sauce and tamarind water. Add lime leaves, green beans, galangal and turmeric. Simmer until thick.

Serve with:
- Raw Vegetables (page 380), such as apple eggplants, 'betel' leaves, cabbage, cucumber, white turmeric
- sprigs of coriander.

CURRY OF ASH MELON

geng krua fak gwio

Geng krua are very varied curries, ranging from straightforward and slightly salty through pleasantly bitter to sweet and sour. The seasoning of this curry is salty and rich, smoky and creamy. The heat is moderate and plays a supporting role to the other ingredients. Although this type of curry is little known in the West, it is the most diverse style of curry throughout Thailand.

What is unusual about *geng krua* is that they rarely use shrimp paste but instead normally include fish to give depth and body to the curry. They are generous and gentle curries that enhance any ingredient – and are mellow, with the fish supporting the structure of the taste and playing as important a role in the curry as the main ingredient. Almost any fish can be used, although traditionally freshwater fish is preferred – fresh, dried, salted, boiled or grilled. I have found that when fish is added to a curry paste it requires longer cooking than usual, at a higher heat, to achieve the desired separation.

1 small ash melon or bottle gourd
1½ cups coconut cream
1 teaspoon palm sugar
2 tablespoons fish sauce
½–1 cup coconut milk
2 kaffir lime leaves, shredded

paste
6 dried long red chillies, deseeded, soaked and drained
large pinch of salt
1 tablespoon chopped galangal
2 tablespoons chopped lemongrass
3 tablespoons chopped red shallot
2 tablespoons chopped garlic
3 tablespoons cooked fish – roasted or boiled – or hot-smoked trout

First, make the paste (see page 280).

Prepare the melon or gourd: peel, cut in half, then deseed with a tablespoon. Wash and dry before cutting the flesh into 2 cm (1 in) cubes. Crack the coconut cream over medium heat, then work in 2 tablespoons of the paste. Add melon or gourd. Fry paste over medium heat for at least 5 minutes until you can smell the fish – and, coincidentally, the melon or gourd will be almost cooked. Season with sugar and most of the fish sauce, leaving some for final seasoning. Moisten with coconut milk and continue to simmer until the melon or gourd is just cooked. Serve sprinkled with lime leaves. Check seasoning before serving.

Accompany with:
- salted fish
- Stir-fried Dried Mussels (page 396)
- Sweet Shredded Skate (page 396).

CURRY OF GRILLED BEEF AND SIAMESE CASSIA
geng kii lek

Mom Leuang Sae Gritsadtagorn was born in 1904. Descended from a second-reign family, she was one of the first of her generation to be educated at a school for girls, rather than in the cool arcades of a palace. Later she married one of the numerous grandsons of Rama IV and lived the conventional and somewhat leisured life of a woman of her class. Hardship, however, struck when her husband died rather young, leaving her to raise their four children. She enterprisingly subdivided her family compound, built several houses and sold them to support and educate her children.

Mom Leuang Sae delighted most in cooking, thus making merit daily with monks – and occasionally cooking for the king and queen, to whom she was a lady-in-waiting. She had filled several plump volumes with her favourite recipes when she died in 1980. This is one of them.

500 g (1 lb) Siamese cassia
200 g (6 oz) beef – rump, for example
1 cup coconut cream
1 tablespoon palm sugar
3 tablespoons fermented fish sauce (*nahm pla raa*)
  or 2 tablespoons fish sauce
2 cups coconut milk or stock
3 tablespoons shredded *grachai* (wild ginger)
3 kaffir lime leaves, torn

paste

9 dried long red chillies, deseeded, soaked and drained

large pinch of salt

1 tablespoon chopped galangal

2 tablespoons chopped lemongrass

3 tablespoons chopped *grachai* (wild ginger)

3 tablespoons chopped red shallot

1 tablespoon chopped garlic

4 tablespoons ground *pla grop* (crisp fish)

Blanch Siamese cassia 3–5 times from a cold-water start with salt and refresh until not so pungently bitter (it should taste like good tea). Reserve a few tablespoons of the final blanching water. Pick the leaves from the stalks – you should have about 1 cup. Once blanched, it will last a week if refrigerated.

Next, make the paste (see page 280).

Grill the beef until rare and set aside to rest well. Bring coconut cream to the boil, turn the heat down to medium and simmer until separated, stirring regularly. Add 3 tablespoons of the paste and fry, stirring regularly, for several minutes until fragrant. Season with palm sugar and simmer until the paste has darkened a little and the *pla grop* is fragrant. Add fish sauce and simmer to evaporate slightly. Add coconut milk or stock, together with the reserved blanching water from the cassia, and simmer for a few minutes. Add Siamese cassia leaves and reduce the heat. Replenish with extra stock if necessary. Slice the beef. Add to the curry with the *grachai* and lime leaves. Remove from the heat immediately – any further cooking would toughen the meat. Check seasoning: it should be salty, slightly bitter and hot. It should also be fragrant from the fish sauce and *grachai*.

Accompany with:

→ pickled red shallots

→ Steamed Eggs (page 388)

→ *pla salit*, grilled.

MANGOSTEEN AND MUSSEL CURRY

geng hoi malaeng puu mangkrut

This is a 'sour' *geng krua*, given an extra dimension by palm sugar and tamarind water. To balance this extra seasoning, the curry paste includes coriander root and kaffir lime zest. In this type of curry, fatty or richly flavoured meat or fish is combined with sweetly sour fruit or unripe sour vegetables – for instance duck with lychees, pork with green tomatoes, crab with pineapple, chicken with sour snakeskin pear.

The primary seasoning is salty, then sweetness or sourness is the next flavour, depending upon the garnish and preference – this can be adjusted by altering the proportions of sugar, tamarind and fish sauce. Take into account, when seasoning, the sourness of the fruit or vegetable that will be added later and do not under-salt, nor over-season with sugar or tamarind.

1½ cups coconut cream
2 tablespoons palm sugar
1 tablespoon fish sauce
1 tablespoon tamarind water
½ cup coconut milk
3 mangosteens, flesh removed from husk
300 g (9 oz) mussels or clams
3 kaffir lime leaves, torn
a few picked 'betel' leaves – optional

paste
8 dried long red chillies, deseeded, soaked and drained
large pinch of salt
1 tablespoon chopped galangal
4 tablespoons chopped lemongrass
1 teaspoon finely chopped kaffir lime zest
1 teaspoon scraped and chopped coriander root
3 tablespoons chopped red shallot
3 tablespoons chopped garlic
1 teaspoon shrimp paste (*gapi*) – optional
4 *pla salit* or 5 *pla grop* (crisp fish) *or* flesh of ½ hot-smoked trout

First, make the paste (see page 280). If using *pla salit* or *pla grop*, lightly grill the fish, fillet, skin and grind before adding to the paste.

Crack the coconut cream over medium heat, add 3 tablespoons of the paste and fry until the fish is fragrant. Season with palm sugar, fish sauce – not too much because of the saltiness of the seafood – and then the tamarind water. (Do not cook the paste for more than a minute or so after adding the tamarind or it will burn.) Moisten with coconut milk, then add mangosteens and mussels or clams. Simmer until the molluscs open (discard any that remain stubbornly closed). Finish with lime leaves and 'betel' leaves. Check seasoning – it may need more fish sauce.

Accompany with:
— *pla grop* (crisp fish)
— grilled pork.

RED CURRY OF PORK AND BAMBOO SHOOTS

geng dtaeng moo gap nor mai

The description 'red curry' (*geng dtaeng*) encompasses the largest range of Thai curries. Put simply, its single defining characteristic is that it is red. A red curry paste usually contains the standard ingredients of dried red chillies, garlic, shallots, lemongrass, galangal and shrimp paste, and is nearly always a fried, coconut-based curry. Almost any type of meat, fish or vegetable can be used, and these can be cooked in a variety of ways – grilled, deep-fried or poached in coconut milk before being added, or simply fried in the paste. Remember that red curry paste takes a while to cook: fry the paste for at least 10 minutes before seasoning – it should smell rich and complex, with hints of galangal and kaffir lime when it is ready. It is usually finished with kaffir lime leaves, sliced fresh chillies and Thai or holy basil.

A red curry should be quite liquid but not too thin, and salty and sweet to varying degrees. The flavour balance of this red curry should tend towards salt, then to sweetness – a little more than other red curries because the slightly bitter quality of the bamboo shoots should be taken into account. The Thai like this bitterness, so they do not reduce this characteristic by repeated blanching; instead they sweeten the curry to balance the bitter taste.

200 g (6 oz) pork ribs

3 cups coconut milk

1½ cups coconut cream

1 tablespoon palm sugar

2 tablespoons fish sauce

extra 2 cups coconut milk – optional

1 cup shredded boiled bamboo shoots

3 kaffir lime leaves, torn

2 long red or green chillies, deseeded and cut into ovals

handful of Thai basil leaves

paste

11 dried long red chillies, deseeded, soaked and drained

large pinch of salt

1 teaspoon chopped galangal

2 tablespoons chopped lemongrass

1 teaspoon finely chopped kaffir lime zest

1 teaspoon scraped and chopped coriander root

4 tablespoons chopped red shallot

6 tablespoons chopped garlic

1 teaspoon shrimp paste (*gapi*)

2 teaspoons coriander seeds, roasted and ground

1 teaspoon cumin seeds, roasted and ground

1 teaspoon white peppercorns

First, make the paste (see page 280).

Prepare pork ribs: blanch from a cold-water start, bring to the boil briefly, refresh in cold water and rinse. Then cut into 1 cm (½ in) strips and poach in the 3 cups of coconut milk until cooked – about 20 minutes.

Simmer coconut cream over medium heat until cracked. Work in 4 tablespoons of the paste and fry over a medium heat for about 10 minutes, until very fragrant and the dried spices predominate. Season, first with palm sugar, cooking for a minute or so to allow the sugar to dissolve and to begin to darken the paste. Then add fish sauce and allow to evaporate slightly. Add pork and moisten with either the poaching liquid or the extra 2 cups of coconut milk and simmer for 1–2 minutes.

Finish with the remaining ingredients, take off the heat and wait for a minute before serving to allow the flavours to ripen. The curry should be rich from the coconut cream, slightly sweet and salty, with only a suggestion of the dried spices – and fragrant from the lime leaves, chillies and basil added at the end.

Accompany with:
- Pickled Vegetables (page 383)
- salted fish
- Salted Beef (page 401).

RED DUCK CURRY

geng dtaeng bpet

This recipe belongs to Khun Sin, who cooked for Mom Chao Niwat Sawati Chirapravati. Little is known of her: consigned to a separate area away from the main house, Khun Sin cooked, and cooked well. Bristling, affable and, I suspect, with a pert efficiency, Sin achieved a rare elegance in her food. The following recipe is an indication of her skill.

The paste contains an inordinate amount of dried spices in proportion to the other ingredients – a few roasted shallots are added to counterbalance the degree of spice. This is a dark, rich and redolent curry that is also excellent made with game, such as venison, squab or even hare.

2 duck legs – about 125 g (4 oz) each

3 cups coconut milk

1 cup coconut cream

1 teaspoon–1 tablespoon palm sugar

2 tablespoons fish sauce

4 kaffir lime leaves, torn

2 long green chillies, diagonally sliced

handful of Thai basil leaves

paste

7 dried long red chillies, deseeded, soaked and drained

large pinch of salt

2 tablespoons chopped lemongrass

½ tablespoon finely chopped kaffir lime zest

2 tablespoons chopped red shallot

1 tablespoon roasted and chopped red shallot

1 tablespoon chopped garlic

½ teaspoon shrimp paste (*gapi*)

10 white peppercorns

1½ teaspoons coriander seeds, roasted and ground

1 teaspoon cumin seeds, roasted and ground

¼ nutmeg, coarsely pounded and briefly roasted

5 cloves, roasted and ground

First, make the paste (see page 280).

Bone the duck and cut the meat into 1 cm (½ in) cubes. Wash the bones, then chop and simmer in the coconut milk for 30 minutes. Strain, add the coconut cream to this coconut milk, bring to the boil and add the meat. Simmer gently until meat is tender and cream is oily – about 10 minutes (it may be necessary to add a little water to ensure that it is not too oily), then remove from the heat.

Spoon about a tablespoon of the coconut cream and oil from this pot into a separate pan. Fry 3 tablespoons of the paste in this, moistening often with more coconut cream from the other pot, until fragrant. Season with palm sugar and fish sauce. Incorporate all the coconut liquid and duck, and simmer for 2–3 minutes. Add lime leaves, chillies and basil. Check the seasoning: this rather rich, oily and spicy curry should taste salty, hot and sweet.

Accompany with:

– pickled ginger

– Steamed Salted Duck Eggs (page 391)

– deep-fried dried fish, such as *pla salit*, *pla grop* or Dried Smoked Trout Fillet (page 179).

STEAMED FISH CURRY

hor mok pla

Because the paste is steamed with coconut cream and egg, this red curry becomes delicate and smooth. When I was first taught to make it, I was told that the coconut cream must be incorporated by stirring only in one direction, clockwise; otherwise the emulsion would break. I suspect I was spun a yarn, akin to never making a mayonnaise during a full moon.

Steam over a moderate heat, as too high a heat will soufflé the mixture, causing it to over-expand and toughen as it cools. Mostly seafood is used in this curry: cooked mussels removed from their shells, added to the mixture and then spooned back into their shells before steaming make a particularly elegant version.

200 g (6 oz) fish fillets – whiting, blue-eye cod or perch

pinch of salt

a little lime juice

2 tablespoons fish sauce

pinch of palm sugar

½ cup coconut cream

1 small egg, lightly beaten

6 kaffir lime leaves, finely shredded

1–2 banana leaves – optional

handful of Thai basil leaves

1 tablespoon thick coconut cream

a few long red chillies, julienned

paste

6–10 dried long red chillies, deseeded, soaked and drained

large pinch of salt

1 tablespoon chopped galangal

2 tablespoons chopped lemongrass

1 teaspoon finely chopped kaffir lime zest

1 teaspoon scraped and chopped coriander root

2 tablespoons chopped red shallot

3 tablespoons chopped garlic

1 teaspoon shrimp paste (*gapi*), roasted

First, make the paste (see page 280).

Wash fish in water with a little salt and squeeze of lime juice. Drain, pat dry and slice finely. In a bowl, season fish with fish sauce and sugar, stirring with a spoon. Gradually and cautiously, work in the coconut cream. Like a mayonnaise, it must not separate; if it does, add a little ice-cold water and stir to incorporate. Fold in 3 tablespoons of the paste and check seasoning: it should be salty and sweet, redolent with coconut cream. Stir in the egg and finish with the lime leaves, reserving a few for garnish.

Cut banana leaves – if using – into large circles, around 12 cm (5 in) in diameter. Wipe them and then put one circle on top of another, shiny sides out, with the grain of the leaves running at right angles to each other. At four evenly spaced intervals crimp the leaves to form a basket, securing with small toothpicks. Flatten the bottom, line with Thai basil leaves and add the curry. (Or, more simply, line a large porcelain bowl with the Thai basil and spoon in the curry.)

Steam over a moderate heat for 15–30 minutes, until the curry has set (this will depend on the amount prepared and the size of the steaming receptacle). Remove carefully and garnish with thick coconut cream, the reserved lime leaves and red chilli julienne.

Accompany with:
— Pickled Vegetables (page 383), especially ginger
— Deep-fried Trout Dumplings (page 395), or any fish dumplings
— Salted Pork with Coconut Milk (page 397)
— Freshly Salted Beef (page 402).

GRILLED PRAWN CURRY

ngob gung

In this type of curry, the paste is generally mixed with coconut cream, seasoned and finished with shredded chillies, kaffir lime leaves and Thai basil. This is then worked into any fish or shellfish, which is wrapped in banana leaves and grilled (*ngob* denotes wrapping in banana leaves). The following version is quite similar, except the curry paste is mixed not with coconut cream but with freshly grated coconut. This creates a textured, nutty finish.

If making this recipe with a large piece of fish that will take some time to cook, it is not necessary to heat the paste with the grated coconut; simply combine, season, wrap and grill.

2 cups freshly grated coconut

3 tablespoons oil

1 tablespoon palm sugar

3 tablespoons fish sauce

6 large uncooked prawns (shrimp), peeled and deveined

6 kaffir lime leaves, shredded

1–2 banana leaves

handful of Thai basil leaves

2 toothpicks, soaked in water for at least an hour

paste

8–10 dried long red chillies, deseeded, soaked and drained

large pinch of salt

1 tablespoon chopped galangal

3 tablespoons chopped lemongrass

1 teaspoon finely chopped kaffir lime zest

1 tablespoon scraped and chopped coriander root

2 tablespoons chopped red shallot

2 tablespoons chopped garlic

First, make the paste (see page 280).

Combine grated coconut with oil and 3 tablespoons of the curry paste. Cook over low heat in a small pan or heavy wok until paste is fragrant and a little oily. Season with sugar and fish sauce and remove from heat. Cool. Stir in prawns and lime leaves. Clean banana leaves and cut into 2 rectangles, 8 cm × 12 cm (3 in × 5 in). Place the leaves on top of each other, shiny sides out. Line with basil leaves and then spread mixture over a third of leaf. Fold to form an envelope and secure with toothpicks. Chargrill over a medium heat for 10 minutes.

BEEF PANAENG

geng panaeng neua

A *panaeng* curry is perhaps one of the most popular in the Thai repertoire. Salty, sweet and redolent of Thai basil, with a background taste of peanuts, the curry is enriched with plenty of coconut cream – and can be improved by roasting one or two of the shallots before adding them to the paste.

This is one of the few curries normally made with beef, although chicken or pork can replace it. Usually the meat is braised before it is added to the curry, because meat in Thailand is so tough that it needs prolonged cooking. Therefore, I think the best cut of beef to use is one that is full-flavoured, has good texture and is able to sustain prolonged cooking – such as shank, rib or brisket. Alternatively, finely sliced meat can be added to the curry after it has been seasoned, to cook quickly.

The peanuts must be thoroughly cooked and cooled before being added to the paste: if they are insufficiently cooked, they will make the curry gritty. I prefer to boil them, as this gives the curry a subtle bitterness. Others may prefer to roast them, which will make the curry toasty and rich.

200 g (6 oz) beef brisket or cheek, sinew removed

4 cups coconut milk

3 cups coconut cream

BEEF PANAENG

1½ tablespoons palm sugar

2 tablespoons fish sauce

extra 3 cups coconut milk – optional (see method)

3 kaffir lime leaves, torn

3 long red or green chillies, cut in half and deseeded

large handful of Thai basil leaves

paste

4 tablespoons peanuts

7 dried long red chillies, deseeded, soaked and drained

large pinch of salt

1 teaspoon scraped and chopped coriander root

1½ tablespoons chopped galangal

1 tablespoon chopped lemongrass

3 tablespoons chopped red shallot

2 tablespoons chopped garlic

½ nutmeg, coarsely pounded and briefly roasted

First, make the paste. Boil the peanuts for at least 30 minutes until very soft, drain and cool. Pound or blend the paste (see page 280), adding peanuts last.

Blanch the meat from a cold-water start (to soften its flavour) and rinse. Bring coconut milk to the boil, add beef, then turn down the heat and braise gently until tender – about 2 hours. Allow to cool in the liquid, then remove and slice.

Crack the coconut cream by simmering over a medium heat, then fry 4 tablespoons of the paste in the coconut cream for 10 minutes. Season first with palm sugar and then, after a minute or so, the fish sauce. Moisten with the 3 cups coconut milk or the same amount of the beef-braising liquid (the latter makes the curry very meaty – it is a matter of preference). Add the sliced beef, simmer briefly to heat through, and finish with the remaining ingredients.

Accompany with:
- pickled ginger
- Steamed Eggs (page 388) or Steamed Egg Mousse (page 390)
- Salted Prawns (page 392)
- deep-fried fish.

GREEN CURRY OF CHICKEN WITH BABY CORN

geng gwio warn gai

Green curry is the most classic of Thai curries – certainly one with which most people are familiar, as it is ubiquitous on Thai restaurant menus. To my understanding, it is the most typical of the central plains curries, being based on coconut cream fried with a paste made from fresh green chillies, sharpened with galangal, shallots and lemongrass. Other ingredients are fish, fowl, meat and vegetables, and these can be grilled, salted or deep-fried, simmered in the curry paste or poached in the coconut milk before being added to the seasoned paste.

The characteristic seasoning of a green curry is quite hot (although the degree may vary) and salty. There is no sugar in the seasoning to mitigate the heat – any sweetness is due to coconut cream and the garnish. Some cooks insist on adding sugar to this curry, but I find the sugar overwhelms the complex array of tastes. Since green curries are more pungent (and thinner) than the gentle red curries, they usually have strongly flavoured meat or fish in them. Firm, slightly bitter vegetables, such as bamboo shoots, banana blossom or apple and pea eggplants are the perfect foil to this curry, giving it an additional breadth of flavour. Corn, young coconut or heart of coconut palm lead the curry's taste elsewhere. The final garnish needs to be crisp and decided in its flavour, so that it improves the curry rather than disappears into it: it almost always includes kaffir lime leaves, fresh chillies and Thai basil and, if the curry is pungent, holy basil, *grachai* (wild ginger) or white turmeric.

2 cups coconut cream

150 g (5 oz) skinless chicken thigh fillets, sliced

2 tablespoons fish sauce

2 cups thin coconut milk or stock

6–10 baby corn

3 kaffir lime leaves, torn

2 long red chillies, diagonally sliced

handful of Thai basil leaves

paste

3 tablespoons green bird's eye chillies (scuds)

large pinch of salt

1 tablespoon chopped galangal

2 tablespoons chopped lemongrass

1 tablespoon finely chopped kaffir lime zest

1 tablespoon scraped and chopped coriander root

1 teaspoon chopped red turmeric

3 tablespoons chopped red shallot

2 tablespoons chopped garlic

1 teaspoon shrimp paste (*gapi*)

10 white peppercorns

½ teaspoon coriander seeds, roasted and ground

¼ teaspoon cumin seeds, roasted and ground

First, make the paste (see page 280).

Crack the coconut cream in a pan and add 2 tablespoons of the paste. Fry over a medium to high heat, stirring regularly to prevent the paste burning. Add chicken and continue to cook, still stirring, until the paste is fragrant. Season with fish sauce and then add coconut milk or stock. Bring to the boil, reduce heat, add corn and simmer. When chicken is cooked (about 3–4 minutes), garnish with lime leaves, chillies and Thai basil.

Accompany with:
— Steamed Salted Duck Eggs (page 391)
— dried fish
— Freshly Salted Beef (page 402).

GREEN CURRY OF TROUT DUMPLINGS WITH APPLE EGGPLANTS

geng gwio warn look chin pla

Jip Bunnark was the niece of the culinary doyenne of Thailand, Thanpuuying Pliang Pasonagorn. Born in 1899, Jip was raised in her aunt's palace, where she learnt the traditional arts of cooking. She became renowned as one of the finest cooks of her generation. After marrying into the illustrious Bunnark family, Jip taught at the prestigious Suan Dusit College for almost a decade during the 1940s, and many of today's respected culinary teachers were her pupils. Later she wrote a cookbook in which she adapted, altered and often simplified recipes for Thai classic dishes to suit modern tastes and circumstances. This is one of them.

While any fish, or seafood, can be puréed to make the dumplings for this recipe, the trout imparts a pleasing hue that contrasts with the green curry. Adding tapioca flour to the dumplings gives them a toothsome quality, but only a little should be used or they become too floury. If time is short, the fish can simply be sliced and added to the finished curry, rather than made into dumplings.

3 cups coconut milk or salted water

2 cups coconut cream

2 tablespoons fish sauce

extra 2 cups coconut milk

3–4 apple eggplants

2 kaffir lime leaves, torn

3 long red or green chillies, deseeded and cut into ovals

handful of Thai basil leaves

1 tablespoon peeled and shredded *grachai* (wild ginger)

paste

2 tablespoons green bird's eye chillies (scuds)

2 tablespoons chopped long green chilli

large pinch of salt

1 tablespoon chopped galangal

3 tablespoons chopped lemongrass

1 teaspoon finely chopped kaffir lime zest

1 tablespoon scraped and chopped coriander root

1 teaspoon chopped red turmeric

1 teaspoon chopped *grachai* (wild ginger)

3 tablespoons chopped red shallot

2 tablespoons chopped garlic

1 teaspoon shrimp paste (*gapi*), roasted

1 teaspoon white peppercorns

1 teaspoon coriander seeds, roasted and ground

1 sheath of mace, roasted and ground – optional

fish dumplings

3 coriander roots, scraped and chopped

1 teaspoon salt

1½ tablespoons chopped garlic

1 tablespoon chopped ginger

5 white peppercorns

200 g (6 oz) filleted, skinned and minced trout flesh

2 tablespoons tapioca flour – optional (increase seasoning slightly if using)

2 tablespoons fish sauce or light soy sauce

1 teaspoon white sugar

First, make the paste (see page 280).

To make the fish dumplings, pound coriander roots in a mortar with salt, garlic, ginger and peppercorns until fine. In a large bowl, combine this coriander paste with the fish and tapioca flour, if using, working until the mixture can be rolled into a ball. Pick it up and then throw it back into the bowl. Repeat the process several times – this slapping improves the texture of the dumplings, making them smoother and firmer. Season with fish sauce or light soy sauce and sugar. Slap several more times. Test by poaching a little of the mixture in some boiling water or coconut milk; adjust seasoning, if necessary, but do not over-season as the dumplings are going into a highly seasoned curry.

Roll, spoon or pinch mixture into 2 cm (1 in) dumplings. Poach in the 3 cups coconut milk or salted water. The dumplings take a surprisingly short time to cook, about 3 minutes, and are ready when they float to the top. Drain and set aside.

Crack the coconut cream and fry 3 tablespoons of the paste, at a brisk pace over a medium to high heat, until the greenness of the raw ingredients has disappeared. The paste must smell cooked, but the fresh chillies should still be fiercely and freshly pungent. Season with fish sauce and moisten with the extra 2 cups coconut milk. Bring to the boil, add apple eggplants and simmer for a few minutes to cook them. Add dumplings, heat through and then finish with kaffir lime leaves, chillies, Thai basil and *grachai*.

Accompany with:
- Steamed Salted Duck Eggs (page 391)
- trout roe
- Freshly Salted Beef (page 402).

FOREIGN CURRIES

Just as Thailand has absorbed many ingredients, so it has absorbed many new dishes. Some were introduced centuries ago and are so incorporated that they are indistinguishable from indigenous dishes. Given that Thailand has been at a crossroads of trade and civilisations, what is uniquely Thai is sometimes rather difficult to discern. However, some curries, like the following few examples, clearly have foreign origins – although they have, of course, been 'Siam-ised'.

SOUTHERN-STYLE CURRY OF MUD CRAB

geng guwa malayu

This curry is quite common in the south of Thailand, and shares many qualities with Malaysian curries.

Any fish – especially the long, silver-skinned ribbon fish – is used there, but scallops or clams are also very good. Although traditionally there is no vegetable garnish in this curry, I think 'betel' leaves, pickled mustard greens or some sour fruit, like santol or *langsart*, are delicious inclusions.

1 large live mud crab – about 1–1½ kg (2–3 lb)

1 cup coconut milk

2 cups stock or water

1 tablespoons white sugar

3 tablespoons fish sauce

2 tablespoons tamarind water

handful of torn 'betel' leaves – optional

1 cup coconut cream

5 kaffir lime leaves, finely shredded

paste

6 dried long red chillies, deseeded, soaked and drained

large pinch of salt

2 teaspoons scraped and chopped coriander root

5 tablespoons chopped lemongrass

3 tablespoons chopped red shallot

3 tablespoons chopped garlic

1 tablespoon chopped red turmeric

1 tablespoon shrimp paste (*gapi*)

First, make the paste (see page 280).

Kill the crab humanely, and rinse off any mud or dirt. Then remove the top of its shell, scrape out any tomalley or roe and chop the crab into bite-size pieces.

Bring coconut milk and stock to the boil and simmer until the liquid has slightly separated – only a matter of moments. Season with sugar, fish sauce and tamarind water, and add 3 tablespoons of the paste. Simmer for a minute before adding the crab and 'betel' leaves. Continue to simmer until cooked. Check seasoning: it should be salty and sour. Finish with coconut cream and serve sprinkled with lime leaves.

Serve with Pickled Vegetables (page 383).

CHIANG MAI PORK CURRY

geng hang lae

This curry comes from the north of Thailand, as the name suggests, and is sometimes called a Burmese curry; it was adopted by the northern Thai when they were under the rule of the Burmese from the sixteenth to eighteen centuries. With the complexities of a *mussaman* – also an imported curry – this thick and oily dish is redolent of spices that suggest an Indian origin, not very far away from the borders of Myanmar (as Burma is now called).

Pork belly and ribs and peanuts are the most consistent ingredients in this curry, which has many variations. On the northern border of Thailand, at Chiang Saen, the local version adds a selection of vegetables – boiled or fermented bamboo shoots, long green and apple eggplants or snake beans – to the requisite pork and peanuts.

Always make more than necessary as this curry keeps well – in fact, it improves in the keeping.

200 g (6 oz) pork belly

200 g (6 oz) pork ribs

3 tablespoons rendered pork fat or oil

12 red shallots, peeled

3 cups coarsely shredded ginger

1 cup pickled garlic, peeled and heads cut in half

1 cup pickled garlic syrup

½ cup roasted peanuts

3 tablespoons palm sugar

4 tablespoons fish sauce

4 tablespoons tamarind water

1–2 cups stock or water

curry paste

10 dried long red chillies, deseeded, soaked and drained

large pinch of salt

1 tablespoon chopped galangal

6 tablespoons chopped lemongrass

2 tablespoons chopped ginger

1 tablespoon chopped red turmeric

8 tablespoons chopped red shallot

6 tablespoons chopped garlic

1 tablespoon coriander seeds, roasted and ground

2 teaspoons cumin seeds, roasted and ground

3 star anise, roasted and ground

2 cm (1 in) piece of cassia bark, roasted and ground

5 cloves, roasted and ground – optional

2 Thai cardamom pods, roasted and seeds ground – optional

garlic and ginger paste

4 garlic cloves, peeled

½ teaspoon salt

2 cm (1 in) piece of ginger, peeled

First, make the curry paste (see page 280). Then make the garlic and ginger paste by pounding the ingredients using a pestle and mortar.

Blanch pork belly and ribs twice from a cold-water start. Refresh and, when cool, cut into 2 cm (1 in) cubes. Heat fat or oil, and fry garlic and ginger paste until golden. Add curry paste and pork and simmer for several minutes, stirring regularly. Add shallots, ginger, pickled garlic, pickled garlic syrup and peanuts. Season with palm sugar, fish sauce and tamarind water. Cover with stock or water and simmer for 1 hour, or until pork is tender. Check seasoning: it should be salty, sweet and sour, with flavours of ginger and star anise. >

Accompany with:

— deep-fried fish
— Crispy Fried Pork (page 399)
— Deep-fried Pork Skin (page 400).

AROMATIC DUCK CURRY
geng gari bpet

Geng gari (aromatic curry) is of Indian origin, as the name suggests – *gari* is the Tamil word from which the English 'curry' is derived. The seasoning is quite salty, and only a little sugar is added to prevent the paste having a bitter edge from the abundance of dried spices; the taste should be redolent of spice, not riddled with it. This type of curry is usually accompanied by pickled vegetables to cut through the coconut cream in the curry and reveal the spice. Poultry or beef are the most common ingredients used in a *geng gari*, together with a starchy vegetable – potato being the most traditional. Occasionally freshwater fish is used, while alternative vegetables include pumpkin, taro, white radish or sweet potato. This recipe comes from Mom Ratchawongse Dteuang Sanitsawongse.

4 cups coconut milk

2 duck legs, cut into 3 pieces – and skin removed, if preferred

3 medium-size potatoes, peeled and quartered

3 cups coconut cream

2 teaspoons palm sugar

3 tablespoons fish sauce

handful of deep-fried shallots

paste

7 dried long red chillies, deseeded, soaked and drained

1 teaspoon salt

1 tablespoon chopped red turmeric

3 tablespoons chopped red shallot

2 tablespoons chopped garlic

1 tablespoon chopped galangal

1 tablespoon chopped lemongrass

2 teaspoons scraped and chopped coriander root

15 white peppercorns

1 tablespoon coriander seeds, roasted and ground

2 teaspoons cumin seeds, roasted and ground

1 teaspoon fennel seeds, roasted and ground

3 sheaths mace, roasted and ground

First, make the paste (see page 280).

Heat coconut milk. Add duck pieces and poach until cooked – about 20 minutes – then set aside. Rinse potatoes under running water to remove any excess starch, then boil in salted water or coconut milk until cooked but still firm.

Meanwhile, crack the coconut cream and fry the paste in it for at least 5 minutes, until fragrant with the spices. Season with palm sugar and fish sauce. Moisten with the duck poaching liquid, ladle by ladle, until a medium-thick curry is achieved. Add duck and potatoes. Check seasoning, then sprinkle with deep-fried shallots.

Serve with:
- pickled red shallots
- Cucumber Relish (page 402)
- *pla grop* (crisp fish).

CHICKEN LIVERS WITH SOUTHERN-STYLE CURRY PASTE

dap pat baep malayuu

This is a southern Muslim curry. Traditionally the livers are poached before being added to the curry as the Thai prefer them completely cooked, but for Western tastes simply simmer the livers in the curry for a few minutes.

200 g (6 oz) chicken livers
½ cup oil
6 red shallots, finely sliced
2 cups chicken stock
1–2 tablespoons white sugar
large pinch of salt
1 tablespoon fish sauce
2 tablespoons white vinegar
1 red shallot, coarsely sliced
1 tablespoon coriander leaves

paste
8 dried long red chillies, deseeded, soaked and drained
large pinch of salt
6 tablespoons chopped red shallot
3 tablespoons chopped garlic
3 tablespoons chopped ginger
1 tablespoon chopped lemongrass
1 tablespoon coriander seeds, roasted and ground
1 teaspoon cumin seeds, roasted and ground

First, make the paste (see page 280).

Clean the livers, discarding any discoloured parts – and, if desired, poach until firm and cooked. Cut into bite-size pieces.

Heat oil and deep-fry the finely sliced shallots until golden, then remove and drain about a third of the shallots. Add paste to the same oil and simmer, stirring regularly, until fragrant. Moisten with stock as required, but don't make it too wet – simmer until any excess has evaporated. Season with sugar, salt, fish sauce and vinegar: the curry should taste rich, spicy and salty; it should also be quite oily. Add liver and simmer for a few minutes. Sprinkle with reserved deep-fried shallots, coarsely sliced shallots and coriander leaves.

Serve with:
— Raw Vegetables (page 380), such as 'betel' leaves, cabbage and cucumber
— Pickled Vegetables (page 383)
— pickled ginger
— Steamed Eggs (page 388)
— Cucumber Relish (page 402).

MUSSAMAN CURRY OF CHICKEN

geng mussaman

A *mussaman* curry is the most complex, time-consuming Thai curry to make; it is also the most delicious. Although now completely incorporated into the Thai repertoire, the *mussaman* is a relatively recent addition. This style of curry is believed to have arrived in Siam with the first Persian envoy to the Court of Ayuthyia in the sixteenth century. Sheik Amed remained in Siam and eventually established the Bunnark family, which, over the centuries, grew in power to rival the royal family. The following recipe is from Jip Bunnark and is much more complicated than the historic recipe that has been suggested as the original *mussaman*, which required only dried spices with some onions and ginger. However, when the Siamese absorb new influences they do so by adapting a novel dish in a peculiarly, ornately Siamese way. A Thai *mussaman* curry is oily, and highly seasoned with tamarind and sugar.

The most common version uses chicken or beef with potatoes and onions, but I have come across many variations, including duck with pieces of pineapple (making unnecessary the final addition of pineapple juice), beef with white radish and even freshwater fish with long eggplants. I have always thought, in deference to its origins, that partridge or pheasant would be pleasing. A starchy vegetable – potato, sweet potato, white radish – is a necessary component. I often marinate the chicken in a sweet soy sauce, such as *kecap manis*, so that when it is fried it has a deep-golden colour.

3 chicken legs

4 medium-size potatoes

oil for deep-frying

8 small pickling onions or red shallots, peeled

4–5 cups coconut milk

5 Thai cardamom pods, roasted

½ cup peanuts, roasted

4 bay leaves, roasted

3 cups coconut cream

2 tablespoons–1 cup palm sugar

3–5 tablespoons fish sauce

2–5 tablespoons tamarind water

1 cup pineapple juice

paste

5 dried long red chillies, deseeded, soaked and drained

4 tablespoons chopped red shallot

5 tablespoons chopped garlic

2 tablespoons chopped galangal

3 tablespoons chopped lemongrass

1 tablespoon scraped and chopped coriander root

large pinch of salt

2 tablespoons peanuts, roasted

1 tablespoon coriander seeds, roasted and ground

1 teaspoon cumin seeds, roasted and ground

5 cloves, roasted and ground

½ nutmeg, coarsely pounded and briefly roasted

2 sheaths of mace, roasted and ground

2 cm (1 in) piece of cassia bark, roasted and ground

4 Thai cardamom pods, roasted and seeds ground

Cut each chicken leg into four, removing skin if desired; wash and dry. Peel and quarter the potatoes, then steep in cold water to leach out any excess starch.

To make the paste, combine the chillies, shallots, garlic, galangal, lemongrass and coriander root, and roast in a wok with a little water until brown and fragrant. Purée these roasted ingredients and work in the salt, peanuts and the combined sieved dried spices until a smooth paste is achieved.

Deep-fry chicken pieces until golden. Remove and drain on absorbent paper. Repeat with potatoes and onions. (Deep-frying seals and firms the chicken and vegetables, as well as enriching the curry.) >

Put chicken in another pan, add sufficient coconut milk to just cover (too much will dilute the intense flavours of the curry), and bring to the boil. Add cardamom pods, peanuts and bay leaves. When chicken is almost cooked, about 10 minutes, add potatoes and onions.

In a medium pot, crack the coconut cream and then add the paste. Turn down the heat and simmer, stirring regularly to prevent burning, for at least 10 minutes – cook until you can smell the dried spices. Be careful, for the paste will be very hot and it splatters. If the paste begins to burn, change the pan. If the paste is not oily enough, moisten with some of the chicken braising liquid. When the paste is oily, hot and sizzling, season with palm sugar and, when that has dissolved, continue to simmer as the sugar begins to caramelise, deepening the colour and flavour of the curry. The amount of sugar required is determined by taste and the accompanying dishes.

Add fish sauce and tamarind water. The amount of these should be increased or decreased according to the amount of sugar being used: the sweeter the curry, the more the sweetness needs to be balanced with salty and sour elements. Do not over-season at this stage – you should be creating a base for the curry with the paste and its initial seasonings and then, when the curry is finished, you can correct the seasoning balance as desired.

Add the cooked paste to the pot containing the chicken, potatoes and onions, stirring it in well. Stir in pineapple juice. Check the seasoning: it should taste sweet, sour and salty.

Serve with:
- fruit, especially watermelon and half-ripe mango
- pickled ginger
- Steamed Salted Duck Eggs (page 391)
- Freshly Salted Beef (page 402).

A SOUTHERN MUSSAMAN CURRY OF BEEF

geng mussaman neua

Another school of thought believes that a *mussaman* curry came from the south of the country where there are many Muslims, perhaps arriving with Indian merchants or Arab traders. Certainly most types of *mussaman* curry have all the hallmarks of southern Muslim food – rich with coconut cream and redolent of spices, especially cassia, cumin and cardamom.

200 g (6 oz) boneless beef shank or flank
4 cups coconut cream
3 tablespoons shredded ginger

¼ cup roasted peanuts

2 cm (1 in) piece cassia bark

3 tablespoons white sugar or palm sugar

2 tablespoons fish sauce

4 tablespoons tamarind water

2 long white eggplants – optional

1 cup coarsely shredded boiled bamboo shoots – optional

paste

15 dried long red chillies, deseeded, soaked and drained

large pinch of salt

½ cup grated coconut, roasted

¼ cup peanuts, roasted

7 Thai cardamom pods, roasted and seeds ground

3 bay leaves, roasted and ground

5 cloves, roasted and ground

First, make the paste (see page 280).

Cut the beef into large cubes – about 'the size of a small chicken egg'. Wash and dry. Bring coconut cream to the boil, add beef and simmer, stirring occasionally, for 2 hours or until tender (you may need to add a little water during the braising). Drain off braising liquid and set aside. Add the paste to the beef in the braising pot, along with the ginger, peanuts and cassia bark. Fry over a low heat, stirring regularly, until fragrant. Add reserved braising liquid to cover, season with sugar, fish sauce and tamarind water, and bring to the boil.

If using eggplants, cut them in half lengthwise, then into three. Add to the curry, along with the bamboo shoots, if using, and simmer until eggplant is cooked. The curry should taste equally sweet, sour and salty.

Serve with Steamed Eggs (page 388).

10

SALADS

Salads (*yam*) are one of the most important yet diverse categories in the Thai culinary repertoire. Although *yam* is often translated as 'salads', in fact it literally means to 'toss' or 'mix together' – a loose description of the manner of their composition. All Thai salads are notable for their distinct flavours and decided textures that tantalise the palate and invigorate the meal.

Yam has none of the connotations of cool green leaves dressed with a mellow vinaigrette that denote a Western salad. Rather a Thai salad is a lively assemblage of ingredients. These can range from the very ancient and simple, like minced meat or fish (*larp dip*), blanched squid dressed with lime, chillies and fish sauce, or a quenching bean sprout salad, to the exceedingly complex, such as a rich and smoky curry-like dressing over shredded vegetables, prawns and chicken.

Thai salads are versatile. They can be enjoyed at any time of the day, in any circumstance: as a snack, an appetiser, or to accompany a bowl of comforting rice soup eaten at night, where the salad's sprightliness adds savour and contrast. Unlike curries, soups and relishes, which are unimaginable without rice, Thai salads can be eaten on their own. But however – or whenever – they are eaten, the cardinal rule is that the dressing must be strongly flavoured, with a highly defined and poised seasoning that complements and unifies all the ingredients it dresses.

Although the main ingredient is often freshly cooked and therefore warm, it is tempered – both in temperature and flavour – by the fresh herbs and the dressing that season it. *Yam* are best eaten just above room temperature when the aromatic red shallots, mint and coriander leaves will not soften, wilt and lose their vibrancy, and the dressing will retain its sharp spiciness.

The very similar techniques employed in salads mean that there is no evolution from simple to complex in this type of dish – although, of course, salads can be made incrementally complex by adding new ingredients.

SALAD INGREDIENTS

Because of their simplicity, it is vital that the ingredients in a salad are fresh and at the peak of their season. Hence the 'principal' ingredient depends on what is available, but most salads include a handful of sliced red shallots, mint and coriander leaves as a consistent garnish.

RED SHALLOTS

Shallots impart a sharp and decisive taste to a salad. They are always cut lengthwise. Thai cooks prefer to use the smallest bulbs, which are sweet, comparatively subtle in flavour, and present a vivid and attractive pink edge.

Shallots are occasionally grilled or roasted before being added to a salad. Traditionally this is done over an open flame, but an easier way is to 'roast' them in a wok with a little water, unpeeled, until the water has evaporated and the skin is charred. This ensures that the shallots are completely cooked and quite smoky but without any bitter, blackened parts that would taint the salad. Either way, once cool they are peeled, sliced and added to the dish.

Deep-fried shallots add a wonderful nuttiness to a salad. Mostly they are sprinkled over the finished salad at the last minute, so they remain crisp.

MINT

The best variety to use is common garden mint. The leaves alone are used – and the smaller they are, the better. Larger leaves need to be torn so that they do not over-whelm the salad; do not cut them with a knife or the leaves will blacken. Mint is used in almost every Thai salad, but with discretion. Its fresh menthol flavour cools and refreshes and is a pleasant respite from the salad's intensity.

CORIANDER

Coriander's spicy and herbaceously sweet leaves give a clean sharpness to the salad. Picking the leaves gives the salad a refinement, but chopping will do. It is important not to add too much coriander – it can so easily take over a salad.

PAK CHII FARANG

Pak chii farang (long-leaf coriander) is almost always shredded before use, although if very young the soft leaves can be torn into salads. For those who are not fond of coriander, this is a more palatable alternative, having a similar but less intense taste. Its enticing fragrance is mostly released on heating, therefore it is used mainly in the warm and spicy salads from the north and north-east, to temper and perfume.

BASIL

Thai basil is an uncommon salad herb. Normally it is served as a side dish with salads, but when it is added to the salad itself it imparts a sweet aniseed flavour. Leaves are added whole or torn; do not cut with a knife or the edges of the leaves will blacken.

Holy basil is only used in a few very pungent, rustic salads from the north. The leaves have a clove-like intensity that can almost numb the tongue.

LEMONGRASS

Lemongrass is usually very finely sliced for salads. This should be done as close as possible to use, as the flavour and fragrance dissipate when exposed to air, and the stalk also discolours and warps. Some cooks plunge the stalk briefly into boiling water to soften it, thus making it easier to slice – and more fragrant.

KAFFIR LIME LEAVES

These should be prepared just before they are needed as they dry so quickly. Fold or roll no more than 3 or 4 leaves lengthwise, then shred as finely as possible. The fastidious remove the central rib by lifting it away from the leaf.

COCONUT

Raw coconut has a soft texture and rich taste. In Thailand, there is a special small, claw-like utensil to remove the coconut flesh from the husk; a zester is a good substitute. Cut the coconut in half and wash the inside and then scrape out the flesh. Using a zester, make long strokes across each half of the coconut, rotating to ensure even scraping, and avoiding the brown skin. It is easier to collect the coconut scrapings if you work over a tea towel. Occasionally, the flesh is grated.

If roasted coconut is required, roast the scraped or grated coconut in a very low oven, checking and turning often. Once it is golden and fragrant, it is ready to use, offering a sweet nuttiness and pleasing textural contrast.

MAKING A DRESSING

I have found the more primitive the techniques employed – such as in a *larp* or a grilled meat salad – and the more robust the 'principal' ingredient (offal, dried fish or sweet prawns, for example), the more pronounced is the seasoning of the dressing.

Most dressings are prepared separately before the salad ingredients are combined, since this takes the briefest of moments. But try not to make the dressing more than an hour or two beforehand. Usually chillies, garlic and perhaps coriander root are pounded before being seasoned with sugar, lime juice and fish sauce to make a dressing, but some dressings are a simple paste of grilled ingredients or some chilli jam, diluted and seasoned. Coconut cream can be used to add a rich body to the dressing. And occasionally, the dressing is made as the salad is assembled, with the juices that exude from the ingredients forming a delicious base for the dressing – for example, Grilled Crayfish and Tomato Salad (page 360).

Salad dressings are traditionally made using a pestle and mortar – and, in this instance, conveniently too, since the ingredients are easily and quickly reduced to a purée. A blender could be used, but it saves little time and does not give the same well-textured finish. The ingredients should be added to the mortar in the following order, beginning with the hardest and most difficult to pound, or those that must be completely puréed.

CORIANDER ROOT

Coriander root is used to counter any strong, earthy tastes – such as shrimp paste or freshwater fish – or gamy, meaty flavours in a dressing. It also counterbalances the raw garlic. Coriander root creates an undercurrent taste – that is, it should never dominate a dressing. Always scrape coriander roots to remove the skin and then soak in water to dislodge any lurking soil. Dry before use.

SALT

Salt is used both as an abrasive and a seasoning element. Use the best quality available, as the taste of good salt improves the salad.

fundamentals of thai cooking | salads

GARLIC

This gives a meaty body to the dressing. Only a few cloves should be used, otherwise the garlic will overwhelm the balance.

CHILLIES

Despite their fierce heat, bird's eye chillies (scuds) lend a delicious floral taste and some pleasing heat to a salad, if not excessively used. Only the most fastidious, or fearful, remove the seeds. Remember that the more puréed the chilli, the greater will be the heat in the dressing. Normally, I prefer to use white sugar in a dressing with scuds, as palm sugar seems to mask their floral taste.

Always deseed fresh long chillies before adding to dressings. I like to remove the white membrane as well, to reduce any excess heat and ensure a cleaner, fruitier taste. Chop or mince before adding to the mortar – this reduces the pounding substantially. With red chillies, I like to use palm sugar, as its richness marries well with the chilli; white sugar, I think, works best with green chillies.

Sometimes, grilled chillies are used whole or torn as an ingredient in the salad itself, but mostly they are pounded into a paste, usually with grilled shallots and garlic, before being dissolved to make a dressing. Normally only red chillies are grilled; green or unripe chillies are harder to peel. The chillies should be grilled, cooled, peeled and deseeded before being added to the dressing. Grilled chillies create a smoky, hot, yet suggestively sweet flavour; they are not as spicy as raw chillies, since the grilling moderates their heat.

SUGAR

Too much sugar cloys the palate, swamping all other tastes and seasonings. Too little and the dressing will be sharp, thin and coarse.

White sugar imparts a clean, sweet flavour to dressings. Although it is fine to use normal sugar, it does take some time to dissolve in a dressing, so the real degree of sweetness it will produce may not be immediately discernible. It is better to use castor (superfine) sugar, which dissolves more quickly, ensuring that the true seasoning can be tasted as the dressing is being made.

Palm sugar imparts a mellow, slightly nutty and richer taste and texture to a dressing. Coconut sugar is normally lighter in colour and, although it has a slightly different taste, can be used interchangeably with palm sugar. Palm sugar can be softened by pounding with a clean pestle and mortar, puréeing in a food processor or melting in a microwave oven. So prepared, it dissolves quickly and a more accurate measure of its sweetness can be gauged.

LIME JUICE

Lime juice is the major souring agent in the dressing. As its flavour, fragrance and colour dissipate quickly, it is important to squeeze the limes only when the juice is needed – and to squeeze by hand (machines tend to rasp at the pith, break the membranes and crush the seeds, imparting a pervasive bitterness). If you must prepare lime juice in advance, store it refrigerated.

Lemons should not be substituted for limes. They have a very different taste and are completely inappropriate. If limes are scarce, a better alternative is good coconut vinegar, used in similar quantities.

VINEGAR

Milder, less acidic coconut vinegars work remarkably well in *yam* dressings. Coarser vinegars should be diluted with a little water or simmered with a little sugar, and perhaps perfumed with pandanus leaves, garlic or coriander roots.

KAFFIR LIME AND OTHER CITRUS JUICES

The juice from the kaffir lime is very pungent and should be used cautiously. A little gives an alluring perfume and yet has a surprisingly pervasive taste. Too much and it overwhelms every other flavour in a dressing, giving it a soapy, bitter taste. When kaffir lime juice is used, it counters robust or coarsely flavoured items, such as pork liver or meaty freshwater fish. Occasionally, the juice is used with salt to cleanse and bleach ingredients like offal before blanching.

The juices of Asian citron, kalamansi lime and unripe Asian orange are rarely used alone in dressings. They are uncommon and seasonal, but are sometimes added for their flavour and perfume; mandarin, orange or tangelo juice make excellent alternatives.

TAMARIND WATER

This is mainly used in cooked dressings, to enrich as well as sour.

GALANGAL WATER

A very pungent liquid of pounded young galangal, mixed with water and strained, this is sharp and slightly astringent: use sparingly. I always pound a little salt with the galangal as this gives a fuller taste. Once pounded, the galangal tends to darken and become bitter; this affects the taste of the water, so it is best to make galangal water only when it is needed. A squeeze of lime juice can help to retain its fresh colour and bracing taste. Galangal water is included in salads where the main ingredient is very strong – liver, for example.

FISH SAUCE

Fish sauce – and salt in general – tightens the taste of the dressing and concentrates its flavours on the palate. Too little and the dressing's taste will be loose, but too much is piercing – and it is hard to retrieve a dressing that is too salty. Always add fish sauce gradually and cautiously, tasting the dressing as you do so, in order not to over-salt.

FERMENTED FISH SAUCE

This pungent sauce is mostly used in north and north-eastern salads. Occasionally the whole fermented fish (*pla raa*) is deep-fried and dressed with lemongrass, shallots and chillies, becoming a salad in itself – a dish for those who pursue authenticity to the extreme. Mostly, however, the whole fish is diluted and simmered with aromatics. Although fermented fish sauce (*nahm pla raa*) is not as salty as fish sauce, it is more obtrusive; use sparingly.

LIGHT SOY SAUCE

I prefer to use the light, Thai version of soy: light both in colour and in body. It has a subtle sweetness and is not too intensely salty, which means it can authentically replace fish sauce. The result will be different, as soy sauce lacks the capacity to 'disappear' in the way that fish sauce does. Slow, naturally fermented soy sauce is the best to use – and the healthiest.

ROASTED DRIED CHILLIES

Almost invariably, dried chillies are grilled or roasted to impart a wonderfully smoky flavour, then ground before being added to a dressing. To roast, simply heat the chillies in a dry wok and stir until they colour and are fragrant; just be careful – the fumes are awesome. I find the rich and toasty heat of dried chillies addictive, but it is best to tread cautiously when adding them to a dressing: more can always be added.

While dried long red chillies are sometimes deseeded before roasting, dried bird's eye chillies are rarely deseeded. Ground to make roasted chilli powder, they are an essential seasoning for spicy *larp* and grilled beef salads. Whole dried chillies can also be deep-fried or caramelised and used as a garnish for a salad.

CHILLI JAM

This rich, nutty relish (page 200) is often used as a dressing for Thai salads. It is normally diluted with a little coconut cream and the seasoning adjusted before use.

COCONUT CREAM

Coconut cream adds a sumptuous quality to dressings. Often the 'principal' ingredient is cooked in coconut cream before the salad is finished and seasoned. Salads of this nature are usually sweeter than other types and are rarely highly spiced.

SEASONING THE DRESSING

Each ingredient needs to be thoroughly incorporated in the dressing before the balance of the seasoning is checked. When seasoning a dressing, sweet ingredients are usually added before souring agents. The salty element – that is, fish sauce – is generally added last, as it is normally the strongest flavour. It needs to be handled carefully and added in proportion to the previous seasoning tastes. Fish sauce can easily upset the intended balance of the seasoning; while increasing the amounts of other seasoning components can restore this, it is difficult to achieve, as the dressing then often becomes too intense.

A clever exercise is to make a sample salad dressing as a helpful teaching method that reveals the dynamics of seasoning. Such a demonstration was proposed by Kasma Loha-unchit in her book, *It Rains Fishes*. Here is my version. It is wise to have a glass of water at the ready.

2 coriander roots, scraped

2 pinches of salt

5 garlic cloves, peeled

6 bird's eye chillies (scuds)

3 tablespoons white sugar

9 tablespoons lime juice

2 tablespoons palm sugar

4 tablespoons fish sauce

Using a pestle and mortar, pound 1 coriander root with a large pinch of salt and 3 garlic cloves. Pound 3 chillies into the paste and sniff: it should be rich with garlic, clean from the coriander root and sharp with chillies, but with no one fragrance overwhelming the others.

Add and purée another 2 cloves of garlic. Notice the subtle change – at first almost indiscernible, but soon it becomes increasingly apparent. To adjust the balance, purée another coriander root, a pinch of salt and another 3 scuds. The dressing will certainly be more pungent now, but the balance should have been restored.

Now add 2 tablespoons of white sugar and use the pestle to grind the granules. Add 2 tablespoons of lime juice and stir with the pestle until the sugar has completely dissolved. Taste the dressing. The sugar dominates, masking the garlic and coriander and even the chillies – well, momentarily at least. The chilli then shines through. Add a tablespoon of palm sugar and notice the mellowness that this sugar imparts, covering the heat once more. Add an extra 4 tablespoons of lime juice; now the dressing should be pleasingly tart. All the ingredients can begin to be tasted as the sweetness recedes.

Add a further tablespoon of lime juice, and the dressing becomes sharp and clean and all the tastes are clear. Add another. Pour in 3 tablespoons of fish sauce, a tablespoon at a time, tasting after each addition. The dressing becomes more defined – tighter, as it were. Surprisingly, it even becomes sweeter. The dressing should be balanced: sour, salty, hot and sweet.

To continue the exercise, add a further tablespoon of fish sauce and see how the dressing becomes unpleasantly salty. This can be adjusted by adding roughly 2 tablespoons of sugar, one white and the other palm – each will result in a slightly different finish – and 1 more tablespoon of lime juice. The balance should be regained.

The effect of each component in a dressing should now be appreciated and, more importantly, it can be seen how they can be manipulated to strike a balance. When making a dressing, assemble the ingredients according to the recipe, but then taste and adjust – according to the seasoning instructions yet modified by one's own preference.

Most traditional Thai dressings have three tastes – hot, salty and sour; these normally contrast with the 'principal' ingredient, which will often give the fourth seasoning. Occasionally, there are four seasonings, with the addition of sugar. Aberrantly, I like to add sugar to most dressings – it is a matter of my taste.

Some salads have an accepted sequence of seasoning. The spicy minced meat salads from the north and north-east (*larp*), for example, are equally hot, salty and sour, whereas the 'cured' salads (*pla*) are decidedly sour, hot then salty. However, with some exceptions, there is rarely a rigorous application of set seasonings. Since there are few rules, individual preference usually prevails, but always within limits. Sweetness gives the dressing body and depth; however, it should never be the dominant seasoning. Saltiness makes flavours more discernible, drawing out especially – yet surprisingly – the sweetness of other ingredients. Sourness cleans, highlighting the other tastes and ingredients. Heat, of course, gives pungency to the dressing, but also helps to clean the other seasonings and flavours, preventing them becoming a clutter of tastes. It also makes the palate more sensitive to texture.

It is important to remember when seasoning a dressing that it is just that. The dressing should be finely honed, encompassing the salad. It must be intensely flavoured since it dresses other, often strongly flavoured ingredients; otherwise, it will taste insipid by comparison and there will be no unifying element to the salad.

DRESSING THE SALAD

There is also a correct proportion of dressing to salad. Too much and it will swamp the salad; too little and the salad will taste dry and disjointed. The correct amount does not just coat the ingredients, as in a Western salad, but liberally anoints. After all, the salad is one of many dishes that accompany and give savour to rice. Perhaps the best way to ensure that the proper amount of dressing is added is to toss the salad with some of its dressing, then put it on a dish or plate and pour a few table-spoons of the remaining dressing over it.

If the dressing has been made in advance, recheck the seasoning just before using, as the balance can change; in particular, the sourness of lime juice quickly dissipates, which means the dressing becomes saltier and sweeter. Always taste and adjust the seasoning, as required.

CLAM SALAD

yam hoi

This salad is an exercise in simplicity and restraint. It is also a generic recipe that can be used as the basis for many salads, using almost any ingredient.

In Thailand, it is made using bloody clams or cockles, which are full of iodine and strikingly red in colour. Cockles, pipis, mussels or any other molluscs can be substituted. The shellfish may need to be purged of grit – check with your seafood supplier. If so, simply cover with plenty of water in which a tablespoon of flour has been dissolved and set aside for an hour or two.

The clams are very quickly blanched in salted water, which can also be infused with some offcuts of lemongrass, galangal or kaffir lime leaves – these help to perfume the salad and 'cleanse' the molluscs as they cook, but are not essential. An excellent Thai technique, used mainly with seafood, is to dip an item in and out of boiling water – *luak* – using a 'spider' (wooden-handled wire strainer). The water should not return to the boil once the ingredient is added; sometimes the pot is even removed from the heat. Cooking this way ensures that the flesh does not overheat or toughen, and results in a silken, yielding texture.

300 g (9 oz) clams, cockles, pipis or mussels in their shells, cleaned

pinch of salt

handful of lemongrass offcuts and galangal peelings – optional

splash of fish sauce

squeeze of lime juice

a few bruised bird's eye chillies (scuds) – optional

3 red shallots, sliced

2 tablespoons finely shredded young ginger (if only old is available, steep for
a minute or so in salted water to remove some of its pungency) – optional

Heat a pan of water until boiling. Add salt and a few offcuts of lemongrass and galangal, if using. Boil for a minute or two, then remove the aromatics; if boiled for too long, they will impart an unnecessarily oily heaviness to the water. Plunge the shellfish into the water and turn down the heat – it is imperative that the water does not come back to the boil. Lift in and out of the water with a strainer, if desired. When the shells open, remove and drain (discard any that remain stubbornly closed).

Dress with a splash or two of fish sauce and lime juice to taste – the exact amount of fish sauce and lime juice is a matter to be decided by the cook and the clams alone, but do remember that the clams are quite salty. Add the remaining ingredients and serve; the clams can be taken out of their shells to serve, but this is a refinement that is not strictly necessary.

SQUID SALAD

yam pla meuk

This salad uses the same light blanching technique as the clam salad opposite. Thai salads are rarely as unadorned as the previous recipe; they normally include other ingredients that highlight the principal ingredient by contrasting with its texture and flavour. However, it is important to remember that a Thai salad is mostly a simple affair. If it is a squid salad, then there is very little else but squid. All other inclusions are ingredients with a subsidiary role and should be used sparingly.

200 g (6 oz) squid
3 red shallots, finely sliced
2 kaffir lime leaves, shredded
1 stalk lemongrass, finely sliced
handful of mixed mint and coriander leaves

dressing
2–4 bird's eye chillies (scuds)
pinch of salt
2 tablespoons lime juice
large pinch of white sugar
2 tablespoons fish sauce

First, make the dressing (see page 338); it should taste salty, sour and hot.

Clean the squid, then score by holding the knife at an angle and making diagonal cuts, taking care not to cut right through. Cut the body into about 2 cm (1 in) strips, scrape the suckers from the tentacles and cut tentacles into 2 cm (1 in) lengths. Blanch the squid briefly in salted boiling water until just opaque. Combine with the remaining salad ingredients, dress and serve immediately.

BEAN SPROUT SALAD

yam tua nork

This salad has its origins in the south of Thailand. For the perfectionist, the bean sprouts look most elegant if they are topped and tailed before being added to the dish, but this is not obligatory.

2 cups bean sprouts
4 tablespoons coconut cream
1–2 tablespoons vinegar
2 red shallots, sliced
1 tablespoon coriander leaves

paste

3 tablespoons grated coconut, roasted

3 tablespoons peanuts, roasted

large pinch of salt

First, make the paste: gradually pound the ingredients together using a pestle and mortar, adding one by one, until smooth. Mix the paste with the bean sprouts and season with coconut cream and vinegar: it should taste smoky, rich, sour and salty. Serve sprinkled with shallots and coriander leaves.

SALAD OF PORK, YOUNG GINGER AND SQUID

yam muu gap king orn lae pla meuk

In this salad, each 'principal' ingredient is as important as the other: the steamed pork brings mellowness that is counterbalanced by the bracing ginger, while the squid has a pleasing texture.

50 g (2 oz) cleaned squid

50 g (2 oz) pork fillet

50 g (2 oz) young ginger, cut into batons

4 red shallots, sliced

handful of mixed mint and coriander leaves

1 tablespoon deep-fried garlic – optional

dressing

1 coriander root, scraped

pinch of salt

1 garlic clove, peeled

3–4 bird's eye chillies (scuds)

1 tablespoon white sugar

2 tablespoons lime juice

1 tablespoon fish sauce

First, make the dressing (see page 338); it should taste hot, salty, sour and just a little sweet.

Score the squid by holding the knife at an angle and making diagonal cuts, taking care not to cut right through. Slice squid into bite-size pieces, then blanch – *luak* (see page 129) – in boiling water. Steam pork for 5–10 minutes, then cut into strips. Combine with the remaining salad ingredients. Dress and serve.

SALTED PRAWN AND WHITE TURMERIC SALAD

yam gung kem gap kamin kao

This salad is an example of how strongly flavoured ingredients counterbalance each other. White turmeric is quite uncommon outside Thailand, but young ginger, blanched long eggplants or even fresh, new-season bamboo shoots can be used as substitutes.

There are many variations on this salad: Dried Squid (page 392) fried until crisp, for example, and then dressed with succulent pineapple; or salted fish, such as salmon, trout or even sardines, with watermelon and deep-fried shallots.

10 Salted Prawns (page 392)
4 tablespoons shredded white turmeric
1 garlic clove, finely chopped
pinch of palm sugar – optional
2 tablespoons lime juice
2–3 bird's eye chillies (scuds), sliced
splash of fish sauce – optional

Mix prawns with turmeric and garlic. Dissolve palm sugar, if using, in lime juice and add chillies. Pour over the prawns. The dressing should be pungently hot, sour and salty. Season further with a few drops of fish sauce, if needed.

OYSTER AND BANANA BLOSSOM SALAD

yam hoi nang rom

This is a gentle, well-balanced salad that is poised between the subtleties of the oysters, banana blossoms and coconut cream. Instead of oysters, scallops, mussels or crayfish can be used with banana blossoms – or with witlof (Belgian endive), bitter melon or just plain Thai basil.

1 banana blossom
a little lime juice or vinegar
12 oysters – unopened, if possible
1 cup coconut cream
1 tablespoon fermented fish sauce (*nahm pla raa*) or fish sauce
pinch of palm sugar
4 red shallots, sliced
2 tablespoons shredded *pak chii farang* (long-leaf coriander)

Prepare banana blossom (see page 142), slice finely on an angle and immerse in water acidulated with lime juice or vinegar. This should be done no more than 30 minutes in advance, as the water retards browning but does not prevent it.

Shuck the oysters, strain their brine, then store them in it.

Heat the coconut cream, and season with either fermented or regular fish sauce and sugar. Drain banana blossom and squeeze dry, then stir into the warm coconut cream, along with oysters and their brine. Remove from heat.

On serving, sprinkle with shallots and *pak chii farang*.

WILD GINGER AND SWEET PRAWN SALAD

yam grachai gap gung warn

The original recipe for this salad from the northern central plains used the whole *grachai* plant, including the young green stalks and fleshy leaves. Unless there is a patch of *grachai* nearby, this is unlikely to be an option, so the rhizomes alone will do, but reduce the quantity as they are more pungent. Ginger – especially ginger flowers – can be used. Sour snakeskin pears are also uncommon, but a shredded tart green mango is a perfect alternative.

Simmering in sugar is another method of food preservation. In the markets of Thailand there are trays of various delicious sweetmeats, including small, unpeeled prawns. The shells present no problem, only a textural interest; if the prawns are large, their shells do become unpleasantly chewy, however, and so should be removed beforehand.

I think Sweet Pork (page 397) would make a very agreeable substitute for the sweet prawns in this salad.

10 medium uncooked prawns (shrimp)
5 tablespoons palm sugar
3 tablespoons fish sauce
1 cup shredded *grachai* (wild ginger)
3 sour snakeskin pears *or* 1 green mango

dressing
5 bird's eye chillies (scuds)
pinch of salt
pinch of shrimp paste (*gapi*)
1 tablespoon fish sauce
2 tablespoons lime juice

Peel and devein the prawns. Heat the palm sugar with the fish sauce, simmer until quite thick and add the prawns. Simmer until they are just cooked. Remove from the heat and cool on a small tray.

Next, make the dressing (see page 338); it should taste hot, mostly sour and just a little salty. The balance will be regained once it is combined with the sweet prawns. >

Wash the *grachai*, peel the rhizome and the lower stalk, then cut elegantly on an angle into 2 cm (1 in) lengths. Peel the sour snakeskin pears or mango, pare the flesh away from the large central seed and slice. Combine with the prawns, dress and serve.

CUCUMBER AND PRAWN SALAD

yam dtaeng gwa

This famous combination of ingredients dates from the time of Ayuthyia and is still very popular today. Because this salad is so elegantly simple, the dried prawns must be of the best quality. Rather than use second-rate dried prawns, fresh prawns can be used, but then there is no need to grind them. Just combine with the cucumber and dress. Cucumber adds a pleasing and crisp coolness to the salad, but shredded small *madan* (sour cucumber), green mango, segments of mangosteen or crunchy lengths of Asian celery are enticing options.

> 2 tablespoons dried prawns (shrimp) – preferably homemade (see page 151)
> 1 small cucumber
> 3 red shallots, sliced
> handful of mixed mint and coriander leaves
>
> **dressing**
> 1 garlic clove, peeled
> pinch of salt
> 2 bird's eye chillies (scuds)
> 1½ tablespoons lime juice
> 1 tablespoon fish sauce
> pinch of white sugar

First, make the dressing (see page 338); it should taste sour, salty and hot.

Purée the dried prawns to a floss – ideally in an electric coffee grinder. A pestle and mortar is a painstaking alternative, as the prawns must be very fine for this salad to work. Wash the cucumber, top and tail then cut in half lengthwise and slice finely on an angle. Combine cucumber, shallots, mint and coriander, then dress. Arrange on a plate and sprinkle over the dried prawn floss.

MANGOSTEEN SALAD WITH ROE

yam mangkut gap kai pla

The Thai approach to combining ingredients in salads can at times be cavalier – whatever is at hand is used – yet the results can be outstanding. This refined recipe came

from Darley Street Thai, where Tanongsak Yordwai, one of the more skillful cooks there (and at nahm), was toying with some sevruga caviar and mangosteens left over from a function. Such a combination may sound improbable, but when assembled so deftly, it proved to be delectable and became an accidental favourite.

Of course any decent-quality fish roe is acceptable, and more realistic – only please do not use lumpfish roe. A few quickly blanched prawns would make an exquisite alternative. Mangosteens are an irritating fruit. They are just so delicious, but the supply can be quite erratic. The trees fruit twice a year and the crop can be either a glut or a dearth. Green star fruit (also known as carambola), *madan* (sour cucumber), or the dependable green mango, are good alternatives.

4 mangosteens
pinch of palm sugar
2 tablespoons lime juice
1 tablespoon fish sauce
3–5 bird's eye chillies (scuds), sliced
4 red shallots, sliced
3 tablespoons fish roe
handful of coriander leaves

Peel the mangosteens and dress the segments with sugar, lime juice and fish sauce. Arrange on a plate, sprinkle with the remaining ingredients and serve.

ROAST DUCK AND LYCHEE SALAD

yam bpet yang

Roast duck can be purchased in Chinatown, or an easy approximation can be made at home. Simply combine sweet soy sauce (*kecap manis*) with some soy sauce, maltose and a pinch of five spice powder, and smear over a cleaned duck. I also like to put a little ginger, orange zest and a pandanus leaf into its cavity before cooking. Roast in a moderate oven (190°C or 375°F) for about 30 minutes. Reserve any juices from the duck, as they give a wonderfully rich body to the dressing. You'll need about a quarter of a duck for this recipe.

200 g (6 oz) roast duck meat, elegantly sliced
15 lychees, peeled and deseeded
3 spring (green) onions, finely shredded
1 tablespoon shredded ginger
1 teaspoon deep-fried garlic
handful of coriander leaves
2 tablespoons deep-fried peanuts
pinch of sesame seeds

dressing

1 tablespoon plum sauce – optional, but delightful

1 tablespoon palm sugar – less if using plum sauce

1 tablespoon Chinese black vinegar

3 tablespoons light soy sauce

2 tablespoons juices from the duck or stock

First, make the dressing (see page 338); it should taste salty, sweet and just a little sour. Combine all remaining ingredients except sesame seeds. Dress salad, sprinkle with sesame seeds and serve.

CURED PORK AND OYSTER SALAD

yam naem gap hoi nang rom

The succulence of the cured pork in this salad is supported and cleaned by the ginger, while the cooling quality and smooth lush texture of the oysters seem to meld everything together. The peanuts add a contrasting crunch. Such is the interplay of ingredients that make Thai salads so memorable.

A couple of alternative combinations are scallops with roast duck and long eggplants, or crabmeat with pork dumplings and Asian celery.

8 oysters

100 g (3 oz) Chiang Mai cured pork (*naem*)

handful of shredded ginger – preferably young

4 red shallots, sliced

handful of mixed mint and coriander leaves

1 tablespoon deep-fried peanuts

dressing

2 coriander roots, scraped

pinch of salt

2 garlic cloves, peeled

3–5 green dragon's eye chillies *or* 2–4 green bird's eye chillies (scuds)

large pinch of white sugar or palm sugar

3 tablespoons lime juice

2 tablespoons fish sauce

First, make the dressing (see page 338); it should taste very hot, sour, salty and sweet.

If the oysters are unopened, shuck them and strain their brine into the dressing. Unwrap the cured pork and chop coarsely. Combine all salad ingredients, dress and serve.

GRILLED EGGPLANT SALAD

yam makreua yao

Long green Thai eggplant is often available in Asian speciality shops. It is quite fleshy and, most importantly, it is not bitter. The nearest approximation is the purple Japanese eggplant. Don't be tempted to use any other kind of eggplant when making this salad: it will be too pungent and bitter, since the dressing makes use of the flavourful juices from the grilled eggplants. This is an attractively smoky salad.

> 4 long green or Japanese eggplants
> 2 tablespoons mint leaves
> 3 red shallots, sliced
> 2 tablespoons chopped spring (green) onion
> large pinch of roasted chilli powder
> 2 tablespoons lime juice
> 1 tablespoon fish sauce
> ½ teaspoon ground dried prawns (shrimp)

Grill the eggplants until charred and soft. Place in a bowl, cover until cool and then peel. Add all the other ingredients except the dried prawns to the bowl with the eggplants and combine. The salad should taste smoky, hot, and equally sour and salty. Arrange on a plate and sprinkle with ground dried prawns.

Serve with Steamed Eggs (page 388).

SALAD OF CRISPY PRAWN CAKES WITH GREEN MANGO AND PEANUTS

yam gung fuu

This salad comes from modern-day Ayuthyia. The city is at the confluence of three rivers, the noble Chao Phraya, the Lopburi and the Pa Sak, effectively making the main part of the ancient city an island. These shallow waters are ideal breeding grounds for freshwater prawns, which often find their way into prawn cakes.

Peanuts are used in many Thai salads, where their crunchy texture and slightly bitter flavour is a welcome addition. They come in many sizes – the smaller, the better. In South East Asia, 'baby' peanuts, about ½ centimetre (¼ inch) long, are often used in salads.

> 1 small green mango, julienned
> 50 g (2 oz) roasted or deep-fried peanuts
> handful of mint leaves
> handful of coriander leaves

GRILLED EGGPLANT SALAD, SERVED WITH STEAMED EGGS (page 388)

3 red shallots, finely sliced

Crispy Prawn Cakes (1 quantity of recipe on page 394)

dressing

2–5 bird's eye chillies (scuds)

2 tablespoons lime juice

2–4 teaspoons white sugar

1 tablespoon fish sauce

First, make the dressing (see page 338).

To assemble the salad, mix the mango with peanuts, mint and coriander, shallots and prawn cakes. Pour dressing over and serve.

CHICKEN, CRAB AND CHINESE BROCCOLI SALAD

yam gai lae bpuu chom chuam

This salad is adapted from a recipe in a book by Archarn Gobgaew Najpinij, coincidentally called *Arharn Thai* ('Thai Food'). She is a culinary consultant for many government functions and the senior lecturer on Thai food at the prestigious Suan Dusit College in Bangkok. The interplay between the bitter crunch of the broccoli, the yielding sweetness and body of the crab and chicken, and the luscious, spicy dressing captures the essence of a good *yam*.

200 g (6 oz) Chinese broccoli

100 g (3 oz) chicken, poached and shredded

50 g (2 oz) cooked crabmeat

1 tablespoon coriander leaves

dressing

2 coriander roots, scraped

pinch of salt

1 small long red chilli

2–4 bird's eye chillies (scuds)

1 small head pickled garlic, excess skin removed

1 tablespoon pickled garlic syrup

1 tablespoon white sugar

3 tablespoons lime juice

3 tablespoons fish sauce

First, make the dressing (see page 338); it should taste salt, sour, hot and sweet.

Wash and peel the Chinese broccoli. Cut into 2 cm (1 in) pieces, blanch in boiling salted water for 3–4 minutes, and refresh in iced water. Combine with all remaining ingredients, dress and serve.

SALAD OF LANGSART AND CARAMELISED PEANUTS

yam langsart

Langsart are deliciously sour, slightly bitter, lychee-like fruit with mottled yellow skin. Any tart, fleshy, small stone fruit, such as longans or loquats, can be used in this recipe in their place.

Pork belly is the preferred cut for this dish, as Thai cooks enjoy the layering of meat, fat and skin. I like to blanch it before poaching it (the resulting stock can be used in soups and curries). Fillet is a more than acceptable, healthy cut but, as it contains little fat, do not blanch or it will be tough and dry. Instead, poach until just cooked – and always let it rest for several minutes before slicing. Chicken can happily replace the pork, and a few prawns or a little squid or crabmeat add a pleasant dimension to this salad.

200 g (6 oz) *langsart*, peeled and stoned

50 g (2 oz) cooked pork, finely sliced

50 g (2 oz) cooked small prawns (shrimp), sliced squid or shredded crabmeat

3 tablespoons grated coconut, roasted

4 long red chillies, grilled, peeled, deseeded and coarsely torn

1 dried long red chilli, julienned and roasted

dressing

3 tablespoons coarsely ground caramelised peanuts

2 tablespoons white sugar

3 tablespoons coconut vinegar

   or 2 tablespoons white vinegar diluted with 1 tablespoon water

1 teaspoon salt

First, make the dressing (see page 338); it should taste sweet, sour and salty.

Combine all the remaining ingredients except the dried chilli, dress and serve sprinkled with the chilli julienne.

SALAD OF CRISP FISH AND ASIAN CITRON ZEST

yam piu som sa gap pla grop

This salad is a classic of the Thai repertoire. The concentrated smokiness of the *pla grop* (crisp fish) contrasted with the slightly bitter quality of the Asian citron is a perfect combination. Often a little shredded boiled pork skin is also added.

The origins of this salad are ancient: preserved fish invigorated with fresh herbs – for example, grilled fish (usually *pla salit*) seasoned with plenty of shredded green mango, shrimp paste and dried chillies, then drizzled with lime juice and fish sauce – would very often be eaten with a side plate of raw vegetables. Any preserved fish or prawns make excellent substitutes, as does lightly cured fish, such as in the next recipe, or even a well-flavoured fresh fish – although the dressing must be altered to take account of the different qualities of these fish and their various states.

If Asian citron is not available, tangelo makes an ideal alternative. Some recipes use watermelon, but this should only be done during the high days of summer when watermelons are at their ruddy best. Lengths of crisp Asian celery are also often included in recipes for this salad.

100 g (3 oz) *pla grop* (crisp fish)
3 tablespoons shredded Asian citron zest
50 g (2 oz) shredded boiled pork skin – optional
2 tablespoons ground roasted peanuts
2 tablespoons deep-fried shallots
1 tablespoon deep-fried garlic

dressing
1 tablespoon Asian citron juice
2 tablespoons fish sauce
1 tablespoon lime juice
1 tablespoon palm sugar
1 tablespoon pickled garlic syrup – optional

First, make the dressing (see page 338); it should taste sour, salty and sweet.

Fillet the fish and deep-fry at a low to medium temperature until crisp and fragrant. Combine with the rest of the ingredients, reserving a little of the deep-fried shallots and garlic for garnish. Dress the salad and serve, sprinkled with reserved deep-fried shallots and garlic.

SALMON AND ROE SALAD

yam pla lae kai pla

Traditionally a strong, oily fish, such as catfish or threadfin, or even Crispy Fish Cakes (page 393), is used in a salad such as this. Although unauthentic, salmon's slightly oily qualities are perfectly consistent with Thai cuisine. Salting and drying concentrates the oils and flavours in the fish, tightening its flesh. Grilling slightly chars the flesh – and especially the skin, imparting a smoky and slightly bitter crunch. This prevents the salmon being overwhelmed by the pungency of the salad. Cooking the salmon to medium is a Western deviation; a Thai would cook the fish completely, but I like the mellowness of this half-cured, not-quite-cooked fish.

Green mango is a traditional companion to fish, especially salted fish, and its succulent, tart flavour would make a refreshing addition to this salad.

200 g (6 oz) salmon fillet

3 tablespoons light soy sauce or fish sauce

pinch of salt

pinch of white sugar

3 red shallots, sliced

2 tablespoons very coarsely ground roasted peanuts

handful of mixed mint and coriander leaves

1 tablespoon shredded *pak chii farang* (long-leaf coriander) – optional

1 teaspoon deep-fried garlic – optional

3 tablespoons salmon roe

dressing

pinch of white sugar

pinch of palm sugar

2 tablespoons lime juice

2 tablespoons fish sauce

large pinch of roasted chilli powder

Marinate the salmon in the soy sauce or fish sauce, salt and white sugar overnight. Dry on a rack for a day. (The fish can be kept for several days at this stage, if refrigerated.)

Make the dressing (see page 338); it should taste equally hot, sour and salty, with just a little sweetness.

Grill salmon over a fierce heat for about 2 minutes each side, until the outside is charred yet the inside is only cooked to rare. Rest for 5 minutes in a warm place.

Combine all the remaining ingredients except salmon and roe. Coarsely flake in the fish, then dress the salad. Sprinkle with the salmon roe just before serving – this prevents the roe reacting to the acid in the dressing and toughening.

GRILLED CRAYFISH AND TOMATO SALAD

yam makreuatet gung nahm jeut pao

Born in the late nineteenth century, Mom Leuang Dtiw Chonlamartpitjarn was an adventurous woman for her time and enjoyed travelling throughout Thailand, especially to remote provinces. Mom Dtiw believed that much could be learnt from nature, and from the often-primitive farmers she encountered. She championed the use of local ingredients, favouring venison, pheasant, rabbit and other game in the mountainous north and isolated north-east. Mom Dtiw had a sense of timeliness and seasonality – knowing when to eat and how to eat, whenever and wherever she might be. After all, she was a Thai.

This salad comes from the north of Thailand and uses the small, quite tart orange tomatoes and mild, plump lime-green chillies of the region. Cherry tomatoes and banana chillies are very similar, and the addition of grilled chillies and lime juice ensures that the salad tastes the same too. Although Mom Dtiw's original recipe called for prawns, I think crayfish are a very appropriate alternative.

10 freshwater crayfish
4 red shallots
6 banana chillies
10 long red or green chillies
100 g (3 oz) cherry tomatoes

dressing
large pinch of palm sugar
2 tablespoons fish sauce
1 tablespoon lime juice

Grill the crayfish until just cooked and the shallots, chillies and tomatoes until soft and charred. Rest the chillies and tomatoes in a covered bowl – the steam will help to lift their skins – and keep the shellfish and shallots apart, to prevent the charred shallot skin from tainting the juices. Reserve all the juices from the tomatoes, chillies and crayfish; these form the basis of the dressing.

When cool enough to handle, shell, devein and slice the shellfish, mixing the meat with any tomalley from their heads. Peel and slice the shallots. Peel and deseed the chillies and tomatoes, then slice the chillies.

To make the salad, simply combine everything in a bowl, adding sugar, fish sauce and lime juice. It should taste salty, hot and slightly sour.

COCONUT CHICKEN SALAD
yam gop gati tian

The Thai name for this salad is 'mock frog salad'. It comes from the informative recipe book of Mom Chao Janjaroen Rachani. Her recipe can serve as the basis for many versions, perhaps using poached shredded chicken, a fillet of freshwater fish, wild mushrooms, or even frog. This cooling salad is the perfect accompaniment to a hot and sour curry or a pungent relish.

At Darley Street Thai, we used cooked crab with great success – omitting the paste, but sprinkling a little julienned chilli over the finished dish.

1 cup coconut cream
pinch of salt
150 g (5 oz) skinless chicken breast fillet

1–2 tablespoons stock or water, if required – see method

large pinch of palm sugar

1 tablespoon fish sauce

½ tablespoon lime juice

2 stalks lemongrass, very finely sliced

3 red shallots, sliced

4 kaffir lime leaves, finely shredded

1 tablespoon shredded *pak chii farang* (long-leaf coriander)

handful of Thai basil leaves

1 tablespoon ground roasted peanuts – optional

paste

3 dried long red chillies, deseeded and grilled

2 garlic cloves, grilled and then peeled

large pinch of salt

First, make the paste: gradually pound the ingredients together, using a pestle and mortar, until smooth.

Heat coconut cream with salt, add chicken breast and simmer very gently until cooked (about 4–5 minutes). If the coconut cream seems about to separate, add a few tablespoons of stock or water. Remove chicken, cool and shred elegantly.

Return 4 tablespoons of the coconut cream to the boil and mix in the paste. Season with the palm sugar, fish sauce and lime juice: it should taste rich, salty, sweet and sour. Mix in all the remaining ingredients except peanuts. Serve – sprinkled with the peanuts, if using.

CRISP FISH AND CHILLI SALAD

yam pla grop gap prik

This recipe is one more from the annals of the peerless Thanpuuying Pliang Pasonagorn. She recommends *pla grop* for its brittle texture and smoky and salty flavour. I think that grilled salmon, fresh or slightly salted, also marries perfectly with this well-textured salad; duck livers, blanched, grilled or even caramelised, are also an excellent possibility. The aromatic ingredients are deep-fried until crisp and golden but not too brown. This can be done some time in advance, as can the simple sweet fish sauce dressing. The original recipe also deep-fried the shredded kaffir lime leaves and coriander; however, they do lose a considerable amount of flavour if this is done, becoming merely textural components. I prefer to leave them fresh, so bringing a vitality to the salad.

A salad such as this, if reduced in size, can easily be served as a complex side dish.

oil for deep-frying

1 tablespoon shredded galangal

1 stalk lemongrass, sliced

5 red shallots, sliced

4 garlic cloves, sliced

2 *pla grop* (crisp fish) – about 150 g (5 oz)

6 green dragon's eye chillies *or* 4 green bird's eye chillies (scuds)

pinch of salt

4 tablespoons palm sugar

2 tablespoons tamarind water

1–2 tablespoons fish sauce

4 kaffir lime leaves, shredded

1 tablespoon coriander leaves

In a small pan over a medium heat, separately deep-fry the galangal, lemongrass, shallots and garlic until fragrant and golden. Remove with a slotted spoon and drain on absorbent paper. Deep-fry the *pla grop* until crisp and golden.

Cut chillies in half lengthwise and scrape out the seeds and white membrane. Steep in salted water for 2–3 minutes. Drain and dry, then cut into small, elongated lozenges.

Heat palm sugar in a small pan and simmer for a minute or so. Add the tamarind water and fish sauce and continue to simmer until quite thick. Taste carefully – it is very hot: it should be sweet, sour and salty. Stir in the deep-fried ingredients and chillies and serve sprinkled with kaffir lime leaves and coriander.

SANTOL SALAD WITH GRILLED PRAWNS
yam grathorn gap gung pao

Santol are pleasantly sour and sweet, slightly astringent fruit that are normally the size of an apple. Alternatives to this fruit are the more familiar green mango and loquats, or the sharp, apple-like hog plum.

This tight, sweet salad dressing reminds me of the base for *miang* (pages 483–6) and, like them, it can be eaten with a few 'betel' leaves, as well as some slices of cucumber to cut its sweet intensity. I like to add a pinch of powdered dried galangal as the palm sugar simmers, to pepper the salad. Any tomalley from the prawns can also be added at this time.

4 tablespoons palm sugar

2 tablespoons fish sauce

3 tablespoons tamarind water

2 santol, cleaned and shredded

50 g (2 oz) cooked pork, sliced

1 tablespoon shredded boiled pork skin – ideally homemade (see page 169)

2 tablespoons deep-fried shallots

1 tablespoon deep-fried garlic

1 tablespoon deep-fried peanuts

3 large prawns (shrimp), grilled, peeled, deveined and shredded

1 tablespoon coriander leaves

Heat palm sugar and simmer until quite thick, but do not allow to caramelise. Add fish sauce and tamarind water and continue to simmer until quite thick once more. It should taste equally sweet, sour and salty. Stir in the santol and cook for about 3–4 minutes. Add pork and pork skin, shallots, garlic and peanuts. Continue to simmer until the sauce has been absorbed – about 2 minutes. Serve sprinkled with the shredded prawns and coriander.

SALADE COMPOSÉE

yam yai

The Thai believe that a good salad demonstrates deft culinary skills, as the cook must balance the tastes well. In complicated salads such as this, it is important to cut all the ingredients to a similar size. The salad can then be dressed evenly and every component can be tasted. This is a salad at its most complex and considerable skill is needed to ensure that the flavours and textures do not explode into a clutter. It may seem difficult to assemble but in fact almost any ingredient can be included, excluded or substituted – judiciously.

50 g (2 oz) cooked pork, sliced

10 cooked small prawns (shrimp), peeled and deveined

2 tablespoons shredded boiled pork skin – ideally homemade (see page 169)

50 g (2 oz) Dried Squid (page 392), shredded

2 tablespoons dried prawns (shrimp), rinsed

2 hard-boiled eggs, shelled and quartered

1 small cucumber, finely sliced

50 g (2 oz) Chinese cabbage, coarsely shredded

5 cloud ear mushrooms, washed and sliced

handful of mint leaves

handful of coriander leaves

1 long red chilli, shredded

dressing

1 coriander root, scraped

pinch of salt

1 garlic clove, peeled

3 tablespoons lime juice

1 tablespoon stock

1 tablespoon white sugar

1 tablespoon fish sauce

Make the dressing (see page 338); it should taste sour, a little salty and sweet. Combine all the other salad ingredients, dress and serve.

SCALLOP SALAD

pla hoi shenn

Pla salads are mostly made with seafood that cooks quite quickly, and their dressings are always sour, hot and salty. They are perfumed by lemongrass and mint and finished with shredded kaffir lime leaves.

Any delicate seafood, such as lobster, prawns, salmon or oysters, can be used in this recipe.

100 g (3 oz) scallops

3 tablespoons lime juice

pinch of salt

1 tablespoon fish sauce

3 bird's eye chillies (scuds), pounded

3 red shallots, sliced

1 stalk lemongrass, finely sliced

4 kaffir lime leaves, shredded

handful of mixed mint and coriander leaves

Clean the scallops. If quite thick, slice them in half crosswise. Knead lime juice and salt into scallops and marinate for 3–4 minutes, until scallops are firm and opaque.

Add fish sauce and scuds. Taste the dressing: it should be sour, hot and salty. Adjust accordingly. Combine with remaining ingredients and serve.

MARINATED BEEF SALAD

pla neua sot

'The savoury dressing, succulent herbs and meat excite the palate like a lover's caress', opined King Rama II about this dish in his evocative Boat Songs – and, when it is prepared correctly, he may well be right. One way to ensure this is to use the best-quality beef and a tender cut, such as fillet; it is also important to work the marinade well into the meat before leaving it for at least 10 minutes so that it cures successfully. Some cooks might prefer to grill the meat to rare, rest it and then slice finely before adding to the lime juice for a few moments only.

150 g (5 oz) beef fillet

large pinch of salt

4 tablespoons lime juice

1 tablespoon kaffir lime juice – optional

pinch of white sugar – optional

3 bird's eye chillies (scuds), pounded – optional

2 tablespoons fish sauce

4 red shallots, sliced

1 stalk lemongrass, finely sliced

3 kaffir lime leaves, finely shredded

1 tablespoon julienned red chilli

handful of mixed mint and coriander leaves

Finely slice the beef across the grain, into slices no thicker than ½ cm (¼ in). Combine salt with lime juice(s) and sugar, if using, stir in the scuds, if using, and vigorously massage into the beef slices. Leave to marinate for at least 10 minutes, until the meat starts to 'cure'. Squeeze the beef to extract the marinade, which is then used to make the dressing. Taste – it should be sour and only slightly salty – and season with fish sauce.

Add all the remaining ingredients and serve, perhaps with a caress.

MARINATED PRAWN SALAD WITH GRATED COCONUT

pla gung mapraow krut

The best prawns to use in this salad are small ones; larger ones can be used, but they should be sliced or chopped beforehand so that they cure quickly in the marinade without breaking down. The marinade should be quite pungent, as it will be countered by the rich and cooling grated coconut.

15 small uncooked prawns (shrimp), peeled and cleaned –
   about 100 g (3 oz) in all

large pinch of palm sugar

1 tablespoon fish sauce

1 cup grated coconut

4 red shallots, sliced

2 stalks lemongrass, finely sliced

handful of mixed mint and coriander leaves

3 kaffir lime leaves, finely shredded

1 tablespoon julienned long red chilli

marinade

1 garlic clove, peeled

large pinch of salt

2–5 bird's eye chillies (scuds)

4 tablespoons kaffir lime juice, or regular lime juice perfumed with a little
   mandarin juice

To make the marinade, pound together the garlic, salt and chillies using a pestle and mortar until you have a fine paste. Transfer to a large bowl and stir in the lime juice. Add prawns and knead vigorously for several minutes. Leave for a further few minutes until the prawns have 'cured'.

Add palm sugar and fish sauce; the marinade should now taste sour, salty, hot and sweet. Work in the coconut. Add remaining ingredients, reserving a little shredded lime leaf and red chilli to garnish.

Serve with:

— Raw Vegetables (page 380), especially young ginger and cucumber

— sprigs of Thai basil, mint and coriander

— Fish Cakes (page 494).

WING BEAN SALAD

yam tua pluu

Mom Leuang Neuang Ninrat was born in the early part of the twentieth century, and was one of the last Thai women to have been educated in the age-old manner of Siam. At 12 months old, she went to live with her grandmother Mom Jao Ying Sabai Ninrat, who was an attendant to one of King Rama V's wives, to learn the traditional fine arts. After the toppling of the absolute monarchy the palace was dissolved and, at the age of 21, Mom Neuang was confronted with the modern world for the first time. She wrote a fascinating account of her time in the palace documenting this extraordinary, but now extinct, way of living. She told of the importance of grace, rigid etiquette and deference, the refined manner of living. She also included many recipes, as food played an important part in the life of the palace – more so than usual for Mom Neuang, since her grandmother was principal cook at Suan Sunanpaa Palace in the north of Bangkok.

The frills on wing beans are delightful, but can turn an unsightly black if kept too long or overcooked. Mom Neuang recommended trimming them.

100 g (3 oz) wing beans, trimmed of any black parts

pinch of salt

50 g (2 oz) cooked pork, elegantly sliced

50 g (2 oz) cooked prawns (shrimp), peeled and cut in half lengthwise

1 tablespoon ground dried prawns (shrimp)

handful of grated coconut, roasted

2 tablespoons coarsely ground roasted peanuts

3 tablespoons coconut cream

dressing

2 tablespoons Chilli Jam (page 200)

1 teaspoon palm sugar

1 teaspoon lime juice

1 tablespoon fish sauce

First, make the dressing (see page 338); it should taste rich, salty, sour and sweet.

Slice wing beans finely. Plunge into boiling salted water, then remove the pot from the heat. Once the beans have changed colour, drain and mix with the dressing. Combine remaining ingredients except coconut cream, arrange salad on a plate and drizzle with the coconut cream.

SMOKED CATFISH SALAD

pla pla lom kwan

This rustic salad comes from the north of Thailand, and is taken from a collection of recipes assembled in the early part of the twentieth century to raise money for the Wat Benchamabopit, the Marble Temple in the north of Bangkok. This was one of the first cookbooks in Thailand; before then, most recipes were published as part of a memorial book.

This particular recipe was donated to the cause by Thanpuuying Wongsanuprapaan, and originally called for a grilled catfish. This oily freshwater fish is normally grilled over embers for so long that it effectively becomes smoked. Any freshwater fish will do – and, while smoking it will render a faithful reproduction, this is not essential. However, the shallots, garlic, eggplants and chillies do need to be grilled, otherwise the salad loses its unique character. They can be grilled in the usual way or, if the fish is being smoked, can be smoked with it.

The base of this salad is rich, slightly bitter and smoky. The kaffir lime juice counters the pungency of fermented fish sauce; if regular fish sauce is used, then normal lime juice should be used instead of kaffir lime juice.

4 red shallots, unpeeled

4 garlic cloves, unpeeled

2 apple eggplants

4 slices galangal

1 catfish, trout or Murray perch – smoked (see page 179), if desired

large pinch of salt

1 hog plum or small green mango, shredded

2 tablespoons kaffir lime juice or lime juice

2 tablespoons fermented fish sauce (*nahm pla raa*) or fish sauce

1 tablespoon ground roasted rice

2 long red chillies, grilled, peeled, deseeded and coarsely torn

handful of holy basil

handful of mint

Grill the shallots, garlic, apple eggplants and galangal until charred and tender. Cool, peel and coarsely slice the shallots, garlic and eggplants. Mince the galangal.

If you are not smoking the fish, poach or chargrill it. Before chargrilling, wrap the fish in banana leaves or oiled foil to prevent the skin from sticking to the grill plate and tearing the flesh.

Fillet the flesh from the fish and coarsely slice. Combine all these ingredients with salt and hog plum or green mango. Season with lime juice and fish sauce: the salad should taste sour and salty. Serve sprinkled with the roasted rice, chillies, basil and mint.

Eat with Raw Vegetables (page 380), such as cucumber, cabbage and green beans.

WILD MUSHROOM SALAD

yam het bpa

Any type of mushroom can be used in this salad; however, I do have a prejudice against flavourless, cultivated varieties. The best way to clean mushrooms is to wipe them to remove any dirt or twigs that may still be attached. Then they are mostly ready to use, although with some varieties the gills or foam underneath the cap is scraped away. Once cleaned, mushrooms should be used quite quickly, as the exposed flesh oxidises, sometimes turning an unsettling colour.

150 g (5 oz) assorted wild mushrooms

2 tablespoons stock

pinch of salt

pinch of white sugar – optional

3 tablespoons lime juice

2 tablespoons fish sauce

large pinch of roasted chilli powder

4 red shallots, sliced

handful of mixed mint and coriander leaves

2 tablespoons shredded *pak chii farang* (long-leaf coriander)

1 tablespoon chopped spring (green) onion

1 tablespoon ground roasted rice

Clean the mushrooms and cut into attractive slices. Heat stock in a small pan, and add salt and sugar (if using). Add the mushrooms and simmer until cooked – the cooking time varies wildly, depending on the variety: pine mushrooms need to be simmered for at least 10 minutes, while the delicate grey ghost mushroom takes mere moments. If using an assortment, add the mushrooms accordingly.

Remove from the heat and season with lime juice, fish sauce and chilli powder; the salad should taste equally hot, sour and salty. Add shallots, herbs and spring onions. Serve sprinkled with ground roasted rice.

Serve with:

— a few sprigs of Thai basil

— sliced cabbage and cucumber.

SPICY MINCED CHICKEN SALAD

larp gai

A *larp* is an ancient salad. Some argue that it has the same origins as steak tartare – raw meat eaten with onions. The merchants of this part of Asia, the Haw, may have helped to spread this dish from the south-west of China and now, throughout northern Thailand, there are adaptations of this style of salad – *larp*, *nahm dtok* and *sup*.

What these diverse styles of *larp* seem to have in common is that the meat is minced or chopped, then cooked in the dressing, which is spicy and based on dried chillies. Sliced red shallots and shredded *pak chii farang* (long-leaf coriander), mint and coriander leaves are invariable aromatic companions in a traditional Thai *larp*. Mostly the salad is bound with ground roasted rice – northern salads are usually thicker than their counterparts from the south. *Larp* and their ilk are always accompanied by a plate of two or three raw vegetables, as befits their rustic simplicity. I find that iceberg lettuce is an ideal, though unorthodox, cooling aside.

Originally from the north-east, this basic, simple style of *larp* is now deservedly popular throughout Thailand.

150 g (5 oz) skinless chicken breast or thigh fillets

50–100 g (2–4 oz) chicken offal, such as liver, heart and giblets – optional

pinch of salt

1 small garlic clove, finely chopped – optional

3 tablespoons stock

extra pinch of salt

pinch of white sugar

3 tablespoons lime juice

large pinch of roasted chilli powder

1 tablespoon fish sauce

3 red shallots, sliced

handful of mixed mint and coriander leaves

1 tablespoon shredded *pak chii farang* (long-leaf coriander)

1 tablespoon ground roasted rice

Mince the chicken (see page 127) with salt and garlic, if using. If using offal, wash in salted and acidulated water to clean and remove any coarseness, then finely slice.

Heat stock and season with salt and sugar. Add mince and offal, if using, and simmer, stirring often, until just cooked (about 3–4 minutes); do not overcook or the meat will toughen. Season with lime juice, chilli powder and fish sauce. Mix in shallots and herbs. Check the seasoning – the salad should taste hot, sour and salty – and adjust accordingly. Sprinkle with roasted rice.

Eat with Raw Vegetables (page 380), such as cabbage, snake beans and cucumber.

CHIANG MAI–STYLE LARP OF PORK

larp chiang mai muu

This *larp* is from the region surrounding Chiang Mai, in the north of Thailand, and is profoundly different from those of other regions. It is like a very thick curry redolent with spices: a mixture of white and black peppercorns are used in the paste – this, and the use of long pepper and *macquem*, are sure indications of the dish's Burmese origins. No lime juice or any other souring agent is used, and this is what makes this style of *larp* so peculiar; if necessary, the paste should be moistened with stock or water to prevent burning.

100 g (3 oz) pork ribs

3 garlic cloves, peeled

pinch of salt

1 tablespoon rendered pork fat or oil

pinch of palm sugar – optional

1–2 tablespoons fish sauce

3 red shallots, sliced

1 tablespoon chopped spring (green) onion

1 tablespoon coriander leaves

paste

5 dried long red chillies, deseeded, soaked and drained

pinch of salt

5 red shallots, peeled

5 garlic cloves, peeled

2 tablespoons chopped galangal

2 tablespoons chopped lemongrass

1 tablespoon cumin seeds, roasted and ground

1 teaspoon *macquem* or Szechuan peppercorns, roasted and ground – optional

2 long pepper, roasted and ground

1 sheath mace, roasted and ground

5 black peppercorns, ground

5 white peppercorns, ground

First, make the paste: gradually pound the ingredients together using a pestle and mortar, adding one by one, until smooth. Coarsely chop the pork ribs and poach in salted water until tender – about 5–10 minutes – perhaps with a few offcuts of galangal and lemongrass from the paste. When cool enough to handle, remove the meat from the bones and roughly chop.

Chop the garlic with the salt. Heat rendered pork fat or oil in a small pan and fry garlic until golden. Add paste and fry until fragrant of the spices. Season with sugar, if using, and fish sauce. Add pork and moisten with a little of its poaching stock or water. Simmer for about 5 minutes, moistening further if necessary.

Add remaining ingredients and serve in a small bowl.

Accompany with:
- Raw Vegetables (page 380), such as cabbage, green beans, banana blossoms and cucumber
- sprigs of mint
- Deep-fried Pork Skin (page 400).

MONKS' OFFERING

yam tawai

This salad blurs the distinction between curries, salads and *nahm prik* relishes. Is it a salad dressed with a rich sauce, vegetables topped with a relish or a dry curry? This is significant because for the Thai there are no firm rules that codify their cuisine; rather it is a happy accumulation of techniques and methods that are used to arrive at a delicious result. This rich and ornate salad was so highly considered it was traditionally offered to monks on ceremonial occasions, most notably on the inauguration of the Temple of the Emerald Buddha in 1809. There are many variations of this recipe, but all specify that the vegetables be cooked separately from the meat or prawns – and sometimes from each other.

2 cups coconut cream

2–3 tablespoons palm sugar

2 tablespoons tamarind water

2 tablespoons fish sauce

½ cup Siamese watercress cut into 1 cm (½ in) lengths, blanched and refreshed

2 long eggplants, grilled, peeled and shredded

2 banana chillies, grilled, peeled and shredded

50 g (2 oz) poached skinless chicken breast fillet, shredded

10 cooked small prawns (shrimp), peeled and deveined

1 tablespoon deep-fried shallots

pinch of sesame seeds

paste

4–8 dried long red chillies, deseeded, soaked and drained

pinch of salt

4 red shallots, grilled and then peeled

4 garlic cloves, grilled and then peeled

3 tablespoons ground *pla grop* (crisp fish)

50 g (2 oz) grilled *pla salit* or hot-smoked trout

First, make the paste: gradually pound the ingredients together using a pestle and mortar, adding one by one, until smooth.

Crack coconut cream over medium heat until separated, add paste and fry until fragrant. Season with palm sugar to taste, tamarind water and fish sauce: it should taste rich, salty, smoky, sweet and sour.

Arrange the vegetables, chicken and prawns on a plate. Partially cover with the sauce, and sprinkle with deep-fried shallots and sesame seeds.

BAMBOO SHOOT SALAD FROM ISARN

sup nor mai

This popular north-eastern dish is very similar to *larp* of this region, except that boiled and shredded bamboo shoots are normally used instead of meat or fish. Consistent with this salad's origins, fermented fish sauce is the main seasoning of this pungent 'wet' salad.

200 g (6 oz) shredded and boiled bamboo shoots

3 red shallots, sliced

2 tablespoons chopped spring (green) onion

2 tablespoons shredded *pak chii farang* (long-leaf coriander)

handful of mint leaves

1 tablespoon ground roasted rice

dressing

4 tablespoons lime juice

3 tablespoons fermented fish sauce (*nahm pla raa*)

2 teaspoons roasted chilli powder

First, make the dressing (see page 338); it should taste hot, sour and salty.

Combine all the ingredients except rice, then serve sprinkled with the ground roasted rice.

Eat with:

— Raw Vegetables (page 380)

— 'betel' leaves and sprigs of coriander.

GRILLED BEEF SALAD

nahm dtok

A *nahm dtok* is another northern salad, and one which shares many characteristics with *larp*. However, it is made with a single piece of grilled meat. The name of this salad comes from the beads of meat juice that form on the side farthest from the heat as the meat grills, which Thai cooks refer to as *nahm dtok* – literally 'water falling'. This is their cue to turn the meat, which is normally cooked to medium-rare. Beef is the most common meat in this salad, although occasionally pork is used. I think venison or hare would be especially good dressed in this manner.

150 g (5 oz) beef rump or sirloin

4 red shallots, sliced

2 tablespoons shredded *pak chii farang* (long-leaf coriander)

handful of mixed mint and coriander leaves

1 tablespoon ground roasted rice

dressing

pinch of white sugar

3 tablespoons lime juice

3 tablespoons fish sauce

very large pinch of roasted chilli powder

First, make the dressing (see page 338); it should be pungently hot, sour and salty.

Chargrill the beef to your taste. For medium-rare, grill beef to rare, then rest in a warm place for at least 10 minutes. Slice the beef, and combine with shallots and herbs. Dress the salad and sprinkle with roasted rice.

Serve with a wedge of cabbage and a few snake beans.

11

AN

SIDE DISHES
ACCOMPANIMENTS

To give further dimension to a meal, the Thai add accompaniments, or *Kreaung kiam*. These pleasant, biting dishes contrast with and parallel the main dish. *Kreaung kiam* cannot be eaten by themselves; their value lies in their effect on the dishes that they are meant to accompany. The idea of complementary dishes counterbalancing each other is not limited to side dishes: each dish must relate to every other one on the table, enhancing by contrast, or reinforcing similar flavours. *Kreaung kiam* thus help to unify the meal.

These accompaniments can be quite simple, such as steamed eggs, or exactingly complicated, such as grilled skate shredded and caramelised in palm sugar. Perhaps the simplest accompaniments are fresh raw vegetables and sour or ripe tropical fruit – to relieve the intense flavours of a relish or the rich sweetness of a coconut-based curry.

Pickled garlic is best accompanying a hot and salty curry like a jungle curry, while pickled ginger is an ideal accompaniment to a sour orange curry or a *mussaman* curry. The more complex *kreaung kiam* of grilled or deep-fried salted fish, clams, eggs or beef are perfect companions to sour orange curries. And the rich saltiness of steamed or deep-fried salted duck eggs is a good foil to a green curry. Curries at the hotter end of the scale, like a southern yellow curry, are eaten with a plate of crisp and cool raw vegetables, like green beans, cucumber and white turmeric, recalling the accompaniments for *nahm prik* relishes.

RAW VEGETABLES
pak dip

Vegetables that are to accompany a relish or the occasional curry need to have some decided texture and flavour to withstand the intensity of these dishes. Cucumber, cabbage and green snake beans are most commonly used. But the list is endless: green tomatoes, young ginger and white turmeric; eggplants and banana blossoms; sour leaves, such as tamarind; or even fruit like green papaya, pomelo, star fruit, hog plum or green mango. Rocket, witlof, spinach and sorrel are certainly less authentic accompaniments, but they work deliciously well.

Raw vegetables should be washed and sliced into aesthetically and appropriately sized pieces (in richer or noble Thai households, they were intricately carved).

selection of vegetables from the following
'betel' leaves, picked
long eggplants, sliced
cucumber, cut into lengths
spring (green) onions, trimmed and cut into lengths
iceberg lettuce, cut into wedges

Siamese watercress, picked

young wing beans or green beans, trimmed

snake beans, cut into 2 cm (1 in) lengths

young ginger, peeled and sliced

white turmeric, peeled and sliced

banana blossoms, separated into leaves and steeped in acidulated water

fennel, trimmed and finely sliced

witlof (Belgian endive), separated into leaves

rocket (arugula), trimmed

sorrel leaves, trimmed

young spinach leaves, trimmed

savoy cabbage, cut into wedges

green tomatoes, cut into chunks

green mango, peeled and sliced

pomelo, separated into segments

rose apple, cut into pieces

Steep vegetables in very cold water before serving. Some cooks add a few ice cubes to ensure that the vegetables are truly quite crisp.

BOILED VEGETABLES

pak dtom

Good vegetables for boiling to serve as a *kreaung kiam* include cabbage, asparagus, green beans, okra and Siamese watercress.

a little 'cracked' coconut cream – optional

selection of vegetables from the following

asparagus, trimmed and boiled for 2–6 minutes

baby corn, boiled for 2–3 minutes

cabbage, cut into fine wedges and boiled for 5 minutes

green beans, cut into 2 cm (1 in) lengths and boiled for 2–4 minutes

okra, trimmed and boiled for 3 minutes

snake beans or wing beans, cut into 2 cm (1 in) lengths and boiled for no more than 1 minute

pumpkin, peeled, sliced and boiled for 5 minutes

Siamese watercress, boiled for 2–4 minutes

Boil the vegetables in salted water for the required time, then refresh by rinsing in cold water. Arrange the vegetables on a plate – and, if desired, drizzle with heated coconut cream that has just begun to separate.

VEGETABLES SIMMERED IN COCONUT MILK

pak dtom gati

2 cups coconut milk

pinch of salt

selection of vegetables from the following

cucumber, sliced

bamboo shoots, cleaned and shredded

Siamese watercress, cut into lengths

snake beans, cut into 2 cm (1 in) lengths

apple eggplants, cut into quarters and steeped in salted water to prevent
  discolouration

banana blossoms, separated into leaves and steeped in acidulated water

pumpkin tendrils

Simmer prepared vegetables in lightly salted coconut milk until tender. Remove vegetables and assemble on a plate before drizzling the almost-separated coconut cream over them.

GRILLED VEGETABLES

pak pao

A traditional manner of grilling vegetables is to cut them to the requisite size before putting them into a length of bamboo covered with coconut cream, then sealing the bamboo with banana leaves and grilling or roasting it in embers for at least 30 minutes, until most of the coconut cream has been absorbed by the vegetables. This imparts a wonderfully resinous taste to green papaya, water mimosa, beans, banana blossoms and eggplants. Bamboo segments can often be purchased at Asian food shops or plant nurseries. Soak them in water before use, as if they are too dry they will burn and impart more than a resinous quality to the vegetables.

The following is a much simpler alternative.

a little coconut cream – optional

selection of vegetables from the following

long eggplants, sliced

bamboo shoots, sliced

mushrooms, sliced

pumpkin, peeled and sliced

banana chilli, cut into strips

The prepared vegetables can be simply chargrilled as they are, but I like to dip them into a little coconut cream before grilling to compound their smoky bite.

DEEP-FRIED VEGETABLES

pak chut blaeng tort

The best vegetables for deep-frying are those that cook quite quickly.

1 cup rice flour or plain (all-purpose) flour
½ cup coconut cream
1 cup hydrolysed lime water – optional
oil for deep-frying

selection of vegetables from the following

Chinese broccoli, peeled (if old) and cut into 5 cm (2 in) lengths
chilli leaves
Siamese watercress, cut into 2 cm (1 in) lengths
banana blossoms, shredded
Asian pennywort leaves
'betel' leaves
sprigs of Thai basil
long eggplants, sliced
snake beans, cut into 2 cm (1 in) lengths

To make batter: combine first three ingredients and rest for at least 30 minutes. Moisten with extra water if too thick. Using hydrolysed lime water makes the batter crisp, despite the coconut cream. If reluctant to use this, or unable to find hydrolysed lime powder, then do not use the coconut cream, as the resulting batter will be gluey and gooey. Use plain water – roughly 1 cup – instead. (Alternatively, an egg can be used instead of batter – simply crack and whisk.)

Dip vegetables in batter (or beaten egg). Deep-fry in a wok or pot in plenty of oil until vegetables are cooked and batter is crisp and golden. If using a selection of vegetables, add according to the cooking time required.

PICKLED VEGETABLES

pak dong

These can be made several hours ahead for convenience.

1 cup white vinegar
1 cup water
1 cup white sugar
2–4 tablespoons liquid from pickled garlic – optional
2 tablespoons salt

selection of 2 or 3 vegetables from the following

Chinese cabbage, cut into fine wedges

onions, peeled and quartered

banana chillies, cut into strips

snake beans, trimmed and cut into 2 cm (1 in) lengths

white radish, peeled and sliced

baby corn, trimmed

Boil vinegar and water with sugar, garlic liquid and salt until sugar and salt have dissolved. When cool, immerse vegetables for at least 30 minutes.

SPICY PICKLED VEGETABLES

pak dong

This is a simple and easy recipe by Mom Leuang Taw Kritakara and Mom Ratchawongse Pimsai Amranand from their cookbook, *Modern Thai Cooking*. Thirty years ago, they ran a fondly remembered restaurant called the Tollgate, on Sukhumwit in Bangkok. Both recommend this recipe to accompany deep-fried meat or fish, but I think it also works well with a *lon* relish.

1 cup small cauliflower florets

1 cup cucumber cut into 1 cm (½ in) cubes

1 cup shredded Chinese cabbage

1 cup corn kernels

2 cups coconut vinegar

pinch of salt

1 cup oil

1–2 cups water, depending on strength of vinegar

pinch of white sugar

1 teaspoon sesame seeds, roasted

paste

1 tablespoon chopped long red chillies

pinch of salt

1 tablespoon chopped red shallot

1 tablespoon chopped garlic

First, make the paste: gradually pound the ingredients together using a pestle and mortar, adding one by one, until smooth.

Blanch vegetables separately in vinegar with salt. Fry the paste in the oil until fragrant. Add vinegar, water and vegetables and return to the boil. Season with sugar to taste. Serve at room temperature, sprinkled with the sesame seeds.

PICKLED GARLIC

gratiam dong

When pickling garlic, it is important to first soak the garlic in salted water overnight to kill the green shoot at its centre, otherwise it will begin to turn an unnerving blue-green colour. In fact, the best garlic to use is young or spring garlic which has not yet begun to sprout. If this is not available, cut each clove in half and carefully remove the sprout without bruising the clove. And if only older heads are available, blanch them in water before soaking to reduce their pungency.

20 garlic cloves *or* 10 small heads young or spring garlic
2 cups water
1 cup white or coconut vinegar
2 tablespoons salt
1 cup white sugar

Peel garlic cloves – or peel excess, but not all, skin from young heads. Soak in salted water overnight.

Next day, drain the garlic, rinse it and place in a sterilised jar. Bring the 2 cups water, vinegar, salt and sugar to the boil. Pour this syrup over the garlic and seal the jar. Leave in the sun or a warm, dry place for at least 15 and up to 30 days. Leave to mature in refrigerator for a further 5 days before use.

PICKLED GINGER

king dong

The best ginger to use for pickling is new season's young or white ginger, which is sometimes available for a couple of months during late summer from Asian food stores. If only mature ginger is available, peel and rub with a little salt and leave for a few hours to leach out some of its pepperiness. Rinse in water before proceeding with the recipe. Do not use gnarled old ginger roots.

2 cups peeled, washed and sliced young ginger
1½ cups white sugar
1 tablespoon salt
1½ cups white vinegar (not too strong)
½ cup water

Steep ginger in salted water for around 1 hour. Drain, rinse, then squeeze out the excess water. Place in bowl.

Make a syrup by dissolving sugar and salt in vinegar and water. Bring to the boil. When the sugar has dissolved, strain over the ginger. Cover and leave for at least a week before use. Store in the refrigerator.

PICKLED RED SHALLOTS

horm dong

The subtle astringency of pickled shallots is used to assuage the sharp heat of a jungle curry, or to cut through the richness of a highly spiced yellow curry.

Although pickled red shallots can be bought at Asian shops, homemade are preferable.

500 g (1 lb) red shallots

2 tablespoons coconut vinegar or white vinegar

2 cups rice-rinsing water

1 tablespoon palm sugar

1 rounded tablespoon salt

1 cup coconut water

1 cup water

Peel the shallots and soak overnight in salted water. Next day, drain, rinse and leave to dry. Combine the remaining ingredients and stir until dissolved. Place the shallots in a sterilised glass jar and pour over the liquid. Cover and leave in the sun or a warm, dry place for at least 4 days. Once sufficiently sour, store refrigerated for another week before use. Refrigerated, these pickled shallots last for a few months.

PICKLED CUCUMBER

dtaeng gwa dong

Pickled cucumber often accompanies sour orange or red curries, especially of chicken or quail.

500 g (1 lb) cucumber

salt

1 cup white vinegar

½ cup white sugar

½ cup water

2 cm (1 in) piece of cassia bark – optional

5 cloves

Top and tail cucumber. Cut into quarters lengthwise and deseed. Rub with salt and leave to drain overnight. Bring vinegar, sugar and water to the boil, add spices and simmer for 5 minutes. Cool and leave overnight. Strain.

The next day, wash cucumber, pat dry and place in a sterilised glass jar. Pour pickling liquid over it and leave for 3 weeks in a warm, dry place before use. Refrigerated, pickled cucumber lasts indefinitely.

PICKLED CABBAGE

galambii dong

> 2 tablespoons salt
>
> 1 tablespoon palm sugar
>
> 1 tablespoon white vinegar
>
> 2 cups water
>
> 1 savoy cabbage

Dissolve salt and sugar in vinegar and water. Remove coarse, outer leaves from the cabbage, then cut into quarters, removing and discarding the core. Cut cabbage roughly into squares. Wash. Place in a sterilised glass jar and cover with the liquid. Leave in the sun or a warm, dry place for 3–5 days, then refrigerate. This keeps for 1 week only.

PICKLED APPLE EGGPLANTS

makruea dong

> 1–2 tablespoons salt
>
> 1 tablespoon sugar – either palm or white, as preferred
>
> 2 cups rice-rinsing water
>
> 1 tablespoon white vinegar
>
> 200 g (6 oz) apple eggplants

Dissolve the salt and sugar in the rice-rinsing water and vinegar. Top the eggplants and cut into sixths. Wash. Place in a sterilised glass jar and cover with the liquid. Leave in the sun or a warm, dry place for 5 days. Refrigerated, this keeps for 1 week.

PICKLED MUSTARD GREENS

pak gart dong

These salty and sour mustard greens can be used as an accompaniment to curries, especially red – either plain or stir-fried with eggs, sugar and deep-fried garlic.

To make a salty and sweet version (to accompany rice soup, or to use in a salad), simply add another 2 tablespoons of sugar.

> 3 bunches mustard greens
>
> 6–8 cups rice-rinsing water
>
> 1 tablespoon salt
>
> 2 tablespoons palm sugar
>
> 1 tablespoon white vinegar

Wash mustard greens and separate the leaves, trimming and discarding any stems and very fibrous parts. Soak in salted water overnight to remove the harsh peppery taste of the raw leaves, then drain. Dry in the sun for a day or leave overnight in an oven with the pilot light on.

Next day, mix all the other ingredients well. When sugar has dissolved, pour the solution over the greens and cover. Allow to ferment for 4–15 days in the sun; the length of time needed is determined by the heat and strength of the sunlight.

Store refrigerated – and rinse before use.

PICKLED SIAMESE WATERCRESS

pak bung dong

> 1 bunch Siamese watercress or any other leafy Chinese greens
> 1 cup white vinegar
> 2 tablespoons salt
> 1 cup white sugar
> 1 cup water

Cut the tough ends from the cress. Wash, removing any wilted or rotting leaves and chop into 2 cm (1 in) lengths. Bring vinegar and salt to the boil in a pan. Briefly blanch the cress, remove and set aside in a bowl. Add sugar and water to the pan and boil until dissolved. Pour over the cress, ensuring that it is completely immersed. This can be eaten when cool, but is best after 1 day. Discard after 3 days.

STEAMED EGGS

kai neung

Steamed eggs are much more tender than boiled eggs – and just as easy to make. I like them soft, so 10 minutes is usually just right. However, if the heat is low, the eggs might need a little longer.

> 2 eggs

Simply steam the eggs for 10 minutes, then leave to cool. Crack the shell carefully by rolling the egg against the top of a table, then gently press against the white, lift the shell off and peel. Rinse the egg to remove any grit.

STEAMED EGGS, PICKLED GINGER (page 385) AND CUCUMBER, ACCOMPANYING FRIED CHILLI RELISH (page 208)

OMELETTE

kai jiaw

Eggs and rice are the perfect foil for any hot food. The following recipe is a very simple way of dealing with eggs. Perhaps by now it is needless to say, but this simplicity can be embellished – with a few sliced red shallots, a little crabmeat or minced pork, some pickled mustard greens or dried prawns.

2 eggs
large pinch of salt
3 tablespoons oil
3 spring (green) onions, finely sliced
pinch of ground white pepper

Whisk eggs with salt. Heat a wok and, when very hot, add the oil. Carefully pour in the egg mixture – the oil will froth up and splatter, but the result is a delicious, crispy-edged omelette. Cook over high heat. Turn the omelette once it has set, and briefly cook the other side. Drain. Serve sprinkled with spring onions and white pepper.

DEEP-FRIED EGGS

kai tort

These really should be tried because they are delicious, and are a particularly good *kreaung kiam* for Prawns and Yellow Beans Simmered in Coconut Cream (page 444). In another version – and this is my favourite way to eat eggs – the deep-fried eggs are dressed with sweetened fish sauce.

2 eggs
oil for deep-frying

Break an egg into a bowl, then carefully roll into a pot of hot oil. Fry for 30 seconds, turn and, after another 30 seconds, remove and drain.

Deep-fried eggs must be eaten hot.

STEAMED EGG MOUSSE

kai dtun

This is a delicious, simple and cooling accompaniment to a fierce relish or a complex curry such as a *panaeng*.

There are many variations to the basic recipe: minced pork, blanched small prawns or crabmeat, sliced chicken or pork liver, and long Thai green eggplants can be included, depending on the relish or curry it is to accompany.

1 large egg

pinch of salt

1 tablespoon fish sauce or light soy sauce

pinch of white sugar

2 red shallots, sliced

handful of coriander leaves

2 tablespoons stock, water or coconut cream

ground white pepper

Whisk the egg, then add all the other ingredients. Pour into a bowl, mould or ramekin. Gently steam until cooked – around 5–10 minutes.

STEAMED SALTED DUCK EGGS

kai kem

Mostly, salted duck eggs are cooked by boiling, but I find that steaming results in a softer, creamier texture.

2 salted duck eggs

Steam the eggs for 20 minutes. Cut the unshelled eggs in half with a sharp knife, then scoop out the halves with a spoon.

DEEP-FRIED SALTED DUCK EGGS

kai kem tort

1 salted duck egg

1 fresh duck or chicken egg white

oil for deep-frying

To make an elegant accompaniment to a curry, separate the salted egg, divide and roll the yolk – which will have become hard during the salting process – into 4 small balls, steam for 10 minutes until cooked.

Combine the white of the salted egg with the white of the fresh egg and mix well. (Occasionally, a little rice flour is added to the egg whites to form a batter.) Dip the cooled yolk pieces into the egg white mixture, then deep-fry in plenty of hot oil until crisp.

SALTED PRAWNS

gung kem

An agreeable accompaniment, this is also the traditional way the Thai keep excess prawns from spoiling. Mixed with sliced red shallots and chillies, the prawns make an excellent, simple salad.

The taste of the prawns is altered to a pungent saltiness and their texture becomes denser, losing the sweet lightness that is favoured in the West – but the Thai consider this a very agreeable transformation.

2 cups water

3 tablespoons salt

2 stalks lemongrass

6 king prawns (jumbo shrimp), peeled and deveined

Put water and salt in a large pot and bring to the boil. When the salt has dissolved, add lemongrass and prawns. Return to the boil, then remove from the heat and leave the prawns to cool in the brine.

Either serve at room temperature or reheat in the brine, but do not boil as this will toughen the prawns.

DRIED SQUID

pla meuk dtat dtiaw

If the squid is to be deep-fried, then it must be completely dried or it will shrink and toughen on cooking.

200 g (6 oz) cleaned squid

4 tablespoons light soy sauce

large pinch of salt

pinch of white sugar

pinch of ground white pepper

Marinate squid in light soy sauce, salt, sugar and pepper overnight. Dry on a rack in a warm place or in the sun for at least a day, until completely dry. Turn the squid at least twice during this time to prevent the flesh being marked by the rack.

Refrigerated, this will keep for a couple of days.

CRISP FISH SKIN

nang pla tort grop

This is a simple accompaniment enjoyed for its texture as much as its taste. Any fish skin will do, although I find salmon, snapper or red emperor the best. Wash and scrape the skin to remove any scales. If using salmon skin, I like to leave a little of the flesh and fat on the inside: once dried and fried it is pleasantly crunchy – but do not leave too much attached or it will not crisp when it fries.

fish skin from a side of fish, such as salmon, snapper or red emperor

large pinch of salt

pinch of white sugar

pinch of ground white pepper

4 tablespoons light soy sauce

oil for deep-frying

Clean the fish skin and marinate in salt, sugar, pepper and soy sauce, working the marinade into the skin. Leave refrigerated overnight, or at room temperature for several hours. Dry on a rack in the sun or a warm place for around 12 hours or until brittle and completely dry, turning once or twice to ensure that it dries evenly and does not become marked by the rack. Cut into 4 cm (2 in) strips.

Heat plenty of clean oil and deep-fry, a few pieces at a time, until the fish skin swells slightly and is crisp. Drain and serve.

CRISPY FISH CAKES

pla fuu

Crispy fish cakes make another very agreeable and common accompaniment. This is a most improbable dish. Traditionally catfish grilled over charcoal is used but in the following recipe the addition of hot-smoked trout replicates its flavour. The collagen in the fish holds the cake together during the frying and rather than falling apart, as one would expect, it sticks together and becomes a crisp crumble of toasted fish. Although this recipe may sound difficult, it is in fact quite easy after one or two attempts at the deep-frying.

Crispy fish cakes keep for a day or so, but the flavour does deteriorate. The cakes can be kept warm for some time after cooking, for instance above an oven.

100 g (3 oz) flathead or gurnard (sea robin)

a little hot-smoked trout

large pinch of salt

oil for deep-frying

Wash the flathead or gurnard. Roast in a moderate oven (190°C or 375°F), on a cake rack set over a tray lined with foil, until quite dry and just beginning to colour. Cool.

Blend with the hot-smoked trout and salt in a food processor until the mixture looks like breadcrumbs. (Do not include any hard or dried bits of fish – by the time they have broken down, the rest of the fish will be over-processed.) If the fish is ground too fine, then it will not 'clump' when it fries; too coarse and when it fries the pieces will harden into little pellets. Err on the side of over-salting the fish crumbs, for the salt will cook during the deep-frying and give the fish a full flavour.

Bring plenty of oil in a wok to a medium to high temperature. The temperature must be just right: if the oil is too hot it will scorch the fish; too cool and the collagen in the fish will not cook quickly enough to hold the fish floss together.

Deep-fry a small handful of the 'crumbs' at a time. Again, be careful: too much added at one time will cool the oil and either prevent the collagen from bonding or saturate the cakes with oil. Too little may scorch the fish or make the cakes too brittle. Rain a small handful into the oil. When it has finished foaming, pull the crumbs from the opposite side of the wok into the centre. Repeat, pushing into the centre from the nearer side. The collagen should now hold the fish cake together and it should smell cooked. Flip over, and when it is slightly golden in colour, remove and drain on absorbent paper. Allow the oil to reheat, then repeat the process until all the mixture is used.

CRISPY PRAWN CAKES

gung fuu

These make a sumptuous alternative to Crispy Fish Cakes (page 393), and are especially agreeable accompanied by Sweet Fish Sauce (page 460), Steamed Eggs (page 388) and sprigs of coriander. They are expensive to make, however, as only fresh prawns should be used; the collagen in frozen prawns will be denatured to the extent that it cannot bind the crumbs together during deep-frying.

12 large uncooked prawns (shrimp)
pinch of salt
oil for deep-frying

Wash the prawns. Combine with salt and 'roast' in a wok until the prawns change colour and are quite dry. Cool, then peel and devein. Pound or purée the prawn meat with the salt from the wok until it has the consistency of fresh breadcrumbs.

In a wok, heat oil until it is medium to hot: if the oil is too hot, it will scorch the crumbs; too cool, and the prawns will be saturated with oil and not form cakes. Rain in a handful of the crumbs – one handful at a time, one cake at a time. When the foaming has stopped, pull the 'raft' together quickly with two fish slices, first away from one side of the wok and then from the other; turn it over and then remove from oil. Drain on absorbent paper. Allow the oil to reheat, then repeat the process until all the prawn mixture is used.

DEEP-FRIED TROUT DUMPLINGS

tort man pla trout

While any fish can be used in this recipe, one of the most common is a whiting-like fish, *pla grai* – which has the unusual but desirable characteristic, as far as the Thai are concerned, of making a very rubbery dumpling. Trout may not be so toothsome, but it makes an attractive dumpling.

2 coriander roots, scraped and chopped
2 garlic cloves, peeled
1 cm (½ in) piece of ginger, peeled
pinch of salt
pinch of white pepper
200 g (6 oz) minced trout – but any fish will do
a little white sugar, to taste
fish sauce, to taste
2 steamed salted duck egg yolks, quartered
oil for deep-frying

Using a mortar and pestle, make a fine paste from the coriander root, garlic, ginger, salt and pepper. Combine with minced trout. Slap the mixture – pick it up and throw it back into the bowl – until it becomes smoother and firmer, then season with sugar and fish sauce. Wrap the trout mixture around the quartered duck egg yolks and deep-fry in medium to hot oil until golden.

MARRON GLACÉ

gung mangkorn warn

A variation on a classic.

1 tablespoon oil
4 tablespoons palm sugar
2 tablespoons fish sauce
1 cooked marron (large freshwater crayfish)
   or 3 large prawns (shrimp), peeled and deveined
2 tablespoons deep-fried shallots

paste
1 coriander root, scraped and chopped
pinch of salt
2 garlic cloves, peeled
5 white peppercorns

First, make the paste: gradually pound the ingredients together using a pestle and mortar, adding one by one, until smooth. Fry the paste in the oil until golden. Add sugar and simmer over a low heat until thick. Moisten with fish sauce and continue to simmer for a moment. Add marron or prawns, coat with the syrup and allow to cool. Serve sprinkled with deep-fried shallots.

STIR-FRIED DRIED MUSSELS

hoi malaeng puu haeng

The most authentic mollusc to use in this recipe is a razor clam, but mussels, scallops or pipis (littleneck clams) are agreeable alternatives. Just make sure the shellfish is completely dry, otherwise it will splutter while frying and become tough.

> 200 g (6 oz) mussels
> pinch of salt
> pinch of white sugar
> 3 tablespoons light soy sauce
> oil for deep-frying
> 2 teaspoons white sugar
> good pinch of salt
> handful of coriander leaves

Shell the mussels. Marinate in salt, sugar and soy overnight. Next day place on a rack and leave for several hours until dry. Heat a wok, add oil and, when hot, add the mussels. When they begin to crisp, remove. Sprinkle with sugar, salt and coriander.

SWEET SHREDDED SKATE

pla graben warn

This is a very complicated *kreaung kiam* that can be served with any curry. It hails from Phetchaburi, to the south-west of Bangkok, where King Rama IV would retire during the wearying April heat. His summer palace was high in the hills and caught all the breezes from the nearby sea.

Dried salted beef is prepared in this manner all over Thailand – and the ladies of the court no doubt employed their refined techniques on local ingredients to produce alternative, intriguing delicacies. This is one of them.

> 1 skate wing, around 300 g (9 oz)
> 2–3 tablespoons light soy sauce
> pinch of white sugar
> 4 tablespoons palm sugar
> 2 tablespoons fish sauce

Wash and dry the fish, then marinate overnight in soy sauce and white sugar. Next day, grill slowly until overcooked but not overly charred. Cool, then pull the flesh apart, picking and shredding it into fine strands.

Bring palm sugar to the boil over a low heat in a heavy small pot or a wok. Add fish and stir constantly to prevent from clumping. Pour in fish sauce and simmer until the syrup evenly coats the fish strands.

SALTED PORK WITH COCONUT MILK

muu kem gati

A perfect accompaniment to a sour orange curry, a jungle curry, or Old-fashioned Tamarind Relish (page 191).

100 g (3 oz) boneless pork leg
good pinch of salt
pinch of white sugar
1–2 tablespoons light soy sauce
pinch of white pepper
½ cup coconut milk
½ cup water or chicken stock

Cut the pork along the grain into ½ cm (¼ in) slices. Marinate overnight in salt, sugar, soy and pepper.

Next day, put pork in pan, cover with coconut milk and water or stock and simmer until quite dry. Remove and cool slightly, then tear coarsely.

SWEET PORK

muu warn

A dish served with many relishes. This is an especially irresistible sweetmeat that warrants this caveat: double the recipe.

300 g (9 oz) steamed or poached pork neck (if the latter, keep the stock)
1 cup white sugar
pinch of salt
a little water or poaching stock
3 tablespoons fish sauce
1 tablespoon sweet soy sauce (*kecap manis*)
3 red shallots, sliced
ground white pepper
handful of coriander leaves, chopped

Slice the pork. In a wok or heavy pot caramelise the sugar with salt. Moisten with water or stock. Add the pork. Season with fish sauce and soy sauce and simmer until thick. Serve sprinkled with red shallots, white pepper and coriander.

SWEET CRISPY PORK

muu grop warn

This is another version of the omnipresent sweet pork, and it is just as irresistible! I think that the pork is improved if it is salted in a cup of light soy sauce and a pinch each of salt and sugar for 2 days before it is steamed. Thus impregnated with salt, it withstands the sweetness of this dish. Sugar plays a vital role in Thai cooking, balancing what might otherwise be an excess of heat, sourness and saltiness.

1 kg (2 lb) pork belly, with bone attached

oil for deep-frying

2 cups palm sugar

½ cup fish sauce

1 tablespoon oyster sauce

3 tablespoons deep-fried shallots

1 tablespoon coriander leaves

paste

3 coriander roots, scraped and chopped

pinch of salt

4 garlic cloves, peeled

1 teaspoon white peppercorns

1 star anise, roasted and ground

Steam pork until well cooked – about 30 minutes. Cool and rest. Lift the meat from the bone, reserving the bone for stock. Cut pork into roughly 1 cm (½ in) cubes and pat dry.

Heat oil and deep-fry pork over a moderate heat until golden brown, then drain.

Next, make the paste: gradually pound the ingredients together using a pestle and mortar, adding one by one, until smooth. Heat a wok, add a little of the deep-frying oil and fry paste until fragrant and golden. Dissolve sugar in fish sauce and oyster sauce, add to wok and, when sticky, add pork and simmer for a few minutes until coated. (Do not simmer for too long, or the meat will toughen.) Serve sprinkled with deep-fried shallots and coriander leaves.

PORK COOKED IN TWO STYLES

muu sorng yang

1 kg (2 lb) pork belly, with bone attached

1 teaspoon oil

3 garlic cloves, pounded

1 bottle (about 220 g or 7 oz) white fermented bean curd

½ cup coconut cream

a little Chinese rice wine

handful of Thai basil leaves

ground white pepper

100 g (3 oz) palm sugar

1 star anise

1 tablespoon oyster sauce

4 tablespoons fish sauce

2 coriander roots, scraped and chopped

handful of deep-fried shallots

handful of coriander leaves, chopped

Steam pork for 1 hour and leave to cool. Cube pork and then divide into two halves. Fry one half in oil until it colours, drain off excess fat, add garlic and continue to fry until fragrant. Add bean curd, coconut cream and rice wine and simmer for several minutes, until thick. Add Thai basil, sprinkle with pepper and set aside.

Melt sugar in a large pan and then add star anise, oyster sauce, fish sauce, coriander root and the rest of the pork. Simmer gently until soft and sticky. Make sure it isn't too sweet – add a little more fish sauce if it is – and sprinkle with deep-fried shallots and coriander before serving.

CRISPY FRIED PORK

muu grop

This is wicked, but it's delicious! Remember to start preparations at least 4 days before it is to be served.

1 kg (2 lb) pork belly

pinch of salt

pinch of white sugar

3 tablespoons light soy sauce

3 tablespoons white vinegar

5 tablespoons salt

oil for deep-frying

Wash the pork. Marinate in salt, sugar and light soy sauce for 2 days.

Remove from marinade and steam until cooked, about 30 minutes. Cool but do not refrigerate. Cut pork into 2 cm (1 in) strips along the grain. With a fork, furiously prick the skin, then vigorously rub with vinegar and salt. Leave to dry at least overnight, but preferably for 48 hours.

Brush off dried salt. Deep-fry in hot, clean oil until pork skin has bubbled and looks like crackling. Remove from oil, drain, cool and slice across the grain.

DEEP-FRIED PORK WITH SPICES

muu tort kreuangthet

A simple side dish that offers a pleasant and spicy contrast to a rich *lon*. Beef, fish or prawns could be used instead of pork, depending on what it accompanies.

It is not necessary to roast the spices beforehand, since they will toast as the pork deep-fries. A little puréed garlic can also be added to the marinade.

large pinch of white peppercorns
large pinch of coriander seeds
large pinch of cumin seeds
pinch of grated nutmeg
seeds from 1 cardamom pod
100 g (3 oz) pork neck
2 tablespoons light soy sauce
pinch of white sugar
oil for deep-frying

Coarsely grind the spices using a pestle and mortar: altogether they should measure a scant tablespoon. Slice the pork quite finely – a little less than ½ cm (¼ in) thick. Work in the spices, soy sauce and sugar and leave for 20 minutes.

Heat oil and deep-fry pork until cooked – about 3–5 minutes. Let pork rest for a moment before serving.

DEEP-FRIED PORK SKIN

kaep muu

The surprising thing about this recipe is the degree to which the shrivelled skin puffs up when deep-fried; boiling it with the lime powder ensures this remarkable response. The skin must be completely dry before frying or it will become sodden with oil and unsatisfyingly limp. It is also important to ensure that the oil is clean and that there is plenty of it. Pork skin treated like this is a steadfast accompaniment to most northern Thai relishes and curries.

100 g (3 oz) pork skin

pinch of hydrolysed lime powder

pinch of salt

2 tablespoons white vinegar

oil for deep-frying

Scrape fat away from the skin and, with sharp scissors, cut pork skin into small pieces – perhaps 2 cm × 3 cm (1 in × 1¼ in) – they expand enormously as they cook. Clean the skin and remove any remaining excess fat. Boil in plenty of water with lime powder, salt and vinegar until the skin is tender and opaque. Drain and dry on a rack in a warm place for at least 2 days, until completely dry.

Deep-fry in plenty of hot oil. When skin puffs and expands, remove and drain on absorbent paper.

SALTED BEEF

neua kem

Salting is a traditional Thai method of preserving meat, usually beef, for long periods of time. The best beef for salting is a coarsely flavoured and stringy-textured cut, such as round, skirt or topside. It is important to cut the meat along its well-defined grain. This is contrary to all Western butchery practice, but allows for easy shredding later.

200 g (6 oz) beef

5 tablespoons fish sauce or light soy sauce

large pinch of salt

pinch of white sugar

pinch of white pepper

Cut meat into long slices, about ½ cm (¼ in) thick, along the grain. Work the fish sauce or soy sauce, salt, sugar and pepper into the beef, then marinate overnight.

Next day, dry beef strips for at least 24 hours on a rack in the sun or a warm airy place until completely dry. The spot should not be too hot, or the meat might cook rather than dry. Make sure the strips are sufficiently spaced for the air to circulate, and turn at least once. Make sure they have completely dried; otherwise they will become mouldy when stored.

Salted beef can be kept for several weeks in the refrigerator.

FRESHLY SALTED BEEF

neua kem sot

This version of salted beef is made during the rainy season in Thailand when there is no guarantee of sufficient sun to dry salted beef in the normal way (see page 401). Any full-flavoured cut of beef that can sustain protracted cooking can be prepared this way. If time is short, some beef rump or sirloin, or even venison, can be briefly marinated before being quickly deep-fried over a high heat until golden.

    200 g (6 oz) beef flank
    pinch of salt
    4–5 tablespoons fish sauce
    pinch of white sugar
    good pinch of ground white pepper
    oil for deep-frying

Cut the beef into ½ cm (¼ in) strips. Vigorously work the salt, fish sauce, sugar and white pepper into the meat, then leave to marinate for half an hour or so. Cover the meat with water and simmer in a pot or wok until all the water has evaporated. Remove and allow to dry.

Heat the oil and deep-fry the meat over a moderate heat until golden, fragrant and crisp.

CUCUMBER RELISH

ajat dtaeng gwa

In many ways, an *ajat* can be seen as a salad of shredded vegetables that is piquantly dressed with a sweet and sour syrup. It helps to cut the richness of coconut-based curries, and makes a simple, refreshing accompaniment to many dishes, including Fish Cakes (page 494), Prawn Cakes (page 495) and Madtarbark (page 530).

Occasionally shredded green papaya, cabbage or even pickled garlic is used in an *ajat*, but mostly it consists of sliced cucumber with a little ginger, red shallot, chilli and coriander. The syrup should be light and savoury. If it is too strong, it overwhelms all the other components of the relish. Often a coriander root is added when making the syrup to bring a pleasantly herbaceous quality to the relish. It is always served at room temperature. The syrup can be made well in advance and keeps indefinitely.

Some cooks prefer to steep the ingredients in the syrup for an hour or so before needed, resulting in a mellow accompaniment, but I like to assemble the *ajat* when required: all the ingredients then retain a crisp integrity of taste.

3 tablespoons coconut vinegar or white vinegar

3 tablespoons white sugar

4 tablespoons water

pinch of salt

1 small cucumber, washed, quartered lengthwise and sliced – about ½ cup

4 red shallots, finely sliced

2 tablespoons julienned ginger

1 long red chilli, julienned or cut into thin rounds

1 tablespoon coriander leaves

Combine vinegar, sugar, water and salt in a small saucepan and bring to the boil. Remove from the heat when sugar has dissolved. Cool. The syrup should taste sour and sweet.

Mix remaining ingredients in a serving bowl and pour the syrup over them.

ROTI

In the south of Thailand, *roti* is often served with curries such as a *mussaman* or *geng gari*. It is also used to dip into any leftover curry for breakfast.

2½ cups plain (all-purpose) flour

large pinch of salt

large pinch of sugar

1 egg, lightly whisked

2 tablespoons water

ghee for frying

Combine flour, salt, sugar, egg and water to make a thick dough. Knead until firm. Divide into small egg-size balls and set aside to rest, covered with a damp tea towel, for at least 30 minutes.

Roll a dough ball into a disc, about ½ cm (¼ in) thick. Pick up the disc and twist to make a rope, then wrap this into a spiral. Now roll the spiral flat again, until it is ½ cm (¼ in) thick. Shallow-fry in the ghee over a low heat for about 4 minutes each side.

Repeat this process with the other dough balls.

12

MENUS

This chapter consists of menus, with recipes, designed to make one traditional Thai meal. The Thai abhor repetition; to them a well-composed meal comprises several dishes. A meal ideally consists of a relish, a soup, a curry and a salad – and perhaps a simple stir-fried, grilled or deep-fried item. And, of course, rice. A meal without rice is inconceivable, and a meal without a choice of dishes is impoverished. Just as the balance of flavours and textures is important in the construction of an individual dish, it is essential when designing a meal. Never is one flavour, taste or seasoning dominant, nor should there be repetition of a style of dish – to the Thai this would be nonsensical and a lapse in taste.

Thai custom dictates that food is never served in the utensil in which it has been cooked. Thai artisans have made beautiful tableware for centuries. Sukothai, for instance, produced a famous style of glazed jade-green ceramic bowl called celadon. A pair of fish, symbolising prosperity and health, was sketched onto the dried but not yet fired clay. Rice plates were – and are – much larger than other bowls or serving dishes. This reflects the primacy of rice in a meal and the auxiliary role of the other elements. Rice plates are wide and shallow, curry plates smaller and deeper. Small soup bowls and their spoons are in the Chinese style. Flat plates were introduced by Europeans as early as the seventeenth century, before which only bowls were used.

For 24 years during the reign of King Rama IV, a Monsignor Pallegoix resided in Siam as the papal nuncio. He had many occasions to observe the Thai and their habits. His *Description of the Thai Kingdom or Siam* is remarkable for these insights and the genial affection he felt towards his 'flock':

> The Thai take all their meals seated on a mat or carpet . . . The dishes are cut in small pieces and the rice is placed aside . . . The diners have neither spoons, nor forks, nor knives. They only use a mother-of-pearl spoon to take from the plates. For all the rest, fingers are sufficient. Only when they are satisfied do they drink pure water or a cup of tea. Among the rich people, the husband usually eats before his wife . . . The dining hour is, so to speak, sacred for the Thai. One never bothers someone who is eating; even masters themselves watch out not to interrupt the meal of their slaves . . . The time of a meal is also a time of silence. Even if one is with ten or twenty people to eat together, one barely hears a few words escape one or the other, so deeply engrossed are they in their business!

While it remains unwise to disturb any Thai while they are eating, silence no longer reigns, except out of respect when eating with a superior. Now, meals are gregarious, filled with laughter, good food and friendly banter.

Until the late nineteenth century, most people ate with their hands: with the fingers of the right hand, keeping either the little or index finger free, rice would be mixed with an accompanying dish, and formed into a small mound on the plate. It was lifted with the four fingers to the mouth, the thumb shifting the food into the mouth to ensure the manoeuvre was clean and successful. Occasionally, in a very casual atmosphere – or upcountry – it is still possible to see people eat in this manner with beguiling grace. The poor ate off banana leaves; the richer from ceramic bowls. The spoon was a familiar serving utensil before it made the crossover to being used to eat rice. Then later, due to continuing European influence, the fork entered the fray, and the rice began to be eaten from a plate instead of a shallow bowl. Chopsticks are used only when eating noodles – a dish of Chinese origin.

A THAI MEAL

Although the Thai are inveterate snackers, there are no appetisers. While there may be a few dishes prior to the meal proper, these are considered to be hors d'oeuvres, literally 'outside the meal'. Most dishes arrive more or less simultaneously. The senior person or host will normally begin the meal or invite others to do so. Rice is served first and only a little is taken from one of the other dishes at a time, using its serving spoon. This portion is then mixed with rice. Once this is eaten, the next dish is moved on to – there is no set sequence in choosing, it is simply a matter of preference. Usually, however, a spicy dish is followed by a cooling one, and a rich, sweet one by a tart one, so that even when eating the meal, a balance is maintained. Food is not piled onto the plate – that would be ill-mannered.

Time is of little consideration and the Thai will while it away amicably. There is little concern if the food becomes cold, or if it is served only warm, as on a traditional stove it was almost impossible for all dishes to be produced hot simultaneously. In the heat of the tropics this is not much of an issue. Moreover, flavour is at its optimum just above room temperature.

Once, only tea or water was consumed. Alcohol was forbidden to the faithful. Green Chinese tea was lightly brewed. Drinking water was perfumed by infusing it with flowers. At sunset, when jasmine was at its most fragrant, the buds were picked and steeped overnight in terracotta urns, giving the water a luscious quality. Notably, it was a breach of etiquette to drink during the meal – only before or after. Soup, a constant companion throughout the meal, served to quench the thirst.

This has changed and the Thai now drink throughout the meal. The problem for a modern diner is often what wine to drink. By its very nature, a Thai meal is full of contrasts, so a wine that might be perfect with one dish is ruined by others – making it difficult to find the right match. A generous wine is best, one with good fruit qualities and a little residual sugar. Wines that are wooded or heavy with tannin taste hollow and bitter when confronted with the swings of seasonings. The wine should not be too fine: such subtlety cannot compete successfully with this strong food – it is a waste of wine and a distraction from the food. The choice of wine is again a matter of taste: a good semillon is ideal with a crispy fish cake and green mango salad; shiraz and *mussaman* curry is often a harmonious affair; a demi-sec champagne and *ma hor* (an hors d'oeuvre of pork, chicken and prawn with pineapple and mandarin) were made for each other. I like pinot noir, a light shiraz, Côtes du Rhône, grenache, an elegant sparkling red wine, unwooded chardonnay, a German spätlese, or a gewürztraminer (especially from Alsace) with this food, but then I like those styles of wines with almost any food. Drink what is preferred. A refreshing beer, of course, is always good.

Cooking a Thai meal can be time-consuming, especially if everything is done alone or on the day of the meal. But the Thai rarely cook or eat alone; they rarely do anything alone. Often the preparation of a meal reflects this sense of social occasion as family or friends are roped in to assist – or at least to chat and lighten the tasks. Moreover, some of the preparation can be done in advance: curry pastes can be made the previous day, coconuts can be husked and so on. Cooking should be enjoyable, not off-putting or mechanical. So before starting, assess the difficulty of the chosen recipes and the time they will take. If unsure of the techniques, or if time is pressing, keep the meal as simple as possible. Stagger the preparation – do not be staggered by it.

The menus that follow may well take some cooks aback with their complexity. But remember, these are models that indicate the extent to which Thai cooking can go, and the range of flavours and textures; there is no obligation to reproduce them in their entirety. A Thai meal is flexible and should reflect the seasonality of ingredients, the time available and the preferences of the cook. By all means, amend or simplify menus, and substitute recipes from previous chapters, but always aim for an authentic balance of flavours and textures.

These menus serve 4–6 people – roughly one dish per person, with rice.
If fewer people are to eat, reduce the quantity of each dish served rather than the number of dishes.

MACKEREL BRAISED WITH GREEN PAPAYA

dtom kem pla insri

This braised dish is cooked over several hours. Since most Thai food was traditionally cooked over open coals – where the temperature could only be adjusted by fanning the embers, or removing them – it was often very hard to avoid prolonged boiling, which toughened the fish. The Thai appreciate such a toothsome texture in their food, but this is perhaps not as palatable to Western tastes. One way to remain faithful to the recipe, and yet retain the fish's succulence, is to cook it in a very low oven – at no more than 90°C (195°F); green papaya also contains enzymes that help to keep the fish tender.

The best fish for this dish is one that is slightly oily or earthy. Thai cooking deals with strongly flavoured fish – or any food – by employing equally strong seasonings, aromatics and spices that counter the robust ingredient. In this recipe the lemongrass, galangal, ginger, shallots and chillies help to remove the muddy taste of the fish – or at least mask it. The seasoning clarifies and defines the flavours used: the tamarind removes any muddiness or oiliness from the dish, while the fish and soy sauces tighten the palate with their salt, and the sugar gives a rich body. Every ingredient, and its proportion, is relative to every other ingredient in the dish. So if a different fish is used or a different taste is desired, adjust accordingly.

Besides mackerel, the best fish for this dish are bonito, swordfish, mahi-mahi, tuna (albacore or bluefin), a small whole tommy ruff, Murray or silver perch, even a small carp. Ideally the fish should be braised on the bone to prevent the flesh shrinking too much but, given the size of some of the suggested fish, this could be unwieldy and over-generous – so braise fillets with the skin attached and remove it afterwards, if desired.

1 small to medium mackerel – about 500 g (1 lb) whole *or* 200 g (6 oz) fillets

salt

lime juice

3–5 long red or green chillies

10 slices galangal

2 stalks lemongrass

5 thick slices ginger

2 coriander roots, scraped

5 red shallots, peeled

5 garlic cloves, peeled

5 pods fresh tamarind *or* 4 tablespoons tamarind pulp

1 very small green papaya – approximately 200 g (6 oz)

2–3 cups stock or water

4 tablespoons palm sugar

2 tablespoons dark soy sauce

2 tablespoons fish sauce or light soy sauce

1 tablespoon coarsely ground white peppercorns

3 red shallots, finely sliced

1 tablespoon coriander leaves

pinch of ground white pepper

Wash the fish scrupulously, rubbing it with salt and lime juice (this removes any loose elements that would cloud the stock, and helps the fish to remain an appetising colour). Rinse and pat dry. Using a pestle and mortar, bruise the chillies, galangal, lemongrass, ginger, coriander roots, shallots and garlic. If using fresh tamarind, peel and bruise or break into pieces. Peel the papaya and cut into 2 cm × 3 cm (1 in × 1¼ in) pieces.

Bring stock or water to the boil, add tamarind, palm sugar, soy and fish sauces and coarsely ground white pepper. When dissolved, add the bruised aromatics and the papaya. Simmer for several minutes.

At this point, Thai cooks would simply simmer the fish and the aromatics in a pot without regard to temperature or time until the flavour is right, but I like slow braising as this leaves the flesh moist and comparatively tender rather than firm. Lay the fish in an appropriately sized ovenproof dish or pan and pour over the boiling broth. Make sure the fish is completely covered, adding more stock or water if required. Bring back to the boil and then cover with a lid or foil and place in a very low oven for 2 hours – set the oven temperature to no hotter than 80°C or 175°F (as the pan is covered, there will be a build-up of heat, so if the thermostat is set at 90°C or 195°F the liquid could boil, toughening the fish). Skim occasionally and check that the fish is still immersed, replenishing with warm water or stock if necessary.

After about 2 hours, remove the fish from its tray very, very carefully. Serve in a deep bowl with some of the braising liquid strained over, sprinkled with sliced shallots, coriander and pepper.

BANANA CHILLI, DRIED FISH AND PORK SALAD

yam sam yang

The success of this salad lies in its diverse and pungent ingredients. Initially, the salad has a broad range of flavours that bursts on the palate. This then resolves into a pointed balance between the *grachai*, green mango, banana chilli and *pla salit*. Thai food is not so much a clutter of tastes and textures as a concerted exercise in pushing the palate to the brink of possible tastes.

Pork shin is hock with the skin removed. It is readily available in Chinese butchers. Although any other cut can be used, I like its rich and subtly gelatinous texture and character, which work well in this salad.

150 g (5 oz) boneless pork shin

2 banana chillies, grilled, peeled, deseeded and torn into strips

2 *pla salit*, grilled, filleted and sliced

2 tablespoons shredded *grachai* (wild ginger)

½ green mango, julienned

2 large red shallots, sliced

1 tablespoon coriander leaves

1 teaspoon deep-fried garlic

dressing

1½ tablespoons lime juice

1½ tablespoons fish sauce

pinch of white sugar

2 bird's eye chillies (scuds), pounded until fine

pinch of roasted chilli powder

Wash pork, steam for 20 minutes, then cool. Shred coarsely and combine with all the salad ingredients. Make the dressing (see page 338), mix into salad, and serve.

KRUA OF SALTED SWORDFISH

krua pla dap

This a rich, pungent and dry relish. The original recipe calls for the paste to be fried in coconut cream that has been squeezed from roasted, grated coconut undiluted by water – a very difficult thing to do, in my experience. An alternative way to approximate the taste is to continue to simmer the separated coconut cream until it becomes golden brown and very nutty, before frying the paste.

I find the best fish to salt for this relish is swordfish, especially the red muscular offcuts, which have a rich taste and a wonderfully grainy texture. However, any oily fish, such as tuna or salmon, can be used in place of the swordfish – as can dried fish, *pla grop* (crisp fish) or dried prawns, which don't need to be salted first.

150 g (5 oz) swordfish
3 tablespoons light soy sauce
pinch of salt
pinch of white sugar
3 cups coconut cream
1–2 tablespoons palm sugar
2 tablespoons fish sauce

paste
6–10 dried long red chillies, deseeded, soaked and drained
pinch of salt
1 tablespoon chopped galangal
3 tablespoons chopped lemongrass
1 teaspoon finely grated kaffir lime zest
2 coriander roots, scraped and chopped
1 tablespoon chopped *grachai* (wild ginger)
4 tablespoons chopped red shallot
3 tablespoons chopped garlic
5 tablespoons salted swordfish or other dried fish (see above)
½ cup grated coconut, roasted

Salt the swordfish by marinating overnight in light soy sauce, salt and sugar and then drying for a day or so. Grill, cool and pound using a pestle and mortar or grind in a spice grinder.

Next, make the paste (see page 280), incorporating the ground salted fish. Crack the coconut cream; it must be quite separated and golden in colour, otherwise the relish will taste dry and musty. Be careful, as it is apt to burn. Spoon the coconut oil into a clean pot and fry the paste until sizzling, oily yet dry, and fragrant with the roast coconut and fish. It may be necessary to moisten the paste with a little water to achieve this. Simmer until the liquid has evaporated, then season with sugar and fish sauce. The relish should taste rich, nutty, slightly salty and just a little sweet.

Serve with a selection from:
— Raw Vegetables (page 380), such as cucumber, hog plum, rose apple and sorrel
— Boiled Vegetables (page 381), especially green beans and apple eggplants

- Vegetables Simmered in Coconut Milk (page 382), especially spinach and baby corn
- Pickled Vegetables (page 383)
- Steamed Eggs (page 388)
- steamed or grilled prawns, mussels or clams
- Sweet Pork (page 397).

RED CURRY OF QUAIL DUMPLINGS

geng ped luk chin nok gradtaa

The original recipe for this curry was in Thanpuuying Pliang Pasonagorn's cookbook *Mae Krua Hua Bark* and called for a turtledove, but a quail or two will do. For her dumplings, Than Pliang used a little tapioca flour, but I think this results in rather heavy, starchy dumplings. Perhaps she used freshly made flour, which would be very similar to using fresh cassava – from which tapioca flour is made. I find fresh cassava even better: it gives the dumplings a toothsome crunch and a slightly tingling, bitter flavour.

It is essential to soak the grated cassava to remove the indigestible – and, in excessively large amounts, poisonous – hydrocyanic acid, which is both water-soluble and rendered harmless by heat. Fresh cassava is not too common; frozen, however, it is always available at African and Pacific Islander food shops. In this instance it may be best to buy frozen, as the longer it has been uprooted and exposed to air, the greater the build-up of acid and the more bitter it becomes. Or, if preferred, just a sprinkling of tapioca flour can be used.

Crushing the quail bones extracts their marrow and imparts a richness to the purée. One variation is to slice the breast meat and poach it in the curry along with the dumplings, or you can just use sliced meat together with some sliced Thai eggplants of any kind.

2 large quail – about 300 g (9 oz) in all
100 g (3 oz) cassava
1–3 teaspoons palm sugar
1–2 tablespoons fish sauce
1 cup coconut cream
extra 1 tablespoon palm sugar
extra 2 tablespoons fish sauce
2 cups coconut milk
3 kaffir lime leaves, torn
2 long red or green chillies, diagonally sliced and deseeded
handful of Thai basil leaves

curry paste

5–10 dried long red chillies, deseeded, soaked and drained

large pinch of salt

2 tablespoons chopped galangal

4 tablespoons chopped lemongrass

1 tablespoon finely grated kaffir lime zest

1 tablespoon scraped and chopped coriander root

3 tablespoons chopped red shallot

4 tablespoons chopped garlic

1 rounded teaspoon shrimp paste (*gapi*), roasted

½ teaspoon white peppercorns

½ teaspoon coriander seeds, roasted

¼ teaspoon cumin seeds, roasted

garlic paste

1 coriander root, scraped and chopped

pinch of salt

2 garlic cloves, peeled

2 slices ginger

pinch of ground white pepper

First, make the curry paste (see page 280), then make the garlic paste by pounding the ingredients together using a pestle and mortar.

Wash and dry the quail. Traditionally the bird is boned, the meat minced, the bones pounded using a pestle and mortar until fine, and then these are combined. In the modern kitchen, the quail can be puréed in a food processor, being careful not to overwork or overheat the meat. It may be necessary to stop halfway through to allow the meat to cool, even refrigerating it for a while. The truly cautious could purée the meat and bones separately. (If the purée does overheat it will be very difficult to sieve and the dumplings will taste oily.) Sieve the purée, working through as much as possible, or put through a small mouli – perhaps the best piece of equipment for this.

Finely grate the cassava. Steep in water for a few minutes, knead vigorously, then squeeze in a tea towel to extract as much water as possible.

In a medium bowl, combine garlic paste, cassava and quail. Season with sugar and fish sauce. Gather into a ball and throw back into the bowl, slapping it several times, until it becomes firmer and quite sticky. Test the seasoning by poaching a small piece: it should taste rich, marrow-like and slightly salty. Make the mixture into small dumplings – about 1–2 cm (½–1 in) diameter.

Crack the coconut cream, and fry 4 tablespoons of the curry paste in it until fragrant of the dried spices, then season with the extra sugar and fish sauce. Meanwhile poach dumplings in the coconut milk for 3–5 minutes. When all are cooked, gradually pour enough coconut milk into the paste to produce a slightly thick sauce. Check the seasoning: the curry should taste salty, hot and a little sweet. Add dumplings, kaffir lime leaves and chillies and simmer for a minute. Add basil and serve.

Eat with one of the following:

— pickled ginger
— Pickled Cucumber (page 386)
— Deep-fried Eggs (page 390), ideally quail eggs
— Salted Prawns (page 392).

SQUID AND PORK SOUP

geng jeut pla meuk yord sai

Although pork is the traditional meat used for stuffing the squid in this recipe, chicken, prawns, crabmeat, or even a combination of these, can be used. If there is no time to stuff the squid, just roll the pork mixture into dumplings and poach in the soup, along with the scored squid and vegetables.

Blanched bitter melon, gourd, cucumber, oyster mushrooms or any wild mushrooms can also be used in this soup – but if the vegetables are quite strongly flavoured, add a little oyster sauce to the stock to give it sufficient depth.

3 cleaned squid – about 150 g (5 oz) in all
100 g (3 oz) minced fatty pork
1 tablespoon light soy sauce
pinch of white sugar
4 cups chicken stock
pinch of salt
pinch of white sugar
a little oyster sauce – optional
2 tablespoons light soy sauce
3 fresh shiitake mushrooms, destemmed and sliced
1 small bunch Asian celery, cut into 2 cm (1 in) lengths
3 spring (green) onions, cut into 2 cm (1 in) lengths
1 tablespoon coriander leaves
pinch of ground white pepper
drizzle of sesame oil

paste
2 coriander roots, scraped and chopped
pinch of salt
3 garlic cloves, peeled
10 white peppercorns

Using a pestle and mortar, pound together the paste ingredients until fine.

Separate squid tentacles from body and chop finely. Mix paste with minced pork and the squid tentacles and season with soy sauce and sugar. Slap the mixture until it becomes firmer and stickier, then stuff inside cleaned squid tubes. Secure ends with toothpicks. (If using large squid, nick the stuffed squid two or three times on each side, only just exposing the meat – this will allow the squid to expand with the stuffing, but do not cut too deeply or the squid will tear.)

Bring stock to the boil. Season with salt, sugar, oyster sauce and light soy sauce to taste. Add squid and mushrooms, return to the boil and then turn down the flame as low as possible. Poach very gently until squid is quite firm – usually around 5 minutes, but longer for large squid. Skim as necessary. Remove squid from soup and rest for a few minutes. If the squid is large, slice into 1 cm (½ in) rounds.

Return stock to the boil, skim, and add celery and spring onions. Simmer for a moment until the vegetables wilt and their flavour infuses the soup. Return squid to the pot, and finish with coriander, pepper and sesame oil.

MENU

Coconut Soup of Salted Beef and Bamboo Shoots

Fried Green Tamarind Relish

Stir-fried Asparagus

Red Curry of Scallops

Steamed Snapper with Ginger

COCONUT SOUP OF SALTED BEEF AND BAMBOO SHOOTS
dtom gati neua kem nor mai dong

This soup is a delectable classic of Thai cooking. Its success relies upon the interplay between the sour, fermented bitterness of the bamboo shoots and the rich saltiness of the beef simmered in coconut cream. The lemongrass, lime leaves, shallots and coriander roots help to counterbalance these robust flavours. The soup is seasoned with a little palm sugar, and plenty of white pepper and fermented fish sauce (*nahm pla raa*). It is not absolutely necessary to add this heady brew to the soup – its addition certainly improves the dish, but its omission does not unduly diminish it. The soup is finished with red shallots and coriander leaves to sharpen and perfume.

This soup can be varied in many ways. For example, finely sliced venison can be briefly marinated in fish sauce before being deep-fried and then combined with sliced white radish; salted fish, bought or made, can be simmered with asparagus, Chinese broccoli or winter melon; fresh fish, such as snapper, can be cooked with pickled mustard greens or Siamese watercress; or pork with whole red shallots, fresh or pickled. Finally, picked *cha-om* or torn 'betel' leaves can also be added at the end to enhance the flavour of this timeless, sumptuous soup.

100 g (3 oz) Salted Beef (page 401)

oil for deep-frying

1 cup stock

2 cups coconut milk

1 cup coconut cream

pinch of salt

large pinch of palm sugar

large pinch of ground white pepper

4 tablespoons fermented fish sauce (*nahm pla raa*) *or* 2 tablespoons fish sauce

4–5 slices galangal

2 stalks lemongrass, trimmed

2 coriander roots, scraped

3 red shallots, peeled

2 kaffir lime leaves, torn

1 cup Fermented Bamboo Shoots (page 152), rinsed

extra 3 red shallots, sliced

1 tablespoon coriander leaves

Rehydrate the salted beef in water for 10–15 minutes, but no longer or the meat will become sodden and splutter incessantly when it is deep-fried. (Soaking swells the meat so that when it is fried it does not toughen; it also dissolves the excess salt that preserves the beef.) Thoroughly dry the meat, then deep-fry for about a minute. Bruise the beef with a pestle and mortar – this opens up the meat and softens the fibres – and repeat the deep-frying and bruising once more. When cool, tear beef into bite-size pieces along the grain.

Bring stock, coconut milk and coconut cream to the boil. Season with salt, sugar, pepper and fish sauce, to taste. Bruise galangal, lemongrass, coriander roots and shallots using a pestle and mortar, and add to soup, along with kaffir lime leaves. Add beef and bamboo shoots. Simmer for at least 5 minutes – until the meat is tender and infused with the coconut and other seasonings.

Replenish with a little stock or coconut cream if the soup is too thick: it should taste creamy, slightly sour and fragrant from the fermented fish sauce. Serve sprinkled with the sliced shallots and coriander leaves.

FRIED GREEN TAMARIND RELISH

nahm prik makam pat

The character of this relish comes from the fruity sourness of fresh tamarind, the smokiness of roasted red shallots and smoked fish, the nuttiness of garlic, the richness of pork fat and the cleansing heat of chillies – all with an undercurrent of pungent shrimp paste.

Fresh tamarind has a sharp, green quality that the mellow sour tamarind water does not, so while tamarind water can be used as a close alternative to the fresh fruit, it is not quite the same. However, if fresh tamarind is unavailable, simply double the quantity of tamarind water used in the final seasoning.

Additional ingredients – from green mango, *madan* (sour cucumber), sorrel, cape gooseberries and pea eggplants to salted crab – may augment and enhance the flavour of this *nahm prik*.

4 tablespoons rendered pork fat or oil

1 tablespoon palm sugar

2–3 tablespoons fish sauce

2 tablespoons tamarind water

nahm prik paste

5 garlic cloves, unpeeled

4 red shallots, unpeeled

4–10 dried long red chillies, deseeded, soaked and drained

pinch of salt

2 tablespoons chopped red shallot

3 tablespoons chopped garlic

4 tablespoons cleaned fresh tamarind – about 8 pods

3 tablespoons ground *pla grop* (crisp fish), dried or smoked fish
  or dried prawns (shrimp)

1 tablespoon shrimp paste (*gapi*)

garlic paste

3 red shallots, peeled

3 garlic cloves, peeled

pinch of salt

First, make the pastes. For the *nahm prik* paste, roast or grill the unpeeled garlic and shallots until the skin is charred and the insides tender. Cool, peel and then gradually pound the ingredients together using a pestle and mortar, adding one by one, until smooth. Make the garlic paste by pounding the ingredients together using a pestle and mortar.

Heat rendered pork fat or oil in a small saucepan and fry garlic paste over a gentle heat, stirring continuously, until nuttily fragrant and golden. Add *nahm prik* paste and cook until fragrant of the fish or prawns – around 10 minutes. It may be necessary to moisten with a little stock or water to ensure that the paste cooks sufficiently without burning. Season with sugar, fish sauce and tamarind water. Simmer until relish is quite dry and just a little oily. (I find that moistening with water or a light stock from the fish bones improves the relish because it allows it to simmer for some time, deepening the taste without introducing additional flavours.) The relish should taste hot and smoky, salty and sour, and redolent of the smoked fish.

Good accompaniments to this relish are:
- Raw Vegetables (page 380), such as sorrel, rocket (arugula) and white turmeric
- Boiled Vegetables (page 381), such as apple eggplants, wing beans and baby corn
- Grilled Vegetables (page 382)
- Pickled Vegetables (page 383)
- Steamed Eggs (page 388)
- Steamed Salted Duck Eggs (page 391)
- Crispy Fish Cakes (page 393)
- steamed or grilled prawns or fish
- Sweet Pork (page 397).

STIR-FRIED ASPARAGUS

pat nor mai farang

A simple dish that prevents the palate – and the cook – from being too overwhelmed by the range of flavours and methods in this menu. If asparagus is not in season, then try bean sprouts with ginger, sugar snap peas or nutty broccoli. Almost any vegetable can be stir-fried successfully, so long as it cooks quickly, or is cut into sufficiently small pieces to ensure that it does.

Some Thai cooks blanch vegetables before stir-frying them.

2 garlic cloves, peeled
pinch of salt
1 tablespoon oil
100 g (3 oz) young asparagus, cut into 2 cm (1 in) lengths
2 tablespoons stock or water
1 tablespoon light soy sauce
pinch of white sugar
pinch of ground white pepper

Pound garlic and salt together using a pestle and mortar. Heat a wok until very hot. Add oil and, when hot, add garlic and asparagus. Stir-fry until asparagus is just tender – about 3–4 minutes. Add stock or water, soy sauce and sugar, and simmer for another minute or so.

When serving, sprinkle with pepper.

RED CURRY OF SCALLOPS

chuu chii hoi shenn

This is an elegant curry: it should not be too thick or intensely flavoured, or the scallops will be overpowered. So, after seasoning the curry, simmer until almost, but not quite, dry – the degree is determined by taste.

If scallops are not available, mussels, clams, prawns or any other seafood make excellent alternatives. This curry can also be made with whole or filleted fish, cooked in the seasoned curry or deep-fried until crisp and crunchy, then added at the end.

2 cups coconut cream

1 tablespoon palm sugar

2 tablespoons fish sauce

1 cup coconut milk or stock

12–16 small scallops, cleaned – about 200 g (6 oz) in all

4 kaffir lime leaves, shredded

1 tablespoon thick coconut cream

a little red chilli, julienned

1 tablespoon coriander leaves

paste

5–8 dried long red chillies, deseeded, soaked and drained

large pinch of salt

5 slices galangal

3 tablespoons chopped lemongrass

4 tablespoons chopped garlic

3 tablespoons sliced red shallot

1 tablespoon scraped and chopped coriander root

10 white peppercorns

1 rounded teaspoon shrimp paste (*gapi*), roasted

First, make the paste (see page 280).

Crack the coconut cream over medium heat, add 3 tablespoons of the paste and fry, stirring regularly, for at least 5 minutes, until fragrant. Season with sugar and fish sauce. Add coconut milk and simmer until reduced, quite thick and separated. Add scallops and half the kaffir lime leaves and continue to simmer briefly, with the scallops immersed, until the flesh is just cooked. (Alternatively, the scallops can be removed from their shells, cooked in the curry, then returned to their shells and the curry poured over them.)

Check seasoning: it should be salty, a little hot and fragrant from the kaffir lime. To serve, arrange scallops on a plate, drizzle over the coconut cream, then sprinkle with the remaining lime leaves, red chilli and coriander.

STEAMED SNAPPER WITH GINGER

pla neung king

Most Thai cooks prefer to use a whole fish, believing it cooks better and has more flavour than fillets. They also share the Chinese belief that, once served on the plate, the fish should always face the same direction. When removing the bones, the fish should be turned over, not around. It is bad luck to do otherwise, as a fish never goes against the flow.

Any fine, white-fleshed fish can be prepared this way; try sea bream, turbot or john dory.

1 whole snapper – around 400 g (12 oz)
3 tablespoons light soy sauce
pinch of white sugar
1 cup shredded ginger
4 spring (green) onions, shredded
large pinch of ground white pepper
1 tablespoon coriander leaves

Clean and score the fish. Place on a plate and cover with the soy sauce, sugar and half the ginger. Steam until just cooked – around 20 minutes – checking the underside of the fish to make sure it is done. When it is, strew with the rest of the ginger and the spring onions and steam for a moment longer, until the onions have softened. Carefully remove the plate from the steamer with tongs, retaining as much of the liquid as possible, and serve sprinkled with pepper and coriander.

MENU

Deep-fried Fish with Pickled Garlic

Salted Beef Stir-fried with Sugar and Shallots

Curry of Pigeon and Herbs

Yabbies Simmered in Coconut Cream

Grilled Banana Chilli Salad

DEEP-FRIED FISH WITH PICKLED GARLIC

pla tort gratiam dong

King Rama V was a renowned gourmet. Yet, like most people in exalted positions, being continually confronted with formal banquets and bound by stringent etiquette, he delighted in the simple. Shrimp paste relish (*nahm prik gapi*) was a perennial favourite. Another dish that renewed his fatigued palate was one such as the following. He wrote longingly about a simple dish like this in his journal during a trip to Europe.

Different types of oil subtly vary the taste of the finished dish. Regular vegetable oil is an easy choice, and it works well, but the perfumed oil that has been used to deep-fry garlic and shallots can be used instead. Traditionally, Thai cooks deep-fry in rendered pork fat or coconut oil: both are distinctly unhealthy. The first is dripping with cholesterol and the second laden with saturated fats. However, if cooked at the right temperature, the fish will be quickly sealed, which prevents it absorbing any of the frying medium. Using pork fat results in a rich silken texture and coconut oil gives a nutty finish. I usually mix a small amount of pork fat or coconut oil with vegetable oil to soften it and give it greater character, without compromising health requirements too much!

Finally, the fish can be cooked for varying lengths of time, depending on the texture preferred. Most Thai cooks have no hesitation in deep-frying a fish at a low heat for an alarmingly long time – sometimes up to 30 minutes. This results in a very crisp, quite dry finish that may be overcooked to Western taste, but offers a wonderfully crunchy textural contrast to a *lon* or another luxuriously flavoured coconut dish. Alternatively, the fish can be quickly deep-fried over very high heat, with a succulent and moist result. Always rest the fish for several minutes before serving, to allow the flesh to relax and make it easier to lift from the bone.

200 g (6 oz) fillet of barramundi, sea bass or salmon

1–2 tablespoons fish sauce or light soy sauce

pinch of salt

pinch of white sugar

large pinch of white pepper

oil for deep-frying

2 heads – about 10 cloves – pickled garlic, sliced

1 tablespoon coriander leaves

Marinate the fish overnight in the fish sauce or soy sauce, salt, sugar and pepper. Remove and leave to dry for an hour or longer, as preferred – I like to leave the fish to dry in a warm place for about 10 hours or overnight.

Deep-fry the fish either at a high temperature for about 4–6 minutes, or over a lower heat for about 10–15 minutes. Drain. Garnish with pickled garlic and coriander.

SALTED BEEF STIR-FRIED WITH SUGAR AND SHALLOTS

neua kem pat wan

This is an ancient dish, dating back to the Court of King Narai in the mid-seventeenth century. It can perform the function of a salad, stir-fry or side dish. The shredded salted beef, deep-fried shallots, garlic and chilli can be prepared a day in advance, making this quite quick to assemble. However, the beef does need to be salted and dried beforehand, which takes at least 48 hours.

200 g (6 oz) Salted Beef (page 401)

oil for frying

1 dried long red chilli, deseeded, soaked and drained, then julienned lengthwise

6 tablespoons palm sugar

2 tablespoons fish sauce

2 tablespoons deep-fried shallots

2 tablespoons deep-fried garlic

1 tablespoon coriander leaves

Rehydrate beef in water for at least 10 minutes (this removes the excess salt necessary to preserve it), drain and pat dry. Deep-fry for about a minute or so, ideally in some of the oil used for deep-frying shallots or garlic. Remove and pat off any excess oil. Pound lightly, using a pestle and mortar, to open up the fibres. Repeat deep-frying and bruising once more, then allow to cool.

Tear or shred the meat, separating each fibre, strand by strand. This can be quite tedious – perseverance results in a fine product – so a coarser tear will do. >

Quickly stir-fry the chilli in a teaspoon of oil until it is toasted and fragrant. Drain on absorbent paper.

Heat palm sugar in a wok. When it has melted, add fish sauce and shredded beef and simmer over a low heat to prevent burning. Stir or toss to ensure that the sugar syrup coats the beef strands and is absorbed evenly. When sticky, remove from the heat. Toss with deep-fried shallots and garlic, chilli and coriander leaves.

CURRY OF PIGEON AND HERBS
geng kae nok pirap

This memorably hot curry from the north of Thailand uses fresh herbs to mitigate the effect of the chillies. In the markets of Chiang Mai, there are stalls that sell the required vegetables and leaves in small bundles wrapped in a bamboo leaf. This curry may include some or all of the following: wing beans, 'betel' leaves, blanched bamboo shoots, various basils, *pak chii farang*, tiny bitter melons and a mixture of eggplants; alternative ingredients are used without compunction, based on their quality. Therefore, for the Western cook, spinach, rocket (arugula), blanched chicory or baby corn are more than suitable. And, instead of pigeon, guinea fowl, quail or wild duck – even rabbit, pork, eel or any freshwater fish or prawns – can be used.

Quality is not the only determining factor when choosing ingredients; whim plays an important part. However, what does remain consistent is the seasoning – this simple curry is hot and salty.

1 large pigeon or squab – around 450 g (14 oz), yielding 150 g (5 oz) meat
oil for frying
pinch of sugar
1 tablespoon fish sauce
1–2 cups stock or water
3 kaffir lime leaves, torn
3 long green chillies, broken in half

a selection of the following – about a handful in total
Thai or holy basil leaves
chilli or 'betel' leaves
pumpkin shoots
coarsely shredded *pak chii farang* (long-leaf coriander)
spinach
pea or apple eggplants

curry paste
10–15 bird's eye chillies (scuds)
large pinch of salt

1 rounded tablespoon chopped galangal – keep offcuts for stock (see method)

3 tablespoons chopped lemongrass – keep offcuts for stock (see method)

3 tablespoons chopped red shallot

2 tablespoons chopped garlic

1 teaspoon shrimp paste (*gapi*), roasted

garlic paste

1 garlic clove, peeled

pinch of salt

2 bird's eye chillies (scuds)

First, make the curry paste (see page 280), then make the garlic paste by pounding the ingredients together using a pestle and mortar.

Bone the pigeon or have it boned at the shop, but ask for the bones and any offal. Cut meat and offal, if available, into fine slices. If you have time, wash bones, blanch them, and then make into a quick stock with galangal and lemongrass offcuts. Otherwise, any stock or just water can be used.

Heat a pan, add oil and, when hot, fry garlic paste over a high heat until golden. Then add curry paste, stirring constantly to prevent scorching, until it sizzles and is explosively fragrant. When you feel compelled to sneeze, season paste with sugar and fish sauce, then turn down the heat and add meat. Continue to fry for a minute, then add 1–2 cups of stock or water. Bring to the boil and add kaffir lime leaves and chillies, along with the selection of herbs and leaves. Simmer until the leaves are wilted and cooked. Check seasoning – it should be hot, salty and floral – a little extra sugar may be added, if desired.

Possible accompaniments to this curry include:
- pickled ginger
- pickled red shallots
- Steamed Salted Duck Eggs (page 391)
- Deep-fried Eggs (page 390) – pigeon eggs would be very apposite
- Salted Prawns (page 392)
- salted fish.

YABBIES SIMMERED IN COCONUT CREAM

lon yabby

Of course there are no yabbies in Thailand, but there are freshwater prawns, and so these delectable crustaceans are perfectly agreeable with the cuisine. This is a rich and creamy relish. Freshwater crayfish, crabmeat, minced prawns, chopped scallops or any fish can also be used as an alternative to the yabbies. Further additions might include shredded ginger, *grachai* (wild ginger) or green mango.

6 large *or* 12 small yabbies or freshwater crayfish

½ cup stock

1 cup coconut cream

1 tablespoon palm sugar

1 tablespoon tamarind water

1–2 tablespoons fish sauce

50 g (2 oz) minced pork – optional

1 tablespoon finely sliced lemongrass

3 red shallots, sliced

1 long red or green chilli, cut into rounds

1 tablespoon coriander leaves

Wash the yabbies or crayfish, place in a large pot of boiling salted water, perhaps with a few offcuts of lemongrass or kaffir lime leaves, and boil for 5 minutes. Remove and plunge into iced water, then shell, scraping out all the flesh and tomalley. Discard the black veins that run along the back, then slice the flesh.

Bring stock and coconut cream to the boil over medium heat. Season with sugar, tamarind water and fish sauce. Add minced pork, if using, stirring to prevent clumping and being careful not to boil. Add yabby or crayfish flesh, tomalley and lemongrass, simmer for a moment, then finish with shallots, chilli and coriander. The relish should taste rich, salty, sweet and sour.

Serve with some of the following:
— Raw Vegetables (page 380), especially rocket (arugula), spinach and cabbage
— Grilled Vegetables (page 382), such as long green eggplants, pine mushrooms and bamboo shoots
— Deep-fried Vegetables (page 383), such as 'betel' leaves and Siamese watercress
— Spicy Pickled Vegetables (page 384)
— Crispy Fish Cakes (page 393)
— Sweet Pork (page 397)
— Deep-fried Pork with Spices (page 400).

GRILLED BANANA CHILLI SALAD

yam prik yuak pao

6 small *or* 4 large banana chillies

4 red shallots, unpeeled

50 g (2 oz) poached or steamed chicken, shredded – optional

a few poached or steamed small prawns (shrimp), shelled and deveined – optional

2 red shallots, sliced

2 tablespoons mint leaves

2 tablespoons chopped spring (green) onion

dressing

1–2 teaspoons palm sugar

squeeze of lime juice

large pinch of roasted chilli powder

1 tablespoon fish sauce

Grill the banana chillies and shallots until charred. Rest, separately, in covered bowls. When cool enough to handle, peel, retaining any liquid from the chillies. Slice shallots and combine with remaining salad ingredients in a bowl.

To make the dressing, dissolve the palm sugar in the chilli liquid, and season with lime juice, chilli powder and fish sauce. It should taste smoky, slightly hot, salty and sweet.

Mix dressing into salad and serve.

MENU

Salad of Murray Cod and Apple Eggplants

Fermented Bean Curd Simmered in Coconut Cream

Red Chicken Curry with Ginger and Green Beans

Prawns Simmered in Caramel and Sugar Cane

Baby Corn, Young Coconut and Shiitake Mushroom Soup

SALAD OF MURRAY COD AND APPLE EGGPLANTS

yam pla gap makreua

The smoky heat and sourness of this salad's dressing offsets the 'earthiness' of the freshwater fish, as well as being a perfect foil to the richness of the fermented bean curd *lon* that is also in this menu. This is yet another example of the dynamics of taste that work within a well-crafted meal – and within each dish – ensuring it is united and balanced, with contrasts and harmonies. This applies to texture as well as taste: the crisp eggplants contrast with the *lon* relish, and the taste and texture of the salad complement the pea eggplants in the curry, which in turn are counterbalanced by the sugar cane in the *dtom kem* of prawns.

Pea and long green eggplants can be used instead of the apple eggplants in this salad, but Western eggplants are not a good substitute.

200 g (6 oz) fillet of Murray cod, perch, trout or zander

2 garlic cloves, peeled

pinch of salt

a little oil or rendered pork fat

3 tablespoons stock or water

2 tablespoons finely sliced lemongrass

2 apple eggplants, halved and then finely sliced

1 tablespoon shredded *pak chii farang* (long-leaf coriander)

2 tablespoons mint leaves, torn

large pinch–½ teaspoon roasted chilli powder

pinch of sugar

1 tablespoon lime juice

1 tablespoon fish sauce

Clean the fish and cut into strips about 1 cm × 2 cm (½ in × 1 in). Pound garlic with salt until fine. Heat oil or rendered pork fat and fry garlic until golden. Add stock or water, then fish. Turn down the heat and simmer for 2 minutes. Remove from heat and add remaining ingredients.

The salad should taste hot, salty, fragrant and a little sour.

FERMENTED BEAN CURD SIMMERED IN COCONUT CREAM

lon dtor huu yii

So many dishes in Thai cuisine have unlikely ingredients – because of their taste, or sometimes just the thought of them. Fermented bean curd exemplifies this: an unusual preparation with an unbecoming name, it is an acquired taste, but after the first few encounters the taste becomes more than acceptable. One quickly appreciates its sumptuous yet slightly musty flavour.

Season this *lon* well with red shallots and white pepper.

1 cup coconut cream

½ cup stock

4 cubes fermented bean curd, plus 4 tablespoons of its liquid

2–3 teaspoons palm sugar

2 teaspoons tamarind water

large pinch of ground white pepper

50 g (2 oz) minced fatty pork

3 large prawns (shrimp), peeled, deveined and minced

4 red shallots, sliced

1 long red or green chilli, sliced into rounds

1 tablespoon coriander leaves

Bring coconut cream and stock to the boil. Add bean curd with its liquid, and simmer until quite thick. Season with sugar to taste, tamarind water and pepper. Add minced pork and prawns, stirring constantly to prevent it clumping.

Finish with remaining ingredients: the relish should taste rich and creamy, salty and just a little sweet and sour.

Serve with some of the following:
— Raw Vegetables (page 380), such as banana blossom, banana chilli, cabbage, white turmeric, cucumber – and, if not serving with Red Chicken Curry with Ginger and Green Beans, plenty of sliced young ginger
— Grilled Vegetables (page 382), ideally bamboo shoots and long eggplants
— Pickled Vegetables (page 383), especially cucumber, Chinese cabbage, Siamese watercress
— Crispy Fish Cakes (page 393)
— deep-fried or grilled fish, squid or prawns (shrimp)
— Salted Beef (page 401), deep-fried.

RED CHICKEN CURRY WITH GINGER AND GREEN BEANS

geng sap nok gai

When it is time to harvest the rice, the once-green paddies sway as the hot breezes rustle through the golden fronds of rice. Hoping to enjoy some of this bounty, the rice-paddy birds raid the fields: intent only on eating rice, the birds are easily snared in nets set up in the paddies. Quickly killed, they are plucked and their remaining down is singed over a few embers. About the size of very small quail, these birds are constantly flying, so their flesh is quite tough. After they have been cleaned and gutted they are washed, then very roughly chopped with their bones – keeping the flesh on the bones prevents it tightening and toughening too much during cooking. The birds are used in a curry like the following recipe, in which their rich, gamy flavour is counterbalanced by earthy pea eggplants and fragrant Thai basil. Minced chicken, quail, duck, pigeon or squab are logical substitutes for this rustic pilferer.

In provinces near Bangkok, shredded young ginger is also added to the curry. Should young ginger be out of season, old ginger can be used, so long as it is first shredded and steeped in salted water for a few minutes to remove some of its pungency.

1 cup coconut cream
1 cup julienned ginger
1–2 teaspoons palm sugar
2 tablespoons fish sauce
1 cup coarsely minced skinless chicken breast or thigh fillets

1 cup coconut milk or stock

3 tablespoons finely cut snake beans or green beans

handful of pea eggplants

2 apple eggplants, sliced

4 kaffir lime leaves, shredded

1 long red chilli, julienned

handful of Thai basil leaves

paste

5–10 dried long red chillies, deseeded, soaked and drained

large pinch of salt

1 tablespoon chopped galangal

3 tablespoons chopped lemongrass

1 teaspoon finely grated kaffir lime zest

2 teaspoons scraped and chopped coriander root

3 tablespoons chopped red shallot

3 tablespoons chopped garlic

1 teaspoon shrimp paste (*gapi*), roasted

10 white peppercorns

½ teaspoon coriander seeds, roasted

First, make the paste (see page 280).

Crack the coconut cream over a medium heat. Add about a third of the ginger and 3 tablespoons of the paste. Fry, stirring regularly, until fragrant with kaffir lime and coriander seed. Season with sugar to taste, then fish sauce. Add chicken and another third of the ginger. Moisten with coconut milk or stock, and add beans and eggplants. Simmer until fragrant and chicken is cooked – about 2 minutes. Finish with the remaining ginger, kaffir lime leaves, chilli and basil.

Serve with astringent *kreaung kiam*, such as:

— pickled red shallots

— Pickled Cucumber (page 386)

— Semi-dried Fish (page 150).

PRAWNS SIMMERED IN CARAMEL AND SUGAR CANE

gung dtom kem sai ooy

This simple and elegant soup relies on the interplay of sugar with salt, and coriander with pepper and garlic. The original recipe came from Mom Ratchawongse Dteuang Sanitsawongse and called for *pla chorn*, a trout-like fish that is unavailable outside Thailand. As with almost every Thai dish, alternatives can be used with an easy versatility – prawns, crayfish, eels or any freshwater fish are happy replacements.

If sugar cane can be found, it really should be used. It imparts a savoury, slightly bitter sweetness to the dish – and the longer it is cooked, the deeper and more complex its flavour becomes. In the south of Thailand, pineapple, green papaya or bamboo shoots are used instead of sugar cane. Mom Dteuang favoured Asian celery, while I like to use long green eggplants or very fresh peanuts.

8 cm (3 in) piece of sugar cane – optional

1 tablespoon oil or rendered pork fat

3 tablespoons palm sugar – or 2 tablespoons, if using sugar cane

3 tablespoons fish sauce or light soy sauce

1–2 cups stock

6–10 large king prawns (jumbo shrimp), peeled and deveined

3 red shallots, sliced

pinch of ground white pepper

1 tablespoon coriander leaves

paste

2 coriander roots, scraped and chopped

pinch of salt

3 garlic cloves, peeled

10 white peppercorns

First, make the paste: gradually pound the ingredients together using a pestle and mortar, adding one by one, until smooth.

If using sugar cane, cut into 2 cm (1 in) lengths, peel and then cut each piece into quarters. Heat oil or rendered pork fat in a pan and fry paste until golden and fragrant. Add palm sugar and heat until just lightly caramelised. Add fish sauce or soy sauce. If using sugar cane, add it now, along with 2 cups stock, and simmer for 20 minutes to extract and develop the flavour. Otherwise, add only 1 cup of stock and simmer for a few minutes only. Either way, skim as necessary. Add prawns and simmer until cooked.

Serve sprinkled with shallots, pepper and coriander.

BABY CORN, YOUNG COCONUT AND SHIITAKE MUSHROOM SOUP

geng jeut kao port orn

This simple soup relies upon the refreshing taste of young coconut and its juice. Young coconuts are often available whole: simply cleave in half over a bowl (to catch the juice) and spoon the soft, gelatinous flesh out of the shell, trimming off any attached skin. Happily, young coconut flesh and juice can also be bought prepared, usually frozen, with their flavour and character unimpaired.

4 cups chicken stock

pinch of salt

pinch of white sugar

2–3 tablespoons light soy sauce

10–12 baby corn, cleaned and cut in half lengthwise

6 fresh shiitake mushrooms, stalks discarded and caps sliced

4 spring (green) onions, cut into 2 cm (1 in) lengths

flesh and juice of 1 young coconut

pinch of ground white pepper

1 tablespoon coriander leaves

Bring stock to the boil. Season with salt, sugar and soy sauce. Add corn, mushrooms and spring onions. Simmer until cooked – about a minute or so – and then finish with coconut flesh and juice. Serve sprinkled with pepper and coriander.

MENU

Prawn and Lemongrass Relish

Egg Mousse with Pineapple, Corn and Salted Duck Eggs

Crispy Fish Cakes and Sweet Pork Salad

Bream and Green Gourd Simmered in Coconut Cream

Deep-fried Bean Curd with Crab, Pork and Spring Onions

Chicken Curry with Holy Basil, Ginger and Peanuts

PRAWN AND LEMONGRASS RELISH

nahm prik dtakrai

This is a sweetly aromatic relish where the floral, citrus-like flavour of the lemongrass is tempered by freshly cooked prawns. One old-fashioned trick to enhance lemongrass is to plunge it into boiling water for a moment after cleaning: this softens the flesh, making it easier to cut, but also invigorates the fragrance of the lemongrass. This should be done only just before adding it to the relish.

Using dried prawns gives body to the relish, but an aromatic alternative is some freshly grilled *pla grop* (crisp fish), or even a little hot-smoked trout. These will alter the original taste, but agreeably so, and a few grilled shallots, chillies or pea eggplants will augment this delicious smokiness. Only use a tiny morsel of shrimp paste, if any, to give a pleasing depth. A little coriander root and a sliver of lime or Asian citron zest can also enhance the character of this relish.

3–4 garlic cloves, peeled

pinch of salt

1 tablespoon ground dried prawns (shrimp)

3 tablespoons finely sliced lemongrass

4–6 bird's eye chillies (scuds)

pinch of shrimp paste (*gapi*) – optional

10 small prawns (shrimp), blanched and peeled

1 tablespoon palm sugar

2 tablespoons lime juice

1–2 tablespoons fish sauce

Pound garlic with salt using a pestle and mortar. Add dried prawns and lemongrass and, when completely puréed, the scuds and shrimp paste, if using. Add fresh prawns and pound until mashed. Season with sugar, lime juice and fish sauce – the relish should taste floral from the lemongrass, hot, sour, salty and sweet. Adjust accordingly.

Serve with one or more of the following:
- Raw Vegetables (page 380), such as cucumber, white turmeric and witlof (Belgian endive)
- Boiled Vegetables (page 381), especially apple eggplants and bamboo shoots
- Grilled Vegetables (page 382), especially long green eggplants
- Deep-fried Vegetables (page 383), ideally 'betel' leaves and Siamese watercress
- Pickled Cabbage (page 387)
- Steamed Eggs (page 388)
- Omelette (page 390), with *cha-om*
- Steamed Salted Duck Eggs (page 391)
- freshly shucked oysters
- *pla grop* (crisp fish), grilled or deep-fried.

EGG MOUSSE WITH PINEAPPLE, CORN AND SALTED DUCK EGGS
kai dtun lert

This is a complex, yet easy-to-assemble accompaniment from Thanpuuying Pliang Pasonagorn. Keep the salted duck egg whites to use in the batter for Deep-fried Bean Curd with Crab, Pork and Spring Onions (page 440).

Sometimes it can be difficult to unmould this mousse, but it can be served unmoulded.

1 corn cob

pinch of salt

pinch of castor (superfine) sugar

1 pandanus leaf – optional

1 cup medium to coarsely minced pineapple

large pinch of cornflour (cornstarch) or rice flour

4 tablespoons coconut cream, stock or water

3 salted duck egg yolks, cut into quarters

pinch of ground white pepper

2 eggs, lightly beaten

Wash and remove all but the innermost leaves of the corn. Boil corn cob in plenty of water with salt and sugar and the pandanus leaf (if using) until corn is tender; this can take a surprisingly long time – up to 20 minutes. Cool, peel and then pare the kernels away from the cob. Squeeze pineapple dry in a clean tea towel, extracting as much juice as possible. (If pineapple is very sweet, rinse it first.)

Mix cornflour or rice flour with coconut cream, stock or water, combine with all the other ingredients and pour into a lightly oiled bowl. Cover with baking (parchment) paper, and steam gently until cooked – about 30 minutes.

CRISPY FISH CAKES AND SWEET PORK SALAD

yam pla fuu muu warn

Thai food abounds in the most eccentric combinations, as exemplified by this salad. Tender fish is grilled or roasted, ground and then deep-fried, forming a crisp and crumbly fish cake, while pork is caramelised with palm sugar, rendering it deliciously soft and yielding. Thus the principal ingredients finish in contrast to their original state. This salad has become a classic in its own right but is also an apposite *kreaung kiam*, especially in the context of this menu.

Traditionally, the fish is grilled over embers, effectively smoking it. In the absence of glowing embers, the addition of smoked fish such as *pla grop*, *pla salit* or even hot-smoked trout gives a similar depth of flavour.

2 red shallots, sliced

oil for deep-frying

extra 2 red shallots, unpeeled

1–2 dried long red chillies *or* 4–5 dried bird's eye chillies

large pinch of white sugar

1 very small green mango, julienned – about ½ cup

handful of mixed mint and coriander leaves

crispy fish cakes

300 g (9 oz) flathead or gurnard (sea robin)

50 g (1½ oz) hot-smoked trout

large pinch of salt

sweet pork

100 g (3 oz) pork neck, belly or shin

4 tablespoons palm sugar

1–2 tablespoons light soy sauce or fish sauce

½ star anise, roasted and ground

1 coriander root, scraped and chopped

2 tablespoons deep-fried shallots

dressing

1 long red chilli, deseeded *or* 3 bird's eye chillies (scuds)

pinch of salt

1 tablespoon white sugar

2 tablespoons lime juice

1 tablespoon fish sauce

Deep-fry the sliced shallots in oil until golden and then drain. Re-use oil for crispy fish cakes.

For the crispy fish cakes, follow the method on page 393. (The proportion of smoked fish is increased here, to give the fish a deeper, more redolent taste, which will ensure it is not overwhelmed by the sweet pork.)

For the sweet pork, steam or poach the pork until cooked (about 20–30 minutes), then cool and cut into 1 cm (½ in) cubes. Melt sugar in a wok. Add pork, soy or fish sauce, star anise and coriander root and simmer gently until quite sticky. (Do not boil as this will toughen the pork.) Finish with deep-fried shallots.

Grill or roast the unpeeled shallots. When cool enough to handle, peel and slice. Wash the dried chillies. Toast them in a wok over a medium heat. When beginning to smoke, add sugar and stir to coat the chillies with caramelised sugar. Cool.

Next, make the dressing (see page 338): it should taste hot, sour, salty and sweet.

To assemble the salad, combine all the ingredients, toss with the dressing and serve. Alternatively, the sweet pork can be heated in a small wok and, when hot, the crispy fish cakes added, before the dish is finished with the remaining ingredients. This method means the salad is served warm.

BREAM AND GREEN GOURD SIMMERED IN COCONUT CREAM

geng liang pla

If buying a whole fish and then filleting it, make a stock from the head and bones using coconut milk – add a few shallots, a piece of lemongrass, the peel from the *grachai* and some salt. Simmer for around 20 minutes before straining. Scrape as much flesh as possible from the head and bones and add it to the paste.

Any fish, crab, scallops or even plump, briny oysters are delicious possibilities for experimentation in this dish, and pumpkin or cucumber can be used instead of gourd.

2 bream fillets, roughly 150 g (5 oz) in all
   or a whole bream, about 300 g (9 oz), filleted
3 cups stock or coconut milk
pinch of salt
pinch of white sugar – optional
100 g (3 oz) green gourd, peeled, deseeded and cut into 2 cm (1 in) cubes
1 tablespoon julienned *grachai* (wild ginger)
1 cup coconut cream
pinch of ground white pepper
handful of lemon basil leaves

paste

3 tablespoons chopped *grachai* (wild ginger)
pinch of salt
2 tablespoons chopped red shallot
15 white peppercorns
2 tablespoons fish retrieved from the stock – if using a whole fish (see above)
   or 1 tablespoon *pla salit*, dried prawns or smoked fish
   or ½ tablespoon shrimp paste (*gapi*), roasted

First, make the paste by pounding the ingredients together using a pestle and mortar until smooth.

Cut the fish into large but elegant pieces. Bring stock or coconut milk to the boil and season with a little salt and sugar, if using. Stir in the paste to dissolve, then add the gourd. When almost cooked (about 5–8 minutes), add fish, *grachai* and coconut cream. Simmer for just a minute or two until the fish is cooked, then finish with the remaining ingredients.

The soup should be salty, peppery and fragrant from the *grachai* and lemon basil.

DEEP-FRIED BEAN CURD WITH CRAB, PORK AND SPRING ONIONS

tor huu yord sai tort

The best bean curd to use for this dish is silken; it is also the most delicate, and therefore needs to be handled very, very carefully. Refrigerate the stuffed bean curd before steaming, and again for at least an hour – even overnight – after steaming but before slicing and deep-frying. If refrigerating for a long time before deep-frying, ensure the stuffing is heated through by deep-frying at a medium heat for slightly longer than if deep-frying from room temperature.

It is important to season the stuffing well – in fact, almost over-season, since it is effectively the only component of the dish that has a decided flavour. The bean curd is, after all, bean curd. Check the flavour by poaching a little of the mixture and adjusting seasoning accordingly. I think coarsely minced fresh-water fish or crayfish make agreeable alternatives to the crab and pork stuffing.

If possible, use leftover salted duck egg whites – perhaps from Egg Mousse with Pineapple, Corn and Salted Duck Eggs (page 435) – when making the batter. They impart a rich and crisp saltiness, but remember to reduce the amount of salt to compensate.

50 g (1½ oz) minced fatty pork
1 tablespoon light soy sauce
drizzle of oyster sauce
pinch of palm sugar
50 g (1½ oz) cooked crabmeat
2 tablespoons chopped coriander leaves
2 spring (green) onions, chopped
300 g (9 oz) silken bean curd
1 banana leaf
1–2 egg whites
pinch of salt
pinch of ground white pepper
drizzle of sesame oil
½ cup plain (all-purpose) flour, seasoned with salt and pepper
oil for deep-frying

paste
1 coriander root, scraped and chopped
pinch of salt
2 garlic cloves, peeled
2 slices ginger
large pinch of ground white pepper

Using a pestle and mortar, pound together the paste ingredients until fine. Combine with pork and season with light soy sauce, oyster sauce and sugar. Slap the mixture – pick it up and throw it back into the bowl – until it becomes firmer and stickier. Work in crabmeat and two-thirds of the coriander and spring onions.

Drain bean curd and slice in half, crosswise. Place one piece of bean curd on the banana leaf. Shape stuffing mixture into an equivalent-size rectangle, carefully place on the bean curd and top with the other half of the bean curd.

Refrigerate for at least an hour, then steam gently on the banana leaf for 25 minutes – it should feel yieldingly firm. Remove, still on the banana leaf, lifting with the aforementioned gentleness. Refrigerate for at least an hour. When required, cut bean curd sandwich into 6 pieces. Beat the egg whites with salt, pepper and sesame oil. Dip bean curd in egg whites then roll in flour. Deep-fry in plenty of clean oil until golden. Drain, and serve sprinkled with the reserved coriander and spring onions.

CHICKEN CURRY WITH HOLY BASIL, GINGER AND PEANUTS

geng gai haeng

2 cups coconut cream

1 tablespoon palm sugar

2 tablespoons fish sauce

1 tablespoon roasted and finely ground peanuts

150 g (5 oz) skinless chicken thigh fillets, sliced

3 tablespoons julienned ginger

4 kaffir lime leaves, shredded

1 long red chilli, julienned

handful of holy basil leaves

1 tablespoon roasted and coarsely ground peanuts

paste

6–10 dried long red chillies, deseeded and soaked

large pinch of salt

1 tablespoon chopped galangal

2 tablespoons chopped lemongrass

1 teaspoon finely grated kaffir lime zest

1 teaspoon scraped and chopped coriander root

3 tablespoons chopped red shallot

4 tablespoons chopped garlic

10 white peppercorns

½ teaspoon coriander seeds, roasted

¼ teaspoon cumin seeds, roasted

1 sheath mace

First, make the paste (see page 280).

Crack coconut cream in a large pan over medium heat. Add 3 tablespoons of the paste and fry over medium heat until fragrant, stirring regularly. Season with sugar, then fish sauce. When the colour has deepened, add finely ground peanuts and fry for a further minute until the curry is oily. Add chicken. Simmer for 4–5 minutes – it may be necessary to add a little water to prevent it burning.

When chicken is cooked, add remaining ingredients. Check the seasoning: it should be salty, spicy, fragrant with holy basil and slightly sweet.

Kreaung kiam to accompany this dish:
- pickled red shallots
- Steamed Egg Mousse (page 390)
- Steamed or Deep-fried Salted Duck Eggs (page 391)
- Stir-fried Dried Mussels (page 396)
- Freshly Salted Beef (page 402).

MENU

Hot and Sour Soup of Crab and Pine Mushrooms

Prawns and Yellow Beans Simmered in Coconut Cream

Braised Quail Eggs with Star Anise and Bamboo Shoots

Aromatic Chicken Curry

Deep-fried Squid with Garlic and Peppercorns

Chilli Sauce

HOT AND SOUR SOUP OF CRAB AND PINE MUSHROOMS
geng dtom yam bpu gap het

In contrast to the complexities of the other dishes in this menu, this unusual *dtom yam* gives sprightly relief. A light broth in this meal would not have sufficient pungency to balance the curry; on the other hand, too complicated a soup could overwhelm and confuse the palate. This soup is simple but is powerfully flavoured.

1 crab, weighing approximately 300 g (9 oz)

6–8 cups stock

pinch of salt

pinch of palm sugar

2 tablespoons tamarind water *or* 1 fresh tamarind pod, bruised – optional

2 stalks lemongrass, bruised

2 tomatoes, deseeded and coarsely chopped

4–6 medium pine mushrooms, wild mushrooms or oyster mushrooms

2 tablespoons fish sauce

2 tablespoons minced deep-fried garlic – optional

2–3 tablespoons lime juice

extra 1 tablespoon fish sauce

4–10 bird's eye chillies (scuds), bruised

1 tablespoon coriander leaves

Clean the crab: remove cap and tail and scrape out tomalley. Cut crab into portions.

Bring stock to the boil, and season with salt, sugar and tamarind, if using. Add lemongrass and tomatoes. Clean mushrooms (if using pine mushrooms, brush off any dirt or pine needles and remove gills) and break into bite-size pieces. Add crab – and pine mushrooms, if using – to boiling stock. Season with fish sauce and deep-fried garlic, if using, then simmer for about 10 minutes, until crab and mushrooms are just cooked. If using wild or oyster mushrooms, add these for the last 30 seconds of the cooking time only.

Mix lime juice, extra fish sauce and chillies in a serving bowl. Ladle in soup and check the seasoning: it should taste hot, salty and sour. Sprinkle with coriander leaves.

PRAWNS AND YELLOW BEANS SIMMERED IN COCONUT CREAM

lon dtao jiaw

The delicious, nutty, miso-like taste of yellow beans predominates in this relish – try to find the finer, creamy white kind. The beans are only slightly bruised in this recipe, giving an agreeable texture.

Reserve any tomalley from the prawn heads and cook as described in the recipe. In some versions of this dish, a dried long red chilli is puréed and fried with the yellow beans to approximate the colour of tomalley and to add piquancy. Shredded ginger and green mango can also be added to the relish along with the sliced red shallots, if desired.

PRAWNS AND YELLOW BEANS SIMMERED IN COCONUT CREAM, SERVED WITH CRISPY FISH CAKES (page 393)

4 tablespoons yellow bean sauce

4 uncooked prawns (shrimp), peeled and deveined, tomalley reserved

1 cup coconut cream

1 tablespoon palm sugar

pinch of ground white pepper

1 tablespoon tamarind water

1 tablespoon fish sauce

½ cup coconut milk or stock

3 red shallots, sliced

a few slices of long red chilli

squeeze of mandarin juice – optional

1 tablespoon coconut cream

1 tablespoon coriander leaves

Rinse yellow beans, strain, then bruise using a pestle and mortar. Coarsely chop the prawns.

In a small pan, crack the coconut cream over medium heat, add yellow beans and cook over a medium heat, stirring regularly, until the beans are fragrant and nutty. Add prawn tomalley and continue to fry until the tomalley loses its raw, eggy smell and appearance. Season with palm sugar, pepper, tamarind water and a little fish sauce, but be careful as the yellow beans are already quite salty. Add prawns and moisten with coconut milk or stock. Simmer briefly until prawns are just cooked – a minute or less. Stir in shallot and chilli slices. Finish with mandarin juice, if using, coconut cream and coriander leaves.

Serve with a selection of the following:
- Raw Vegetables (page 380), such as cucumber, fennel, sorrel, green tomatoes and white turmeric
- Boiled Vegetables (page 381), especially green beans
- Deep-fried Eggs (page 390)
- *pla grop* (crisp fish)
- Crispy Fish Cakes (page 393)
- Sweet Pork (page 397).

BRAISED QUAIL EGGS WITH STAR ANISE AND BAMBOO SHOOTS

kai parlow

The size of quail eggs makes them perfect for a *kreaung kiam*. Rinsed and sliced, salted white radish or dried lily stalks are good alternatives to the bamboo shoots.

    8 quail eggs
    2 coriander roots, scraped
    pinch of salt
    2 garlic cloves, peeled
    1 slice ginger
    10 white peppercorns
    1 star anise, roasted and ground
    1 tablespoon oil
    3 tablespoons palm sugar
    2 tablespoons fish sauce or light soy sauce
    1 cup stock
    1 tablespoon oyster sauce
    1 cup peeled, shredded and boiled bamboo shoots

Steam or boil the eggs for 4–5 minutes, allow to cool, then shell and set aside.

Using a pestle and mortar, pound coriander roots, salt, garlic, ginger, peppercorns and star anise into a fine paste. Fry paste in oil until golden. Add palm sugar and, when beginning to caramelise, add fish sauce or soy sauce, stock and oyster sauce. Add bamboo shoots and simmer for about 3 minutes, skimming as required. Add quail eggs and continue to simmer for another minute or so.

There should be some liquid, but not too much, and it should taste salty and sweet and slightly bitter.

AROMATIC CHICKEN CURRY

geng gari gai

In the past, most spices were considered to have medicinal properties; even today, if unprocessed spices are required in a recipe, the Thai will go to a Chinese medicine shop to buy them – where the best quality can be found. These shops are normally dark, cool and fitted out in wood. There are drawers upon drawers of spices, all of which are medicinal, and some culinary, such as white and black peppercorns, cumin and fennel seeds, long pepper and cardamom. Each spice is carefully weighed and separately wrapped, as befits these little gems of more than culinary savour.

This curry is liltingly spiced – the spices support the whole, and their effect is in the aftertaste.

200 g (6 oz) skinless chicken thigh fillets, cut into 1 cm (½ in) cubes

4 kipfler, pink eye, maris piper or other waxy potatoes

4 cups coconut milk

pinch of salt

2 cups coconut cream

1 tablespoon palm sugar

2 tablespoons fish sauce

extra 3 tablespoons coconut cream

½ cup deep-fried shallots

marinade

1 tablespoon chopped ginger

1 tablespoon chopped garlic

pinch of salt

½ cup coconut cream

paste

6–10 dried long red chillies, deseeded, soaked and drained

large pinch of salt

1 tablespoon chopped red turmeric

4 tablespoons chopped red shallot

3 tablespoons chopped garlic

1 coriander root, scraped and chopped

1 teaspoon white peppercorns

1 tablespoon coriander seeds, roasted

a little grated nutmeg – optional

For the marinade make a very fine paste from the ginger, garlic and salt. Add the coconut cream, and marinate the chicken cubes in it for at least 2 hours, preferably overnight.

Next, make the curry paste (see page 280). Peel and quarter potatoes and steep in water for a few hours to remove any excess starch. Simmer in 3 cups of the coconut milk, with a pinch of salt, until cooked, adding water if more liquid is needed. Drain. Meanwhile, poach chicken in 1 cup each of the coconut milk and cream until cooked – about 6 minutes. Drain and reserve most of the poaching liquid, keeping enough in the pot just to cover the chicken.

In a smaller pan, simmer the remaining cup of coconut cream until it separates, then fry the curry paste in it over a medium heat for not less than 5 minutes, stirring regularly to prevent scorching, until fragrant with pepper and coriander seed. Do not worry if the paste has separated or is oily – it is meant to be like that – and it should really sizzle. Season with palm sugar and stir until it has melted into the paste and changed colour, then add fish sauce. Simmer for a further minute or so.

Pour paste back over the chicken. Make sure the curry covers the chicken; if not, add more of the chicken poaching liquid. (Do not add any coconut milk from the potatoes as it will be too starchy; it is for this same reason that the potatoes are cooked separately from the chicken.)

Add potatoes to the curry. Shake the pot to ensure that everything is well incorporated but do not use a spoon as this could break up the potatoes. Allow to rest for a few minutes to enable the spices to ripen and the flavours to meld. Bring the curry gently to the boil, then check the seasoning: it should taste a little salty, rich from the coconut cream and spicy. Finish with the extra coconut cream and the deep-fried shallots.

This curry is traditionally accompanied by Cucumber Relish (page 402).

DEEP-FRIED SQUID WITH GARLIC AND PEPPERCORNS
pla meuk tort gratiam prik thai

The combination of garlic, coriander and pepper is classically Thai – perhaps one of the most ancient. Normally the garlic is peeled and pounded into a fine paste with the other ingredients. However, this version is one I once had in Phuket, in which whole, unpeeled heads of garlic were pounded to make a coarse paste. Since Thai garlic is a little finer than most Western garlic, it is best to remove some of the excess skin and central stalk when pounding.

200 g (6 oz) cleaned squid, scored
1 tablespoon fish sauce or light soy sauce
pinch of white sugar
3 coriander roots, scraped and chopped
pinch of salt
1 teaspoon white peppercorns
2 heads garlic, unpeeled
oil for deep-frying
1 tablespoon coriander leaves

Marinate squid in fish sauce or soy sauce and sugar for half an hour or so.

Using a pestle and mortar, pound coriander roots with salt and peppercorns. Add garlic and continue to pound into a coarse paste, removing some of the garlic's excess skin, core and hard base as you go.

Mix paste with squid. Heat plenty of oil in a wok and, when sufficiently hot, deep-fry squid over a high heat, stirring regularly. When golden, remove and drain; be careful not to overcook the squid – it may be necessary to remove the cooked garlic (which will separate from the squid) and the squid at different times. Sprinkle with coriander and serve a bowl of the following chilli sauce on the side.

CHILLI SAUCE

sauce prik

Grilled and deep-fried dishes are often accompanied by this delicious chilli sauce (sometimes called Sauce Siracha). Red in colour and full-bodied in flavour, it is readily available and comes in varying degrees of heat; the following version can be made as hot or as mild as desired. Once made, this will last indefinitely in the refrigerator.

> 1 cup garlic cloves, peeled
>
> pinch of salt
>
> 5–10 dried long red chillies, deseeded and soaked
>
> 2 tablespoons white sugar
>
> 1 cup water

Combine all the ingredients in a small saucepan and cover. Simmer until garlic and chilli are tender, replenishing with a little water, if necessary. Cool and purée.

MENU

Salted Beef Simmered in Coconut Cream

Relish of Peanuts

Steamed Chicken with Mushrooms

Oyster Salad

Pork and Green Peppercorn Curry

Grilled Squid

SALTED BEEF SIMMERED IN COCONUT CREAM

neua kem pat gati

Grilling the beef imparts a nutty, slightly smoky, resinous quality. A few slices of white radish or even a couple of whole red shallots can also be simmered in the coconut cream.

> 100 g (3 oz) Salted Beef (page 401)
>
> 1 cup coconut cream
>
> pinch of palm sugar
>
> fish sauce – optional
>
> pinch of ground white pepper
>
> 3 red shallots, sliced
>
> 1 tablespoon coriander leaves

Rehydrate the beef in cold water for around 5 minutes, then drain and pat dry. Grill beef over a medium heat until slightly charred, remove and cool. Bruise the meat using a pestle and mortar, to soften, then shred coarsely.

Bring coconut cream to the boil. Add beef and simmer until almost dry. Season with palm sugar, fish sauce (if necessary) and pepper. Serve sprinkled with red shallots and coriander.

RELISH OF PEANUTS

nahm prik tua pat

1 tablespoon palm sugar

2 tablespoons tamarind water

2–3 tablespoons fish sauce

2 tablespoons oil or rendered pork fat

paste

9–12 dried long red chillies, deseeded, soaked and drained

pinch of salt

4 tablespoons chopped garlic

2 tablespoons ground dried prawns or ground dried fish

1 tablespoon shrimp paste (*gapi*)

½ cup peanuts, roasted

First, make the paste: gradually pound the ingredients together using a pestle and mortar, adding one by one, until smooth. Season paste with palm sugar, tamarind water and fish sauce: it should taste hot, sour, salty and sweet.

Heat oil or rendered pork fat in a wok or pan, add paste and fry over a low heat until invitingly fragrant and smelling of peanuts – around 10 minutes.

Serve with a selection of the following:

— Raw Vegetables (page 380), such as cucumber, sorrel and witlof (Belgian endive)

— Vegetables Simmered in Coconut Milk (page 382), such as green beans, baby corn, long green eggplants, bamboo shoots and bitter melon

— Grilled Vegetables (page 382)

— Deep-fried Vegetables (page 383)

— Pickled Vegetables (page 383)

— steamed fish or prawns (shrimp)

— Crispy Fish Cakes (page 393)

— Sweet Pork (page 397).

STEAMED CHICKEN WITH MUSHROOMS

gai dtun het

The technique of double-steaming is Chinese, and allows prolonged cooking without the ingredients becoming dry or tough. Such extended cooking ensures the flavours ripen and mingle. Any well-flavoured meat or salted fish that can sustain prolonged cooking can be treated this way. A variation of this recipe that has become a favourite of mine is to marinate a very good-quality chicken in light soy sauce, salt and white sugar for 2–4 days. This tightens the fibres in the meat, giving it a firm texture almost like cooked ham. It is then washed, dried and steamed as described below.

The skin can be removed from the chicken before steaming; however, the rich body it lends the stock is much appreciated by Thai diners. I think it best to steam with the skin on and then remove once cooked, skimming off any oil at the same time. In order to ensure this is completely done, allow to cool for at least 30 minutes. The skin and any excess fat can then be rendered and used to make the deep-fried minced garlic.

If fresh pine mushrooms are available, they can be steamed with the chicken, or by themselves; the prolonged, gentle cooking makes a tea-like bouillon. I also like to include a few chunks of peeled melon or gourd, a few pieces of dried orange zest and a tablespoon of red dates. Cooking the chicken in stock gives a rich flavour and gives body to the broth, but many versions simply use water, as a delicate and flavoursome stock is made during the cooking.

4 large pine mushrooms, brushed and cleaned

  or 8 best-quality dried shiitake mushrooms

2–3 tablespoons oyster sauce

1 tablespoon palm sugar

2 pieces of ginger, bruised

3 corn-fed chicken legs

  or 1 small corn-fed chicken – approximately 400 g (12 oz)

large pinch of salt

1–2 tablespoons lime juice

a few outer leaves of cabbage

2 tablespoons light soy sauce

3 coriander roots, scraped

1 star anise

8 cups chicken stock or water

pinch of ground white pepper

1 tablespoon coriander leaves

½ teaspoon minced deep-fried garlic – optional

If using dried shiitakes, rinse, cover with water and add 2 tablespoons of the oyster sauce, a pinch of the palm sugar and the smaller of the 2 pieces of ginger. Simmer, covered, until the mushrooms are tender – around 10 minutes. Strain, keeping the stock, and when cool snip off the stalks. Return the mushroom caps to the stock.

Cut each chicken leg into three pieces; if using a whole chicken, take off the legs and cut each into three. Remove backbone and trim breast cage of excess bones. Cut each breast in half lengthwise and then cut each half into three. Trim the wings. Remove any excess skin and fat, as desired. Wash chicken in several changes of water, dry and marinate in salt and lime juice for a few minutes – this keeps the chicken skin white and firm during the cooking. Rinse and dry.

Line a bowl that will fit into the steamer with cabbage leaves. Combine chicken, mushrooms, 1–2 tablespoons oyster sauce (1 tablespoon only, if using shiitakes), light soy sauce, the larger piece of ginger, coriander roots, star anise and remaining palm sugar. Cover with boiling stock or water, cover bowl with foil, and steam for 3 hours, regularly checking the water level in the steamer.

When ready to serve, carefully remove from steamer and allow to cool slightly. Skim off any excess fat and check seasoning: the broth should be rich and mellow. Serve in a large bowl, sprinkled with pepper, coriander – and garlic, if using.

OYSTER SALAD

yam hoi nang rom

12 oysters – unshucked, if possible
1 cup chopped Asian celery
1 stalk lemongrass, sliced
3 red shallots, sliced
handful of mint leaves
handful of coriander leaves
2 tablespoons deep-fried shallots – optional

dressing
½ long red chilli, deseeded and chopped
pinch of salt
1–2 teaspoons white sugar
2 tablespoons lime juice
1 tablespoon fish sauce

First, make the dressing (see page 338); it should taste hot, sour, salty and a little sweet. Shuck oysters, retaining any juices. Strain oyster juices and mix into the dressing. Combine oysters with remaining ingredients, dress and serve sprinkled with deep-fried shallots, if using.

PORK AND GREEN PEPPERCORN CURRY

geng muu prik thai orn

This is an extraordinary curry: the paste contains neither garlic nor red shallots, it has an inordinate amount of cumin and no shrimp paste – it simply should not work. When I first came across this recipe in the memorial book of Thanpuuying Pliang Pasonagorn, I thought that there had been a misprint – there so often are in very old, privately published books. But it is, in fact, an explosively fragrant curry aromatic with lemongrass and cumin. It is quite oily, as it requires a lot of cracked coconut cream to help prevent the paste being too sharp and pungent. The curry needs to be well seasoned to ensure that there is a balance between the heat of the paste and the salt.

Fresh green peppercorns are an essential component: they complete the curry and without them it is truly diminished. A meaty freshwater fish, like Murray perch, brown trout or *pla grop* (crisp fish), or seafood such as blood clams, swordfish or bonito, are all excellent alternatives to the pork, as are venison shanks and duck liver.

I like to double-blanch the pork from a cold-water start before braising in the coconut milk. This gives the meat a rich yet clean subtlety.

150 g (5 oz) boneless pork shin

2 cups coconut milk

lemongrass offcuts (from paste – see below)

pinch of salt

1½ cups coconut cream

1 teaspoon palm sugar

2 tablespoons fish sauce

2 tablespoons picked green peppercorns

3 kaffir lime leaves, shredded

handful of holy basil leaves

1 long red chilli, deseeded and julienned

paste

6–10 dried long red chillies, deseeded, soaked and drained

large pinch of salt

6 tablespoons chopped lemongrass

1 tablespoon finely grated kaffir lime zest

2 tablespoons scraped and chopped coriander root

1 teaspoon coriander seeds, roasted

1 teaspoon cumin seeds, roasted

First, make the paste (see page 280).

Wash pork. Bring coconut milk to the boil in a pan. Add pork, lemongrass offcuts and salt. Add water to cover, if necessary. Simmer until pork is tender – around 30 minutes – and leave to cool in stock. When cool, remove, reserving the stock, and trim and slice the meat into 1 cm (½ in) pieces.

Crack the coconut cream over medium heat, and fry the paste in the coconut oil until fragrant (this takes only a few minutes because all the paste ingredients are dry), then season with palm sugar and fish sauce. Add pork. Moisten, if necessary, with a little of the reserved stock. Finish the curry with the remaining ingredients and check seasoning: it should taste hot and salty, aromatic from the basil and pungent with pepper.

Good accompaniments for this curry are:
- *grachai* (wild ginger)
- pickled ginger
- Steamed Salted Duck Eggs (page 391)
- Salted Prawns (page 392)
- Stir-fried Dried Mussels (page 396)
- Braised Quail Eggs with Star Anise and Bamboo Shoots (page 447).

GRILLED SQUID

pla meuk yang

A simple dish, and a respite after the complexities of previous recipes. The Thai enjoy grilled seafood, and in any restaurant the menu will include grilled whole fish, prawns, crabs or clams, eaten with either a sweet or sour, but usually hot, dipping sauce. Normally, when the Thai grill, they tend – at least to my taste – to overcook. I think they often appreciate ingredients equally for their texture and their taste.

1 medium squid or cuttlefish – around 200 g (6 oz) – cleaned and scored
1 tablespoon fish sauce
3 tablespoons coconut cream
1 tablespoon coriander leaves

sauce
1 coriander root, scraped
pinch of salt
3 garlic cloves, peeled
3–5 bird's eye chillies (scuds)
1 tablespoon white sugar
2 tablespoons lime juice
1 tablespoon fish sauce

Cut squid into bite-size pieces. Marinate in fish sauce and 2 tablespoons of the coconut cream for at least 30 minutes.

To make the sauce, pound coriander root with salt using a pestle and mortar until fine. Add garlic and scuds and continue pounding until you have a coarse paste. Season with sugar, lime juice and then fish sauce. The sauce should be hot, sour, salty and sweet.

Grill the squid, drizzling with the remaining coconut cream as it cooks – this caramelises and enhances the flavour. Serve sprinkled with coriander leaves, and with a bowl of the sauce on the side.

MENU

Pickled Ginger with Yellow Beans

Salted Beef Ribs Braised in Coconut Cream

Sweet Fish Sauce with Grilled Fish

Sour Orange Curry of Prawns and Siamese Watercress

Bean Curd Stir-fried with Bean Sprouts

PICKLED GINGER WITH YELLOW BEANS

king dong dtow jiaw

Peel the ginger following the shapely contours of the hand: slice elegantly along the length of the rhizome, being careful not to slice all the way through. This will hold the ginger together and yet expose the maximum area to the pickling liquid. Young ginger is the best type for this preserve – it is not so peppery and has an inviting colour and tender flesh.

200 g (6 oz) ginger
2 tablespoons salt
3 tablespoons yellow bean sauce, rinsed
2 tablespoons white sugar
1 cup water

Peel and slice the ginger almost all the way through. Rub with salt and after 20 minutes work gently to extract as much liquid as possible. Rinse in plenty of water. Bring the remaining ingredients to the boil. Cool completely before pouring over the ginger. Leave in the sun or a warm place in an airtight container for at least 2 weeks before use. This lasts for 2 months unrefrigerated, or indefinitely chilled.

SALTED BEEF RIBS BRAISED IN COCONUT CREAM

neaua kem sot

In this version of salted beef, the salted meat is braised in coconut cream and milk, the fat renders as it simmers and, when the liquid evaporates, the meat begins to fry. The sugar from the coconut and marinade then caramelises and the meat becomes salty, succulent and savoury.

Meat cooked in this way must be eaten hot, otherwise it will taste oily. It can be served in many ways: as a salad with handfuls of fresh herbs, dressed with lime juice and chillies; in a curry, especially a green curry with lots of pea egg-plants and *grachai* (wild ginger); or in small amounts as an accompaniment.

500 g (1 lb) beef ribs
1 tablespoon salt
3 tablespoons white sugar
1 teaspoon ground white pepper
3–4 cups light soy sauce
3 stalks lemongrass
1 cup coconut cream
5 cups coconut milk
4 red shallots, sliced
handful of mixed mint and coriander leaves
3–4 bird's eye chillies (scuds), finely sliced
2 limes, cut into quarters

Rinse the meat, then marinate in salt, sugar and pepper, adding enough light soy sauce to cover. Leave for 3–5 days.

Finely slice the lemongrass, retaining the offcuts. Drain the marinated beef, then braise with the lemongrass offcuts in coconut cream and milk for 3 hours, turning regularly to prevent burning and to ensure an even and attractive honey-gold colour. When most of the liquid has evaporated and the meat is tender and has begun to caramelise, carefully remove from the pan, rest for a few minutes, then remove the bones and slice the meat.

Serve sprinkled with shallots, mint and coriander leaves and chillies, and garnished with quartered limes.

SWEET FISH SAUCE WITH GRILLED FISH

nahm pla warn pla yang

This relish balances the other dishes in the menu well. Traditionally, the fish that accompanies the relish is grilled so slowly over a few embers that it in fact becomes slightly smoked and, as the excess fat renders, it drips onto the embers, making the smoke even more pungent and giving the fish a glorious honey-coloured skin and a redolently smoky flavour. It can be on the grill for up to 2 hours – wildly over-cooked by Western standards, but it works deliciously with the sweet fish sauce.

This dish can be made well in advance. The sauce can be served in a bowl with both vegetables and fish on the side, poured over the fish with the vegetables alongside, or all tossed together like a salad. Bitter or sour vegetables and fruit offer a balance to the sweetness of this dish. In Thailand a very bitter vegetable called *sadao* or neem plant, which can sometimes be found in Asian shops, is its regular partner. It needs to be blanched two or three times from a cold-water start to leach out its excessive bitterness. Alternatively, and more conveniently, witlof can be used, either raw or blanched.

> 1 whole fish – about 250 g (8 oz) – ideally freshwater, such as trout or catfish
> about 2 cups fish sauce or light soy sauce
> ½ cup palm sugar
> extra 3 tablespoons fish sauce
> 2 tablespoons tamarind water
> 1 tablespoon deep-fried shallots
> 1 teaspoon deep-fried garlic
> a few dried long or bird's eye chillies, deep-fried
> 1 tablespoon coriander leaves

Clean fish and marinate in fish sauce – enough to cover. Melt palm sugar in a small pan and simmer with the extra 3 tablespoons fish sauce for a few minutes. Add tamarind water and continue to simmer for a minute or so, until thick. (Do not simmer the sauce for too long or the sugar will caramelise and, when cool, it will become a sticky rock.) Skim, strain and cool. The relish should taste salty, sweet and slightly sour.

Grill the fish. Mix the sweetened fish sauce with deep-fried shallots and garlic, chillies and coriander and serve in a bowl to accompany the fish, with vegetables on the side.

Serve with a selection of vegetables and herbs:
— Raw Vegetables (page 380), such as witlof (Belgian endive), young ginger, white turmeric, cucumber and cabbage
— sprigs of coriander, Thai basil and mint
— Boiled Vegetables (page 381), especially cabbage.

SOUR ORANGE CURRY OF PRAWNS AND SIAMESE WATERCRESS

geng som gung sy pak bung

A sour orange curry is a boiled curry, using ingredients that are readily available and techniques that are time-honoured, easy and convenient.

Although I prefer to use a light chicken stock, a prawn stock can be made from the prawn shells: just simmer in water with a few aromatics, such as off-cuts of galangal and lemongrass, and salt until a pink hue is achieved – to ensure this, add a tomato or two to the stock. Be sure to extract the tomalley from the prawn heads beforehand to make a paste (page 183), which can be used to enhance this curry or other dishes.

6–8 large uncooked prawns (shrimp), unpeeled

3 cups stock

2 tablespoons fish sauce

2 tablespoons tamarind water

pinch of white sugar – optional

1 small bunch Siamese watercress, choy sum or Chinese cabbage,
    washed and cut into bite-size pieces

paste

5–10 dried long red chillies, deseeded, soaked and drained

large pinch of salt

3 tablespoons chopped red shallot

1 tablespoon shrimp paste (*gapi*)

3 tablespoons steamed fish, cooked prawn meat or dried prawns

First, make the paste (see page 280).

Peel and devein the prawns, leaving their tails intact. Bring stock to the boil, add paste and when it has returned to the boil, season with most of the fish sauce, half the tamarind water and the sugar, if using. Add the vegetables and prawns. Simmer until cooked. Finish with another tablespoon of tamarind water and a little more fish sauce, if required.

Check the seasoning: the curry should be salty, sour and hot.

Kreaung kiam for this curry might include:

— Raw Vegetables (page 380), especially cabbage and white turmeric

— Pickled Cucumber (page 386)

— pickled red shallots

— Omelette (page 390)

— Steamed Salted Duck Eggs (page 391)

— Sweet Pork (page 397).

BEAN CURD STIR-FRIED WITH BEAN SPROUTS

tor huu pat tua nork

This is a simple stir-fry. I prefer to use silken bean curd; there is no need to cut or slice it into pieces, as it will break up once it is stir-fried.

The fastidious can nip off the slightly discoloured tops and tails of the bean sprouts. Chinese chives or spring onions can be used in place of the bean sprouts, if preferred.

300 g (9 oz) silken bean curd
2 garlic cloves
pinch of salt
1 tablespoon oil
50 g (2 oz) bean sprouts
2 tablespoons light soy sauce
1 teaspoon white sugar
a little oyster sauce – optional
2 tablespoons stock
1 tablespoon coriander leaves
pinch of white pepper

Drain bean curd. Pound garlic with salt. Heat a wok and, when hot, add oil. Fry garlic paste until beginning to colour, then turn up the heat to very high and add bean curd. Toss for a few minutes before adding bean sprouts – but do not stir too often or the bean curd will become an unsightly mash. Season with soy sauce, sugar and the oyster sauce, if using, then moisten with the stock.

Serve sprinkled with coriander and pepper.

MENU

Relish of Garlic and Chillies

Grilled Lobster or Prawns

Stir-fried Banana Chillies

Jungle Curry of Fish with Deep-fried Shallots

Salmon and Coconut Soup

RELISH OF GARLIC AND CHILLIES (page 464), SERVED WITH GRILLED LOBSTER (page 465)

RELISH OF GARLIC AND CHILLIES

nahm prik gratiam suk

The traditional recipe from which this is derived calls for boiling the garlic in water. However, I have found the relish is greatly improved by gently simmering the garlic in a light syrup with a little lime juice or vinegar. The lime juice imparts a slight bitterness but, I think, pleasantly so. The relish should not be too wet, and it should have quite a tight texture and flavour.

10 garlic cloves, peeled
1 tablespoon palm sugar
pinch of salt
dash of lime juice or vinegar – optional
1 cup water
5 dried long red chillies, deseeded, soaked and drained
salt or fish sauce, to taste
1 tablespoon tamarind water
a little lime or mandarin juice

Simmer garlic with sugar, salt, lime juice or vinegar, if using, and water in a small pan, covered, for 20 minutes or until soft. Cool.

Purée chillies with the cooled garlic, plus a few tablespoons of the garlic-simmering liquid, in a blender. Or, if using a pestle and mortar, pound chillies with garlic until fine and then moisten with some of the liquid. Season with tamarind water and lime or mandarin juice: the relish should be salty, hot, sour and sweet.

Serve the relish in a bowl, with a selection of the following on the side:
– Raw Vegetables (page 380), such as cabbage, cucumber, 'betel' leaves and witlof (Belgian endive)
– sprigs of Thai basil
– Boiled Vegetables (page 381), especially baby corn
– Vegetables Simmered in Coconut Milk (page 382), especially witlof (Belgian endive)
– Deep-fried Vegetables (page 383), ideally Chinese broccoli
– Pickled Vegetables (page 383)
– *pla grop* (crisp fish)
– Dried Squid (page 392).

GRILLED LOBSTER OR PRAWNS

gung mangkorn pao

> ½ lobster *or* 2–3 king prawns (jumbo shrimp)
>
> 2–4 tablespoons coconut cream
>
> 2 tablespoons fish sauce or light soy sauce
>
> pinch of white sugar

> Marinate lobster or prawns in coconut cream, fish sauce or soy sauce and sugar for a few minutes. Chargrill until just cooked.

STIR-FRIED BANANA CHILLIES

pat prik yuak

The chillies need to be almost burnt to bring out their smoky flavour. The sauce is thickened with tapioca flour, mixed with water and then briskly stirred into the simmering liquid. Once it has thickened, the dish should be served immediately; if the sauce is cooked for too long, the flour begins to break down and the sauce thins.

> 4–6 small banana chillies
>
> 2 garlic cloves, peeled
>
> pinch of salt
>
> 1 tablespoon oil
>
> 1 cup stock
>
> 1 tablespoon oyster sauce
>
> 1 teaspoon palm sugar
>
> 1 tablespoon Chinese black vinegar
>
> 1 teaspoon tapioca flour mixed with 1 tablespoon water
>
> 1 tablespoon light soy sauce – optional
>
> pinch of ground white pepper
>
> 1 tablespoon coriander leaves

Break or crush chillies using a pestle and mortar – this prevents them exploding during cooking. Heat a wok, add chillies and 'roast', tossing occasionally to prevent burning.

Meanwhile, make a coarse paste from the garlic and salt. When chillies are almost cooked and quite charred, add oil and, when hot, the garlic paste. Fry until golden and fragrant, then moisten with stock. Season with oyster sauce, palm sugar and vinegar. Simmer until chillies are tender, adding a little more stock or water, if necessary, to ensure that the chilies cook through and that there is sufficient liquid to make the sauce. Add tapioca flour mixture and simmer until thickened. Check seasoning – add a little light soy sauce, if desired.

Serve sprinkled with pepper and coriander.

JUNGLE CURRY OF FISH WITH DEEP-FRIED SHALLOTS

geng bpa pla sai

This spicy curry comes from the northern Thai city of Lampang. It originally called for a catfish caught from one of the many rivers that cascade through this mountainous region, but almost any freshwater fish will work happily in this dish.

Deep-fried shallots impart a deliciously nutty taste and perfume to the curry. They should be added just before serving, so they do not thicken the curry.

oil for deep-frying

6 red shallots, sliced

pinch of white sugar – optional

1 tablespoon fish sauce

1 cup stock

100 g (3 oz) fillet of catfish, Murray perch or trout, sliced

2 tablespoons shredded *pak chii farang* (long-leaf coriander)

curry paste

10–15 green bird's eye chillies (scuds)

large pinch of salt

1 tablespoon chopped galangal

2 tablespoons chopped lemongrass

1 teaspoon finely grated kaffir lime zest

1 teaspoon chopped coriander root

3 tablespoons chopped red shallot

2 tablespoons chopped garlic

1 teaspoon shrimp paste (*gapi*), roasted

garlic paste

2 garlic cloves, peeled

pinch of salt

3 bird's eye chillies (scuds)

First, make the curry paste (see page 280), then make the garlic paste by pounding the ingredients together using a pestle and mortar until smooth.

Heat oil in a wok, deep-fry shallots until golden, remove and set aside. Pour off all except 1 tablespoon of oil, add garlic paste and fry over a high heat, stirring regularly, until golden. Add curry paste and continue to fry over a high heat until fragrant enough to produce a sneeze. Season with sugar, if using, and then fish sauce. Add stock and, when boiling, the fish. Simmer until just cooked – about 1 minute. Finish with shallots and *pak chii farang*. This curry should taste hot and salty, nutty from the shallots and aromatic from the *pak chii farang*.

SALMON AND COCONUT SOUP

dtom khaa pla salmon

2 cups stock

2 cups coconut cream

pinch of salt

pinch of palm sugar

pinch of ground white pepper

10 slices galangal

2 stalks lemongrass

2 coriander roots, scraped

4 red shallots, peeled

4 kaffir lime leaves, torn

200 g (6 oz) salmon fillet, cubed

50 g (2 oz) oyster mushrooms

3 tablespoons lime juice

2 tablespoons fish sauce

3–10 bird's eye chillies (scuds)

1 tablespoon coriander leaves

Bring stock and coconut cream to the boil. Season with salt, sugar and pepper. Bruise galangal, lemongrass, coriander roots and shallots in a pestle and mortar, and then add, along with the lime leaves, to the simmering liquid. Add salmon and mushrooms and gently simmer until just cooked – about 3 minutes.

Combine lime juice, fish sauce and chillies. Pour into a serving bowl, and ladle in the soup. Check the seasoning – it should be salty, sour, creamy and hot – and adjust accordingly. Serve sprinkled with the coriander.

MENU

Salad of Dried Squid and Green Mango

Bean Curd and Bean Sprout Soup

Red Curry of Pork and Pumpkin

Crab Steamed with Ginger

Lon of Salted Duck Eggs

SALAD OF DRIED SQUID AND GREEN MANGO

yam pla meuk dtat dtiaw

This rustic salad comes from southern Thailand, where the coastline is scattered with fishing villages. The fishermen live a hard but simple life – little has changed in the last 50 years. At night, their boats leave the piers at sunset to trawl for squid in seas that teem with life. Stationing themselves some distance from the shore, the fishermen wait with blazing lights to snare the squid, which swim in massive shoals. Although vividly coloured when alive, the squid's colour fades once caught and soon becomes the more familiar opaque, porcelain white. While much of the fishermen's catch is sold fresh, some is preserved by being dried in the sun.

100 g (3 oz) Dried Squid (page 392)

oil for deep-frying

1 small green mango, shredded

4 red shallots, sliced

handful of mixed mint and coriander leaves

dressing

pinch of white sugar

3 tablespoons lime juice

2 tablespoons fish sauce

large pinch of roasted chilli powder

First, make the dressing (see page 338); it should taste sour, hot and salty.

Quickly deep-fry the squid in plenty of hot oil until crisp and golden, then drain. Combine with all remaining ingredients, dress and serve.

BEAN CURD AND BEAN SPROUT SOUP

geng jeut tor huu orn

3 garlic cloves, peeled

large pinch of salt

1 tablespoon oil

5 cups stock

1–2 tablespoons oyster sauce

2 tablespoons light soy sauce

pinch of white sugar

100 g (3 oz) fresh shiitake or oyster mushrooms, sliced

50 g (2 oz) bean sprouts

300 g (9 oz) silken bean curd

1 tablespoon coriander leaves

pinch of ground white pepper

Pound garlic with salt until you have a fine paste. Heat oil in a small pan, and fry garlic paste until fragrant and golden. Pour in the stock, season with oyster sauce, light soy sauce and sugar, and bring to the boil. Add sliced mushrooms, then bean sprouts and bean curd, and simmer for 2–3 minutes. On serving, sprinkle with coriander and pepper.

RED CURRY OF PORK AND PUMPKIN
geng krua muu gap fak leuang

This is a rather thick curry in which the paste should be cooked at a higher heat than normal until the fish is smokily fragrant. Any fish, boiled, smoked or dried, can be used in the paste – even *pla grop* (crisp fish), dried oysters or dried mussels.

Blanching the pork ensures its taste does not dominate the curry. Skate, with its rich, gelatinous texture, is a perfect alternative, especially if a few torn 'betel' or lemon basil leaves are added at the end. And any type of pumpkin or gourd can be used.

200 g (6 oz) pumpkin, peeled and cut into 2 cm (1 in) pieces
200 g (6 oz) pork ribs
3 cups coconut milk
2 cups coconut cream
1 tablespoon palm sugar
2 tablespoons fish sauce
3–4 kaffir lime leaves, torn
4 long green chillies, diagonally sliced and washed in salted water

paste
8 dried long red chillies, deseeded, soaked and drained
large pinch of salt
2 tablespoons chopped galangal
3 tablespoons chopped lemongrass
4 tablespoons chopped red shallots
3 tablespoons chopped garlic
4 tablespoons *pla salit* or any cooked fish

First, make the paste (see page 280).

Wash pumpkin pieces in several changes of water to remove some of the starch that could unduly thicken and mar the curry. Blanch pork ribs from a cold-water start, then rinse. Cut into 2 cm (1 in) pieces. Remove the hard bones but keep the softer cartilage, which adds a pleasing texture to the finished curry. Cover with coconut milk, topping up with water if necessary – and adding a few offcuts of galangal, lemongrass, red shallots and kaffir lime leaves, if desired. Simmer until cooked – about 10 minutes. Drain pork, reserving the coconut milk, then slice against the grain into 1 cm (½ in) pieces.

Heat coconut cream in a pan, stirring constantly to prevent it scorching. When it has separated, add paste and fry over a medium heat, stirring constantly. After about 5 minutes or so, the paste should be fragrant and sizzling in the coconut oil. It may be necessary to moisten with some of the reserved coconut milk, if it is too dry; this will increase the separation, but that is a desired characteristic. Simmer until oily, then season with palm sugar and continue to fry for another minute before adding fish sauce. Add pumpkin and continue to fry; after a few minutes, moisten with 2 cups of the reserved coconut milk. Simmer until pumpkin is tender (about 5 minutes), then add pork.

Finish with kaffir lime leaves and chillies. Remove from the heat, but leave to stand in warm place for a few minutes before serving, to allow the flavour of the curry to develop and ripen. The curry should taste salty and hot, and sweet and creamy from the coconut cream and pumpkin.

Some good accompaniments include:

- pickled ginger
- pickled red shallots
- dried fish, grilled or deep-fried
- Dried Squid (page 392)
- Salted Beef (page 401), grilled.

CRAB STEAMED WITH GINGER

bpu tarlae neung

The most famous area for catching mud crabs is in the province of Chonburi, on the east coast of the Gulf of Thailand, around Pattaya. Along the coastal road are many villages; their houses often jut out over the water and mangrove swamps, which are the best places to find the crabs the locals catch and sell. In markets throughout Thailand, there are always one or two stalls that sell crabs; they are very popular and the best crabs are sold by mid-afternoon.

The most sought-after crabs are those that are heaviest for their size. Prospective buyers will always scrutinise several crabs, weighing each in their hands, turning it over and inspecting the belly to determine the sex – the tail flap is always broader in a female so it can protect the fertilised eggs safely. They will inquire of the vendor when and where it was caught and if it contains any precious eggs. The price for a female crab laden with roe will be markedly higher than for a mere male. When the right crab is chosen, the haggling begins. This time-honoured rite is expected, even encouraged, by both vendor and buyer. It is entertainment that engages, delights and diverts.

Once a price is agreed, the purchase is made and the crab goes home. The crab is almost always dispatched on the day it is bought. If it is kept for too long – and as far as the Thai are concerned overnight is too long – then the crab begins to digest itself. The Thai poetically describe this as 'the meat of the crab returning to the sea'.

Thai cooks prefer the gentle technique of steaming to all others when dealing with crabs. They often eat them strewn with ginger and celery, which they believe will remove any strong fishy flavours, or with a *nahm jim* – a garlic, chilli and lime sauce.

1 mud crab or other type of crab – about 600 g (1¼ lb)
2 stalks lemongrass, bruised
3 tablespoons light soy sauce
pinch of white sugar
2 cups julienned ginger
1 cup finely sliced spring (green) onions
1 bunch Asian celery, cut into 2 cm (1 in) lengths
pinch of ground white pepper
1 tablespoon coriander leaves

Kill the crab humanely, then rinse away any mud. Remove carapace, scrape out and set aside any roe and tomalley. With a cleaver or heavy knife, cut crab into portions. Lay lemongrass on a plate and place crab on top, seasoning with light soy sauce and sugar. Strew over 1 cup of ginger and the reserved roe and tomalley. Steam over a high heat for 15 minutes, or until cooked. Add remaining ginger, spring onions and celery, and steam for a further minute until the greens have just wilted. Remove from steamer, then sprinkle with pepper and coriander leaves.

LON OF SALTED DUCK EGGS

lon kai kem

Mostly just the yolks of the salted duck eggs are used, but I like the saltiness of the whites and so use all of the eggs. It is a matter of economy, I suppose – and taste. If just using the yolks in this recipe, use 4 eggs instead of 2 and keep the whites to make a batter.

This richly flavoured *lon* can be embellished with some shredded green mango and ginger, as well as shallots, chillies and *grachai*.

2 salted duck eggs *or* 4 salted duck egg yolks
1 cup coconut cream
½ cup stock
1 tablespoon fish sauce

50 g (2 oz) minced fatty pork

large pinch of palm sugar

1 tablespoon tamarind water

100 g (3 oz) minced prawns (shrimp)

2–3 tablespoons coconut milk or stock

3 stalks *grachai* (wild ginger), julienned – optional

1 tablespoon finely sliced lemongrass

1 long red or green chilli, cut into rounds

3 kaffir lime leaves, torn

2 red shallots, sliced

pinch of ground white pepper

1 tablespoon coriander leaves

Steam salted duck eggs or yolks for around 20 minutes, then leave to cool. If using whole eggs, cut in half and scoop out of shell. Crumble yolks – and white, if using all of the eggs.

Heat coconut cream and stock in a small pot to just boiling, then season with fish sauce. Mix in minced pork and continue to simmer for 1–2 minutes, stirring regularly, to prevent it clumping. Season with palm sugar and tamarind. Work in minced prawn and salted eggs or yolks, and stir for 2 minutes, being careful not to overcook. You may need to add a little coconut milk or stock. Add *grachai*, if using, lemongrass and chillies, moistening with a little more coconut milk or stock, if necessary. Check the seasoning: the *lon* should taste salty, rich from the egg and a little sour. Finish with lime leaves, shallots, pepper and coriander.

Serve with some of the following:

- Raw Vegetables (page 380), such as cucumber, white turmeric and cabbage
- Deep-fried Vegetables (page 383), especially 'betel' leaves and basil sprigs
- Pickled Vegetables (page 383)
- steamed or grilled mussels
- Crispy Fish Cakes (page 393)
- Sweet Pork (page 397).

part three

food 'outside
the meal'

part three food 'outside the meal'

The meal proper starts and finishes with rice and its accompanying dishes. Everything else is 'outside the meal' – in Thai called *arharn wang*. But, to the Thai, a life without snacks is as inconceivable as a meal without rice. Throughout the day, various dishes placate any hunger. Unlike most traditional food, snacks are rarely prepared at home but are normally purchased from a nearby market or a wandering hawker.

Before the nineteenth century, food was generally prepared in households, although it might be eaten elsewhere, in paddies or on a rare journey. But wherever the Thai congregate there is food. In larger towns, enterprising women began to set up market stalls offering snacks to itinerant workers – although the food served could be rather rustic, such as *miang* (sweetmeats rolled in 'betel' or other leaves). In parts of Bangkok where government bureaucrats were to be found, ladies of the palace catered for the stalls, so the food there was inevitably more refined, even complex.

Later, as more people moved to the city, the demand became greater, although it was still mainly concentrated around the markets. The influx of Chinese migrants brought a range of new dishes to the Thai market stalls; and still most snacks and street food are of Chinese origin – only a few, like green papaya salad (*som dtam*), are truly Thai. Hawkers soon left the market place and sought their customers elsewhere: on the canals, in the streets, in boats; with bamboo poles slung over their shoulders, and later wheeling their wares on carts. They can sometimes be seen carrying a pot of glowing embers, the sign of their trade. Curry shops appeared in the second half of the nineteenth century. Originally such shops were makeshift, operating under the shade of a tree, with one or two specialities, but today they offer a huge array of dishes: curries, salads and stir-fries, prepared earlier and served at room temperature – fast, easy food that is delicious to eat and yet offers the possibility of a full meal.

Day in and day out, the Thai always seem to be eating sweets but, like snacks, these are considered to be outside the meal proper. Some believe desserts are the pinnacle of Thai cookery, employing techniques as complex as those used when preparing savoury food, if not more so. There are elaborate methods of simmering and clarifying syrups and perfuming sugars. Although confections may not be prepared following exact recipes, they are made according to traditional practices – and with an alchemist's devotion and precision.

13 SNACKS

AND STREET FOOD

The Thai eat all day long – it would appear they do not stop. Breakfast is usually a simple affair: steamed banana or pumpkin sprinkled with grated coconut, sesame seeds, salt and sugar. Rice left from the previous night's meal might be simmered in water or stock to make rice soup, which may be accompanied by stir-fried fish, an omelette or some curry. In the Muslim south, such curries are eaten with *roti*. Truly delicious fresh tropical fruit, such as pineapple, red papaya with lime juice, mangosteen and star fruit, are also served for breakfast. Lunch presents few of the complexities of the main, nightly meal. It can consist of noodles stir-fried or in a soup, Thai noodles with a pungent sauce and a plate of vegetables, or fried or seasoned rice with a *nahm prik* relish. During the afternoon and into the early evening, sweet morsels and delicate savouries, such as curry puffs, *madtarbark* or tapioca dumplings, may be enjoyed until dinner. Supper usually means a trip to Chinatown for a calming bowl of rice soup or porridge accompanied by several plates of highly seasoned dishes, or yet more sweets.

HORS D'OEUVRES AND SNACKS

In the palaces of Siam, snacks were delicious diversions to delight and idle away the time. Complex dishes were designed to stimulate the palate after the heat of the day. Most traditional Thai hors d'oeuvres are therefore quite complicated, befitting the accomplishments of these rarefied cooks. Even though these dishes might precede a meal, they still were not considered a part of it. More often they were consumed mid-afternoon, or whenever hunger beckoned. According to some of the older memorial books, these hors d'oeuvres were surprisingly substantial which, given the light eating habits of the Siamese, suggests that they were offered a good time before the commencement of the meal proper.

Usually a pair of hors d'oeuvres were served, one wet and the other dry. These might include seasoned minced chicken rolled around baby corn, encased with the kernels of sweetcorn and steamed; rice porridge with shredded chicken and prawns; and steamed tapioca dumplings filled with a minced pork relish or even 'macaroni' stir-fried with peanuts and spring onions. Delicious no doubt, but an overwhelming introduction to a meal, and so very much at odds with the delicacy that is the hallmark of good Thai cooking.

Appetisers as we know them do not exist in traditional Thai cooking. Spring rolls, 'money bags', satay and their ilk are not truly Thai – they belong to a general South East Asian cuisine spread by the Chinese. Their inclusion in the Thai repertoire is yet another example of the way the Thai accommodate and incorporate foreign cuisines into their cooking. There are, however, apposite dishes that can precede a Thai meal extremely well. A *miang* or some ground fish with fruit would be a very agreeable beginning indeed; an egg net offers as much joy and comfort now as it did to King Rama II when he wrote of it in his Boat Songs.

CHILLI WITH SALT

prik gap gleua

This ancient preparation is an accompaniment to fresh or pickled fruit. I prefer this to taste salty, hot and sweet; others may think differently. Roasted chilli powder now often replaces the scuds to make this, together with sour fruit, the quintessential Thai snack.

4–10 bird's eye chillies (scuds) *or* 1 teaspoon roasted chilli powder
2 tablespoons salt
3–4 tablespoons white sugar

Pound the chillies, or mix the chilli powder, with the salt. Stir in sugar to taste – usually at least 3 tablespoons.

ANCIENT CHILLI RELISH WITH SALT AND COCONUT

prik gap gleua

Given the irrepressible nature of Thai cooks, alternatives to rudimentary Chilli with Salt were soon developed. Chillies were pounded with a little salt and mixed with shrimp paste and some palm sugar to form a murky mass, just perfect for tart fruit. Or palm sugar would be simmered with chillies to make a tight, thick sauce that could be kept for some time. This is a modern, urbane version of such a rustic relish.

Traditionally it was stored in bamboo segments for up to a month, making it easy to transport. At its simplest, the relish was sprinkled on, or stirred through, warm rice. Now it is usually eaten with fresh vegetables and tender leaves, but it was once popular with half-ripe mango and pieces of watermelon.

2 cups shredded coconut
5–10 dried bird's eye chillies
pinch of salt
3 tablespoons palm sugar

Dry coconut in the sun for a day, or in a slow oven (150°C or 300°F) for an hour or so, then roast in a wok or heavy pan until golden – to yield 1 cup roasted coconut. Pound chillies into a fine paste with the salt. Add coconut and keep pounding until you have a coarse paste. Season with palm sugar; the relish should taste rich and nutty, sweet and salty – and just a little hot.

This keeps indefinitely.

SWEET FISH SAUCE

nahm pla warn

A sauce such as this is eaten with crisp, tart or full-flavoured fruit, such as green mango, guava, rose apple, even watermelon. It is particularly satisfying with pickled fruit.

2 cups palm sugar

1 cup fish sauce

4–10 bird's eye chillies (scuds), chopped

4 red shallots, sliced

2 tablespoons dried prawns (shrimp)

Simmer palm sugar with fish sauce until reduced and sticky. Sprinkle with chillies, shallots and whole or ground dried prawns. This keeps for a few days unrefrigerated.

PICKLED GREEN MANGO

mamuang dong

Pickled fruit is popular with all Thai, its succulence being a welcome and cooling respite in the heat of the day. This recipe works for most close-textured fruit.

1 cup salt

2 tablespoons palm sugar

5 cups water

4 green mangoes

5 cups hydrolysed lime water

Combine salt, sugar and water. Bring to the boil, strain and cool. Peel mangoes and cut into quarters, then soak in hydrolysed lime water for around an hour. Rinse and dry thoroughly. Put into a sterilised jar and cover with the syrup, making sure the mango is completely immersed. Cover and leave in a warm, dry place for 15–20 days. This keeps indefinitely and does not need to be refrigerated.

PICKLED GREEN MANGO WITH HONEY

mamuang dong nahm peung

Pickled mango can be eaten as is, but is delicious infused with honey.

1 quantity Pickled Green Mango (above)

5 cups hydrolysed lime water

2 cups honey

Rinse mango, then soak in hydrolysed lime water for 6–8 hours. Rinse again and dry thoroughly. Cover mango with honey and leave in a warm, dry place for 4 days. This keeps indefinitely and does not need to be refrigerated.

MIANG LAO

The first time I came across this common snack was in one of the fast-disappearing markets of Bangkok. An old woman sitting on her haunches behind a small table was selling what seemed to be a very odd array of food. In bowls made from folded banana leaves were chopped shallots, dried prawns, roasted coconut and 'betel' leaves; by her side was a large earthenware pot filled with a dark, sticky sauce. She pulled out a banana leaf and spooned the various components onto it in separate mounds, and in the centre ladled a dollop of thick, toasty caramel. A small amount of each ingredient was placed on a 'betel' leaf, topped with some sauce and then the leaf was rolled up and eaten. It was truly sensational, the array of ingredients became a myriad tastes and textures bound together by the sauce and the herbaceous nuttiness of the leaf. It is no surprise, then, that *miang* is so popular.

The original *miang* came from the north of Thailand, near the Burmese border, where wild tea leaves were fermented and chewed with salt. The taste was quite bitter and tannic, but came with a mildly pleasant narcotic effect. Gradually other ingredients – ginger, red shallots and palm sugar – were included and rolled into the folds of leaves in this dizzyingly satisfying, rustic wad. This version is said to be Laotian; however, I suspect it is a central plains Thai interpretation of the northern original. The salty dried turnips can be found at Chinese food shops.

2 tablespoons oil

6 red shallots, sliced

4 garlic cloves, sliced

200 g (6 oz) minced pork

3 tablespoons fish sauce

3 tablespoons palm sugar

2 tablespoons tamarind water

2 tablespoons shredded ginger

1 tablespoon salty dried turnips, rinsed and dried – optional

1 teaspoon ground white pepper

2 tablespoons ground roasted peanuts

1 cup pickled mustard greens

Heat the oil in a wok; fry the shallots and garlic until golden. Add the pork and stir to prevent from clumping. Season with both the fish sauce and palm sugar then, after a minute, the tamarind water. Work in the ginger, turnip (if using), pepper and peanuts. Simmer, while continuing to stir regularly, until it becomes a sticky paste. Allow to cool. Separate the leaves of the mustard greens and rinse; or, if particularly strong, blanch and refresh them. Roll the paste into small balls – about 2 cm (1 in) diameter – and wrap with the mustard green leaves. >

Serve with:

— Rice Cakes (page 486)
— a few bird's eye chillies (scuds)
— coriander sprigs
— sliced red shallots.

MIANG OF POMELO WITH PRAWNS

miang som

This version of *miang* is merely the base from which many variations spring. Crab-meat, cured pork, salted beef or oysters all sit happily on leaves – whether these are 'betel', *bai tong lang* (as opposite), or even spinach.

The sauce can be made several days in advance – it keeps indefi-nitely. All the tastes should be of equal strength, therefore the most pungent ingredients need to be cut into small pieces to ensure this balance: the lime should be cut into minuscule cubes, the ginger slightly larger and the red shallots into roughly ½ centimetre (¼ inch) pieces. I prefer to slice the chillies finely, too, but others – daredevils – eat them coarsely chopped or whole.

2 tablespoons grated coconut, roasted

1 teaspoon finely diced lime

1 tablespoon diced young ginger

2 tablespoons diced red shallot

handful of coriander leaves

1–3 bird's eye chillies (scuds), finely sliced

4 prawns (shrimp), blanched, peeled, deveined and sliced

1 cup pomelo flesh

16 *bai tong lang*, 'betel' or spinach leaves

paste

4 slices galangal, roasted

large pinch of salt

3 bird's eye chillies (scuds)

large pinch of shrimp paste (*gapi*), roasted

1 tablespoon dried prawns (shrimp)

3 tablespoons grated coconut, roasted

1 tablespoon peanuts, roasted

sauce

1 cup palm sugar

¼ cup water

4 tablespoons fish sauce

3 tablespoons tamarind water

First, make the paste: gradually pound the ingredients together using a pestle and mortar, adding one by one, until smooth.

For the sauce, heat sugar with water. When dissolved, simmer for several minutes until syrup is quite thick. Add fish sauce, then stir in the paste and continue to simmer for a few minutes, until the galangal can be smelt. Add tamarind, but do not simmer for too long or it will scorch – and do not reduce too much or the dressing will harden on cooling. Remove from the heat. When cooled a little, check the seasoning: it should taste sweet, rich, sour and salty.

Combine remaining ingredients except *bai tong lang,* 'betel' or spinach leaves. Dress with the sauce and serve on the leaves.

RICE CAKES WITH CHILLI, PRAWN AND PORK SAUCE

kao dtang nar dtang

Rice is never wasted. For the many temple festivals and family gatherings in Thailand, there has to be sufficient rice to feed large numbers, and it is normally cooked in a huge and heavy pot. Even with somebody stirring attentively, the weight of the rice presses against the bottom of the wok and it sticks. As more begins to catch, it forms a crust. Usually by this stage the rice is cooked. Once the rice has been served the crust at the bottom is scraped out in large pieces and dried in the sun over a few days. I find that adding a proportion of sticky rice, soaked overnight, helps to bind the rice sheet as it dries. These dried cakes keep indefinitely; when they are needed, they are deep-fried in plenty of hot, clean oil.

Rice cakes are used mainly as a snack, or even as a makeshift appetiser – historically, they were used as the basis of soldiers' rations – and can be served with this rich coconut sauce of minced prawns and pork, or simply smeared with Chilli Jam (page 200).

3 cups jasmine rice

½ cup soaked white sticky rice – optional

oil for deep-frying

sauce

8 dried long red chillies, deseeded, soaked and drained

pinch of salt

3 coriander roots, scraped and chopped

3 tablespoons chopped red shallot

3 tablespoons chopped garlic

15 white peppercorns

1 cup coconut cream

3 tablespoons palm sugar

3 tablespoons fish sauce

100 g (3 oz) minced uncooked prawns (shrimp)

50 g (2 oz) minced pork

1 cup coconut milk

3 red shallots, sliced

2 tablespoons ground roasted peanuts

1 tablespoon coriander leaves

Start preparation of the rice cakes a day or two in advance. If using two kinds of rice, mix and cook together. Allow the rice to cool a little, but do not let it become too cold, as cold starch will not bond. Thoroughly clean a rectangular metal tray about 30 cm (12 in) long: there must be no residue of oil or soap, or the rice cakes will not 'pop' when fried. Press the rice onto the tray, and sprinkle with a little water. Press down firmly using a spatula or fish slice until the rice forms an even sheet – it should be no thicker than ½ cm (¼ in). Dry in a warm place overnight or for several nights: it must be completely dry or, again, the rice will not pop. As the sheet dries, it will crack and break up into large pieces. When completely dried and semi-translucent, peel off and store in an airtight container.

For the sauce, make a paste from the chillies, salt, coriander roots, shallot, garlic and peppercorns by pounding with a pestle and mortar, adding one by one, until smooth.

Simmer the coconut cream until it separates or 'cracks'. Add paste and fry over a medium heat until fragrant. Season with palm sugar and continue to simmer for about 3 minutes, then add fish sauce, minced prawns and pork. Simmer for a few minutes, stirring regularly to prevent clumping. Moisten with coconut milk and simmer for another minute or so. Check the seasoning: the sauce should taste salty and sweet. Stir in shallots, peanuts and coriander.

When required, deep-fry rice cakes in plenty of clean oil until they have puffed to almost triple their original size and are just beginning to colour lightly. Serve with the sauce.

MINCED PORK, CHICKEN AND PRAWN PASTE WITH PINEAPPLE AND MANDARIN

ma hor

This dish's Thai name whimsically means 'galloping horses'. It is a perfect hors d'oeuvre because of the wonderful interplay between the sweet, nutty and salty relish, the sweet and sour pineapple and the succulent mandarin. This recipe has been adapted from one belonging to the woman who first introduced me to Thai cooking, Khun Sombat Janphetchara, and although there are many versions of this dish, I still find hers one of the best. *Ma hor* stimulates and teases the palate, in readiness for the meal to follow.

Do not fill the pieces of fruit too far in advance as the acids in the fruit break down the paste and the sugars in the paste will make the fruit weep.

100 g (3 oz) minced pork

100 g (3 oz) minced skinless chicken breast or thigh fillets

100 g (3 oz) minced uncooked prawns (shrimp)

¼ teaspoon salt

oil for frying

1 cup palm sugar

½ cup fish sauce

½ cup deep-fried shallots

½ cup deep-fried garlic

4 tablespoons ground roasted peanuts

¼ pineapple, peeled, core removed and sliced crosswise

10 mandarin segments

handful of coriander leaves

1 long red chilli, cut in half lengthwise, deseeded and shredded

paste

4 coriander roots, scraped and chopped

pinch of salt

5 garlic cloves, peeled

15 white peppercorns

Fry the minced pork, chicken and prawns separately, each with a pinch of salt, in a little oil, then drain and cool.

Next, make the paste by pounding the ingredients using a pestle and mortar until fine. Fry paste in 3 tablespoons of oil until golden and fragrant. Add palm sugar and fish sauce, and simmer gently for a few minutes until quite thick. >

Add the pork, chicken and prawns and simmer for a few minutes, stirring to prevent the meat from clumping. Add half of each of the deep-fried shallots and garlic and the roasted peanuts, and simmer until reduced to a sticky paste: it should taste sweet, nutty and salty. Remove from heat and finish with the remaining deep-fried shallots and garlic and roasted peanuts. Put to one side to cool – the mixture will solidify considerably.

Prepare the fruit: slice pineapple crosswise into triangles; remove the top of each mandarin segment, extract any seeds and form a pocket. When ready to serve, roll pieces of the mixture into small balls and use to fill the pockets in the mandarin segments and to top the pineapple slices. Finish with coriander and shredded chilli.

CHICKEN DEEP-FRIED IN PANDANUS LEAVES

gai hor bai dtoei

Wrap chicken as follows: hold base of leaf in left hand and tip in right hand, form a cup by bringing base of leaf across front of top part of leaf; place chicken inside, then bring the long section of leaf around, over and under chicken, now tuck it under the leaf and tighten. It is exactly the same process as knotting a tie.

3 skinless chicken thigh fillets
2 coriander roots, scraped and chopped
pinch of salt
3 garlic cloves, peeled
2 cm (1 in) piece of ginger, peeled
pinch of ground star anise – optional
10 white peppercorns
½ cup sweet soy sauce (*kecap manis*)
5 tablespoons palm sugar
3 tablespoons Chinese red vinegar
2 tablespoons sesame oil
2 tablespoons Worcestershire sauce
15 large pandanus leaves
oil for deep-frying
pinch of sesame seeds, roasted

Cut each chicken fillet into 5 pieces.

Using a pestle and mortar, pound coriander roots with salt, garlic, ginger, star anise, if using, and peppercorns into a fine paste. Stir in the soy sauce, palm sugar, vinegar, sesame oil and Worcestershire sauce. Use half of this to marinate the chicken, leaving overnight, or for up to 3 days – refrigerated. Reserve the other half of the mixture to make a sauce, keeping it in the refrigerator.

When ready to cook, dilute the reserved marinating mixture with a tablespoon or so of water to make a dipping sauce. Remove chicken from marinade, and wrap each piece of chicken in a pandanus leaf. Deep-fry in oil over a medium heat, being careful not to burn. Drain and rest for a minute or so, then serve with a bowl of sauce sprinkled with a few sesame seeds.

MOM LEUANG NEUANG'S FAMOUS SATAY

satay leu

Although the dish is probably of Muslim origin, 'satay' is a Chinese word meaning 'three pieces'. Usually satay is eaten with Cucumber Relish (page 402); however, Mom Leuang Neuang suggests eating this with fresh raw vegetables, such as cucumber and green beans, and a chilli and shallot sauce.

200 g (6 oz) fillet of beef, pork or chicken

½ cup coconut cream

1 teaspoon turmeric powder

1 tablespoon condensed milk

1 tablespoon palm sugar

pinch of white sugar

2 tablespoons fish sauce

a little Thai whisky – Mekong or Santip – or bourbon

12–16 bamboo skewers, soaked in water for 1 hour

paste

4 tablespoons chopped red shallot

pinch of salt

3 tablespoons ground roasted peanuts

1 tablespoon coriander seeds, roasted

1 teaspoon cumin seeds, roasted

sauce

5–6 long red chillies, deseeded and rinsed

pinch of salt

3 red shallots, peeled and chopped

½ cup white vinegar

1–2 tablespoons castor (superfine) sugar

First, make the paste: gradually pound the ingredients together using a pestle and mortar, adding one by one, until smooth. Cut meat into strips about 5 cm × 2 cm (2 in × 1 in). Mix paste with the coconut cream, turmeric, condensed milk, palm sugar and white sugar, fish sauce and whisky, and work this marinade into the meat until absorbed. Put to one side for a few hours.

For the sauce, purée chillies with salt and shallots. Season with vinegar and sugar to taste: the sauce should be sweet, sour, hot and salty.

Thread 3 pieces of meat onto each bamboo skewer, pushing down tightly. Repeat until all the meat is used. Grill over charcoal, sprinkling the satays with any excess marinade as they cook. Serve with a bowl of sauce on the side.

EGG NETS

latiang

The base for this dish is merely minced pork and prawns, seasoned with garlic, pepper and coriander. But what lifts it from the norm is the way it is dressed – with egg nets. King Rama II compared these little morsels to the pillow upon which he dreamed. I guess it depends on how the egg rolls.

Note that you need to start preparations the day before; the eggs are whisked, strained and rested overnight so that they can be poured or drizzled quickly and smoothly, like a thick cream – this ensures that the egg nets are thin and elegant.

> 3 eggs
> oil for frying
> 3 coriander roots, scraped
> pinch of salt
> 4 garlic cloves, peeled
> 10 white peppercorns
> 50 g (2 oz) minced pork
> 100 g (3 oz) minced uncooked prawns (shrimp)
> 2 tablespoons fish sauce
> 3 tablespoons palm sugar
> 1 tablespoon finely sliced lemongrass
> 3 red shallots, sliced
> 1 tablespoon julienned red chilli
> handful of coriander leaves

Whisk the eggs lightly to combine. Do not over-beat, as this will make the eggs difficult to strain; it also incorporates too much air, which makes the eggs 'bubble' slightly on cooking, and then become tough. Strain the whisked eggs through a fine sieve to remove filaments and membranes, and to help break down the protein. Rest eggs overnight in a glass or plastic container, which must be scrupulously clean (they are very susceptible to absorbing other flavours). As the mixture is also an ideal environment for bacteria, it is wise to refrigerate it. >

Next day, pour the eggs into a bowl wide enough for your hand, and leave to reach room temperature. Dip the tops of your fingers (up to the first joint) of one hand into the bowl, stir through the mixture, then lift your hand from the bowl. The egg mixture will dribble and drip back into the bowl. Try this a few times to become accustomed to its flow.

Half fill a wok with oil and heat it up to medium, then maintain this temperature over a low flame. Now dip your hand into the egg mixture and quickly wave across the wok, so that the egg drizzles into the oil. Move your hand backwards and forwards, then from side to side, to form the net. Do not move too quickly, or the strands will be too thin to form a net and too brittle to fold when cooked and cooled. It will be necessary to re-dip your hand into the egg mixture once or twice to form sufficient strands to make a net. Circle the perimeter of the net with more egg mixture to form a border.

Watch the temperature: if the oil is too hot, the eggs cook too quickly and the nets become brown and brittle. If the oil is too cool, then the net becomes sodden with the oil. Remove net and drain on greaseproof paper. Repeat until all the mixture is used (normally 1 egg makes 2 nets). Cool. The nets can be made several hours in advance.

Using a pestle and mortar, pound coriander roots, salt, garlic and peppercorns into a paste. Heat oil in a pan or wok and fry paste until fragrant and golden. Add pork and, after a minute or so, the minced prawns, stirring regularly to prevent clumping. Season with fish sauce and palm sugar, and set aside. When cool, mix with lemongrass, shallots, chilli and coriander.

Lay out one net. Spread some of the mixture on the lower third of the net. Roll the net, gathering in its ends to form a cigar. Repeat with the remaining nets and mixture. On serving, slice into pieces with a sharp knife.

FISH CAKES

tort man pla

A great snack, especially after a trip to the market. In the south of Thailand, the mixture is occasionally wrapped around a small chilli before being deep-fried.

300 g (9 oz) fish fillets, such as whiting or orange roughy

4 tablespoons Red Curry Paste (page 149)

1 egg, lightly beaten

3 tablespoons fish sauce

1 teaspoon castor (superfine) sugar

5 kaffir lime leaves, shredded

2 tablespoons finely cut snake beans or green beans

oil for deep-frying

Wash fish in cold, salted water. Combine fish, curry paste and egg in a food processor, blend well and season with fish sauce and sugar. (If you do not have a food processor, first mince the fish and then pound together with the curry paste, egg, fish sauce and sugar using a pestle and mortar.) In a large bowl, gather the fish purée up into a ball and throw back into the bowl; continue this slapping until the mixture becomes firmer and stickier (this aerates the ingredients and makes the cakes puff up when deep-fried). Mix in lime leaves and beans. Mould into small discs, then deep-fry in a wok with plenty of oil over a medium heat.

Serve immediately – the cakes toughen as they cool – with Cucumber Relish (page 402).

PRAWN CAKES

tort man gung

A traditional accompaniment to Thai Noodles with Crab, Prawn and Chilli Jam (page 578), these can also be eaten in the same way as fish cakes (see previous recipe), accompanied by Cucumber Relish (page 402).

> 2 coriander roots, scraped and chopped
> pinch of salt
> 3 garlic cloves, peeled
> 1 slice ginger
> large pinch of ground white pepper
> 150 g (5 oz) minced uncooked prawns (shrimp), with any tomalley reserved
> large pinch of palm sugar
> 1–2 tablespoons light soy sauce
> oil for deep-frying

Pound coriander roots, salt, garlic, ginger and pepper into a paste. Combine with minced prawns and tomalley (if any), then slap the mixture against the side of the bowl until it becomes firmer and stickier. Season with sugar and soy sauce. Test a little by poaching in water – it should taste slightly salty and sweet – and adjust seasoning, if necessary. Roll into 2 cm (1 in) balls, flatten into cakes and deep-fry in plenty of medium to hot oil.

STICKY RICE TOPPED WITH PRAWNS

kao niaw nar gung

At around four o'clock in the afternoon, this unusual sweetmeat would be served to revive the ladies of the Thai royal palaces. Shredded dried fish, minced chicken or pork were also prepared in this manner and served atop rice.

1 coriander root, scraped and chopped

pinch of salt

2 garlic cloves, peeled

10 white peppercorns

1 tablespoon oil

½ cup minced uncooked prawns (shrimp)

1 tablespoon fish sauce

1 tablespoon white sugar

pinch of salt

2 tablespoons shredded kaffir lime leaves

1 tablespoon coriander leaves

1 cup cooked Sweetened White Sticky Rice (page 616), coloured after cooking with a little saffron or turmeric

Using a pestle and mortar, pound coriander root, salt, garlic and peppercorns into a paste. Heat oil in a wok, fry paste until golden, then add minced prawns. Season with fish sauce and sugar and continue to simmer for a minute or so, until the prawn meat is just cooked. Adjust the seasoning with salt, mix in lime leaves and coriander, and set aside. When cool, spoon over sticky rice and serve.

SMOKED SAUSAGE

sai grop

Traditionally this sausage is grilled, but I have found that its redolent complexity is best reproduced by smoking in a wok; this gives it an authentic Thai taste.

250 g (8 oz) minced fatty pork

4 tablespoons fish sauce

2 tablespoons palm sugar

1 egg

½ cup coconut cream

2 tablespoons shredded kaffir lime leaves

3 tablespoons chopped coriander leaves

1 metre (3 feet) thick sausage casing

3–4 cups grated coconut

3–4 tablespoons white sugar

2–3 tablespoons tea leaves

1 banana leaf – optional

a few slices young ginger

a few coriander sprigs

a few bird's eye chillies (scuds)

SMOKED SAUSAGE, SERVED WITH SMOKED FISH PASTE (page 498)

paste

4 dried long red chillies, deseeded, soaked and drained

large pinch of salt

2 tablespoons chopped lemongrass

1 tablespoon chopped galangal

1 tablespoon chopped coriander root

1 teaspoon finely grated kaffir lime zest

3 tablespoons chopped garlic

4 tablespoons chopped red shallot

1 teaspoon shrimp paste (*gapi*)

½ cup ground roasted peanuts

First, make the paste: gradually pound the ingredients together using a pestle and mortar, adding one by one, until smooth. Mix paste with minced pork, seasoning with fish sauce and palm sugar. Add egg, coconut cream, kaffir lime leaves and coriander. Rest, refrigerated, for an hour or two.

Clean sausage casing by rubbing with a little salt and vinegar. Rinse in running water. Feed one end of the casing onto a tap and run water through it. If there are any holes in the casing, discard the offending piece. Fit a wide nozzle to a piping bag, wipe the nozzle with a little oil and feed the casing onto it. Tie a knot in the end of the casing and slowly force the pork mixture into it. When filled, knot the other end. Rest for an hour or so.

Mix grated coconut, sugar and tea leaves, then pour into a foil-lined wok. Curl the sausage onto a banana leaf, if using, and place in a bamboo steamer inside the wok. Cover the wok. Turn the heat to high, and when the coconut mixture begins to smoke, turn it down. Smoke gently for 25 minutes, replenishing the mixture or turning up the heat if it stops smoking.

Rest for at least 20 minutes before slicing. Serve with ginger, coriander sprigs and scuds.

SMOKED FISH PASTE

pla naem

This is the traditional accompaniment to smoked sausage. The fish should be smoky, while the piquancy of fresh shallots and the citrus of the Asian citron or mandarin should balance and toy with the fish.

200 g (6 oz) Smoked Fish (page 179)

4 tablespoons Asian citron, mandarin or orange juice

1 tablespoon pickled garlic syrup

1 teaspoon salt

1 tablespoon palm sugar

100 g (3 oz) shredded boiled pork skin – ideally homemade (see page 169)

1 tablespoon ground roasted peanuts

6 red shallots, sliced

2 tablespoons sliced pickled garlic

1 tablespoon shredded Asian citron or mandarin zest

200 g (6 oz) ground roasted rice

6–10 'betel' leaves

1 long red or green chilli, shredded

1 tablespoon coriander leaves

Scrape the flesh from the smoked fish, making sure no bones remain. Moisten fish with citrus juice and pickled garlic syrup. Season with salt and palm sugar. Combine with pork skin, peanuts, shallots, pickled garlic and citrus zest. Finish with the ground roasted rice. Serve on 'betel' leaves, sprinkled with chilli and coriander.

GROUND FISH

pla bon

This is a very ancient snack, the original of which goes back to the mid-seventeenth century and the court of King Narai the Great. The ladies of the court were experimental and inventive. A basic dried fish paste – not dissimilar to one that might be added to a curry paste or to a *nahm prik* relish – they deep-fried instead. Any recipes from that time which specify white sugar denote wealth, and a recipe like this indicates the truly exotic tastes and opulent nature of Thai cooking.

200 g (6 oz) fish fillets – traditionally *pla chorn*, but salmon makes
   a good alternative

1 tablespoon salt

1 cup oil

3 slices galangal

3–5 tablespoons white sugar

large pinch of salt

½ cup deep-fried shallots

4 red shallots, sliced

3 tablespoons fish roe (perhaps salmon, which is sumptuous if not
   exactly authentic) – optional

Roast or grill fish until well cooked. Grind or pound with the tablespoon of salt until it looks like breadcrumbs. Heat the oil (ideally that used to deep-fry shallots),

add galangal slices to perfume it, then pour in the fish crumbs. Stir constantly over a medium heat – the stirring prevents the fish from scorching and clumping. When the fish has lost its raw smell and is golden, strain and smooth the crumbs over absorbent paper to cool. (At this stage, the cooked fish crumbs will keep for a few days unrefrigerated.)

When ready to serve, combine fish crumbs with sugar, the pinch of salt and the deep-fried shallots in a small bowl. The mixture should taste equally sweet and salty – adjust, if necessary. Finish with fresh shallots and roe, if using.

Serve surrounded by:
- segmented and sliced fruit – mandarin, pomelo, watermelon, half-ripe mango
- 'betel' leaves
- sprigs of coriander.

FOOD WITH DRINKS

While Buddhism recommends abstention from alcohol, many Thai men discreetly ignore this tenet of their faith. Groups of men gather in restaurants, nightclubs or even in the street to drink whisky, gossip and eat. So much so that Thailand is the fifth-ranking country, per capita, in consumption of alcohol. Mostly Mekong or Santip whisky, with soda and plenty of ice, is drunk.

There is a whole style of Thai food prepared specifically as an accompaniment to drinking, called *gap klaem*. These dishes are rarely eaten with rice but they line the stomach, and plate after plate arrives to be eagerly consumed by ever-more-appreciative drinkers. *Gap klaem* are always intensely flavoured and include such dishes as stir-fries with incendiary chillies, garlic and holy basil ('drunken stir-fry') – hot enough to sober up the dead; sliced grilled beef with chilli sauce ('crying tiger'); and the perennial favourite, grilled chicken.

Other dishes that may appear are Chiang Mai cured pork (*naem*), served with young ginger and peanuts; *miang*; a sour orange curry with water mimosa; an array of hot and sour soups; and fish simmered over coals. Salads are especially welcomed – of crisp smoked fish and shredded green mango; salted or thousand-year-old duck eggs dressed with ginger; *larp* of various kinds; or marinated prawns (shrimp) with coriander, garlic and a stupefying amount of chopped chillies.

All these are single-plate dishes: they are not shared and people order individually, although the Thai will still eat together. There is also no assumption that rice will be served with them – but it might be.

GROUND FISH (page 499)

MARINATED PRAWNS

gung dong

Some Thai prefer to eat these prawns just briefly marinated, in effect raw. Others prefer longer, so the acid can 'cure' the prawns. All shellfish can be treated in this way.

2–3 tablespoons lime juice

10 bird's eye chillies (scuds), bruised

3 garlic cloves, sliced

2 tablespoons fish sauce

large pinch of castor (superfine) sugar – optional

100 g (3 oz) peeled uncooked prawns (shrimp), chilled

handful of mixed mint and coriander leaves

Combine lime juice, chillies and garlic with fish sauce; stir in sugar, if using, until dissolved. Pour over prawns and marinate for about 5 minutes before sprinkling with mint and coriander.

Serve with icy-cold beer.

MUSSELS WITH CHILLI JAM

hoi malaeng puu nahm prik pao

Almost any seafood can be cooked in this way, but most Thai prefer mussels or, at a pinch, clams. I find it best to cook the mussels before adding the chilli jam, which all too easily catches and burns.

2–3 tablespoons stock or water

200 g (6 oz) mussels, scrubbed and debearded

1 stalk lemongrass, bruised

3–4 slices galangal

2 kaffir lime leaves, torn

1 teaspoon palm sugar

1 tablespoon fish sauce

1 tablespoon tamarind water

2 tablespoons Chilli Jam (page 200)

1 long red or green chilli, diagonally sliced and deseeded

handful of Thai basil leaves

In a wok, bring stock or water to the boil. Add mussels, lemongrass, galangal and half the lime leaves. Cover and simmer until the mussels have opened. (Discard any that remain closed.) Season with palm sugar, fish sauce and tamarind water. When dissolved, stir in chilli jam. Finish with the remainder of the lime leaves, and the chilli and basil.

GRILLED CHICKEN

gai yang

This is the basic recipe for a dish that allows great variation. Some cooks add a large pinch of powdered turmeric to the paste; others add some fresh lemongrass or a little black pepper. To my mind, the best version comes from a village called Si Saket, in the north-east of Thailand.

> 3 coriander roots, scraped and chopped
> pinch of salt
> 4 garlic cloves, peeled
> 10 white peppercorns
> 1 small chicken – about 400 g (12 oz)
> 3 tablespoons fish sauce
> large pinch of palm sugar

> **sauce**
> ½ cup scraped and chopped coriander root
> pinch of salt
> ½ cup garlic cloves, peeled
> 1 cup long red chillies, deseeded if desired
> 4 cups white vinegar
> 3 cups white sugar
> 4 cups water
> large pinch of salt

Using a pestle and mortar, pound coriander roots, salt, garlic and peppercorns into a fine paste. Cut chicken in half along the breastbone. Flatten out, wash and dry. Work in the paste, fish sauce and sugar and leave to marinate for a few hours.

For the sweet chilli sauce, pound coriander root, salt, garlic and chillies into a paste. Combine vinegar, sugar, water and salt in a pot and bring to the boil. Add paste and stir to dissolve. Simmer sauce until reduced by half, skimming as necessary, then set aside to cool.

Chargrill chicken for about 15–20 minutes, turning regularly. Serve with a bowl of the sauce.

Eat with Raw Vegetables (page 380), especially cucumber.

GRILLED LIVER

dap warn

In Thailand, pork liver is favoured; however, to me, this tastes too much of what it is, so I suggest calves' liver. The Thai also tend to grill liver until well done, but again this is a matter of personal preference.

200 g (6 oz) calves' liver

½–1 teaspoon roasted chilli powder

2 tablespoons lime juice

1 tablespoon fish sauce

handful of mint leaves

handful of holy basil leaves – optional

3 tablespoons chopped spring (green) onion

1 tablespoon ground roasted rice

Clean liver and cut into ½ cm (¼ in) slices. Dip in and out of gently simmering water several times, until just cooked. Combine chilli with lime juice and fish sauce. Dress the liver with this and add the remaining ingredients.

Serve with Raw Vegetables (page 380), such as cucumber and cabbage.

GRILLED BEEF

neua yang

This grilled beef is simple and honest. In Thailand, when accompanied by this chilli sauce, it is called 'crying tiger' (*seua hay rong*) – no doubt a reference to the heat of the sauce, which sometimes includes ground roasted rice and shredded *pak chii farang* (long-leaf coriander).

150 g (5 oz) rump steak

3–4 tablespoons light soy sauce

sauce

3 tablespoons lime juice

2 tablespoons fish sauce

pinch of white sugar – optional

very large pinch of roasted chilli powder

1 red shallot, finely sliced

1 tablespoon chopped coriander leaves

Clean the beef and remove excess fat, as preferred. Marinate in the light soy sauce for an hour or so. Drain and pat dry.

To make the chilli sauce, combine ingredients and check seasoning: the sauce should taste hot, sour and salty.

Grill beef over a high heat for 5–10 minutes, until cooked to the preferred degree, then rest for the same amount of time in a warm place. Slice and serve with the chilli sauce.

SEMI-DRIED BEEF

neua dtaet dtiaw

3 coriander roots, scraped and chopped

pinch of salt

4 garlic cloves, peeled

10 white peppercorns

200 g (6 oz) rump of beef – but in fact any cut of beef will do

2 tablespoons light soy sauce

a little oyster sauce – optional

2 tablespoons white sugar

a splash of whisky – authentically Mekong or, more conveniently, bourbon
or even sherry

oil for deep-frying

Using a pestle and mortar, pound coriander roots, salt, garlic and peppercorns into a fine paste.

Cut beef across the grain into slices about ½ cm (¼ in) thick. In a bowl, combine paste with light soy sauce, oyster sauce (if using), sugar and whisky or sherry. Work this marinade into the beef slices and leave for several hours. Dry in the sun for at least a day, or in a warm, airy place for 2 nights and 1 day; the beef should not be *too* dry.

Deep-fry in plenty of oil over a moderate heat, then drain and serve with a chilli sauce, normally Siracha (see page 145).

HEAVENLY BEEF

neua sawarn

This is great served with chilli sauce and an ice-cold beer. I remember catching an upcountry train in Thailand many years ago – in fact, on my first trip there – and being impressed that, even in third class, such delicious food as this was available.

1 tablespoon scraped and chopped coriander root

large pinch of salt

2 tablespoons chopped garlic

15 white peppercorns

500 g (1 lb) rump of beef

4 tablespoons palm sugar

3 tablespoons light soy sauce

2 tablespoons coriander seeds, lightly crushed

oil for deep-frying

Using a pestle and mortar, pound coriander root, salt, garlic and peppercorns into a fine paste. Cut beef into slices ½ cm (¼ in) thick. Work paste into beef, along with sugar and light soy sauce, then marinate for 3 hours.

Press crushed coriander seeds into the beef, then leave to dry in the sun (or a warm place) until almost, but not quite dry – normally around 1 full day.

Deep-fry in moderately hot oil until golden and fragrant.

STIR-FRIED CRISP FISH WITH HOLY BASIL AND CHILLIES

pla grop pat pet

1 *pla grop* (crisp fish) – preferably homemade from trout or perch (see page 168)

3 tablespoons oil or rendered pork fat

1 teaspoon palm sugar

1–2 tablespoons fish sauce

3 long red or green chillies, diagonally sliced

5 kaffir lime leaves, shredded

1 tablespoon shredded *grachai* (wild ginger) – optional

handful of Thai basil or holy basil leaves, deep-fried

paste

10–15 dried long red chillies, deseeded, soaked and drained

large pinch of salt

1 tablespoon chopped galangal

3 tablespoons chopped lemongrass

1 teaspoon shredded kaffir lime leaves

3 tablespoons chopped red shallot

2 tablespoons chopped garlic

1 rounded teaspoon shrimp paste (*gapi*)

First, make the paste: gradually pound the ingredients together using a pestle and mortar, adding one by one, until smooth.

Remove bones from the fish, if preferred. Heat oil or rendered pork fat and fry paste until fragrant over a medium heat. Season with palm sugar and fish sauce. Add fish and fry, incorporating the paste but taking care not to break up the fish. Add chillies, kaffir lime leaves and *grachai*, if using. Serve sprinkled with the deep-fried basil. This stir-fry should taste hot, aromatic and salty.

STIR-FRIED MINCED BEEF WITH CHILLIES AND HOLY BASIL

neua pat bai grapao

Serve this rustic stir-fry with plenty of steamed rice and a bowl of fish sauce spiked with finely sliced chillies, garlic and a squeeze of lime juice. Often this dish is topped with a fried egg.

3 garlic cloves, peeled

large pinch of salt

2 long red or green chillies

4 bird's eye chillies (scuds)

1 tablespoon oil or rendered pork fat

100 g (3 oz) minced beef, chicken or pork

3 tablespoons stock or water

large pinch of white sugar

1 tablespoon light soy sauce

1 tablespoon dark soy sauce

handful of holy basil leaves

Pound garlic, salt and both kinds of chillies into a paste.

Heat a wok over a very high heat. Add oil or rendered pork fat, then fry the paste for a minute. Add minced meat and continue to stir-fry for a minute. Add stock, sugar and both kinds of soy sauce. Sprinkle over the holy basil and serve.

THREE WAYS WITH CHICKEN

gai sahm yang

This has nothing to do with chicken; and I remember several years ago ordering this dish, in my rudimentary Thai, and being disappointed and confused. I thought it should have included at least some chicken, as the name suggested, but my then-inadequate Thai prevented me from saying so.

5 lemongrass stalks, finely sliced

5 tablespoons shredded young ginger

5 large red shallots, sliced

2 limes, diced

10 coarsely chopped bird's eye chillies (scuds)

½ cup dried prawns (shrimp)

½ cup deep-fried cashew nuts

Arrange all ingredients in separate piles on a platter and serve.

STIR-FRIED QUAIL EGGS WITH EGGPLANTS

pat pet kai nok gradtaa

oil for deep-frying

10 quail eggs, boiled and shelled

large pinch of palm sugar

1–2 tablespoons fish sauce

4 long green eggplants, cut into 2 cm (1 in) discs

   or 5 apple eggplants, cut into sixths and steeped in salted water

2 long red or green chillies, diagonally sliced and, if preferred, deseeded

paste

7–10 dried long red chillies, deseeded, soaked and drained

pinch of salt

2 teaspoons chopped galangal

3 tablespoons chopped lemongrass

1 teaspoon kaffir lime zest

1 tablespoon chopped red shallot

2 teaspoons chopped garlic

1 teaspoon shrimp paste (*gapi*)

First, make the paste: gradually pound the ingredients together using a pestle and mortar, adding one by one, until smooth.

Heat oil in a wok and deep-fry eggs until golden. Remove eggs and drain off all but 3 tablespoons of oil. Add paste and fry until fragrant. Season with sugar and fish sauce. Add eggplants and simmer until cooked – about 4 minutes. Return quail eggs to wok and add chilli.

Check seasoning: this dish should taste slightly salty, nutty from the eggplants and hot.

STIR-FRIED WATER MIMOSA WITH MINCED PORK AND PEANUTS

pat pak grachet

1 tablespoon oil

1 garlic clove, minced with a pinch of salt

2 cups cleaned water mimosa or choy sum

3 tablespoons stock

50 g (2 oz) minced fatty pork

pinch of castor (superfine) sugar

1–2 tablespoons light soy sauce

1 tablespoon roasted peanuts

Heat a wok. Add oil, garlic and water mimosa or choy sum. Stir-fry until garlic is golden and the greens have wilted. Moisten with stock, turn down the heat and simmer for a moment. Add pork, stirring to prevent it clumping. Season with sugar and soy, then add peanuts and serve. This stir-fry should taste nutty, slightly sour and salty.

SALAD OF DEEP-FRIED RICE WITH SAVOURY MINCE

yam kao tort naem sot

This salad is a popular dish to serve with alcohol.

3 tablespoons Red Curry Paste (page 149)

1 cup cooked jasmine rice

1 egg, lightly beaten

3–4 tablespoons fish sauce

oil for deep-frying

2 tablespoons stock

pinch of salt

100 g (3 oz) minced fatty pork

2 tablespoons lime juice

1–2 tablespoons fish sauce

large pinch of roasted chilli powder

2 tablespoons shredded boiled pork skin – ideally homemade (see page 169)

3 red shallots, sliced

handful of mixed mint and coriander leaves

1 tablespoon shredded *pak chii farang* (long-leaf coriander) – optional

1 tablespoon deep-fried dried bird's eye chillies

1 tablespoon coarsely ground deep-fried peanuts

1 small cucumber, sliced

Mix curry paste, rice and egg together. Season with fish sauce. Form into small dumplings, about 1 cm (½ in) in diameter, and deep-fry until golden.

Heat stock with salt and add minced pork, stirring to prevent it clumping. Cook for about 2–3 minutes, then season with lime juice and fish sauce. Add chilli powder, pork skin, shallots, mint, coriander and *pak chii farang*, if using.

Break open the rice dumplings and arrange on a plate. Cover with the savoury mince and serve sprinkled with chillies and peanuts. Accompany with a plate of cucumber slices.

Every town and village in Thailand, no matter what size, has a market. They are at the core of the community – the place to find goods and provisions, the source of information and the font of all gossip. Without them, the Thai simply would not have as much enjoyment of life as they do.

Walking through a market in upcountry Thailand is always an adventure. A cornucopia unfolds in front of you, spilling out onto the ground – and usually underfoot: prawns of various sizes and crabs, miraculously still alive, catfish and frogs urgently convulsing with the fury of life, soon to be brutally shortened. The most remarkable fresh, succulent and young vegetables offer a gentle respite as stall upon stall reveals different types of ginger, young white galangal and hands of *grachai*. Siamese watercress, water mimosa, asparagus appear so moist, fresh and green, as if just picked – in stark contrast to the oppressive humidity that wilts the people. There is fruit of staggering variety, from the familiar apple and lychee to the obscure snake-skin pear and the heavenly, malodorous durian. Fresh coconuts are husked, crushed and squeezed, and bucket after bucket is filled with pickles, ginger, garlic, mustard greens and bamboo shoots. There are prepared goods like curry pastes (which is a blessing indeed), made freshly that morning; shrimp pastes from various parts of Thailand, each with its own discernible taste; rice of differing vintages, regions and varieties; fish sauce and bags of sugar – the storehouse of life at hand.

Along the alleys of markets and the canals, there are always stalls selling prepared food to other stallholders, shoppers and dawdlers. A whole meal, from curries to soups and relishes, can be bought, making Thai cooking an easy pleasure. While such convenient purchases are made, a snack or two is always eaten . . .

Food of this kind is strongly flavoured, not using rare ingredients that have been delicately seasoned, but rough and rank ones, rudely dressed. These are bitingly pungent and raw flavours, needing only a small bowl mixed with rice.

GREEN PAPAYA SALAD WITH SWEET CRISPY PORK

som dtam malakor gap muu warn grop

This dish is one of the most loved in the Thai repertoire. Originally a market-place snack or lunchtime dish from the north-east, it proved so irresistible that it is now eaten throughout Thailand and has become a signature dish. Fermented fish sauce is sometimes used to season the papaya rather than fish sauce. A wedge of lime can also be included in the paste before adding the green papaya. In the markets of Bangkok, I have even seen some hawkers slice a ripe hog plum into the mortar.

The traditional method of shredding a green papaya is quite easy. The hard, green fruit is peeled with a sharp knife, then it is held in one hand while the other cuts and shreds the flesh, before it is sliced away from the fruit. A more modern and convenient method is to use a mandoline.

3 garlic cloves, peeled

pinch of salt

4–6 bird's eye chillies (scuds)

1 heaped tablespoon roasted peanuts

2 tablespoons dried prawns (shrimp)

1 slice lime – optional

4 cherry tomatoes, quartered

2 snake beans, cut into 1 cm (½ in) lengths

1 cup shredded green papaya

2 tablespoons palm sugar

1 tablespoon lime juice

1 tablespoon tamarind water

1–2 tablespoons fish sauce

sweet crispy pork

1 cup palm sugar

½ cup sweet soy sauce (*kecap manis*)

3 tablespoons oyster sauce

pinch of salt

pinch of ground star anise – optional

200 g (6 oz) pork neck

oil for deep-frying

Prepare the sweet crispy pork a day in advance. Make a syrup by simmering the palm sugar with soy sauce, oyster sauce, salt and star anise (if using) until quite reduced – about 3 minutes. Be careful – the sugar and oyster sauce burn easily. Cool. Slice pork into 5 cm × 2 cm (2 in × 1 in) pieces and marinate overnight in this syrup. Dry on a rack for a day until almost dry.

For the salad, pound garlic with salt and chillies in a pestle and mortar. Add peanuts and dried prawns, and pound into a coarse paste. Add lime, if using, then add cherry tomatoes and beans to the mortar, and gently mash together. Add green papaya and bruise. Season with palm sugar, lime juice, tamarind water and fish sauce.

Deep-fry the pork in plenty of oil over a medium heat until mahogany-coloured and fragrant, and serve alongside the salad.

Eat with wedges of cabbage, cucumber slices and snake beans. Coconut Rice (page 514) is also a classic accompaniment to this salad.

GREEN PAPAYA SALAD WITH SWEET CRISPY PORK (page 511)

COCONUT RICE

hung kao man gati

This rice is usually served alongside Green Papaya Salad (page 511), although occasionally it is eaten with a hot curry garnished with a few pickled or salted condiments. It is not served instead of plain cooked rice at a normal meal, for its richness might cloy and interfere with the balance of the dishes.

Following is a traditional method of cooking coconut rice, although now many cooks simply stir a few tablespoons of coconut cream through freshly cooked rice. Some also include a handful of sticky rice (soaked overnight), which imparts a more toothsome texture.

Very often coconut rice is served sprinkled with deep-fried shallots, while the Muslim version includes ginger water, cloves, cardamom and cassia bark, making a delicious counterfoil to the spicy heat of southern Thai food.

> 2 cups jasmine rice
> 2 cups coconut cream
> 1 cup water
> pinch of salt
> 1–2 tablespoons white sugar or palm sugar
> 2 pandanus leaves, tied in small knots

Rinse rice, then soak in plenty of water for at least 2 hours. Drain rice and put into a heavy-based pan. Mix coconut cream with 1 cup water. Add salt and sugar, stir until dissolved, then add pandanus leaves. Pour this over the rice and bring slowly to the boil, stirring to prevent cream separating. When it has just come to the boil, cover and turn down the heat. After 15 minutes, check to make sure it is not burning. If cooked, remove from the heat; if not, stir and leave on the heat for another minute or two. Before serving, allow rice to rest off the heat for another 5 minutes.

POMELO SALAD

dtam som oo

In the north, pomelo is sometimes used in a salad similar to the classic green papaya salad, with the addition of lemongrass. Shredded cucumber, green mango, green beans and even jackfruit are also often prepared in the same manner.

> 1 garlic clove, peeled
> pinch of salt
> 3–7 bird's eye chillies (scuds)
> 1 tablespoon ground dried prawns (shrimp)
> ¼ teaspoon land crab paste (*nahm bpuu*) – optional
> 1 stalk lemongrass, finely sliced

2 apple eggplants, sliced

1 cup pomelo segments, peeled and torn into pieces

a few small cooked prawns (shrimp), peeled and deveined

2 teaspoons palm sugar

1 tablespoon fish sauce

1 tablespoon lime juice

Pound garlic with salt and chillies in a pestle and mortar. Add dried prawns and pound until you have a coarse paste. Add crab paste, if using, lemongrass and apple eggplants. Mash together carefully. Add pomelo and fresh prawns. Season with palm sugar, fish sauce and lime juice.

Eat with:

— Raw Vegetables (page 380), especially 'betel' leaves, Chinese cabbage and green beans

— Deep-fried Pork Skin (page 400)

— Grilled Chicken (page 503)

— steamed white sticky rice (see page 172).

PINEAPPLE AND WHITE GUAVA SALAD

som dtam sapparot

Many kinds of fruit can be used in this salad from upcountry Thailand: plantain or star fruit with dried prawns; or banana blossom with ground fish.

½ small pineapple

1 white guava

3 garlic cloves, peeled

pinch of salt

5–10 bird's eye chillies (scuds)

1 tablespoon castor (superfine) sugar

1 tablespoon fermented fish sauce (*nahm pla raa*) – optional

2 tablespoons fish sauce – or more, to taste, if not using fermented fish sauce

Peel and remove the core from the pineapple. Wash and then coarsely chop the flesh – there should be about 150 g (5 oz). Peel the guava and shred coarsely.

Pound garlic with salt, then add chillies and pound into a coarse paste. Add pineapple and guava and mash gently. Season with sugar and fish sauce(s).

Serve with a selection from:

— Raw Vegetables (page 380), such as 'betel' leaves, lotus shoots, cabbage and green beans

— Salted Beef (page 401)

— Semi-dried Beef (page 505).

BLACK FRIED SQUID

pla meuk pat

This dish comes from the deep south of Thailand, around the Muslim province of Satun. The use of squid ink is quite unusual; in fact, I haven't come across it in any other Thai recipe. Carefully extract the ink sac when cleaning the squid. If the squid is already cleaned, then purchase a small sachet of ink separately – about a teaspoon is enough.

300 g (9 oz) squid

4 red shallots, sliced

pinch of salt

2 tablespoons oil

large pinch of roasted chilli powder

1 tablespoon castor (superfine) sugar

1–2 tablespoons tamarind water

1 spring (green) onion, finely sliced

handful of coriander leaves

Clean the squid, reserving its ink. Pound the shallots with the salt.

Heat oil and fry shallots until golden, then add squid, the reserved ink and the chilli powder and cook until almost burnt. Reduce the heat and season with sugar and tamarind. Serve sprinkled with spring onion and coriander.

MUSSELS WITH THAI BASIL

hoi malaeng puu bai horapha

200 g (6 oz) mussels

2 stalks lemongrass

½ cup chicken stock

1 small bunch Thai basil, chopped

Clean and debeard the mussels. Add lemongrass to stock, bring to the boil and steam mussels, covered, until they open. (Discard any that remain closed.) Sprinkle with Thai basil and serve.

SMOKED CHIANG MAI SAUSAGE

sai ouah

Sausages are popular throughout Thailand. There are many variations: those from the east are sometimes made with beef and liver, while in the north a curry paste might be included.

300 g (9 oz) coarsely minced fatty pork
pinch of salt
large pinch of palm sugar
2 tablespoons soy sauce
1 tablespoon fish sauce
2 tablespoons shredded kaffir lime leaves
handful of chopped coriander leaves
1 metre (3 feet) sausage casing
2 cups grated coconut – in this instance, desiccated will do
1 banana leaf – optional

paste
6–10 dried long red chillies, deseeded, soaked and drained
pinch of salt
3 tablespoons chopped lemongrass
1 tablespoon chopped galangal
3 tablespoons chopped red shallot
2 tablespoons chopped garlic
1 tablespoon chopped long pepper
   or 2 teaspoons ground white pepper and 1 teaspoon ground black pepper
2 cm (1 in) piece of cassia bark, roasted and ground

First, make the paste: gradually pound the ingredients together using a pestle and mortar, adding one by one, until smooth. Combine paste with minced pork, seasoning with salt, sugar, soy sauce and fish sauce. Slap the mixture against the side of the bowl until it becomes firmer and stickier. Check seasoning: it should be salty and hot. Add lime leaves and coriander.

   Scrupulously, but gently, wash the casing inside and out with salted, acidulated water. Dry. Knot one end. Fill a forcing bag with the mixture and squeeze into the casing – the sausage should naturally fall into coils. Knot the other end.

   Put coconut into a foil-lined wok. Place sausage on a banana leaf, if using, and place in a bamboo steamer inside the wok. Cover the wok. Turn the heat to high, and when the coconut begins to smoke, turn it down. Smoke gently for an hour or so, replenishing the coconut or turning up the heat if it stops smoking. Allow to cool.

   This can either be eaten as it is, or reheated by deep-frying in plenty of oil.

Accompany with slices of ginger and sprigs of coriander.

FERMENTED PORK SAUSAGES

sai grop brio

All over the country, there are stalls selling this type of sausage, which can be cooked fresh or fermented. I prefer the latter, but care must be taken during this process. Rice is used as the catalyst for fermenting a whole range of products in Thailand, from bamboo shoots and Siamese watercress to pork and fish.

100 g (3 oz) white sticky rice, soaked overnight

2 metres (6 feet) sausage casing

5 coriander roots, scraped and chopped

2 tablespoons salt

10 garlic cloves, peeled

500 g (1 lb) minced fatty pork

1 tablespoon palm sugar

2–3 tablespoons fish sauce

Drain the rice, steam for 20–25 minutes, then set aside to cool. Scrupulously, but gently, wash the casing inside and out with salted, acidulated water. Dry.

Using a pestle and mortar, pound coriander roots with salt and garlic, add rice and continue pounding until smooth. Alternatively, these ingredients can be combined in a food processor, so long as the coriander roots, salt and garlic are puréed before the rice is added. (This prevents the gluten in the rice from being over-worked and knotting as it purées; if this happens, it is almost impossible to incorporate the rice into the pork and it may be necessary to start again.)

Mix this paste with the pork, making sure it is well combined. Season with palm sugar and, if necessary, fish sauce. Fry a little of the mixture to check the seasoning, and adjust accordingly.

Knot casing at one end. Fill a forcing bag with the mixture and squeeze into the casing, ideally turning or linking the sausages into 5 cm (2 in) lengths. If cooking 'fresh', refrigerate overnight before grilling.

If fermenting, hang the sausages in a warm, airy place for 4–7 days; put a tray underneath, as they tend to weep. The length of time you need to leave them depends on the temperature and the desired degree of sourness: test after the fourth day by grilling one and tasting. Once sufficiently soured, the fermented sausages will then keep for several days refrigerated.

When ready to cook, grill or fry over low to medium heat for around 5 minutes. Allow to cool slightly.

Serve with:

— slices of young ginger and wedges of cabbage

— bird's eye chillies (scuds)

— sprigs of coriander.

CRAB STIR-FRIED WITH CURRY POWDER

bpuu pat pong garee

> 1 male crab – about 500 g (1 lb)
>
> 2 garlic cloves, peeled
>
> pinch of salt
>
> 1 long red chilli
>
> 2 cm (1 in) piece of ginger, peeled
>
> 2 tablespoons oil
>
> 2 heaped tablespoons curry powder
>
> 1 tablespoon fish sauce
>
> pinch of white sugar
>
> 1 egg, lightly beaten
>
> 2–4 tablespoons chicken stock, coconut cream or milk, or water
>
> 1 small bunch spring (green) onions or Asian celery,
>   cut into 2 cm (1 in) lengths – about 1 cup
>
> 1 small pickling onion, sliced
>
> 3 tablespoons chopped coriander leaves

Kill the crab humanely. Clean by lifting off its carapace, scraping out any mustard and roe, and removing its tail. Wash then quarter the crab.

Using a pestle and mortar, pound garlic, salt, chilli and ginger into a rather coarse paste. Heat a wok, add oil and then the paste. When paste is beginning to colour, add curry powder and, when fragrant, season with fish sauce and sugar. Stir in the egg and cook for a moment. Add crab and simmer over a low heat until the crab is done – about 5 minutes – moistening, as necessary, with a little stock, coconut cream or milk, or water. Mix in spring onions or celery and the sliced onion. Check seasoning, then serve sprinkled with chopped coriander.

STEAMED WHITING OR TURBOT WITH CHILLIES AND LIME JUICE

pla neung manao

> 1 whiting or turbot – around 400 g (12 oz)
>
> 4 tablespoons lime juice
>
> 2 tablespoons fish sauce
>
> 2 tablespoons finely chopped Asian celery
>
> 1–2 tablespoons chopped bird's eye chillies (scuds)
>
> 3 tablespoons chopped garlic

Score the fish and steam until just cooked, about 10–12 minutes. Mix lime juice with fish sauce, then stir in celery, chillies and garlic. Pour over the fish and serve.

CRAB STIR-FRIED WITH CURRY POWDER

CHIANG MAI CURED PORK

naem

This cured pork, made by fermenting pork and sticky rice with garlic, is perhaps the most famous preserved meat from Chiang Mai province. The best was made by an old lady called Bpa Yon, who sold her wares near Chiang Mai railway station. Travellers would purchase some *naem* for the journey to Bangkok and soon her fame, and the cured pork, spread throughout Thailand. Although it can be purchased in most Thai food shops, store-bought lacks the robust depth of flavour of homemade. I always make more than is strictly necessary – it lasts as long as it can be resisted.

Curing pork can be an adventure, but should really only be done during the warmer months when the rapid fermentation preserves the meat before it spoils. The bruised chillies release flavour, as well as enzymes that help to stop the meat from spoiling. All utensils must be scrupulously clean.

2 tablespoons salt

2 cups coarsely minced lean pork

½ cup white sticky rice

⅓ cup garlic cloves, pounded

½ teaspoon salt

½ cup shredded boiled pork skin – ideally homemade (see page 169)

5 bird's eye chillies (scuds), bruised

1 or 2 banana leaves – optional

Mix the 2 tablespoons salt into the pork. Press into colander and leave overnight, refrigerated. Steep sticky rice in water overnight.

Next day, remove pork from refrigerator and allow to come to room temperature. Meanwhile, steam rice until cooked (around 20 minutes) and set aside to cool to room temperature.

Purée the garlic with the ½ teaspoon salt and the steamed sticky rice. If using a food processor, purée garlic and salt first, then add rice. Take care not to over-process the rice – although there should be no discernible grains in the purée, otherwise the *naem* will be tough and distasteful. Thoroughly combine the rice purée with pork and shredded pork skin.

Insert the chillies into the meat and wrap in banana leaves or plastic wrap, or force into a plastic container, ensuring that there are no trapped air bubbles. Leave in indirect sun or at warm room temperature for up to a week, checking after 3 and 5 days. When the meat has successfully fermented it will be moist, firm, succulent and sour – and should be stored in the refrigerator, where it will keep for a few weeks.

The traditional Thai way to eat this delicious cured meat is sliced on a plate with slices of ginger, red shallots, scuds, limes, roasted peanuts, raw vegetables and coriander sprigs.

But in the region of its origin there are many other ways of serving it: grilled; mixed in a salad; stir-fried with chanterelles; even *naem* and eggs. *Naem* is one of the best things that can be eaten on a hot day with a cold beer.

STUFFED BAMBOO SHOOTS

nor ouah

This recipe comes from Khun Pen, 'Aunty Moon', who made this dish every day in her restaurant in Chiang Mai. Other stuffings, such as prawns, freshwater fish or the mixture used to make Smoked Chiang Mai Sausage (page 518), can also be used.

4 whole bamboo shoots

4 coriander roots, scraped and chopped

pinch of salt

4 garlic cloves, peeled

100 g (3 oz) minced fatty pork

2–3 tablespoons soy sauce

pinch of palm sugar

½ cup rice flour

3–4 tablespoons hydrolysed lime water

oil for deep-frying

handful of chopped coriander leaves

Clean the bamboo shoots. Keeping the shoots whole, blanch them from a cold-water start, repeating as necessary.

Pound coriander roots, salt and garlic into a paste. Combine this with the pork, slapping the mixture against the side of the bowl until it becomes firmer and stickier. Season with soy sauce and sugar, then divide into four.

From the side, insert a small bamboo skewer into the middle of one of the bamboo shoots. Pull it up to the top third of the shoot and then drag it down to the bottom third. Repeat several times, in effect coarsely shredding the middle portion of the bamboo shoot, yet keeping it intact. This forms a 'cage' into which the meat can be stuffed. Push the ends of the bamboo shoot towards the centre to expand the cage, insert a quarter of the pork mixture, then gently pull the ends of the shoot taut. Repeat with the other shoots.

Make a thick batter with rice flour and lime water. Heat oil in a wok. Roll shoots in batter and deep-fry over a medium heat until the meat is cooked and the batter golden. Remove, drain and serve sprinkled with the chopped coriander.

BREAM STEAMED WITH GINGER, CELERY AND PICKLED PLUMS

pla neung buay king cheun chai

The best type of pickled plums to buy are the plump Chinese ones that are about the size of chestnuts and come in a salty, sour brine.

1 bream – about 400 g (12 oz) – cleaned
½ lime
2 coriander roots, scraped and bruised
½ cup shredded ginger
½ cup shredded Asian celery
6 pickled plums
4 tablespoons pickled plum juice
1 cup chicken stock
pinch of salt
2 tablespoons light soy sauce
pinch of castor (superfine) sugar
handful of coriander leaves

Score the fish on both sides and rub with the lime. Place in a shallow bowl and push coriander roots into its cavity. Cover fish with ginger, celery and pickled plums. Mix pickled plum juice with stock, salt, soy and sugar and pour over fish. Cover and steam for 10–15 minutes. Sprinkle with coriander leaves and serve.

CUCUMBER AND PORK STIR-FRIED WITH EGG

kai pat dtaeng gwa sai muu

100 g (3 oz) pork belly
2 tablespoons oil
2 cloves garlic, crushed with a pinch of salt
1 small cucumber, diagonally cut into chunks about 5 cm × 2 cm (2 in × 1 in)
2 eggs
1 tablespoon fish sauce
1 teaspoon white sugar
large pinch of ground white pepper
handful of coriander leaves

Steam pork belly for 10–15 minutes, allow to cool and then cut into 2 cm (1 in) cubes. Heat oil in a wok and fry garlic until beginning to colour. Add pork and fry for 4 minutes over a high heat. Add cucumber and stir-fry until it begins to turn translucent – about 3 minutes. Add eggs and stir-fry for a further 2 minutes, then season with fish sauce and sugar. Serve sprinkled with pepper and coriander leaves.

BREAM STEAMED WITH GINGER, CELERY AND PICKLED PLUMS

PORK BRAISED WITH STAR ANISE

muu parlow

Cauldrons of this soup are found in almost every market place in Thailand. *Parlow* originates from China, and probably arrived in the nineteenth century with the wave of Chinese migration to Siam.

Pork is most commonly found bubbling away in the large vats. However, duck, chicken and even goose are occasionally prepared in this manner, according to the time of year or the affluence of the area. Whatever the soup is made from, there is a certain comfort in the pervasive aniseed perfume that wafts through a shop in which it is served. Mostly, it is eaten with a plate of rice – in small quantities as a snack or in a larger bowl as a substantial meal.

2 pork hocks

oil for deep-frying

300 g (9 oz) firm bean curd, cut into 2 cm (1 in) cubes

2 coriander roots, scraped and chopped

large pinch of salt

5 cloves garlic, peeled

10 white peppercorns

2 tablespoons oil

2 star anise

5 cm (2 in) piece of cassia bark

2 tablespoons palm sugar

3 tablespoons fish sauce

8 cups stock

2 tablespoons oyster sauce

2 tablespoons sweet soy sauce (*kecap manis*)

4–6 boiled eggs, shelled

5 cloves garlic, unpeeled

2 cm (1 in) piece of ginger, peeled and bruised

handful of coriander leaves

ground white pepper

Bring the hocks to the boil in plenty of salted water. Refresh. Repeat. Dry.

Deep-fry the hocks until they are quite brown. Soak them in water for 5 minutes. Dry and deep-fry again until coloured. (This process makes the skin swell, which helps prevent it stretching and breaking during the long braising, but is also time-consuming. If time or inclination do not permit, then much of this can be left out; some Thai cooks simply deep-fry the hocks to colour before adding to the braise.)

Deep-fry the bean curd until golden.

Using a pestle and mortar, pound coriander roots, salt, garlic and pepper-corns into a paste. Heat the 2 tablespoons of oil in a large pot and fry this paste, with the star anise and cassia, until light golden and fragrant. Season with sugar and fish sauce. Continue to fry for a few more moments, then add stock, oyster sauce and sweet soy sauce. Bring to the boil, add pork hocks and simmer for 1 hour, or until the hocks are just cooked, skimming often. Add bean curd and eggs and continue to simmer for another 10 minutes. Remove from the heat, add garlic and ginger to the pot and rest for 30 minutes to allow the flavours to mature.

To serve, bring back to the boil and sprinkle with coriander leaves and white pepper.

STIR-FRIED BEEF WITH SPICES
neua pat nahm prik pao kaek

1 teaspoon coriander seeds

1 teaspoon cumin seeds

pinch of salt

3–4 tablespoons fish sauce

200 g (6 oz) rump of beef, sliced into strips 5 cm × 2 cm (2 in × 1 in)

1–2 tablespoons oil

2–3 tablespoons Chilli Jam (page 200)

5 tablespoons deep-fried shallots

large pinch–1 teaspoon roasted chilli powder

pinch of ground white pepper

extra 1 tablespoon fish sauce

1 tablespoon chopped coriander leaves

Lightly roast the coriander and cumin seeds, then grind them. Mix with salt and fish sauce, and marinate beef in this for a few hours.

Heat oil in a wok and stir-fry beef until cooked as preferred – about 2–3 minutes for medium-rare. Turn down the heat and add chilli jam and deep-fried shallots, adding a little water if necessary. Season with chilli powder, pepper and extra fish sauce. Check the seasoning: it should be hot, salty, aromatic from the spices, and sweet and nutty from the deep-fried shallots.

Serve sprinkled with chopped coriander leaves.

DEEP-FRIED FISH WITH THREE-FLAVOURED SAUCE

pla tort sahm rot

1 tablespoon oil

½ cup palm sugar

2–3 tablespoons water

2 tablespoons tamarind water

1 tablespoon fish sauce

1 ocean perch or gurnard – about 400 g (12 oz)

1 tablespoon fish sauce or light soy sauce

oil for deep-frying

2 long red chillies, deep-fried

handful of holy basil or Thai basil leaves, deep-fried

paste

1 tablespoon scraped and chopped coriander root

pinch of salt

3 long red or green chillies, deseeded and coarsely chopped

4 garlic cloves, peeled

3 red shallots, peeled

First, make the paste: gradually pound the ingredients together using a pestle and mortar, adding one by one, until smooth. Fry the paste in a tablespoon of oil for several minutes until fragrant. Season with palm sugar, then add 2 or 3 tablespoons of water and simmer until thick. Add tamarind water and fish sauce and continue to simmer until reduced once more. Check the seasoning: the sauce should be sweet, sour, hot and salty.

Marinate the fish in fish sauce or light soy sauce for 10 minutes only. Drain and deep-fry until crisp. To serve, coat the fish with the sauce, crush the chillies then sprinkle them and the basil over the fish.

STEAMED FISH WITH VERMICELLI AND THAI BASIL

pla bae sa

The charcoal brazier this is cooked on, with its fish-shaped tray, is called a *bae sa* and is of Chinese origin. In many restaurants in Thailand, this popular dish cooks slowly over embers, simmering throughout the meal and thus concentrating the flavours. Occasionally the fish is steamed, or even grilled or deep-fried, before the prolonged poaching. This dish is especially popular with hot and sour soups, and sour orange curries.

½ cup dried rice vermicelli

1 silver perch or whiting – about 400 g (12 oz)

2 tablespoons lime juice

large pinch of salt

1 or 2 cabbage leaves

1 tablespoon shredded *grachai* (wild ginger)

4 red shallots, sliced

3 tablespoons sliced lemongrass

1 tablespoon shredded *pak chii farang* (long-leaf coriander)

5–10 bird's eye chillies (scuds) – optional

handful of Thai basil leaves

3 kaffir lime leaves, shredded

3 cups chicken stock

pinch of salt

4 tablespoons tamarind water

2 tablespoons fish sauce

3 tablespoons pickled garlic syrup – optional

Soak the rice vermicelli in water for 5 minutes. Meanwhile, clean the fish and score the flesh on both sides. Rub with lime juice and salt. Line a bowl with cabbage leaves and lay fish on top. Drain vermicelli and cut into roughly 5 cm (2 in) lengths. Mix together *grachai*, shallots, lemongrass, *pak chii farang*, chillies (if using), vermicelli, basil and lime leaves and scatter over fish. Bring stock to the boil and season with salt, tamarind water, fish sauce and pickled garlic syrup, if using. Pour stock over fish and steam for 10–15 minutes, then carefully ease into a serving bowl and pour the broth over the fish.

MADTARBARK

These Muslim pastries are eaten throughout South East Asia. Hawkers offer a variety of fillings, such as lamb (actually mutton) and beef. I like to make the filling mixture quite spicy, although this would not usually be the case in Asia.

100 g (3 oz) Roti dough (⅓ of recipe on page 403)

oil for frying

filling

2 tablespoons chopped red shallot

pinch of salt

1 tablespoon chopped garlic

1 teaspoon coriander seeds, roasted

½ teaspoon cumin seeds, roasted

2 teaspoons curry powder

2 tablespoons oil or ghee

100 g (3 oz) minced skinless chicken thigh fillets

2 tablespoons fish sauce

pinch of white sugar

1 pickling onion, sliced

2 tablespoons chopped spring (green) onion

2 tablespoons chopped coriander leaves

1 egg, lightly beaten

For the filling, make a paste from the shallot, salt, garlic, coriander and cumin seeds and curry powder, using a pestle and mortar. Heat oil or ghee and fry paste until fragrant. Add chicken and cook, stirring to prevent it clumping. Season with fish sauce and sugar: the filling should taste salty and aromatic. Cool, then stir in sliced onion, spring onion and coriander. Mix in the egg.

Roll out the dough until it is very thin (in Asia it is tossed, slapped and stretched by hand to form a paper-thin, elastic film, but this can only be done with a lifetime's experience). Heat oil in a large, heavy pan, add thinly rolled pastry and spread the filling in the centre. Fold the sides of the pastry into the centre and then fold in the flaps at either end to make a parcel. When golden on one side, turn and cook the other side. Remove, cool slightly and then cut into quarters.

Serve with Cucumber Relish (page 402).

CHINESE CHIVE CAKES

kanom guay chai

The stuffing for these cakes can also be made from spring onions or shredded, cooked bamboo shoots.

½ cup tapioca flour

2 tablespoons oil

200 g (6 oz) Chinese chives, cut into 2 cm (1 in) lengths

pinch of salt

pinch of castor (superfine) sugar

pastry

2 cups rice flour

½ cup tapioca flour

¼ cup white sticky rice flour

¼ cup arrowroot flour

1 teaspoon salt

1 tablespoon oil

3 cups water

sauce

4 tablespoons dark soy sauce

dash of vinegar

1 long red chilli, chopped

First, make the pastry: mix flours with salt. Work in oil and then water to form a thick paste. Put the pastry in a pot or wok and stir firmly over a low heat until almost cooked – the pastry will start to become slightly translucent and very sticky. Remove and cool for a few minutes only. Spread the ½ cup of tapioca flour on a board and work into the warm pastry until comparatively firm and clean to touch. Roll into balls 4 cm (1½ in) in diameter and let rest for at least 10 minutes.

Heat oil and fry chives. When wilted, season with salt and sugar. Cool, then drain. Roll out pastry balls into thin discs – about ¼ cm (⅛ in) – and slightly thinner at the edges. Place about 2 tablespoons of the garlic chives in the centre of each disc, fold pastry up and over. Seal, pinching the edges together. Repeat with the rest of the pastry and chives – you should have about 10 cakes.

Steam for 20 minutes, then cool. Often the cakes are reheated by shallow-frying until golden. Combine sauce ingredients and serve with the cakes.

STIR-FRIED SIAMESE WATERCRESS WITH YELLOW BEANS, GARLIC AND CHILLIES

pak bung fai dtaeng

This simple dish can be enhanced with a little shrimp paste and a few small prawns, or with roast duck and fermented bean curd. In Phitsanulok, the night markets specialise in this dish, which is served in a memorable way: a waiter armed with a plate crosses the street and the cook tosses the finished dish from the wok, it flies across the street and lands on the plate – mostly.

2 garlic cloves, peeled

pinch of salt

oil for frying

200 g (6 oz) Siamese watercress

3 tablespoons yellow bean sauce, rinsed

1 long red chilli, crushed

pinch of white sugar

½ cup stock

2 tablespoons light soy sauce

Crush garlic with salt. Heat a wok, add oil and throw in watercress, garlic, yellow beans, chilli and sugar. When wilted, add stock and season with soy sauce. Serve.

STIR-FRIED SIAMESE WATERCRESS WITH YELLOW BEANS, GARLIC AND CHILLIES

CURRY PUFFS

kari buff

These wonderful pastries are sold at virtually every market in Thailand. The more discriminating prefer very small versions, but clearly such connoisseurs have never had to make these little beauties themselves!

Although the preparation may seem daunting initially, it is well worth the effort. The filling can be made in advance. I have always thought that duck and sweet potato would make a delicious alternative to the stuffing recipe given below.

2 coriander roots, scraped and chopped

1 teaspoon salt

3 garlic cloves, peeled

large pinch of ground white pepper

3 tablespoons oil

2 heaped tablespoons curry powder

3 tablespoons white sugar

2 tablespoons light soy sauce

200 g (6 oz) coarsely minced skinless chicken thigh fillets

1 onion, coarsely cubed

500 g (1 lb) boiled potatoes, cooled, peeled and coarsely cubed

a little stock or water

chopped coriander leaves

extra oil for deep-frying

outer pastry

1 tablespoon ghee or butter

2 cups plain (all-purpose) flour

2 tablespoons cornflour (cornstarch)

1 teaspoon salt

1 tablespoon oil

½ cup water

inner pastry

5 tablespoons oil

1 cup plain (all-purpose) flour

1 tablespoon cornflour (cornstarch)

For the filling, make a paste from the coriander roots, salt, garlic and pepper, using a pestle and mortar. Heat oil and fry paste until fragrant and golden. Turn down heat, add curry powder and, when very fragrant, season with sugar and light soy sauce.

Add chicken, onion and potatoes and simmer for about 10 minutes, until onion is cooked and all is tender and mellow. If necessary, moisten with a little stock or water to prevent it drying out and burning. The filling should taste rich, slightly sweet and salty, perfumed by the curry powder; it needs to taste quite strong or the puffs will be bland. Allow to cool, then stir the coriander through.

For outer pastry, rub ghee or butter into flour and cornflour. Rest for 30 minutes. Combine remaining ingredients and work in. Knead until smooth and well incorporated. Rest for at least 30 minutes. Roll into small balls 4 cm (1½ in) in diameter – you should have about 12–16.

For inner pastry, work oil into flour and cornflour. Knead until wet, then rest for 20 minutes or so. Roll into the same number of 2 cm (1 in) balls.

Roll each ball of outside pastry into a disc. Place an inner pastry ball at the top of the disc and, with your fingers, roll the outside pastry over it to make a shape like a cigar. Turn cigar by 90° and, with a rolling pin, flatten from centre out into an elliptical shape. Roll up with your fingers again and then turn another 90°; roll flat with a pin again, keeping the rough oval shape. Repeat turning and rolling up once more, and then leave to rest for a few minutes.

Cut pastry rolls into discs a little more than ½ cm (¼ in) thick. Roll these out into ovals about 6 cm (2½ in) long and 4 cm (1½ in) wide. Place a tablespoon of the stuffing just forward of the centre. Fold pastry over and seal, making a semi-circle. The traditional way to seal the edge is by folding about ½ cm (¼ in) of the edge over itself and crimping to form an attractive, bead-like finish. Refrigerate for about 30 minutes.

Deep-fry in plenty of oil over a medium heat until the pastry is golden and crisp. Serve hot or at room temperature.

CUP CAKES
kanom krok

These delicious little Thai pastries are sold throughout the kingdom. They are eaten as snacks, but frankly make the most excellent desserts. Usually they are sold plain, however some vendors occasionally top them with a few steamed corn kernels and some chopped spring onions; in the palaces of Siam, they were topped with a spoonful of curry, such as *pat prik king* or even a red peanut-based *panaeng* curry.

The correct mould for these cup cakes is a flat, lidded, heavy cast-iron pan with many small hemispheres about 1½ centimetres (¾ inch) in diameter – and like any mould the older and more seasoned it is, the better. This recipe makes about 20 cup cakes. They should be eaten hot, but not straight from the mould as they are molten.

batter

½ cup rice flour

¾ cup water

2 tablespoons cooked jasmine rice

¼ cup finely grated coconut

¼ cup hydrolysed lime water

pinch of salt

topping

2 tablespoons castor (superfine) sugar

pinch–½ teaspoon salt

¾ cup coconut cream

For the batter, sieve flour and mix with about ¼ cup of the water to form a malleable paste. Knead until firm but elastic. Allow to rest for 30 minutes, then combine with remaining batter ingredients and blend in a food processor until fine.

For the topping, stir sugar and salt into the coconut cream until dissolved.

Oil the mould, heat over a medium flame and then oil again; traditionally, rendered pork fat was used, but an oiled cloth will suffice. Carefully pour in the batter, filling the hemispheres three-quarters full (canny Thai cooks use two old teapots to dispense a steady, even stream of batter). Cover with the lid and cook over a medium heat until the sides have firmed and are beginning to colour – about 2 minutes.

Pour a tablespoon of the topping over each cake, cover again and cook for another 2 minutes or so.

Remove from the mould with a spoon. Serve hot – and serve a lot.

SOUTHERN MUSLIM CHICKEN

gai gorla

This dish can be made with liver, fish or even large clams instead of chicken. You'll need to start preparations a day in advance.

1 spatchcock, poussin or small chicken, about 400–500 g (12 oz–1 lb)

2 cups coconut cream

2 tablespoons palm sugar

2 tablespoons fish sauce

1 tablespoon tamarind water

SOUTHERN MUSLIM CHICKEN, SERVED WITH STEAMED EGGS (page 388)

paste

7 dried long red chillies, deseeded, soaked and chopped

1 tablespoon scraped and chopped coriander root

5 tablespoons chopped red shallot

5 tablespoons chopped garlic

5 tablespoons chopped ginger

5 tablespoons grated coconut

large pinch of salt

2 tablespoons roasted peanuts – optional

marinade

1 tablespoon chopped garlic

1 tablespoon chopped red shallot

large pinch of salt

1 tablespoon chopped ginger

1 teaspoon scraped and chopped coriander root

large pinch of ground white pepper

4 tablespoons coconut cream

For the paste, lay out chopped chilli, coriander root, shallot, garlic, ginger and coconut in a warm place to dry for a day.

For the marinade, pound the garlic, shallot, salt, ginger, coriander root and pepper into a paste, then add the coconut cream. Cut down the breastbone of the chicken and flatten, removing excess bones. Wash and dry, then marinate overnight.

Next day, pound all the paste ingredients together until smooth. Heat the 2 cups coconut cream and, when well separated, add paste and fry until fragrant, stirring constantly, over a low heat. Season with sugar, fish sauce and tamarind water: it should taste rich, smoky, salty and sweet.

Grill chicken until it colours and the marinade smells cooked. Dip chicken into the coconut curry and return to the grill. Repeat, so that the chicken slowly cooks and its curry coating caramelises, forming a crust.

Serve with:

- pickled ginger
- sprigs of coriander
- Steamed Eggs (page 388)
- Cucumber Relish (page 402).

Rice feeds the Thai from dawn until dusk and beyond. Breakfast is sometimes simply leftover rice simmered in water or stock to make rice soup; lunch may be little more than fried or seasoned rice enlivened with a pungent relish; and long evenings often end with a bowl of easily digestible rice soup or porridge.

SEASONED RICE *klut gap kao*

Seasoned rice is a truly ancient Thai dish. It uses ingredients always at hand in the Thai kitchen – shrimp paste, dried prawns or fish, garlic, shallots and green mango. Originally it must have been just fresh warm rice put on a plate and mixed with a spoonful of fresh and fragrant shrimp paste and a few aromatics, then seasoned with lime juice, and perhaps palm sugar and fish sauce. The method has remained simple.

Traditionally, shrimp paste is the main seasoning in seasoned rice, but it is not used heavily, just enough to perfume the rice. A basic garlic paste might be added to enhance the dish, with perhaps a little scraped coriander root or a slice of galangal, and sometimes ground dried prawns, smoked and dried fish (*pla grop*, *pla salit* or *pla haeng*), or prawn tomalley. Occasionally, the pastes are briefly fried in a wok before being mixed with the rice: this invigorates the shrimp paste and softens its flavour. Sometimes a leftover *nahm prik* will form the base and most relishes, especially Nahm Prik of Fresh Tamarind, Prawns and Pork (page 202), Embarking Relish (page 204) and Seasoned Prawn Relish (page 220), are ideal; and their relevant accompaniments make appropriate garnishes for the rice. Such relishes or pastes are thoroughly mixed into warm rice – traditionally with the hands, which would often be moistened with a little oil to prevent the grains sticking – and then the aromatic ingredients are carefully incorporated to ensure they maintain their texture. These might include sliced red shallots, sliced garlic or shredded ginger, along with some shredded tart fruit, such as green mango. Crisp-fried dried prawns, deep-fried dried bird's eye chillies, chopped fresh scuds, salted duck eggs and Chinese Dried Shredded Pork (page 550). Traditionally the remnants from rendering pork fat, the scratchings, were sometimes added, moistened with a little of the fat itself, but now sliced cooked pork meat is more commonly used.

The rice is then seasoned with lime juice. Taste the rice before adding any fish sauce or sugar: most of the ingredients are either quite salty or sweet, so these are not always required. After seasoning, the rice is usually pressed into a small, wet Chinese soup bowl and unmoulded onto an individual plate, with sliced raw vegetables – such as cucumber, 'betel' leaves, sprigs of coriander and Thai basil – on the side. Sweet and textured condiments often accompany this delicious rice: Prawn Crackers (page 542), Sweet Pork (page 542) and Crisp Pork Sheets (page 543). More elaborate versions of seasoned rice merge with the classic Chinese and Muslim braised chicken and rice dishes, especially in the south of Thailand.

RICE SEASONED WITH SHRIMP PASTE

kao klut gapi

Mom Leuang Dterb Chomsai was a famous cook during the middle of the twentieth century. She was from a family renowned for its culinary distinction and helped to promote Thai cooking overseas. Although she followed traditional practices, Mom Dterb attempted to modernise Thai cooking and make it more accessible, especially for those living outside Thailand. She suggests this dish might also include some shredded green mango, ginger or *grachai* (wild ginger) – and crisp-fried whole dried prawns or *pla grop* (crisp fish) as possible substitutes for the crispy fish cake.

This recipe makes enough for 2 people.

4 tablespoons oil

1 tablespoon minced garlic

1 tablespoon shrimp paste (*gapi*)

2 cups warm, freshly cooked jasmine rice

½ cup Sweet Pork (1 quantity of recipe on page 542)

1 large Crispy Fish Cake (page 393)

¼ cup ground dried prawns (shrimp)

3 tablespoons sliced red shallots

2 tablespoons lime juice

Heat oil in a wok or pan. Add garlic and fry until golden. Stir in shrimp paste and, when fragrant, add rice and mix through. Add sweet pork, crispy fish cake, dried prawns and shallots; when everything is incorporated, season with lime juice.

RICE SEASONED WITH PRAWN AND TOMALLEY

kao klut man gung

Traditionally, dried prawns were coarsely ground and fried with a tablespoon of sugar before being added to this recipe. However, fresh prawns can be used instead.

This recipe makes 1 serving.

1 coriander root, scraped and chopped

pinch of salt

2 garlic cloves, peeled

pinch of ground white pepper

3 uncooked prawns (shrimp), unpeeled

oil for frying

1 tablespoon castor (superfine) sugar

3 tablespoons fish sauce

1 cup warm, freshly cooked jasmine rice

3 red shallots, sliced

½ cup shredded green mango or *madan* (sour cucumber)

1–3 bird's eye chillies (scuds), finely sliced

1 tablespoon pork scratchings (see page 171) – optional

1 tablespoon deep-fried garlic

squeeze of lime juice

Make a paste from the coriander root, salt, garlic and pepper, using a pestle and mortar. Peel, devein and mince the prawns, reserving any tomalley from their heads. Heat oil and fry paste until golden and fragrant. Add tomalley and fry until deep red in colour, then add minced prawns. Season with sugar and fish sauce, and simmer until cooked – about a minute or so. This prawn paste should taste rich, salty and sweet. Combine with all remaining ingredients, seasoning to taste with lime juice.

SEASONED RICE WITH CHILLI JAM, SALTED DUCK EGG AND SMOKED FISH

kao klut rajchagarn thii hok

This recipe, attributed to Mom Leuang Bong Malakul, comes from a dusty memorial book, where it is more poetically called 'Seasoned Rice in the Style of the Sixth Reign'. She suggests that Prawn Crackers (page 543) are an ideal accompaniment.

This amount is for 5 people.

4 cups warm, freshly cooked jasmine rice

3 tablespoons Chilli Jam (page 200)

1 tablespoon palm sugar

2 tablespoons lime juice

2 tablespoons fish sauce

2 Steamed Salted Duck Eggs (page 391) – yolks only

100 g (3 oz) warm Sweet Pork (1 quantity of recipe on page 542)

2 tablespoons shredded steamed chicken breast fillets

100 g (3 oz) fillet of Smoked Fish (page 179)

1 green mango, shredded

1 teaspoon deep-fried garlic

1 tablespoon fresh green peppercorns

1 small cucumber, shredded

Mix rice with chilli jam. Season with sugar, lime juice and fish sauce. It should taste rich, slightly sour, salty and sweet. Crumble in salted duck egg yolks. Stir in sweet pork, chicken, smoked fish and green mango. Serve sprinkled with deep-fried garlic, green peppercorns and cucumber.

PRAWN CRACKERS

kao kriap gung

The best prawns for this recipe are ones that are a little too old to use for anything else – these will purée easily and produce lighter, airier crackers. Once dried, prawn crackers last indefinitely. While they can just be deep-fried in plenty of hot oil, they will be lighter if they are first fried in medium to hot oil, drained and then re-fried in very hot oil. Do not fry too many at one time, or they will be difficult to manage as they expand.

1 tablespoon chopped garlic

1 tablespoon salt

1 teaspoon ground white pepper

100 g (3 oz) minced uncooked prawns (shrimp)

2 tablespoons fish sauce

pinch of castor (superfine) sugar

1¾ cups tapioca flour

1 tablespoon plain (all-purpose) flour

4 tablespoons boiling water

oil for deep-frying

Pound garlic, salt and pepper into a paste. Pound prawns until smooth and sticky. Add garlic paste and season with fish sauce and sugar.

Sieve flours together, then divide into two halves. Work one half into the prawn paste and knead until sticky. Moisten the remainder with the boiling water to form a tight paste. Add prawn paste and knead vigorously. If too dry, add a little more water; if too wet, a little extra flour. Continue to knead for 5 minutes until quite firm. Roll into a cylinder about 4 cm (1½ in) in diameter. Steam for at least 20 minutes or until cooked. Remove and cool, then slice into very thin discs and dry thoroughly in the sun or a warm, dry place. Store in an airtight container and, when required, deep-fry in plenty of hot oil.

SWEET PORK

muu warn

There are many recipes for sweet pork. This easy version is part of Mom Leuang Dterb's Rice Seasoned with Shrimp Paste (page 540).

100 g (3 oz) pork belly

3–4 cups water or stock

4 tablespoons palm sugar

2 tablespoons fish sauce

2 tablespoons water

Simmer pork in water or stock until tender, drain, cool and slice into ½ cm (¼ in) cubes. Heat sugar in a heavy pan and, when caramelised, add fish sauce and water. Add pork and simmer until coated, golden and quite dry – about 15 minutes.

CRISP PORK SHEETS

muu paen

Once cooked, these pork sheets will last for a week in an airtight container. They make a fine accompaniment to seasoned rice.

> 200 g (6 oz) lean pork, such as loin or fillet
> 4 tablespoons light soy sauce
> 3 tablespoons palm or white sugar

> Clean pork, slice very thinly and marinate in soy sauce and sugar overnight. Lay pork between two pieces of plastic and press as thinly as possible with a rolling pin. Dry in the sun or in a warm, dry place.
> Grill very slowly until the sugar has caramelised.

HAINANESE POACHED CHICKEN AND RICE

kao man gai

This recipe, using a whole chicken, feeds five people happily; a chicken leg will be sufficient for two. Often the chicken is simply poached in water to make its own stock, but in that case I like to add some coriander stalks, a few pieces of ginger peel and pandanus leaves to enhance the flavour. Traditionally the chicken is only just cooked, with the bones still red. This is done by poaching the chicken briefly and then covering the pan, removing it from the heat and leaving to cool in the stock; this method cooks the chicken very slowly. However, a safer option – and one more suited to Western tastes – is to cook the bird for longer, as in this recipe.

The classic accompaniment is a gourd soup made from the stock, which is generally served warm, not piping hot. Make sure the gourd is cooked – almost dissolved – and the soup is properly seasoned. I find a little oyster sauce enriches it perfectly, but do not use too much or the light, clear broth will be marred.

The best rice to use for this dish is old rice. It has a somewhat heavier flavour, takes longer to cook and absorbs more water than young rice. Adding a little sticky rice also improves the dish, giving the rice an agreeable texture.

Any excess fat and skin from the chicken should be rendered with a little salt and then used to fry the garlic, along with a little sesame oil. The rice is seasoned *before* it is cooked with salt and perhaps sugar – one of the few times this occurs in Thai cooking.

1 corn-fed, free-range chicken – about 1¼ kg (2½ lb)

3–4 litres (3–4 quarts) chicken stock or water

pinch of salt

3 cups old rice or jasmine rice

½ cup white sticky rice, soaked overnight

3 garlic cloves, minced with a pinch of salt

4 tablespoons oil or rendered chicken fat

pinch of salt

pinch of white sugar – optional

stock from the chicken

1 small cucumber, sliced

handful of chopped coriander leaves

soup

1 small green gourd, peeled, deseeded and cut into 2 cm (1 in) cubes

1 tablespoon light soy sauce

1 teaspoon deep-fried garlic

pinch of ground white pepper

1 tablespoon chopped spring (green) onion

1 tablespoon chopped coriander leaves

Wash and clean the chicken. Poach in stock or water, seasoned with salt. Simmer, skimming as required, for 25–30 minutes. Turn off the heat and allow to cool in the stock.

Combine the two kinds of rice, rinse in several changes of water and drain. Heat oil or chicken fat in a wide pot over a medium heat, add garlic and fry until golden and fragrant. Add rice and continue to fry for a further few minutes. Add salt and sugar, if using. Ladle in strained stock to cover rice to a depth of a little more than the first joint of your index finger. Stir, cover with a lid and cook over a very low heat for 20 minutes. If, at the end of the cooking time, the top of the rice is a little dry, ladle over an extra tablespoon or two of stock or water, cover and leave over the heat for a few minutes longer.

Remove chicken from pot. To make the soup, bring stock back to the boil, add gourd and simmer until soft – about 5–8 minutes. Add soy sauce, garlic, pepper, spring onion and coriander.

When ready to serve, lift chicken meat from bones and slice. For each portion, quickly press some rice into a wet Chinese soup bowl, then unmould onto a plate and lay the chicken over or alongside the mound of rice. Garnish with cucumber and coriander – and accompany with a bowl of the refreshing gourd soup.

This dish is usually served with a spicy dipping sauce, such as Yellow Bean and Ginger Sauce (next recipe).

YELLOW BEAN AND GINGER SAUCE

nahm jim dtow jiaw

In Thailand, Hainanese Poached Chicken and Rice (page 543) is always served with a spicy sauce to prevent the whole dish from being bland. Here is one version.

 2 coriander roots, scraped and chopped

 pinch of salt

 2 garlic cloves, peeled

 3 tablespoons chopped ginger

 pinch of ground white pepper

 1 tablespoon castor (superfine) sugar

 1 tablespoon white vinegar

 1 tablespoon yellow bean sauce, rinsed

 1 tablespoon light soy sauce

 1 tablespoon dark soy sauce

 1 long red chilli, cut into rounds

 1 tablespoon chopped coriander leaves

Pound coriander roots, salt, garlic, ginger and pepper into a paste. Season with sugar, vinegar, yellow beans and soy sauces, then add chilli and coriander. The sauce should taste salty, hot, slightly sweet and sour.

CHICKEN BRAISED IN RICE WITH TURMERIC AND SPICES

kao mok gai

This is a very old recipe from Mom Chao Wimonrat Jinprawit, who recommends the addition of saffron to the paste.

In Pattani, in the Muslim south of Thailand, I once had a pilaff like this with a bowl of spicy but plain broth, perfumed with deep-fried shallots.

 3 chicken legs, each cut into 3 pieces

 oil for deep-frying

 10 red shallots, sliced

 pinch of salt

 3 cups jasmine rice, rinsed and drained

 4 cups stock

 2 cassia leaves or bay leaves

 1 small piece cassia bark, roasted

 2 Thai cardamom pods, roasted

paste

1 tablespoon chopped garlic

pinch of salt

2 tablespoons chopped ginger

1 tablespoon chopped turmeric

1 teaspoon coriander seeds, roasted

1 teaspoon cumin seeds, roasted

seeds of 2 Thai cardamom pods, roasted

2 cloves, roasted

1 cm (½ in) piece cassia bark, roasted

First, make the paste: gradually pound the ingredients together using a pestle and mortar, adding one by one, until smooth. Marinate the chicken in this paste for a few hours.

Heat oil in a pot and deep-fry the shallots, remove and then deep-fry the chicken. Combine shallots, salt and chicken with rice and add sufficient stock to cover to a depth of the first joint of your index finger; bring to the boil. Cover pot and turn down heat to very low. When rice is cooked (about 20–25 minutes), so should the chicken be. Add cassia leaves or bay leaves, cassia bark and cardamom pods and leave to infuse for 5 minutes before serving.

FRIED RICE *kao pat*

Fried rice is the most versatile of dishes. It is of Chinese origin – as is the vital piece of equipment needed to make it, the metal wok. Although fried rice was known to the Thai for many centuries, it was not until the nineteenth century, with extensive Chinese immigration into Siam and the development of food stalls, that it entered the Thai culinary repertoire. And it is now a firm favourite – eaten as a snack, for lunch, a fast dinner or a late supper – but never in place of steamed rice as the basis of a meal.

There are certain guidelines that need to be followed to ensure the success of the dish. The rice used should be slightly dry. If cooking rice specifically to fry, then use a little less water than usual. Mostly, however, fried rice is made from leftover rice. Ideally the rice should be at room temperature: if it is too cold, the rice will retain an unpleasant hardness, be difficult to break up when added to the wok – and be mashed in the attempt to succeed; if the rice is freshly cooked and piping hot, it will stick to the wok, overcook and turn into mush.

Fried rice should always be cooked in a wok, to ensure that the rice cooks properly – and it needs plenty of oil to moisten and flavour it, and to help keep the grains separate. Use good-quality oil; I like to use oil that has been used to deep-fry shallots or garlic – it is pleasantly perfumed, but without too forceful a character. Mince garlic with a little salt (this seems to sweeten it), then fry in a little oil over a medium heat until it begins to colour and become fragrant, before adding the next ingredient. The scrupulous cook would remove the garlic to prevent it overcooking, but this is an uncommon safeguard.

An egg is usually added, and this should be cooked at a slightly higher heat than other ingredients: allow the white to firm and colour around the edges before scrambling the egg. It is important that the egg is almost cooked before adding the next ingredient – this gives the rice an egg colour, taste and texture, as well as the capacity to absorb other liquids, thus helping to bind it. The same scrupulous cook would remove the egg before adding the next ingredient. If meat or fish is to be cooked, it can be added now, although some cooks prefer to add it before the egg. Often a few slices of white or brown onion are added. When an ingredient is added to the wok really depends on how long it takes to cook. However, when fried rice is cooked at the street stalls of Thailand, little time is wasted in considering the niceties of technique.

When the rice is added, turn down the heat to ensure that nothing burns while the rice is warming. Separate the grains with a spoon, so that each one gets coated with the oil, egg and seasoning. If the rice begins to stick, pour an extra tablespoon or two of oil around the sides of the wok – often this is added as a matter of course. The rice is seasoned with white sugar (normally a large pinch is sufficient), light soy sauce and perhaps a little oyster sauce; fish sauce is rarely used. The degree of seasoning is a matter of taste but fried rice is a mild dish. It should taste just a little salty and rich – never bland. The seasoning should be mixed through the rice by stirring and tossing to ensure that it is thoroughly incorporated. Then the final ingredients are added, any cooked meats and aromatics, mostly spring onions and coriander.

Almost any ingredient can be used in fried rice, and it is an ideal way to make small amounts of leftovers feed several people. Deep-fried fish, pork deep-fried with garlic and peppercorns; chilli jam and dried prawns; Chiang Mai cured pork (naem) and shredded ginger; squid and Chinese chives; salted beef; bitter melon and crab, fish or prawn dumplings with Thai basil, a few bulbs of pickled garlic or a few pickled mustard greens and chicken are only some possibilities that can quickly be turned into a plate of fried rice. Leftover curries, especially red ones, can also be added to fried rice: only a little of the curry is necessary – a few tablespoons to a cup of rice. Occasionally nahm prik relishes are fried with rice, being mixed into the rice before it is added to the wok.

Fried rice is one dish that is never shared; each person has their own plate. It is almost invariably garnished with a few slices of cucumber, sprigs of coriander and wedges of lime. A small bowl of prik nahm pla – fish sauce and chopped bird's eye chillies seasoned with lime – is often served with it; I also like to add a few slices of garlic.

All the following fried rice recipes are sufficient for 1 person.

FRIED RICE WITH LONGANS AND ROAST DUCK

kao pat lamyai bpet yang

2 garlic cloves, peeled

large pinch of salt

4 tablespoons oil

1 egg

100 g (3 oz) Chinese roast duck, finely sliced

large pinch of white sugar

pinch of ground white pepper

3 tablespoons light soy sauce

1 cup cooked jasmine rice

2 tablespoons chopped spring (green) onion

6 longans, peeled and deseeded

1 tablespoon coriander leaves

lime wedges

1 tablespoon deep-fried shallots – optional, but delightful

Chop garlic with salt. Heat oil in a wok, add garlic and, when fragrant, crack in the egg, allowing the white to firm before scrambling. Add roast duck and season with sugar, pepper and light soy sauce. Add rice, turn down the heat, mix and toss. Stir in spring onion, longans and coriander. Serve garnished with lime wedges and deep-fried shallots, if using.

FRIED RICE WITH CHINESE SAUSAGE

kao pat gunchiang

3 tablespoons oil

1 Chinese sausage

2 garlic cloves, peeled

pinch of salt

1 cup cooked jasmine rice

large pinch of white sugar

2 tablespoons light soy sauce

2 tablespoons Asian celery cut into 1 cm (½ in) lengths

1 tablespoon coriander leaves

Heat oil in a wok. Fry the sausage over a moderate heat until lightly coloured. Remove, cool slightly and slice on the diagonal. Mince garlic with salt. Reheat oil and fry garlic until coloured. Add rice and sliced sausage, toss until warmed through, then season with sugar and light soy sauce. Add Asian celery and coriander. Serve.

FRIED RICE WITH PINEAPPLE, PRAWNS AND CURRY POWDER

kao pat sapparot

Some cooks add a few chicken livers as well as the prawns.

2 garlic cloves, peeled

pinch of salt

3 tablespoons oil

1 teaspoon curry powder

1 tablespoon chopped onion

3 medium uncooked prawns (shrimp), peeled and deveined

1 egg

large pinch of white sugar

2 tablespoons light soy sauce

¼ cup minced pineapple

1 cup cooked jasmine rice

2 tablespoons Chinese Dried Shredded Pork (below)

2 tablespoons chopped spring (green) onion

1 tablespoon coriander leaves

Chop garlic with salt. Heat oil in a wok and fry garlic over a medium heat until fragrant and just starting to colour. Add curry powder and onion and, when fragrant, the prawns. When the prawns are almost cooked (about 4 minutes), add egg and scramble for a minute, then season with sugar and soy sauce. Add pineapple and rice, turn down the heat, mix and toss. When everything is hot, stir through the shredded pork and spring onion. Serve sprinkled with coriander.

CHINESE DRIED SHREDDED PORK

muu yong

This keeps for several weeks in an airtight container.

1 kg (2 lb) lean pork, such as loin or fillet

½ cup light soy sauce

1 tablespoon white sugar

Cut pork into 2 cm (1 in) cubes. In a small pot, cover pork with water and add light soy sauce and sugar. Cover and simmer until the water has almost evaporated, then leave to cool in the pot. Remove, then tear and shred the meat, sprinkling with any residual sauce from the pot. Fry meat in a wok over low heat, stirring regularly and very carefully to ensure that strands do not stick together or break up.

DEEP-FRIED RICE

kao tort

This recipe is like rice rissoles! There are many variations of this classic lunchtime dish, which can include chicken, crab, bean curd or prawns (shrimp).

1 cup coconut cream
100 g (3 oz) Chinese sausage, sliced
3 tablespoons fish sauce
1 tablespoon palm sugar
100 g (3 oz) minced pork
1 egg, lightly beaten
3 cups cooked jasmine rice
4 egg whites
1 cup plain (all-purpose) flour, sieved
pinch of salt
pinch of ground white pepper
oil for deep-frying
handful of coriander leaves

paste
7 dried long red chillies, deseeded, soaked and drained
pinch of salt
2 teaspoons chopped galangal
1 tablespoon chopped lemongrass
1 teaspoon finely grated kaffir lime zest
2 teaspoons scraped and chopped coriander root
2 tablespoons chopped red shallot
2 tablespoons chopped garlic
10 white peppercorns
2 tablespoons ground roasted peanuts

First, make the paste: gradually pound the ingredients together using a pestle and mortar, adding one by one, until smooth.

Simmer coconut cream for a moment, then add paste. Add Chinese sausage and simmer for 3–4 minutes. Season with fish sauce and palm sugar, then add minced pork, stirring to prevent it clumping. The mixture should taste rich, sweet and salty. Stir in the egg and, after a moment, the rice. Incorporate everything thoroughly; check seasoning and adjust to taste. Allow to cool, then roll into 2 cm (1 in) dumplings. Put egg whites and flour in separate bowls, and season each with salt and pepper. Dip dumplings into egg whites and then into flour. Deep-fry in medium to hot oil until golden. Drain and sprinkle with coriander leaves.

Serve with Cucumber Relish (page 402).

FRIED RICE WITH CRAB

kao pat bpuu

1–2 garlic cloves, peeled

large pinch of salt

3 tablespoons oil

1 egg

1 cup cooked jasmine rice

large pinch of ground white pepper

larger pinch of white sugar

2 tablespoons light soy sauce

3 spring (green) onions, cut into 1 cm (½ in) lengths

100 g (3 oz) cooked crabmeat

1 tablespoon coriander leaves

Mince garlic with salt. Heat oil in a wok and fry garlic until fragrant and beginning to colour. Crack in the egg, allowing the white to firm before scrambling. Add rice and turn down the heat. Fry gently, mixing and tossing. Season with pepper, sugar and light soy sauce: the rice should be well seasoned, but not too salty. Add spring onions and, after a moment, the crabmeat, reserving a little to sprinkle over the finished dish, along with coriander.

RICE SOUPS *kao dtom lae joek*

These one-bowl dishes are often eaten at night but sometimes at breakfast. It is believed that rice cooked in this way is easily digestible, and so it is often eaten by invalids and those recuperating from illness – or from the night before. In Thai rice soup (*kao dtom*), the rice grains remain quite distinguishable. The Chinese version (congee or *joek*) is usually made from broken grains of rice simmered for hours, resulting in a purée or porridge-like soup. The Thai version is derived from Chinese rice porridge: evidence for this is the many ingredients that season the soup and also the manner in which it is eaten – in a large bowl with chopsticks and a Chinese soup spoon.

The following recipes assume that there is no leftover rice – an unimaginable thing in Thailand – and the rice is cooked from scratch. Very often, however, leftover rice is simply reheated in stock. These soups might be finished with duck and shredded ginger, abalone simmered in oyster sauce, or prawns and their tomalley with spring onions. Mom Leuang Neuang Ninrat suggests that cooked rice be simmered in seasoned coconut milk with pandanus then sprinkled with crispy dried fish or shredded salty beef, or even deep-fried squid.

Given the comforting nature of these rice soups, pungent side dishes and sauces are often served with them. These can be as simple as chillies steeped in vinegar, some puréed yellow beans or deep-fried peanuts. Normally *kao dtom* has a few pungent accompaniments like freshly shredded ginger, Spicy Yellow Bean Sauce (page 558), Preserved Cabbage (page 558), Steeped Chinese Broccoli (page 559), Salted Prawn Salad (page 559), or Steamed Salted Duck Eggs (page 391). Chinese congee, however, can sometimes just be plain rice soup. Its accompaniments can be as unassuming as the Thai versions, or they can be a whole banquet of dishes – from pork ear jelly to steamed fish or Seaweed and Shiitake Mushrooms (page 560). Usually they too are pungent – especially when congee is served at supper time, to ensure the dish is a satisfying and agreeable end to the day.

All these rice soup recipes make enough for 4 people.

RICE CONGEE

joek

Only broken rice is used for this recipe, and it is cooked for much longer than usual to ensure it is a delicious gruel. Traditionally the rice was left to cook overnight in the dying embers so that by morning it was ready for breakfast.

> 3 cups broken rice
> 12 cups water
> large pinch of salt
> 2 pandanus leaves
> 6–8 tablespoons light soy sauce
> large pinch of ground white pepper
> 3 tablespoons chopped spring (green) onion
> 3 tablespoons coriander leaves

Rinse rice, and put into a large, heavy pot. Add water, salt and pandanus, and bring to the boil. Reduce heat and simmer at a very low temperature, stirring regularly to prevent sticking and to assist in breaking up the rice. It will take at least an hour to cook, and perhaps longer.

Season with light soy sauce, pepper, spring onion and coriander.

Congee is mostly eaten with pork or pork products – like sliced liver, kidneys or Chinese sausage – cooked in the gruel. Some cooks like to add eggs. Other accompaniments often include deep-fried bread, shredded ginger and a small bowl of sliced chillies steeped in vinegar.

RICE SOUP WITH CONDIMENTS

kao dtom gap

For a delicious result, a rich, full-flavoured stock is essential – one that is made from chicken bones simmered with Asian celery, white radish, cracked white peppercorns and salt. If fish is used to make the stock, then sliced galangal is also added to the aromatics. Sometimes finely sliced fish or prawns, chicken breast, pork kidneys or minced beef, which need very little cooking time, are poached with the rice. If the fish or meat is cooked separately – for instance, prawns, fish, chicken or pork – it is often marinated beforehand in a mixture of coriander root, powdered dried galangal, garlic and ground white pepper before being stir-fried and added to the rice.

3 cups jasmine rice
4½ cups stock

condiments
soy sauce
minced deep-fried garlic
Preserved Cabbage (page 558)
ground white pepper
coriander leaves
Asian celery, finely sliced
spring (green) onions, finely sliced
sliced long red chillies
vinegar
fish sauce

Cook rice using any method. Bring stock to the boil, add rice to it and simmer briefly. Ladle into a bowl, then season with various condiments, such as soy sauce, minced deep-fried garlic and preserved cabbage. Sprinkle with pepper, coriander leaves, and perhaps some finely sliced Asian celery and spring onions.

Accompany with a small dish of chillies in vinegar and a bowl of fish sauce.

RICE PORRIDGE

kao dtom kreuang

This is a prolonged method of cooking rice and a gentle way to eat it. Remarkably the rice retains its shape and each grain remains distinct amid a thick broth. New rice is preferred for this recipe as it is more fragrant than older rice, contains more starch and is softer when cooked. If the rice is old, then add a little sticky rice to soften and thicken the soup. Traditionally this rice is cooked gently in an earthenware pot, as it is believed that by doing so the rice soup picks up the flavour of the earth.

3 cups jasmine rice

10 cups water or stock

1–2 pandanus leaves

1–2 slices ginger, bruised

Rinse the rice well. Cover with plenty of water or stock, add pandanus and ginger, and bring to the boil, then reduce heat and simmer over a low heat. Skim off the froth. Stir occasionally, but not too often or the grains will be broken. Simmer for about an hour, until rice is translucent and very tender. Set aside for an hour or so for the grains to swell.

When ready to serve, reheat, replenishing with extra water if necessary.

There are myriad accompaniments to this rice porridge:
— peanuts
— spring (green) onions, chopped
— salted white radish
— deep-fried fish, pork or squid with garlic and peppercorns
— Chinese roast duck
— Salted Prawn Salad (page 559)
— Stir-fried Siamese Watercress with Yellow Beans, Garlic and Chillies (page 532)
— Bean Curd Stir-fried with Bean Sprouts (page 462)
— Pork Braised with Star Anise (page 526).

SQUID AND EGG RICE SOUP

kao dtom pal meuk sy kai

3 cups jasmine rice

7 cups chicken stock

200 g (6 oz) cleaned and sliced squid

2–3 tablespoons light soy sauce

1 egg, lightly beaten

2 tablespoons chopped Asian celery

1 tablespoon minced deep-fried garlic

1 tablespoon chopped coriander leaves

pinch of ground white pepper

Cook rice in stock for 20 minutes, add squid and simmer until cooked – about 2 minutes. Season with light soy sauce, stir in egg and simmer for another minute or so. Finish with Asian celery, deep-fried garlic, coriander leaves and pepper.

RICE SOUP WITH MUD CRAB

kao dtom bpuu tarlae

3 coriander roots, scraped and chopped

pinch of salt

1 tablespoon chopped ginger

4 garlic cloves, peeled

10 white peppercorns

3 cups jasmine rice

6 cups stock

4 tablespoons oil

1 mud crab, around 600 g (1¼ lb), cleaned and chopped into 2 cm (1 in) pieces

3 tablespoons fish sauce or light soy sauce

pinch of sugar

4 tablespoons dried prawns (shrimp), rinsed

3 tablespoons chopped Asian celery

1 tablespoon Preserved Cabbage (page 558), rinsed

Using a pestle and mortar, pound coriander roots, salt, ginger, garlic and peppercorns into a paste. Cook rice in stock. Heat oil, add paste and fry until fragrant. Add crab and fry until cooked (4–6 minutes), taking care that the garlic in the paste does not burn. Season with fish sauce or light soy sauce and sugar. Stir crab mixture through the soup. Add dried prawns and Asian celery, and sprinkle with preserved cabbage.

OYSTER AND PORK RICE SOUP

kao dtom hoi nang

3 garlic cloves, peeled

pinch of salt

3 cups jasmine rice

6 cups stock or water

large pinch of salt

4 tablespoons oil

200 g (6 oz) minced fatty pork

2 eggs, lightly beaten

24 oysters, shucked (reserve any liquid)

a little fish sauce – optional

½ teaspoon powdered galangal

2 tablespoons chopped spring (green) onion

2–3 tablespoons chopped coriander leaves

pinch of ground white pepper

OYSTER AND PORK RICE SOUP

Pound garlic and salt into a paste. Cook the rice for 20 minutes in the stock or water, with a large pinch of salt. Heat oil and fry garlic paste until golden, then add minced pork and fry until cooked – about 3–5 minutes. Add to rice and return to the boil. Stir in the eggs and then add the oysters. Season, if necessary, with fish sauce. Serve sprinkled with galangal, spring onions, coriander and pepper.

SPICY YELLOW BEAN SAUCE

nahm jim dtow jiaw

> 3 coriander roots, scraped and chopped
> pinch of salt
> 3 garlic cloves, chopped
> 1 tablespoon chopped ginger
> 3 tablespoons yellow bean sauce, rinsed
> 1 long red chilli, deseeded if preferred
> large pinch of palm sugar
> 1 tablespoon white vinegar

Gradually pound the ingredients together using a pestle and mortar, adding one by one, until smooth. It should taste salty, hot, sweet and sour. (For a less fiery sauce, the chilli can be sliced into the sauce afterwards.)

PRESERVED CABBAGE

dtang chai

> 500 g (1 lb) Chinese cabbage
> 1 tablespoon chopped galangal
> 1 tablespoon chopped garlic
> 1 tablespoon chopped ginger
> 3 tablespoons salt
> ¼ cup white sugar
> 1 tablespoon Chinese rice wine

Cut cabbage into roughly 1 cm (½ in) strips and leave in the sun (or a warm place) until wilted and beginning to colour. Pound galangal, garlic and ginger with salt. Combine this paste with the cabbage, sugar and rice wine, and work vigorously. Put into a sterilised jar, seal, and leave in the sun or a warm, dry place for 3 days. Open and stir the cabbage, re-seal and leave in the sun or a warm, dry place for a further 2 weeks. This preserve keeps indefinitely, and does not need to be refrigerated.

STEEPED CHINESE BROCCOLI

pak kanaa dong kem

> 1 bunch (about 250–300 g or 8–10 oz) Chinese broccoli
>
> 2 cups fish sauce or light soy sauce
>
> 4 tablespoons palm sugar

Peel the broccoli, and slice into ½ cm (¼ in) pieces. Dry in the sun until wilted. Bring fish sauce or light soy sauce to the boil and add palm sugar. Add broccoli and simmer for a moment. Remove from heat and allow to cool. Store in a sterilised glass jar for a week or so before use.

SALTED PRAWN SALAD

yam gung kem

> 10 Salted Prawns (page 392)
>
> a little fish sauce or light soy sauce – to taste
>
> 1 teaspoon white sugar
>
> 2 tablespoons lime juice
>
> 1 garlic clove, finely sliced
>
> 2–5 bird's eye chillies (scuds), sliced

Combine all and serve.

PICKLED CRAB

bpuu dong sahm rot

> 3 blue swimmer crabs – about 200 g (6 oz) each
>
> ½ cup white sugar
>
> 1 cup water
>
> ¼ cup white vinegar
>
> 1 cup fish sauce
>
> 2 tablespoons coriander seeds, roasted

Clean the crabs, blanch briefly and then rinse. Simmer remaining ingredients together for 5 minutes, skim and strain. Return to the boil and add the crabs. Simmer until cooked – about 10 minutes.

SEAWEED AND SHIITAKE MUSHROOMS

sarai het horm nahm dtaeng

12 best-quality large dried shiitake mushrooms

2 cups stock

1 cup coarsely chopped cabbage

3 spring (green) onions, cut into 2 cm (1 in) lengths

1 tablespoon tapioca flour

50 g (2 oz) seaweed, such as *nori*

a little light soy sauce

a drizzle of Chinese black vinegar

handful of coriander leaves

pinch of ground white pepper

mushroom stock

3 slices old ginger

3 coriander roots, scraped

3 tablespoons oyster sauce

pinch of palm sugar

1 star anise

piece of dried orange peel

small piece of pork fat – optional

1 pandanus leaf – optional

3 cups water

Soak the shiitake mushrooms in warm water for 5 minutes. Combine the mushroom stock ingredients, add the shiitakes and simmer for 10 minutes, skimming as necessary. Cool, strain, snip off and discard the mushroom stalks and return the mushroom caps to the liquid.

Bring the 2 cups of stock to the boil. Add cabbage and simmer until wilted, then add spring onions. Pour in 1 cup of the mushroom stock and return to the boil. Skim. Mix the tapioca flour with 2 tablespoons of the mushroom stock and stir in; when stock has thickened, add seaweed and shiitakes. Skim again and check seasoning – add a little light soy sauce, if required. Serve drizzled with vinegar and sprinkled with coriander and pepper.

It sometimes seems that there is a noodle shop or stall on every corner of every street in Thailand – from the hub of Bangkok's business centre, Silom Road, to the dustiest village. Once there were hawkers who plied their wares along the streets of Bangkok, and even along the canals, where customers would perch on the banks as they ate their noodles. They are ubiquitous: it was even said that during one of the coups d'état in the early 1980s, noodle stalls were set up near the scene of the confrontation, to cater to the opposing factions and the spectators.

Noodles are eaten with fervour in Thailand at any time of the day, and in an extraordinary range of styles. There are various types of noodles (see pages 163–4) – fresh and dried, made from wheat and rice flour – and there are as many ways to eat them: blanched and dressed, in stir-fries and in soups. Most noodles are interchangeable; at noodle stalls one is always asked what noodles are preferred, and they are produced accordingly.

Stir-fried noodles are cooked in a wok: some dishes are cooked rapidly over a fierce heat, in order to colour, even char, the noodles; others are cooked more gently, with the noodles being cooked and then incorporated into the well-seasoned dish. If egg noodles are used in a stir-fried dish, they need to be blanched in boiling water and drained before being added to the wok. Fresh rice noodles are simply added.

Blanched noodles – which are dipped in boiling water or a light stock – can either be served in a soup (in Thailand described as 'wet') or merely seasoned and served 'dry' in a bowl. Noodles intended for soups are placed in a bowl and a ladle of broth is poured over; the stock must be full-flavoured, or the dish will be bland and insipid. Such stocks are often made with pork and duck bones and strong aromatics such as white radish, cabbage, spring onions, star anise and pandanus. The stock is then seasoned with oyster sauce and soy sauce, giving a deep, inviting depth to the taste and appearance of the soup.

In deference to their origins, noodles are generally eaten in the Chinese manner – in a bowl with chopsticks and a Chinese soup spoon – although some stir-fried noodle dishes are served on flat plates and eaten with a spoon and fork.

At the table, noodles are served with an assortment of condiments, *kreuang brung*: roasted chilli powder, ground galangal, Asian celery, sliced red chillies steeped in vinegar, ground deep-fried peanuts, white sugar and fish sauce. Some more elaborate garnishes could include Chinese Dried Shredded Pork (page 550) and Preserved Cabbage (page 558).

All the following noodle recipes are sufficient for 1 person.

PAT THAI

pat thai

This simple, tasty noodle dish is enjoyed throughout Thailand and is famous all over the world. For a more luxurious version, fresh prawns can be used: simply fry a few peeled prawns in the wok with the shallots, then proceed with the rest of the recipe.

a good handful of dried thin rice noodles

1 tablespoon palm sugar

1 tablespoon white sugar

1 tablespoon tamarind water

2 tablespoons fish sauce

1 small bunch Chinese chives

1 teaspoon oil

2 red shallots, coarsely chopped with a pinch of salt

1 egg

50 g (2 oz) firm bean curd, deep-fried and cut into
    ½ cm (¼ in) cubes

1 tablespoon dried prawns (shrimp), rinsed and dried

1 teaspoon shredded salted white radish, rinsed and dried

pinch of roasted chilli powder

handful of bean sprouts

1 tablespoon crushed roasted peanuts

1 lime wedge

extra 1 teaspoon roasted chilli powder

Soak noodles in water for 2 hours until soft. Drain. Simmer palm sugar and white sugar with tamarind water and fish sauce for 1–2 minutes, until dissolved. Chop most of the Chinese chives into 2 cm (1 in) lengths, reserving a few – chopped into 5 cm (2 in) lengths – for garnish.

Heat oil in a wok over a medium heat and fry shallots until fragrant and beginning to colour. Crack in egg, turn down the heat and stir. Mix in bean curd, dried prawns and white radish, then add noodles. Turn up the heat and stir-fry for about a minute, allowing the noodles to colour a little. Add the prepared sauce and the pinch of chilli powder, then simmer for another 30 seconds–1 minute, adding a little more oil if necessary. Finally, add most of the bean sprouts and Chinese chives, and cook for another 30 seconds, until wilted. Check seasoning: the noodles should taste sweet, sour and salty.

Pile on a plate and top with the reserved bean sprouts and Chinese chives. Serve with crushed roasted peanuts, a lime wedge and roasted chilli powder on the side of the plate.

CRISPY NOODLES

mii grop

There are many versions of these deep-fried noodles coated with a thick, sweet dressing. The following recipe dates from the middle of the twentieth century. Another version, by Khun Sombat Janphetchara, the woman who first introduced me to Thai cooking, uses minced pork, chicken and prawns and deep-fried red shallots. An alternative, far more common, dressing for *mii grop* is made from a cup each of plum sauce, mild chilli sauce and palm sugar, mixed together and reduced down to a thick syrup.

The sauce given here is equally sweet, sour and salty. It lasts indefinitely when refrigerated. If making in advance, do not add the lime and mandarin juices, or their flavours will dull; finish the reheated sauce with them. Serve the noodles as quickly as possible, since the garnishes will wilt quickly in such amounts of sugar. For an elegant presentation, cover the finished dish with a small egg net (see page 492).

½ packet (about 100 g or 3 oz) dried thin rice noodles

1 small egg, beaten

oil for deep-frying

1 cup bean sprouts, topped and tailed

1 tablespoon julienned mandarin zest

1 tablespoon shredded long red chilli

2 tablespoons peeled and chopped pickled garlic

2 tablespoons chopped Chinese chives

1 tablespoon coriander leaves

sauce

2 coriander roots, scraped and chopped

4 garlic cloves, peeled

10 white peppercorns

pinch of salt

2 tablespoons oil

1 cup yellow bean sauce, rinsed and puréed

½ cup prawn (shrimp) tomalley – optional, but desirable

1 cup white sugar

2 eggs, lightly beaten

½ cup lime juice

3 tablespoons mandarin juice

Soak noodles in warm water for 10 minutes then drain and mix with the beaten egg. Leave to dry overnight. (This seals the noodles, so they remain quite crisp, and also helps the sauce to coat them.)

For the sauce, pound coriander roots, garlic, pepper and salt into a paste, then fry in oil until golden. Add yellow beans and fry until fragrant. Add prawn tomalley (if using) and, when thick and red, season with sugar. Gradually add eggs, stirring vigorously to prevent them curdling. Simmer until thick, then add lime and mandarin juices, and simmer for a moment only before removing from heat. Cool.

Heat plenty of oil in a wok and deep-fry the noodles, gradually removing them as they become slightly puffed and lightly coloured. This can be done some time in advance. In another wok or pan, carefully reheat the sauce – it burns easily – and add to the crisped noodles. Coat with sauce and stir in remaining ingredients, combining well to ensure they are evenly distributed.

STIR-FRIED RICE NOODLES WITH CHICKEN AND CHINESE BROCCOLI

gai pat sii uuu

2 tablespoons oil

3 garlic cloves, crushed

200 g (6 oz) skinless chicken thigh fillets, sliced

2 handfuls fresh wide rice noodles

50 g (2 oz) Chinese broccoli, cut into 2 cm (1 in) lengths

1 egg

1 teaspoon dark soy sauce

2 tablespoons light soy sauce

a little oyster sauce – optional

1 teaspoon castor (superfine) sugar

a few tablespoons chicken stock or water

pinch of ground white pepper

handful of bean sprouts

Heat a wok, add oil and then garlic. When garlic is beginning to colour, add chicken and continue to fry until the chicken is almost cooked. Add noodles and broccoli and, once these are cooked (about 4 minutes), the egg, stir-frying to scramble it. Season with the soy sauces, oyster sauce, if using, and sugar, then moisten with stock or water. Serve sprinkled with pepper and garnished with bean sprouts.

RICE NOODLES AND PORK WITH THICKENED 'GRAVY'

raat nar muu

This is my favourite noodle dish. It is best when the noodles are coloured before-hand in a well-seasoned wok with the dark soy and a little oil; should they begin to stick, drizzle a few extra tablespoons of oil down the sides and toss.

Occasionally, the pork is marinated in a little oyster sauce before it is cooked. If the broccoli is old, it should be blanched before it is added to the simmering stock, otherwise the pork will be tough by the time the broccoli is cooked.

Sliced chicken or squid can be used instead of pork, if desired.

good handful of fresh wide rice noodles

1 tablespoon sweet soy sauce (*kecap manis*)

4 tablespoons oil

2 garlic cloves, minced with a pinch of salt

50 g (2 oz) pork fillet, sliced

½ cup stock

1 cup chopped young Chinese broccoli

1 tablespoon yellow bean sauce, rinsed

1 tablespoon dark soy sauce

1 tablespoon light soy sauce

1 tablespoon tapioca flour, mixed with 1 tablespoon water

Rub the noodles with the sweet soy sauce and leave to dry for about 10 minutes. Heat 2 tablespoons of the oil in a wok, stir-fry noodles until coloured, then remove and keep warm.

In a small pot – or the cleaned wok – heat the other 2 tablespoons of the oil and fry the garlic until beginning to colour. Add pork and fry until the garlic is golden. Add stock and broccoli, then season with yellow beans and dark and light soy sauces. Simmer for a moment. Add tapioca slurry and stir. Once it has thickened, serve as soon as possible (the sauce starts to break down after a minute or so), poured over the noodles.

Serve with:

— fish sauce

— roasted chilli powder

— white sugar

— sliced long red chillies in vinegar.

COCONUT NOODLES

mii gati

Tomalley traditionally gives this mild noodle dish its ruddy colour; however, most modern cooks use a little tomato paste to approximate the colour, if not the taste.

1½ cups coconut cream

1 tablespoon yellow bean sauce, rinsed

1 tablespoon palm sugar

1 tablespoon tamarind water

1 tablespoon fish sauce

4 uncooked prawns (shrimp), peeled, deveined and minced –
    reserve any tomalley

50 g (2 oz) minced fatty pork

50 g (2 oz) silken bean curd, cut into small rectangles

2 red shallots, sliced

large pinch of roasted chilli powder

pinch of castor (superfine) sugar

2–3 tablespoons fish sauce

50 g (2 oz) dried thin rice noodles, blanched and refreshed

handful of bean sprouts

1 tablespoon chopped Chinese chives

Simmer the coconut cream until thick and beginning to separate. In another pan, bring 4 tablespoons of the cracked coconut cream to the boil and add yellow beans, palm sugar, tamarind water and fish sauce. Add minced prawns, pork, bean curd, shallots and chilli powder, and simmer for 4–5 minutes. Check seasoning: the sauce should taste quite strongly salty, sweet and sour.

Heat the remaining coconut cream, add prawn tomalley (if any), and fry until pink and cooked. Add sugar and fish sauce, then the noodles, stirring to ensure that the noodles are coated evenly. Add bean sprouts and Chinese chives, simmer for a moment until wilted, then remove from the heat.

Arrange the noodles in a loose coil on a plate, and either pour over the sauce or serve in a small bowl alongside.

Serve with:

— quarters of cleaned banana blossoms

— sprigs of coriander or Asian pennywort

— a few leaves of young rocket (arugula).

DRY NOODLES WITH PICKLED MUSTARD GREENS, PRAWNS AND BEAN SPROUTS

gwi dtiaw haeng

handful of dried thin rice noodles

handful of bean sprouts

2 tablespoons chopped pickled mustard greens, rinsed

50 g (2 oz) minced cooked prawns (shrimp), mixed with 1 tablespoon fish sauce

50 g (2 oz) shredded poached chicken

50 g (2 oz) firm bean curd, sliced crosswise

1 tablespoon castor (superfine) sugar

2 tablespoons fish sauce

2 tablespoons lime juice

large pinch of roasted chilli powder

1 tablespoon ground roasted peanuts

1 teaspoon minced deep-fried garlic

1 tablespoon chopped coriander leaves

Briefly blanch the noodles, bean sprouts and mustard greens together. Drain. Combine with the minced prawns, chicken and bean curd. Season with sugar, fish sauce, lime juice and chilli powder. Mix thoroughly.

Serve sprinkled with peanuts, garlic and coriander.

RICE NOODLE AND MINCED PORK SOUP

gwio sen mii muu sap

Traditionally, this soup was garnished with pork scratchings, and one source even suggests some coarsely ground Crisp Fish Skin (page 392).

2 cups stock

3 tablespoons light soy sauce

pinch of white sugar

100 g (3 oz) good-quality minced pork

1 cup *bai dtamleung*, snow pea shoots or young spinach leaves

50 g (2 oz) dried thin rice noodles, blanched and drained

large pinch of minced deep-fried garlic

large pinch of ground white pepper

handful of chopped coriander leaves or Asian celery

Bring stock to the boil, and season with soy sauce and sugar. Add pork and *bai dtamleung*, snow pea shoots or spinach. Simmer briefly, stirring to prevent the pork from clumping and overcooking. Put the blanched noodles into a bowl, pour over the stock and garnish with garlic, pepper and coriander or celery.

BEEF AND NOODLE SOUP

gwio tio neua

50 g (2 oz) rump of beef, finely sliced

2 tablespoons chopped Asian celery

handful of bean sprouts

50 g (2 oz) fresh wide rice noodles, blanched

stock

1 kg (1 lb) beef bones

pinch of salt

1 beef shank

stock or water, to cover

2 tablespoons dark soy sauce

pinch of sugar

5 slices galangal

1 stalk lemongrass

handful of coriander stalks

1 star anise

1 piece dried orange peel

2 pandanus leaves

1 teaspoon cracked pepper – both white and black – perhaps even
    including a few Szechuan peppercorns

dumplings

50 g (2 oz) minced lean beef

large pinch of salt

pinch of ground white pepper

2 tablespoons crushed ice

Put all the stock ingredients in a large pot, bring to the boil and simmer for
2–3 hours, skimming as required. Strain the stock, reserving the beef shank.
Check seasoning – the stock should be full-flavoured and well-seasoned. Remove
meat from the shank and slice finely.

To make the dumplings, purée the beef with salt and pepper. Knead
and slap the mixture against the side of the bowl until quite sticky. Work in the
ice, a little at a time, kneading to ensure it is completely absorbed. Roll into
4–5 dumplings and poach in salted water. Refresh and drain.

Bring stock back to the boil. Add dumplings, the meat from the beef
shank and the sliced beef. Simmer briefly and then finish with the Asian celery.

Put bean sprouts and noodles into a bowl, then pour over the soup.

Serve with:

- ← white sugar
- ← fish sauce
- ← roasted chilli powder
- ← Chilli and Vinegar Sauce (below).

CHILLI AND VINEGAR SAUCE

prik dong nahm som

A simple way to enliven a noodle soup is to serve this sauce alongside. The seeds should be removed from the long chillies – unless a truly memorable sauce is desired.

1 cup long green chillies, deseeded
a few bird's eye chillies (scuds) – to taste
1 garlic clove, peeled
about 1 tablespoon salt
1 cup white vinegar

Break and bruise the chillies using a pestle and mortar. Steep in salted water for an hour, then drain. Purée the chillies with garlic, salt and vinegar. Pour into a sterilised glass jar and set aside.

The sauce will be ready after a few hours;however, it improves – well, mellows – after a few days, and then can be kept indefinitely, unrefrigerated. It should taste sour, hot and salty.

CHIANG MAI CURRIED NOODLE AND CHICKEN SOUP

kao soi gai

This dish is enjoyed throughout the ancient northern city of Chiang Mai, and is believed to have travelled there from the south of China with the Haw, Muslim traders who plied that route.

The best noodles to use are the somewhat flat egg noodles, about ½ centimetre (¼ inch) wide. Deep-fry a few of them in very hot, clean oil to use as a garnish, but be careful – they splatter as they expand and become crisp. Beef is often used in the soup in place of chicken.

4 tablespoons coconut cream

1 small chicken leg – about 100 g (3 oz) – quartered

1 tablespoon palm sugar

2 tablespoons light soy sauce

1 teaspoon dark soy sauce

2 cups stock or water

handful of fresh egg noodles

a few deep-fried egg noodles

1 tablespoon chopped spring (green) onion

1 tablespoon chopped coriander leaves

paste

3 dried long red chillies, deseeded, soaked and drained

4 red shallots, unpeeled

3 garlic cloves, unpeeled

1 tablespoon chopped turmeric

2 tablespoons chopped ginger

pinch of salt

3 coriander roots, scraped and chopped

1 teaspoon coriander seeds, roasted and ground

First, make the paste: roast chillies, shallots, garlic, turmeric and ginger; when they are cool enough to handle, peel chillies, shallots and garlic. Gradually pound all the paste ingredients together, using a pestle and mortar, until smooth.

Simmer the coconut cream until thick and beginning to separate. Fry the paste in the cracked coconut cream until fragrant – about 5 minutes. Add chicken, turn down the heat and simmer for a few minutes. Season with palm sugar, then add the light and dark soy sauces. Moisten with stock or water and continue to simmer until chicken is cooked – about 20 minutes. Check seasoning: the soup should taste salty and slightly sweet from the coconut cream.

Blanch the fresh egg noodles. Put into a bowl and pour the curried chicken soup over them. Garnish with deep-fried noodles, spring onion and coriander.

Serve with:
- sliced red shallots
- wedges of lime
- pickled mustard greens
- Roast Chilli Sauce (next recipe).

ROAST CHILLI SAUCE

prik bon pat

A dark, flavourful chilli sauce to accompany rich dishes, such as Chiang Mai Curried Noodle and Chicken Soup (page 571).

oil for deep-frying
3 red shallots, chopped
2 garlic cloves, chopped
4–10 dried bird's eye chillies
large pinch of salt
pinch of palm sugar – optional

Heat oil and deep-fry the shallots and garlic until golden. Remove and drain. Deep-fry the chillies, then drain. Pound shallots, garlic and chillies into a coarse paste. Season with salt and sugar, if using, then moisten with a little of the deep-frying oil. The sauce should taste hot and salty.

ROAST DUCK AND EGG NOODLE SOUP

ba mii nahm bpet yang

With a duck bought from a barbecue shop in Chinatown, this recipe becomes quick and easy. To make the duck easier to eat, remove the bones, then simmer them in some stock with a little light soy sauce and a pinch of sugar to make a delicious soup base.

2 cups stock
large pinch of salt
pinch of white sugar
1 teaspoon oyster sauce
100 g (3 oz) fresh egg noodles
a few pieces of Chinese broccoli, chopped
100 g (3 oz) Chinese roast duck, sliced
1 tablespoon chopped spring (green) onion
1 tablespoon chopped coriander leaves
a sprinkle of Preserved Cabbage (page 558), rinsed
a little minced deep-fried garlic
pinch of ground white pepper

Bring stock to the boil, and season with salt, sugar and oyster sauce. Briefly blanch the noodles and broccoli in water. Place these in a bowl and top with the duck. Cover with the boiling stock, then serve sprinkled with spring onion, coriander, cabbage, garlic and pepper.

BARBECUED PORK AND CRAB WONTON SOUP

gwio bpuu lae muu dtaeng

Prawns, chicken or fish can also be used to make wontons, so long as the filling is well seasoned. Barbecued pork can be bought from Chinese barbecue shops.

2 cups stock

2 tablespoons light soy sauce

pinch of sugar

a little oyster sauce – optional

1 cup *bai dtamleung* or snow pea shoots or young spinach leaves

50 g (2 oz) sliced barbecued pork

1 teaspoon minced deep-fried garlic

1 tablespoon chopped spring (green) onion

1 tablespoon chopped coriander leaves

pinch of ground white pepper

wontons

1 coriander root, scraped and chopped

pinch of salt

1 garlic clove, peeled

1 slice ginger

pinch of white pepper

30 g (1 oz) minced fatty pork

pinch of white sugar

1 tablespoon light soy sauce

30 g (1 oz) cooked crabmeat

1 teaspoon chopped coriander leaves

1 teaspoon chopped spring (green) onion

8 wonton skins

1 egg white

First, make the wontons. Pound coriander root, salt, garlic, ginger and pepper into a paste. Mix in the pork and slap the mixture against the side of the bowl until it becomes firmer and stickier. Season with sugar and light soy sauce. Mix in crab, coriander and spring onion. Lay out the wonton skins. Place a quarter of the crab and pork mixture in the centre of each one. Smear the edges with egg white. Gather up the edges and twist to seal. Cook the wontons in plenty of salted water for about 3–4 minutes at a rolling boil.

Meanwhile, bring stock to the boil and season with soy sauce, sugar and oyster sauce, if using. Add *bai dtamleung* or other greens and simmer for a few moments, until wilted. Place wontons in a bowl, and pour over the stock. Add barbecued pork and sprinkle with garlic, spring onion, coriander and pepper.

KANOM JIN

These traditional Thai noodles translate, literally, as 'Chinese dessert' or 'pastry'. Certainly they are derived from Chinese rice noodles – being spaghetti-like in shape and length – but the Thai version is usually served at room temperature. Often *kanom jin* are included in a celebratory meal, especially at a wedding, as noodles symbolise long life.

Kanom jin are eaten throughout Thailand, especially at lunch. Sometimes they are eaten with curries, normally red and green curries, taking the place of rice. Usually, however, a small bowl of rich and often spicy sauce is served alongside a few loose coils of noodles, or the sauce may be poured over them. There are many kinds of sauces that dress *kanom jin*, and these reflect regional differences: in the north, they are based on pork and simmered in stock, perhaps with tomatoes and pickled mustard greens; further south, they are often rich with coconut cream and include seafood, especially prawns. Side dishes can be as simple as a plate of raw vegetables and fresh herbs (especially lemon basil), or they can extend to vegetables that have been pickled, deep-fried in batter or simmered in coconut; steamed eggs and curries; and fish dumplings simmered in coconut cream.

Normally two coils of fresh noodles are served per person – that is, roughly, a good handful. More should always be available. If using dried noodles, follow the instructions on the packet.

KANOM JIN FROM THE SHANS

kanom jin nahm ngiaw

This sauce comes from Chiang Rai, in the mountainous far north of Thailand, and is believed to have originated among the Shan, one of the region's ethnic groups.

Often minced beef is used instead of pork. The blood cakes are optional; for the adventurous, they are usually available at Chinese butchers.

200 g (6 oz) pork ribs, cut into 2 cm (1 in) lengths and rinsed

pinch of salt

2–3 cups stock

2 tablespoons oil or rendered pork fat

pinch of palm sugar

3–4 tablespoons light soy sauce

2 cups coarsely chopped, deseeded tomatoes

2 blood cakes, cut into 2 cm (1 in) cubes – optional

150 g (5 oz) minced fatty pork

1 teaspoon deep-fried garlic

1 tablespoon chopped spring (green) onion

1 tablespoon chopped coriander leaves

2 coils – about 100 g (3 oz) – fresh *kanom jin* rice noodles

garlic and chilli paste

2 garlic cloves, peeled

pinch of salt

1 long red chilli

shallot paste

6–10 dried bird's eye chillies

pinch of salt

4 tablespoons chopped red shallot

3 tablespoons chopped garlic

1 tablespoon chopped red turmeric

1 teaspoon fermented soy beans (*tua nao*) or shrimp paste *(gapi)*

First, make the two pastes separately by gradually pounding the ingredients together using a pestle and mortar, adding one by one, until smooth.

Put pork ribs in a pot, add salt and enough stock to cover. Bring to the boil and simmer until tender (about 15–20 minutes), skimming as required. In a wok, heat oil or rendered pork fat and fry garlic and chilli paste until golden. Add the shallot paste and fry until fragrant. Season with palm sugar and soy sauce, then add tomatoes. Simmer for several minutes and then add blood cakes, if using, and minced pork, stirring to prevent it clumping. Pour this over the pork ribs and simmer for 4–5 minutes. Check seasoning: it should be rich and salty, a little hot, sour and sweet. Sprinkle with garlic, spring onion and coriander, and serve in a bowl alongside the noodles.

Serve with:

- bean sprouts
- snake beans, finely cut
- pickled mustard greens, shredded
- dried bird's eye chillies, deep-fried
- Deep-fried Pork Skin (page 400).

PINEAPPLE AND DRIED PRAWNS WITH THAI NOODLES

kanom jin sao nahm

2 coils – about 100 g (3 oz) – fresh *kanom jin* rice noodles

2 cups minced pineapple

2 tablespoons shredded ginger – optional

4 garlic cloves, sliced

½ cup ground dried prawns (shrimp)

dressing

3 tablespoons palm sugar

4–5 tablespoons lime juice

4 tablespoons fish sauce

5–20 bird's eye chillies (scuds)

First, make the dressing (see page 338): it should taste sour, salty and sweet. Depending on the number of chillies, it will be quite hot or very, very hot.

Place the noodles on a plate and top with the pineapple, ginger, if using, and garlic. Spoon over the dressing and sprinkle with the ground dried prawns.

Serve with:

— sprigs of lemon basil

— Steamed Eggs (page 388)

— Fish Dumplings Simmered in Coconut Cream (below).

FISH DUMPLINGS SIMMERED IN COCONUT CREAM

jaeng lorm luk chin pla

A sumptuous foil to the astringent flavours of Pineapple and Dried Prawns with Thai Noodles (previous recipe).

2 coriander roots, scraped and chopped

pinch of salt

2 garlic cloves, peeled

large pinch of ground white pepper

150 g (5 oz) fish fillets – such as whiting – finely minced

pinch of castor (superfine) sugar

pinch of salt

1 tablespoon water

2 cups coconut cream

1 teaspoon palm sugar

2 tablespoons fish sauce

Pound coriander roots, salt, garlic and pepper into a paste. Add fish and pound until puréed. Season with sugar and salt, then add the tablespoon of water. Gather and roll into small dumplings – roughly 1 cm (½ in) in diameter.

Heat coconut cream, and season with palm sugar and fish sauce. Add fish dumplings and simmer until cooked – about 5–6 minutes. (You may need to add a little more water to prevent the coconut cream from separating.)

THAI NOODLES WITH CRAB, PRAWN AND CHILLI JAM

kanom jin nahm prik

This is a favourite of Archarn Gobgaew Najpinij, head teacher of Suan Dusit College.

3 cups coconut cream

3 tablespoons roasted and ground mung beans

2 tablespoons Chilli Jam (page 200)

3 tablespoons palm sugar

2 tablespoons tamarind water

3 tablespoons fish sauce

100 g (3 oz) minced uncooked prawns (shrimp)

50 g (2 oz) cooked crabmeat

3 tablespoons shredded sour snakeskin pear or green mango

2 tablespoons kaffir lime juice

1 kaffir lime, cut in half

1 tablespoon deep-fried shallots

1 tablespoon deep-fried garlic

2 coils – about 100 g (3 oz) – fresh *kanom jin* rice noodles

paste

3 red shallots, unpeeled

4 cloves garlic, unpeeled

2 slices galangal, chopped

pinch of salt

2 coriander roots, scraped and chopped

1 teaspoon shrimp paste (*gapi*), roasted

First, make the paste: roast shallots, garlic and galangal; when cool enough to handle, peel shallots and garlic. Gradually pound all the paste ingredients together using a pestle and mortar, adding one by one, until smooth.

Bring coconut cream to the boil and add paste, ground mung beans and chilli jam. Simmer for a few minutes, then season with sugar, tamarind water and fish sauce. The sauce should taste smoky, rich, salty and sweet. Add minced prawns and stir to prevent from clumping. When cooked (about 5 minutes), add crab, snakeskin pear or green mango, kaffir lime juice and kaffir lime. The sauce should now taste fragrantly sour, salty, sweet, yet slightly bitter. Pour into a bowl, sprinkle with deep-fried shallots and garlic, and serve alongside the noodles.

Accompany with some of the following:

— Raw Vegetables (page 380), such as green papaya, banana blossom, green beans and cucumber >

THAI NOODLES WITH CRAB, PRAWN AND CHILLI JAM, SERVED WITH DEEP-FRIED VEGETABLES (page 383)

- deep-fried dried long red chillies
- Deep-fried Vegetables (page 383)
- Steamed Eggs (page 388)
- Steamed Fish Curry (page 314)
- Fish Cakes (page 494) or Prawn Cakes (page 495)
- Prawn Fritters (below)
- Chicken Simmered in Coconut Cream (below)
- Banana Fritters (page 598).

PRAWN FRITTERS

gung chut blaeng tort

Normally unpeeled small prawns are used in this recipe; however, peeled prawns can easily be used if less 'crunch' is desired.

2 tablespoons rice flour

3 salted duck egg whites *or* 3–4 regular egg whites mixed with a pinch of salt

100 g (3 oz) small uncooked prawns (shrimp)

oil for deep-frying

Mix flour with egg whites, add prawns and deep-fry spoonfuls in plenty of oil until golden and crisp.

CHICKEN SIMMERED IN COCONUT CREAM

jaeng lorm gai

A mild, soothing accompaniment to Thai Noodles with Crab, Prawn and Chilli Jam (page 578).

2 coriander roots, scraped and chopped

pinch of salt

2 garlic cloves, peeled

pinch of ground white pepper

1 cup coconut cream

1 cup coconut milk

1 tablespoon palm sugar

2 tablespoons fish sauce

100 g (3 oz) minced skinless chicken breast or thigh fillets

Pound coriander roots, salt, garlic and pepper into a paste. Bring coconut cream and milk to the boil, add paste and stir to dissolve. Season with palm sugar and fish sauce. Add chicken and simmer until cooked (about 3 minutes), stirring to prevent it clumping. The sauce should taste creamy, salty and sweet.

THAI NOODLES WITH WILD GINGER

kanom jin nahm yaa

There are versions of this particular noodle sauce throughout the country. In the northeast, it is made with dried bird's eye chillies and not coconut cream; in the north, with pork instead of fish; and in the south, with turmeric and dried prawns.

1 cup water

1 cup *pla chorn* or trout flesh

2 cups water or stock

½ cup coconut cream

large pinch of white sugar

3 tablespoons fish sauce

pinch of roasted chilli powder – optional

2 coils – about 100 g (3 oz) – fresh *kanom jin* rice noodles

paste

5 dried long red chillies

pinch of salt

1 tablespoon chopped galangal

3 tablespoons chopped lemongrass

5 tablespoons chopped *grachai* (wild ginger)

5 tablespoons chopped red shallot

4 tablespoons chopped garlic

3 tablespoons dried fish

First, make the paste. Combine all paste ingredients and simmer in a cup of water until tender, then purée using a pestle and mortar or a blender.

Poach *pla chorn* or trout in the 2 cups of water or stock until cooked – about 10 minutes. Pound fish and add to paste, reserving the stock. Simmer coconut cream until slightly thickened but not separated, dissolve the paste in it and simmer gently until fragrant. Season with sugar and fish sauce: it should taste hot and salty and fragrant with *grachai*. Add 1 cup of the reserved stock, simmer for a few minutes and check seasoning. Dust with chilli powder, if using, and serve in a bowl alongside the noodles.

Serve with some of the following:

- bean sprouts
- sprigs of lemon basil
- long red and green chillies, diagonally sliced
- Boiled Vegetables (page 381), such as bitter melon and Siamese watercress
- Vegetables Simmered in Coconut Milk (page 382), especially shredded bamboo shoots
- Steamed Eggs (page 388).

14

DESSERTS

There is a natural inclination to salve the palate with something sweet after a pungent meal. In the mountains of the north of Thailand, this could mean a simple ball of glistening palm sugar. Although this is certainly primitive, it is nonetheless delicious, much as fresh, unprocessed honey is. There is an ancient dessert, as old as Sukothai – perhaps even older – where a little of the sticky rice freshly cooked for the meal is reserved and sprinkled with palm sugar, salt, grated coconut and roasted sesame seeds. This simple sweet is still served today.

Given the incremental nature of Thai cooking, it should come as no surprise that although desserts can be quite rustic, such as boiled red beans sweetened with sugar, they can also be extraordinarily intricate. The traditional palace kitchen was divided into savoury and sweet sections, each independently controlled by their respective chef. The head dessert cook was a specialist. She would have spent years in training and daily practices to refine her art, and was held in great respect. Annually a special ceremony acknowledged her skills: incense, candles and flowers were presented to her with hands joined and raised in a *wai*; offerings were made to the Buddha in her name; food was given to monks to accumulate merit for her; and special desserts, trimmed sugar bananas and young coconut were given to the gods and spirits to thank them for providing such a talented cook.

Fresh tropical fruit (*polamai*) has always had a place at the Thai table, being an ideal way to finish a Thai meal. Fruit not only relieves the palate after the rigours of intensely flavoured dishes, but also gives the cook a reprieve. Mostly fruit is eaten fresh and simply peeled; however, in the palaces of Siam fruit was carved into intricate shapes. This practice evolved into a highly regarded and sophisticated art where fresh produce was elaborately transformed into exquisite, decorative flowers, bundles of leaves, uncommon fruit and sometimes bizarre animals. Although many hours were lavished in their production, little more than a selection of small, brass, curled knives was used to carve them. In many ways, this is the essence of Thai desserts, where the most extraordinary – and at times whimsical – results come from simple ingredients and utensils; all that is needed is a steady hand and patience.

Over the centuries, the frugal Siamese developed many ways to preserve their fruit. Over-ripe bananas were once simply dried in the sun and then eaten as a snack. Later, during the Ayuthyian period, they were finely sliced, deep-fried until very crisp and then rolled in sugar. This evolved into a style of dessert where the fruit was simmered with sugar until glacéd. While sweet fruit was preserved in syrup, sour fruit – like tamarind, star fruit, green mangoes and limes – was just dried and sprinkled with white sugar.

Then there were the very sweet desserts, *kanom* – a term which probably derives from the Mon (the indigenous inhabitants of the central plains), being their word for dense, even crystallised, sugar syrup; it has come to mean 'sweet to taste' in modern Thai. Other early desserts were made from boiled rice pounded to a paste with palm sugar and perhaps enriched with some grated coconut, or later with coconut cream. This rustic combination formed the basis of most desserts in Siam.

As the Thai became more sophisticated they began to enjoy a diverse array of savoury foods with rice, but desserts remained surprisingly primitive, often just a sweet paste. Stalls selling such pastes were first reported during the Ayuthyian period, and soon these snacks were enjoyed on their own, at any time of the day. There was a market in the city called *bpaa kanom*, 'dessert forest' – in an area that specialised in making and selling desserts. Historically, selling – and making – such desserts was the province of women. They would layer them on trays and either stroll along streets or paddies, or board small boats and row along canals, hawking their wares.

The arrival of the Portuguese in the mid-sixteenth century did more than introduce the chilli to Thailand. Like most Europeans, the Portuguese considered Siamese food abominable, so they employed many servants, but no Thai cooks. At first they had their own cooks, although they sometimes engaged Chinese cooks. One dessert that was popular with the Portuguese of that time was an egg custard called *ovos moles*, made by mixing egg yolks with cream and flour and then stirring over a low heat until set – a method of cooking with which the Thai were already familiar. Very soon, the Thai were making a version of *ovos moles* from coconut cream, egg yolks and rice flour: it was called *tong ek*, 'golden ones', and is still popular today. Similarly, Thai cooks, with their love of complexity, seized upon the Portuguese confection of *ovos de frios* (egg noodles), transforming it into *foi tong* ('golden strands') and overshadowing its Iberian ancestor. These intricate desserts fashioned from egg yolks joined the Thai repertoire in the late seventeenth century, and it is believed they were introduced by Thao Thong Giip Ma, the half-Portuguese, half-Japanese Christian wife of Constantine Faulkon. Her life was a sad one. Her family was expelled from Japan due to their belief in Christianity and, like many Japanese before them, they fled to Siam, where she married the Greek adventurer Faulkon. After his execution in 1688, she was enslaved and spent the remainder of her life in the kitchens of the new king, her husband's enemy, Phra Phetracha.

The Portuguese made many desserts with egg yolks, as egg whites were used to clarify wine on the Iberian peninsula and such confections made good use of the surplus yolks. Since wine was not clarified in Siam, the Thai gradually omitted egg yolks from their versions of Portuguese recipes, but they continued to develop them. At first, coconut cream was churned with fresh rice flour, and perhaps was coloured with ripe bananas, tamarind or even flavoured with the ash of burnt coconut husks.

In the early Bangkok period, a letter describing a temple festival recorded some of the snacks and sweets produced for the occasion. They included crisp crystallised bananas, sweet prawn-filled egg nets, various egg-based custards, 'golden strands', sweetened sticky rice and a sweetmeat with minced chicken. King Rama II was moved to write some 30 stanzas describing individual desserts and their allure:

Pon plap haeng cheuam	Crystallised persimmon
Plap jin jak duay mit	The Chinese fruit sliced and fanned
Tahm pranit nahm dtarn guan	Gorgeous and swathed in sugar
Kit oidt orn yim yuan	Its sweetness draws me to smile
Yon ying plap yap yap paan	Mesmerised by its sparkling lustre

To the south-west of Bangkok lies Phetchaburi, 'the city of diamonds'. Situated at a crossroads of ancient trade routes, this city has been a centre of dessert-making for several centuries. Around the town, groves of sugar palm and coconut trees supply the many confectioners who specialise in yellow bean pudding, made from the exquisitely flavoured local sugar, and crystallising the many varieties of fruit that flourish in this fertile region. In the mid-nineteenth century, King Mongkut established a summer palace on one of the surrounding hills to escape the heat of the capital. The enterprising ladies of his court became renowned for their skills, refining local dishes, such as green mango with rambutans, and creating elaborate new desserts.

Sweet snacks are the type of food that is most associated with Thai ceremonies, often having their origins in the past. Offerings, full of arcane symbolism, were made to placate the gods, goddesses and spirits of Siam – sweets were used to sweeten their temper. Topknot lollies are presented to the gods at the end of Brahmin rites; yellow bean pudding was recommended to placate malevolent spirits and a piece was left at many countryside altars; and coconut and rice sweetmeats were offered to departed ancestors during the Thai New Year festival, Songkran. Many desserts are also associated with Buddhism, with special sweets being made to honour monks after ceremonies.

Desserts were once made to mark a special occasion, to commemorate an event, or according to the seasons. Regrettably, little of this traditional culture – a culinary calendar – remains, but a few desserts still retain symbolic elements and timing. During September, for example, rice caramel with sesame seeds and peanuts is a favoured offering, having the auspicious number of seven ingredients. In October, steamed sticky rice and banana in banana leaves, is offered at the end of Buddhist Lent. At Songkran, coconut ash pudding and red-coloured sticky rice is served.

During the marriage ceremony special desserts are prepared, some to offer to the gods, but also as gifts between bride and groom, and for each respective family member. Such desserts include the aptly named young girl's cake and lady's fingers. 'Golden strands' and 'golden flowers' are included on many occasions, their colour being considered especially auspicious. These are all traditional, but not necessarily indigenous, desserts. Chinese desserts, such as bird's nests and sesame seed biscuits, are also served at a wedding banquet, perhaps due to the considerable influence of Chinese culture in Thailand and the importance it places on family, marriage and children.

When significant and elaborate ceremonies were to be performed and therefore feasts had to be prepared, often the dessert cooks would begin their tasks a week beforehand. The importance of the occasion was gauged by the amount of ingredients used – eggs determined this for the desserts and poultry or meat for the savoury dishes.

The annual temple fair at Wat Tanlom, which is held on a full moon in July, in the province of Chonburi, captures the spirit of many Thai desserts. The purpose of the festival is to commemorate a well-loved abbot, Phra Phipatanasirikul. He set up the school, was their doctor and confessor. It is said that he had a sweet tooth – most Thai do. In order to commemorate him, and to raise money for the temple, the monks and all the villagers from the surrounding district join together to cook various dishes, especially desserts.

The work is divided into teams, by districts, to share the toil. And it is hard work. One dessert alone calls for mixing 65 kilograms (more than 140 lb) of coconut, 20 kilograms (44 lb) of palm sugar and 16 kilograms (35 lb) of glutinous rice flour; this sticky mass must be churned for up to five hours in the tropical heat. No one shirks the work, since it is believed those who contribute will make merit. All the dessert is then sold to the villagers and visitors to the three-day temple fair. So far, a new pavilion and prayer hall have been built as a result of the villagers' hard work and a revered monk's sweet tooth.

As with savoury food, there are traditional combinations of desserts – tapioca, for example, being paired with bananas simmered in coconut cream, or with black sticky rice. Thanpuuying Pliang Pasonagorn, my steadfast guide to most traditional culinary customs, includes two types of desserts to finish her menus, one 'wet' and one 'dry': that is, one served in a liquid (often iced and perfumed syrup) or simmered in sweetened coconut cream; and the other a pastry or egg-yolk confection.

Utensils are an important consideration in dessert-making. I have found it is best to use a brass wok (see page 126) for Thai desserts – although if a dessert is simmered briefly it is of slight benefit only. But it is vital to use glass or porcelain containers to store desserts, as they will pick up flavours or react unfavourably with anything else. In any case, all utensils must be thoroughly clean to ensure that they do not impart any undesirable flavours.

Each recipe in the chapter makes enough for a single plate, which may be combined as part of a dessert platter. Ideally, two desserts, with an accompanying plate of fruit, would be prepared for 4–6 people.

The ancient practices of smoking and perfuming water, coconut cream or desserts at various stages of their production give a distinctive character to Thai desserts. I suspect that plain desserts were once offered to the gods, along with incense and flowers, which purified and perfumed the sweets.

A subtle balance must be achieved when using these heady and pungent ingredients. The result of perfuming or smoking food should be to enhance it, not to smother with the cloying fragrance of jasmine or the unctuous resin of a candle. Therefore discretion is required.

SMOKING WITH CANDLES

Perhaps unique to Thai cuisine, many desserts are 'smoked' using highly resinous candles, to imbue them with an incense-like character. Occasionally water used to extract coconut cream or for steeping is also smoked. Once, the smoke may have been used to purify ingredients and, while smoking may not preserve food, I have found it certainly masks slightly soured flavours.

Traditionally these candles were elaborately prepared, being progressively layered with many perfumes. The thick wick, made of many entwined cotton strands, was heavily perfumed with sandalwood oil. This was surrounded by a thick, soft, mottled brown and black paste and then rolled into a horseshoe-shaped candle. The best were made from beeswax, paraffin and camphor-like resinous gums; inferior versions often used rendered pork fat.

As far as I know, these unusual candles can be found only in Thai specialty shops – and then only after asking. They should be kept refrigerated in a small, airtight container. There is no substitute for these aromatic candles, but they are not essential to make Thai desserts. While they do impart a unique perfume, the flavour they produce is an acquired taste.

To smoke desserts in the traditional manner, the wick of the candle, exposed at both ends, is lit and after a few moments extinguished. It is then placed in a heavy container, carefully set amid the pastries and sweets, which is sealed with a lid. The desserts are left for a few hours to become suffused with the aroma. Cautiously, I prefer to put the candle in a small bowl and then place it among the desserts, since an exposed candle can easily fall over and burn rather than smoke the sweets.

SMOKED WATER

nahm op tian

A glass or enamel bowl is best for this procedure. It should be quite wide in diameter, maximising the area of water exposed to the smoke. The candle is not very heavy so it can be floated on a small glass disc or a piece of foil. If this is too tenuous, then place a small upturned bowl or disc for the candle on a stand in the centre of the larger bowl or jar. Make sure the candle does not touch the lid. It should smoke for several minutes after being extinguished. Should the smoke be insufficient – that is, if it only smokes for a minute or so before the air clears – then relight and blow out again, otherwise the water will be insipid. An alternative method is to gently blow the smoke from the extinguished candle onto the surface of the water.

> 4 cups water
> 1 Thai candle
>
> Bring water to the boil. Cool and pour into a wide bowl. Light the candle at both ends. When well alight, blow flames out. Place it on a shallow bowl and float on top of the water. Cover quickly and leave, covered, for at least an hour.

PERFUMING WITH FLOWERS

Usually the highly aromatic Thai jasmine flowers are used in this simple technique. Aberrantly, they are known in English as 'Arabian jasmine' and have little to do with common jasmine. The flowers are usually made into garlands and bouquets that are offered to the Buddha or given to monks and elders, as their white colour and pleasing aroma are considered auspicious.

In the more mundane world of desserts, the flowers are picked at sunset, when their piercing fragrance is at its best, and then steeped in water overnight to produce perfumed water. They are never boiled in water or syrup as this would ruin their ethereal scent. They may also perfume sugar (either white or palm) or a finished dessert, such as 'golden strands' or mock jackfruit seeds, in an enclosed container – again usually overnight.

Traditionally other flowers can also be used, such as ylang ylang, a burnt-cream coloured flower with four thick, elongated petals and a rich, almost fatty, fragrance. Ylang ylang flowers profusely throughout the year in the tropics, but elsewhere only during a humid summer. Like jasmine, its pervasive fragrance quickly dissipates and within a day it is spent, stale and hollow – a shadow of its former self.

But, in fact, any deliciously fragrant flower can be used: a quick raid on the garden will do. It is important to ensure that the blooms have not been sprayed with any chemicals; if ordering from a florist, insist on organic flowers. Old-fashioned or tea roses, geraniums and frangipanis (bled of their sap beforehand) are all ideal. A heady scent is what is required, so use whatever is at its most fragrant. I have found the intensely fragranced small dried buds of red roses, which are readily available in Chinese shops, work admirably.

While temperate flowers have an undeniably different fragrance from lush jasmine, they are decidedly better to use for perfuming than any chemical essences. Should such essences be the only choice, use them cautiously (a drop or two only), for they have the capacity to dominate any dessert.

PERFUMED WATER

nahm dork mai

Water that has been boiled and then cooled picks up more fragrance than water straight from the tap. Only steep blossoms overnight, as their fragrance is volatile and dissipates quickly, becoming flat and dull within 24 hours. Traditionally a lidded, earthenware jar is used, but any sealable glass or porcelain jar will do, or even a bowl covered with plastic wrap.

Occasionally, smoked water is used instead of plain water; there is no need to boil this first.

> 4 cups water
>
> 10 jasmine flowers *or* 1 cup less pungent flowers
>
> 2 ylang ylang flowers – optional

> Bring water to the boil. Cool and pour into a wide bowl.
>
> Clean jasmine or other flowers and add to the water. If using ylang ylang flowers, briefly wilt them over a flame – this helps to release their perfume – before placing them in a small dish and floating them on the water. Seal bowl and leave overnight. Remove flowers before use.

DESSERT INGREDIENTS

The rustic combination of palm sugar, rice flour and coconut formed the basis of most desserts in Siam. Although these desserts may have had very limited ingredients, their quality and vibrant freshness lent them surprising dimensions of flavour, belying their simplicity. The palm sugar would have been freshly boiled sap – sweet, but slightly bitter from impurities. The rice flour would have been freshly milled and soaked overnight to remove any excess starch; during the tropical night, the starch would slightly ferment. Fresh grated coconut would have been squeezed without the addition of water, to make an incomparably luscious cream.

PANDANUS LEAVES

These blade-like leaves release their resinous flavour only on heating. They can be boiled whole – although they are usually knotted to make them easier to remove – in syrups and other desserts. However, they should only be simmered briefly, for if stewed they impart an oily, sallow quality. Pandanus leaves are also used to wrap or package small sweetmeats, and occasionally the leaves are blended with a little water to colour and perfume pastries.

SAFFRON

Although not a traditional Thai flavouring, I find saffron adds depth to syrups and a golden hue to egg desserts that can normally be obtained only by using duck eggs.

COCONUT

The coconut is indispensable in making Thai desserts, and it is used in all stages of development – young, intermediate and old – and even the husk is employed.

However, the best coconut cream is made from old, 'dry' coconuts; it is essential to peel the brown skin to obtain a pristinely white cream. Ideally, coconut cream for desserts should be extracted from coconut alone, without adding water to dissolve it in, but it takes a massive amount of strength to wring out the cream this way. Frankly, I have never been able to achieve this successfully. Instead, aim to extract the cream for desserts using a minimal amount of water – about 1 cup to 2 cups grated coconut – following the method given on page 148. This will yield a heavy, thick cream. Then wait for 30 minutes or so to allow the cream to rise to the top and skim off this even more concentrated cream. Coconut cream intended for desserts is immeasurably improved by being prepared with perfumed water, or smoked and perfumed water (see pages 588–90). The result is a cream of incomparable quality and resonance – fresh, rich, luscious, slightly resinous and aromatic. Although it is possible to smoke and perfume the cream after it has been made, it does not taste the same, being rawer in taste and not as deep.

After the coconut cream has risen to the top of the bowl and been removed, what remains is coconut milk, which can be used to poach fruit. If more is needed, simply mix the squeezed coconut flesh with additional water and extract again. Although a small amount of cream will be produced, the result will be mostly milk. When 'cracked' or separated coconut cream (see page 148) is allowed to cool, the cream separates into the oil and solids. The oil is used to deep-fry peanuts, shallots, lotus seeds and bananas. It is a heavy oil which imparts a sharp, rather peppery flavour, and I like to cut it with some good flavourless vegetable oil. Undiluted, a little can be smeared in moulds to prevent desserts sticking to them. The oil lasts indefinitely and, if strained, can be re-used many times. The residue that remains after the clear oil is removed from separated cream is coconut solids or curds, which are used to give body and moisture to some desserts.

SALT

This is used in many desserts to varying degrees, mostly in minuscule amounts. Salt draws out the flavour of the other ingredients and has the effect of countering extremes of taste, tempering sweetness and reducing the unctuousness of coconut cream. Sometimes it is used as a strong flavour in itself. Salt can come as a surprise to the unsuspecting, and is an acquired taste in desserts; it may initially have been employed as a preservative.

SUGAR

Often sugar – of whatever kind – to be used in desserts is perfumed with flowers overnight before use the next day; the elusive perfume dissipates after a day or so.

In Thailand, white sugar is produced by simmering and clarifying sugar cane with hydrolysed lime water. This results in a clean, but not always ultra-purified, sugar that is normally used to make syrups. For those who do not wish to clarify their own, either castor (superfine) or regular granulated sugar can be used.

Moist, soft, honey-golden granules of Thai palm sugar are indispensable when making these desserts. Different grades are used for different desserts as each imparts a distinct colour and flavour. The best quality comes from Phetchaburi, a renowned centre of dessert-making. When fresh, palm sugar is ambrosial, but regrettably it is often adulterated with cheaper cane sugar. Accomplished Thai dessert chef Tanongsak Yordwai suggests that one way to invigorate it is to dissolve it in a little mixed coconut cream and milk, then simmer, stirring regularly to prevent scorching and promote its re-crystallisation. I think some young coconut water with a few pandanus leaves would also be an excellent liquid to use for this purpose. Remember, however, that sugar treated in this way will be denser and wetter than just-bought sugar, so reduce any other liquids in the recipe accordingly. Palm sugar treated like this can also ferment, so make only as required.

Coconut sugar shares many properties with palm sugar, although the aroma is creamier. Once, many desserts specified coconut sugar in their ingredients, but this is now rare.

SUGAR SYRUP

Originally a basic syrup was made by stirring – traditionally with a few folded pandanus leaves – sugar with cold water until it had dissolved. This takes little time if palm sugar is used, especially if the hands are employed, but slightly longer with white sugar. Now, more often sugar syrup is made by simmering white sugar (rarely palm sugar) in perfumed water. The simmering clarifies the sugar, giving the resultant syrup an alluring sheen. Once the sugar has dissolved, the syrup is strained.

Sometimes the syrup is simmered with crushed eggshells and egg whites to further clarify it and capture any impurities that tend to lurk in the not-so-refined Thai white sugar. The syrup is allowed to cool slightly before the coagulated egg whites and shells are carefully lifted from the liquid. Then it is strained through several layers of damp muslin or a few times through a very fine sieve. This process endows the syrup with a greater lustre and suppleness.

Normally the proportions are 1 part sugar to 1 part water, by volume or weight, but this proportion, and thus the density of the syrup, is very much a matter of personal choice. Some prefer lighter syrups made with 1 part sugar to 2 parts water; others like their syrup a little denser. Generally it is of little importance if the syrup is to be used to finish dishes or macerate fruit. However, when a dessert calls for an item to be poached or simmered in a syrup, it is imperative that the syrup is of the correct density. If palm sugar or coconut sugar is dissolved in water to make a syrup, be careful, for it will scorch and taint if simmered too long.

MALTOSE

This can be added as a safeguard when making concentrated sugar syrups and thick palm sugar candies, as its chemical composition retards crystallisation. It retains its distinctive taste when used with white sugar, but becomes indistinguishable when combined with palm sugar. Maltose also softens caramels and candies, helping them to remain pliable once cool.

HONEY

It is uncommon to include honey in Thai desserts, although it can be used as a substitute for maltose. It also makes an ambrosial dipping sauce for fruit or pastries, perhaps tempered by lime juice.

STICKY RICE

The best white sticky rice to use for desserts is from the previous year's harvest. It has a deeper taste than new rice and, while it takes longer to cook, the grains retain a pleasing toothsome character. Sticky rice is usually soaked overnight in cold water before use – if this is forgotten, it can be soaked in warm, but not hot, water for 30 minutes or so. Black sticky rice has a tinted bran, and is used only for desserts. It must be soaked overnight in plenty of water before it is cooked and then boiled until completely tender. Otherwise, when sugar is added, any uncooked starch in the rice toughens.

FLOUR

Whatever it is made from – rice, tapioca, arrowroot or mung beans – flour can be prepared fresh or bought dried. All dried flour should be sieved before use in desserts.

The most fastidious cooks will grind their own fresh flour. While time-consuming, this is not difficult. The rice (long-grain or sticky) is first soaked in plenty of water for a few hours, then it is milled – traditionally in a heavy, granite affair. A modern reprieve is to blitz the rice in a blender or food processor, with a little water to facilitate the process, until it is truly puréed. The resulting paste is collected in a cloth bag, which is weighed down overnight to extract any excess liquid; it may slightly ferment during the night, but this only adds to its character. The paste retains some moisture – in fact, it is crumbly – and must be used within a day, otherwise it will have soured too much. It is nutty and less starchy than dried flour and imparts an indefinable subtlety and finesse to desserts. In pastries, it makes a softer dough and, while allowing other ingredients to shine, it also retains its own nutty rice flavour. If using fresh flour, take into account the extra moisture it contains and alter recipes accordingly.

Using completely dry flour means that pastries do lose some complexity of taste, but it is unquestionably more convenient. Some Thai cooks perfume dried flour with jasmine as a matter of course. Recipes may call for smoking the flour, others require it to be roasted: each process gives it a different, yet enhanced, taste.

Rice flour is most commonly used in Thai desserts. The best quality is very white and absorbs a surprising amount of liquid. It cooks quite quickly and contains no gluten, so when cooked it yields a thick paste with a short 'crisp' texture and a good sheen. White sticky rice flour results in a rather heavy, densely textured pastry when cooked. It can be used alone, but more often is added in combination with rice flour, each imparting its own qualities to the finished dessert. Black sticky rice flour has the same properties as white sticky rice flour, but it turns a deep purple when cooked and is not commonly used.

Tapioca flour, extracted from the cassava root, gives a malleable, silken and dense texture to pastries. It is rarely used alone, but rather to lend elasticity to rice flour pastry. Thai arrowroot flour is often quite lumpy: it needs to be ground and sieved before being added to other flour. It softens and lightens pastry, giving a crunchy texture.

Mung bean flour is made from blanched or roasted mung beans, with their skins being removed before grinding. When cooked alone with water, mung bean flour becomes a translucent, tasteless paste; hence it is generally used with other flours.

MUNG BEANS
Yellow mung beans form the basis of several classic Thai desserts, especially yellow bean pudding. Roasted and ground mung beans (see page 163), or occasionally roasted sesame seeds, may be used as a garnish.

Mung bean flour (see above) is also used in some desserts.

EGGS
Duck eggs are ideal for use in Thai desserts; they are available from some delicatessens and specialist butchers. They are larger than chicken eggs and richer in flavour, with a deeper-coloured yolk and a more viscous white.

Unless otherwise specified, the recipes here are for large chicken eggs, so remember to compensate for the difference in size if using duck eggs: a duck egg is roughly 25 per cent larger than a large chicken egg.

HYDROLYSED LIME WATER
Tender fruit is often soaked in hydrolysed lime water (see page 159) to tighten its cell membranes, enabling it to survive prolonged simmering without dissolving or toughening. Once soaked, the fruit must be thoroughly rinsed in running water.

AGAR-AGAR
This flavourless, seaweed-derived setting agent gives a crisp crunchiness to desserts that is unique. It is normally used to make a pleasant and cooling jelly flavoured with coconut, pandanus or eggs.

GRILLED BANANAS WITH GRATED COCONUT AND SALT

gluay pao

Fruit makes up a huge part of Thai desserts. Bananas, for example, can be dried, grilled, simmered in perfumed syrups or coconut cream, puréed and then churned.

5 ripe sugar bananas or plantains

½ cup grated coconut

large pinch of salt

1 tablespoon white sugar – optional, but preferable for the modern palate

Grill bananas or plantains in their skin. When the skin begins to split while cooking, slit it open with a sharp knife (this prevents the bananas steaming). Grill until the skin is charred and the inside is tender.

Mix grated coconut with salt and, if desired, sugar. Sprinkle this into the split and eat while hot, scooping out the banana and coconut together.

GRILLED BANANAS WITH COCONUT CREAM AND TURMERIC

gluay yang kamin

5 small bananas

1–2 tablespoons lime juice

Sweetened White Sticky Rice (1 quantity of recipe on page 616)

3–4 tablespoons coconut cream

syrup

2 cups coconut cream

pinch of salt

2 cups palm sugar

1½ cups black coconut sugar

1–2 pandanus leaves, knotted

2 tablespoons finely chopped turmeric

Peel bananas and steep in water acidulated with lime juice to prevent discolouration. Combine syrup ingredients and simmer over a medium heat until thick – about 7–10 minutes. Grill bananas, press between two weights to flatten, then immerse in syrup for at least 10 minutes.

When ready to serve, remove bananas from syrup and slowly grill until golden, caramelised and fragrant. Serve over sticky rice, with the coconut and turmeric syrup and coconut cream.

GREEN MANGO WITH RAMBUTANS

som chum

In Thailand, some fruit is available throughout the year, like pineapples, bananas and papayas. Other fruit is seasonal, like mangosteens and rambutans – about which King Rama II soberly observed that although ugly on the outside, the inside was delectable and one should therefore not be fooled by appearance.

Here the interplay of sweet syrup and sour fruit is enhanced with the nutty and crunchy character of deep-fried shallots. King Rama II compared the succulence and perfume of this dish to the pleasing tones of a lover's voice.

1 cup white sugar

1½ cups water

1 pandanus leaf, knotted

pinch of salt

20 rambutans

1 small green mango, shredded

a little crushed ice

3 tablespoons deep-fried shallots

Make a syrup by simmering the sugar and water, adding pandanus leaf and salt. Cool and remove pandanus. Peel the rambutans, prise out their seeds, then combine with green mango. Pour the syrup over the fruit, add crushed ice and sprinkle with deep-fried shallots to serve.

SANTOL IN SYRUP

grathorn loy gaew

Literally translated, *loy gaew* means 'floating gems'. In fact the technique is very simple: fresh fruit macerated in syrup. The syrup is often iced, and such desserts are particularly relished in the heat of the tropics. A *loy gaew* relies on prime produce – whatever seasonal fruit is at its best should be used. The fruit must be perfectly ripe and the syrup delicately perfumed. Mostly a single fruit is macerated, although a medley would be just as welcome. Slightly tart fruit helps to balance the cool sweetness of the dish: pineapple, young coconut, boiled sugar cane or lotus seeds, grapes, Asian citrus fruit, rambutans, sweet tamarind flesh, lychees, longans, ripe papaya or watermelon. I think tamarillo, peaches, prickly pears, apricots and apples are also good candidates. Salt is sometimes added to the syrup or sprinkled over the finished compôte to further accentuate the taste, and occasionally a little coconut cream or milk is added to enrich the dish.

This classic recipe comes from Praya Manit Manidtayagun. Born in 1879, he was the son of a high-ranking government official who sent his son abroad to study in England when he was just 13. There he attended a public school and later read law and was admitted to one of the Inns of Law, the Inner Temple, specialising in constitutional law. On his return to Thailand he began a steady rise at the Ministry of Law, culminating in his appointment as a Privy Councillor during the sixth reign. He died in 1940.

Than Manit enjoyed cooking both Western and Thai food. His slim memorial book contains many complicated recipes – not surprising, given his background and rank. The following recipe, however, is elegant, brief and simple.

1 cup white sugar
1 cup Perfumed Water (page 590)
4 santol
pinch of salt
ice shavings – optional

Simmer sugar and water to make a syrup. Strain and cool.

Peel santol and cut into sixths. Steep in salted water for several minutes to remove some of its astringency and to prevent the thick, white pith from discolouring. Remove seeds from the flesh, then squeeze santol dry, extracting as much water as possible.

Stir the fruit into the cold syrup and serve sprinkled with a little salt and perhaps some ice shavings.

BANANA FRITTERS

kao mao tort

The best type of banana to use for this dessert is the small sugar banana, sometimes known as Ducasse. These bananas are rather small, so if using a different, larger variety, cut each into lengths about 2 cm (1 in) long. Once fried, the banana fritters can be eaten hot, just out of the oil, or can be kept for a few hours. In the markets of most Thai towns, several stalls sell these delicious fritters. They are prepared in the morning – and usually sold out by the afternoon.

1 cup grated coconut
1 cup palm sugar
3 cups roasted and crushed flattened rice
5 bananas, peeled
1 egg, beaten
oil for deep-frying

batter

1 cup rice flour

½ cup water

1 cup hydrolysed lime water

1 egg, lightly beaten

1 teaspoon salt

Knead grated coconut with palm sugar, then simmer in a saucepan until it is quite sticky. Add 2 cups of the flattened rice and stir until fragrant. Allow the mixture to cool, divide into 5 balls, flatten into discs and wrap around the bananas. The recipe can be prepared ahead to this stage.

Make batter by kneading flour with water to form a heavy dough. Leave to rest for 30 minutes, then work in lime water, coconut cream (if using), egg and salt. When ready to eat, dip coated bananas in beaten egg, then roll in the remaining cup of flattened rice and finally dip into batter. Deep-fry until golden and crisp.

GLACÉD GINGKO NUTS IN PERFUMED SYRUP

bpae guay cheuam nahm horm

Glacéing is a method of preserving fruit – and occasionally vegetables, especially tubers – by simmering in a dense sugar syrup. The syrup should be simmered gently, so as not to overly reduce it. This also helps prevent the fruit or vegetable from disintegrating, and ensures that the syrup is thoroughly absorbed. Sometimes a little lime juice or citric acid is added to prevent the syrup crystallising and to give the finished dish a gleam. A pinch of salt helps to bring out the sweetness of the sugar and stops the syrup being too cloyingly sweet. Once glacéd, a preserved item can be kept for a week.

Gingko nuts – from the maidenhair tree – are believed to increase circulation and be efficacious for the lungs, bladder and urinary system. They are readily obtainable from most Chinese medicine shops.

40 gingko nuts

1 cup white sugar

2 cups Perfumed Water (page 590)

Shell the nuts and peel their skins; it may be necessary to steep the shelled nuts in hot water to lift this skin. Bring to the boil in plenty of cold water and simmer until tender. Drain and cool. Remove green germ by pushing it out from the centre of the nut with a small skewer or toothpick. (If cooked further with the germ, the nuts turn an attractive pale jade colour, but become bitter.)

Melt sugar in perfumed water and simmer the nuts gently until the sugar has been absorbed. The nuts can be eaten hot or allowed to cool and served with ice.

GLACÉD POMELO PEEL

bliak som oo cheuam

This is an excellent way to use the large amount of often-discarded pomelo peel. The method is very simple; the preliminary soaking, blanching and squeezing mitigates the inherent bitterness of the peel. Some cooks remove the zest, considering that the white, fleshy pith alone yields a superior result. The peel can be simmered until the sugar syrup begins to crystallise, but I prefer a slightly moister result, and so remove the peel while there is still some syrup remaining. Some cooks roll the glacéd peel in perfumed sugar before drying.

Many peeled fruit and vegetables can also be treated in this pleasingly simple way – honeydew melon, pineapple, jackfruit, cassava, even potato.

pomelo peel
hydrolysed lime water
1–2 teaspoons salt
white sugar
Perfumed Water (page 590)

Cut the peel into elegantly shaped pieces. Wash and steep in plain water for around 3 hours to remove some of its bitterness. Rinse and squeeze dry and then steep once more, this time in hydrolysed lime water, for a further 3 hours. Drain, rinse and dry thoroughly.

Blanch peel four times in salted water from a cold-water start, refreshing and squeezing the pith each time to extract any further bitterness. Weigh the peel. For every 250 g (8 oz) of prepared peel, make a syrup with 750 g (1½ lb) sugar and 3½ cups perfumed water. Simmer over a medium heat until syrup has reduced slightly. Add peel, turn heat to low and simmer. Turn the peel regularly and baste constantly with the syrup until it has all been absorbed.

When ready, the peel will be translucent and have a wonderful sheen. Remove and drain on a rack in the sun or a warm, airy place until quite dry.

PANDANUS AND COCONUT AGAR-AGAR

wun bai dtoei lae gati

This dessert is normally poured into small metal moulds, but any mould can be used as long as it is very clean – any residual oil or detergent will mar the clarity of the agar-agar. There is no need to refrigerate this jelly, which will begin to set once the liquid cools. However, it is essential that the first layer has not set too firmly before the next layer is poured over it, or they will not gel together. If preferred, only one type of mixture can be made or the mixtures can be set in separate moulds.

Sometimes shredded young coconut is served alongside; Tanongsak Yordwai make an excellent version with coffee added to the jelly.

These types of desserts are best eaten on the day they are made. If kept, the agar-agar continues to work, and the jelly becomes increasingly tough.

15 g (½ oz) agar-agar

4 cups water – ideally including some coconut water

2 cups white sugar

½ cup water blended with 3 pandanus leaves, then strained

2 cups coconut cream

pinch of salt

Stir agar-agar into water, bring to the boil and simmer for at least 10 minutes, stirring regularly. Pour in sugar and simmer until dissolved. Divide this syrup in half. Mix one half with the pandanus water and heat slowly, but do not allow to boil. Pour the hot pandanus syrup into a clean tray or 10 individual moulds. Combine the remaining syrup with the coconut cream and salt. Slowly bring to the boil, stirring constantly. When the pandanus layer is just beginning to set, pour in the coconut syrup. (If intending to serve unmoulded, reverse the order of these layers.)

Leave to cool, and serve when fully set. To unmould, run a small knife around the edges of the agar-agar and gently shake free.

POMEGRANATE AGAR-AGAR

wun tap tim

4 pomegranates

20 g (⅔ oz) agar-agar

3 cups water

1 pandanus leaf – optional

1 cup white sugar

½ cup pomegranate syrup or molasses

Quarter the pomegranates, remove 1 tablespoon whole seeds and set aside. Rub the pomegranate quarters against a sieve, then let the fruit rest in the sieve over a bowl, so the juice 'bleeds' out – yielding about ½ cup of juice.

Mix the agar-agar with the water and bring to the boil with the pandanus leaf, if using. Allow to simmer, stirring constantly, for at least 10 minutes. Add sugar and, once dissolved, add pomegranate juice and syrup. Bring almost to the boil, stirring regularly. Remove from the heat and add reserved pomegranate seeds, then pour into a tray or 7 individual moulds and leave to cool.

To unmould, run a small knife around the edges of the agar-agar and gently shake free.

RUBIES

tap tim grop

A highly coloured root, *klang*, was traditionally used to colour this well-known dessert. Most Thai cooks now use red food colouring, but pomegranate juice (see previous recipe for an easy way of extracting this) is a natural substitute.

½ cup water chestnuts
½ cup pomegranate juice
1 cup tapioca flour
3 cups Perfumed Water (page 590)
1 cup cold sugar syrup (see page 592), made from 1 cup sugar and
   1 cup perfumed water
shaved or cracked ice
½ cup coconut cream

Peel and clean the water chestnuts and cut into roughly ¼ cm (⅛ in) cubes. Soak overnight in pomegranate juice. Remove and drain. Roll in tapioca flour, then place in a sieve and shake to remove excess flour. Bring perfumed water to the boil, add coated water chestnuts and simmer until cooked – about 2 or 3 minutes; the 'rubies' float to the surface when they are ready. Remove and steep in cold water. Drain and combine equal amounts of the water chestnuts, syrup and ice, then serve drizzled with the coconut cream.

GOLDEN TEARDROPS

tong yord

This dessert, 'golden strands' and 'golden flowers' are all made from duck egg yolks: the difference lies in the density of the sugar syrup they are cooked in.

When the 'golden teardrops' are dropped into the syrup, one side should be rounded and the other elongated. The syrup should be boiling, but not so dense as to be close to crystallising. It is imperative that perfumed water is sprinkled over the syrup once the teardrops are removed, and once more after the syrup has boiled, to restore the proper density and prevent the sugar crystallising.

If the teardrops are flat after cooking, it may be that the egg yolks were over-beaten, and thus unable to expand to their optimum once heated. Or perhaps not enough flour, which stabilises the dumplings during cooking, was folded in. Or there may have been insufficient syrup, so the batter had too little space to cook and expand. Or the dumplings may have hit the bottom of the wok when added to the simmering syrup. Or the syrup was too light or had begun to crystallise. If they are too hard, perhaps the teardrops were too large, which means that too much air might have escaped from them during cooking. Or perhaps the syrup was too dense . . .

It is important to place the teardrops in the cool, lighter syrup while they are still hot so that it can be drawn into the dumplings by osmosis, ensuring that they will be moist and glistening.

4–5 tablespoons rice flour

1 Thai candle and/or fragrant flowers

5 cups white sugar

8 cups Perfumed Water (page 590)

3 pandanus leaves, knotted

10 duck egg yolks *or* 13–14 large chicken egg yolks

Lightly roast the flour in a brass wok until light gold and then smoke with a candle (see page 588), perfume with flowers (see page 589) – or both – for an hour or so.

Simmer sugar with 6 cups of the perfumed water and pandanus leaves until dissolved and then strain. Bring two-thirds of the syrup to the boil and simmer gently until it reaches 'soft ball' stage – until there are small bubbles. Refrigerate the remaining third.

Meanwhile beat the egg yolks until pale – almost at a 'ribbon' stage. (The yolks should not be too pale or over-beaten, otherwise they will absorb too much flour and the teardrops will be heavy. If under-beaten, however, the teardrops will be lumpen and will soufflé when poached and then become crumbly when cooled in the syrup.) In a small bowl, gradually fold flour into the yolks until well incorporated – the proportion by volume of yolks to flour should be about 2:1. Spoon a teaspoon of the mixture at a time into the boiling syrup. Traditionally this is done with the fingers, deftly rolling and shaping the mixture into a teardrop shape about 1–2 cm (½–1 in) long. Drop into the rapidly boiling syrup and repeat with several more teardrops. After a minute, sprinkle the syrup with a little water – no more than 2 tablespoons – to reduce the heat and frothing, then turn the teardrops. Simmer for another few moments then remove. Steep in the reserved light syrup for 5 minutes, ideally with a few extra flowers.

Replenish the simmering syrup with some of the remaining perfumed water to ensure that it remains at the 'soft ball' stage and repeat the process until all the mixture is used up.

GOLDEN STRANDS

foi tong

Duck eggs are the best to use for this, as they have the most attractive colour, the richest flavour and sufficient protein to make the strands. Chicken eggs can be used but they do not have the same colour and flavour. Often the syrup is perfumed with a few

GOLDEN TEARDROPS (page 603), GOLDEN STRANDS (above) AND GOLDEN FLOWERS (page 607)

pandanus leaves to prevent the strands from being too rich. I think saffron can perform the same task and has the added benefit of giving chicken egg yolks a gorgeous colour. The freshest eggs are best — and if they have not been refrigerated, so much the better.

It takes a few attempts to get this classic example of a complex Thai dessert right; patience and skill are required.

6 duck eggs or 8 chicken eggs
1½ kg (3 lb) castor (superfine) sugar
11 cups Perfumed Water (page 590)
10 fragrant flowers, preferably Thai jasmine — optional

Separate the eggs, saving a couple of the eggshells. Strain the yolks through a fine sieve or damp muslin, then stir in the thick egg white that remains attached to the shell and rest this mixture overnight in the refrigerator. In a separate bowl, refrigerate a tablespoon of the egg white (reserve the rest of the egg whites for other uses — such as Egg White Custard with Young Coconut, page 623).

Make a syrup with sugar and 10 cups of the perfumed water, ideally in a brass wok. Let it boil for 1 minute, add ½ cup of water to arrest the boiling, then add the reserved tablespoon of egg white and a few crushed eggshells. Bring back to the boil and, after syrup clarifies, lift off the resulting foam. Skim the syrup regularly with a clean, hot spoon: ensure there is a bowl of hot water nearby to keep the spoon clean and hot, otherwise it will reintroduce impurities. Always have a small bowl of cold water nearby too, ready for sprinkling into the simmering syrup to ensure that it remains at a reasonably constant sugar density: the strands will be brittle if the syrup is too heavy, but the required filaments will not form if it is too thin. When the syrup is totally clean, strain through a fine sieve.

Return syrup to the boil. Pour the yolks into an icing bag with the finest nozzle. Stream the equivalent of a few tablespoons of the mixture in a circular motion about 10 cm (4 in) above the hottest part of the syrup where it is bubbling; turn the heat down to medium. Allow to cook for 1 minute, then turn heat to very low and drag a long chopstick or skewer through the syrup to collect the strands. (Turning the heat to very low before removing the strands allows the eggs to relax and the syrup to settle and makes it easier to collect and 'comb' the strands.) Drag backwards and forwards, collecting all the strands, and teasing and unknotting them. Lay on a plate, folding the threads over into thirds. Add ½ cup more perfumed water to syrup, return to boil, skim surface, then add more yolk mixture.

Once cooked, the strands are often moistened with a little syrup to give them an alluring gleam. They can also be perfumed with jasmine flowers (see page 589) for a few hours, if desired.

GOLDEN FLOWERS

tong yip

In this recipe, make sure the syrup is not boiling when the egg is added, to ensure an even spread. A steady hand helps, too! If the syrup is too dense, then the discs will not spread sufficiently and will themselves be dense. Conversely, if too light, then the discs will be too wet. Traditionally the cooled discs are moulded in small cups, about 1½–2 centimetres (¾–1 inch) in diameter and pinched (*yip* in Thai) into flower-like shapes. More skilled confectioners can create five, even seven, petals. For the less adroit, like myself, three or four is a triumph.

> 10 duck egg yolks
> 1–2 cups Perfumed Water (page 590)
>
> **heavy syrup**
> 4 cups white sugar
> 7 cups Perfumed Water (page 590)
> 1 egg white
> a few eggshells, crushed
>
> **light syrup**
> ½ cup white sugar
> 1 cup Perfumed Water (page 590)

First, make the heavy syrup by simmering sugar with perfumed water. Boil for 1 minute, add 2 tablespoons water to arrest the boiling, then add a tablespoon of egg white and the crushed eggshells. Bring back to the boil, reduce the heat to a simmer and, after syrup clarifies, lift off the resulting foam. Skim often with a ladle kept in hot water. When the syrup is totally clean, strain through a fine sieve.

Make the light syrup by simmering the sugar and perfumed water. Sieve and set aside. Meanwhile, pass the egg yolks through a fine sieve or damp muslin and then beat until frothy and beginning to whiten. Cover and rest for a few minutes.

Over a medium heat, return the heavy syrup to the boil in a brass wok, then turn down the heat and drop a tablespoon of the egg mixture into the syrup. (Be careful not to stir too much when spooning out the mixture for poaching – if too much air is removed, the resulting confection will be tough and dense.) It will expand into a disc about 4 cm (1½ in) across. Repeat 5 or 6 times to fill the wok. Turn up the heat until syrup begins to bubble, then turn discs over and ladle boiling syrup over them; they will begin to swell. After a minute or so, remove and steep in the cool light syrup. Repeat until all the mixture has been used. Replenish the heavy syrup with ¼ cup of perfumed water after each batch is cooked.

Once cooled, remove a disc from the syrup, pinch the edges to form a 'flower' and press into a small cup to shape. Repeat with the remaining discs – or at least as many as you can be bothered to do.

GOLDEN ONES

tong ek

Surprisingly, it is best to use coconut cream that is not too thick for this dessert; otherwise it will taste too oily. For the same reason, duck eggs are considered too strongly flavoured. Ground lotus or melon seeds, cashews or peanuts, even ground almonds, can be used to thicken this delicate paste in place of the flour. Since there is such a high proportion of egg and coconut cream with little to stabilise them, it is wise to cook the paste over a very low heat. Tanongsak Yordwai recommends cooking it over a pot of boiling water rather than a direct flame.

½ cup coconut cream
½ cup white sugar
1½ tablespoons arrowroot flour
½ tablespoon rice flour – roasted or perfumed, if desired
5 egg yolks
gold leaf – optional
Thai candle to smoke – optional

Combine and simmer coconut cream with sugar until quite thick. Allow to cool. Sieve flours together.

Add egg yolks to syrup and stir constantly over a low heat, while very slowly adding the flour – over a 10-minute period – until it is thick and cooked, but still quite moist. When it is ready, there should be no taste of flour. Check this by smearing a bit of the paste on the tongue and across the upper palate: if any grains of flour can be felt, continue to cook.

Allow to cool slightly before pressing into small moulds or spooning into oval shapes. Top with gold leaf and smoke the finished desserts with a candle (see page 588), if desired.

COCONUT ASH PUDDING

kanom bliak bun

This ebony-like sweet is eaten wrapped in banana leaves during the celebration of Songkran, Thai New Year. Untraditionally, I like to give the cooked paste a whirl in a food processor to break down the gluten, rendering it wonderfully tender and slippery. To accentuate the perfume of this dessert, a pinch of ground star anise or cassia can be added to the raw paste.

What makes this pudding so peculiar yet delicious is the coconut ash. This is made from the husk of young coconut, left to dry in the sun or a warm place for several days. It is then set alight in a bowl (be careful, for it burns fiercely) and the cooled cinders are sieved.

1 cup white sticky rice flour

¼ cup rice flour

2 tablespoons arrowroot flour

2 cups young coconut water

1 cup coconut cream

2½–3 cups hydrolysed lime water

¾ cup palm sugar

3 tablespoons coconut ash

2 pandanus leaves – optional

2 tablespoons coarsely crushed deep-fried peanuts

2 tablespoons shredded young coconut

extra 2 tablespoons coconut cream

Sieve the flours together, then mix with 1 cup of the young coconut water and knead to a fine, firm dough. Rest for around 30 minutes. Mix coconut cream, 2 cups of the hydrolysed lime water, the remaining cup of coconut water and the palm sugar. Stir until dissolved, then mix in the coconut ash. Combine thoroughly with the dough, then strain the mixture 3–4 times through a very fine sieve, working the residue through with a ladle. Some fastidious cooks sieve it through muslin (cheesecloth) one final time.

Add pandanus, if using, to mixture and bring to the boil in a brass wok or wide pot, stirring regularly. Simmer over a low to medium heat until thick and sticky – this can take up to 30 minutes. It should taste rich, liquorice-like and sweet. There should be no taste – or texture – of uncooked flour. Check this by smearing a bit of the paste on the tongue and across the upper palate: if any grains of flour can be felt, continue to cook. If the mixture becomes too dry, moisten with a little hydrolysed lime water.

When the pudding is ready, remove pandanus leaves (if using) and pour into a tray, spreading it evenly with a spatula. Allow to cool. To serve, spoon onto plates, sprinkle with peanuts and young coconut, and drizzle with coconut cream.

BANANA PASTE

gluay guan

Churned desserts use sugar to preserve fruit or vegetables. Salt draws out the other component flavours, enhancing mango, pineapple, bananas, tomatoes and *madan* (sour cucumber). It also serves to preserve the confection: churned desserts keep for a few days only; after this time, the coconut cream spoils and the starch swells.

Use over-ripe bananas for this recipe: their pronounced sugar will produce a luscious paste.

2 cups coconut cream

1 cup palm sugar

large pinch of salt

2 cups puréed banana

½ cup hydrolysed lime water

In a wok – ideally a brass one – simmer coconut cream until it begins to separate. Add palm sugar and salt, stirring to dissolve. Stir in banana purée and then gradually add hydrolysed lime water. Gently fold over a low to medium heat until the banana paste pulls away from the sides of the wok.

In Thailand, this dessert is often pressed into a small metal tray to cool and then cut into squares to serve. More conveniently, the paste can be simply spooned into a small bowl.

TAMARIND PASTE

makaam guan

It may seem extraordinary to add chillies to a dessert, but they impart a sharpness to the paste and prevent the tamarind being too sour. The amount of salt used depends on the quality of the tamarind used – some brands are quite salty and therefore require no extra salt. The best-quality tamarind pulp is prunishly sour and needs a little salt to create an intriguingly complex taste.

Use granulated sugar to finish the dish – its larger grains lend an interesting texture.

2 cups thick tamarind water

2 cups chopped tamarind pulp, seeds and fibre removed

1½ cups white sugar

4 bird's eye chillies (scuds), pounded with a pinch of salt

½ cup perfumed white sugar (see page 589)

Mix tamarind water and pulp, sugar and chillies together. Work with a wooden spoon over a low heat until thick and sticky – about 15–20 minutes. Set aside until lukewarm, then shape into oval balls and roll in perfumed sugar.

MOCK JACKFRUIT SEEDS

met kanun

Various starchy tubers or pulses can be used in this luscious and playful dessert, such as taro or even jackfruit seeds themselves. The best eggs to use are duck eggs, as their density ensures the 'seeds' will be thickly covered and their colour gives a depth to the dessert. Chicken yolks do not work as well: they create a limp coating and impart little colour; if using, at least enhance the colour by adding a pinch of saffron to the yolks. Dipping the 'seeds' in egg before poaching gives them a little topknot, which is significant as this dessert is served during the tonsure ceremony (see page 626) and on other auspicious occasions.

10 or so fragrant flowers
1 cup Perfumed Water (page 590)

paste
2½ cups steamed and puréed pumpkin
½ cup grated coconut
1½ cups thick coconut cream
1¼ cups white sugar – perhaps perfumed with
   a few jasmine flowers (see page 589)

syrup
2 cups white sugar
1 egg white
2 eggshells, crushed
1½ cups Perfumed Water (page 590)

coating
10 duck egg yolks

For the paste, combine ingredients and stir over a very low heat until quite firm. The longer it takes to cook the purée, the deeper and sweeter will be its flavour, but it should not be too reduced or the finished dessert will be dry. Cool before rolling into small ovals – about 1½ cm (¾ in) long and 1 cm (½ in) wide – keeping your hands wet to prevent the paste sticking to them.

For the syrup, combine sugar with egg white and eggshells, mixing well. Add this to the perfumed water and bring slowly to the boil, stirring to ensure the egg white is well dispersed. When the syrup has simmered and the egg white has coagulated, turn off the heat, leave a minute to settle, then carefully lift off the 'raft' of egg white and eggshells. Return the syrup to the boil, skim, then strain through damp muslin (cheesecloth) or a very fine sieve. >

Bring back to the boil over a medium heat and simmer, skimming regularly, until slightly reduced and at the 'light thread' stage: if measured with a sugar thermometer, this is about 104°C (220°F). A manual test is to remove a teaspoon of the simmering syrup, wet the thumb and index finger, and take a pinch of the syrup; when the finger and thumb are slightly pulled apart, a fine thread should stretch between them. (It is important to get the temperature, and thus the density of the syrup, correct. If it is too hot or dense, the egg coating will crinkle; if too cold or too light, it will not stick to the 'seeds'.)

For the coating, pass the yolks through a sieve and then set aside to rest for a few minutes.

Pierce each pumpkin oval with a toothpick and swirl through the egg yolks to coat liberally. Poach a few at a time in the hot – but not boiling – syrup over a low heat for 2 minutes. Carefully turn the 'seeds' and bring back to the boil very, very slowly. Barely simmer for a minute, before removing from the syrup and allowing to cool. They can then be further perfumed with flowers for a few hours (see page 589).

If re-using the syrup for another batch, replenish with perfumed water before use and bring back to the 'light thread' stage.

CARAMELISED COCONUT RICE

kao niaw dtaeng guan

This sweetmeat is traditionally served during Songkran (Thai New Year) festivities.

2 cups white sticky rice
3–5 pandanus leaves, cut into 2 cm (1 in) pieces
2 cups palm sugar
1 cup coconut cream
2 tablespoons maltose
pinch of salt
1 teaspoon roasted sesame seeds – optional

Soak rice overnight. Next day, drain rice, place in a clean bamboo steamer with the pandanus leaves and steam at a rolling boil for 25–30 minutes until the rice is just cooked, but still has a little bite to it. Remove and spread out on a plate to cool.

In a brass wok or clean stainless-steel pan, heat palm sugar with coconut cream, maltose and salt until bubbling. Add the rice and stir – or churn, as the Thai would say – over a medium to low heat until the mixture is sticky and the syrup has been absorbed by the rice. Remove from the heat and spread onto a small tray, forming a layer 2 cm (1 in) thick.

Sprinkle the rice with roasted sesames seeds as it cools, if desired.

RICE CARAMEL WITH SESAME SEEDS AND PEANUTS

grayasart guan

In his pioneering book of the 1930s, *Siamese State Ceremonies*, Quaritch Wales described an arcane, now discontinued, ritual where 32 young virgins of high rank stirred 8 pans that contained 60 of the grains, fruits and sugars grown in the Kingdom of Siam. It was called 'mixing heavenly rice', and the resulting confection resembled 'something like a mince pie'. After being blessed by monks, this ambrosia was fed to the king, his family, high-ranking officials and monks attached to the palace and royal monasteries. Some was also left at crossroads to feed and appease ancestors and wandering ghosts.

There are seven ingredients that are believed to satisfy even the most rapacious of ghosts, and these are combined in this dessert, which is traditionally served at weddings and is also often eaten during Buddhist celebrations.

2½ cups palm sugar

1 cup coconut cream

½ cup maltose or honey

4 cups flattened rice, roasted

3½ cups popped rice

1 cup sesame seeds, roasted

1 cup peanuts, roasted

Combine sugar with coconut cream and maltose or honey in a wok or pan. Simmer until reduced by a third. Mix remaining ingredients, pour into the syrup and stir to coat evenly. Press into a lightly oiled tray. When cooled, cut into 1 cm × 4 cm (½ in × 1½ in) sweetmeats.

JADE RICE WITH ROASTED WATERMELON SEEDS

kao niaw gaew

You can buy watermelon seeds at Chinese supermarkets. Alternatively, dry some fresh seeds in the sun over several days – they will then keep indefinitely. For this recipe, roast them in a dry, heavy-based pan for a minute or so.

10 pandanus leaves

½ cup water

1 cup coconut cream

2 cups white sugar

pinch of salt

2 cups steamed white sticky rice, cooled

1 tablespoon watermelon seeds, roasted

Chop and purée the pandanus leaves with the water. Combine with coconut cream in a brass wok or enamel pan. Heat, adding sugar and salt, and simmer for a few minutes until thickened. Add rice and stir constantly to coat each grain. Once cream is completely absorbed, remove from the heat and rest in a glass bowl, covered.

To serve, coarsely grind the watermelon seeds and sprinkle over the rice.

SWEETENED WHITE STICKY RICE

kao niaw muun

This classic recipe is the basis for the most popular of Thai desserts, sticky rice. Make the sweetened coconut cream while the rice is steaming, as once the grains are cooked they must be immediately covered by the cream. Often a knotted pandanus leaf is added to further perfume the rice. The bowl is then covered, even wrapped in a towel, and allowed to rest in a warm place to absorb the cream completely.

Occasionally this rice is eaten by itself, and sometimes – quite bizarrely – with dried fish or prawns. More often, it is eaten with tropical fruit such as jackfruit or custard apples – and is most famously paired with mango. Often the dessert is garnished with some ground roasted yellow mung beans or sesame seeds.

2 cups white sticky rice
2 cups coconut cream
2 cups castor (superfine) sugar
large pinch–2 teaspoons salt

Soak rice overnight. Next day, drain, rinse and steam until tender – about 20 minutes. Make sure rice is not piled too high in the centre, so that it cooks evenly: test some grains from the thickest area. Meanwhile, stir coconut cream with sugar and salt until dissolved.

When rice is cooked, remove from steamer and pour prepared coconut cream over rice. Stir to incorporate thoroughly, then cover and set aside for 15 minutes in a warm place before serving – either as it is, or accompanied by slices of fresh fruit and blanketed with Sweet Coconut Cream (page 618).

SWEETENED WHITE STICKY RICE, SERVED WITH MANGO AND SWEET COCONUT CREAM (page 618)

SWEET COCONUT CREAM

gati lart naa kanom

This cream is used as a topping for desserts.

> 2 cups coconut cream
> 1 pandanus leaf
> 2 teaspoons rice flour, mixed with a little water or coconut cream to form a paste
> large pinch of salt
> ¾–1 cup white sugar

Heat coconut cream with pandanus leaf, then stir in flour paste and salt. When thick, add sugar and stir until dissolved. (Do not add sugar before flour has thickened the cream or it will lose its sheen, becoming an unappetising grey.) Strain before serving.

STEAMED BLACK STICKY RICE

kao niaw kao muun

Black sticky rice takes an inordinately long time to steam – as long as 3 hours. Be sure to replenish the water in the steamer, otherwise it will be blacker than the rice.

Egg White Custard with Young Coconut (page 623) or Jackfruit Custard (also page 623) can be served with this delicious rice. The coconut candy used in the recipes for Caramelised Coconut Dumplings in Coconut Cream (page 621) and Coconut Caramel Pastries (page 628) is also a wonderful accompaniment.

> 1 cup black sticky rice
> 1 cup white sticky rice
> 1 cup white sugar
> pinch of salt
> a few pandanus leaves – optional
> 1 cup coconut cream

Soak the two kinds of rice together overnight. Next day, drain rice, rinse, put in a bowl and steam for 3 hours. When the rice is soft, stir in the sugar, salt and pandanus leaves, if using. Allow to rest for 10 minutes, or until all the sugar has dissolved and the pandanus leaves have begun to release their fragrance. Pour the coconut cream over.

This dessert can be served warm or at room temperature.

RICE CUSTARD

kao mart song kreuang

This is one of the most delicious rice custards I know. It is rich and very sweet. The lychees help to counter the sugar and the apricot kernels impart a pleasing bitterness. Apricot kernels and dried longans are normally available in Chinese medicine shops, while fermented rice is sold in most Asian shops.

1 cup fermented rice

½–1 cup white sugar

1 egg, lightly beaten

2 pandanus leaves, knotted

3 tablespoons shredded young coconut

1 teaspoon apricot kernels, blanched

3 tablespoons corn kernels, pared from a freshly steamed cob

10 fresh lychees, peeled and deseeded

a few dried longans

Bring fermented rice to the boil. Add sugar to taste, egg and pandanus leaves and gently simmer, stirring constantly, until thickened. Test by coating the back of a spoon with the custard and then running a finger across it: if the finger mark remains, the custard is cooked. Remove pandanus leaves.

When cool, add remaining ingredients and serve in a small bowl.

BANANAS SIMMERED IN COCONUT CREAM

gluay buat chii

Fruit, such as bananas, jackfruit or durian, simmered in pure white coconut cream are always prepared for the ceremonial banquet after the ordination of a monk or a nun. In fact, the Thai name of this dish means 'to ordain a nun' – a reference to the colour of the nuns' habits: they are swathed in white, as is this dessert.

Apart from bananas, peanuts, cashews, custard apple, breadfruit, durian or jackfruit work well. Try to use the thickest coconut cream for the sauce: it should be simmered gently and stirred regularly to prevent it coagulating and forming lumps. But be careful not to break up the fruit – some cooks soak the bananas in hydrolysed lime water for several minutes before cooking to help prevent this. Often a pandanus leaf is added to perfume the simmering cream.

This dessert is always eaten warm, sometimes straight from the stove, and is normally served in a bowl. Often a few spoonfuls of fresh, unseasoned coconut cream are drizzled over the finished dish to further enrich it.

6 small sugar bananas

1 cup coconut milk

1 cup white sugar

large pinch of salt

2 cups coconut cream

Peel bananas and cut each into 4 pieces. Bring coconut milk to the boil. Add bananas and simmer until tender, skimming and reserving any 'foam'. Once bananas are cooked (about 2–3 minutes), add sugar and salt, swirling gently to dissolve without breaking up the bananas. It should taste rich, sweet and salty. Simmer for a few more minutes until the bananas have begun to absorb the sugar, then remove from the heat.

Meanwhile, bring coconut cream to the boil, stirring constantly to prevent from separating, until thickened. Remove from the heat and allow to cool. Skim off the cream that will have floated to the top and add to the bananas. Also stir in the reserved coconut 'foam' to enrich and thicken the dessert.

CUSTARD APPLES SIMMERED IN COCONUT CREAM

buat chii noi naa

As custard apples discolour quickly (rubbing cut surfaces with a little lime juice retards this), it is best to peel and deseed just as needed. Some ancient and indubitably fanatical cooks used to replace the seeds with deep-fried peanuts!

The degree of sweetness and saltiness required is entirely personal. The result should be an agreeable balance of rich coconut cream, sugar and meaty but slightly tart custard apple. The salt should add a cleansing note to the dessert, preventing it being too rich and sweet.

1 ripe custard apple

2 cups coconut cream, smoked and perfumed (see pages 588–9)

1 pandanus leaf, knotted

pinch of salt

3–5 tablespoons white sugar

Peel and deseed the custard apple. Bring 1½ cups of the coconut cream to the boil, adding the pandanus leaf. Season with salt and sugar. Add custard apple and simmer for a moment. Finish with the remaining coconut cream and serve.

CARAMELISED COCONUT DUMPLINGS IN COCONUT CREAM

kanom koh

Instead of using perfumed water in these dumplings, some cooks add a little puréed pandanus to the water when making the pastry, to give the dumplings an attractive jade hue. Other cooks use black sticky rice flour to obtain a purple colour. Make sure the dumplings are not too big, or they will lose much of their delicacy and will not make for pleasant eating. Likewise the pastry should not be too thick, or the dumplings will be doughy. Some cooks like to stabilise the coconut cream by adding a little rice flour; while this does prevent the cream from separating, it can make for a rather heavy dessert.

Traditionally, both the candy and the pastry are rolled into balls of the same size to ensure there is the right proportion of each.

3 cups coconut cream

1 pandanus leaf, knotted – optional

2 tablespoons rice flour mixed with a little water to form a paste – optional

3 tablespoons white sugar

large pinch of salt

coconut candy

1 cup palm sugar

1½ cups grated coconut

1 Thai candle

10 or so fragrant flowers

pastry

¾ cup sticky rice flour – ideally freshly made

pinch of salt

about 6 tablespoons warm Perfumed Water (page 590)

For the coconut candy, melt palm sugar in a brass wok. Add grated coconut and stir over a low heat until sugar has been absorbed by coconut. Allow to cool and then roll into balls about 1 cm (½ in) in diameter. Smoke and perfume in a sealed container for several hours or overnight (see pages 588–9).

To make the pastry, sieve flour with salt. Gradually pour in warm perfumed water, gathering and kneading to form a smooth and malleable paste. (It is difficult to give an accurate measurement for the water, as it depends on the quality of the flour: if the paste is too dry or firm, add a little more water; if too wet, incorporate more flour.) Roll into a cylinder, about 2 cm (1 in) in diameter, and rest for a few minutes. >

Slice pastry into ½ cm (¼ in) discs and wrap each around a coconut candy ball, rolling into a seamless dumpling. Repeat until all the candy and pastry is used. Cook in plenty of boiling water for 1–2 minutes: when they float to the top, the dumplings are cooked. Remove and refresh in iced water. Drain.

Over a low heat, gently bring coconut cream and pandanus leaf, if using, to the boil, stirring regularly. Stir in rice flour paste, if using, and, once the cream has thickened, the sugar and salt. It should taste rich, a little sweet and pleasantly salty. Strain. Slowly return coconut cream to the boil. Add dumplings and simmer until warmed through, stirring to ensure that the coconut cream does not separate. Serve in bowls.

PANDANUS TAPIOCA

saku song kreuang

Tapioca pearls have been used in desserts since the time of Ayuthyia, when commercial letters record ships arriving with sugar and tapioca from the south. During this period, monks and novices are known to have eaten tapioca pudding. It was also served during convalescence.

12 lychees, rambutans or longans
1 cup tapioca pearls
4 cups water
6 pandanus leaves
½ cup water
2 cups white sugar
shredded flesh of 1 young coconut

Cut lychees, rambutans or longans in half, prise out seeds and remove shells. Winnow any dust and husks from the tapioca. Cook in boiling water for about 15 minutes, stirring regularly to prevent it burning, until almost transparent. Drain, refresh in cold water, then drain again. Purée pandanus leaves in ½ cup water, then simmer for a minute until pandanus is cooked. Add sugar and, when completely dissolved, the coconut and fruit. Combine with tapioca and serve.

EGG WHITE CUSTARD WITH YOUNG COCONUT

sangkaya mapraow orn

This classic custard, eaten throughout Thailand, is normally based on egg, coconut cream and sugar. Sometimes it is plain, perhaps perfumed with pandanus; at other times pieces of fruit, such as coconut, jackfruit and rambutan – or even starchy ingredients, such as blanched peanuts and sliced taro – are used. However, the following recipe is based on egg whites, which you may have conveniently left over after making any of the egg yolk desserts – 'golden ones', 'golden strands', 'golden teardrops' or 'golden flowers' (see pages 603–8). The custards are normally steamed over a surprisingly high heat until firm. One classic recipe calls for the custard to be steamed inside a pumpkin, which makes for a sumptuous finish to a meal, or it can be eaten with Sweetened White Sticky Rice (page 616).

1 cup egg white – from about 6 eggs
¾ cup white sugar
1 cup palm sugar
½ teaspoon salt
¾ cup coconut cream
1 cup shredded young coconut

Combine all ingredients. Whisk until slightly frothy. Strain. Pour into a hot mould or, even better, the husk of the young coconut. Stir gently to help remove any bubbles from the custard and skim any bubbles that float to the top. Steam for 20–25 minutes. Allow to cool before serving.

JACKFRUIT CUSTARD

sangkaya kanun

4–5 jackfruit seeds – optional
2¼ cups shelled raw eggs, preferably duck – about 12 eggs
1⅓ cups thick coconut cream
2 cups palm sugar – ideally perfumed (see page 589)
½ cup ripe jackfruit flesh

Boil the seeds, if using, until tender. Peel and cut into thin slices.

Combine eggs with coconut cream and sugar, but do not over-whisk or the custard will be full of bubbles. Strain, skim off any froth and leave to rest for a few minutes. Skim once more, then stir in jackfruit flesh. Pour into a hot mould or cup, stir and skim once more. Place the sliced jackfruit seeds on top (if using), cover with paper and steam over a high heat for 15 minutes, reduce heat to low and steam for a further 30 minutes or until firm. Allow to cool before serving.

YELLOW BEAN PUDDING

kanom gumapa geng tua

This rich pudding can be made with almost any starchy vegetable or fruit, like pumpkin, breadfruit, yellow beans or even peanuts. An older or mature vegetable is preferable, as it results in a denser, more flavoursome purée. The best palm sugar to use is the darkest – not the dark, almost mahogany sugar from Malaysia, but a deep, honey-coloured sugar from Thailand. Do not over-beat the eggs, otherwise too much air is introduced, and the pudding will swell and 'soufflé' as it cooks and then fall and toughen once it cools. Some recipes add a few tablespoons of rice flour to stabilise and thicken the mixture.

Deep-fried shallots may seem an unusual garnish for this dessert; however, they enhance the dish with their crisp, fragrant nuttiness. Boiled apricot kernels, lotus seeds, peanuts or cashew nuts can also be used as a base for this delicious pudding, garnished with a handful of the same ingredient deep-fried or roasted.

½ cup yellow mung beans, soaked overnight and drained

10 eggs, lightly beaten

½ cup coconut curds – the residue of cracked cream

2 cups very thick coconut cream – the topmost layer

2 cups palm sugar

1 tablespoon coconut oil

4 tablespoons white sugar or coconut cream – optional

handful of deep-fried shallots

Wrap the mung beans in a clean tea towel and steam for about 35 minutes or until tender. Purée and sieve. In a brass wok or a heavy-based pan, stir the purée over a very low heat until dry, but not too dry (if the purée is too wet, the pudding will be heavy and soggy) – this may take as long as 10 minutes. Do not allow to scorch.

Combine eggs with coconut curds, coconut cream and sugar; strain. In a wok or pot, combine bean purée with egg mixture and stir constantly over a low to medium heat until it begins to boil and has thickened substantially – enough to hold its shape. (If it is insufficiently cooked at this stage, the pudding will be heavy, crumbly and wet; if overdone, it will be dry and brittle.) Lightly oil a mould with coconut oil and heat until quite hot: this will create a good, fragrant crust and ensure that the pudding does not stick to the sides. Pour in the batter, smoothing the surface with an oiled spatula or hand. If desired, sprinkle the pudding with white sugar or coconut cream – these will caramelise to create an inviting, crisp crust. >

Heat a chargrill and, when the coals are glowing, remove them. Cover the mould with a baking sheet and then with the hot coals; cook for around 30 minutes. Alternatively, the pudding can be baked, uncovered, in a hot oven – 220°C (425°F) – until golden, fragrant and just slightly pulling away from the sides of the mould.

To serve, sprinkle with deep-fried shallots.

WHITE AND RED SWEETS OR TOPKNOT LOLLIES

kanom dtom kao lae dteang

These sweetmeats use the trilogy of sweet ingredients: coconut cream, rice flour and sugar. Ancients believed that these ingredients recall the three cornerstones of Buddhism: the Buddha himself, his sayings and the monkhood. Brahmin priests, on the other hand, believed that this dessert was the favourite of Ganesha, the Hindu elephant-god of honesty, good fortune and art. Whatever its religious significance, this dish from the Sukothai period was considered auspicious when eaten during the tonsure ceremony, a Brahmin ceremony that marked the end of childhood.

Until the age of 11 or 13, a child would have a peculiar hairstyle, shaved except for a tuft or topknot on the head that grew uncut. As the girl or boy grew, it was knotted. When of age, monks would arrive and, after chanting, duly cut the knot. In a palace it was celebrated with great pomp, befitting such a momentous occasion. Elsewhere it was much simpler but, like all ceremonies in Thailand, the event finished with 'making merit' by feeding the monks. The last royal-sponsored ceremony was held just before the toppling of the absolute monarchy in 1932 and the practice is now all but extinct – although occasionally a young child with a distinct tuft can be seen in the more remote provinces.

Full of meaning, these confections are thoroughly delicious.

white sweet

1 cup palm sugar

4 tablespoons Perfumed Water (page 590)

2 cups grated coconut

about ¼ cup Perfumed Water (page 590)

1 cup white sticky rice flour, sieved

pinch of salt

red sweet

2 cups white sticky rice flour, sieved

1 cup Perfumed Water (page 590)

1 cup palm sugar

2 cups grated coconut

For the white sweet, bring palm sugar and perfumed water to the boil. When sugar has dissolved, add 1 cup of the grated coconut and simmer until sticky. Allow to cool, then roll into small balls about 1 cm (½ in) in diameter.

Gradually work the ¼ cup of perfumed water into the sieved flour and knead for a minute or so until you have a malleable pastry (you may need more or less water, depending on the flour). Roll into a cylinder – about 3 cm (1¼ in) in diameter. Cut into 1 cm (½ in) slices and press into thin discs. Place a cooled coconut ball in the centre of each pastry disc and wrap. Repeat until all pastry and coconut balls are used up. Boil in plenty of water until the sweets float to the top. Drain and serve rolled in the remaining grated coconut mixed with salt.

For the red sweet, gradually stir ½ cup of perfumed water into the sieved flour and then knead into a pastry. Roll into a cylinder 1½ cm (¾ in) in diameter and rest for about 30 minutes or so. Cut into ½ cm (¼ in) slices and then press into thin discs.

Bring the remaining ½ cup of perfumed water to the boil with the palm sugar and, when sugar has dissolved, add grated coconut and simmer, stirring regularly, until golden and caramelised. Set side.

Boil 'red sweet' discs in plenty of water until they float to the top. Drain and roll in the caramelised coconut.

The white and red sweets are always served together.

BIRD'S NESTS

kanom rang nok

500 g (1 lb) taro or cassava
oil for deep-frying
¾ cup palm sugar
1 tablespoon maltose

Peel and wash taro or cassava in water, then cut into coarse julienne. Soak in water for 10 minutes to remove any bitter starch. Drain and pat dry.

Heat the oil to medium. Rain in the taro and, when beginning to crisp and colour, stir so that it cooks evenly. Drizzle in palm sugar and continue to stir until it melts; as the sugar begins to caramelise and the taro begins to colour, add the maltose and stir vigorously to fully incorporate. Remove with a strainer and allow to cool slightly on a tray before forming into nest-like mounds.

COCONUT AND RICE SWEETMEATS

kao mao bot

These sweetmeats were originally made for the spirits of ancestors.

½ cup white sugar

½ cup Perfumed Water (page 590) or young coconut water

½ cup coconut cream

½ cup grated young coconut

½ cup grated regular coconut

1 cup flattened rice, roasted, ground and sieved

10 or so fragrant flowers

1 Thai candle

Combine sugar with perfumed water or young coconut water and bring to the boil. When sugar has completely dissolved, strain. Add coconut cream and simmer, stirring regularly, until reduced to a thick cream. Stir in grated young and regular coconut. Continue to simmer until coconut cream is thick and coconut is soft and glistening, but do not let it caramelise; if necessary, add a little extra water.

Allow to cool for a moment. Scoop out 1 teaspoon of the mixture and roll in the ground flattened rice. Shape into a small ball – traditionally the size and shape of a small turtle egg – and repeat until all the mixture is used.

Perfume the sweets for several hours with fragrant flowers (see page 589), smoke with a candle (see page 588) – or both.

COCONUT CARAMEL PASTRIES

kanom sort sai

If fresh flour is used for the pastry, then only a little water is required to make it into a malleable pastry. The water can be coloured green with pandanus purée, if desired.

Traditionally this dessert is elaborately wrapped in banana leaves.

coconut candy

1½ cups grated coconut

½ cup Perfumed Water (page 590)

1½ cups palm sugar

1 tablespoon white sticky rice flour

¼ cup coconut cream

pastry

1 cup white sticky rice flour – ideally fresh

about ¼ cup Perfumed Water (page 590)

topping

2 cups thick coconut cream

¼ cup rice flour

pinch of salt

For the coconut candy, mix coconut with perfumed water and palm sugar and simmer, stirring and turning over, until golden. Mix sticky rice flour with coconut cream, pour into caramelised coconut mixture and continue to stir until thick and sticky. Allow to cool, then roll into small balls around 1 cm (½ in) in diameter.

For the pastry, combine flour with just enough perfumed water to make a thick paste, then knead until it becomes a thick, malleable dough. Rest, covered, for around 30 minutes. Shape pastry into balls of 1½ cm (¾ in) diameter, then press each ball into a disc roughly ¼ cm (⅛ in) thick. Place a coconut candy onto the pastry, roll and seal. Repeat until all the pastry and candy has been used.

For the topping, sprinkle a little of the coconut cream onto the rice flour in a wok or pot, and work for a moment to mix thoroughly. Add the remaining coconut cream and salt and simmer, stirring constantly, until thickened. Set aside to cool.

Place each dumpling in a small cup, such as a Chinese tea cup (traditionally, a small banana-leaf cup would have been crafted), cover with the topping and steam for 30 minutes. Allow to cool before serving.

YELLOW BEAN DUMPLINGS

kanom tua baep

This is quite a versatile recipe. The dumplings are often eaten for breakfast or as a snack, and may even be filled with small prawns instead of mung beans to make an appetiser.

¼ cup yellow mung beans, soaked overnight and drained

½ cup grated coconut

pinch of salt

2 tablespoons sesame seeds, roasted

3 tablespoons white sugar

pastry

½ cup white sticky rice flour

¼ cup black sticky rice flour

scant ½ cup warm Perfumed Water (page 590)

Steam the beans for 40 minutes, then add all except 2 tablespoons of the coconut and steam for a further 5 minutes. Set aside to cool. >

Meanwhile, make the pastry. Combine and sieve the flours. Sprinkle with the perfumed water and knead to form a fairly dense pastry. Roll into balls 2 cm (1 in) in diameter. Bring a large pot of water to the boil and boil the pastry balls until they float to the top. Remove and allow to cool slightly. While still warm, roll out on plastic wrap to form flat discs about 4 cm (1½ in) in diameter and ½ cm (¼ in) thick.

Mix the cooled mung bean and coconut mixture with the salt, 1½ tablespoons of the sesame seeds and 2 tablespoons of the sugar. Place a little of the filling on the front third of each pastry circle, fold over and seal.

Combine the remaining grated coconut, sesame seeds and sugar and sprinkle over the top of the pastries to serve.

SELECT BIBLIOGRAPHY

BOOKS IN ENGLISH

PRIMARY SOURCES

anon. *An Englishman's Siamese Journals: 1890–1893*, Siam Media International Books, Bangkok.

Bock, Carl, *Temples and Elephants*, first published London, 1884; White Orchid Press, Bangkok, 1985.

Buls, Charles, *Siamese Sketches*, first published Brussels, 1901; (transl. Walter E. J. Tips), White Lotus Press, Bangkok, 1994.

Carter, A. Cecil, *The Kingdom of Siam 1904*, The Siam Society, Bangkok, 1988.

Choisy, Abbé de (transl. and with an introduction by Michael Smithies), *Journal of a Voyage to Siam: 1685–1686*, Oxford University Press, Kuala Lumpur, 1993.

Crawfurd, John, *Journal of an Embassy to the Courts of Siam and Cochin China*, first published 1828; Oxford University Press, Singapore, 1988.

Finlayson, George, *The Mission to Siam and Hué: 1821–1822*, Oxford University Press, Singapore, 1988.

Gervais, Nicolas, *The Natural and Political History of the Kingdom of Siam*, first published Paris, 1688; (transl. and ed. John Villiers), White Lotus Press, Bangkok, 1989.

Jottrand, Mr & Mrs Émile (transl. and with an introduction by Walter E. J. Tips), *In Siam: The Diary of a Legal Advisor of King Chulalongkorn's Government*, White Lotus Press, Bangkok, 1996.

Kaempfer, Engelbert, *A Description of the Kingdom of Siam 1690*, first published London, 1727; White Orchid Press, Bangkok, 1996.

Leonowens, Anna, *The English Governess at the Siamese Court*, first published England, 1870; Oxford University Press, Singapore, 1988.

Loubère, Simon de la, *The Kingdom of Siam*, first published London, 1693; Oxford University Press, Singapore, 1986.

Neale, Fred Arthur, *Narrative of a Residence at the Capital of Siam*, first published London, 1852; White Lotus Press, Bangkok.

Pallegoix, Monsignor Jean-Baptiste, *Description of the Thai Kingdom or Siam: Thailand under King Mongkut*, first published 1854; (transl. Walter E. J. Tips), White Lotus Press, Bangkok, 2000.

Sivaram, M., *The New Siam in the Making*, Stationers Printing Press, Bangkok, 1936.

Smith, Malcolm, *A Physician at the Court of Siam*, first published 1952; Oxford University Press, Singapore, 2nd imprint 1985.

Smithies, Michael (ed. and, in part, transl.), *The Chevalier de Chaumont and the Abbé de Choisy: Aspects of the Embassy to Siam 1685*, Silkworm Books, Chiang Mai, 1997.

—— (ed.), *The Discourses at Versailles of the First Siamese to France: 1686–7*, The Siam Society, Bangkok, 1986.

—— (ed.), *The Siamese Memoirs of Count Claude de Forbin: 1685–1688*, Silkworm Books, Chiang Mai, 1996.

Sommerville, Maxwell, *Siam on the Meinam from the Gulf to Ayuthia*, first published London, 1897; White Lotus Press, Bangkok, 1985.

Tachard, Guy, *A Relation of the Voyage to Siam*, first published 1688; White Orchid Press, Bangkok, 1985.

Ta-Kuan, Chou (transl. Paul Pelliot & J. Gilman d'Arcy Paul), *The Customs of Cambodia*, The Siam Society, 3rd edition, Bangkok, 1993.

Thompson, P. A., *Siam: An Account of the Country and the People*, first published USA, 1910; White Orchid Press, Bangkok, 1987.

Wales, H. G. Quaritch, *Siamese State Ceremonies*, first published London, 1931; Curzon Press, London, 1992.

SECONDARY SOURCES

Achaya, K. T., *Indian Food: A Historical Companion*, Oxford University Press, New Delhi, 1994.

Akin Rabibhadana, *The Organization of Thai Society in The Early Bangkok Period 1782–1873*, Wisdom of The Land & Thai Association of Qualitative Researchers, Bangkok, 1996.

Anderson, Edward F., *Plants and People of the Golden Triangle: Ethnobotany of the Hill Tribes of Northern Thailand*, Dioscrides Press, 1993.

Brown, Ian, *The Élite and the Economy in Siam c. 1890–1920*, Oxford University Press, Singapore, 1988.

Bulan Phithakpol, Waunee Varanyaanond, Suparat Reungmaneepaitoon & Wood, Henry, *The Traditional Fermented Foods of Thailand*, ASEAN Food Handling Bureau, Kuala Lumpur, 1995.

Chaiyan Rajchagool, *The Rise and Fall of the Thai Absolute Monarchy*, White Lotus Press, Bangkok, 1994.

Chatthip Nartsupha, *The Thai Village Economy in the Past*, Silkworm Books, Chiang Mai, 1999.

Clifford, Hugh, *Further India*, first published London, 1904; White Lotus Press, Bangkok, 1990.

Davidson, Alan, *The Oxford Companion to Food*, Oxford University Press, Oxford, 1999.

Dhida Saraya, *(Sri) Dvaravati – The Initial Phase of Siam's History*, Muang Boran Publishing House, Bangkok, 1999.

Finestone, Jeffrey, *The Royal Family of Thailand: The Descendants of King Chulalongkorn*, Phitsanulok Publishing, Bangkok, 1989.

Forbes, Andrew & Henley, David, *Khon Muang: People and the Principalities of North Thailand*, Asia Film House/Sollo Development Limited, 1997.

Fukai, Hayao (transl. Peter Hawkes), *Food and Population in a Northeast Thai Village*, University of Hawaii Press, Honolulu, 1993.

Gerson, Ruth, *Traditional Festivals in Thailand*, Oxford University Press, Kuala Lumpur, 1996.

Girling, John L. S., *Thailand: Society and Politics*, Cornell University Press, New York, 1987.

Gosling, Betty, *Sukothai: Its History, Culture, and Art*, Oxford University Press, Singapore, 1991.

Greene, Stephen L. W., *Absolute Dreams: Thai Government under Rama VI, 1910–1925*, White Lotus Press, Bangkok, 1999.

Higham, Charles & Rachanie Thosarat, *Prehistoric Thailand: From Early Settlement to Sukothai*, River Books, Bangkok, 1998.

Ho, Alice Yen, *At the South-East Asian Table*, Oxford University Press, Kuala Lumpur, 1995.

Hosking, Richard, 'The Candle-scented Cakes and Sweets of Thailand', *Studies in the Humanities and Sciences*, Vol. XXXIII, No. 2 (2), Offprint, Hiroshima Shudo University, Japan, 1993.

Hunter, Eileen, with Narisa Chakrabongse, *Katya & the Prince of Siam*, River Books, Bangkok, 1994.

Hutchinson, E. W., *Adventurers in Siam in the Seventeenth Century*, DD Books, Bangkok, 1985.

Jacquat, Christine & Bertossa, Gianni, *Plants from the Markets of Thailand*, Editions Duang Kamol, Bangkok, 1990.

McGee, Harold, *On Food and Cooking: The Science and Lore of the Kitchen*, Charles Scribner's Sons, New York, 1984.

Mom Leuang Manich Jumsai, *History of Laos*, Wacherin Publishing, Bangkok, 1994.

—— *History of Thailand and Cambodia*, Wacherin Publishing, Bangkok, 1996.

—— *Thai Folktales*, Chalermint, Bangkok, 1999.

Marks, Tom, *The British Acquisition of Siamese Malaya (1896-1909)*, White Lotus Press, Bangkok, 1997.

Morson, Ian, *Four Hundred Years: Britain and Thailand*, Nai Suk's Editions, Bangkok, 1999.

Mowe, Rosalind (ed.), *Southeast Asian Specialities*, Culinaria Könemann, Cologne, 1998.

Mulder, Dr Niels, *Everyday Life in Thailand: An Interpretation*, Editions Duang Kamol, Bangkok, 1985.

Paiboon Suthasupa, Viboon Rattanapanpone & Sompong Shevasunt, *Protein Food Production in Thailand*, Institute of Southeast Asian Studies, Singapore, 1982.

Phya Anuman Rajadhon, *Essays on Thai Folklore*, Sathirakoses Nagapradipa Foundation, Bangkok, 1986.

—— *Popular Buddhism in Siam and Other Essays on Thai Studies*, Sathirakoses Nagapradipa Foundation, Bangkok, 1986.

—— *Some Traditions of the Thai*, Sathirakoses Nagapradipa Foundation, Bangkok, 1987.

Piper, Jacqueline M., *Rice in South-East Asia: Cultures and Landscapes*, Oxford University Press, Kuala Lumpur, 1993.

Prasert Na Nagara & Griswold, A. B., *Epigraphic and Historical Studies*, The Historical Society, Bangkok, 1992.

Reichart, P. A. & Philipsen, H. P., *Betel and Miang: Vanishing Thai Habits*, White Lotus Press, Bangkok, 1996.

Rogers, Peter, *A Window on Isan: Thailand's Northeast*, Editions Duang Kamol, Bangkok, 1989.

—— *Northeast Thailand from Prehistoric to Modern Times: In Search of Isan's Past*, Editions Duang Kamol, Bangkok, 1996.

Rong Syamananda, *A History of Thailand*, Thai Watana Panich, Bangkok, 1986.

The Royal Kingdom of Thailand, Tourism Authority of Thailand, 1997.

Ruohamäki, Olli-Pekka, *Fisherman No More? Livelihood and Environment in Southern Thai Maritime Villages*, White Lotus Press, Bangkok, 1999.

Schliesinger, Joachim, *Ethnic Groups of Thailand: Non-Tai-Speaking Peoples*, White Lotus Press, Bangkok, 2000.

Segaller, Denis, *Thai Ways*, Post Publishing Company, Bangkok, 1987.

—— *More Thai Ways*, Allied Newspapers Limited, Bangkok, 1982.

Smithies, Michael, *Old Bangkok*, Oxford University Press, Singapore, 1986.

—— (ed.), *Descriptions of Old Siam*, Oxford University Press, Kuala Lumpur, 1995.

Stobart, Tom, *The Cook's Encyclopedia: Ingredients and Processes*, B. T. Batsford Ltd, London, 1980.

Sumet Jumsai, *Naga: Cultural Origins in Siam and the West Pacific*, Chalermint Press and DD Books, Bangkok, 1997.

Suthon Sukphisit, *The Vanishing Face of Thailand*, Post Books, Bangkok, 1997.

Tannahill, Reay, *Food in History*, Penguin Books, London, revised edition 1988.

Terwiel, B. J., *A Window on Thai History*, Editions Duang Kamol, Bangkok, 2nd revised edition 1991.

Thanapol Chadchaidee, *Essays on Thailand*, D. K. Today, Bangkok, 1994.

Thongchai Winichakul, *Siam Mapped: A History of the Geo-body of a Nation*, Silkworm Books, Chiang Mai, 1994.

Tips, Walter E. J., *Gustave Rolin-Jaequemyns and the Making of Modern Siam*, White Lotus Press, Bangkok, 1996.

Toussaint-Samat, Maguelonne (transl. Anthea Bell), *History of Food*, Blackwell Publishers, Oxford, 1992.

Van Esterik, Penny, *From Marco Polo to McDonald's: Thai Cuisine in Transition*, Food and Foodways, Harwood Academic Publishers, United Kingdom, 1992.

Visser, Margaret, *Much Depends on Dinner*, Penguin Books, London, 1989.

—— *The Rituals of Dinner*, Penguin Books, London, 1992.

Warren, William, *The Grand Palace*, The Grand Palace, Bangkok, 1988.

Waugh, Alec, *Bangkok: The Story of a City*, reissued Orientations, Bangkok, 1987.

Wyatt, David K., *Thailand: A Short History*, Yale University Press, London, 1984.

—— *Studies in Thai History*, Silkworm Books, Chiang Mai, 1994.

Yee, Kenny, Gordon, Catherine & Win, Sun, *Thai Hawker Food*, BPS Publications, Bangkok, 1993.

COOKBOOKS

Brennan, Jennifer, *Thai Cooking*, Futura Publications, London, 1984.

Chalie Amatyakul, *The Best of Thai Cooking*, Travel Publishing Asia, Hong Kong, 1987.

Cost, Bruce, *Foods from the Far East*, Century, London, 1990.

Cotterell, Yong Yap, *The Chinese Kitchen: A Traditional Approach to Eating*, Weidenfeld & Nicolson, London, 1986.

Esbensen, Mogens Bay, *Thai Cuisine*, Viking O'Neil, Melbourne, 1990.

Leeming, Margaret & Man-hui, May Huang, *Chinese Regional Cookery*, Rider and Company, London, 1983.

Loha-Unchit, Kasma, *It Rains Fishes: Legends, Traditions and the Joy of Thai Cooking*, Pomegranate Press, San Francisco, 1995.

Owen, Sri, *The Rice Book: The Definitive Book on the Magic of Rice Cookery*, Doubleday, London, 1993.

Phia Sing, *Traditional Recipes of Laos*, Prospect Books, London, 1981.

Sibpan Sonakul, *Everyday Siamese Dishes*, Pracand Press, Bangkok, first published 1952, 5th edition 1969.

Solomon, Charmaine, *Charmaine Solomon's Encyclopedia of Asian Food*, Hamlyn Australia, Melbourne, 1997.

Taik, Aung Aung, *Under the Golden Pagoda: The Best of Burmese Cooking*, Chronicle Books, San Francisco, 1993.

Mom Leuang Taw Kritakara & Mom Ratchawongse Pimsai Amranand, *Modern Thai Cooking*, Editions Duang Kamol, Bangkok, 1977.

Thompson, David, *Classic Thai Cuisine*, Simon & Schuster, Sydney, 1993.

Vatcharin Bhumichitr, *The Taste of Thailand*, Pavilion, London, 1998.

Wandee Na Songkhla, *The Thai Cuisine Book*, Bangkok.

—— *The Royal Favourite Dishes*, Bangkok.

Warren, William, *Thailand the Beautiful Cookbook*, Weldon Owen, Sydney, 1992.

THAI SOURCES

One of the unusual characteristics of Thai bibliographies is that the first name determines alphabetical ordering – although those with honorific titles are always listed first. Before the sixth reign, few people had acknowledged surnames. Today, even the Thai telephone book registers people by their first name.

COOKBOOKS

Although it is unlikely that these references will be available to the English reader, I feel nonetheless that they should be acknowledged. Only the author and date of publication – if known – are given.

Mom Chao Ying Janjaroen Rachani, 1951

Mom Chao Ying Jongjittanorm Disakul, 1958

Mom Ratchawongse Dteuang Sanitsawongse (editor of *Dtamrap Saiyaowapaa* – the first cookbook anthology with recipes donated by many famous cooks), 1930s

Mom Ratchawongse Kukrit Pramoj, 1979

Mom Ratchawongse Ying Reuang Orranop Wijidtrarnnon, 1944

Mom Leuang Dterb Chomsai, 1953, 1976

Leuang Witaya Nukgongrawiim, 1937

Khun Ying Suratsiang Mongkolgarn, 1968

Thanpuuying Pliang Pasonagorn, 1910

Archarn Janyaasudtbarn, 1982

Professor Sisamorn Kongpan & Manii Suwannapong & Aacharah Tinarai, 1992

Khun Anongnart Puangpayorm, 1969

Chalosii Jidtagidt, 1965

Nangsao Chaluay Gandtaworanii, 1934

Nang Dtaenggwa Iamgrasin, 1956

Khun Gidtjaa Tiansawadtgit, 1989

Gingranok Garnjanaapaa, 1938

Khun Gobgaew Najpinij, 1899

Khun Gopkaew Artpinit, 1999

Hae Jantaburii, 1942

Hayii Hiproham, 1929

Jamnong Rasamiinawanapanit, 1930

Janaet, 1963

Jantorn Tadsanon, 1981

Jariyaa & Sanomwangnai, 1970

Khun Jarutwarn Noppaen, 1982

Khun Jip Bunnark, 1951

Khun Jitsamarn Gomormtidi, 1960

Nii Jong Suwasang, 1933

Law Paydtararat, 1925

Mae Bunrort, 1962

Khun Mae Ok, 1927

Mae Pron, 1988

Khun Nalin Kuuamornpatana, 1993

Khun Narinoparat, 1925

Payao Thaiwatcharaaramart, 1989

Khun Pradit Suppachang, 1985

Pradit Thaiyaanon, 1961

Prasit Prapadtanan & Rasanii Mayaa, 1967

Sermporn Sadtdapan, 1992

Sor Banyaamart, 1968

Sor Priinoi, 1994

Khun Wacharipan Pinarkha

Nai Waet Wor Sarakarm, 1939

Wandee Na Songkhla, 1987

Worn Wannasawarn, 1924

MEMORIAL BOOKS

Mom Chao Raohinaowadi Disakul, 1912–1984

Professor Mom Ratchawongse Bunranapork Gasamsii, 1925–1977

Mom Ratchawongse Dteuang Sanitsawongse, 1883–1968

Jao Jorm Mom Ratchawongse Sadap Ratchagarn tii haa, 1986

Mom Leuang Kleuawarn Prasitsongkarm, 1891–1969

Mom Leuang Neuang Ninrat, 1994

Mom Leuang Pidakmanusard, 1899–1981

Mom Leuang Ying Sae Gritsadtagorn, 1904–1980

Mom Leuang Ying Lek Taepawarn, 1857–1958

Mom Grasamsiisudtpawongse, 1923–1970

Mom Raruaai Gasamesan, 1897–1964

Thanpuuying Gleeb Mahiton, 1876–1961

Thanpuuying Pliang Pasonagornrawongse & Khunying Praditamornpiiman, 1925

Khunying Aap Mannitgunlapat, 1895–1972

Khunying Daeng Nawisaetiyon, 1881–1966

Khunying Muang Wipapuwadon, 1884–1958

Khunying Pradit Amoronpimarn, 1926

Khunying Siisurasongklarm, 1896–1978

Khunying Wibunluk Chunhawarn, 1898–1955

Nang Banchaa Piichitrart, 1889–1963

Nang Bannagorngowidt, 1902–1965

Nai Chalong Bposayanon, 1922–1970

Nai Chamni Winitparn, 1896–1974

Nai Dtragun Amartdayartgun, 1871–1951

Nang Jamniang Mirinatangun, 1908–1971

Nai Juseuken Judtrageun, 1884–1967

Nai Kam Ponghiran, 1914–1972

Nang Kleuang Siibunruang, 1882–1971

Nang Lek Na Songkhla, 1893–1953

Nai Lek Puwatsaet, 1900–1971

Nang Linchii Nakkawatjana, 1892–1956

Khun Mae Choi and Khun Saipim Surawantana, 1881–1966

Khun Mae Ju Bunranasing, 1878–1971

Naawaeat Chitchusii, 1903–1963

Nang Nipat Pantumasadt, 1900–1972

Nang Niranaa Bpraemwatana, 1919–1963

Nang Nit Suwawarnnasang, 1890–1965

Nang Nornlak Suridyatkam, 1941–1975

Nang Nuangsii Jikdtiwarn, 1928–1969

Nang Oonreuan Pipadtanagun, 1908–1989

Praya Manit Manidtayagun, 1879–1940

Pandtiiying Pradap Gidtiijarn, 1918–1979

Nang Pard Anusorn, 1892–1970

Nai Pondtamruttor Khunjannonraksaa, 1901–1960

Ponargarttor Mondtrii Harnwichai, 1913–1989

Pontor Chalerm Mahatanaanon, 1910–1991

Prabamonbunyaa, 1896–1970

Praniigorn Bodhi, 1897–1971

Nang Rareung Na Talan, 1906–1980

Nang Rat Naetmukdaa, 1900–1969

Nang Saengiam Dtraisorat, 1990

Nangsao Sanguan Ramsam, 1909–1942

Nang Sap Potpaarnit, 1895–1972

Nang Sawai Taephadtsadin Na Ayuthyia, 1905–1968

Nang Sayimart Madtayomjan, 1901–1960

Nai Siihanat Sanitwongse naa Ayuthyia, 1928–1972

Nang Sontisaaranan, 1888–1964

Nang Taet Praniprachachon, 1887–1964

Nang Tet Praniiprachachon, 1888–1984

Nang Tongkarm Pidtaksrgorn, 1884–1969

Nang Warnaa Gardtsakun, 1910–1972

Nai Wichit Wichaidtit, 1942–1991

Nang Wong Jandtramart Amartdayartgun, 1891–1978

Nai Yord Chanayut, 1899–1981

Nai Yoy Jidtranon, 1885–1970

Nang Yudtigidtdtamrongsarn, 1906–1978

INDEX

INDEX

Numbers in **bold** indicate photographs.